Logic, Second Edition, is the first text to make logic relevant, interesting, and accessible to today's students by bridging both formal and informal logic to real life.

Here's what some of your colleagues are saying about this exceptional text:

"*Logic* is terrific. We have needed a text with this approach [more effective in bridging formal to informal logic and logic to real-life situations] for a long time."

—William S. Jamison, *University of Alaska Anchorage*

"The author succeeds brilliantly in presenting the essence of logical reasoning throughout the text as a dynamic, integral part of daily human interaction rather than simply an academic discipline."

—Joia Lewis Turner, *St. Paul College*

"The writing style is perfect."

—Thompson M. Faller, *University of Portland*

"Outstanding. Written in clear language, with wit and imagination. Baronett takes students through the theory of sound reasoning, types of logics, and logic applications in almost every kind of human discourse. This text is a useful, viable tool for building a bridge between formal logic and real-life situations."

—Merle Harton, *Everglades University*

"The well-chosen and relevant examples are a major selling point. This book looks terrific."

—Aeon Skoble, *Bridgewater State University*

"The exposition is delightfully clear. The examples are thought-provoking, topical, copious, and well gradated by level of difficulty."

—Frank X. Ryan, *Kent State University*

Please read on to see how *Logic,* Second Edition, addresses *your* course needs.

The Perfect Text for Your Course . . .
No Matter How You Teach It

Your course is unique; you have your own teaching philosophy and style.
Whether you teach traditional Introduction to Logic, Critical Thinking/
Informal Logic, or Formal Logic, Baronett: *Logic,* Second Edition, can be
tailored to fulfill your course needs.

We'll make it easy for you; choose one of our Alternate Editions or build
the book you want, chapter by chapter.

Option 1. Author Stan Baronett has suggested four Alternate Editions
that may work for you. Each Alternate Edition comes in full color, with
answers to problems, a full glossary, and an index. The books are in stock
and available for ordering. Please see the ISBN information below.

> *Logic: Concise Edition*
> Chapters 1, 3, 4, 5, 6, 7, 8
> Order using ISBN: 978-0-19-994129-2
>
> *Logic: An Emphasis on Critical Thinking and Informal Logic*
> Chapters 1, 2, 3, 4, 10, 11, 12, 13 A–E, 14, 15
> Order using ISBN: 978-0-19-994128-5
>
> *Logic: An Emphasis on Formal Logic*
> Chapters 1, 5, 6, 7, 8, 9
> Order using ISBN: 978-0-19-994126-1
>
> *Logic: With Diagramming in Chapter 4 Informal Fallacies*
> Full text (examples of diagramming on facing page)
> Order using ISBN: 978-0-19-997081-0

Option 2. Create your own customized textbook by choosing the specific
chapters that you need for your course. Please contact your Oxford
University Press Sales Representative or call 800.280.0280 for details.

Informal Fallacies
With or Without Diagramming . . .
Which Would You Prefer?

2. Tu Quoque

A variety of the *ad hominem* fallacy known as **tu quoque** (meaning "you, too" or "look who's talking") is distinguished by the specific attempt of one person to avoid the issue at hand by claiming the other person is a hypocrite. For example:

> [1] You have been lecturing me about not joining a gang. But Dad, [2] you were a gang member, and [3] you never went to jail. So, [4] I'll make my own decision about joining a gang.

Premises 1, 2, and 3 are used to imply the following: [5] *Dad, you are a hypocrite.* This result is then used to reject Dad's arguments: [6] *I can disregard your lectures.* The reconstructed argument can be diagrammed as follows:

```
1   2   3
    ↓
   [5]

   [6]        This conclusion is the result of a tu quoque fallacy; the at-
    ↓         tack is aimed at Dad, not Dad's arguments. Since [6] is not
    4         justified, it cannot support 4.
```

**Chapter 4.
Informal Fallacies
(With Diagramming)**

**Chapter 4.
Informal Fallacies
(Standard Text)

No Diagramming**

2. Tu Quoque

A variety of the *ad hominem* fallacy known as **tu quoque** (meaning "you, too" or "look who's talking") is distinguished by the specific attempt of one person to avoid the issue at hand by claiming the other person is a hypocrite. For example:

> You have been lecturing me about not joining a gang. But Dad, you were a gang member, and you never went to jail. So, I'll make my own decision about joining a gang.

The premises are used to imply the following: *Dad, you are a hypocrite.* This result is then used to reject Dad's arguments: *I can disregard your lectures.* As we can see from the reconstructed argument, the conclusion is the result of a *tu quoque* fallacy. The fallacy occurs because the argument attacks Dad; therefore it fails to address Dad's arguments.

Another example comes from the political world. If a U.S. senator criticizes the human rights failings of China by offering a detailed description of recorded UN inquiries, a Chinese representative might say the following:

To view the complete Chapter 4 with diagramming, please turn to the back of your Instructor's Edition.

Incorporating 2600 exercises— more than 1000 of them new—author Stan Baronett breathes new life into logic with a wealth of real-world examples and exercises . . .

For example, suppose you read the following:

> The Senate recently held hearings on for-profit colleges, investigating charges that the schools rake in federal loan money, while failing to adequately educate students. Critics point to deceptive sales tactics, fraudulent loan applications, high drop-out rates, and even higher tuitions. In response, the Department of Education has proposed a "gainful employment" rule, which would cut financing to for-profit colleges that graduate (or fail) students with thousands of dollars of debt and no prospect of salaries high enough to pay them off.
>
> Jeremy Dehn, "Degrees of Debt"

If the information in this passage is accurate, then government decisions might affect thousands of people. On reading this, you would probably search for related material, to determine whether the information is correct. However, you would be concerned for more than just accuracy. You would also be asking what it means for you. Are the critics correct? Are the new rules justified, and do they address the criticism? You are seeing competing claims.

Real-world examples help bring logic down to earth for students

"Profiles in Logic" provide short sketches of logicians, philosophers, mathematicians, and others associated with logic

PROFILES IN LOGIC
Augusta Ada Byron

Ada Byron (1815–52) was the daughter of the poet Lord Byron, but she never got to know her father. Her parents separated when Ada was only a month old. When she was 18, she met Charles Babbage, the inventor of the "analytical engine," an elaborate calculating machine. Ada Byron worked with Babbage for the next 10 years, trying to solve the complex problems associated with what we now call computer programming. How can we get a machine to do complex mathematical calculations and analysis? A major problem for Babbage was to get a machine to calculate Bernoulli numbers (special sequences of rational numbers). Ada Byron's work on this difficult problem culminated in her breakthrough—the first

computer program ever. What she created was an *algorithm*, a series of steps that achieve a final result. The analytic engine could do its calculations step by step, and so can modern computers.

But Ada Byron envisioned machines that could do far more than just calculate numbers. She wrote of a machine that could "compose elaborate and scientific pieces of music of any degree of complexity or extent." In the late 1970s, the United States Department of Defense began work on a programming language capable of integrating many complex embedded computer applications. The successful program bears the name *Ada*, in recognition of Ada Byron's achievements.

PROFILES IN LOGIC
John Venn

Although many people applied the ideas of Boolean algebra, perhaps the most useful contribution was that of John Venn (1834–1923), who created what we now call *Venn diagrams*. If we want to analyze categorical syllogisms, we start by simply drawing circles. Venn's system uses three overlapping circles of identical size. Each circle represents one of the three terms in the syllogism: the subject term of the conclusion, the predicate term of the conclusion, or the middle term—the term that occurs only in the premises. The distinct areas of the circles can then display the claims of the categorical syllogism. For example, shading an

area indicates an empty class and is used for universal categorical statements. The letter "X" indicates that a class is not empty; it is used for particular categorical statements.

Venn diagrams have the advantage of uniformity: They offer a mechanical method for determining the validity (or invalidity) of any categorical syllogism. Venn diagrams are also used in the branch of mathematics called *set theory*. Just as two circles may overlap only a bit, two sets may have just some members in common, called their intersection. Together, the areas of both circles represent the union of sets, or all their members taken together.

. . . and makes it easier for your students to understand and relate to logic.

CHECK YOUR UNDERSTANDING 13E

Analyze the statistical reasoning in each passage.

1. In general, however, the financial odds still greatly favor a person with a college degree. The Bureau of Labor Statistics estimates that median weekly earnings for a person with a bachelor's degree was $1,025 in 2009, compared with just $626 for those with only a high school diploma.

Allison Linn, "Is It Worth It to Go to College?"

Answer:

Since the Bureau of Labor Statistics has access to large amounts of data, we can assume that the size of the data set is adequate. The *median* weekly income for persons with a bachelor's degree was $1,025 (in 2009); therefore we know that 50% of that data set made more than that amount and 50% made less. For those with only a high school diploma, 50% of that data set made more than $626 a week and 50% made less.

On the surface, the difference between $1,025 and $626 is substantial. However, we are not told either the *mean* or the *standard deviation* in the two sets of data. Without that information, we cannot determine the amount of diversity in the sets. In addition, people with bachelor's degrees in engineering and computer science average three to four times the yearly salary of many social science majors. The article does not distinguish between majors. It therefore may misleadingly suggest that any kind of bachelor's degree puts you in a position to make substantially more than a person with only a high school diploma.

A unique, extended explanation or model of the answer to the first question of each "Check Your Understanding" section shows students what is expected of their answers

An additional 25% of the exercises are answered at the back of the book

"Logic Challenge" problems present puzzles and paradoxes that end each chapter on a fun note

precision. A claim is made that appears to be
significant, but which, upon analysis, is not.

CHAPTER 5

Check Your Understanding 5A

5. Subject term: *malicious murderers*
Predicate term: *evil people*

This is an example of an A-proposition.

9. Subject term: *lottery winners*
Predicate term: *lucky people*

This is an example of an E-proposition.

13. Subject term: *amendments to the U.S. Constitution*
Predicate term: *unconstitutional acts*

This is an example of an E-proposition.

Check Your Understanding 5B

5. Universal negative; subject term distributed; predicate term distributed.

9. Universal affirmative; subject term distributed; predicate term undistributed.

13. Universal negative; subject term distributed; predicate term distributed.

Check Your Understanding 5C

I.
5. True.

II.
5. a. True. Since these fall under *subalternation*, if the universal (in this case an E-proposition) is true, then the corresponding particular (in this case an O-proposition) must be true, too.

III.
5. Undetermined. No immediate inference can be made about the subaltern of a false A-proposition.

IV.
5. c. Undetermined. Since these fall under *subalternation*, if the universal is false, then the corresponding particular could be either true or false.

9. a. True. Since these fall under *subalternation*, if the universal is true, then the corresponding particular must be true.

13. c. Undetermined. Since these fall under *subalternation*, if the particular is true, then the corresponding universal could be either true or false.

17. a. True. Since they are *contradictories*, if one is false, then the other must be true.

21. c. Undetermined. Since they are *subcontraries*, they can both be true at the same time.

Check Your Understanding 5D

5. A. Converse: No people likely to go to prison are greedy politicians.
   B. Obverse: All greedy politicians are non-people likely to go to prison.
   C. Contrapositive: Some non-people likely to go to prison are not non-greedy politicians. (*Valid by limitation*)

9. A. Converse: Some days when banks close are public holidays. (*Valid by limitation*)
   B. Obverse: No public holidays are non-days when banks close.
   C. Contrapositive: All non-days when banks close are nonpublic holidays.

13. A. Converse: No diet-busters are ice cream toppings.
   B. Obverse: All ice cream toppings are non-diet-busters.
   C. Contrapositive: Some non-diet-busters are not non-ice cream toppings. (*Valid by limitation*)

17. A. Converse: Some grease-laden products are French fries. (*Valid by limitation*)
   B. Obverse: No French fries are non-grease-laden products.
   C. Contrapositive: All non-grease-laden products are non-French fries.

21. A. Converse: Some great works of art are tattoos.
   B. Obverse: Some tattoos are not non-great works of art.
   C. Contrapositive: Not valid for I-propositions.

25. A. Converse: No acts left unrewarded are good deeds.
   B. Obverse: All good deeds are non-acts left unrewarded.
   C. Contrapositive: Some non-acts left unrewarded are not non-good deeds. (*By limitation*)

Check Your Understanding 5G

5. Let S = *psychics*, and P = *frauds*. All S are P.

9. Let S = *teachers*, and P = *miserable wretches*. All S are P.

13. Let S = *sea creatures*, and P = *bivalves*. All S are P.

17. Let S = *scientific researchers*, and P = *people with impeccable credentials*. Some S are P.

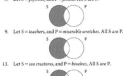

LOGIC CHALLENGE: A RELATIVE PROBLEM

At a party you overhear two conversations. In the first conversation you hear this:

Stu: Who is that man sitting on the couch, the one with the red sweater?
Lou: His name is Drew and he is my nephew.
Sue: He is definitely not my nephew.

You walk over to the couch and hear this:

Pru: By the way, is Lou married?
Drew: No, he is single. He is Sue's biological brother.

No two people at the party have the same name, so each of the conversations are referring to the same persons. The question is: How are Sue and Drew related?

Additional pedagogical elements make the material even more accessible.

A. NATURAL DEDUCTION

Natural deduction is a proof procedure by which the conclusion of an argument is validly derived from the premises through the use of rules of inference. The function of **rules of inference** is to *justify* the steps of a proof. A **proof** (also called a *deduction* or a *derivation*) is a sequence of steps in which each step is either a premise or follows from earlier steps in the sequence according to the rules of inference. A justification of a step includes a rule of inference and the prior steps that were used to derive it. This procedure guarantees that each step follows validly from prior steps. A proof ends when the conclusion of the argument has been correctly derived.

There are two types of rules of inference: *implication rules* and *replacement rules*.

> **Implication rules** are *valid argument forms*. When the premises of a valid argument form occur during a proof, then we can validly derive the conclusion of the argument form as a justified step in the proof. (*Modus ponens* and *modus tollens* are two examples of valid argument forms.)

> **Replacement rules** are *pairs of logically equivalent statement forms*. Whenever one pair member of a replacement rule occurs in a proof step, then we can validly derive the other pair member as a justified step in the proof. For example, the statement form, $\sim (p \cdot q)$ is logically equivalent to $(\sim p \vee \sim q)$.

Both types of rules of inference have the same function—*to ensure the validity of the steps they are used to justify*. A natural deduction proof can begin with any number of

Marginal definitions

Natural deduction
A proof procedure by which the conclusion of an argument is validly derived from the premises through the use of rules of inference.

Rules of inference
The function of rules of inference is to justify the steps of a proof.

Proof A sequence of steps (also called a deduction or a derivation) in which each step is either a premise or follows from earlier steps in the sequence according to the rules of inference.

Implication rules Valid argument forms that are validly applied only to an entire line.

Replacement rules Pairs of logically equivalent statement forms.

KEY TERMS

term 46	definiens 51
intension 47	intensional definition
extension 47	synonymous definition
class 47	operational definition 53
empty class 47	definition by genus and
increasing intension 48	difference 56
decreasing extension 48	extensional
decreasing intension 48	definition 56
increasing extension 48	ostensive definition 56
definition 51	enumerative definition 57
definiendum 51	definition by subclass 58

precising definition 64
theoretical definition 65
persuasive definition 67
cognitive meaning 79
emotive meaning 79
value claim 79
factual dispute 82
verbal dispute 83

Key Terms

Inconsistent statements: Two (or more) statements that do not have even one line on their respective truth tables where the main operators are true (but they can be false) at the same time.

Increasing extension: In a sequence of terms where each term after the first denotes a set of objects with more members than the previous term.

Increasing intension: In a sequence of terms where each term after the first connotes more attributes than the previous term.

Independent premises: Premises are indepen-

Instantial letter: The letter (either a variable or a constant) that is introduced by universal instantiaton or existential instantiation.

Instantiation: When instantiation is applied to a quantified statement, the quantifier is removed, and every variable that was bound by the quantifier is replaced by the same instantial letter.

Intension: The intension of a term is specified by listing the properties or attributes that the term connotes—in other words, its sense.

Intensional definition: Assigns a meaning to a term by listing the properties or attributes

M

Main operator: The operator that has in its range the largest component or components in a compound statement.

Major premise: The first premise of a categorical syllogism (it contains the major term).

Major term: The predicate of the conclusion of a categorical syllogism.

Material equivalence: A rule of inference (replacement rule).

Material implication: A rule of inference (replacement rule).

Glossary

STRATEGIES AND TACTICS

Strategy 1: Simplify and isolate
  Tactical Moves—Try using any of the following:
    A. *Modus ponens* (MP)
    B. *Modus tollens* (MT)
    C. *Disjunctive syllogism* (DS)

Strategy 2: Look for negation
  Tactical Moves—Try using any of the following:
    A. *Modus tollens* (MT)
    B. *Disjunctive syllogism* (DS)

Strategy 3: Look for conditionals
  Tactical Moves—Try using any of the following:
    A. *Modus ponens* (MP)
    B. *Modus tollens* (MT)
    C. *Hypothetical syllogism* (HS)

Strategy 4: Look at the conclusion
  Tactical Moves—Try anticipating what you need.
    Try working backward from the conclusion by imagining what the next to last line of the proof might be. Use this to help determine a short-term strategy to derive that line.

Reference Boxes

Summary

- Class: A group of objects.
- Categorical proposition: Relates two classes of objects.
- Subject term: The term that comes first in a standard-form categorical proposition.
- Predicate term: The term that comes second in a standard-form categorical proposition.
- A-proposition: Asserts that the entire subject class is included in the predicate class ("All S are P").
- I-proposition: Asserts that part of the subject class is included in the predicate class ("Some S are P").
- E-proposition: Asserts that the entire subject class is excluded from the predicate class ("No S are P").
- O-proposition: Asserts that part of the subject class is excluded from the predicate class ("Some S are not P").

Bulleted Chapter Summaries

The final step is the horseshoe:

R	S	P	R ⊃ (S v ~ P)
T	T	T	T T F
T	T	F	T T T
T	F	T	F F F
T	F	F	T T T
F	T	T	T T F
F	T	F	T T T
F	F	T	T F F
F	F	F	T T T

Constructing truth tables for compound propositions requires a step-by-step approach. It is best to be methodical and not try to do more than one thing at a time. First, calculate the number of lines needed. Second, place the T's and F's under the columns for all the simple propositions in the guide. Third, identify the main operator and the order of operations. Fourth, apply your knowledge of the five operators to fill in the truth values according to the order of operations. In the final step, fill in the truth values for the main operator.

Detailed guides help students learn to create "truth tables" and Venn diagrams.

Diagramming A-propositions

We can start by diagramming **A**-propositions. Suppose the major premise is "All P are M." Following Chapter 5, we need to shade the areas of P that are outside of M:

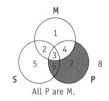
All P are M.

The S circle makes things look more complicated, but it does not change the basic principle. Since all the areas of P outside M must be shaded, we just need to shade both Areas 6 and 7.

Since the major premise must contain the major term and the middle term, the only other possible A-proposition for it is "All M are P." To diagram this, we need to shade all the areas of M that are outside of P:

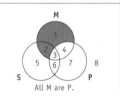
All M are P.

Since all the areas of M outside P must be shaded, we need to shade both Areas 1 and 2. The same principle applies to the minor premise. In fact, there are only two more possible diagrams to consider for **A**-propositions. The minor premise can be either "All S are M" or "All M are S."

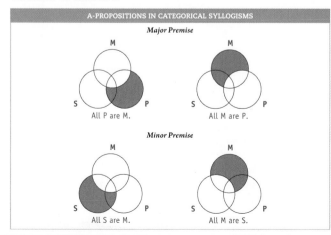

A-PROPOSITIONS IN CATEGORICAL SYLLOGISMS
Major Premise
All P are M.   All M are P.
Minor Premise
All S are M.   All M are S.

A rich set of supplemental resources is available to support teaching and learning in this course.

The Instructor's Manual with Computerized Test Bank on CD includes:

- Solutions to all exercises in the book, enhanced by explanations and answers that elucidate the details of the correct answers

- A summary of each chapter

- Key Terms

- A customizable Computerized Test Bank—with multiple-choice, true/false, and fill-in-the-blank questions—that allows instructors to give **exams or homework problems that can be auto-graded**

- A traditional "pencil-and-paper" Test Bank and answer key containing the same questions as the Computerized Test Bank

- PowerPoint-based lecture outlines

The Instructor's Manual with Computerized Test Bank and the traditional Test Bank are also available in printed format.

The Companion Website offers:

Instructor Resources (password-protected):

- A downloadable version of the Instructor's Manual (except for the Test Bank and the exercise solutions)

- PowerPoint-based lecture outlines

Student Resources

- Brief chapter summaries

- Interactive Flash Cards with key terms and definitions

- Web Links and other media resources

- Practice quizzes with answers and explanations (includes questions answered in the book *and* new, original questions)

The Learning Management System Cartridges include, in a fully downloadable format:

- Instructor's Manual and Computerized Test Bank (**exams and homework problems can be auto-graded**)

- Student material from the companion website

The Best Book . . . at the Best Price

Oxford University Press, a not-for-profit organization in the U.S., produces high-quality scholarship at the best possible prices for your students. We invite you to compare the price and quality of our full-color comprehensive book to other textbooks published for your course.
At only **$89.95,** *Logic*, Second Edition, is the best value of any full-color text on the market.

* Price as of August 1, 2012 and subject to change.

Logic

Logic

Second Edition

Stan Baronett

New York   Oxford
Oxford University Press

Oxford University Press is a department of the University of Oxford. It furthers the University's
objective of excellence in research, scholarship, and education by publishing worldwide.

Oxford New York
Auckland Cape Town Dar es Salaam Hong Kong Karachi
Kuala Lumpur Madrid Melbourne Mexico City Nairobi
New Delhi Shanghai Taipei Toronto

With offices in
Argentina Austria Brazil Chile Czech Republic France Greece
Guatemala Hungary Italy Japan Poland Portugal Singapore
South Korea Switzerland Thailand Turkey Ukraine Vietnam

For titles covered by Section 112 of the US Higher Education Opportunity
Act, please visit www.oup.com/us/he for the latest information about
pricing and alternate formats.

Published by Oxford University Press.
198 Madison Avenue, New York, New York 10016
http://www.oup.com

Library of Congress Cataloging-in-Publication Data

Baronett, Stan.
    Logic / by Stan Baronett. — Second Edition.
        pages cm.
    Includes index.
    ISBN 978-0-19-984631-3
    1. Logic. I. Title.
    BC108.B26 2012
    160—dc23
                              2012014438

Printing number: 9 8 7 6 5 4 3 2 1

Printed in the United States of America
on acid-free paper

Brief Contents

Contents

Part III Formal Logic

Part IV Inductive Logic

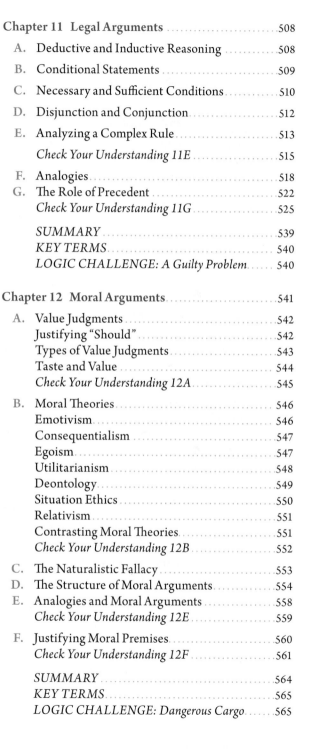

Preface

Today's logic students want to see the relevance of logic to their lives. They need motivation to read a logic textbook and do the exercises. Logic and critical thinking instructors want their students to read the textbook and to practice the skills being taught. They want their students to come away with the ability to recognize and evaluate arguments, an understanding of formal and informal logic, and a lasting sense of **why they matter**. These concerns meet head-on in the classroom. This textbook is designed to help alleviate these concerns.

THE BACKSTORY

The driving force behind writing this book was the belief that **logic can be made relevant, interesting, and accessible to today's students**, without sacrificing the coverage that instructors demand and expect. An introduction to logic is often a student's only exposure to rigorous thinking and symbolism. It should prepare them for reasoning in their lives and careers. It must balance careful coverage of abstract reasoning with **clear, accessible explanations and vivid everyday examples**.

This book was written to meet all those challenges. **Relevant examples provide a bridge between formal reasoning and practical applications of logic, thereby connecting logic to student lives and future careers.** Each chapter opens with a discussion of an everyday example, often taken directly from contemporary events, to pose the problem and set the narrative tone. This provides an immediate connection between logic and real-world issues, motivating the need for logic as a tool to help with the deluge of information available today.

The challenge of any introduction to logic textbook is to connect logic to students' lives. Yet existing texts can and should do more to reinforce and improve the basic skills of reasoning we all rely on in daily life. Relevant, real-life examples are essential to making logic accessible to students, especially if they can mesh seamlessly with the technical material. To accomplish this, quotes and passages from modern and classic sources illustrate the relevance of logic through some of the perennial problems that impact everyone's lives. Examples from the workplace, careers, sports, politics, movies, music, TV, novels, new inventions, gadgets, cell phones, transportation, newspapers, magazines, computers, speeches, science, religion, superstition, gambling, drugs, war, abortion, euthanasia, capital punishment, the role of government, taxes, military spending, and unemployment are used **to show how arguments, and thus the role of logic, can be found in nearly every aspect of life.** The examples were chosen to be interesting, thought-provoking, and relevant to students. The voice of the book strives to engage students by connecting logic to their lives.

AN INCLUSIVE TEXT

The fifteen chapters are designed to provide a comprehensive logic textbook, but also one that can be tailored to individual courses and their needs. To that end, several topics that were previously squeezed into one chapter or an appendix in the first edition have been given their own chapters, each with additional explanations and examples to facilitate student comprehension. The additional explanations enable students to gain a deeper understanding of the logical concepts, and the new examples help flesh out the different settings in which the logical apparatus can be found.

The result is a full five chapters on deductive logic, but also a uniquely applied six-chapter part on inductive logic. Here separate chapters on analogical arguments, legal arguments, moral arguments, statistical arguments, scientific arguments, and analyzing a long essay get students to apply the logical skills learned in the earlier parts of the book. They show students that the logical skills they are learning do in fact have practical, real-world application. The new material also provides more experience to help students when they do the exercise sets.

These additions also provide far greater flexibility to instructors. Chapters and many sections can easily be skipped in lecture, without loss of continuity. In addition, those wishing a briefer text can choose a text tailored to their course. They may choose to emphasize or omit certain chapters on formal logic or critical reasoning. They may choose a selection of the concluding applied chapters to reflect their and their students' interest.

ALTERNATE AND CUSTOM EDITIONS

Because every course and professor is unique, Alternate and Custom Editions are available for this book. Each Alternate Edition comes in full color, with answers to problems, a full glossary, and an index. The books are in stock and available for ordering. Please see the ISBN information below:

Logic: Concise Edition
Chapters 1, 3, 4, 5, 6, 7, 8
Order using ISBN: 978-0-19-994129-2

Logic: An Emphasis on Critical Thinking and Informal Logic
Chapters 1, 2, 3, 4, 10, 11, 12, 13 A–E, 14, 15
Order using ISBN: 978-0-19-994128-5

Logic: An Emphasis on Formal Logic
Chapters 1, 5, 6, 7, 8, 9
Order using ISBN: 978-0-19-994126-1

Logic: With Diagramming in Chapter 4 Informal Fallacies
Full text
Order using ISBN: 978-0-19-997081-0

It is also possible to create a customized textbook by choosing the specific chapters necessary for a course. Please contact your Oxford University Press Sales Representative or call 800.280.0280 for details.

For more information on Alternate and Custom Editions, please see the insert in the Instructor's Edition of this book.

NEW TO THIS EDITION

Great care has been given to retain the style of presentation and the voice of the first edition, since considerable evidence exists that students have responded well to the manner of presentation. Yet this is a major revision, and the changes are wide and deep. For example, the original book did not provide a comprehensive treatment of several topics that many instructors need. The revision addresses that specific problem, but there are many other equally important improvements in this edition. The substantive changes are not solely in the direction of greater rigor, but enhance this text's overriding goal of **relevance, accessibility, and student interest** as well. They include the adoption of more standard terminology, clearer and more accurate definitions of terms and concepts, three completely new chapters, more thorough explanations, added examples from real-life sources, and over 1000 new exercises, bringing the total to nearly 2600 exercises.

- Based on instructors' and reviewers' suggestions, Chapter 1, *What Logic Studies*, now concentrates on a few core topics such as statements and arguments, argument recognition, truth and logic, deductive and inductive arguments, and the role of counterexamples. In addition, a focused discussion of logical necessity for understanding validity is offered.
- The material in Chapter 2, *Language Matters*, has been given its own chapter and has been extensively rewritten. Its position in the book falls in line with the order of presentation by many instructors. The discussion of types of definitions is now more comprehensive and is connected directly to real-life examples. New discussions of cognitive and emotive meaning, as well as factual and verbal disputes, flesh out the practical applications of the topics. Chapter 3, *Diagrams and Analysis*, now has complementary topics, such as paraphrasing and diagramming arguments. Since paraphrasing a statement, argument, or passage sometimes requires altering words or phrases, it is a skill that can benefit from following on the heels of a study of definitions. Also, diagramming some arguments often requires paraphrasing, so it complements the overall discussion. Finally, a discussion of incomplete arguments and rhetorical language rounds out the chapter. Chapter 4, *Informal Fallacies*, contains many new explanations and additional examples. The new explanations help clarify the fallacies and provide information to assist in understanding the subtle distinctions that occur between the various subsets of fallacies. The additional examples illustrate the many settings in which informal fallacies occur. The examples illustrate the

analysis of the specific fallacy involved and the effect that the fallacy has on our understanding of arguments. As a result, the range of fallacies discussed once again exceeds that in any other text—as does their application to everyday life and critical reasoning.

- Chapter 5, *Categorical Propositions*, and Chapter 6, *Categorical Syllogisms*, originally appeared as an appendix in the first edition. The display of Venn diagrams has been redesigned to provide a clearer model for students to follow. The two chapters combine to provide detailed coverage of both Aristotelian and Boolean interpretations of categorical propositions and syllogisms. Chapter 5 generates the reasoning behind the traditional and modern squares of opposition. Existential import is introduced and explained in Chapter 5 and additional discussion in included Chapter 6, where Venn diagrams and rules for determining the validity of categorical syllogisms are presented. Chapter 7, *Propositional Logic*, now presents a simplified way to construct truth tables. The truth table model provides the basic tools that students need to build and analyze truth tables. Students are able to grasp quickly the method and to begin applying it to the analysis of statements and arguments. Students are also given ample opportunity to translate ordinary language statements and arguments using logical operators. Finally, a section on indirect truth tables is provided for those instructors who want to present a shorter method. The rules of inference presented in Chapter 8, *Natural Deduction*, now follow the order found in most textbooks. The rules are fully explained, and examples are presented of some incorrect moves often made by students. Emphasis has been placed on translating ordinary language using symbols in order for students to have additional experience with logical operators. To this end, many new examples have been included, and exercise sets now contain more proofs of varying lengths for student practice. In addition, conditional proof and indirect proof procedures are presented. Chapter 9, *Predicate Logic*, has been greatly expanded. The chapter now begins with an extended discussion of translating ordinary language and it provides numerous exercises. The rules of inference have been rewritten to provide more clarity, and conditional proof and indirect proof methods are applied. Methods for proving invalidity include the counterexample method and the finite universe method. Finally, two new sections are included—on relational predicates and identity.
- In Chapter 10, *Analogical Arguments,* the discussion of analogies is given its own chapter with added discussion and examples. A novel way of diagramming analogical arguments is presented, allowing students to visually explore how these kinds of arguments work. Chapter 11, *Legal Arguments*, and Chapter 12, *Moral Arguments*, are completely new. Both chapters introduce their respective topics by way of skills already learned in earlier chapters, such as analogies and the use of logical operators. This direct and sustained application of logical skills provides students with another view of the connection between logic, reasoning, and real-world issues. Chapter 13, *Statistical Arguments and Probability,* has been

given its own chapter. It has been substantially expanded to include presentations of statistical averages and an extensive discussion of standard deviation. Many real-life examples of statistical reasoning are illustrated along with specific criteria that can be applied directly to the appraisal of statistical arguments. New illustrations have been designed to facilitate student understanding. The chapter also contains the fundamentals of probability theory. This information can be useful to those instructors who like to introduce some probability calculation techniques to their students, depending on the needs of the course. Chapter 14, *Causality and Scientific Arguments*, has been given its own chapter. It provides an introduction to causality by providing descriptions, explanations, and applications of five of Mill's methods for investigating cause-effect relationships. Many unique illustrations have been created to enrich student comprehension of these topics. In addition, this chapter now includes discussions of two new topics—*inference to the best explanation* and *science and superstition*. Students are provided the tools needed to analyze scientific reasoning and to recognize its importance and relevance to modern life. Also, students can gain an appreciation of the difference between scientific and superstitious thinking, and how to apply consistent methods of analysis to hypotheses and theories.

- Chapter 15, *Analyzing a Long Essay*, is new, to provide students with a long, journal-type paper for analysis. The essay concerns Semmelweis's discovery of the cause of childbed fever. The story is interesting in its own right, so students are apt to read it on that level first. Afterward, they can apply the skills learned throughout the book in order to experience an in-depth analysis of an extended piece of reasoning. For example, the essay contains numerous examples of analogical, statistical, and cause-effect arguments. It also touches on some legal and ethical issues which can be subjected to critical appraisal.

SPECIAL FEATURES

The features that instructors found most useful in the first edition have been retained, and some new features have been added:

- Each chapter opens with a **preview**, beginning with real-life examples and outlining the questions to be addressed. It thus serves both as motivation and overview, and wherever possible it explicitly bridges both formal and informal logic to real life. For example, Chapter 1 starts with the deluge of information facing students today, to show the very need for a course in logic or critical thinking.
- **Marginal definitions of key terms** are provided for quick reference. Of course, key terms appear in boldface when they are first introduced.
- The use of **reference boxes** has been expanded, since they have proven useful to both students and instructors. They capture material that is spread out over a number of pages in one place for easy reference.

- *Profiles in Logic* are short sketches of logicians, philosophers, mathematicians, and others associated with logic. The men and women in these sketches range in time from Aristotle and the Stoics to Christine Ladd-Franklin, the early ENIAC programmers, and others in the past century.
- **Bulleted summaries** are provided at the end of each chapter, as well as a list of key terms.
- The much **expanded exercise sets** have been renamed *Check Your Understanding*. This emphasizes to students that they should use these sections to see what they have learned and where they need to do more work.
- The *Check Your Understanding* sets include a **solution to the first problem in each set**. Explanations are also provided where additional clarity is needed. This provides a model for students to follow, so they can see what is expected of their answers. An additional 25% of the exercises have answers provided at the back of the book.
- End-of-chapter *Logic Challenge* problems are included for each chapter. These are the kind of puzzles—like the problem of the hats, the truth teller and the liar, and the scale and the coins—that have long kept people thinking. They end chapters on a fun note, not to mention with a reminder that the challenges of logic are always lurking in plain English.
- A **full glossary and index** are placed at the end of the book.

STUDENT AND INSTRUCTOR RESOURCES

A rich set of supplemental resources is available to support teaching and learning in this course. These supplements include an **Instructor's Manual with Computerized Test Bank on CD**, downloadable **Learning Management System Cartridges**, and a **Companion Website** for instructors and students available online at www.oup.com/us/baronett.

The **Instructor's Manual with Computerized Test Bank on CD** includes:

- Solutions to all exercises in the book
- Summary of each chapter
- Key Terms
- A customizable Computerized Test Bank with multiple-choice, true/false, and fill-in-the-blank questions to allow instructors to give both Exams and Homework Problems. If you are interested in receiving auto-graded feedback on these questions, please contact Wimba customer service at 706-802-1713.
- A traditional Test Bank and answer key for instructors to give "pencil-and-paper" Exams and Homework using the identical questions that are found on the Computerized Test Bank
- **The Instructor's Manual with Computerized Test Bank and the traditional Test Bank are also available in printed format**
- PowerPoint-based lecture outlines

The **Learning Management System Cartridges** include:

- Instructor's Manual and Computerized Test Bank, as well as student-material from the companion website, in a fully downloadable format for instructors using a learning management system in their courses. For more information on this, please contact your Oxford University Press Sales Representative at 1-800-280-0280.

The **Companion Website** includes the following material:

- Introduction to Book/Authors
  - Table of Contents
  - About the Authors
- Instructor's Resources (password protected)
  - A downloadable version of the Instructor's Manual (excepting the Test Bank and the Solutions to exercises, which are only available in CD or printed format)
  - PowerPoint-based lecture outlines
- Student Resources
  - Brief Summary of each chapter
  - Interactive Flash Cards with key terms and definitions
  - WebLinks and other media resources
  - Practice quizzes with answers and explanations

ACKNOWLEDGMENTS

For their very helpful suggestions throughout the writing process, I would like to thank the following reviewers:

- Guy Axtell, Radford University
- Joshua Beattie, California State University–East Bay
- Bernardo Cantens, Moravian College
- Darron Chapman, University of Louisville
- William Devlin, Bridgewater State University
- David Lyle Dyas, Los Angeles Mission College
- David Elliot, University of Regina
- Thompson M. Faller, University of Portland
- Matthew Frise, University of Rochester
- Dimitria Electra Gatzia, University of Akron
- Cara Gillis, Pierce College
- Matthew W. Hallgarth, Tarleton State University
- Anthony Hanson, De Anza College
- Merle Harton, Jr., Everglades University
- Jeremy D. Hovda, Minneapolis Community & Technical College
- Debby D. Hutchins, Gonzaga University

- Will Heusser, Cypress College
- Daniel Jacobson, University of Michigan–Ann Arbor
- William S. Jamison, University of Alaska Anchorage
- Benjamin C. Jantzen, Virginia Polytechnic Institute & State University
- William M. Kallfelz, Mississippi State University
- Lory Lemke, University of Minnesota–Morris
- David Liebesman, Boston University
- Ian D. MacKinnon, University of Akron
- Erik Meade, Southern Illinois University Edwardsville
- James Moore, Georgia Perimeter College
- Allyson Mount, Keene State College
- Joseph B. Onyango Okello, Asbury Theological Seminary
- Greg Rich, Fayetteville State University
- Linda Rollin, Colorado State University
- Frank X. Ryan, Kent State University
- Eric Saidel, George Washington University
- Kelly Salsbery, Stephen F. Austin State University
- Stephanie Semler, Virginia Polytechnic Institute & State University
- Robert Shanab, University of Nevada–Las Vegas
- David Shier, Washington State University
- Aeon J. Skoble, Bridgewater State University
- Joshua Smith, Central Michigan University
- Paula Smithka, University of Southern Mississippi
- Deborah Hansen Soles, Wichita State University
- James S. Taylor, The College of New Jersey
- Joia Lewis Turner, St. Paul College
- Patricia Turrisi, University of North Carolina–Wilmington
- Mark C. Vopat, Youngstown State University
- Mia Wood, Pierce College
- Kiriake Xerohemona, Florida International University
- Jeffrey Zents, South Texas College

Many thanks also to the staff at Oxford University Press, Robert Miller, executive editor; John Haber, development editor; Thom Holmes, development editor; Kristin Maffei, associate editor; Barbara Mathieu, production editor, and Kim Howie, senior designer, for their work on the book. The *Profiles in Logic* portraits were drawn by Andrew McAfee.

Part I

Chapter 1

What Logic Studies

We live in the Information Age. The Internet provides access to millions of books and articles and thousands of newspapers from around the world. Personal websites, blogs, and chat rooms contain instant commentary about events around the world. Cell phones allow mobile access to breaking stories and worldwide communication. Cable television stations provide local news and world news 24 hours a day. Some of the information is simply entertaining. However, we also find stories that are important to our lives. In fact, they may do more than just supply facts. They may make us want to nod in agreement or to express disbelief.

For example, suppose you read the following:

> The Senate recently held hearings on for-profit colleges, investigating charges that the schools rake in federal loan money, while failing to ad-equately educate students. Critics point to deceptive sales tactics, fraudu-lent loan applications, high drop-out rates, and even higher tuitions. In response, the Department of Education has proposed a "gainful employment" rule, which would cut financing to for-profit colleges that graduate (or fail) students with thousands of dollars of debt and no prospect of salaries high enough to pay them off.   Jeremy Dehn, "Degrees of Debt"

If the information in this passage is accurate, then government decisions might affect thousands of people. On reading this, you would probably search for related material, to determine whether the information is correct. However, you would be concerned for more than just accuracy. You would also be asking what it means for you. Are the critics correct? Are the new rules justified, and do they address the criticism? You are seeing competing claims.

Other types of information make claims of their own. For example, you might read the following:

> Although there are tens of thousands of applications written for Windows Mobile, they won't work on Windows Phone 7; so Microsoft has to recruit a whole new base of developers.
>
> "Microsoft Bets Big on New Phone Software," Newsystocks.com

The information in this passage not only concerns a different topic; it also contains an argument. An **argument** is a group of statements of which one (the conclusion) is claimed to follow from the others (the premises). A **statement** is a sentence that is either true or false. **Premises** contain information intended to provide support or reasons to believe a **conclusion**, the statement that is claimed to follow from the premises. In the example just mentioned, the conclusion is "Microsoft has to recruit a whole new base of developers." The premises are "there are tens of thousands of applications written for Windows Mobile" and "they won't work on Windows Phone 7."

It is quite common for people to concentrate on the individual statements in an argument and investigate whether they are true or false. Since everyone wants to know things about the world, the actual truth or falsity of statements is important; but it is not the only important question. Equally important is the question, "Assuming the premises are true, do they support the conclusion?" This question offers a glimpse of the role of **logic**, which is the study of reasoning.

Arguments can be simple, but they can also be quite complex. In the argument regarding Microsoft, the premises and conclusion are not difficult to recognize. However, this is not always the case. Here is an example of a complex piece of reasoning taken from the novel *Catch-22*, by Joseph Heller:

> There was only one catch and that was Catch-22, which specified that a concern for one's own safety in the face of dangers that were real and immediate was the process of a rational mind. Orr was crazy and could be grounded. All he had to do was ask; and as soon as he did, he would no longer be crazy and would have to fly more missions. Orr would be crazy to fly more missions and sane if he didn't, but if he was sane he had to fly them. If he flew them he was crazy and didn't have to; but if he didn't want to he was sane and had to. Yossarian was moved very deeply by the absolute simplicity of this clause of Catch-22 and let out a respectful whistle.

This passage cleverly illustrates complex reasoning. Once you know how to tease apart its premises and conclusions, you may find yourself as impressed as Yossarian.

Logic investigates the level of correctness of the reasoning found in arguments. There are many times when we need to evaluate information we are receiving. Although everyone reasons, few stop to think about reasoning. Logic provides the skills needed to identify other people's arguments, putting you in a position to offer coherent and precise analysis of those arguments. Learning logical skills enables you to subject your own arguments to that same analysis, thereby anticipating challenges and criticism. Logic can help, and this book will show you how. It introduces the tools of logical analysis and presents practical applications of logic.

Argument A group of statements of which one (the conclusion) is claimed to follow from the others (the premises).

Statement A sentence that is either true or false.

Premise The information intended to provide support for a conclusion.

Conclusion The statement that is claimed to follow from the premises of an argument.

Logic The study of reasoning.

A. STATEMENTS AND ARGUMENTS

The terms "sentence," "statement," and "proposition" are related, but distinct. Logicians use the term "statement" to refer to a specific kind of sentence in a particular language—a *declarative sentence*. As the name indicates, we declare, assert, claim, or affirm that something is the case. In this sense every statement is either true or false, and these two possibilities are called **truth values**. For example, the statement "Water freezes at 32° F." is in English, and it is true. Translated into other languages we get the following statements:

Truth value Every statement is either true or false; these two possibilities are called *truth values*.

El agua se congela a 32° F. (Spanish)
Wasser gefriert bei 32° F. (German)
Pānī 32 ḍigrī ēpha mēṁ freezes. (Hindi)
L'eau gèle à 32° F. (French)

Nu'ó'c đóng băng ó' 32° F. (Vietnamese)
Tubig freezes sa 32° F. (Filipino)
Air membeku pada 32° F. (Malay)
Maji hunganda yapitapo nyuzi joto 32° F. (Swahili)

The foregoing list contains eight *sentences* in eight different languages that certainly look different and, if spoken, definitely sound different. Since the eight sentences are all declarative sentences, they are all *statements*. However, the eight statements all *make the same claim*, and it is in that sense that logicians use the term "proposition." In other words, a **proposition** is the information content imparted by a statement, or simply put, its meaning. Since each of the eight statements makes the same claim, they all have the same truth value.

Proposition The information content imparted by a statement, or, simply put, its meaning.

It is not necessary for us to know the truth value of a proposition to recognize that it must be either true or false. For example, the statement "There is a diamond ring buried fifty feet under my house" is either true or false regardless of whether or not anyone ever looks there. The same holds for the statement "Abraham Lincoln sneezed four times on his 21st birthday." We can accept that this statement must be true or false, although it is unlikely that we will ever know its truth value.

Many perfectly acceptable sentences do not have a truth value. Here are some examples:

What time is it? (Question)
Clean your room now. (Command)
Please clean your room. (Request)
Let's do lunch tomorrow. (Proposal)

None of these sentences make an assertion or claim, so they are neither true nor false. Quite often we must rely on context to decide whether a sentence is being used as a statement. For example, the opening sentence of a poem by Robert Burns is "My love is like a red, red rose." Given its poetic use, we should not interpret Burns as making a claim that is either true or false.

Inference A term used by logicians to refer to the reasoning process that is expressed by an argument.

The term **inference** is used by logicians to refer to the *reasoning process* that is expressed by an argument. The act or process of reasoning from premises to a conclusion is sometimes referred to as *drawing an inference*. Arguments are created in order to establish support for a claim, and the premises are supposed to provide good reasons for accepting the conclusion.

Arguments can be found in almost every part of human activity. Of course, when we use the term in a logical setting, we do not mean the kinds of verbal disputes that can get highly emotional and even end up with acts of violence. Logical analysis of arguments relies on rational use of language and reasoning skills. It is organized, is well thought-out, and appeals to relevant reasons and justification. Unfortunately, many arguments fail in these respects, like the following quote:

> Most of the arguments to which I am party fall somewhat short of being impressive, owing to the fact that neither I nor my opponent knows what we are talking about.   Robert Benchley, *After 1903—What?*

Of course, arguments arise where we expect people to know what they are talking about, as in a legal or a medical situation. Car mechanics, plumbers, carpenters, electricians, engineers, computer programmers, accountants, nurses, office workers, and managers all use arguments regularly. Arguments are used to convince others to buy, repair, or upgrade a product. Arguments can be found in political debates, and in ethical and moral disputes. Although it is common to witness the angry, emotional type of arguments when fans discuss sports, nevertheless there can be logical arguments even in that setting. For example, if fans use statistics and historical data to support their position, then they can create rational and logical arguments.

B. RECOGNIZING ARGUMENTS

Studying logic enables us to master many important skills. It helps us to recognize and identify arguments correctly, in either written or oral form. In real life, arguments are rarely found in nice neat packages. We often have to dig them out, like prospectors searching for nuggets of gold. We might find the premises and conclusions occurring in any order in an argument. In addition, we often encounter incomplete arguments, so we must be able to recognize arguments even if they are not completely spelled out.

An argument offers reasons in support of a conclusion. However, not all groups of sentences are arguments. A series of sentences that express *beliefs* or *opinions*, by themselves, do not constitute an argument. For example, suppose someone says the following:

> I wish the government would do something about the unemployment situation. It makes me angry to see some CEOs of large corporations getting huge bonuses while at the same time the corporation is laying off workers.

The sentences certainly let us know how the person feels about issues. However, none of the sentences seem to offer any support for a conclusion. In addition, none of the sentences seem to be a conclusion. Of course it sometimes happens that opinions are meant to act as premises of an argument. For example, suppose someone says the following:

> I don't like movies that rely on computer-generated graphics to take the place of intelligent dialogue, interesting characters, and an intricate plot. After watching the ads on TV, I have the feeling that the new movie *Bad Blood and Good Vibes* is not very good. Therefore, I predict that it will not win any Academy Awards.

Although the first two sentences express opinions and feelings, they are offered as reasons in support of the last sentence, which is the conclusion.

Many newspaper articles are good sources of information. They are often written specifically to answer the five key points of reporting: *who, what, where, when,* and *why*. A well-written article can provide details and key points, but it need not conclude anything. Reporters sometimes simply provide information, with no intention of giving reasons in support of a conclusion. On the other hand, the editorial page of newspapers can be a good source of arguments. Editorials generally provide extensive information as *premises*, meant to support a position strongly held by the editor. The editorial page usually contains letters to the editor. Although these pieces are often highly emotional responses to social problems, some of them do contain arguments.

When people write or speak, it is not always clear that they are trying to conclude something. Written material can be quite difficult to analyze because we are generally not in a position to question the author for clarification. We cannot always be certain that what we think are the conclusion and premises are, in fact, what the author had intended. Yet we can, and should, attempt to provide justification for our interpretation. If we are speaking with someone, at least we can stop the conversation and seek clarification. When we share a common language and have similar sets of background knowledge and experiences, then we can recognize arguments when they occur by calling on those shared properties.

Since every argument must have a conclusion, it sometimes helps if we try to identify that first. Our shared language provides **conclusion indicators**—useful words that nearly all of us call on when we wish to conclude something. For example, we often use the word "therefore" to indicate our main point. Here are other words or phrases to help recognize a conclusion:

Conclusion indicator
Words and phrases that indicate the presence of a conclusion (the statement claimed to follow from premises).

CONCLUSION INDICATORS

Therefore	Consequently	It proves that
Thus	In conclusion	Suggests that
So	It follows that	Implies that
Hence	We can infer that	We can conclude that

We can see them at work in the following examples:

1. Salaries are up. Unemployment is down. People are happy. *Therefore,* reelect me.

2. Salaries are down. Unemployment is up. People are not happy. *Consequently,* we should throw the governor out of office.
3. The book was boring. The movie based on the book was boring. The author of both the book and the screenplay is Horst Patoot. *It follows that* he is a lousy writer.

Although conclusion indicators can help us to identify arguments, they are not always available to us, as in this example:

> We should boycott that company. They have been found guilty of producing widgets that they knew were faulty, and that caused numerous injuries.

If you are not sure which sentence is the conclusion, you can simply place the word "therefore" in front of each of them to see which works best. In this case, the second sentence seems to be the reason offered for why we should boycott the company: *because* the company has been found guilty, *therefore* we should boycott it.

In addition to identifying the conclusion, our analysis also helped reveal the premise. As here with "because" in this example, a **premise indicator** distinguishes the premise from the conclusion. Here are other words or phrases that can help in recognizing an argument:

Premise indicator Words and phrases that help us recognize arguments by indicating the presence of premises (statements being offered in support of a conclusion).

PREMISE INDICATORS

Because	Assuming that	As indicated by
Since	As shown by	The fact that
Given that	For the reason(s) that	It follows from

When premise and conclusion indicators are not present, you can still apply some simple strategies to identify the parts of an argument. First, to help locate the conclusion, try placing the word "therefore" in front of the statements. Second, to help locate the premise or premises, try placing the word "because" in front of the statements.

In some cases you will have to read a passage a few times in order determine whether an argument is presented. You should keep a few basic ideas in mind as you read. For one thing, at least one of the statements in the passage has to provide a reason or evidence for some other statement; in other words, it must be a premise. Second, there must be a claim that the premise supports or implies a conclusion. If a passage *expresses a reasoning process*—that the conclusion follows from the premises—then we say that it makes an **inferential claim**. The inferential claim is an objective feature of an argument, and it can be *explicit* or *implicit*. Explicit inferential claims can often be identified by the premise and conclusion indicator words and phrases discussed earlier (e.g., "because" and "therefore"). On the other hand, while implicit inferential claims do not have explicit indicator words, they still contain an inferential relationship between the premises and the conclusion. In these cases we follow the advice given earlier by supplying the words "therefore" or "because" to the statements in the passage in order to help reveal the inferential claim that is implicit.

Inferential claim If a passage expresses a reasoning process—that the conclusion follows from the premises—then we say that it makes an inferential claim.

Of course determining whether a given passage in ordinary language contains an argument takes practice. Like all tools, our strategies and indicator words take practice in order to use them correctly. Even the presence of an indicator word may not by itself mean that the passage contains an argument:

> He climbed the fence, threaded his stealthy way through the plants, till he stood under that window; he looked up at it long, and with emotion; then he laid him down on the ground under it, disposing himself upon his back, with his hands clasped upon his breast and holding his poor wilted flower. And *thus* he would die—out in the cold world, with no shelter over his homeless head, no friendly hand to wipe the death-damps from his brow, no loving face to bend pityingly over him when the great agony came.   Mark Twain, *Tom Sawyer*

In this passage the word "thus" (my italics) is not being used as a conclusion indicator. It simply indicates the manner in which the character would die. Here is another example:

> The modern cell phone was invented during the 1970s by an engineer working for the Motorola Corporation. However, the communications technologies that made cell phones possible had been under development *since* the late 1940s. Eventually, the ability to make and receive calls with a mobile telephone handset revolutionized the world of personal communications, with the technology still evolving in the early 21st century.
>
> Tom Streissguth, "How Were Cell Phones Invented?"

Although the passage contains the word "since" (my italics), it is not being used as a premise indicator. Instead, it is used to indicate the period during which communications technology was developing.

We pointed out that *beliefs* or *opinions* by themselves do not constitute an argument. For example, the following passage simply *reports* information, without expressing a reasoning process:

> Approximately 2,000 red-winged blackbirds fell dead from the sky in a central Arkansas town. The birds had fallen over a 1-mile area, and an aerial survey indicated that no other dead birds were found outside of that area. Wildlife officials will examine the birds to try to figure out what caused the mysterious event.
>
> "Why Did 2,000 Dead Birds Fall From Sky?" Associated Press

The statements in the passage provide information about an ongoing situation, but no conclusion is put forward, and none of the statements are offered as premises.

A noninferential passage can occur when someone provides *advice* or words of wisdom. Someone may recommend that you act in a certain way, or someone may give you advice to help you make a decision. Yet if no evidence is presented to support the advice, then no inferential claim is made. Here are a few simple examples:

> In three words I can sum up everything I've learned about life: it goes on.
>
> Robert Frost, as quoted in *The Harper Book of Quotations* by Robert I. Fitzhenry

> People spend a lifetime searching for happiness; looking for peace. They chase idle dreams, addictions, religions, even other people, hoping to fill the emptiness that plagues them. The irony is the only place they ever needed to search was within.   Ramona L. Anderson, as quoted in *Wisdom for the Soul* by Larry Chang

The passages may influence our thinking or get us to reevaluate our beliefs, but they are noninferential. The same applies to *warnings*, a special kind of advice that cautions us to avoid certain situations:

- Dangerous currents. No lifeguard on duty.
- All items left unattended will be removed.
- Unauthorized cars will be towed at owner's expense.

The truth value of these statements can be open to investigation, but there is no argument. No evidence is provided to support the statements, so the warnings, however important they may be, are not inferential.

Sometimes a passage contains *unsupported* or *loosely associated statements* that elaborate on a topic but do not make an inferential claim:

> Coaching takes time, it takes involvement, it takes understanding and patience.
> Byron and Catherine Pulsifer, "Challenges in Adopting a Coaching Style"

> Our ability to respect others is the true mark of our humanity. Respect for other people is the essence of human rights.   Daisaku Ikeda, "Words of Wisdom"

The passages lack an inferential claim. The statements in the passage may elaborate a point, but they do not support a conclusion.

Some passages contain information that illustrates how something is done, or what something means, or even how to do a calculation. An *illustration* may be informative without making an inferential claim:

> To lose one pound of fat, you must burn approximately 3500 calories over and above what you already burn doing daily activities. That sounds like a lot of calories and you certainly wouldn't want to try to burn 3500 calories in one day. However, by taking it step-by-step, you can determine just what you need to do each day to burn or cut out those extra calories.
> Paige Waehner, "How to Lose Weight: The Basics of Weight Loss"

The passage provides information about calories, fat, and weight loss. It illustrates what is required in order to lose one pound of fat, but it does not make an inferential claim. For another example, the definition of a technical term:

> In order to measure the performance of one investment relative to another you can calculate the "Return on Investment (ROI)." Quite simply, *ROI* is based on returns over a certain time period (e.g., one year) and it is expressed as a percentage. Here's an example that illustrates how to perform the calculation: A 25% annual ROI would mean that a $100 investment returns $25 in one year. Thus, in one year the total investment becomes $125.
> "How to Calculate a Return on an Investment," eHow, Inc.

The passage defines "Return on Investment" and illustrates how to do a simple calculation. However, even though the word "thus" occurs at the beginning of the last statement, it is not a conclusion indicator in this context.

A passage might combine several of the things we have been describing—a report, an illustration, and an example—making the decision to interpret it as an argument a bit more challenging. Let's look at a long passage:

> All life on Earth—from microbes to elephants and us—requires the element phosphorus as one of its six components. But now researchers have discovered a bacterium that appears to have replaced that life-enabling phosphorus with its toxic cousin arsenic, raising new and provocative questions about the origins and nature of life. News of the discovery caused a scientific commotion this week, including calls to NASA from the White House asking whether a second line of earthly life has been found. A NASA press conference Thursday and an accompanying article in the journal *Science* said the answer is "no." But the discovery opens the door to that possibility and to the related existence of a theorized "shadow biosphere" on Earth—life evolved from a different common ancestor from all we've known so far.
>
> Marc Kaufman, "Bacteria Stir Debate About 'Shadow Biosphere'"

The passage provides information about the chemical basis used for defining "all life on Earth." It then goes on to report some interesting findings regarding a living organism that apparently does not fit the usual definition. The passage reports that the scientific community at large does not think that the discovery by itself shows that a second line of earthly life has been found. However, the passage ends by noting the possibility of a "shadow biosphere" on Earth. This can be the basis for interpreting the passage as expressing an implicit inferential claim.

There is one more topic regarding noninferential passages that needs to be explored—the role of *explanations*. That discussion will be presented in the next section.

CHECK YOUR UNDERSTANDING 1B.1

Pick out the premises and conclusions of the following arguments. (A complete answer to the first problem in each *Check Your Understanding* section is given as a model for you to follow. The problems marked with a star are answered in the back of the book.)

1. Exercise helps strengthen your cardiovascular system. It also lowers your cholesterol, increases the blood flow to the brain, and enables you to think longer. Thus, there is no reason for you not to start exercising regularly.

Answer:
Premises:

    (a) Exercise helps strengthen your cardiovascular system.
    (b) It (exercise) also lowers your cholesterol.
    (c) (Exercise) increases the blood flow to the brain.
    (d) (Exercise) enables you to think longer.

Conclusion: There is no reason for you not to start exercising regularly. The indicator word "Thus" helps identify the conclusion. The other statements are offered in support of this claim.

2. If you start a strenuous exercise regimen before you know if your body is ready, you can cause serious damage. Therefore, you should always have a physical checkup before you start a rigid exercise program.

3. Since television commercials help pay the cost of programming, and because I can always turn off the sound of the commercials, go to the bathroom, or get something to eat or drink, it follows that commercials are not such a bad thing.

4. Since television commercials disrupt the flow of programs, and given that any disruption impedes the continuity of a show, consequently we can safely say that commercials are a bad thing.

5. We should never take our friends for granted. True friends are there when we need them. They suffer with us when we fail, and they are happy when we succeed.

6. They say that "absence makes the heart grow fonder," so my teachers should really love me, since I have been absent for the last 2 weeks.

7. I think, therefore I am.

René Descartes

8. I believe that humans will evolve into androids, because we will eventually be able to replace all organic body parts with artificial parts. In addition, we will be able to live virtually forever by simply replacing the parts when they wear out or become defective.

9. At one time Gary Kasparov had the highest ranking of any chess grand master in history. However, he was beaten in a chess tournament by a computer program called Deep Blue, so the computer program should be given a ranking higher than Kasparov.

10. It is true that $1 + 4 = 5$, and it is also true that $2 + 3 = 5$. Thus, we can conclude with certainty that $(1 + 4) = (2 + 3)$.

11. The digital camera on sale today at Cameras Galore has 5.0 megapixels and costs $200. The digital camera on sale at Camera Warehouse has 4.0 megapixels and it costs $150. You said that you did not want to spend over $175 for a camera, so you should buy the one at Camera Warehouse.

12. You should buy the digital camera at Cameras Galore. After all, you did say that you wanted the most megapixels you can get for up to $200. The digital camera on sale today at Cameras Galore has 5.0 megapixels and costs $200. But the digital camera on sale at Camera Warehouse has only 4.0 megapixels and it costs $150.

13. The world will end on August 6, 2045. I know this because my guru said it would, and so far everything he predicted has happened exactly as he said it would.

14. Fast-food products contain high levels of cholesterol. They also contain high levels of sodium, fat, and trans fatty acids. These things are bad for your health. I am going to stop eating in fast-food places.

15. You should eat more vegetables. They contain low levels of cholesterol. They also contain low levels of sodium, fat, and trans fatty acids. High levels of those things are bad for your health.

CHECK YOUR UNDERSTANDING 1B.2

Determine whether the following passages contain arguments. Explain your answers.

1. Our company has paid the highest dividends of any Fortune 500 company for the last 5 consecutive years. In addition, we have not had one labor dispute. Our stock is up 25% in the last quarter.

Answer: Not an argument. The three propositions can be used to support some other claim, but together they simply form a set of propositions with no obvious premise or conclusion.

2. Our cars have the highest resale value on the market. Customer loyalty is at an all-time high. I can give you a good deal on a new car today. You should really buy one of our cars.

3. I hate the new music played today. You can't even find a station on either AM or FM that plays decent music anymore. The movies are no better. They are just high-priced commercials for ridiculous products, designed to dupe unsuspecting, unintelligent, unthinking, unenlightened consumers.

4. We are going to have a recession. For 100 years, anytime the stock market has lost at least 20% of its value from its highest point in any fiscal year, there has been a recession. The current stock market has lost 22% of its value during the last fiscal year.

5. She doesn't eat pork, chicken, beef, mutton, veal, venison, turkey, or fish. It follows that she must be a vegetarian.

6. It seems as if everyone I know has a computer or cell phone. The electronics industry is making better and better products every year.

7. The cost of electronic items, such as televisions, computers, and cell phones, goes down every year. In addition, the quality of the electronic products goes up every year. More and more people throughout the world will soon be able to afford at least one of those items.

8. There is biological evidence that the genetic characteristics for nonviolence have been selected over time by the species, and the height and weight of humans have increased over the centuries.

9. She won the lottery, so she will quit her job soon.

10. Income tax revenues help pay for many important social programs, and without that money some of the programs would have to be eliminated. If this happens, many adults and children will suffer needlessly. That is why everyone, individuals and corporations, should not cheat on their income taxes.

11. All living things (plants, animals, humans) have the ability to absorb nourishment, to grow, and to propagate. All "living creatures" (animals and humans) have in addition the ability to perceive the world around them and to move about. Moreover, all humans have the ability to think, or otherwise to order their perceptions into various categories and classes. So there are in reality no sharp boundaries in the natural world.   Jostein Gaarder, *Sophie's World*

12. *Veidt*: Will you expose me, undoing the peace millions died for? Kill me, risking subsequent investigation? Morally you're in checkmate.
    Jon: Logically, I'm afraid he's right. Exposing this plot, we destroy any chance of peace, dooming Earth to worse destruction. On Mars, you demonstrated life's value. If we would preserve life here, we must remain silent.
    Alan Moore and Dave Gibbons, *Watchmen*

★ 13. The officer shook his head, perplexed. The handprint on the wall had not been made by the librarian himself; there hadn't been blood on his hands. Besides, the print did not match his, and it was a strange print, the whorls of the fingers unusually worn. It would have been easy to match, except that they'd never recorded one like it.   Elizabeth Kostrova, *The Historian*

14. Johnny wondered if the weather would affect his plans. He worried that all the little fuses and wires he had prepared might have become damp during the night. Who could have thought of rain at this time of year? He felt a sudden shiver of doubt. It was too late now. All was set in motion. If he was to become the most famous man in the valley he had to carry on regardless. He would not fail.
    Tash Aw, *The Harmony Silk Factory*

15. It may be no accident that sexual life forms dominate our planet. True, bacteria account for the largest number of individuals, and the greatest biomass. But by any reasonable measures of species diversity, or individual complexity, size, or intelligence, sexual species are paramount. And of the life forms that reproduce sexually, the ones whose reproduction is mediated by mate choice show the greatest biodiversity and the greatest complexity. Without sexual selection, evolution seems limited to the very small, the transient, the parasitic, the bacterial, and the brainless. For this reason, I think that sexual selection may be evolution's most creative force.   Geoffrey Miller, *The Mating Mind*

16. Sue hesitated; and then impulsively told the woman that her husband and herself had been unhappy in their first marriages, after which, terrified at the thought of a second irrevocable union, and lest the conditions of the contract should kill their love, yet wishing to be together, they had literally not found the courage to repeat it, though they had attempted it two or three times. Therefore, though

in her own sense of the words she was a married woman, in the landlady's sense she was not. *Thomas Hardy, Jude the Obscure*

17. The idea that space and time may form a closed surface without boundary also has profound implications for the role of God in the affairs of the universe. So long as the universe had a beginning, we could suppose it had a creator. But if the universe is really completely self-contained, having no boundary or edge, it would have neither beginning nor end; it would simply be. What place, then, for a creator? *Stephen W. Hawking, A Brief History of Time*

18. After supper she got out her book and learned me about Moses and the Bulrushers, and I was in a sweat to find out all about him; but by and by she let it out that Moses had been dead a considerable long time; so then I didn't care no more about him, because I don't take no stock in dead people. *Mark Twain, Huckleberry Finn*

19. I don't know when children stop dreaming. But I do know when hope starts leaking away, because I've seen it happen. Over the years, I have spent a lot of time talking with school children of all ages. And I have seen the cloud of resignation move across their eyes as they travel through school without making any real progress. They know they are slipping through the net into the huge underclass that our society seems willing to tolerate. We must educate our children. And if we do, I believe that will be enough. *Alan Page, Minnesota Supreme Court Justice, NFL Hall of Fame Induction Speech*

20. To me the similarities between the *Titanic* and *Challenger* tragedies are uncanny. Both disasters could have been prevented if those in charge had heeded the warnings of those who knew. In both cases, materials failed due to thermal effects. For the *Titanic*, the steel of her hull was below its ductile-to-brittle transition temperature; and for the *Challenger*, the rubber of the O-rings lost pliability in sub-freezing temperatures. And both tragedies provoked a worldwide discussion about the appropriate role for technology. *Mark E. Eberhart, Why Things Break*

21. Project Gutenberg eBooks are often created from several printed editions, all of which are confirmed as Public Domain in the U.S. unless a copyright notice is included. Thus, we do not necessarily keep eBooks in compliance with any particular paper edition. *Project Gutenberg website*

22. Stepan Arkadyevitch had learned easily at school, thanks to his excellent abilities, but he had been idle and mischievous, and therefore was one of the lowest in his class. *Leo Tolstoy, Anna Karenina*

23. We are intelligent beings: intelligent beings cannot have been formed by a crude, blind, insensible being: there is certainly some difference between the ideas of Newton and the dung of a mule. Newton's intelligence, therefore, came from another intelligence. *Voltaire, Philosophical Dictionary*

24. Churches are block-booking seats for *March of the Penguins*, which is apparently a "condemnation of gay marriage" and puts forward the case for "intelligent design," i.e., Creationism. To be honest, this is good news. If American Christians want to go public on the fact that they're now morally guided by penguins, at least we know where we all stand.   Caitlin Moran, "Penguins Lead Way"

25. Authoritarian governments are identified by ready government access to information about the activities of citizens and by extensive limitations on the ability of citizens to obtain information about the government. In contrast, democratic governments are marked by significant restrictions on the ability of government to acquire information about its citizens and by ready access by citizens to information about the activities of government.
                    Robert G. Vaughn, "Transparency—The Mechanisms"

26. *Charlie Brown:* Why would they ban Miss Sweetstory's book?
    Linus: I can't believe it. I just can't believe it!
    Charlie Brown: Maybe there are some things in her book that we don't understand.
    Sally: In that case, they should also ban my Math book!
                    Charles M. Schulz, *Peanuts*

27. Here's the narrative you hear everywhere: President Obama has presided over a huge expansion of government, but unemployment has remained high. And this proves that government spending can't create jobs. Here's what you need to know: The whole story is a myth. There never was a big expansion of government spending. In fact, that has been the key problem with economic policy in the Obama years: we never had the kind of fiscal expansion that might have created the millions of jobs we need. Ask yourself: What major new federal programs have started up since Mr. Obama took office? Health-care reform, for the most part, hasn't kicked in yet, so that can't be it. So are there giant infrastructure projects under way? No. Are there huge new benefits for low-income workers or the poor? No. Where's all that spending we keep hearing about? It never happened.   Paul Krugman, "Hey, Small Spender"

28. The '80s debaters tended to forget that the teaching of vernacular literature is quite a recent development in the long history of the university. (The same could be said about the relatively recent invention of art history or music as an academic research discipline.) So it is not surprising that, in such a short time, we have not yet settled on the right or commonly agreed upon way to go about it.
                    Robert Pippin, "In Defense of Naïve Reading"

29. The greatest tragedy in mankind's entire history may be the hijacking of morality by religion.   Arthur C. Clarke, *Collected Essays*

30. Jokes of the proper kind, properly told, can do more to enlighten questions of politics, philosophy, and literature than any number of dull arguments.
                    Isaac Asimov, *Treasury of Humor*

31. The aim of argument, or of discussion, should not be victory, but progress.

    Joseph Joubert, *Pensées*

32. Whenever I hear anyone arguing for slavery, I feel a strong impulse to see it tried on him personally.   Abraham Lincoln, Speech to 14th Indiana regiment, March 17, 1865

⋆ 33. The most important thing in an argument, next to being right, is to leave an escape hatch for your opponent, so that he can gracefully swing over to your side without too much apparent loss of face.   Sydney J. Harris, as quoted in *Journeys 7*

34. The logic of the world is prior to all truth and falsehood.

    Ludwig Wittgenstein, *Notebooks 1914–1916*

35. I am aware that the assumed instinctive belief in God has been used by many persons as an argument for His existence. But this is a rash argument, as we should thus be compelled to believe in the existence of many cruel and malignant spirits, only a little more powerful than man; for the belief in them is far more general than in a beneficent Deity.   Charles Darwin, *The Descent of Man*

36. The most perfidious way of harming a cause consists of defending it deliberately with faulty arguments.   Friedrich Nietzsche, *The Gay Science*

⋆ 37. For nothing requires a greater effort of thought than arguments to justify the rule of nonthought. I experienced it with my own eyes and ears after the war, when intellectuals and artists rushed like a herd of cattle into the Communist Party, which soon proceeded to liquidate them systematically and with great pleasure. You are doing the same. You are the brilliant ally of your own gravediggers.

    Milan Kundera, *Immortality*

38. When you plant lettuce, if it does not grow well, you don't blame the lettuce. You look for reasons it is not doing well. It may need fertilizer, or more water, or less sun. You never blame the lettuce. Yet if we have problems with our friends or our family, we blame the other person. But if we know how to take care of them, they will grow well, like the lettuce. Blaming has no positive effect at all, nor does trying to persuade using reason and argument. That is my experience. If you understand, and you show that you understand, you can love, and the situation will change.   Thich Nhât Hanh, *Peace Is Every Step*

39. Your friends praise your abilities to the skies, submit to you in argument, and seem to have the greatest deference for you; but, though they may ask it, you never find them following your advice upon their own affairs; nor allowing you to manage your own, without thinking that you should follow theirs. Thus, in fact, they all think themselves wiser than you, whatever they may say.

    Viscount William Lamb Melbourne, *Lord Melbourne's Papers*

40. Violence and lawlessness spread across London . . . property and vehicles have been set on fire in several areas, some burning out of control. One reporter

pointed out that in Clapham where the shopping area had been picked clean, the only shop left unlooted and untouched was the book shop.

Martin Fletcher, "Riots Reveal London's Two Disparate Worlds," NBC News

⭐ 41. The only people who really listen to an argument are the neighbors.

42. I've put in so many enigmas and puzzles that it will keep the professors busy for centuries arguing over what I meant, and that's the only way of insuring one's immortality.

James Joyce, as quoted in James Joyce by Richard Ellmann

43. The Keynesian argument that if the private sector lacks confidence to spend, the government should spend is not wrong. But Keynes did not spell out where the government should spend. Nor did he envisage that lobbyists can influence government spending to be wasteful. Hence, every prophet can be used by his or her successors to prove their own points of view. This is religion, not science.

Andrew Sheng, "Economics Is a Religion, Not a Science"

44. All true wisdom is found on T-shirts. I wear T-shirts, so I must be wise.

⭐ 45. The National Biosafety Board has approved the release of genetically modified mosquitoes for field testing. This particular type of mosquito can spread the dengue fever and yellow fever viruses. Clinical trial at the laboratory level was successful and the biosafety committee has approved it for testing in a controlled environment. The males would be genetically modified and when mated with female mosquitoes in the environment, it is hoped the killer genes would cause the larvae to die. The regional director cautioned that care be taken in introducing a new species to the environment.

Newspaper article, "Field Testing Approved for Genetically Modified Mosquitoes"

46. It may not always be immediately apparent to frustrated investors—they wish management would be more frugal and focus more on the stock price—but there's usually some calculated logic underlying Google's unconventional strategy. Google's brain trust—founders Larry Page and Sergey Brin, along with CEO Eric Schmidt—clearly think differently than most corporate leaders, and may eventually encourage more companies to take risks that might not pay off for years, if ever. Page and Brin warned potential investors when they laid out their iconoclastic approach to business before Google sold its stock in an initial public offering. "Our long-term focus may simply be the wrong business strategy," they warned. "Competitors may be rewarded for short-term tactics and grow stronger as a result. As potential investors, you should consider the risks around our long-term focus."

Michael Liedtke, "Calculated Risks? Making Sense of Google's Seemingly Kooky Concepts"

47. Tribalism is about familiarity within the known entity. It's not about hatred of others, it's about comfort within your own, with a natural reluctance to expend the energy and time to break across the barriers and understand another group. Most of what we're quick to label racism isn't really racism. Racism is

premeditated, an organized class distinction based on believed superiority and inferiority of different races. That "ism" suffix makes racism a system, just like capitalism or socialism. Racism is used to justify exclusion and persecution based on skin color, things that rarely come into play in today's NBA.

J. A. Adande, "LeBron James, Race and the NBA"

48. Kedah Health Department employees who smoke will not be eligible for the annual excellence performance awards even if they do well in their work. The Director said, "Thirty percent or 3,900 of our 13,000 department personnel are smokers. As staff representing a health department, they should act as role models. Thus, I hope that they will quit smoking."

Embun Majid, "Health Department Snuffs Out Excellence Awards for Smokers"

★ 49. Even though testing in horse racing is far superior in many respects to testing in human athletics, the concern remains among horse racing fans and industry participants that medication is being used illegally.

Dr. Scott Palmer, "Working in the Light of Day"

50. I stated above that I am among those who reject the notion that a full-fledged human soul comes into being the moment that a human sperm joins a human ovum to form a human zygote. By contrast, I believe that a human soul—and, by the way, it is my aim in this book to make clear what I mean by this slippery, shifting word, often rife with religious connotations, but here not having any—comes slowly into being over the course of years of development. It may sound crass to put it this way, but I would like to suggest, at least metaphorically, a numerical scale of "degrees of souledness." We can initially imagine it as running from 0 to 100, and the units of this scale can be called, just for the fun of it, "hunekers." Thus you and I, dear reader, both possess 100 hunekers of souledness, or thereabouts.

Douglas Hofstadter, *I Am a Strange Loop*

C. ARGUMENTS AND EXPLANATIONS

We saw that, in some contexts, words such as "since" or "thus" are not used as premise or conclusion indicators. In much the same way, the word "because" is often placed in front of an **explanation**, which provides reasons for why or how an event occurred. To see the difference between an *argument* and an *explanation*, imagine that a student's cell phone starts ringing and disturbs everyone's concentration during an exam. After class, one of the students might complain:

> *Because* you failed to turn off your cell phone before entering the classroom, I think it is safe to say that your behavior shows that you are self-centered, inconsiderate, and rude.

The speaker concludes that the cell phone owner's lack of consideration reveals character flaws—"self-centered, inconsiderate, and rude." In this setting, the word "because"

Explanation An explanation provides reasons for why or how an event occurred. By themselves, explanations are not arguments; however, they can form part of an argument.

is used to indicate that evidence is being offered in support of a conclusion; so we have an argument.

Now, as it happens, the student whose cell phone started ringing responds using the word "because," too:

> I forgot to turn off my cell phone *because* I was almost in a car accident on my way to take the exam this morning, and I was completely distracted thinking about what happened.

In this setting, however, the word "because" is used to indicate an *explanation*. This speaker does not dispute the fact that the cell phone went off during the exam; rather, he is attempting to explain *why* it happened.

Here are two more examples to consider:

A. Because you started lifting weights without first getting a physical checkup, you will probably injure your back.

B. Your back injury occurred because you lifted weights without first getting a physical checkup.

The first passage contains an inferential claim. In this context the word "because" indicates that a statement is used as support for the conclusion "you will probably injure your back." The premise uses the accepted fact that the person has started lifting weights, so the premise is not in dispute. Since the person has not yet injured his or her back (and might not in the future), the conclusion can turn out to be either true or false.

However, in the second passage the word "because" is not used to indicate support for a conclusion. From the context it appears that the back injury is not in dispute, so what the passage contains is an explanation for the back injury. The explanation may be correct, or it might be incorrect, but in either case there is no argument in the second passage.

Let's work through another example. Suppose your car does not start. A friend might say, "Your car doesn't start *because* you have a dead battery." If you thought that the word "because" is acting as a premise indicator ("you have a dead battery"), then the conclusion would be, "Your car doesn't start." The problem with treating this example as an argument is that the alleged conclusion is not in doubt; it has already been established as true. We generally construct arguments in order to provide good reasons (premises) to support a proposition (the conclusion) *whose truth is in question*. But in this example you do not need any reasons to believe that your car doesn't start: you already know that. In general, explanations do not function directly as premises in an argument if they explain an already accepted fact.

Your car does not start, *because* → your battery is dead.
you are out of gas.
your starter is defective.
someone stole your engine.

Accepted Fact

Explanations
(each may be true or false)

However, explanations can also be used to construct arguments—the goal being to *test* the explanation, to see if it is correct. Chapter 14 further develops the relationships between explanations, experiments, and predictions.

CHECK YOUR UNDERSTANDING 1C

Determine whether each of the following passages contains an *argument* or an *explanation*. Explain your answer.

1. Luke must have found a better job; that's why he didn't come to work today.
Answer: Explanation. It is a fact that he did not come to work today; so an explanation is being offered.

2. In platonic love there can be no tragedy, because in that love all is clear and pure.

Leo Tolstoy, *Anna Karenina*

3. For the last 10 years the best picture Oscar has gone to a drama. A comedy has no chance of winning the Oscar for best picture this year.

4. The job of arguing with the umpire belongs to the manager, because it won't hurt the team if he gets thrown out of the game.

Earl Weaver, as quoted in *Home Plate* by Brenda Berstler

5. Many independent candidates won recent elections, even beating out strong incumbents. It must be because voters are disappointed with the two-party system.

6. People generally quarrel because they cannot argue.

Gilbert K. Chesterton, *The Collected Works of G. K. Chesterson*

7. An independent candidate will never win the presidency of the United States. This is because the two-party system of Democrats and Republicans is too powerful to let a third party get any wide base of support among the American voting public.

8. That God cannot lie is no advantage to your argument, because it is no proof that priests can not, or that the Bible does not.

Thomas Paine, *The Life and Works of Thomas Paine*

9. Welcome to the fall of Les Miles. That sentence is all about context—because I mean fall as a season, not as a drop from grace.

Bruce Feldman, "Les Miles Is on a Heck of a Run," ESPN

10. There has been an overall decrease in violence among humans worldwide throughout recorded history. Some biologists claim that this is because the genetic characteristics for nonviolence have been selected over time by the species.

11. Project Gutenberg is synonymous with the free distribution of electronic works in formats readable by the widest variety of computers including obsolete, old, middle-aged and new computers. It exists because of the efforts of hundreds of volunteers and donations from people in all walks of life.

From Project Gutenberg website

12. Since there is biological evidence that the genetic characteristics for nonviolence have been selected over time by the species, we should see an overall decrease in violence among humans worldwide in the coming centuries.

⭐ 13. To make Windows Phone 7 a success, Microsoft has to win over not just phone manufacturers and phone companies, but software developers. The iPhone and Android are popular in part because of the tens of thousands of tiny applications, or "apps," made by outside software developers.

Newspaper article, "Microsoft Bets Big on New Phone Software"

14. Presently I began to detect a most evil and searching odor stealing about on the frozen air. This depressed my spirits still more, because of course I attributed it to my poor departed friend.   Mark Twain, *How to Tell a Story, and Other Essays*

15. While it is true that science cannot decide questions of value, that is because they cannot be intellectually decided at all, and lie outside the realm of truth and falsehood. Whatever knowledge is attainable, must be attained by scientific methods; and what science cannot discover, mankind cannot know.

Bertrand Russell, *Religion and Science*

16. "You must understand," said he, "it's not love. I've been in love, but it's not that. It's not my feeling, but a sort of force outside me has taken possession of me. I went away, you see, because I made up my mind that it could never be, you understand, as a happiness that does not come on earth; but I've struggled with myself, I see there's no living without it. And it must be settled."

Leo Tolstoy, *Anna Karenina*

⭐ 17. Years ago I used to think sometimes of making a lecturing trip through the antipodes and the borders of the Orient, but always gave up the idea, partly because of the great length of the journey and partly because my wife could not well manage to go with me.   Mark Twain, *How to Tell a Story, and Other Essays*

18. Briefly, Cosmic Consciousness, according to Bucke, is a higher form of consciousness that is slowly but surely coming to the entire human race through the process of evolution. The mystics and religious leaders of the past were simply ahead of their time. Bucke believes that Cosmic Consciousness is the real source of all the world's religions. He did not believe that the cosmic state is necessarily infallible. Like the development of any faculty, it takes a long time to become perfected. And so, just because Cosmic Consciousness is the root of religious beliefs, it doesn't follow that the beliefs are necessarily correct.

Raymond Smullyan, *Some Interesting Memories: A Paradoxical Life*

19. It's nothing or everything, Culum. If you're prepared to be second-best, go topside now. What I'm trying to make you understand is that to be *the* Tai-Pan of The Noble House you have to be prepared to exist alone, to be hated, to have some aim of immortal value, and to be ready to sacrifice anyone you're not sure

of. Because you're my son I'm offering you today, untried, a chance at supreme power in Asia. Thus a power to do almost anything on earth.

James Clavell, Tai-Pan

20. All the big corporations depreciate their possessions, and you can, too, provided you use them for business purposes. For example, if you subscribe to the Wall Street Journal, a business-related newspaper, you can deduct the cost of your house, because, in the words of U.S. Supreme Court Chief Justice Warren Burger in a landmark 1979 tax decision: "Where else are you going to read the paper? Outside? What if it rains?"

Dave Barry, "Sweating Out Taxes"

D. TRUTH AND LOGIC

Determination of the truth value of a statement is distinct from analysis of the logic of the argument. *Truth value* analysis determines if the information in the premises is accurate, correct, or true. *Logical* analysis determines the strength with which the premises support the conclusion. If you are not aware of the difference between the truth value and the logic of an argument, then confusion can arise. Suppose you hear that the book you are now reading weighs 2000 pounds. If you are like most people, you immediately know the statement to be false. Your decision happens so fast you could not stop it if you tried. This shows that one part of our mind is constantly analyzing information for truth value. We must recognize that our minds are constantly working on two different levels, and we must learn to keep those levels separate. In order to evaluate the logic of an argument, we must often temporarily ignore the truth values— not because they are unimportant, but simply because an analysis of the logic requires us to focus on an entirely different question. We must learn to not be distracted by trying to determine the truth value of the statements—just as when we close our eyes to concentrate on hearing something.

Of course it is important that our statements be true. However, a thorough analysis of arguments requires an active separation of the truth value from the logic. Think of what happens when children begin learning addition. For example, an elementary teacher gave two cookies to each student at the beginning of the class. "Okay Sam," she said, "you have two cookies, and Sophie has two cookies. How many cookies do you have together?" At that point Sam started to cry. The teacher thought that Sam was embarrassed because he didn't know the answer. In fact, Sam had already eaten his two cookies. His reaction was based on knowing that the teacher's statement that he had two cookies was false, so perhaps he thought he would be in trouble for having eaten the cookies. It is easy to forget that it often takes time to learn to think abstractly.

E. DEDUCTIVE AND INDUCTIVE ARGUMENTS

Logical analysis of an argument is concerned with determining the strength of the *inference*—the claim that the conclusion follows from the premises. We start with a working definition of two main classes of arguments: deductive and inductive.

A **deductive argument** is one in which it is claimed that the conclusion follows *necessarily* from the premises. In other words, it is claimed that under the assumption that the premises are true it is *impossible* for the conclusion to be false.

An **inductive argument** is one in which it is claimed that the premises make the conclusion *probable*. In other words, it is claimed that under the assumption that the premises are true it is *improbable* for the conclusion to be false.

To help identify arguments as either deductive or inductive, one thing we can do is look for key words or phrases. For example, the words "necessarily," "certainty," "definitely," and "absolutely" suggest a deductive argument:

> **A.** Jupiter is a planet in our solar system. Every planet in our solar system is smaller than the Sun. Therefore, it follows necessarily that Jupiter is smaller than the Sun.

The indicator word "necessarily" suggests that the argument can be classified as deductive.

On the other hand, the words "probably," "likely," "unlikely," "improbable," "plausible," and "implausible" suggest inductive arguments:

> **B.** Some parts of the United States have had severe winters for the last 10 years. The *Farmer's Almanac* predicts another cold winter next year. Therefore, probably some parts of the United States will have a severe winter next year.

The indicator word "probably" suggests that the argument can be classified as inductive. Of course we have to remember that specific indicator words or phrases may not always occur in ordinary language. In addition, although a passage may contain an indicator word or phrase, the person using the phrase may be misusing the term. In some instances people overstate their case, while in other instances they may not be aware of the distinction between deductive arguments and inductive arguments, so they might use terms indiscriminately. However, looking for indicator words can help in understanding an argument by letting you see how the information is arranged.

Another factor to consider when determining whether an argument is deductive or inductive is the strength of the inferential connection between the premises and the conclusion. In other words, if the conclusion does follow *necessarily* from premises that are assumed to be true, then the argument is clearly deductive. Here is an example:

> **C.** All vegetables contain vitamin C. Spinach is a vegetable. Therefore, spinach contains vitamin C.

Assuming the premises are true, the conclusion is necessarily true. In other words, if we assume that it is true that all vegetables contain vitamin C, and if we also assume that it is true that spinach is a vegetable, then it is impossible for spinach not to contain vitamin C. Therefore, this argument can be classified as deductive. Notice once again the importance of disregarding the truth value of the premises at this point in our analysis. We are *not* claiming that the premises are in fact true. Instead, we are claiming that *under the assumption that the premises are true* it is impossible for the conclusion to be false.

Deductive argument
An argument in which it is claimed that the conclusion follows *necessarily* from the premises. In other words, it is claimed that under the assumption that the premises are true it is *impossible* for the conclusion to be false.

Inductive argument An argument in which it is claimed that the premises make the conclusion *probable*. In other words, it is claimed that under the assumption that the premises are true it is *improbable* for the conclusion to be false.

There is another result of examining the actual strength of the inferential connection between the premises and the conclusion. If we determine that the conclusion of an argument follows probably from premises that are assumed to be true, then it is often best to consider the argument as inductive. Here is an example:

> **D.** The majority of plasma TVs last for 5 years. Chris just bought a new plasma TV. Therefore, Chris's new plasma TV will last 5 years.

Let's examine argument D. Under the assumption that the premises are true, the conclusion is highly likely to be true; however, it is possible that it is false. In other words, if we assume that it is true that the vast majority of plasma TVs last for 5 years, and if we also assume that it is true that Chris just bought a new plasma TV, then it is probable that Chris's new plasma TV will last 5 years. Therefore, this argument can be classified as inductive. Again, we are disregarding the truth value of the premises. We are not claiming that the premises are in fact true. Instead, we are claiming that, *under the assumption that the premises are true*, it is probable that the conclusion is true. Therefore, argument D can be classified as inductive.

Inductive arguments amplify or enlarge the scope of the information in the premises. For example, the first premise in example D provides information about plasma TVs, but it does not make a claim about every plasma TV. Nor does it make a claim about any specific TV (including Chris's TV); instead, it only states something about the majority of plasma TVs. It is in this sense that we say that the conclusion regarding Chris's TV goes beyond the information in the premises; hence it is possible that the conclusion is false even under the assumption that the premises are true.

However, this does not take away from the value of strong inductive arguments. In fact, we rely on them nearly every day. For most practical purposes, we do not have sufficient knowledge of the world to make predictions with certainty, so we rely on evidence and experience to make many decisions. That's why knowing the likelihood of something happening can assist our rational decision making. Inductive arguments play a crucial role in our lives.

There are many kinds of inductive arguments, such as many *analogical arguments*, *legal arguments*, *moral arguments*, *statistical arguments*, and *scientific arguments*. (More on these kinds of inductive arguments can be found in Part IV of this book.) Analogical arguments are based on the idea that when two things share some relevant characteristics, they probably share other characteristics as well. Here is an example:

> I previously owned two Ford station wagons. They both got good gas mileage, both needed few repairs, and both had a high resale value. I just bought a new Ford station wagon, so it will get good gas mileage, need few repairs, and have a high resale value.

Statistical arguments are based on our ability to generalize. When we observe a pattern, we often create an argument that uses a statistical regularity:

> In a survey of 1000 university students in the United States, 80% said that they expect to make more money in their lives than their parents. Therefore,

the vast majority of all university students expect to make more money in their lives than their parents.

Causal arguments are arguments based on knowledge of either causes or effects. For example, a team of medical scientists may conduct experiments to determine if a new drug (the potential cause) will have a desired effect on a particular disease. In a different setting, a forensic expert might do a series of tests to determine the cause of a person's death. Causal arguments can even be found in everyday occurrences. For example, someone might say the following:

> The lamp in my room does not work. I changed the light bulb, but it still did not work. I moved the lamp to another room just in case the wall outlet was defective, but the lamp still did not work. So, it must be the wiring in the lamp that is defective.

We defined a deductive argument as one in which it is claimed that the conclusion follows necessarily from the premises. If we look once again at example C, then we can see that the conclusion does not amplify or expand the scope of the information in the premises. The first premise provides information about *every* vegetable, and the second premise states that spinach is a vegetable. Therefore, under the assumption that the premises are true, the conclusion does not go beyond what is already contained in the premises.

It should not be surprising to find deductive arguments in mathematics and geometry. Even simple arithmetical calculations are deductive. For example, if you assume that you can save $50 a week, then you can conclude that after 1 year (52 weeks) you will have saved $2600. When we encounter an argument that is based on mathematics, we can consider it to be deductive.

Earlier we said that many statistical arguments can be classified as inductive. Of course, there are statistical calculations that are purely mathematical in nature; in those cases the calculations are deductive. However, when the conclusion goes beyond what is provided by the premises, the statistical argument is inductive, like our survey of 1000 university students. Since the conclusion stated something about all university students, it went beyond the scope of the premises.

Another type of deductive argument relies on the definition of a key term. For example, suppose someone were to say, "Since Sam is an unmarried male, Sam is a bachelor." The terms "unmarried male" and "bachelor" have the same meaning. Therefore if the premise is assumed to be true, then the conclusion is necessarily true. Here is another argument that relies on words that are synonymous: "My sister has a chronic inability to sleep, so she has insomnia." Since the phrases "a chronic inability to sleep" and "insomnia" mean the same thing, if the premise is assumed to be true, then the conclusion is necessarily true.

Your ability to classify an argument as deductive or inductive will continue to grow as you have the opportunity to analyze many different arguments.

CHECK YOUR UNDERSTANDING 1E

The following exercises are intended to apply your understanding of the difference between deductive and inductive arguments. Determine whether the following arguments are best classified as being deductive or inductive. Explain your answers.

1. Every insect has six legs. What's crawling on me is an insect. So what's crawling on me has six legs.

Answer: Deductive. The first premise says something definite about every insect. The second premise says that an insect is crawling on me. If both premises are assumed to be true, then the conclusion is necessarily true.

2. Most insects have six legs. What's crawling on me is an insect. Therefore, what's crawling on me probably has six legs.

3. The exam's range of A scores is 90–100. I got a 98 on the exam. It follows necessarily that I got an A on the exam.

4. The exam's range of A scores is 90–100. I got an A on the exam, thus I got a 98 on the exam.

5. All fires need oxygen. There is no oxygen in that room. So there is no fire in that room.

6. Some fires need no oxygen. There is no oxygen in that room. So there is no fire in that room.

7. Carly tossed a coin ten times, and in each case it came up heads. I have a feeling that it is a trick coin. I predict the next toss will be heads.

8. Carly tossed a coin ten times, and in each case it came up heads. The law of averages says that this cannot go on indefinitely. I predict the next toss will be tails.

9. All elements with atomic weights greater than 64 are metals. Z is an element with an atomic weight of 79. Therefore, Z is a metal.

10. The majority of elements with atomic weights greater than 64 are metals. Z is an element with an atomic weight of 79. Therefore, Z is probably a metal.

11. Antibiotics have no effect on viruses. You have a disease that is caused by a virus. You are taking the antibiotic Q. Thus the antibiotic you are taking will have no effect on your disease.

12. Some antibiotics are effective for treating certain bacterial infections. You have a bacterial infection. You are taking the antibiotic Q. Thus the antibiotic you are taking will be effective in treating your bacterial infection.

13. Anyone over 21 years of age can legally play the slot machines in Las Vegas. Sam is 33 years old. Sam can legally play the slot machines in Las Vegas.

14. Anyone over 21 years of age can legally play the slot machines in Las Vegas, unless they are a convicted felon. Sam is 33 years old. Sam can legally play the slot machines in Las Vegas.

15. Every orange has seeds. I am eating an orange, so I am eating something with seeds.

16. Most fruit have seeds. I am eating an orange. All oranges are fruit, so I am eating something with seeds.

⭐ 17. Most Doberman dogs bark a lot. My cousin just got a Doberman dog. Therefore, my cousin's Doberman dog will probably bark a lot.

18. The vast majority of a survey of 600 people who identified themselves as being very religious reported that they were against capital punishment. It is safe to say that the vast majority of all Americans think the same way.

19. Last week, when my car would not start, Mom took me to get a new battery. As soon as I installed it, my car started right up. So my old battery was probably defective.

20. No car battery that has at least one defective cell can be repaired. Your car battery has at least one defective cell, so it cannot be repaired.

F. DEDUCTIVE ARGUMENTS: VALIDITY AND TRUTH

Logical analysis of a deductive argument is concerned with determining whether the conclusion follows necessarily from the premises. Placed in the form of a question, logical analysis of a deductive argument asks the following: "Assuming the premises are true, is it possible for the conclusion to be false?" Answering this question will provide us with some key terms with which we can dig deeper into deductive arguments.

A **valid deductive argument** is one in which, assuming the premises are true, it is *impossible* for the conclusion to be false. In other words, the conclusion follows necessarily from the premises. On the other hand, an **invalid deductive argument** is one in which, assuming the premises are true, it is *possible* for the conclusion to be false. In other words, the conclusion does not follow necessarily from the premises.

Determining the validity or the invalidity of an argument rests on logical analysis. We rely on the assumption that the premises are true in order to determine whether the conclusion necessarily follows. However, truth value does have a role in the overall analysis of deductive arguments. The determination that a deductive argument is valid rests on the *logical assumption* that the premises are true. A valid deductive argument can have premises or a conclusion whose actual truth value is false. This possibility is exactly why we apply truth value analysis *after* we determine that a deductive argument is valid. Combining logical analysis with truth value analysis provides us with two more definitions. First, when logical analysis shows that a deductive argument is valid, and when truth value analysis of the premises shows that they are all true, then the argument is **sound**. However, if the deductive argument is invalid, or if at least one of the premises is false, then the argument is **unsound**.

Valid deductive argument An argument in which, assuming the premises are true, it is *impossible* for the conclusion to be false. In other words, the conclusion follows necessarily from the premises.

Invalid deductive argument An argument in which, assuming the premises are true, it is *possible* for the conclusion to be false. In other words, the conclusion does not follow necessarily from the premises.

Sound argument
When logical analysis shows that a deductive argument is valid, and when truth value analysis of the premises shows that they are all true, then the argument is sound.

Unsound argument If a deductive argument is invalid, or if at least one of the premises is false (truth value analysis), then the argument is unsound.

To determine whether a deductive argument is valid or invalid, we apply logical analysis by assuming the premises are true. If logical analysis determines that the argument is valid, then we apply truth value analysis in order to determine whether the argument is sound or unsound. The following flow chart illustrates the process:

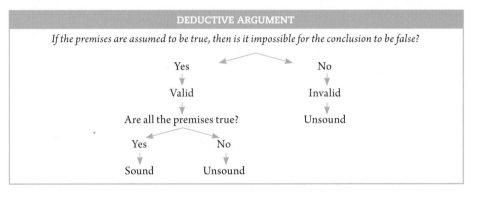

Logical Form

It is easy to confuse the question of the truth value of statements with the logical question of what follows from the statements. To keep the two questions clear and distinct when you analyze arguments, it can help to think about logical possibilities. Consider two examples:

A. All dogs are cats. All cats are snakes. Therefore, all dogs are snakes.
B. No mammals are beagles. No mammals are dogs. Therefore, no beagles are dogs.

Since we are discussing the logical question of validity, we do not want to get bogged down in complicated truth value analysis. Fortunately, it should be easy to determine that all the premises and the conclusions in both A and B are false. What we need to do is reveal the *logical form* of the arguments. The first premise in argument A is "All dogs are cats." We can use letters to stand for the terms "dogs" and "cats" while keeping the words "all" and "are" in place to reveal the logical form of the statement. For example, if we let D = *dogs*, and C = *cats*, then the form is the following: "All D are C." Applying this technique reveals the logical forms of arguments A and B, which we will then label FA and FB. Let D = *dogs*, C = *cats*, S = *snakes*, M = *mammals*, and B = *beagles*.

FA. All D are C.
All C are S.
All D are S.

FB. No M are B.
No M are D.
No B are D.

Notice that we introduced a horizontal line to separate the premises from the conclusion. This technique allows us to eliminate the word "Therefore." We know that an argument is constructed entirely of statements, and we know that each of the premises and the conclusion have two possible truth values (true or false). Recall that a valid argument is a deductive argument in which, assuming the premises are true, it is *impossible* for the conclusion to be false. An invalid argument is a deductive argument in which, assuming the premises are true, it is *possible* for the conclusion to be false.

We initially used the letters D, C, S, M, and B to stand for *dogs, cats, snakes, mammals,* and *beagles.* However, we can substitute any class or group terms we wish for the letters, *as long as we keep the logical form of the argument intact.* What we want to do is to determine whether it is *possible* that either argument A or argument B, or both, can have true premises and a false conclusion. The following table supplies substitution instances for both FA and FB:

Argument Form FA—VALID	Argument Form FB—INVALID

1. T All beagles are dogs.
   T <u>All dogs are mammals</u>
   T All beagles are mammals.
	1. T No dogs are snakes.
	   T <u>No dogs are cats.</u>
	   T No snakes are cats.

2. T
   T Not Possible
   F
	2. T No cats are beagles.
	   T <u>No cats are dogs.</u>
	   F No beagles are dogs.

3. T All beagles are mammals.
   F <u>All mammals are dogs.</u>
   T All beagles are dogs.
	3. T No beagles are cats.
	   F <u>No beagles are dogs.</u>
	   T No cats are dogs.

4. T All dogs are mammals.
   F <u>All mammals are snakes.</u>
   F All dogs are snakes.
	4. T No cats are dogs.
	   F <u>No cats are mammals.</u>
	   F No dogs are mammals.

5. F All dogs are cats.
   T <u>All cats are mammals.</u>
   T All dogs are mammals.
	5. F No beagles are dogs.
	   T <u>No beagles are cats.</u>
	   T No dogs are cats.

6. F All cats are beagles.
   T <u>All beagles are dogs.</u>
   F All cats are dogs.
	6. F No cats are mammals.
	   T <u>No cats are dogs.</u>
	   F No mammals are dogs.

7. F All beagles are cats.
   F <u>All cats are dogs.</u>
   T All beagles are dogs.
	7. F No mammals are cats.
	   F <u>No mammals are dogs.</u>
	   T No cats are dogs.

8. F All dogs are cats.
   F <u>All cats are snakes.</u>
   F All dogs are snakes.
	8. F No mammals are beagles.
	   F <u>No mammals are dogs.</u>
	   F No beagles are dogs.

No matter what we substitute into the form FA it is logically impossible for a false conclusion to follow from true premises. In other words, form FA can result in arguments that correspond to every combination of truth values in the table, *except number 2.* On the other hand, it is logically possible to substitute into form FB and get a false conclusion following from true premises. Form FB can result in arguments that correspond to every combination in the table, *including number 2.*

Even though the actual truth value of the original statements in both argument A and argument B were the same (false premises and a false conclusion), argument A is valid, but argument B is invalid. It is important to remember that when we evaluate arguments, we must always distinguish truth value analysis from the logical analysis.

Counterexamples

The overall analysis of a deductive argument requires two things: logical analysis and truth value analysis. Based on logical analysis deductive arguments are either valid or invalid. When we add the results of truth value analysis, deductive arguments are either sound or unsound. Most people have more experience in evaluating the truth value than the logic of an argument, simply because our formal education is heavily devoted to what is known to be true. A large part of education is the teaching of facts.

The difference between logical analysis and truth value analysis can be illustrated by the role of **counterexamples.** A counterexample to a *statement* is evidence that shows the statement is false, and it concerns truth value analysis. Suppose someone says, "No human is taller than eight feet." If we are able to find a human who is taller than eight feet, then we have evidence that the statement is false. The evidence can be considered to be a counterexample to the statement, "No human is taller than eight feet."

Statements that use the words "never," "always," or the phrase "every time" are often subject to simple counterexamples. Here are some examples of statements and counterexamples:

> *Statement:* "I never get to stay home from school."
> *Counterexample:* "You stay home from school when you are sick and when we go on vacation."
> *Statement:* "He always gets to go first."
> *Counterexample:* "You went first when we rode on the roller-coaster at the park last week."
> *Statement:* "The phone rings every time I'm taking a shower."
> *Counterexample:* "But you took a shower last night and the phone didn't ring."

A counterexample to an *argument* plays a different role. It shows that the premises assumed to be true do not make the conclusion necessarily true. A single counterexample to a deductive argument is enough to show that the argument is invalid. This should not be surprising. If you recall, every deductive argument is either valid or invalid. Therefore, it is not necessary to find more than one counterexample to a deductive argument because there are no degrees of invalidity. In other words, deductive arguments cannot be classified as *partially valid* or *semi-valid*.

Let's consider the following deductive argument:

C. All bomohs are scam artists.
All grifters are scam artists.
All bomohs are grifters.

You do not need to know what either a bomoh or a grifter or a scam artist is in order to determine if the argument is valid or invalid. Whatever those things are we can begin by thinking about the argument in a logical way. The argument relates two things (bomohs

---

Counterexample A counterexample to a statement is evidence that shows the statement is false. A counterexample to an argument shows the possibility that premises assumed to be true do not make the conclusion necessarily true. A single counterexample to a deductive argument is enough to show that the argument is invalid.

and grifters) to a third thing (scam artists). Now even if we assume that every bomoh and every grifter is a scam artist, is it necessarily true that every bomoh is a grifter? The first step of the analysis is to reveal the logical form of the argument. Let's substitute letters for the terms in order to reveal the argument form. (B = *bomohs*, S = *scam artists*, and G = *grifters*)

FC. All B are S.
<u>All G are S.</u>
All B are G.

The second step is to substitute three terms for the letters, such that the substitution instance will be a counterexample. Let's try the following: B = *beagles*, S = *mammals*, and G = *dogs*.

D. All beagles are mammals.
<u>All dogs are mammals.</u>
All beagles are dogs.

Truth value analysis shows that the premises and the conclusion are true, so this substitution instance is not a counterexample. At this point it can help to change our strategy, so that our thinking does not get stuck in a loop. Repeating the same approach to a problem may cause us to miss other possibilities. We might fail to see alternative paths because our minds are locked into one way of analysis. Sometimes, however, all at once the light bulb goes on and we instantly see the answer (the *Aha!* experience). A puzzle illustrates how this can happen.

Imagine that you are given a knife and are told to cut a cake (with no icing) into two equal pieces with one slice. You must always cut the cake in straight lines; you cannot stop a cut halfway through the cake and resume it at another place; and you cannot touch the cake in any other way. This is easily accomplished as follows:

Once you have successfully cut the cake into two equal pieces, you are then asked to cut the cake into four equal pieces with one more slice. You should be able to do this quite easily:

At this point, you are now asked to cut the cake into eight equal parts with just one more slice. Remember the rules: you must cut the cake in straight lines; you cannot start a cut in one place and resume it somewhere else; and you cannot touch the cake in any other way. Can you do it? Do you think it is impossible?

Before reading further, you should have struggled with the problem for a while in order to experience fully the possibility of attacking the problem in only one way. The puzzle, as stated, has set your mind thinking in one direction by imagining the cake as a two-dimensional object. But the cake is a three-dimensional object. It can be cut in half through its middle, leaving four pieces on top and four on the bottom, all equal to each other.

If our search for a counterexample starts with the premises, then we start by making the premises true and then seeing if the conclusion turned out to be false. Although it is generally easier to think of things that would make the premises true, we could get stuck in a loop.

However, there is a way to shorten the amount of time needed to find a counterexample, and that is to analyze an argument from the bottom up. This technique temporarily ignores the premises and instead concentrates on the conclusion. For our current example, the conclusion is "All B are G." Since we are searching for a counterexample, we must substitute terms that make the conclusion false. It helps to choose simple terms that will make the conclusion obviously false. For example, let's try the following substitutions: B = *men*, G = *women*.

> All men are S.
> All women are S.
> All men are women.

The conclusion is clearly false. Now if we can substitute a term for the "S" in the premises, and have the premises be true, then this will produce a counterexample. But before we simply start randomly trying different terms, we should think of what we are trying to accomplish. We need to substitute something for "S" such that both premises are true. That means that we have to think of something that both men and women have in common. Well, since every man and every woman is a human being, we can try that and see what happens.

> **E.** All men are human beings.
> All women are human beings.
> All men are women.

The premises of this argument are true and the conclusion is false, so we have created a counterexample. The counterexample shows that the argument is invalid.

Let's look at another example:

> **G.** All bomohs are scam artists.
> All scam artists are grifters.
> All bomohs are grifters.

Here we have switched the order of the terms in the second premise. Once again, the first step is to reveal the logical form of the argument. Let's substitute the same letters we used earlier for the terms in order to reveal the argument form. (B = *bomohs*, S = *scam artists*, and G = *grifters*)

> **FG.** All B are S.
> All S are G.
> All B are G.

This has the same general logical form that we encountered in example FA:

FA. All D are C.
<u>All C are S.</u>
All D are S.

Since we already said that FA is a valid form, FG is valid as well. However, let's work through the argument using the bottom up technique for additional practice. We can use the same substitutions as before: B = *men*, S = *human beings,* and G = *women.*

All men are human beings.
<u>All human beings are women.</u>
All men are women.

The conclusion is false and the first premise is true. However, the second premise is false. Therefore, this particular substitution instance is not a counterexample. At this point we can take another look at the form of argument FG. If we assume that every B is an S (premise 1), and every S is a G (premise 2), then it seems to follow that every B must be a G. However, we might want to try another substitution instance. Let's use these: B = *women*, S = *human beings,* and G = *mammals.*

All women are human beings.
<u>All human beings are mammals.</u>
All women are mammals.

The premises are true, but so is the conclusion. This particular substitution instance is also not a counterexample. This brings up an interesting point. The counterexample method can be effectively used to show that an argument is invalid, but it cannot show that an argument is valid. If you think about this, it begins to make sense. Invalid arguments have counterexamples, but valid arguments do not.

In order to create a counterexample it helps to use simple terms with which you are familiar. This helps ensure that the truth value of the statements you create are generally well known to everyone. If you noticed, we used terms such as *men, women, cats,* and *dogs.* Although counterexamples are a good way to identify invalid arguments, they are sometimes difficult to create. If we are unable to create a counterexample, then this by itself does not show that the argument is valid; instead it might be that we just failed to find a counterexample. (Part III introduces additional techniques of logical analysis that are capable of showing validity.)

Since many real-life arguments do not fall easily into a form like the examples we have been examining, we sometimes have to be creative in finding a counterexample. For example, consider this argument:

Every student in my daughter's psychology class has at least a 3.0 average. But all the students in her calculus class have at least a 2.0 average. So it has to be that every single student in my daughter's psychology class has a higher average than every single student in my daughter's calculus class.

The first two statements are premises, and the third statement is the conclusion. Another way to create a counterexample to an argument is to construct a *model* that shows the possibility of true premises and a false conclusion.

Suppose that a particular student from the psychology class just mentioned has a 3.2 average. This possibility would make the first premise true. Now suppose that a particular student from the calculus class just mentioned has a 3.6 average. This is possible because the claim in the second premise is that the students have at least a 2.0 average. In this case, the second premise is true, too, but the conclusion is false. We have created a counterexample that shows the argument is invalid. Once again, we can determine whether an argument is valid or invalid without knowing the truth value of the statements involved. There are other methods of translating arguments to reveal the form, as we will see in Part III. For now, though, you can use your practical knowledge of counterexamples to help analyze arguments.

SUMMARY OF DEDUCTIVE ARGUMENTS

Valid argument: A deductive argument in which, assuming the premises are true, it is *impossible* for the conclusion to be false.

Invalid argument: A deductive argument in which, assuming the premises are true, it is *possible* for the conclusion to be false.

Sound argument: A deductive argument is sound when both of the following requirements are met:

1. The argument is valid (logical analysis).
2. All the premises are true (truth value analysis).

Unsound argument: A deductive argument is unsound if either or both of the following conditions hold:

1. The argument is invalid (logical analysis).
2. The argument has at least one false premise (truth value analysis).

CHECK YOUR UNDERSTANDING 1F

I. Create a counterexample or model to show that the following deductive arguments are invalid.

1. All towers less than 200 years old are skyscrapers. All buildings made of steel are skyscrapers. Therefore, all buildings made of steel are towers less than 200 years old.

Answer: If we let T = *towers less than 200 years old*, S = *skyscrapers*, and B = *buildings made of steel*, then the argument form is the following:

All T are S.
<u>All B are S.</u>
All B are T.

The following substitutions create a counterexample: let T = *cats*, S = *mammals*, and B = *dogs*.

> All cats are mammals.
> <u>All dogs are mammals.</u>
> All dogs are cats.

Both premises are true, and the conclusion is false. Therefore, the counterexample shows that the argument is invalid.

2. No skyscrapers are buildings made of steel. No skyscrapers are towers less than 200 years old. Therefore, no buildings made of steel are towers less than 200 years old.

3. All Phi Beta Kappa members are seniors in college. All Phi Beta Kappa members are liberal arts majors. Therefore, all liberal arts majors are seniors in college.

4. No Phi Beta Kappa members are seniors in college. No Phi Beta Kappa members are liberal arts majors. Therefore, no liberal arts majors are seniors in college.

★ 5. All computers are electronic devices. All things that require an AC adapter are electronic devices. Therefore, all computers are things that require an AC adapter.

6. No computers are electronic devices. No electronic devices are things that require an AC adapter. Therefore, no computers are things that require an AC adapter.

7. All skateboards are items made of wood. All items made of wood are flammable objects. Therefore, all flammable objects are skateboards.

8. No skateboards are items made of wood. No items made of wood are flammable objects. Therefore, no flammable objects are skateboards.

★ 9. No unicorns are immortal creatures. No centaurs are immortal creatures. It follows that no unicorns are centaurs.

10. Book A has more than 200 pages. Book B has more than 500 pages. Therefore, book B has more pages than book A.

11. Book A has more than 200 pages. Book B has more than 500 pages. Therefore, book A has more pages than book B.

12. Barney was born before 1989. Hazel was born before 1959. Thus, Hazel was born before Barney.

★ 13. Fidelix was born before 1990. Gil was born before 1991. Thus, Fidelix was born before Gil.

14. Michelle spent 1/3 of her yearly income on her car. Jerzy spent 1/2 of his yearly income on his car. Therefore, Jerzy spent more money on his car than Michelle.

15. Wayne spent 1/2 of his yearly income on his car. Joseph spent 1/3 of his yearly income on his car. Therefore, Joseph spent more money on his car than Wayne.

16. All psychiatrists are people with medical degrees. All people who can prescribe drugs are people with medical degrees. Therefore, all psychiatrists are people who can prescribe drugs.

★ 17. All strawberries are fruit. All strawberries are plants. It follows that all fruit are plants.

18. All members of the U.S. Congress are citizens of the United States. All people under 21 years of age are citizens of the United States. Therefore, no people under 21 years of age are members of the U.S. Congress.

19. All humans are things that contain carbon. All inanimate objects are things that contain carbon. Therefore, all humans are inanimate objects.

20. No coal mines are dangerous areas to work. All dangerous areas to work are places inspected by federal agencies. Therefore, no coal mines are places inspected by federal agencies.

G. INDUCTIVE ARGUMENTS: STRENGTH AND TRUTH

Often our arguments are not expected to achieve validity. As we shall see, the results of analysis of inductive arguments are not all-or-nothing. If you recall, deductive arguments can be only valid, invalid, sound, or unsound. In addition, one deductive argument cannot be more valid (or invalid) than another deductive argument. In contrast to this, one inductive argument can be classified as *stronger* or *weaker* than another inductive argument. We can compare them by determining the probability that their respective conclusions are true, under the assumption that the premises are true.

Logical analysis of an inductive argument asks, "If the premises are assumed to be true, then is it *improbable* for the conclusion to be false?" We start by offering some working definitions. A **strong inductive argument** is an argument such that if the premises are assumed to be true, then the conclusion is probably true. In other words, if the premises are assumed to be true, then it is *improbable* that the conclusion is false. On the other hand, a **weak inductive argument** is an argument such that if the premises are assumed to be true, then the conclusion is not probably true.

When we add truth value analysis to the results of the logical analysis, we get two additional classifications. An inductive argument is **cogent** when the argument is strong and the premises are true. On the other hand, an inductive argument is **uncogent** if either or both of the following conditions hold: the argument is weak, or the argument has at least one false premise. The following flow chart illustrates the process:

Strong inductive argument An argument such that if the premises are assumed to be true, then the conclusion is probably true. In other words, if the premises are assumed to be true, then it is improbable that the conclusion is false.

Weak inductive argument An argument such that if the premises are assumed to be true, then the conclusion is not probably true.

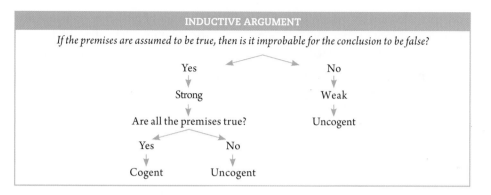

Cogent argument An inductive argument is cogent when the argument is strong and the premises are true.

Uncogent argument An inductive argument is uncogent if either or both of the following conditions hold: the argument is weak, or the argument has at least one false premise.

Techniques of Analysis

Imagine that you have the following information: An opaque jar contains exactly 100 marbles. There are 99 blue marbles in the jar, and there is 1 red marble in the jar. Next, you are told that someone has reached into the jar and picked one marble, and you and a friend are going to guess what color it is. You choose blue and your friend chooses red. We can use this case to create two inductive arguments:

A. An opaque jar contains exactly 100 marbles.
There are 99 blue marbles in the jar.
<u>There is 1 red marble in the jar.</u>
The marble picked is blue.

B. An opaque jar contains exactly 100 marbles.
There are 99 blue marbles in the jar.
<u>There is 1 red marble in the jar.</u>
The marble picked is red.

Using the definitions for inductive arguments, a logical analysis shows that argument A is strong and argument B is weak. In fact, based on the assumption that the premises are true we can calculate that the conclusion of argument A has a 99/100 chance of being true, while the conclusion of argument B has only a 1/100 chance of being true. Given this, we can say that argument A is much stronger than argument B.

Now suppose we are shown the actual marble that was picked and it is red. Is this a counterexample to argument A that would make argument A weak? And would this result suddenly render argument B strong? The answer to both questions is *No*. We determined that the premises, *if they are assumed to be true*, make the conclusion of argument A *probably true*. On the other hand, the premises, *if they are assumed to be true*, make the conclusion of argument B *not probably true*. Therefore, the single result of a red marble does not change our mind.

However, at some point new evidence can become a factor in our overall assessment. Suppose that the red marble is returned to the jar, the jar is shaken, and a second pick yields a red marble again. Since we are assuming that there is only one red marble in the jar, the probability of this happening is $1/100 \times 1/100 = 1/10{,}000$—which is very small, *but not impossible*. In fact, in a very long series of picks, we would eventually expect this to happen. But now suppose that the next five picks all result in a red marble, and each time the red marble is returned and the jar shaken. The probability is now 1/100 multiplied by itself seven times (that is, the original two picks plus five more, all resulting in red). Faced with the new evidence, we may need to explain why we are getting these unexpected results.

We still assume that the premises are true; this is how we are coming up with the probabilities. But at some point the evidence—the actual results—may cause us to *question the truth of the premises*. We might begin to question the proportion of red to blue marbles. We might even doubt that there are any blue ones at all, or if there are 100 marbles. It could even be that this is a scam; the person picking the marble palms a red one and never really puts it back. In other words, we might start doubting the truth of any or all of the premises.

As this example shows, determining whether an inductive argument is strong or weak is not an all-or-nothing thing. Also, a single counterexample does not have the same effect on an inductive argument that it has on a deductive argument. The goals of inductive arguments and deductive arguments are simply different.

Here is another example for analysis:

C. Most National Basketball Association players of the year were at least six feet tall.
The next National Basketball Association player of the year will be at least six feet tall.

As before, logical analysis begins by assuming that the premise is true. Based on this assumption, the conclusion is probably true; therefore, the argument is strong. Furthermore, a truth analysis of the premise reveals that it is true; therefore, the argument is strong and cogent.

Since inductive arguments and deductive arguments have different goals, they cannot be judged in the same manner. There are two goals of a deductive argument: (1) Under the assumption that the premises are true, it is *impossible* for the conclusion to be false (logical analysis); (2) the premises are true (truth value analysis). Given the first goal, it is not surprising that, for a deductive argument, a single counterexample is enough to render the deductive argument invalid. Given the second goal, even one false premise will render a valid deductive argument unsound.

In contrast to this, the logical goal of an inductive argument is different, but the truth value goal is the same: (1) Under the assumption that the premises are true it is *improbable* for the conclusion to be false; (2) the premises are true (truth value analysis). Given the logical goal of an inductive argument, the counterexample method is not by itself enough to render an inductive argument weak. After all, we already accept that it is logically possible for the conclusion to be false while the premises are true. What is important for us to determine about an inductive argument is how *probable* the conclusion is, assuming the premises are true. Given the second goal of an inductive argument, even one false premise will render a strong inductive argument uncogent.

As we saw earlier, there are many types of inductive arguments. In Part IV (Inductive Logic) we introduce techniques of analysis for several types of inductive argument. In addition, Chapter 3 will provide some additional opportunity to work with inductive arguments.

SUMMARY OF INDUCTIVE ARGUMENTS

Strong argument: An inductive argument such that if the premises are assumed to be true, then the conclusion is probably true.

Weak argument: An inductive argument such that if the premises are assumed to be true, then the conclusion is not probably true.

Cogent argument: An inductive argument is cogent when both of the following requirements are met:
1. The argument is strong (logical analysis).
2. All the premises are true (truth value analysis).

Uncogent argument: An inductive argument is uncogent if either or both of the following conditions hold:
1. The argument is weak (logical analysis).
2. The argument has at least one false premise (truth value analysis).

CHECK YOUR UNDERSTANDING 1G

I. Determine whether the following inductive arguments are *strong* or *weak*.

1. Most insects have six legs. What's crawling on me is an insect. So what's crawling on me has six legs.

Answer: Strong. If we assume the premises are true, then the conclusion is probably true.

2. The exam's range of A scores is 90–100. I got an A on the exam, thus I got a 98 on the exam.

3. The exam's range of A scores is 90–100; B scores are 80–89; C scores are 70–79; D scores are 60–69; and F scores are 0–59. I did not get a 98 on the exam. Therefore, I probably did not get an A on the exam.

4. Shane tossed a coin ten times, and in each case it came up heads. Therefore, the next toss will be tails.

5. Shane tossed a coin ten times, and in each case it came up heads. Therefore, the next toss will be heads.

6. Most elements with atomic weights greater than 64 are metals. Z is an element with an atomic weight of 79. Therefore, Z is a metal.

7. Most elements with atomic weights greater than 64 are metals. Z is an element with an atomic weight less than 64. Therefore, Z is a metal.

8. Most antibiotics are effective for treating bacterial infections. You have a bacterial infection. You are taking the antibiotic Q. Thus, the antibiotic you are taking will be effective in treating your bacterial infection.

★ 9. Most fruit have seeds. I am eating an orange, so I am eating something with seeds.

10. Most Doberman dogs bark a lot. My cousin just got a Doberman dog. Therefore, my cousin's Doberman dog will probably bark a lot.

Summary

- Argument: A group of statements of which one (the conclusion) is claimed to follow from the others (the premises).
- Statement: A sentence that is either true or false.
- Premises: Contain information intended to provide support or reasons to believe a conclusion, the statement that is claimed to follow from the premises.
- Logic is the study of reasoning. Logic investigates the level of correctness of the reasoning found in arguments.
- Every statement is either true or false; these two possibilities are called "truth values."
- Proposition: The information content imparted by a statement, or, simply put, its meaning.
- Inference: The term used by logicians to refer to the reasoning process that is expressed by an argument.
- In order to help recognize arguments, we rely on premise indicator words and phrases, and conclusion indicator words and phrases.
- If a passage expresses a reasoning process—that the conclusion follows from the premises—then we say that it makes an inferential claim.
- If a passage does not express a reasoning process (explicit or implicit), then it does not make an inferential claim (it is a noninferential passage).
- Explanation: Provides reasons for why or how an event occurred. By themselves, explanations are not arguments; however, they can form part of an argument.
- Deductive argument: One in which it is claimed that the conclusion follows necessarily from the premises. In other words, it is claimed that under the assumption that the premises are true it is impossible for the conclusion to be false.
- Inductive argument: One in which it is claimed that the premises make the conclusion probable. In other words, it is claimed that, under the assumption that the premises are true, it is improbable for the conclusion to be false.

- Valid deductive argument: One where, assuming the premises are true, it is impossible for the conclusion to be false. In other words, the conclusion follows necessarily from the premises.
- Invalid deductive argument: One where, assuming the premises are true, it is possible for the conclusion to be false. In other words, a deductive argument in which the conclusion does not follow necessarily from the premises is an invalid argument.
- When logical analysis shows that a deductive argument is valid, and when truth value analysis of the premises shows that they are all true, then the argument is sound.
- If a deductive argument is invalid, or if at least one of the premises is false (truth value analysis), then the argument is unsound.
- Revealing the logical form of a deductive argument helps with logical analysis.
- A counterexample to a statement is evidence that shows the statement is false, and it concerns truth value analysis. A counterexample to an argument shows the possibility that premises assumed to be true do not make the conclusion necessarily true. A single counterexample to a deductive argument is enough to show that an argument is invalid.
- Strong inductive argument: An argument such that if the premises are assumed to be true, then the conclusion is probably true. In other words, if the premises are assumed to be true, then it is improbable that the conclusion is false.
- Weak inductive argument: An argument such that if the premises are assumed to be true, then the conclusion is not probably true.
- An inductive argument is cogent when the argument is strong and the premises are true. An inductive argument is uncogent if either or both of the following conditions hold: the argument is weak, or the argument has at least one false premise.

KEY TERMS

argument 3	premise indicator 7	sound argument 27
statement 3	inferential claim 7	unsound argument 27
premise 3	explanation 18	counterexample 30
conclusion 3	deductive argument 23	strong inductive
logic 3	inductive argument 23	argument 36
truth value 4	valid deductive	weak inductive
proposition 4	argument 27	argument 36
inference 4	invalid deductive	cogent argument 36
conclusion indicator 6	argument 27	uncogent argument 36

LOGIC CHALLENGE: THE PROBLEM OF THE HATS

Scientists, philosophers, mathematicians, detectives, logicians, and physicians all face logical problems. How do they go about solving them? For insights, try your own hand at a challenge, the *problem of the hats*. Once you are given the facts of the case, be aware of how you attack the problem, how you take it apart, what you place emphasis on, your avenues of pursuit, and plausible conjectures. The answer requires "seeing" a key move.

Here is the challenge: A teacher comes to class with a box and shows the contents of the box to the students. It contains three white hats, two red hats, and nothing else. There happen to be only three students in this class, and the teacher tells them that he is going to blindfold each one and then place one of the five hats on each of their heads. The remaining two hats will then be placed back in the box, so no one can see them once the blindfolds are removed. If anyone can tell what color hat they have on their heads, then the teacher will give that student an A. But the students are not allowed to guess: they must be able to *prove* they have that color hat.

The teacher removes the blindfold from the first student, who is now able to see the color of the hats on the other two students—but not his own. The first student looks carefully at the other two hats, thinks silently for a while, and says he does not know the color of his hat. The teacher then removes the blindfold from the second student. He, too, looks at the hats on the other two students, thinks for a while, and says he does not know the color of his hat. (As before, this student does *not* say aloud the color of the hats he sees on the other two students' heads.) Now, just as the teacher is about to remove the blindfold from the third student, she says that she knows exactly the color of the hat on her head. In fact, she doesn't even need to see the hats of the other two students to know this.

Can you see how she did it? No information is being held back, no tricks are being played, and no word games are used. All the information necessary to solve the problem is contained in its description. There are three possibilities for you to consider. Which is correct?

1. She cannot possibly know what color hat she has on her head.
2. She has a red hat and can prove it.
3. She has a white hat and can prove it.

Part II

INFORMAL LOGIC

Chapter 2

Language Matters

Words are powerful. They can incite riots and move people to revolt, or they can create calm and soothe those in pain. They take on the aura of "magic words," like secret spells, or they can harm others by their very meaning, such as racial or religious slurs. Words can also fail us. Visiting someone in a hospital or attending a funeral is uncomfortable if we don't know what to say. Even asking for a date can be a frightening experience. We imagine that there are perfect sentences, and if we were lucky enough to utter them, then the person of our dreams would fall in love.

Skill and practice are essential in order to use language effectively—and so are clear, unambiguous, and precise definitions. Most words have multiple meanings, which helps explain why communication can misfire. A misunderstanding can occur even among those we meet every day. Hearing or reading something in context can help, and in conversation we can often ask for clarification. But misunderstandings can have serious consequences, and a choice between two meanings of a single word can affect the course of history.

> A Japanese word, *mokusatsu*, may have changed all our lives. It has two meanings: (1) to ignore, (2) to refrain from comment. The release of a press statement using the second meaning in July 1945 might have ended the war then. The Emperor was ready to end it, and had the power to do so. The cabinet was preparing to accede to the Potsdam ultimatum of the Allies—surrender or be crushed—but wanted a little more time to discuss the terms. A press release was prepared announcing a policy of *mokusatsu*, with the *no comment* implication. But it got on the foreign wires with the *ignore* implication through a mix-up in translation: "The cabinet *ignores* the demand to surrender." To recall the release would have entailed an unthinkable loss of face. Had the intended meaning been publicized, the cabinet might have backed up the Emperor's

decision to surrender. In which event, there might have been no atomic bombs over Hiroshima and Nagasaki, no Russian armies in Manchuria, no Korean war to follow. The lives of tens of thousands of Japanese and American boys might have been saved. One word, misinterpreted.

Stuart Chase, *Power of Words*

Definitions play an important part in analyzing statements and arguments because terms often have numerous meanings. They do, in fact, in the title of this chapter. In "Language Matters," the word "matters" has two legitimate interpretations. It can refer to the subject of the chapter—*the use of language*—or it can refer to the significance of that subject. As we'll see, language is an important topic for the study of logic.

Ambiguity can serve a purpose, just as in the chapter title, and it can also be a great source for jokes. A *double entendre* can be funny when we recognize that a key word has both a common meaning and a risqué or suggestive one. However, when it comes to arguments, *vague, ambiguous,* or *imprecise* terms can reduce the clarity of statements and so get in the way of our understanding of an argument.

A term is *vague* whenever there is no clear or distinct meaning that is attached to it. For example, the phrases "a rich person," "a fair price," and "natural preservatives" remain vague until we are given precise information regarding their intended meaning. In some cases, vagueness occurs because a term is relative to a given situation. For example, you might be considered rich in one country, but not in another. Here is another statement that uses a vague term: "The amount of nuclear waste material in the United States is quite small." What counts as "quite small"? Would the nuclear waste material fit in a tractor trailer, or would it fill up a football stadium? Descriptions like these can clarify a term's meaning.

A term is *ambiguous* if it has several meanings (each of which can be clear and distinct). For example, in the statement "He just bought a light suit," the term "light" might mean either the color of the suit or the weight of the material. We normally rely on context to alert us to which meaning is intended. For example, the terms "left" and "right" are ambiguous unless we are told which direction we are facing. In the following three examples, the term "premises" has multiple distinct meanings, but each is used in a way that eliminates ambiguity:

A. "Premises" means statements that are offered in support of a conclusion.
B. "These premises are off-limits" means that only police authorities are permitted to enter.
C. In a bill of equity case, "premises" means the preliminary or explanatory statements or facts of a document, as in a deed.

In each instance, the term "premises" was defined in a way that eliminates ambiguity, vagueness, and imprecision. Throughout this chapter, we will illustrate how language is used, along with methods that are available to clarify the words in statements and arguments. We hope you gain an appreciation of the relationship between language and logic.

A. INTENSION AND EXTENSION

Term A single word
or a group of words
that can be the subject
of a statement; it can
be a common name, a
proper name, or even a
descriptive phrase.

Clarifying the meaning of statements requires a close look at the meaning of the terms. A **term** is either a single word or a group of words that can be the subject of a statement. A term can be a common name, a proper name, or even a descriptive phrase:

Common Names	Proper Names	Descriptive Phrases
plant	Cleopatra	registered voters
building	Los Angeles	purple flowers
car	Mars	the director of *Inception*
mammal	Moby Dick	military personnel
money	Michael Jordan	Nobel Prize winners

In this section, we look closely at two kinds of meaning: *intension* and *extension*. First, however, we need to be sure we know what we mean by using a term.

Terms, Use, and Mention

Not all words are terms. Generally speaking, prepositions, adverbs, some adjectives, conjunctions, and ungrammatical phrases are not considered to be terms, because they are not the subject of a statement. Here are some examples:

Prepositions	**Adverbs**	**Conjunctions**
in, on, by, since	*quickly, very happily, easily*	*and, but, because, however*

Certain Adjectives	**Ungrammatical Phrases**
good, wise, another, rotten	*a heavily into pothole thus*

We can also distinguish the *use* of a word from the *mention* of a word. This distinction is helpful because it introduces a method that helps clarify some written language. Three sentences can help illustrate the difference:

- John is my brother.
- "John" is a four-letter word.
- "John" means a toilet or bathroom; it can also mean a prostitute's customer.

The first statement *uses* the word "John" as the subject. (Notice that the term does not appear in quotes in that statement.) Thus we say that the first statement *uses* the word "John" (without quotes) to refer to a person. However, in the second example it is not the term itself that is the subject. Instead, it is the term that appears within quotation marks that is the subject. We say that it is being *mentioned*. In other words, the subject of the first statement is a *person*, while the subject of the second statement is the *word* that appears within quotation marks. The subject of third sentence is also the word appearing within quotation marks.

Earlier we described a word such as "because" as not being a term. However, it can still be the subject of a statement when it is enclosed in quotes and is being mentioned. Consider the following two examples:

A. The word "because" is a good premise indicator.

B. I will vote for her because she has outlined a clear strategy for economic recovery.

In the first example the word "because" (appearing in quotes) is being *mentioned*; the quoted word is the subject of the statement. However, in the second example the word "because" (appearing without quotes) is being *used*; it is not a subject.

Two Kinds of Meaning

Two kinds of meaning are associated with terms. The first is the **intension** of a term, which is specified by listing the properties or attributes that the term connotes—in other words, its *sense*. (Do not confuse the term "intension" with "intention." *Intension* is the connotation of a term, whereas *intention* is a mental determination, the intent or purpose of an action.) For example, to specify the intensional meaning of the term "automobile," you might provide a (partial) list of properties: passenger vehicle; powered by an engine; used for traveling on roads and highways.

The second kind of meaning associated with a term is the **extension**—the **class** or collection of objects to which the term applies. In other words, what the term denotes (its *reference*).

> **Intension** The intension of a term is specified by listing the properties or attributes that the term connotes—in other words, its sense.

> **Extension** The class or collection of objects to which the term applies. In other words, what the term denotes (its reference).

> **Class** A group of objects.

The term "automobile" and its meanings

Intension *(connotation):*
The properties:
passenger vehicle; powered by an engine; used for traveling on roads and highways.

Extension *(denotation):*
The class members:
All the cars in the world.

Some terms have intension but no extension. For example, the term "centaur" connotes the following properties: a creature that has a man's head, torso, and arms, but the body and legs of a horse. However, the term "centaur" has no extension; it denotes an **empty class**, or one that has zero members. We get the same result for all mythological creature terms and fictional terms.

> **Empty class** A class that has zero members.

The intension of the term "dinosaurs" is the following: various carnivorous or herbivorous reptiles that lived mostly on land and existed during the Mesozoic Era. The extension of the term is all the dinosaurs that once existed. Although dinosaurs did exist, the term "currently living dinosaurs" denotes an empty class, as does any term that connects the phrase "currently living" with any other extinct animal. This illustrates an important general rule: *Extension is determined by intension.* The intension of the term "currently living dinosaurs" is such that it connotes an attribute that has no reference (i.e., an empty class). On the other hand, the term "currently living cows" has extension, since it refers to all the cows alive today, while the term "cows" refers to all cows living or dead.

To see what effect intension has on extension, take a simple example:

water; ocean; Pacific Ocean

Increasing intension
In a sequence of terms where each term after the first connotes more attributes than the previous term.

Decreasing extension
In a sequence of terms where each term after the first denotes a set of objects with fewer members than the previous term.

Decreasing intension
In a sequence of terms where each term after the first connotes fewer attributes than the previous term.

Increasing extension
In a sequence of terms where each term after the first denotes a set of objects with more members than the previous term.

This sequence of terms has **increasing intension**, meaning that each term after the first connotes more attributes than the previous term. Simply put, the series of terms displays an increase in specific attributes. On the other hand, the sequence of terms has **decreasing extension**, meaning that each term after the first denotes a set of objects with fewer members than the previous term. The extension of the term "water" is all the water in the world; the extension of the term "ocean" is the five recognized oceans (Arctic, Atlantic, Indian, Pacific, and the Southern or Antarctic Ocean); the extension of the term "Pacific Ocean" is one specific ocean.

Let's look at another example:

banana; fruit; food; commodity

This sequence of terms has **decreasing intension**, meaning that each term after the first connotes fewer attributes than the previous term. In other words, the series of terms displays a decrease in specific attributes. However, the sequence of terms has **increasing extension**; each term after the first denotes a set of objects with more members than the previous term. The extension of the term "banana" is all the bananas in the world; the extension of the term "fruit" includes all types of fruit (including bananas); the extension of the term "food" is to all kinds of food (including fruit); and finally, the extension of the term "commodity" is to any kind of product or article of trade or commerce (including food).

Generally speaking, we will find the following to be the case:

- A series of terms that has *increasing intension* has *decreasing extension*.
- A series of terms that has *decreasing intension* has *increasing extension*.
- A series of terms that has *increasing extension* has *decreasing intension*.
- A series of terms that has *decreasing extension* has *increasing intension*.

Of course, these general rules have some exceptions. If a term denotes an empty class, then a series of terms with increasing (or decreasing) intension will not affect the extension (it will remain empty). Here is an example:

leprechaun; leprechaun with red hair; leprechaun with red hair and a green hat

The series of terms regarding leprechauns displays increasing intension, but each term in the sequence denotes an empty class. Another exception to the general rule is when the series of terms has increasing intension but the extension, while not empty, nevertheless remains the same throughout the series. Here is an example:

living horse; living horse with DNA; living horse with DNA and a central nervous system

The series of terms displays increasing intension, but all the terms in the series have the same (non-empty) extension.

Proper Names

One further point needs to be clarified. Since proper names, such as "Cleopatra," can refer to different people, they require a slightly different type of analysis. One way to think about a proper name is that it is simply a shorthand way of describing a person. The descriptions we attach to proper names are, therefore, a special kind of intension, and again will determine the extension of the term. Here is an example:

> After Julius Caesar's assassination, Cleopatra, the Queen of Egypt who died in 30 BC, aligned with Mark Antony instead of Caesar's son Augustus.

Since there are typically many different descriptions that can be used to identify the denotation of a proper name, context and a familiarity with their descriptions can help clear up any confusion. Here is another example that uses the term "Cleopatra":

> Cleopatra, the Los Angeles based record company, recently announced that it signed Huw Lloyd-Langton to a long-term record deal.

Once again, the description attached to the proper name is used to clarify the intended denotation. Whereas the proper name "Cleopatra" denotes a person in the first example, it denotes a record company in the second example. These examples illustrate how relevant descriptions can be used to help determine the extension of a proper name.

The next two sections will explore some specific techniques used to produce definitions. We will begin by describing four intensional definition techniques—*synonymous definitions*, *etymological definitions*, *operational definitions*, and *definition by genus and difference*. This will be followed by an examination of three extensional definition techniques—*ostensive definitions*, *enumerative definitions*, and *definition by subclass*.

CHECK YOUR UNDERSTANDING 2A

I. List some of the properties connoted by the following terms.

1. athlete

Answer: strong, fast, agile, stamina, skilled, competitor

2. country

3. animal

4. game

⭐ 5. president

6. mammal

7. book

8. planet

⭐ 9. plant

10. teacher

11. computer

12. city

II. Name three things denoted by the following terms.

   1. athlete
Answer: Tiger Woods, Shaquille O'Neal, Tom Brady

   2. magazine

   3. movie

   4. U.S. senator

★ 5. philosopher

   6. novelist

   7. Nobel Prize winner

   8. jazz musician

★ 9. lake

  10. extinct animal

III. Name all the things denoted by the following terms.

   1. capital city of California
Answer: Sacramento

   2. Nobel Prize winner in two fields

   3. Earth continent

   4. first person to step on the Moon

★ 5. Seven Wonders of the Ancient World

   6. person who won the most Best Actress Academy Awards

   7. tallest mountain on Earth

   8. planet in our solar system

★ 9. month with 31 days

  10. first person to fly solo across the Atlantic Ocean

IV. The following will require you to apply your knowledge of intension and extension to a sequence of terms.

Put the following series of terms in the order of *increasing intension.*

   1. mammal, animal, pediatrician, physician, human
Answer: animal, mammal, human, physician, pediatrician

   2. American sports car, Corvette, car, sports car, vehicle

   3. shrub, Portland rose, plant, perennial, rose

Put the following series of terms in the order of *increasing extension*.

4. polygon, equilateral triangle, isosceles triangle, convex polygon, triangle

⭐ 5. robin, animal, thrush, flying animal, bird

6. skyscraper, office building, building, New York City skyscraper, Empire State Building

Put the following series of terms in the order of *decreasing intension*.

7. Usain Bolt, human, track and field athlete, athlete, Olympic Gold Medal winner

8. printing, book, 20th-century fictional book, *The Grapes of Wrath*, fictional book

⭐ 9. chilled dessert, dessert, Jell-O, food, Cherry Jell-O

Put the following series of terms in the order of *decreasing extension*.

10. *In the Heat of the Night*, dramas, entertainment, Sidney Poitier movies, movies

11. painting, Vincent van Gogh's *Still Life with Flowers*, still life, art, 19th-century still life

12. human, *Apollo 11* crew member, pilot, Neil Armstrong, astronaut

B. USING INTENSIONAL DEFINITIONS

Part of the analysis of statements and arguments is evaluating the clarity of the terms involved. We saw earlier that the term "matters" can convey two meanings, as in the chapter title. In that setting the ambiguity is not out of place. However, when it comes to arguments, ambiguity should be eliminated. Much of ordinary language contains ambiguous or imprecise political terms, such as "liberal" and "conservative." Typically, statements containing these political labels suffer from being unclear. Consider the following argument:

> My opponent for governor is a liberal, so you should vote against her.

Since we have no idea what the speaker means by the term "liberal," our understanding of the argument is hindered—precisely because of the lack of clarity. An important requirement for a good argument, then, is that all the terms have an acceptable, clear, and unambiguous meaning. This is also a simple but crucial requirement for all communication; its strict adherence would eliminate many confusions and controversies. Problems related to unclear terms can lead to difficulty in determining the truth content of individual statements. In turn, these individual statement problems sometimes lead to *informal fallacies* (the subject of Chapter 4).

A **definition** assigns a meaning to a word, phrase, or symbol. Logicians use the term **definiendum** to refer to that which is being defined, and the term **definiens** to refer to that which does the defining. For example, if you look in a normal dictionary for the definition of the term "book" (the definiendum), you might find the following partial entry: "a printed work of fiction or nonfiction" (the definiens). In one sense then, what

Definition A definition assigns a meaning to a word, phrase, or symbol.

Definiendum Refers to that which is being defined.

Definiens Refers to that which does the defining.

the definiens does is provide an alternative symbolism that has the same meaning as the definiendum. It is in this manner that we say that the definition has assigned a meaning to the definiendum. Here are some examples:

DEFINITIONS

Definiendum	Definiens
e-book	short for "electronic book"; any book published in digital form
dog-eat-dog world	ruthless competition; looking out for your own self-interest
shaman	a person claiming to use magic to cure diseases or predict the future

Intensional definition

Assigns a meaning to a term by listing the properties or attributes shared by all the objects that are denoted by the term.

Synonymous definition

Assigns a meaning to a term by providing another term with the same meaning; in other words, by providing a synonym.

An **intensional** (connotative) **definition** assigns a meaning to a term by listing the properties or attributes shared by all the objects that are denoted by the term. We will examine some of the different strategies that are used for intensional definitions.

Synonymous Definitions

As the name indicates, a **synonymous definition** assigns a meaning to a term by providing another term with the same meaning; in other words, by providing a synonym. This can be a very simple and effective technique to convey the meaning of a term, as long as the synonym is readily understood. Here are a few examples of synonymous definitions:

- "Honest" means trustworthy.
- "Attorney" means lawyer.
- "Feckless" means irresponsible.
- "Adversity" means misfortune.

Since many words cannot be defined accurately by a synonym, this technique has its limitations. For example, someone might try defining "obscene" as "indecent," "offensive," or "depraved." But this word cannot be easily captured by a mere synonym, partly because of the moral and legal issues connected with its use. The Supreme Court has wrestled with trying to define the term "obscene" for legal purposes. In the case of *Miller v. California* (1973), a decision to adopt a definition had five justices in agreement. The majority opinion stated that there were three basic guidelines: "(a) whether 'the average person, applying contemporary community standards' would find that the work, taken as a whole, appeals to the prurient interest; (b) whether the work depicts or describes, in a patently offensive way, sexual conduct specifically defined by the applicable state law; and (c) whether the work, taken as a whole, lacks serious literary, artistic, political, or scientific value." Four justices dissented.

As you can see, these "guidelines" are filled with terms that themselves need to be defined. "Average person," "contemporary community standards," "prurient interest," "sexual conduct," and "serious literary, artistic, political, or scientific value" all need to be clarified.

Word Origin Definitions

A meaning can be assigned to a term by investigating its origin. Since most ordinary English words originated in older languages, such as Latin, Greek, and Arabic, we can often trace the current meaning back to its original sources to see how it has changed through time. The study of the history, development, and sources of words is called *etymology*. For example, the word "etymology" itself comes from the Greek word "etymologia," which combines two root words—"etymo," meaning *true sense*, and "logos," meaning *word*. The suffix "-logy" has another common meaning—*the study of*. Although the term "etymology" originally meant *the true sense of a word*, it now means *the study of the origin of words*. The importance of investigating the origin of words is expressed by the following quote:

> The older a word, the deeper it reaches.   Ludwig Wittgenstein, *Notebooks*

Knowing the origin of a word can sometimes illustrate why the term was chosen. Here is one example:

> "Malaria" means an infectious disease characterized by recurring attacks of chills and fever. The term derives from the Italian "mala," meaning bad, and "aria," meaning air. The term was used because of the mistaken belief that the disease was caused by the bad air in swampy districts. It was only during the 1890s that experiments revealed that the disease was caused by mosquitoes.

Many familiar terms use the common suffix "-logy." For example, "psychology" is now defined as the science or study of human and animal behavior. The term is derived from two Greek words: "psyche," meaning *soul*, and "logia," meaning *the study of*. The term "biology" is now defined as the science or study of living organisms. The term is derived from two Greek words: "bios," meaning *life*, and "logia," meaning *the study of*. Here is one more example of a word origin definition:

> "Philosophy" means love of wisdom. It derives from the Greek word "philosophia" which is a combination of the two root words "philo," meaning *loving*, and "sophia," meaning *wisdom or knowledge*.

Word origin definitions have a practical value as well. Anyone who has watched the National Spelling Bee will recognize the common strategy of not only asking for the definition of a word, but also asking for the language of origin of a word. Contestants who have studied the root words of a given language can use that knowledge to break down a complex word into its component parts. This can help them decide which prefix or suffix to try when piecing together the spelling of a word.

Operational Definitions

An **operational definition** defines a term by specifying a measurement procedure. For example, academic achievement is very important for many people in the field of education, including teachers, administrators, test developers, and students. An operational definition of "academic achievement" might use grade point average (GPA) as a measuring procedure. This measuring device is *quantitative* because it provides us

Operational definition Defines a term by specifying a measurement procedure.

with a range of numerical values. In most colleges, the range is from 4.0 to 0.0, with the highest (4.0) for all A's, to the lowest (0.0) for all F's. Every student who has finished at least one semester has a place on the scale from the highest to the lowest.

An alternative operational definition for "academic achievement" might use letters of recommendation written by teachers. This measuring device is quite different from a GPA; it is *qualitative* because its range of values is open-ended. Letters of recommendation may state the grades you received, as well as an assessment of your position relative to other students (for example, the top 10% of the class). It might also mention other important factors, such as your ability to write original essays, self-discipline, willingness to help other students, the ability to ask relevant questions and grasp abstract material, and the prospects for graduate work, to name a few.

We could rank each student in order, from those with the strongest letters of recommendation to those with the weakest. This would not be easy because we are not dealing with a straightforward quantitative method. For example, the terms "strongest" and "weakest" need to be defined. For the same reason, if we then compare two sets of student rankings for the same student body, we might be surprised to see a large variation. The two lists might not match up very well at all. Therefore, the kind of operational definition we give to a term may affect the strength of the argument in which it plays a part.

Many terms denote phenomena that can only be observed indirectly, such as radioactivity. We cannot see radioactivity. We do, however, have powerful ways of measuring it, as with a Geiger counter, an instrument designed to detect radioactive particles. As in this example, we need some empirical means of measuring or performing experiments on many phenomena in order to obtain objective evidence about them. Scientists can study electrons and other subatomic particles only indirectly, in a device called a "cloud chamber," which is a sealed container containing alcohol vapor. The electrons traveling through the chamber condense the vapor, much like the vapor trails you see in the sky behind a jet airplane. In each of these examples, we are offered strong evidence that these terms denote something that can be physically observed, albeit indirectly.

Since many terms require extraordinary evidence to convince us that they denote actually existing objects, researchers must develop strong methods of gathering indirect evidence. To help us determine if a term truly refers to objects that we can observe only indirectly, we rely on measurement, prediction, and explanation.

First, if a claim uses a term to denote a part of the physical world (however invisible it might be to our five senses), the person asserting the claim must be able to provide strong, credible evidence to back it up. This has been accomplished by devices that can detect and measure what we cannot directly observe. For example, scientists have developed barometers, thermometers, Geiger counters, cloud chambers, and cyclotrons, to name just a few inventions, in order to gather evidence. Second, these measuring devices must allow the accurate prediction of future experimental results. Finally, we must be able to explain how and why the events occur as they do. In other words, the explanations require a theoretical framework or model, as we explore in detail in Chapter 14.

Definition by Genus and Difference

We saw that an intensional definition specifies the attributes that a term connotes, and in this way it determines the class denoted by the term. Any class that has members can be divided into smaller classes called *subclasses*. For example, the class of fruit has many subclasses, such as cherries, strawberries, and apples. And each of those subclasses can be further divided. For example, the subclass of apples has several subclasses of its own, such as McIntosh, Rome, and Granny Smith. We refer to any class of objects that is being divided as the *genus* and the subclasses as *species*. (You can think of the "genus" as *general*, and the "species" as *specific*.)

The terms "genus" and "species" have a slightly different meaning in logic than they do in biology. Biological classifications are ways to relate all life in a hierarchy. For example, humans, whales, dolphins, wolves, and dogs are all members of the class *mammals*. However, humans belong to the order (subclass) *primates*; whales and dolphins belong to the order *cetacea*; wolves and dogs both belong to the order *canidae*. The biological hierarchy is sometimes referred to as the *tree of life* on which all living organisms have a specific place in the hierarchy.

Ludwig Wittgenstein

What would you do if you wrote a book in which you thought you had answered all philosophical questions? Give away the substantial fortune that you inherited? Go teach primary school in a small village? That's exactly what Ludwig Wittgenstein did.

Ludwig Wittgenstein (1889–1951) came from one of the wealthiest families in Vienna. The children all seemed to be gifted with various talents. His brother Paul, for example, was a concert pianist who lost his right arm in WWI. The composer Ravel in fact wrote the *Piano Concerto for Left Hand* for him.

Ludwig also served in the Austrian army during World War I. During his time as a prisoner of war, he began writing what came to be known as *Tractatus Logico-Philosophicus*, one of the most influential books of the last century. In it, Wittgenstein applied recent advances in logic to traditional philosophical questions—and declared them over and done.

As he wrote in the preface, "I am, therefore, of the opinion that the problems have in essentials been finally solved."

The *Tractatus* is a difficult book, subject to many interpretations. Wittgenstein himself said, "I should not like my writing to spare other people the trouble of thinking." For him, the limits of thought are established by clarifying the limits of language: "What we cannot speak about we must pass over in silence."

But Wittgenstein did return to philosophy. He gave lectures to small groups of students, many of whom went on to become influential philosophers themselves. He also wrote a substantial amount of his thoughts in a series of notebooks. Although he withheld publishing anything else during his lifetime, his *Philosophical Investigations* became enormously influential. Despite Wittgenstein's best efforts, philosophical questions are still being asked.

Logic uses the terms "genus" and "species" in a more flexible way, so classes and subclasses do not need to remain in a rigid hierarchy. A person can be placed in many different classes and subclasses, which do not need to have a sense of higher or lower. It is possible for a person to be a mother, daughter, sister, cousin, aunt, professor, scientist, Pulitzer Prize winner, and skier. In fact, it is possible for a class to be a genus relative to one species, and yet that same class can be a species relative to a different genus. For example, the class of siblings is a genus in relation to the species sister. But the class of siblings happens to be a species in relation to the genus offspring. For our purposes, a *genus* is simply any class that is larger than any of its subclasses (*species*).

We can distinguish the different species (subclasses) of a genus by listing the attribute or attributes that indicates the *difference* (or specific difference) between each species. For example, consider the genus *offspring* and two species, *son* and *daughter*. When we qualify the genus offspring by adding the term "male" we supply the difference. The combination of a term denoting the genus (in this example "offspring") with a term that connotes a specific difference (in this example "male") creates the meaning of the term that denotes the species. Here are five examples that illustrate the complete process:

DEFINIENDUM		DEFINIENS	
Species		**Difference + Genus**	
• "Mother"	means	female	parent
• "Bachelor"	means	unmarried	adult male
• "Igloo"	means	snow	house
• "Triangle"	means	three-sided	polygon
• "Gelding"	means	castrated	male horse

Definition by genus and difference Assigns a meaning to a term (the species) by establishing a genus and combining it with the attribute that distinguishes the members of that species.

As the examples illustrate, a **definition by genus and difference** assigns a meaning to a term (the *species*) by establishing a *genus* and combining it with the attribute (the specific *difference*) that distinguishes the members of that species.

C. USING EXTENSIONAL DEFINITIONS

Extensional definition Assigns meaning to a term by indicating the class members denoted by the term.

An **extensional** (denotative) **definition** assigns meaning to a term by indicating the class members denoted by the term. We will describe three ways of assigning meaning by extensional definitions—*ostensive definitions, enumerative definitions,* and *definitions by subclass.*

Ostensive Definitions

Ostensive definition Involves demonstrating the term—for example, by pointing to a member of the class that the term denotes.

An **ostensive definition** involves demonstrating the term—for example, by pointing to a member of the class that the term denotes. (The word "ostensive" comes from the Latin word "ostendere," which means *to show.*) Suppose a car mechanic tells you that you need a new alternator, but you have never seen one. The mechanic could provide an ostensive definition by either pointing to the alternator (if it is still attached to the engine) or letting you see the alternator (if it has been detached from the engine).

The act of showing someone an object or pointing to it is the basis for most ostensive definitions in everyday life.

Ostensive definitions are used to introduce children to many terms by showing some examples of what the term denotes. Many children's television programs introduce words by repeatedly connecting a word to pictures or drawings of the objects denoted by the term. Parents often teach children many terms by a similar procedure—repeating a word while showing an object or a series of similar objects to a child. Ostensive definitions are also used to teach a foreign language by pointing to an object and repeating a word. An ostensive definition is called for whenever you hold an object or point to it and ask, "What is this called?" The answer to the question will be a term associated with that class of objects.

Ostensive definitions require nonverbal behavior—pointing, gesturing, drawing a picture, or showing a photograph. However, since ostensive definitions do not provide alternative words to define an object the way a dictionary definition does, they do not facilitate the creation of new sentences using alternative words for the object. Ostensive definitions show what an object looks like, but they do not provide synonyms or redefine the term by giving alternate meanings. Ostensive definitions are used typically when only a small number of the members of a class are available; this sets limitations on their effectiveness. For example, it is possible that a child who has learned the term "deer" through an ostensive definition will then point to a moose and say "deer." Similarly, when we point to an object, it is not always apparent what we are emphasizing. Is it the shape of the object, or its color, or the material out of which it is made? Although ostensive definitions provide some information regarding the extension of a term, they do not provide information regarding the intension of a term.

Enumerative Definitions

An **enumerative definition** assigns meaning to a term by naming the individual members of the class denoted by the term. Here are a few examples:

- "New England" means Connecticut, Maine, Massachusetts, New Hampshire, Rhode Island, and Vermont.
- "The Knights of the Round Table" means someone such as Sir Galahad, Sir Lancelot, or Sir Gawain.

Enumerative definition
Assigns meaning to a term by naming the individual members of the class denoted by the term.

The first example illustrates a complete enumeration of the members of the class that the term "New England" denotes because every member of the class is included in the definition. The second example, however, provides only a partial enumeration of the members of the class denoted (many members of the class are left out of the definition).

Both partial and complete enumerations can be useful; the context in which the definition occurs provides direction as to which type is appropriate. For example, a complete enumeration of all the members of the class of stars is impractical since there are hundreds of billions of stars in our galaxy alone. However, a complete enumeration of the members of the class of U.S. senators who voted for (or against) a particular bill is something that would be easy to do and may be important for deciding future elections.

Definition by Subclass

A **definition by subclass** assigns meaning to a term by naming subclasses (*species*) of the class denoted by the term. (This differs from an enumerative definition where individual members were named.) A definition by subclass can be partial or complete (it is complete only when the subclasses named include the entire extension). Here are a few examples:

- "Music" means rock, blues, jazz, hip-hop, country, classical, and so forth.
- "Movie genre" means comedy, action, drama, film noir, romance, horror, along with others.
- "Coal" means lignite, subbituminous, bituminous, and anthracite.

The subclasses named in the first definition, when taken together, do not include all the members of the class, so it is a partial definition. The same is true of the second definition. However, the subclasses named in the third definition, when taken together, do include all the members of the class, and therefore is a complete definition.

As we saw with enumerative definitions, both partial and complete definitions by subclass can be useful. Once again, the context in which the definition occurs can provide a direction as to which type is appropriate. For example, a complete definition by subclass of all the species of insects is impractical. After all, there are more than a million species, with probably a lot more yet to be discovered. However, a complete definition by subclass of the members of the class of coal might be useful in determining how much of each type exists and its potential as future sources of energy.

CHECK YOUR UNDERSTANDING 2C

Determine whether the following are synonymous definitions, word origin (etymological) definitions, operational definitions, definitions by genus and difference, ostensive (demonstrative) definitions, enumerative definitions, or definitions by subclass.

1. "Felony" means murder, rape, arson, among other things.
Answer: Subclass

2. "Dentist" is a term derived from the Latin word "dens," meaning *tooth*.

3. "Typhoon" means a tropical hurricane that occurs in Asia and the Pacific Ocean.

4. See that big green thing in front of you? That's an oak tree.

⭐ 5. "Hat" means headgear.

6. "Intelligence" means the score a person receives on the Stanford-Binet I.Q. Test.

7. "Country" means something such as United States, Mexico, Italy, Indonesia, or Japan.

8. "Epistemology" is a term derived from the Greek word "episteme," meaning *knowledge*, and the suffix "-ology," meaning *the study of.*

⭐ 9. "Natural language" means something such as English, Spanish, French, Chinese, or Hindi.

10. Look where I'm pointing; that's your car's alternator.

11. "Novice" means beginner.

12. "Piano" means a musical stringed instrument set in a vertical or horizontal frame, played by depressing keys that cause hammers to strike the strings and produce audible vibrations.

⭐ 13. "Virus" means chicken pox, smallpox, measles, polio, and the like.

14. "Atmospheric pressure" means the reading found on a barometer.

15. The plant next to the shed is a bougainvillea.

16. "Abode" means residence.

⭐ 17. "Construction equipment" means bulldozer, crane, pile driver, dredger, grader and the like.

18. "Metaphysics" comes from the Greek words "meta," meaning *after,* and "physika," meaning *natural things.* The name was used by Andronicus of Rhodes in 70 BC simply as a reference to the books written by Aristotle that happened to be placed in order after his works on physics. It has since come to mean the study of first principles and is even used by some to refer to any investigation that is outside the physical realm.

19. "Biomass" means organic materials used as renewable energy sources, such as wood, crops, and waste.
Clean-energy-ideas.com

20. "Element" means something such as hydrogen, helium, carbon, or oxygen.

⭐ 21. There is a question that some people use to summarize the concerns of Medieval scholars: "How many angels can dance on the head of a pin?" Wendell Johnson is credited with offering this answer: "Bring me a pin, and some angels, and we'll soon find out."

22. "Goods and services" means (in the area of trademarks) chemicals, machinery, hand tools, advertising, transportation, storage, to name only a few.
Adapted from About.com

23. "Laborer" means worker.

24. If I know that someone means to explain a color-word to me, then "That is called 'sepia'" will help me to understand the word.
Ludwig Wittgenstein, *Philosophical Investigations*

⭐ 25. "Rock opera" means something such as *Quadrophenia, The Wall, The Rise and Fall of Ziggy Stardust and the Spiders from Mars*, or *Operation: Mindcrime.*

26. The popular definition of tragedy is heavy drama in which everyone is killed in the last act; comedy being light drama in which everyone is married in the last act.
George Bernard Shaw, "Tolstoy: Tragedian or Comedian?"

27. "Logic" can be defined as the study of the methods of reasoning and the evaluation of arguments. The term is derived from the Greek word "logikos," which means *pertaining to speaking or reasoning.* In turn, the word "logikos" was derived from the word "logos," which means *word, idea,* or *reason.*

28. To find the length of an object, we have to perform certain physical operations. The concept of length is therefore fixed when the operations by which length is measured are fixed: that is, the concept of length involves as much as and nothing more than the set of operations by which length is determined.
Percy W. Bridgman, *The Logic of Modern Physics*

⭐ 29. If one tried to make a man know what the word "pleasantness" meant by producing a rose and letting him smell it, and then producing chocolate and letting him taste it.
Richard Robinson, *Definition*

30. "Patent classification system" means Class 2 Apparel; Class 7 Compound tools; Class 14 Bridges, and many others.
Adapted from the U.S. Patent Office

31. The most common way to find out whether you're overweight or obese is to figure out your body mass index (BMI). BMI is an estimate of body fat, and it's a good gauge of your risk for diseases that occur with more body fat. The overweight group is anyone with a BMI over 25.
U.S. Department of Health and Human Services

32. "President of the United States" means someone such as George Washington, Abraham Lincoln, Franklin D. Roosevelt, or John F. Kennedy.

⭐ 33. "Salary" means wages.

34. "O.K." means acceptable or agreeable (also spelled *okay*). It is a facetious phonetic spelling of *oll korrect* which was meant to represent *all correct.* It was first used in Boston in 1839, then used in 1840 by Democrat partisans of Martin Van Buren during his election, who allegedly named their organization the *O.K. Club* in allusion to the initials of "Old Kinderhook," Van Buren's nickname, derived from his birthplace Kinderhook, New York.
Adapted from *The Random House Dictionary*

35. White lies are at the other end of the spectrum of deception from lies in a serious crisis. They are the most common and the most trivial forms that duplicity can take. The fact that they are so common provides their protective coloring. And their very triviality, when compared to more threatening lies, makes it seem unnecessary or even absurd to condemn them. Some consider all well-intentioned lies, however momentous, to be white; I shall adhere to the narrower usage: a white lie, in this sense, is a falsehood not meant to injure anyone, and of little moral import.
Sissela Bok, *Lying: Moral Choice in Public and Private Life*

D. APPLYING DEFINITIONS

The techniques so far also apply to how definitions can be used in ordinary language. However, many examples found in newspapers, magazines, novels, and other sources do not typically follow the format used in this chapter. In fact, they often make a point of the ambiguity that our techniques so far are designed to avoid.

Generally speaking, many everyday sources do not use quotation marks to indicate that a term is being defined. In addition, by convention some writers use quotation marks differently from how they were introduced in this chapter. For example, an author might use quotation marks to emphasize that a word is being used sarcastically: *That was certainly a "beautiful" dress she had on tonight.* Or a writer might use scare quotes around a phrase to indicate irony. In spoken language, we may even use our hands to mimic the appearance of written scare quotes—the gesture referred to as "air quotes."

Later in this chapter, we introduce techniques that can help clarify statements and arguments in ordinary language. These techniques, such as paraphrasing, will incorporate ideas that you have learned thus far, such as intension, extension, and definitions. For now, though, we need to look more closely at definitions from sources as they typically appear.

Stipulative Definitions

Stipulations help avoid mistakes in interpretation by specifying precise points of reference or measuring devices. A **stipulative definition** does more: it introduces an entirely new meaning. When the new meaning applies to a familiar term or symbol, confusion can easily occur. For example, if a child says, "These pants are tight!" the parent might naturally think the following: "I'm glad you told me. I will take them back and get you a larger size." From the child's perspective, the parent is woefully out of touch. The child then enlightens the parent by exclaiming, "You don't get it. *Tight* means *cool*!"

> **Stipulative definition**
> Introduces a new meaning to a term or symbol.

People using a new term for the first time establish the meaning. Yet the term and its meanings can still be modified by others for their own purposes. For example, when Apple introduced the iPod, it coined a new word and at the same time provided a stipulative definition: a portable digital audio player with the capacity to store thousands of music tracks. Since that time, Apple has introduced even more new words with stipulative definitions. For example, you can now get at least four types of iPods: shuffle, nano, classic, and touch.

Whenever scientists discover new things about the world, they may create new terms or symbols, along with new definitions, or they may use old terms but provide new stipulative definitions. For example, Nobel Prize laureate Murray Gell-Mann coined the term "quark" to refer to the elementary particles that combine to make up protons, neutrons, and other subatomic particles. The six kinds of quarks make a great illustration of the arbitrary nature of stipulative definitions. Physicists refer to them as having six "flavors": *up, down, charm, strange, top,* and *bottom*. Of course, the playful nature of these names also shows the importance of having easy to remember terms if we are to communicate at all.

In addition to intensional definition techniques, stipulative definitions can also use all three types of extensional definitions of a term. For example, a speaker can assign the new meaning of a term by pointing to an object denoted by the term (an ostensive definition). On the other hand, an enumerative definition may be offered, identifying individual members either partially or completely. Finally, a definition by subclass may be given (again, either partial or complete).

Stipulative definitions are proposals to create a new term or to use an old term in a new way. The proposals can be accepted, rejected, modified, or even ignored. However, there are some drawbacks to excessive stipulations of a term. If the meaning of a term is stretched so that it denotes nearly anything, then the term loses its informative value. For example, if everything is "tall," then the term provides no information. For another example, "awesome" means something that inspires a sense of wonder or reverence. But this colloquial meaning can easily mean anything that is great or excellent. In an interview (adapted slightly here), a U.S. Olympic Gold Medal winner managed to apply it to everything from a *game* and his *teammates* to *feelings*, a *crowd*, *opponents*, and an *experience*:

The game was awesome.	My teammates were awesome.
It felt awesome.	The crowd was awesome.
The other team was awesome.	The whole experience was awesome.

At some point the term "awesome" loses its informative power, and it winds up having no more meaning than "Wow!"

Since stipulative definitions are specific but arbitrary, care must be taken when introducing them in an argument. The possibility of confusion can compound mistakes in interpretation, analysis, understanding, and the evaluation of an argument containing stipulated terms. That is why all terms in a good argument are clearly understood or expressly defined, given the context in which the argument occurs. For example, the most modern meaning of the word "mouse" began as a stipulative definition among computer users. Given the widespread acceptance of the new meaning and the reference of the term, and the hundreds of millions of computer users around the world, the directive "Move the mouse to position the cursor at the beginning of the word you want to delete" would rarely be understood as telling you to manipulate a small rodent.

Lexical Definitions

Like the definition of a mouse as a device to position the cursor, over time a stipulative definition can go from being used by a small group of people to widespread acceptance. At this point the term is included among *lexical definitions*.

Lexical definition A definition based on the common use of a word, term, or symbol.

A **lexical definition** is a definition based on the common use of a word, term, or symbol. The definitions found in dictionaries provide the common meanings of terms and are examples of lexical definitions. "Lexical" means the common vocabulary of a given language as determined by the actual use in a community of speakers and writers. Unlike stipulative definitions, a lexical definition is useful if it accurately reports the way a term is commonly used; otherwise it is not very useful.

Since most terms have multiple meanings, we often rely on lexical definitions to clear up any ambiguity that can lead to a misunderstanding. For example, a lexical definition of "career" might include "a way of making a living" or "a paid occupation"; but it can also mean the general progress of a part of life, such as "my career as a student." A lexical definition of "ornament" might be "a decorative object." However, the term "ornament" can be used to indicate an inanimate object (such as a piece of jewelry), or it can be used to indicate an attractive person who accompanies someone to a function.

The lexical definitions found in many dictionaries often use all four types of intensional definitions. First, a lexical definition might provide information regarding the intension of a term by genus and difference. For example, a dictionary might provide the following information for the term "puppy": *genus*—dog; *difference*—very young. Second, since lexical definitions sometimes offer synonyms as part of the definition, they facilitate the creation of new sentences using alternative words for the term being defined. Third, lexical definitions found in dictionaries typically supply the etymology of a term. And finally, a lexical definition might provide an operational definition.

In addition to intensional definitions, many dictionaries often use all three types of extensional definition techniques. First, they might provide an ostensive definition by an illustration or a picture of the objects denoted by the term. Second, an enumerative definition may identify the individual members (again, either partial or complete). Third, a dictionary may supply a definition by subclass.

When we consult a lexical definition, we have the opportunity to clear up any ambiguity—and we should, whenever we encounter ambiguity in statements and arguments. We rely on lexical definitions to provide accurate guidelines to correct and incorrect usage as determined by a community using a common language.

Functional Definitions

A **functional definition** specifies the *purpose* or *use* of the objects denoted by the term. For example, a functional definition of the term "cup" can be "a small open container used to hold liquid or solids." Although cups are used mostly for liquids (e.g., coffee, tea, juice, or water), they are also used in cooking (e.g., a cup of sugar or flour). Since a functional definition concentrates on specifying how something is used, it often omits any mention of the material out of which the object is composed. For example, a cup can be made of glass, plastic, cardboard, wood, and many other materials, as long as it performs its function correctly. In fact, you can always *cup your hands* temporarily to hold water.

We use functional definitions to define the normal use of objects that have been created or designed for specific purposes. For example, if you have your car inspected, you might be told that you need a new alternator. If you have no idea what an alternator does, you can ask the mechanic. She probably will tell you that the alternator supplies electrical power throughout the car. Also, the alternator is necessary to recharge the battery after you start the car, since power is temporarily taken from the battery. This intensional definition does not tell you what an alternator looks

Functional definition
Specifies the purpose or use of the objects denoted by the term.

like. Still, it provides an adequate description of the function of an alternator. Of course, if you ask to see an alternator, the mechanic can point to it in the engine compartment or show you one that is not already connected to an engine. In fact, a functional definition of many simple objects, unlike an alternator, can be given by extension. For example, the best way to illustrate the function of a saw, a hammer, or a doorstopper is to see the tool in action.

Precising Definitions

Precising definition
Reduces the vagueness and ambiguity of a term by providing a sharp focus, often a technical meaning, for a term.

A **precising definition** reduces the vagueness and ambiguity of a term by providing a sharp focus, often a technical meaning, for a term. The precision of this kind of definition eliminates any potential vagueness or ambiguity and thus clears up any problems in understanding. Precising definitions can be found in settings that require very distinct and specific meanings of terms, such as science, law, medicine, or manufacturing.

A legal setting might rely on a precise definition of what constitutes a "dangerous weapon" or "illegal drug." A different legal situation might rely on a precising definition of "burglary": *the breaking and unwarranted entry into the dwelling place of another person with the intention of committing a felony.* Law enforcement officers can use this definition in meeting the requirements for arresting a suspect. At a trial, debate over technical matters internal to the definition may continue as well. For example, the word "breaking" seems to imply the use of force. Nevertheless, some states have interpreted it loosely to include any fraudulent entry—for example, telling the person at the door that you are from the gas company and are there to check for leaks. (Notice the similarity of the words "intension" and "intention." As we saw, "intension" refers to the meaning of a term, while "intention," in a legal setting, means what a person has set his or her mind to doing.)

In science, terms such as "energy," "momentum," and "mass" must have precise definitions. A scientific definition of "energy" includes some discussion of how "*matter* can do *work* by its *mass, electric charge,* or *motion.*" The italicized terms would themselves need precising definitions to convey a complete understanding.

Doctors must often make ethical decisions regarding the status of a critically ill patient. And that can require a precise determination of when a human being is dead. Although this is a highly controversial topic, nevertheless there have been attempts to offer precise definitions of the term "dead" as it pertains to humans. (You can imagine a similar debate over the definition of when human life begins.) Here is one example:

> The National Conference of Commissioners on Uniform State Laws in 1980 formulated the Uniform Determination of Death Act. It states that: "An individual who has sustained either (1) irreversible cessation of circulatory and respiratory functions, or (2) irreversible cessation of all functions of the entire brain, including the brain stem is dead. A determination of death must be made in accordance with accepted medical standards." This definition was approved by the American Medical Association in 1980 and by the American Bar Association in 1981.
>
> MedicineNet, Inc.

This precising definition is an operational definition. It specifies medical procedures that are to be used to determine if the term "dead" applies. Precising definitions are used in many other areas as well. For example, the U.S. Census Bureau has crafted a precising definition of "poverty" based on family income. The definition was used in 2010 to determine the poverty rate in the United States.

> Size of family unit: 1 person—$11,136; 2 people—$14,220; 3 people—$17,378 (the list continues at roughly $3000–$4000 increments per added person).

The Census Bureau also provides the method that they used to calculate the different thresholds:

> The preliminary estimates of the weighted average poverty thresholds for 2010 are calculated by multiplying the 2009 weighted average thresholds by a factor of 1.016403, the ratio of the average annual Consumer Price Index for All Consumers (CPI-U) for 2010 to the average annual CPI-U for 2009.

Once again, we can see that this kind of precising definition is an operational definition. It establishes the meaning of the term "poverty" by specifying monetary thresholds that will be used to determine the number of households in each category, and thus the overall poverty rate in the United States in the year 2010.

As the examples illustrate, precising definitions clarify meaning by eliminating vagueness and ambiguity. Extensional definitions are not useful as precising definitions, because they do not eliminate the potential for vagueness. That is because intension determines extension—and not the other way around.

Since precising definitions are not simply arbitrary assignments of meanings, they differ from stipulative definitions. A stipulative definition can be a way of hiding your intended meaning from those not in your small group. When used this way, a stipulative definition is meant to exclude others from understanding what you mean. In contrast, a precising definition is meant to include as many people as possible by focusing on legitimate, useful, accurate, clear, and direct meaning.

Theoretical Definitions

A **theoretical definition** assigns a meaning by providing an understanding of how the term fits into a general theory. Take some illustrations from science. For example, the term "inheritance" can mean *the estate that passes to an heir,* or it can mean *the characteristics transmitted from parents to their offspring.* The second meaning concerns biology and has been the subject of both theoretical and experimental research for centuries. One of the first modern biological theories of inheritance was formulated by Gregor Mendel in the 19th century. It illustrates the role of theoretical definitions:

Theoretical definition
Assigns a meaning to a term by providing an understanding of how the term fits into a general theory.

- "Factor" means the hereditary unit in which a characteristic (trait) is transmitted from one generation to the next.
- "The first principle of inheritance" means that each individual inherits two factors, one from each parent.

- "The second principle of inheritance" means that the factors are inherited randomly from each parent.
- If two traits are inherited that cannot both be displayed, then the trait that is displayed is called "dominant" and the other is called "recessive."

Mendel's theoretical definitions clearly provide intensional meanings for terms. But the terms could just as well have denoted classes with zero extension. Mendel himself could not know for sure until he began his experiments. In fact, we now use the term "allele" in place of Mendel's term "factor," and the resulting pair of alleles (one from each parent) is now called a "gene." This illustrates an important connection between theoretical definitions and precising definitions. If a theory is successful, then scientists can develop precise definitions for many of the concepts suggested by the theory (e.g., the modern precising definitions of "gene"). The resulting precising definitions (using operational techniques) then pave the way for additional specific ways to measure the objects, which in turn open up new avenues for testing.

Not all theoretical definitions stand the test of time. For example, the term "phlogiston" was originally defined as "the element or particles that exist in a physical body and which are released during combustion." Part of the reasoning behind theorizing that such an element existed was that most material gives off heat and smoke during combustion, so something has to be released into the atmosphere. Also, it was known that if you place a candle in an enclosed space, then the candle soon stops burning. The phlogiston theory explained this by claiming that phlogiston saturates the enclosed space until no more room is available for the release of new particles. This sounds entirely plausible. However, you probably have never heard of phlogiston because we now know that the term denotes an empty class; there is no phlogiston. The discovery of oxygen signaled the end of the phlogiston theory. The candle goes out in an enclosed space not because phlogiston fills the space, but rather because fires need oxygen and all the available oxygen has been used up.

Scientific theories can be understood as *sets of abstract theoretical definitions*. For example, Isaac Newton's definition of the term "gravity" is "an attractive force between bodies that have mass." One of the component terms in this definition is "force," which itself needs defining. Newton's definition of "force" is contained in his three laws of motion. (The first law is "Every object in a state of uniform motion tends to remain in that state of motion unless an external force is applied to it.") Newton's theory is, therefore, the complete set of related theoretical definitions.

A close look at theoretical definitions reveals their main purpose—to provide a way of imagining consequences that can be experimentally tested. It is in this capacity that theoretical definitions can be fruitful. In other words, a theoretical definition can only plant a seed in our imagination. But a precising definition is created in order to be directly applied. Precising definitions offer direct procedures and criteria for determining whether something falls under a certain category. (Who, for example, meets the criteria that define "poverty"?) Theoretical definitions do not function that way. They do not provide a means of direct application. In fact, some highly abstract theories cannot be tested because the technical apparatus has not yet been invented. It took many decades to invent the necessary machinery required to test much of quantum theory. More recently, some physicists, including Stephen Hawking, believe that M-theory will be the final "theory of everything." As of now, however, M-theory remains purely theoretical.

If a theoretical definition is fruitful, then scientists can gain knowledge of how a particular part of the world works. They can attain varying degrees of usefulness or they can be completely useless, as many theories have proven to be. Therefore, we can speak of a theoretical definition as being like an abstract tool. And just as many tools turned out to have no significant utility and were soon discarded, the same fate has befallen on many theories. This is why experimentation is so important in helping us learn about the world. What experiments and testing do is to provide the means of determining the success, failure, or limitations of a theory. We can learn from success, but also from failure. (Chapter 14 returns to how theories are tested.)

Persuasive Definitions

A **persuasive definition** assigns a meaning to a term with the direct purpose of influencing attitudes or opinions. The goal is to persuade the listener or reader to adopt either a favorable or unfavorable response toward whatever is denoted by the term. We will discuss two types of persuasive definitions, those that use *emotional language*, and those that use *figurative language*.

> **Persuasive definition**
> Assigns a meaning to a term with the direct purpose of influencing attitudes or opinions.

Let's start with a few examples that illustrate opposite sides of a contentious issue:

- "National health care" means that the government decides whether you live or die.
- "National health care" means that we get the same medical care that greedy politicians get.

Both definitions fail to offer specific information about the actual policies behind the health-care program. Instead, each definition is crafted to influence a specific attitude and arouse a particular emotional response toward the issue. Let's look at another example.

> Life seems to be an experience in ascending and descending. You think you're beginning to live for a single aim—for self-development, or the discovery of cosmic truths—when all you're really doing is to move from place to place as if devoted primarily to real estate.   Margaret Anderson, *The Fiery Fountains*

The writer is presenting a persuasive definition. It is meant to get us to see that our so-called progress through life may not be as wonderful as might appear. It offers an alternative vision of life that might cause us to rethink our attitude toward our goals and dreams.

We might come across a persuasive definition that is very subtle, especially if the writer is very gifted and creative. Although the definition might be hidden inside the passage, it can be quite powerful. Here is an example:

> I thought if war did not include killing, I'd like to see one every year.
>
> Maya Angelou, *Gather Together in My Name*

The author presents an interesting way of defining the term "war." Angelou's way of presenting the issue is meant to get us to realize that, among other things, wars cause death; and she believes that should be enough to persuade us to abandon the practice.

A persuasive definition might be offered as a way to *reinforce* an opinion or to *change* an opinion. Political speeches are often laced with persuasive definitions that are meant either to create a positive attitude toward a position (or group) or else to disparage the opposing position (or group). However, some debates concern the definition of "politics" itself:

- Politics is the art of the possible.   Otto Von Bismarck, *Complete Works*, vol. 7

- Politics is not the art of the possible. It consists in choosing between the disastrous and the unpalatable.

    John Kenneth Galbraith, *Letter to President Kennedy*

Von Bismarck's definition is meant to place the practice of politics in a positive light. The word "art" suggests that politics is something that skilled artisans can perfect in order to create beneficial results through negotiation. In contrast, Galbraith's definition casts politics in a negative light. Galbraith contradicts Von Bismarck's claim and elaborates directly on the shortcomings of politics. He specifies that the results of negotiation can only be disastrous or unpalatable.

The overall goal of a persuasive definition is not to provide direct or accurate information regarding the intension or extension of a term, but instead to influence our thinking about an issue. This is why persuasive definitions are used extensively in politics. Given this, it is not surprising to find that people who rely on a persuasive definition are rarely interested in whether the definition is accurate; they are concerned simply with the definition's effectiveness as persuasion.

Figurative definitions offer metaphors in place of the attributes normally given through an intensional meaning. They function differently than an informative definition, which provides accurate information regarding how a term is normally used. Consider this definition of "accordion":

Accordion: An instrument in harmony with the sentiments of an assassin.

    Ambrose Bierce, *The Devil's Dictionary*

Bierce's definition relies on your being familiar with the way an accordion looks and sounds. It is humorous only if you already understand the lexical definition:

"Accordion" means a portable wind instrument having a large bellows for forcing air through small metal reeds, a keyboard for the right hand, and buttons for sounding single bass notes or chords for the left hand.

    The Random House Dictionary

Here is another definition that uses both figurative and emotional language.

Religion is the sigh of the oppressed creature, the heart of a heartless world, and the soul of soulless conditions. It is the opium of the people.

    Karl Marx, *A Contribution to the Critique of Hegel's Philosophy of Right*

The terms "sigh," "oppressed," "heartless," and "soulless" are emotionally charged. And the term "opium" is used figuratively; it is meant to evoke a hopeless addiction to the "drug" of religion.

CHECK YOUR UNDERSTANDING 2D

Determine whether the following definitions are stipulative, lexical, precising, theoretical, functional, or persuasive.

1. "Mouse" means a small rodent, or a device for moving the cursor across a computer monitor.

Answer: Lexical

2. Properly speaking, history is nothing but the crimes and misfortunes of the human race.
Pierre Bayle, "Manicheans"

3. "Horn" means a device on a moving vehicle used to get the attention of people and animals.

4. "n00b" means a novice gamer or a newcomer to video games.

⭐ 5. "Momentum" means the impetus of an object in motion.

6. But if you want to be free, you've got to be a prisoner. It's the condition of freedom—true freedom.
Aldous Huxley, *Eyeless in Gaza*

7. "Water molecule" means two atoms of hydrogen and one atom of oxygen.

8. "Scissors" means a device used to cut material or paper.

⭐ 9. "Love" means a strong attraction, devotion, or attachment to a person.

10. "Area of a triangle" means 1/2 base × height.

11. From now on, "late" means anytime after 10:30 PM.

12. "Freedom" is just another word for nothing left to lose.
From the song "Me and Bobby McGee"

⭐ 13. "Right to privacy" means the control of access to undocumented personal information.

14. "Barometer" means an instrument that measures atmospheric pressure.

15. "Purr" means a low, murmuring sound expressive of satisfaction.

16. "E-cigarettes" means plastic and metal devices that heat a liquid nicotine solution in a disposable cartridge.
Adapted from the Associated Press

⭐ 17. "No" means no.

18. No one is more dangerous than he who imagines himself pure in heart: for his purity, by definition, is unassailable.
James Baldwin, *Nobody Knows My Name*

19. "Substance" means the fundamental constituent of existence.

20. "Science" means the systematic knowledge gained through observation and experiment.

⭐ 21. A "derivative" is the rate of change of a function at a specific value of x.

Lawrence Spector, "The Math Page"

22. Definition of a classic: a book everyone is assumed to have read and often thinks they have.

Alan Bennett, *Independent*

23. "Semantics" means the study of the meaning or the interpretation of words and sentences in a language.

24. The difference between gratitude and attribution is not negligible; one displays humility, the other hubris. It seems like a basic tenet of Christianity to give glory to God, quite another to pronounce that God was giving glory to *you*.

Tim Keown, ESPN

⭐ 25. "Fraud" is the intentional use of deceit, a trick or some dishonest means to deprive another of his/her/its money, property or a legal right.   Law.com

26. "Grue" is the property of an object that makes it appear green if observed before some future time t, and blue if observed afterward.

Nelson Goodman, *The New Riddle of Induction*

27. Freedom is nothing else but a chance to be better.

Albert Camus, *Resistance, Rebellion, and Death*

28. "Biofuel" means fuel produced from renewable biomass material, commonly used as an alternative, cleaner fuel source.   Clean-energy-ideas.com

⭐ 29. "Passer rating" (also known as "passing efficiency" or "pass efficiency") is a measure of the performance of quarterbacks and is calculated using each quarterback's completion percentage, passing yardage, touchdowns, and interceptions.

30. A colorimeter is a machine that measures the way an object either reflects or transmits light across the visible spectrum, and records the values which correlate with the way the human eye sees color.

Technical Definition, Sample 1, quoted at www.engl.nie.edu

31. A Coffee Dialogue:
Customer: I'll have a small coffee.
Salesperson: I'm sorry; we only have *Tall*, *Grande*, *Venti*, or our newest size, *Trenta*.
Customer: What's the smallest?
Salesperson: That would be *Tall*.
Customer: So "Tall" means small?
Salesperson: In a manner of speaking.

32. "Alternator" means a device used for producing electrical current.

⭐ 33. "Microscope" means an instrument invented to magnify objects too small to be seen under normal conditions.

34. It's a rare parent who can see his or her child clearly and objectively. At a school board meeting I attended . . . the only definition of a gifted child on which everyone in the audience could agree was "mine."   Jane Adams, *I'm Still Your Mother*

35. "Malaria" means the disease caused by the bite of an anopheles mosquito infected with any of four protozoans of the genus *Plasmodium*.   *Collins Dictionary*

36. Psycho-analysis pretends to investigate the Unconscious. The Unconscious by definition is what you are not conscious of. But the Analysts already know what's in it—they should, because they put it all in beforehand.

    Saul Bellow, *The Dean's December*

⭐ 37. "Syntax" means the study of the grammatical rules of a language.

38. There are two words in the English language that the sports world just can't seem to get right. The first is "ironic," which often gets confused with "coincidental." The second is "redemption," which often gets confused with "The guy who got in trouble in the offseason is playing really well now."

    LZ Granderson, "Ben Roethlisberger's Redemption"

39. Absolute, True, and Mathematical Time, of itself, and from its own nature flows equally without regard to anything external, and by another name is called Duration.   Isaac Newton, *Principia*

40. History for multiculturalists is not a succession of dissolving texts, but a tense tangle of past actions that have reshaped the landscape, distributed the nation's wealth, established boundaries, engendered prejudices, and unleashed energies.

    Joyce Appleby, "Recovering America's Historic Diversity"

⭐ 41. Virus and spyware definitions are files that Security Essentials uses to identify malicious or potentially unwanted software on your computer.

    Microsoft Security Essentials

42. A jerk, then, is a man (or woman) who is utterly unable to see himself as he appears to others. He has no grace, he is tactless without meaning to be, he is a bore even to his best friends, he is an egotist without charm. All of us are egotists to some extent, but most of us—unlike the jerk—are perfectly and horribly aware of it when we make asses of ourselves. The jerk never knows.

    Sydney J. Harris, "A Definition of a Jerk"

43. "Life" means the property or quality that distinguishes living organisms from dead organisms and inanimate matter, manifested in functions such as metabolism, growth, reproduction, and response to stimuli or adaptation to the environment originating from within the organism.

    The American Heritage Dictionary of the English Language

44. An electronic message is "spam" if (A) the recipient's personal identity and context are irrelevant because the message is equally applicable to many other potential recipients; and (B) the recipient has not verifiably granted deliberate, explicit, and still-revocable permission for it to be sent.   The Spamhaus Project Ltd.

⭐ 45. Religion can be defined as a system of beliefs and practices by means of which a group of people struggles with the ultimate problems of human life. It expresses their refusal to capitulate to death, to give up in the face of frustration, to allow hostility to tear apart their human aspirations.

J. Milton Yinger, *The Scientific Study of Religion*

46. "Dementia" is the significant loss of intellectual abilities such as memory capacity, severe enough to interfere with social or occupational functioning. The criteria for diagnosis of dementia include impairment of attention, orientation, memory, judgment, language, motor and spatial skills, and function.

Adapted from Medterms.com

47. The effect is further enhanced because human lips are "everted," meaning that they purse outward. This trait sets us apart from other members of the animal kingdom. Unlike other primates, the soft, fleshy surface of our lips remains exposed, making their shape and composition intensely alluring.

Sheril Kirshenbaum, *The Science of Kissing*

48. Challenged with a 100 million euro ($133 million) deficit, one western German city has introduced a day tax on prostitutes to help whittle down its budget gap. The new "pleasure tax" requires prostitutes in Dortmund to purchase a 6 euro "day ticket" for each day they work, or face a potential fine. Such taxes are not unusual in Germany where prostitution is legal and sex workers must pay tax on their income. Cologne introduced a 150 euro "pleasure tax" on sex workers in 2004 and later added a 6 euro day tax option for part-time prostitutes.   Reuters

⭐ 49. There was a time when "universe" meant "all there is." Everything. The whole shebang. The notion of more than one universe, more than one everything, would seemingly be a contradiction in terms. Yet a range of theoretical developments has gradually qualified the interpretation of "universe." To a physicist, the word's meaning now largely depends on context. Sometimes "universe" still connotes absolutely everything.   Brian Greene, *The Hidden Reality*

50. Civil disobedience is a moral weapon in the fight for justice. But how can disobedience ever be moral? Well I guess that depends on one's definition of the words. In 1919, in India, ten thousand people gathered in Amritsar to protest the tyranny of British rule. General Reginald Dyer trapped them in a courtyard and ordered his troops to fire into the crowd for ten minutes. Three hundred seventy-nine died—men, women, children, shot down in cold blood. Dyer said he had taught them "a moral lesson." Gandhi and his followers responded not with violence, but with an organized campaign of noncooperation. Government buildings were occupied. Streets were blocked with people who refused to rise, even when beaten by police. Gandhi was arrested. But the British were soon forced to release him. He called it a "moral victory." The definition of moral: Dyer's "lesson" or Gandhi's victory. You choose.

James Farmer, Jr., "Resolved: Civil Disobedience Is a Moral Weapon in the Fight for Justice"

E. GUIDELINES FOR INFORMATIVE DEFINITIONS

Ordinary language relies heavily on lexical definitions. Conversations between friends and relatives assume, for the most part, a common agreement on the everyday meaning of words. If a misunderstanding occurs because a term is ambiguous or vague, then the people involved can often clarify the intended meaning. A conversation among coworkers can be informal, regarding non-work-related topics, or it can include technical terms that rely on precise definitions (e.g., a medical procedure to be performed).

Since definitions are used in a variety of settings and for many different purposes, there is no single rule to which every definition must conform. For example, definitions used in poetry, novels, music, or in jokes often use metaphors. They do not have to be truthful, informative, or even accurate in order to be effective. However, if our goal is to impart correct and accurate information, then our definitions should follow definite guidelines. Also, if definitions are to play a role in arguments, then ambiguity, vagueness, and any other source of imprecision need to be eliminated. Fortunately, eight guidelines can make the construction of informative definitions easier.

1. An informative definition should use quotation marks appropriately.

We have already offered a few examples from written sources that did not use quotation marks around a term being defined. However, definitions that are meant to be informative should follow the pattern used in this chapter. Here is an example:

> Life is the sum of the forces that resist death.
>
> Gustav Eckstein, *The Body Has a Head*

This can be easily changed to match the format we have used:

> "Life" means the sum of the forces that resist death.

Here are a few more examples:

- A Sicilian pizza is made with a thick crust.
- "Sicilian pizza" means a pizza made with a thick crust.
- A dune buggy is a small open vehicle with low-pressure tires for riding on sandy beaches.
- "Dune buggy" means a small open vehicle with low-pressure tires for riding on sandy beaches.

In each instance the ordinary language sentence was rewritten in order to place the definiendum within quotation marks. This lets the reader know that the term is being mentioned (the quoted term is the subject).

2. An informative definition should include the essential meaning of a term.

If a definition is to impart information, then it should include the fundamental attributes associated with the objects denoted by the term. The essential properties are what distinguish the objects being referred to from other things. Consider the following example.

> "Television" means plasma, LCD, or LED.

Although the definition does provide extensional meaning through subclasses, it does not give any information about the essential properties of a television (intensional meaning). The next example provides an intensional meaning of the term.

> "Television" means a device for receiving electrical signals and converting them into moving images and sound.

There are many other objects that require a functional definition to provide the essential meaning (e.g., pneumatic jackhammer, computer, and cyclotron). However, an essential definition of "child" would not include a functional definition because we do not define humans by specifying that they serve any distinct purpose.

3. An informative definition should not be too broad or too narrow.
Definitions that are too broad will allow things to be included that should be excluded. For example,

> "Horse" means a large animal that humans often ride.

The definition is too broad. It allows camels and elephants to be included, since they both fit the definition provided. Here is another example of the same term.

> "Horse" means a stallion.

This definition is too narrow. It eliminates females and the young of both sexes. Once again, if a definition is to provide accurate information, then it needs to be such that it includes all and only those objects that are correctly associated with the term's denotation. The following example illustrates this point.

> "Horse" means a quadruped belonging to the same family as zebras and donkeys; individuals typically have a long mane along the back of the neck; a few of the many breeds are appaloosa, mustang, and thoroughbred.

4. An informative definition should not be circular.
In order for a definition to be informative, it must provide substantial material that enlarges our understanding of a term. Some ordinary language definitions fail because they define a term by using the term itself.

> "Addict" means someone who is addicted to a drug.

The definition is circular because it uses the term "addict" as part of the definition. If you do not know already what the term "addict" means, then the proposed definition is not informative. Here are a few more examples:

- "Chemist" means someone who studies chemistry.
- "Length" means how long something is.

Both of these definitions are circular because they assume as part of the definition the very thing they are meant to define. The following are examples of how the three examples can be rewritten to eliminate the circularity:

- "Addict" means someone who is physiologically or psychologically dependent on a substance or activity; some examples of addiction are drug, alcohol, and gambling.

- "Chemist" means someone who studies the properties, composition, reactions, and transformations of elementary substances; inorganic chemistry studies all compounds except those containing carbon; organic chemistry is the study of substances found in living organisms.
- "Length" means the extent of something when measured from end to end (also called "linear," meaning *represented by a line*); some common measuring devices for length are feet and inches, yards, centimeters, and meters.

Since the definition of "length" included measuring devices, it illustrates how an operational definition can help clarify the meaning of certain terms.

5. An informative definition should be affirmative and not negative.

We can convey some meaning by contrasting the objects denoted by a term with other objects. For example:

"Honest" means someone who is not a cheat.

Yet such a definition fails to provide intensional meaning. A definition should make sure to include relevant properties normally associated with the objects it denotes, like this:

"Honest" means someone who is trustworthy and reliable in their intentions and actions.

Let's look at another negative definition.

"Normal" means someone who is not insane.

It can be rewritten as follows:

"Normal" means conforming to a certain standard or convention; in medicine, it refers to someone free from disease; in psychiatry or psychology, it refers to someone free from any mental disorders.

Of course there are exceptions to this rule; in ordinary language situations, a negative definition can be quite adequate to the task. Here are a few simple examples.

- "Dead" means no longer living.
- "Bald tire" means a tire that does not have any tread.

The context in which the definition is used should provide a guide to the appropriateness of a negative definition.

6. An informative definition should not use ambiguous or vague language.

We have seen how ambiguity and vagueness can make a definition less effective and how we can avoid those mistakes. Ambiguity arises when a definition can be reasonably interpreted in more than one way. Here is an example:

"Fanatic" means true believer.

The term "true believer" can mean a person with deep, genuine, and sincere beliefs. However, it can also mean a person whose belief is simply true. The first interpretation emphasizes the sincerity of the belief; the second interpretation emphasizes the truth value of the belief. The definition does not provide a sufficient context to eliminate the ambiguity.

Vagueness results from a definition that fails to delineate precisely what objects are denoted by a term. For example:

> "Capitalism" means the economic system whereby individuals control the wealth.

The term "individuals" is vague in this definition. Does it refer only to individuals, or are small companies and large corporations included? Does the term "wealth" include property as well as money? What role, if any, does a government have in the economic system defined? The definition is not very informative because it leaves too many unanswered questions.

7. An informative definition should not use emotionally charged or figurative language.

Definitions that rely on emotionally charged language generally fail to provide the essential attributes that are required for intensional meaning. The next example illustrates this point:

> To establish justice in a sinful world is the whole sad duty of the political order.
> Reinhold Niebuhr, *On Politics*

The definition uses the words "sinful" and "sad" to establish an emotional response in the reader. The definition may be effective for its intended purpose, but it does not provide either intensional or extensional meaning for the term "political order."

Let's look at another example:

> Ask any die-hard what conservatism is; he'll tell you that it's true socialism.
> Aldous Huxley, *Eyeless in Gaza*

The definition contains the term "die-hard," which is usually associated with a person who holds stubbornly to a position; it is intended to elicit an emotional response. Also, the term "true" in this setting is used to assert that there is only one correct interpretation of the terms involved.

Figurative definitions offer metaphors in place of the essential attributes normally given through an intensional meaning. Consider this example:

> Art is a fruit that grows in man, like a fruit on a plant, or a child in its mother's womb.
> Jean Arp, "Art Is a Fruit"

The use of figurative language is intended to be evocative and poetic; it is not intended to be informative. Therefore, it functions differently from a lexical definition.

8. An informative definition should include a context whenever necessary.

Many common words have more than one meaning. In order to avoid misunderstanding, it sometimes helps to provide the context, often in parentheses:

- "Bank" means (in geography) the dry land bordering a stream or river.
- "Bank" means (in flying) an aircraft's angle of inclination during a turn.

- "Bank" means (in finance) a business involved in saving and lending people's money.
- "Bank" means (in pool or billiards) a cue shot that strikes a side or end cushion.

Once again, the setting in which the definition occurs should provide you with clues regarding whether or not you should include an explicit reference to a context.

CHECK YOUR UNDERSTANDING 2E

Analyze the following passages using the *Guidelines for Informative Definitions*. Explain why you think that one, more than one, or none of the guidelines are applicable to each passage.

1. Reality is that which, when you stop believing in it, doesn't go away.

   Philip K. Dick, *How to Build a Universe That Doesn't Fall Apart Two Days Later*

Answer: The definition uses irony to make its point, so it does not attempt to be informative by providing a lexical or precising definition. However, we can add quotation marks (using Guideline 1): "Reality" means "that which, when you stop believing in it, doesn't go away."

2. One definition of man is "an intelligence served by organs."

   Ralph Waldo Emerson, "Works and Days"

3. "Politician" means an elected official who likes to spend other people's money.

4. The definition of the individual was: a multitude of one million divided by one million.   Arthur Koestler, *Darkness at Noon*

⭐ 5. It is from the womb of art that criticism was born.

   Charles Baudelaire, "Salon of 1846"

6. A philanthropist is a man whose charity increases directly as the square of the distance.   George Eliot, *Middlemarch*

7. I guess the definition of a lunatic is a man surrounded by them.

   Ezra Pound, Quoted in *Charles Olson and Ezra Pound*

8. Retaliation is related to nature and instinct, not to law. Law, by definition, cannot obey the same rules as nature.   Albert Camus, *Resistance, Rebellion and Death*

⭐ 9. Grade point average (GPA) means the number determined by dividing the total grade points achieved by the number of credits earned.

10. It is the greatest happiness of the greatest number that is the measure of right and wrong.   Jeremy Bentham, *Fragment of Government*

11. Tall means anyone who can eat peanuts off my head.

12. To be "conscious" means not simply to be, but to be reported, known, to have awareness of one's being added to that being.

    William James, "How Two Minds Can Know the Same Thing"

13. To say the word Romanticism is to say modern art—that is, intimacy, spirituality, color, aspiration towards the infinite, expressed by every means available to the arts.
Charles Baudelaire, "Salon of 1846"

14. Journalists write news stories based on the material, and then provide a link to the supporting documentation to prove our stories are true.
Charlie Savage, "U.S. Tries to Build Case for Conspiracy by WikiLeaks"

15. The human mind is so complex and things are so tangled up with each other that, to explain a blade of straw, one would have to take to pieces an entire universe.... A definition is a sack of flour compressed into a thimble.
Rémy De Gourmont, "Glory and the Idea of Immortality"

16. If a thousand men were not to pay their tax-bills this year, that would not be as violent and bloody measure as it would be to pay them and enable the State to commit violence and shed innocent blood. This is, in fact, the definition of a peaceable revolution, if any such is possible.
Henry David Thoreau, *On the Duty of Civil Disobedience*

17. Whereas Smith noted that renegotiations or extensions of rookie contracts were "banned" until after the third year, a management official said the proposal "allows" for those renegotiations or extensions after the third year.
Chris Mortensen and Adam Schefter, "Sources: Sides Could Talk This Week"

18. By intuition is meant the kind of intellectual sympathy by which one places oneself within an object in order to coincide with what is unique in it and consequently inexpressible. Analysis, on the contrary, is the operation which reduces the object to elements already known, that is, to elements common both to it and other objects.
Henri Bergson, *An Introduction to Metaphysics*

19. The needs of a society determine its ethics, and in the Black American ghettos the hero is that man who is offered only the crumbs from his country's table but by ingenuity and courage is able to take for himself a Lucullan feast.
Maya Angelou, *I Know Why the Caged Bird Sings*

20. Physics is experience, arranged in economical order.
Ernst Mach, "The Economical Nature of Physics"

F. COGNITIVE AND EMOTIVE MEANING

We saw in Chapter 1 that sentences can be used for a variety of reasons, such as asking a question, providing information, making a request, or giving an order. Language also serves as a vehicle for expressing feelings through songs, poetry, stories, proverbs, jokes, and even lies. We will focus on two functions of language—to convey information and to express emotion.

Language that is used to convey information has **cognitive meaning**, while language that is used to express emotion or feelings has **emotive meaning**. Consider two examples:

A. It's already 7:00. He is late for the appointment.
B. It's already 7:00. He is late for the appointment. I am fed up with his nonsense; he is completely untrustworthy, self-centered, and useless.

The two statements in A convey information, so they both have cognitive meaning. Although the first two statements in B convey information, the third statement is more complex. The phrase "I am fed up with his nonsense" has emotive meaning, and the terms "completely untrustworthy, self-centered, and useless" are value claims. A **value claim** is a judgment that someone (or something) is good or bad, moral or immoral, or better or worse than another person (or thing). However, the value claim that the person referred to in B is "completely untrustworthy, self-centered, and useless" has terms that are vague and that need to be clearly defined. In addition, we are provided with no evidence to support the value claim, other than that the person was once late for an appointment. Therefore, the value claim and the cognitive meaning are obscured by the emotive language.

Let's look at two more examples:

A stem cell is an unspecialized cell found in fetuses, embryos, and some adult body tissues that has the potential to develop into specialized cells or divide into other stem cells. Stem cells from fetuses or embryos can develop into any type of differentiated cells, while those found in mature tissues develop only into specific cells. Stem cells can potentially be used to replace tissue damaged or destroyed by disease or injury, but the use of embryonic stem cells for this purpose is controversial.   *The American Heritage Science Dictionary*

[This] would allow scientists to create an embryonic clone for the purposes of extracting the stem cells from that embryo, a procedure that will cause the embryo's immediate demise. The stem cells may then be used for experimental treatments on another human being with a disease. Let's see, creating a human being for the purposes of killing that person for another human being's health, sounds an awfully lot like cannibalism, only worse. . . . [T]he procedure would not merely use tissue from human embryos, it would destroy them. That's like saying removing someone's heart is just using their tissue.
C. Ben Mitchell, "Biotech Cannibalism"

The first passage provides a definition of the term "stem cells" (an unspecialized cell) and also provides information regarding its sources (fetuses, embryos, and some adult body tissues). There is also information regarding the potential uses of the different kinds of stem cells. The passage illustrates an extended use of cognitive meaning.

The second passage also has examples of cognitive meaning—for example, "The stem cells may then be used for experimental treatments on another human being with a disease." However, it also has examples of emotive meaning—for example, "the embryo's immediate demise," "sounds an awfully lot like cannibalism, only worse," and

---

Cognitive meaning
Language that is used to convey information has cognitive meaning.

Emotive meaning
Language that is used to express emotion or feelings has emotive meaning.

Value claim A judgment that someone (or something) is good or bad, moral or immoral, or better or worse than another person (or thing).

"it would destroy them." There is even sarcasm laced with emotion: "That's like saying removing someone's heart is just using their tissue."

These two passages again illustrate that statements can contain both cognitive and emotive meaning. Look again at "[This] would allow scientists to create an embryonic clone for the purposes of extracting the stem cells from that embryo, a procedure that will cause the embryo's immediate demise." The first part of the sentence has cognitive meaning, and the second part contains both cognitive and emotive meaning. However, the emotional force of the language can sometimes make it difficult to distinguish or extract the cognitive meaning. We can extract the cognitive meaning of the phrase "a procedure that will cause the embryo's immediate demise" by looking closely at certain key words. The term "embryo" can be defined as the stage of development (in humans) up to the second month in the womb. The term "fetus" can be defined as the stage of development (in humans) occurring after the second month in the womb. The term "demise" is a euphemism for the term "death." A more neutral phrase that would extract the cognitive meaning is "arrested development." The cognitive meaning can then be distinguished by paraphrasing the original: "a procedure that causes the arrested development of the embryo."

There is another important use of emotive language in the second passage. The author first uses the term "embryo" but then switches to the term "human"—"Let's see, creating a human being for the purposes of killing that person." The author has maneuvered the reader from "the embryo's immediate demise" to "creating a human being." Since the status of an embryo is a point of controversy, the author is unjustified in simply substituting the term "human" for "embryo." (The terms are not synonymous.)

Since we want to focus on the informational content of the statements in an argument, emotionally charged language interferes with analysis. The emotive meaning of a statement can sometimes override and obscure the cognitive meaning and any value claims that are made. Also, a vague claim can hide behind the emotionally charged language with the result that the evidence needed to support the claim is overlooked. (Chapter 12 offers a detailed discussion of value judgments.)

CHECK YOUR UNDERSTANDING 2F

Determine whether the following passages contain phrases expressing cognitive meaning, emotive meaning, or both. Explain your answers.

1. Americans gave nearly $300 billion to charities last year, a 1% increase when adjusted for inflation.

Answer: Cognitive meaning. The passage provides information regarding the percentage of increase in charitable contributions.

2. Gambling is for suckers. As P. T. Barnum said, "There's a sucker born every minute." State lotteries bleed hard-earned money from those least able to afford

it. The corrupt officials who voted to allow those obscene games should be sent to jail. I'll be happy to turn the key and lock them up.

3. The two new integrated resorts and casinos in Singapore have each generated over $100 million in profits per month since they opened. At this rate they will each be able to pay off their start-up costs in 5 years.

4. The independent assessment committee was satisfied that adequate measures were taken by the local authorities to meet all foreseeable contingencies.

⭐ 5. The Great Pyramid of Giza is the only thing that still exists among the Seven Wonders of the Ancient World.

6. The powers-that-be were ridiculously unprepared for the huge crowd last night. The resulting chaos caused immense suffering and put precious lives in extreme peril. Some heads should roll over this tragedy.

7. At some point, if you don't want to worry about teams in minor markets, don't put teams in minor markets, or don't leave teams in minor markets if they're truly minor. Socialism, communism, whatever you want to call it, is never the answer.   Hank Steinbrenner, owner of the New York Yankees, quoted in the Associated Press

8. It is the business of thought to define things, to find the boundaries; thought, indeed, is a ceaseless process of definition.
                                    Vance Palmer, in *Intimate Portraits*, ed. H. P. Heseltine

⭐ 9. As much as we want to keep everybody, we've already made these guys very, very rich, and I don't feel we owe anybody anything monetarily. Some of these players are wealthier than their bosses.   Hank Steinbrenner, quoted at CBSSports.com

10. It brings us one step closer to the brink of war, because I don't think the North would seek war by intention, but war by accident, something spiraling out of control has always been my fear.   Peter Beck, quoted at Guardian.co.uk

11. The utopian male concept which is the premise of male pornography is this— since manhood is established and confirmed over and against the brutalized bodies of women, men need not aggress against each other; in other words, women absorb male aggression so that men are safe from it.
                                    Andrea Dworkin, *The Root Cause*

12. By contrast with history, evolution is an unconscious process. Another, and perhaps a better way of putting it would be to say that evolution is a natural process, history a human one. . . . Insofar as we treat man as a part of nature—for instance in a biological survey of evolution—we are precisely not treating him as a historical being. As a historically developing being, he is set over against nature, both as a knower and as a doer.   Owen Barfield, *History, Guilt, and Habit*

⭐ 13. The man who can roust the excitement and the enthusiasm of the coordination of the players is the one who will come through, the one that can bring their team to that high expectation of unity, solidarity and togetherness and performing above and beyond the call of duty, he will be the big, big winner Sunday.

Don King, boxing promoter, quoted at ESPN.go.com

14. Ah, California, my home sweet home. Did anyone catch the California Horse Racing Board's meeting the other day, during which the commissioners were asked to choose between bald-faced corporatism and open-handed charity? Okay, maybe it wasn't as simple as that, but contrary conclusions are hard to draw.

Jay Hovdey, *Daily Racing Form*

15. Choosing the wrong policy can have consequences. For example, when comparing breast cancer treatment coverage under three California policies, the study found that a patient would spend nearly $4,000 for a typical treatment under one policy or as much as $38,000 under another even though both policies had similar deductibles and out-of-pocket limits.

Susan Jaffe, "Speak Plain English, Health Insurers Told," *Kaiser Health News*

G. FACTUAL AND VERBAL DISPUTES

Factual dispute Occurs when people disagree on a matter that involves facts.

A **factual dispute** occurs when people disagree on the facts. For example, one person might claim that Benjamin Franklin must have been a U.S. president because his picture is on the $100 bill, while another person claims that Franklin was not a U.S. president. This dispute can be resolved by consulting historical or biographical sources. Here is another example of a factual dispute:

- Our state legislature should pass a law authorizing capital punishment because it is an effective deterrent to violent crime.
- Our state legislature should not pass a law authorizing capital punishment because it has not been shown to be an effective deterrent to violent crime.

The dispute concerns the factual question of whether or not capital punishment is an effective deterrent to violent crime. Each side in the dispute needs to provide relevant scientific evidence in support of its position.

A factual dispute can involve emotional language. It occurs when people agree on certain facts and terms but express their feelings toward the facts in different ways. For example:

- Executing violent criminals is morally acceptable because those people are worthless and commit despicable acts against peace-loving, innocent humans.
- Executing violent criminals is morally unacceptable because even though those people are as bad as you say, we should open our hearts, and learn to love and forgive.

The disputants seem to agree on the terms "worthless," "despicable acts," and "peace-loving." However, their emotional responses to these terms differ, as do their value judgments regarding how we should act toward violent criminals.

A **verbal dispute** occurs when a vague or ambiguous term results in a linguistic misunderstanding. In other words, statements that are thought to be about the objects denoted by certain key terms instead involve a dispute about the terms themselves. These kinds of disputes are not resolved by investigating the facts, but by an investigation of the definitions. Suppose someone is a "small bookmaker." Is his occupation illegal? Since the term "bookmaker" can mean either "a person who makes books" or "a person who accepts illegal wagers on sporting events" (often referred to as a "bookie"), the dispute hinges on an ambiguity arising from an unclear context. Disputes of this nature are easily cleared up once the correct meaning is identified.

Verbal dispute
Occurs when a vague or ambiguous term results in a linguistic misunderstanding.

However, there are more complicated kinds of verbal disputes. A term might be used when there is some overall agreement on its intension, but disagreement as to its extension. For example, some disputes have involved the question of whether a certain belief system qualifies as a "religion." Legal, governmental, and moral issues are all involved. A religion that is recognized by the government has certain privileges, such as being exempt from paying taxes. The disputes can sometimes be resolved by clarifying the intension of the term (which will further determine the extension), so that the court can make a decision. However, deciding the legal question will not necessarily satisfy everyone, because religious issues often evoke emotional responses.

Sometimes the parties involved cannot agree on a definition. Although most governments condemn acts of terrorism, we often hear that "one person's terrorist is another person's freedom fighter." In more formal language, a UN report in 2010 stated that "some delegations pointed out the necessity to distinguish between acts of terrorism and the legitimate struggle of people in the exercise of their right to self-determination."

In a report to the United Nations General Assembly, the Secretary-General offered this definition:

> Any action constitutes terrorism if it is intended to cause death or serious bodily harm to civilians or non-combatants with the purpose of intimidating a population or compelling a Government or an international organization to do or abstain from doing any act.
>
> *In Larger Freedom: Towards Development, Security and Human Rights for All,* March 21, 2005

The United Nations has still not adopted a definition of "terrorism." The contentious issues involving the term "terrorism" are not merely verbal. However, even if a verbal agreement could be reached, the emotive meaning, political divisions, and value judgments that get attached to the term still need to be settled.

CHECK YOUR UNDERSTANDING 2G

Determine whether the following disputes are factual, verbal, or some combination of the two. Also, point out any emotional language that might be involved.

1. A: Drinking one glass of red wine a day has been linked with a lower risk of heart disease.
   B: Excessive alcohol consumption has been linked to liver disease.

Answer: Verbal dispute. Person A talks about the effects of "drinking one glass of red wine a day," while person B talks about the effects of "excessive alcohol consumption." The dispute is not about the facts related to their respective claims.

2. A: All humans are created equal.
    B: That can't be. We all have a unique DNA profile.

3. A: You were fired because of your poor work performance.
    B: I was fired because the supervisor didn't like me.

4. A: My parents are in heaven.
    B: There is no heaven.

⭐ 5. A: The capital city of Korea is Seoul.
    B: You are wrong. The capital city of Korea is Pyongyang.

6. A: There is a higher incidence of child leukemia near nuclear power plants compared to the rest of the United States.
    B: Nuclear power plants provide the best opportunity to free ourselves from oil dependency.

7. A: Here, have a martini.
    B: It's not a martini because it was not made with dry vermouth.
    A: But a martini doesn't have to be made with dry vermouth.

8. A: This is my new car.
    B: That's not new. It's at least 5 years old.

⭐ 9. A: Don't ask her whether you should take the job or not—make your own decision.
    B: I am making my own decision—I have decided to ask her what I should do.

10. A: Sales will increase if we upgrade customer service because customers will feel that we care about their satisfaction.
    B: I disagree. Sales will decrease if we upgrade customer service because it will make it too easy for customers to return products after they used them for a while.

11. A: Our business is booming. Total sales are up 13% over last year.
    B: Our business is not booming. Profit is down 3% from last year.

12. A: Did you see his last movie? What an actor; he's a genius.
    B: I read somewhere that his I.Q. is only 110, so he's definitely not in the genius range.

⭐ 13. A: I don't think, I know.
    B: I don't think you know either.

14. A: The contract proposal offered by the company is reasonable.
    B: The contract proposal is just their way of further exploiting the working class.

15. A: No radio station east of the Mississippi can use the letter "K" as its first call letter.

    B: Oh really; then what about KDKA? It's in Pittsburgh, Pennsylvania.

16. A: The proposed tax hike is too high. The individuals who invest their hard-earned money in businesses that provide all the jobs are being robbed of that which is their sacred right to keep. The government is like a thief who steals rather than works. Taxes are immoral because they take what rightfully belongs to someone and give it to those too lazy or not talented enough to compete. We should be able to do whatever we want with what we earn instead of being subjected to onerous taxation spiraling out of control. The government wants higher and higher taxes the way an addict tries to satisfy an insatiable desire.

    B: The proposed tax hike is not too high. In fact, it is not enough. The rich people in this country are getting away with murder when it comes to paying their fair share. Big corporations need to fleece the public to ensure obscene profits for their shareholders, who then turn around and purchase luxury items that flaunt their wealth with lifestyles that rival the most decadent periods in human history.

17. Juror #3: It's these kids—the way they are nowadays. When I was a kid I used to call my father, 'Sir'. That's right . . . 'Sir'. You ever hear a kid call his father that anymore?

    Juror #8: Fathers don't seem to think it's important anymore.

    From the movie *12 Angry Men*

18. In his System of Nature, A.D. 1776, Linnaeus declares, "I hereby separate the whales from the fish." . . . The grounds upon which Linnaeus would fain have banished the whales from the waters, he states as follows: "On account of their warm bilocular heart, their lungs, their movable eyelids, their hollow ears." . . . I take the good old fashioned ground that the whale is a fish, and call upon holy Jonah to back me. This fundamental thing settled, the next point is, in what internal respect does the whale differ from other fish. Above, Linnaeus has given you those items. But in brief, they are these: lungs and warm blood; whereas, all other fish are lungless and cold blooded.   Herman Melville, *Moby Dick*

19. M: An argument isn't just contradiction.

    A: It can be.

    M: No it can't. An argument is a connected series of statements intended to establish a proposition.

    A: No it isn't.

    M: Yes it is! It's not just contradiction.

    A: Look, if I argue with you, I must take up a contrary position.

    M: Yes, but that's not just saying 'No it isn't.'

    A: Yes it is!

M: No it isn't!

A: Yes it is!

M: Argument is an intellectual process. Contradiction is just the automatic gainsaying of any statement the other person makes. *(short pause)*

A: No it isn't.

M: It is.

A: Not at all.   Monty Python, "The Argument Sketch"

20. A: In 1982, 82 percent of college graduates read novels or poems for pleasure; two decades later, only 67 percent did. And more than 40 percent of Americans under 44 did not read a single book—fiction or nonfiction—over the course of a year. The proportion of 17-year-olds who read nothing (unless required to do so for school) more than doubled between 1984 and 2004. This time period, of course, encompasses the rise of personal computers, Web surfing and video games.   Susan Jacoby, "The Dumbing of America"

B: Susan Jacoby presents a compelling, though perhaps naïve and myopic, view of intellectualism and the persistence of literature in the 21st century. Like so many nervous academics of our age, Jacoby provides a view compounded by urgent pollster data, alarming statistics, and factoids heralding in the age of ignorance at the hands of the digital revolution. A concern about whether young people are wasting their minds has been intermittently fashionable throughout history. If Jacoby contends that "video" is eroding our intellect, I encourage her to immerse herself in the story of Wikipedia. This is a place where today's youth, in phenomenal numbers, are helping professors and graduate students to build a repository of living knowledge from all corners of this planet. This is not a project for the next decade or the century. It is a project for all time.

Jimmy Wales, the founder of Wikipedia, "We're Smarter than You Think"

Summary

- Term: A single word or a group of words that can be the subject of a statement; it can be a common name, a proper name, or even a descriptive phrase.
- Clarifying the meaning of a statement requires a close look at the meaning of the terms involved. Vague, ambiguous, or imprecise terms can reduce the clarity of individual statements and arguments.
- Intension: The intension of a term is specified by listing the properties or attributes that the term connotes—in other words, its sense.
- Class: A group of objects.
- Extension: The class or collection of objects to which the term applies. In other words, what the term denotes (its reference).

- A sequence of terms can have increasing intension, decreasing intension, increasing extension, or decreasing extension.
- Empty class: A class that has zero members.
- A definition assigns a meaning to a word, phrase, or symbol. Logicians use the term "definiendum" to refer to that which is being defined, and the term "definiens" to that which does the defining.
- Intensional definition: Assigns a meaning to a term by listing the properties or attributes shared by all the objects that are denoted by the term.
- Synonymous definition: Assigns a meaning to a term by providing another term with the same meaning; in other words, by providing a synonym.
- Etymology: The study of the history, development, and sources of words.
- Operational definition: Defines a term by specifying a measurement procedure.
- Definition by genus and difference: Assigns a meaning to a term (the species) by establishing a genus and combining it with the attribute that distinguishes the members of that species.
- Extensional definition: Assigns meaning to a term by indicating the class members denoted by the term.
- Ostensive definition: Involves demonstrating the term—for example, by pointing to a member of the class that the term denotes.
- Enumerative definition: Assigns meaning to a term by naming the individual members of the class denoted by the term.
- Definition by subclass: Assigns meaning to a term by naming subclasses (species) of the class denoted by the term.
- Stipulative definition: Introduces a new meaning to a term or symbol.
- Lexical definition: A definition based on the common use of a word, term, or symbol.
- Functional definition: Specifies the purpose or use of the objects denoted by the term.
- Precising definition: Reduces the vagueness and ambiguity of a term by providing a sharp focus, often a technical meaning, for a term.
- Theoretical definition: Assigns a meaning to a term by providing an understanding of how the term fits into a general theory.
- Persuasive definition: Assigns a meaning to a term with the direct purpose of influencing attitudes or opinions.
- There are eight guidelines which are meant to facilitate the construction of informative definitions.
- Cognitive meaning: Language that is used to convey information.
- Emotive meaning: Language that is used to express emotion or feelings.
- Value claim: A judgment that someone (or something) is good or bad, moral or immoral, or better or worse than another person (or thing).
- Factual dispute: Occurs when people disagree on a matter which involves facts.
- Verbal dispute: Occurs when a vague or ambiguous term results in a linguistic misunderstanding.

KEY TERMS

term   46
intension   47
extension   47
class   47
empty class   47
increasing intension   48
decreasing extension   48
decreasing intension   48
increasing extension   48
definition   51
definiendum   51

definiens   51
intensional definition   52
synonymous definition   52
operational definition   53
definition by genus and
    difference   56
extensional
    definition   56
ostensive definition   56
enumerative definition   57
definition by subclass   58

stipulative definition   61
lexical definition   62
functional definition   63
precising definition   64
theoretical definition   65
persuasive definition   67
cognitive meaning   79
emotive meaning   79
value claim   79
factual dispute   82
verbal dispute   83

LOGIC CHALLENGE: THE PATH

A person walks up a mountain path in Tibet to visit a monastery in order to gain en-
lightenment. She starts out on her journey at 7:00 AM and arrives at the monastery 8
hours later. A monk hands her a note and tells her not to read it until she returns to the
bottom of the mountain. The next morning she starts down the path at 7:00 AM. She is
anxious to read the note, and since she is able to walk downhill very fast, she arrives at
the bottom in 4 hours. She opens the note and reads the following:

> On your journey down the path you passed one spot at the exact same time
> that you passed it when you went up the path.

Is the note correct? Explain your answer.

Chapter 3

Diagrams and Analysis

A. *The Basics of Diagramming Arguments*
B. *Incomplete Arguments*
C. *Rhetorical Language*
D. *Necessary and Sufficient Conditions*

A diagram of an argument, like a road map, is a visual tool. It offers a graphic depiction of the argument's structure, and it allows us to follow a path from point A (the premises) to point B (the conclusion). It highlights connections—the connections between the statements that make up the argument. It takes a passage and extracts all the premises, numbers them, and then connects them to the conclusion. You can consult the numbers as you make those connections in the passage yourself.

Maps are especially helpful for long trips, and diagrams are especially useful for extended arguments. If you are on a road trip, you might find that you can get to your destination by several different routes, each through a different city. Similarly, an argument might contain premises that work independently of each other in support of the conclusion. On the other hand, when tracing a route on a map, you might find there is only one way to get where you want to go, and the route takes you through several stops along the way. In the same way, you might need all the premises of an argument, because they work together to support the conclusion.

A road map might show that you cannot get to your destination—or at least not easily, because some roads are not yet completed. In the same manner, some arguments are missing a premise or a conclusion, either intentionally or unintentionally. In those cases, we need to add the missing information based on our overall understanding. If we add a missing premise, then we are building a bridge, to connect the existing premises to the conclusion. If we add a missing conclusion, then we are providing a final destination. Of course, our diagram will have to distinguish the information we are given from what we have added to complete the argument.

Some maps have insets, such as pictures of cities or flights of fancy. We might appreciate seeing a hint of where we are going—or we might just wish we could get on with finding our route. And some passages use rhetorical language, which is designed to have a dramatic effect of its own. When this occurs, language is used to imply things that are not said explicitly. For example, a rhetorical question guides and persuades the reader or the listener. It engages us in a dialogue, but there is only one right answer, and the writer is clever enough to know how we will answer it:

Using rhetorical questions in speeches is a great way to keep the audience involved. Don't you think those kinds of questions would keep your attention?

Bo Scott Bennett, *Year to Success*

This chapter applies diagramming to both simple and extended arguments. We will see how to reconstruct incomplete arguments and to analyze rhetorical arguments. These will introduce us to another kind of statement, called a conditional. We will also encounter informal fallacies, the topic of Chapter 4.

A. THE BASICS OF DIAGRAMMING ARGUMENTS

Once we have analyzed an argument, we can create a diagram—a map of the premises and conclusion. There are a few basic techniques for creating diagrams, and they can be used as building blocks for diagramming extended arguments. For example, suppose you read this simple argument: "You do not take care of your dog. Therefore, you will not be able to accept the responsibility of owning a car." The first step in creating a diagram is to number the statements as they appear (disregarding, at this point, whether they are premises or conclusions).

¹ You do not take care of your dog. Therefore, ² you will not be able to accept the responsibility of owning a car.

The passage contains the conclusion indicator "therefore," so we can determine that statement 2 is the conclusion. The next step is to diagram the argument by connecting the premise to the conclusion with an arrow:

1
↓
2

When there is more than one premise, the premises may act independently in support of the conclusion. **Independent premises** are such that the falsity of one does not nullify the support the others give to the conclusion. We can illustrate this by adding other premises to our example:

Independent premises
Premises are independent when the falsity of one would not nullify any support the others would give to the conclusion.

¹ You will not be able to accept the responsibility of owning a car because ² you do not take care of your dog, ³ you don't clean your room, and ⁴ you do not handle your money responsibly.

Convergent diagram
A diagram that reveals the occurrence of independent premises.

Independent premises can be captured in a **convergent diagram**. Here is the convergent diagram for our example:

2 3 4

1

Each of the three premises has its own arrow, because each premise offers independent support for the conclusion. In other words, each premise, by itself, offers a reason to accept the conclusion. Even if one or two of the premises are shown to be false, an arrow would remain.

Other arguments have two or more premises that act together to support a conclusion. The falsity of one **dependent premise** weakens the support that the other premises give to the conclusion, as in this example:

> [1] The movie version of *The Lord of the Rings* used some of the original dialogue from the books, [2] it used the language Tolkien invented, [3] it used the characters he created, [4] it kept the overall plot, and [5] the settings were the same as in the books. Therefore, [6] the movie trilogy *Lord of the Rings* captured most of the spirit of the original books.

Dependent premises
Premises are dependent when they act together to support a conclusion.

Here 1 through 5 *conjoin* to support the conclusion, that the movies captured most of the spirit of the original books. The dependent premises create a **linked diagram**:

Linked diagram A diagram that reveals the occurrence of dependent premises.

It is also possible that one premise supports more than one conclusion. Consider this argument:

> [1] The new movie *Son of Avatar* will be the highest grossing movie in history. Therefore, [2] it is sure to win multiple Academy Awards, and [3] some of the actors will be among the highest paid in the industry. We can also conclude that [4] the director will get to do anything he wants in the near future.

In this passage, one premise is being used to support three separate conclusions, resulting in a **divergent diagram**:

Divergent diagram A diagram that shows a single premise supporting independent conclusions.

```
      1
     /|\
    ↙ ↓ ↘
   2  3  4
```

Finally, some passages contain a series of arguments, in which a conclusion from one argument becomes a premise in the next one. For example:

> [1] The government just cut taxes and [2] put a freeze on the minimum wage. [3] This combination is sure to create higher unemployment. Of course, [4] that will lead to a drop in gross domestic sales. [5] This will surely cause a recession.

This results in a **serial diagram**:

```
   1   2
    \_/
     ↓
     3
     ↓
     4
     ↓
     5
```

Serial diagram A diagram that shows that a conclusion from one argument is a premise in a second argument.

Statements 1 and 2 are linked (conjoined) to support 3, which is an intermediate conclusion. Statement 3 then is a premise for statement 4, which is another intermediate conclusion. Finally, 4 is a premise for 5, the conclusion of the argument.

Extended arguments often require diagrams that combine two or more of our diagramming techniques, as in this example:

> [1] My working overtime each day for the next three weeks, and [2] my coming in on weekends, [3] will guarantee that I will finish the report early. Of course, [4] it is also possible that working a normal 40-hour week will lead to the same result. Therefore, [5] finishing the report early will lead to a bigger paycheck. [6] It could also lead to a promotion.

(A) The arrow from 1 and 2 to 3 indicates the presence of a linked diagram (dependent premises).
(B) The two arrows, one from 1 and 2 to 3, and the other from 4 to 3, indicate the presence of a convergent diagram (independent premises).
(C) The two arrows, one leading from 3 to 5, and the other from 3 to 6, indicate the presence of a divergent diagram.
(D) The entire diagram reveals the presence of a serial diagram.

CHECK YOUR UNDERSTANDING 3A

I. Diagram the following arguments using the techniques described in this section. (The first fifteen arguments are from *Check Your Understanding 1B.1.* If you worked out answers for that set, then you have already identified the premises and the conclusions.)

1. Exercise helps strengthen your cardiovascular system. It also lowers your cholesterol, increases the blood flow to the brain, and enables you to think longer. Thus, there is no reason for you not to start exercising regularly.

Answer: [1] Exercise helps strengthen your cardiovascular system. [2] It also lowers your cholesterol, [3] increases the blood flow to the brain, and [4] enables you to think longer. [5] There is no reason for you not to start exercising regularly.

2. If you start a strenuous exercise regimen before you know if your body is ready, you can cause serious damage. Therefore, you should always have a physical checkup before you start a rigid exercise program.

3. Since television commercials help pay the cost of programming, and because I can always turn off the sound of the commercials, go to the bathroom, or get something to eat or drink, it follows that commercials are not such a bad thing.

4. Since television commercials disrupt the flow of programs, and given that any disruption impedes the continuity of a show, consequently we can safely say that commercials are a bad thing.

★ 5. We should never take our friends for granted. True friends are there when we need them. They suffer with us when we fail, and they are happy when we succeed.

6. They say that "absence makes the heart grow fonder," so my teachers should really love me, since I have been absent for the last 2 weeks.

7. I think, therefore I am.   René Descartes

8. I believe that humans will evolve into androids, because we will eventually be able to replace all organic body parts with artificial parts. In addition, we will be able to live virtually forever by simply replacing the parts when they wear out or become defective.

★ 9. At one time Gary Kasparov had the highest ranking of any chess grandmaster in history. However, he was beaten in a chess tournament by a computer program called Deep Blue, so the computer program should be given a ranking higher than Kasparov.

10. It is true that $1 + 4 = 5$, and it is also true that $2 + 3 = 5$. Thus, we can conclude with certainty that $(1 + 4) = (2 + 3)$.

11. The digital camera on sale today at Cameras Galore has 5.0 megapixels and costs $200. The digital camera on sale at Camera Warehouse has 4.0 megapixels and it costs $150. You said that you did not want to spend over $175 for a camera, so you should buy the one at Camera Warehouse.

12. You should buy the digital camera at Cameras Galore. After all, you did say that you wanted the most megapixels you can get for up to $200. The digital camera on sale today at Cameras Galore has 5.0 megapixels and costs $200. But the digital camera on sale at Camera Warehouse has only 4.0 megapixels and it costs $150.

★ 13. The world will end on August 6, 2045. I know this because my guru said it would, and so far everything he predicted has happened exactly as he said it would.

14. Fast-food products contain high levels of cholesterol. They also contain high levels of sodium, fat, and trans fatty acids. These things are bad for your health. I am going to stop eating in fast food places.

15. You should eat more vegetables. They contain low levels of cholesterol. They also contain low levels of sodium, fat, and trans fatty acids. High levels of those things are bad for your health.

II. Identify and number the premises and conclusions in the following passages, and then diagram the argument.

1. We will soon get more oil from areas of our country that were once protected by law. However, it has been projected that the amount of oil will be too small to have any serious effect on the overall oil supply. Although coal production will be raised, the amount will not meet the increased amount of energy that will be needed. In addition, new legislation has eliminated the requirement for the automobile industry to increase gas mileage in their new cars. So, it seems that gasoline prices will not go down in the near future.

Answer: [1] We will soon get more oil from areas of our country that were once protected by law. However, [2] it has been projected that the amount of oil will be too small to have any serious effect on the overall oil supply. [3] Although coal production will be raised, [4] the amount will not meet the increased amount of energy that will be needed. In addition, [5] new legislation has eliminated the requirement for the automobile industry to increase gas mileage in their new cars. So, [6] it seems that gasoline prices will not go down in the near future.

2. Driving a car without a seatbelt is dangerous. Statistics show you are 10 times more likely to be injured in an accident if you are not wearing a seat belt. Besides, in our state you can get fined $100 if you are caught not wearing one. You ought to wear one even if you are driving a short distance.

3. Jean studied at least 10 hours for the exam, and she got an A. Bill studied at least 10 hours for the exam, and he got an A. Sue studied at least 10 hours for the exam, and she got an A. Jim studied at least 10 hours for the exam. Jim probably got an A on the exam.

4. Fathers and mothers have lost the idea that the highest aspiration they might have for their children is for them to be wise—as priests, prophets or philosophers are wise. Specialized competence and success are all that they can imagine.

    Allan Bloom, *The Closing of the American Mind*

5. Death is not an event in life: we do not live to experience death. If we take eternity to mean not infinite temporal duration but timelessness, then eternal life belongs to those who live in the present. Our life has no end in just the way in which our visual field has no limits.   Ludwig Wittgenstein, *Tractatus Logico-Philosophicus*

6. But while college debt has proven a financial chokehold for some people, a four-year degree is still great insurance, especially in a tough job market: The unemployment rate for people with a bachelor's degree or higher was 4.5 percent in July, compared to 10.1 percent for those with only a high school diploma.

    Allison Linn, "Is It Worth It to Go to College?"

7. We measure the success of schools not by the kinds of human beings they promote, but by whatever increases in reading scores they chalk up. We have allowed quantitative standards, so central to the adult economic system, to become the principal yardstick for our definition of our children's worth.

Kenneth Keniston, "The 11-Year-Olds of Today Are the Computer Terminals of Tomorrow"

8. We have discovered dozens and dozens of artfully disguised items that have posed a risk. The threats are real, the stakes are high, and we must prevail. When it comes to the Transportation Security Administration (TSA), we are the last line of defense. Therefore, full-body scanners and enhanced pat-downs are necessary to catch nonmetallic security threats.

John Pistole, Head of the TSA, quoted at Washingtonpost.com

9. Because there is a law such as gravity, the universe can and will create itself from nothing. Spontaneous creation is the reason there is something rather than nothing, why the universe exists, why we exist. It is not necessary to invoke God to light the blue touch paper and set the universe going.

Stephen Hawking and Leonard Mlodinow, *The Grand Design*

10. Because robots can stage attacks with little immediate risk to the people who operate them, opponents say that robot warriors lower the barriers to warfare, potentially making nations more trigger-happy and leading to a new technological arms race. "Wars will be started very easily and with minimal costs" as automation increases, predicted Wendell Wallach, a scholar at the Yale Interdisciplinary Center for Bioethics and chairman of its technology and ethics study group.

John Markoff, "U.S. Military Recruits Robots for Combat"

11. Although we like to think of young children's lives as free of troubles, they are in fact filled with disappointment and frustration. Children wish for so much, but can arrange so little of their own lives, which are so often dominated by adults without sympathy for the children's priorities. That is why children have a much greater need for daydreams than adults do. And because their lives have been relatively limited they have a greater need for material from which to form daydreams.

Bruno Bettelheim, "Children and Television"

12. I know that this world exists. That I am placed in it like my eye in its visual field. That something about it is problematic, which we call its meaning. This meaning does not lie in it but outside of it. That life is the world. That my will penetrates the world. That my will is good or evil. Therefore that good and evil are somehow connected with the meaning of the world.

Ludwig Wittgenstein, *Journal*

13. The line that I am urging as today's conventional wisdom is not a denial of consciousness. It is often called, with more reason, a repudiation of mind. It is indeed a repudiation of mind as a second substance, over and above body. It can be described less harshly as an identification of mind with some of the faculties, states, and activities of the body. Mental states and events are a special subclass of the states and events of the human or animal body.

Willard Van Orman Quine, *Quidities*

14. During the next few decades, many Haitian species of plants and animals will become extinct because the forests where they live, which originally covered the entire country, are nearly gone. The decline of frogs in particular, because they are especially vulnerable, is a biological early-warning signal of a dangerously deteriorating environment. When frogs start disappearing, other species will follow and the Haitian people will suffer, as well, from this environmental catastrophe. "Scientists: Haiti's Wildlife Faces Mass Extinction," *Our Amazing Planet*

15. In fact, in a backward way, Vick has been the best thing to happen to pit bulls. "It's very true," says John Goodwin of the Humane Society of the United States. "For the big picture, Michael has been a tipping point. Since his case, there have been 30 new laws enacted all over the country toughening dog fighting penalties. Raids [on dog fighting rings] were up twice as much in 2008—after Vick—as they were in 2006, before him. There's much more awareness. People see it now and call it in." Rick Reilly, "Time to Forgive Vick Is Here"

16. Institutionalized rejection of difference is an absolute necessity in a profit economy which needs outsiders as surplus people. As members of such an economy, we have all been programmed to respond to the human differences between us with fear and loathing and to handle that difference in one of three ways: ignore it, and if that is not possible, copy it if we think it is dominant, or destroy it if we think it is subordinate. But we have no patterns for relating across our human differences as equals. As a result, those differences have been misnamed and misused in the service of separation and confusion.

Audre Lorde, "Age, Race, Class, and Sex: Women Redefining Difference"

⭐ 17. It has only just begun to dawn on us that in our own language alone, not to speak of its many companions, the past history of humanity is spread out in an imperishable map, just as the history of the mineral earth lies embedded in the layers of its outer crust. But there is this difference between the record of the rocks and the secrets which are hidden in language: whereas the former can only give us knowledge of outward dead things—such as forgotten seas and the bodily shapes of prehistoric animals—language has preserved for us the inner living history of man's soul. It reveals the evolution of consciousness.

Owen Barfield, *History in English Words*

18. Logic is not concerned with human behavior in the same sense that physiology, psychology, and social sciences are concerned with it. These sciences formulate laws or universal statements which have as their subject matter human activities as processes in time. Logic, on the contrary, is concerned with relations between factual sentences (or thoughts). If logic ever discusses the truth of factual sentences it does so only conditionally, somewhat as follows: if such-and-such a sentence is true, then such-and-such another sentence is true. Logic itself does not decide whether the first sentence is true, but surrenders that question to one or the other of the empirical sciences. Rudolf Carnap, "Logic"

19. We learned that in addition to the noxious chemicals in our pricey blowouts, there were sketchy ingredients in just about everything we used—from our daily shampooing to our biweekly manicures. We also learned that only 11 percent of the 10,500 ingredients determined by the Food and Drug Administration (FDA) to be in use by the cosmetics industry have been tested for safety by a publicly accountable agency. Of the ones we do know about, some are flat-out dangerous to our health, others are questionable at best, and most are doing almost nothing to improve the quality, feel, and health of our skin and hair. So not only are these products wreaking some unspeakable havoc on our bodies, they're also making us look worse.

Siobhan O'Connor and Alexandra Spunt, *No More Dirty Looks*

20. All logical truth and all truths that logic can warrant must turn upon meaning in the sense of intension. Because logic and the logically certifiable comprise only such facts as are independent of all particular experience and are capable of being known with certainty merely through clear and cogent thinking. The same must hold of any analytic truth: if it is capable of being known by taking thought about it, then it must be independent of meaning in the sense of extension and turn upon meanings only in the sense of intension.

Clarence Lewis, "The Modes of Meaning"

⭐ 21. It is a commonplace that all religion expresses itself in mythological or metaphorical terms; it says one thing and means another; it uses imagery to convey truth. But the crucial fact about religion is not that it is metaphor, but that it is unconscious metaphor. No one can express any thought without using metaphors, but this does not reduce all philosophy and science to religion, because the scientist knows that his metaphors are merely metaphors and that the truth is something other than the imagery by which it is expressed, whereas in religion the truth and the imagery are identified. To repeat the Creed as a religious act it is necessary not to add "All this I believe in a symbolical or figurative sense": to make that addition is to convert religion into philosophy.

R. G. Collingwood, "Outlines of a Philosophy of Art"

22. Leprosy is a disease caused by the bacteria *mycobacterium leprae*, which causes damage to the skin and the peripheral nervous system. Unfortunately, the history of leprosy and its interaction with man is one of suffering and misunderstanding. The newest research suggests that at least as early as 4000 B.C. individuals had been infected with the bacteria, while the first known written reference to the disease was found on Egyptian papyrus in about 1550 B.C. The disease was well recognized in ancient China, Egypt, and India, and there are several references to the disease in the Bible. Because the disease was poorly understood, very disfiguring, slow to show symptoms, and had no known treatment, many cultures thought the disease was a curse or punishment from the gods. Consequently, leprosy was left to be "treated" by priests or holy men, not physicians.   Adapted from "Leprosy (Hansen's Disease)," MedicineNet, Inc.

23. The biggest misconception when discussing Los Angeles' attractiveness as a market is thinking every NFL owner would salivate at the prospect of having a team in the second biggest media market in the country and the entertainment capital of the world. That is simply not the case in the NFL's egalitarian model, in which all national revenues are equally divided among the 32 teams. In the NFL, the amount of money a team can generate from its stadium with as little risk as possible is what NFL owners are after. So if they can get their state, city, or county to completely subsidize the stadium while giving 100 percent of the revenue to the owner, as is the case in many NFL cities, that's the best possible deal. That would never happen in Los Angeles, and therefore moving an NFL team to L.A. has never made financial sense for an owner with a better deal in a smaller market.

Arash Markazi, "A 16-Year Rocky Relationship"

B. INCOMPLETE ARGUMENTS

It is not unusual to find arguments that appear to be missing some important information. Some people purposely leave out information because they assume we will fill in the missing parts. For example, someone might say the following:

> The novel I just bought is by Judy Prince, so I'm sure I'm going to like it.

Even if the speaker is not someone you know quite well, you can probably supply the missing premise:

> The novel I just bought is by Judy Prince. *I liked every novel of hers that I have read so far,* so I'm sure I'm going to like it.

Arguments with missing premises, missing conclusions, or both are called **enthymemes**. This term derives its meaning from the two roots, "en," meaning *in*, and "thymos," which refers to the mind. It means, literally, "to keep in the mind." The missing information is therefore implied. Enthymemes are context-driven. Our recognition and subsequent reconstruction of the argument depends on the setting in which the information appears. However, sometimes we are expected to supply missing information with which we are not necessarily familiar. For example, suppose someone says this:

> I have a Cadillac; therefore I don't have to spend much on maintenance.

The assumption is that we will supply something like the following:

> [1] I have a Cadillac. [2] *Cadillacs require very little maintenance*; therefore, [3] I don't have to spend much on maintenance.

Notice that we placed brackets around the numeral used for the missing premise. This ensures that we include the additional statement in our diagram and indicates that it was not part of the original argument. The diagram can be displayed as follows:

Enthymemes Arguments with missing premises, missing conclusions, or both.

Advertisements sometimes are effective because they are really enthymemes with missing conclusions. A billboard ad once had the following message:

> Banks lend money. We're a bank.

The advertisers were clever enough to know that most people would easily fill in the conclusion: "We lend money." Some slick television ads say very little, but they imply a lot. The visual nature is created in order for you to mindlessly fill in the missing conclusion: "If I buy this product, I will live the kind of life depicted on the screen." (Of course, nobody falls for this.)

Sometimes we must add both a premise *and* a conclusion. Suppose a professional boxer is asked if he will win his upcoming fight. Displaying an air of confidence, he replies,

> The only way I can lose is if I die.

The boxer expects that we will fill in the missing information: "I don't intend to die" (*Missing premise*); and "I will win" (*Missing conclusion*). The reconstruction can now be completed:

> [1] The only way I can lose is if I die. [2] I don't intend to die. [3] I will win.

Since we added both a premise and the conclusion, the resulting diagram should reflect those additions.

$$1 \quad [2]$$
$$\downarrow$$
$$[3]$$

What we choose to supply as a missing premise or conclusion can affect the subsequent evaluation of the argument. For example, suppose someone says the following:

> My horse is fast, because she is a thoroughbred.

We might fill in the missing information in two different ways:

(1) My horse is fast, because she is a thoroughbred, and *all thoroughbreds are fast*.
(2) My horse is fast, because she is a thoroughbred, and *most thoroughbreds are fast*.

The words "fast" and "most" are vague, so we need to provide some working definitions. Let's arbitrarily stipulate that "fast" in this context means able to run a mile in under 1 minute 50 seconds. Furthermore, we can stipulate that "most" means "at least 70%."

Reconstruction (1) makes the argument deductive. Given the stipulated definitions of the words, and assuming the premises are true, the argument is valid. On the other hand, reconstruction (2) makes the argument inductive. Given the stipulated definitions of the words, and assuming the premises are true, the argument is strong. One way to decide which of the two reconstructions is more appropriate is by analyzing the truth value of the statements. In reconstruction (1), the added premise, "all thoroughbreds are fast," is false if even one thoroughbred is not able to run a mile in the stipulated time. It should not be difficult to find at least one thoroughbred that is not capable of meeting the requirement. If so, the argument would still be valid, but it would be unsound because at least one of the premises was false.

For reconstruction (2), the added premise, "most thoroughbreds are fast," is probably true. Now if the remaining premise is true—if the horse in question is in fact a thoroughbred—then the argument is cogent (i.e., strong and containing all true premises). Given both analyses, we should choose the reconstructed argument that gives the benefit of the doubt to the person presenting the argument. This is sometimes referred to as the **principle of charity**. In this case, reconstructing the argument as inductive is the better choice.

Let's analyze the following argument:

> Bill Gateway is rich; it follows that he cheats on his taxes.

We can fill in the missing premise in these two ways:

(1) Bill Gateway is rich, and *since all rich people cheat on their taxes*, it follows that he cheats on his taxes.
(2) Bill Gateway is rich, and *since most rich people cheat on their taxes*, it follows that he cheats on his taxes.

Since the term "rich" is vague, we need to define it for purposes of analysis. We can arbitrarily stipulate that "rich" means any individual whose income exceeds $250,000 a year. In addition, we can reuse the definition of "most" that was given in the previous example.

Let's do a logical analysis first. Reconstruction (1) makes the argument deductive, and assuming the premises are true, it is valid. Reconstruction (2) makes the argument inductive, and assuming the premises are true, it is a strong argument. Now let's do a truth value analysis. In reconstruction (1), the added premise, "all rich people cheat on their taxes," is false if even one rich person does not cheat on his or her taxes. It seems likely that at least one rich person has successfully gone through an exhaustive tax audit and has not cheated. Thus, the argument is valid, but unsound.

For reconstruction (2), the truth value of the added premise, "most rich people cheat on their taxes," is not so obvious. While many people probably have strong feelings regarding the truth or falsity of this added premise, what is needed is objective evidence to decide the issue. For example, suppose the Internal Revenue Service (IRS) published a report stating that approximately 70% of all "rich" people (using our stipulated definition of the term) who have been audited have been found to cheat on their taxes, then this could be used as objective evidence to show the premise is true. If

Principle of charity
We should choose the reconstructed argument that gives the benefit of the doubt to the person presenting the argument.

so, the argument is cogent. However, if the IRS published a report stating that only around 15% of all "rich" people who have been audited have been found to cheat on their taxes, then this could be used as objective evidence to show the premise is false. If so, we would classify the argument as uncogent, because at least one premise is false.

Another interesting point to consider regarding inductive arguments was mentioned in Chapter 1. New information (premises) can sometimes seriously affect their strength. By adding an additional premise or premises to a weak inductive argument, we can often create a new argument that is strong. On the other hand, it is also possible to add an additional premise or premises to a strong inductive argument and thereby create a new argument that is weak. For example, consider the following argument:

> I just drank a bottle of Sunrise Spring Mineral Water. Since it has been shown that most bottled water is safe, I can conclude, with some confidence, that the water was safe.

Assuming the premises are true, this is a strong argument. However, suppose we pick up the newspaper and read an article reporting the following:

> Happy Sunshine Manufacturing Corporation has announced that it is recalling all of its Sunrise Spring Mineral Water due to a suspected contamination occurring in one of its bottling facilities. Anyone having purchased this product is advised to return it to the store of purchase for a full refund.

When added as additional premises, this new information makes the original conclusion unlikely to be true; thus its addition creates a weak argument.

Of course, not all additional information will affect an inductive argument. For example, if new information is added as a premise, but it is irrelevant to the conclusion, then it has no effect on the strength of the argument. In addition, since an irrelevant premise has no bearing on the strength of an inductive argument, it does not affect the truth value analysis of the argument.

Concerning deductive arguments it is often quite easy to add a premise to an invalid argument and create a new valid argument. For example, consider the following argument:

> Frank committed a murder. Therefore, Frank committed a felony.

The argument is invalid. It requires an added premise to make it valid, as the following reconstruction shows:

> Frank committed a murder. Every murder is a felony (*Missing premise*). Frank committed a felony.

If we add a premise to make an argument valid, we must make sure that the new premise does not create an unsound argument. For example,

> Frank committed a felony. Therefore, Frank committed a murder.

This is an invalid argument. It can be made valid by adding a new premise:

> Frank committed a felony. Every felony is a murder (*Missing premise*). Frank committed a murder.

This is a valid argument. However, the new premise is false, because not every felony is a murder. (For example, selling illegal drugs is a felony.) So we must be careful to add premises that not only logically support the conclusion, they are also true.

Additional premises can affect a deductive argument, but only in one direction. As we saw, it is possible to add premises to an invalid argument and create a new valid argument. However, the opposite result cannot happen. Since the original premises of a valid argument provide the necessary support to ensure that the argument is valid, no additional premise or premises can affect that outcome.

CHECK YOUR UNDERSTANDING 3B

I. For each of the following enthymemes, supply either the missing premises or the missing conclusion. Apply the *principle of charity* to your reconstructions. Evaluate the resulting arguments and explain your answers.

1. I am talking to a human; therefore, I am talking to a mammal.

Answer:

Reconstruction 1: Missing premise: *All humans are mammals.*

This makes the argument deductively valid. Since the added premise is true, if the first premise is true, then it is a sound argument.

Reconstruction 2: Missing premise: *The vast majority of humans are mammals.*

This makes the argument inductively strong. But since we know that all humans are mammals, this reconstruction would not be the best choice.

2. I am talking to a mammal; therefore, I am talking to a human.

3. Shane owns a Honda, so it must be a motorcycle.

4. Shane owns a motorcycle, so it must be a Honda.

⭐ 5. I have a headache. I just took two aspirins. Aspirins relieve headaches.

6. The office laser printer can print twenty pages a minute in black and white or ten pages a minute in color. It took 1 minute to print John's ten-page report on the office laser printer.

7. Vincent just had a big lasagna dinner, so I know he is very happy now.

8. Since Vincent just had a big lasagna dinner, it follows that he will soon be looking for the antacid tablets.

⭐ 9. Jake has a viral infection. He decided to take some penicillin pills he had sitting in the medicine cabinet. But he doesn't realize that penicillin has no effect on viruses.

10. Jake has a bacterial infection. He decided to take some penicillin pills he had sitting in the medicine cabinet. Penicillin can be effective when treating bacteria.

11. Frances must be an honest person, because she is an educated person.

12. There are ten marbles in the jar: nine red and one blue. I picked, at random, one of the marbles from the jar.

⭐ 13. Jamillah is a safe driver, so her insurance rates are low.

14. Walter has an expensive camera, therefore he takes perfect pictures.

15. Shane is a well-prepared and diligent student. Teachers respect students who are well prepared and diligent.

16. Perform at your best when your best is required. Your best is required every day.

Adapted from John Wooden's *Pyramid of Success*

⭐ 17. Sen. Tom Coburn said earmarks can create "a conflict of interest that benefits just those we represent from our states or just those who help us become senators. All we have to do is look at campaign contributions and earmarks, and there is a stinky little secret associated with that."

Andrew Taylor, "Senate Shuns GOP Push to Nix Pet Projects," Associated Press

18. When drunk in excess, alcohol damages nearly all organ systems. It is also connected to higher death rates and is involved in a greater percentage of crime than most other drugs, including heroin. But the problem is that "alcohol is too embedded in our culture and it won't go away," said Leslie King, an adviser to the European Monitoring Centre for Drugs.

Adapted from "Alcohol More Lethal Than Heroin, Cocaine," Associated Press

19. Some 80,000 Western-trained Chinese scientists have returned to work in the pharmaceutical and health-care industries in China since the mid-1980s. In addition to the accelerated return of Chinese scientists, the Chinese government and private industry have instituted a surge in investment in research and development in the above mentioned fields.

Adapted from the article "China as Innovator," *Straits Times*

20. There are some things in our society and some things in our world of which I'm proud to be maladjusted, and I call upon all men of goodwill to be maladjusted to these things until the good society is realized. I must honestly say to you that I never intend to adjust myself to racial segregation and discrimination. I never intend to adjust myself to religious bigotry. I never intend to adjust myself to economic conditions that will take necessities from the many to give luxuries to the few, and leave millions of God's children smothering in an airtight cage of poverty in the midst of an affluent society.   Martin Luther King, Jr., 1963 speech

II. The following problems are designed to get you to evaluate the strength of inductive arguments as the result of adding new information. You will be given an inductive argument, and then additional information will be provided. Determine whether the new information strengthens or weakens the original argument. Evaluate each piece of new information independently of the others. Here is the argument:

The lamp in your room does not work.
The light bulb is defective.

1. The ceiling light works.

Answer: Strengthens the argument. If the ceiling light works, then there is electricity available in the room.

2. The lamp is plugged into the wall socket correctly.

3. Your radio is working, and it is connected to the same outlet as the lamp.

4. The ceiling light does not work.

⭐ 5. The lamp is not plugged into the wall socket correctly.

6. Your radio is not working, and it is connected to the same outlet as the lamp.

7. You replace the light bulb, and the lamp now works.

8. You replace the light bulb, and the lamp does not work.

⭐ 9. Every other electrical fixture in the room works.

10. No electrical fixture in the room works.

Apply the same kind of analysis to the next inductive argument. Evaluate the additional information to decide if that particular piece of information strengthens or weakens the argument. Treat each new piece of information independently of the others.

Your car won't start.
Your battery is dead.

11. The headlights don't work.

Answer: Strengthens the argument. Headlights draw their power from the battery; therefore, this new evidence strengthens the argument.

12. The headlights do work.

⭐ 13. The battery is 5 years old.

14. The battery is 3 months old.

15. The horn works.

16. The horn does not work.

⭐ 17. The battery terminal clamps are loose.

18. The battery terminal clamps are tight.

19. When you jump-start the car, it starts.

20. When you jump-start the car, it does not start.

C. RHETORICAL LANGUAGE

As we saw with enthymemes, context can influence our recognition and reconstruction of arguments, which is why interpretations of statements and arguments must be justified. Since it is easy to take a statement out of context and give it any interpretation we please, we need the original context to help us settle disagreements. The more we know about the setting in which the statements and arguments were made, the people involved, and the issues at hand, the more accurate our interpretations, analyses, and evaluations will be. But not all uses of language are transparent. Sometimes we speak or write for dramatic or exaggerated effect. When this occurs, we can be using **rhetorical language**; that is, the language we employ may be implying things that are not explicitly said. We must be careful when we interpret what appears to be rhetorical language, and we need to justify our reconstructions of arguments. This section will explore three uses of rhetorical language: rhetorical questions, rhetorical conditionals, and rhetorical disjunctions.

Rhetorical language
When we speak or write for dramatic or exaggerated effect; that is, the language we employ may be implying things that are not explicitly said.

Rhetorical Questions

Although arguments are constructed out of statements, sometimes a premise or conclusion is disguised as a question. For example, suppose someone says the following:

> You have not saved any money, you have only a part-time job, and at your age car insurance will cost you at least $2000 a year. Do you really think you can afford a car?

Although the last sentence poses a question, it should be clear from the context that the speaker's intention is to make an assertion: "You can't afford a car." This is an example of a **rhetorical question**, a statement disguised in the form of a question. We can reconstruct the argument as follows:

Rhetorical question
When a statement is disguised in the form of a question.

> [1] You have not saved any money. [2] You have only a part-time job. [3] At your age car insurance will cost you at least $2000 a year. [4] You can't afford a car.

Since we changed the rhetorical question into a statement, we placed the corresponding numeral in brackets. This is reflected in the resulting diagram:

In some arguments, both a premise and a conclusion appear as rhetorical questions. For example, suppose a disgruntled teenager says the following:

> I do my share of work around this house. Don't I deserve to get something in return? Why shouldn't I be allowed to go to the *Weaknotes* concert today?

The speaker is using the two rhetorical questions for dramatic effect. Our reconstruction should then reveal the assertions implied by the speaker, as follows:

> [1] I do my share of work around this house. [2] I deserve to get something in return. [3] I should be allowed to go to the *Weaknotes* concert today.

The reconstruction gives us a clearer understanding of the argument, and helps in determining the type of diagram to use.

1
↓
[2]
↓
[3]

Here is another example of a rhetorical question appearing as part of an argument:

> Why do you waste your time worrying about your death? It won't happen during your lifetime.

The reconstructed argument is as follows:

> Your death won't happen during your lifetime. Stop wasting your time worrying about it.

Rhetorical Conditionals

The statement "If you live in New Jersey, then you live in the United States" is an example of a *conditional statement*. The first part, which follows the word "if," is a statement, and it is referred to as the *antecedent*. The second part, which follows the word "then," is also a statement, and it is referred to as the *consequent*. A common error is to think of conditional statements as complete arguments in themselves. But this is incorrect. A conditional statement does not assert that either the antecedent or the consequent is true. What is asserted is that *if* the antecedent is true, *then* the consequent is true. Therefore, a conditional statement by itself is not an argument; however, it can certainly be used as part of an argument. (Conditional statements will be discussed again in Chapter 7.)

Under normal circumstances, then, a conditional statement would not be an argument. However, in the appropriate setting, an argument can be disguised as a rhetorical conditional statement. For instance, suppose you tell a friend that you are trying to lose 25 pounds. The friend might say the following:

> If you were really serious about losing weight, then you would not be eating that large pepperoni pizza all by yourself.

From the context, it should be clear that the speaker is observing you eating a pizza, so that fact is not in dispute. The observation is then used as the basis on which a conclusion is said to follow. In this example, the consequent of the conditional statement contains the intended premise, while the antecedent contains the intended conclusion. The reconstructed argument is as follows:

> You are eating that large pepperoni pizza all by yourself. Therefore, you are not really serious about losing weight.

Rhetorical conditional
A conditional statement that is used to imply an argument.

A conditional statement that is used to imply an argument is called a **rhetorical conditional**. We must take care to reconstruct a conditional statement as an argument only when we are reasonably sure that the conditional is being used rhetorically. A correct reconstruction of a conditional statement as an argument requires a good understanding of the context in which the conditional appears.

Some rhetorical conditionals can even occur in the form of questions. For example, a newspaper editorial page might contain an article written by a pundit who opposed the war in Iraq. At some point in the article we might find this passage:

> If Saddam Hussein did not have weapons of mass destruction, then how can anyone still claim the war was justified?

The rhetorical conditional takes the form of a question, by means of which the author makes two assertions. We can reconstruct the argument as follows:

> Saddam Hussein did not have weapons of mass destruction. Thus, no one can still claim the war was justified.

Depending on the context, a rhetorical conditional can be reconstructed in different ways. For example, suppose we encounter this sentence:

> If you truly care about your children, then why are you neglecting them?

If the speaker happens to be a close friend or relative whose intent is to change someone's behavior, the argument might be reconstructed as follows:

> I know you care about your children. So, you have to stop neglecting them.

On the other hand, if the speaker is a social worker who has observed repeated instances of child neglect, the argument might be reconstructed differently:

> You repeatedly neglect your children. Therefore, you do not truly care for them.

In this case, the social worker may be using the rhetorical conditional as part of a more extended justification for removing the children from a negligent parent.

The next example adds a new dimension to our discussion of rhetorical conditionals. Suppose a parent says this to a child:

> If you are smart, and I know you are, then you will do the right thing.

It is possible to reconstruct the argument and yet retain a conditional as a premise. We might want to allow the phrase "I know you are" to play a key role in our reconstruction. If so, the argument can be displayed as follows:

> If you are smart, then you will do the right thing. I know that you are smart. Thus, you will do the right thing.

Alternatively, we might reconstruct the argument by eliminating the conditional aspect. If we interpret the phrase, "I know you are" as directly asserting the antecedent, then we can place emphasis on the purely rhetorical nature of the conditional. The new reconstruction might look like this:

> You are smart; therefore, you will do the right thing.

Whichever way we decide to reconstruct an argument, we should be prepared to justify our reconstruction by reference to the context in which it originally occurred.

Rhetorical Disjunctions

The statement "Green tea contains antioxidants, or ginseng is a natural herb" is an example of a *disjunction*, because it contains the word "or." The individual statements on either side of the word "or" are called *disjuncts*. The logical commitment asserted by way of a disjunction requires that at least one of the disjuncts be true in order for the disjunction to be true. In our example, if "Green tea contains antioxidants" is true, and "ginseng is a natural herb" is false, then the disjunction is true. Similarly, if "Green tea contains antioxidants" is false, and "ginseng is a natural herb" is true, then the disjunction is true. (As here, it is often the case that both disjuncts can be true at the same time.) Therefore, the only way for a disjunction to be false is if both disjuncts are false. (Disjunctions are also discussed in detail in Chapter 7.)

Rhetorical disjunction A disjunction that is used to disguise a statement or an implied argument.

A **rhetorical disjunction** is a disjunction that is used to disguise a statement or an implied argument. Some disjunctions are used rhetorically in various contexts. These instances can be reconstructed to reveal the implied argument. For example, you ask a friend what kind of ice cream cone he is getting. The reply might be this:

> They only have two kinds, vanilla or chocolate, and you know how much I dislike vanilla.

The reconstructed argument with the missing conclusion can be displayed as follows:

PROFILES IN LOGIC

Augusta Ada Byron

Ada Byron (1815–52) was the daughter of the poet Lord Byron, but she never got to know her father. Her parents separated when Ada was only a month old. When she was 18, she met Charles Babbage, the inventor of the "analytical engine," an elaborate calculating machine. Ada Byron worked with Babbage for the next 10 years, trying to solve the complex problems associated with what we now call computer programming. How can we get a machine to do complex mathematical calculations and analysis? A major problem for Babbage was to get a machine to calculate Bernoulli numbers (special sequences of rational numbers). Ada Byron's work on this difficult problem culminated in her breakthrough—the first computer program ever. What she created was an *algorithm*, a series of steps that achieve a final result. The analytic engine could do its calculations step by step, and so can modern computers.

But Ada Byron envisioned machines that could do far more than just calculate numbers. She wrote of a machine that could "compose elaborate and scientific pieces of music of any degree of complexity or extent." In the late 1970s, the United States Department of Defense began work on a programming language capable of integrating many complex embedded computer applications. The successful program bears the name *Ada*, in recognition of Ada Byron's achievements.

> They only have two kinds, vanilla or chocolate. You know how much I dislike vanilla. So I'm getting chocolate.

There is an important logical connection between rhetorical disjunctions and rhetorical conditionals. The philosopher Arthur Schopenhauer offers numerous examples of incorrect reasoning in everyday rhetoric. We will modify one of his examples. Schopenhauer tells us that it is common to hear people say the following:

> If you don't agree with our country's policies, then why don't you go live in another country?

The first step in our reconstruction is to turn the rhetorical question into a conditional statement:

> If you don't agree with our country's policies, then you should go live in another country.

The implied argument can be easily revealed:

> You don't agree with our country's policies. Therefore, you should go live in another country.

We can turn the conditional statement into a disjunction by revealing the two possibilities that are being asserted:

> Either you agree with our country's policies or you should go live in another country.

The conditional statement asserts that anyone who doesn't agree with the country's policies should go live in another country. On close inspection, we can see that the disjunction makes the identical assertion. Therefore, in this reconstruction the conditional statement and the disjunction are logically equivalent statements. (For a detailed discussion of *logical equivalence*, see Chapter 7.) We can now complete the argument reconstruction using the disjunction:

> Either you agree with our country's policies or you should go live in another country. You don't agree with our country's policies. Therefore, you should go live in another country.

Some rhetorical disjunctions, such as the one just analyzed, are actually examples of the *fallacy of false dichotomy*, which assumes that only two possibilities exist when in fact more than two exist. In our example, only two choices are given: (1) You agree with our country's policies. (2) You should go live in another country. But surely these are not the only two possibilities. A concerned citizen has the right and obligation to try to change a country's policies if they are illegal, immoral, or at least not in the best interests of the country. Certainly not every political decision will turn out to be the best for a particular country.

As we saw earlier, definitions can affect our understanding of statements and arguments. For example, the term "social activist" is sometimes used in a negative way, as if any suggested change to a country's policies were a threat to the country. Hence, a third possibility can be added to the example: (3) You disagree with the country's policies, and you want to change them peacefully and legally. Informal fallacies are discussed more fully in the next chapter.

CHECK YOUR UNDERSTANDING 3C

Reconstruct arguments based on your understanding and interpretation of the rhetorical aspect of the passages that follow. In each case be prepared to offer justification for your reconstruction and interpretation.

1. Would you like to open a new subscription to our Internet service, or do you already subscribe?

Answer: In most cases there is more than one way to reconstruct and evaluate the statements and arguments. As a suggestion, we can reconstruct the argument two ways:

(A) Either you would like to open a new subscription to our Internet service or you already subscribe. You do not already subscribe to our service. Therefore, you would like to open a new subscription to our Internet service.

(B) Either you would like to open a new subscription to our Internet service or you already subscribe. You would not like to open a new subscription to our Internet service. Therefore, you already subscribe.

Both reconstructed arguments are instances of a *false dichotomy* because it is possible that the disjuncts are false in the first premise of each argument.

2. You already ate more than your fair share of our limited food supply; do you really want more?

3. Capital punishment sometimes leads to the execution of innocent humans. As a society we cannot continue to perform such brutal acts of inhumanity. Isn't it time to change the existing laws?

4. You are not happy at your job, so why not quit?

5. Either you love me or you hate me. Which is it?

6. If he is being accused of taking steroids now, then why has he hit approximately the same number of home runs each year since he first started playing professional baseball?

7. If you are correct that he has not taken steroids, then how can you explain his suddenly gaining 40 pounds of muscle and doubling his average home run total?

8. If the United States cannot find the number one terrorist on the list, then it cannot ever hope to eliminate the large number of cells of anonymous terrorists.

9. If you want to get in shape, then why do you sit around the house all day doing nothing?

10. If the Catholic Church really believed in the equality of women, then why aren't there any women priests?

11. If he committed suicide by shooting himself, then why is there no trace of gunpowder on his hands?

12. If U.S. international policy is not to be a nation builder, then we wouldn't keep overthrowing governments we don't like and installing puppet leaders.

⭐ 13. Either we cut school funding or we raise taxes.

14. Would you rather have the government decide which doctor you can see or keep the current health-care system that gives you the freedom of choice?

15. Either you are with us or you are against us.

16. Either you love your country or you are a traitor.

⭐ 17. If you want to be financially secure in your retirement years, then why don't you have a retirement counselor?

18. You hate getting prank phone calls, so why don't you get an unlisted phone number?

19. Would you rather have a foot-long chili-cheese hotdog or two chili-cheese burgers?

20. If you want to get rich quick, then why don't you buy more lottery tickets?

⭐ 21. Does any wrong-headed decision suddenly become right when defended with religious conviction? In this age, don't we know better? If my God told me to poke the elderly with sharp sticks, would that make it morally acceptable to others?
    Rick Reilly, "Wrestling with Conviction"

22. When I was a kid in Dublin, I watched in awe as America put a man on the moon. We thought, you know, this is "mad." Nothing is impossible in America. In America, they can do anything over there. Nothing was impossible—only human nature. Is that still true? Tell me it's true. It's true isn't it? And if it isn't, you of all people can make it true again.
    Bono, 2001 Harvard Commencement Address

23. Ohio State lists 458 people in its athletic department. Included are the athletic director (who's also a vice president of the university), four people with the title senior associate athletic director, 12 associate athletic directors, an associate vice president, a "senior associate legal counsel for athletics," plus a nine-person NCAA compliance office. NCAA rules are complex, to be sure, but does Ohio State really need nine people who do nothing but push NCAA paperwork?
    Gregg Easterbrook, "Why Are Athletic Departments So Big?"

24. Now I know I'm fighting an uphill battle in some sense. If someone willingly chooses to be illogical, how to do you argue with them? Through logic? Clearly you cannot, because they don't subscribe to this. If someone maintains that the

world is 6,000 years old and that any evidence otherwise is just a trick by God to make us think the world is older, how do I argue against this?

Tony Piro, interview at "This Week in Webcomics"

25. The third lesson I teach kids is indifference. I teach children not to care about anything too much, even though they want to make it appear that they do. How I do this is very subtle. I do it by demanding that they become totally involved in my lessons, jumping up and down in their seats with anticipation, competing vigorously with each other for my favor. . . . But when the bell rings I insist that they stop whatever it is that we've been working on and proceed quickly to the next work station. . . . Indeed, the lesson of the bells is that no work is worth finishing, so why care too deeply about anything? Years of bells will condition all but the strongest to a world that can no longer offer important work to do. Bells are the secret logic of schooltime; their argument is inexorable. Bells destroy the past and future, converting every interval into a sameness, as an abstract map makes every living mountain and river the same even though they are not. Bells inoculate each undertaking with indifference.   John Taylor Gatto, "The 7-Lesson Schoolteacher"

D. NECESSARY AND SUFFICIENT CONDITIONS

A basic knowledge of conditional statements can help in the overall understanding of necessary and sufficient conditions. If you recall, the statement used earlier to introduce conditional statements was the following:

> If you live in New Jersey, then you live in the United States.

Sufficient condition
Whenever one event ensures that another event will happen.

Necessary condition
When one thing is essential, mandatory, or required in order for another thing to be realized.

A **sufficient condition** occurs whenever one event ensures that another event will happen. Another way of saying that something is a sufficient condition is to think of the phrases "is enough for" or "it guarantees." In our statement, living in New Jersey is sufficient for living in the United States. Of course, if you live in any of the other 49 other states, then you also live in the United States. Nevertheless, living in New Jersey is sufficient (is enough) to guarantee that you live in the United States.

On the other hand, a **necessary condition** means that one thing is *essential, mandatory,* or *required* in order for another thing to be realized. Given this, in the foregoing statement, living in the United States is necessary for living in New Jersey. In other words, if you do not live in the United States, then you do not live in New Jersey.

A diagram shows one way to picture the logic of necessary and sufficient conditions.

If X, then Y

Y

X

If not Y, then not X

The diagram places the smaller X box within the larger Y box. As the diagram shows, being in X is sufficient for being in Y. Of course, you can be in Y without being in X. In other words, although it is not necessary for you to be in X in order to be in Y, being in X is sufficient for being in Y. On the other hand, as the picture illustrates, you cannot be in X unless you are in Y. In other words, it is necessary to be in Y in order to be in X.

These ideas can also be expressed in the following ways:

Sufficient condition: If you live in New Jersey, then you live in the United States.
Necessary condition: If you do not live in the United States, then you do not live in New Jersey.

Here are some more examples of necessary and sufficient conditions:

Sufficient condition: If you have a gerbil for a pet, then you have an animal for a pet.
Necessary condition: If you do not have an animal for a pet, then you do not have a gerbil for a pet.
Sufficient condition: If there is a fire in the room, then there is oxygen in the room.
Necessary condition: If there is not oxygen in the room, then there is a not a fire in the room.

There are other kinds of relationships that we might find when we analyze for necessary and sufficient conditions. For example:

A. If today is Friday, then tomorrow is Saturday.
B. If today is not Friday, then tomorrow is not Saturday.

Upon analysis, we see that today's being Friday is both sufficient and necessary for tomorrow being Saturday. A little reflection will reveal how this result comes about. The days of the week follow each other in a standard, accepted, and stipulated pattern. Therefore, if today is Friday, then of course tomorrow must be Saturday. In addition, if today is not Friday, then tomorrow cannot possibly be Saturday. (We must also stipulate that we are referring in these cases to one place and not to different places of the world, which have different time zones.)

Now let's analyze two more statements:

C. If today is Friday, then I am 6 feet tall.
D. If today is not Friday, then I am not 6 feet tall.

Upon analysis we see that today's being Friday is neither sufficient nor necessary for my being 6 feet tall. These results should not be surprising if we look at the relationship between the things talked about in C and D. There is no connection between the two that would make the truth or falsity of one somehow dependent on the other.

We can examine a situation that has several necessary and sufficient ingredients. Universities and colleges have specific requirements that must be met in order to get a bachelor's degree. To simplify the discussion, let's consider a hypothetical situation where a university lists the following four requirements that need to be fulfilled in order to get a bachelor's degree:

1. A recognized major
2. A recognized minor (must be different from the major)
3. An overall grade point average (GPA) of at least 2.00
4. A passing grade in at least 125 credits

The university stipulates that each of these four requirements is necessary (you cannot get a bachelor's degree unless you fulfill all four requirements). The university also lists the options that are available to satisfy each of the four requirements. For example, the university lists twenty recognized majors, such as psychology, history, physics, economics, and English. Therefore, majoring in psychology is sufficient to fulfill requirement 1 (as would be majoring in history or physics). The university also lists the recognized minors (where we can use the same list as the majors for our purposes). Therefore, minoring in history is sufficient to fulfill requirement 2 (as would be minoring in physics or economics). An overall GPA of 2.75 is sufficient to fulfill requirement 3 (as would be a GPA of 3.00 or 3.98). Finally, a total of 128 credits with a passing grade is sufficient to fulfill requirement 4 (as would be 126 or 130). A diagram provides a graphic look at the relationship between the necessary and sufficient conditions in this example:

Sufficient Conditions	Psychology history physics economics (etc.)	Psychology history physics economics (etc.)	2.00 2.50 3.23 (etc.)	125 126 130 (etc.)
	↓	↓	↓	↓
Necessary Conditions	Major +	Minor +	Minimum 2.00 GPA +	Minimum 125 credits = Bachelor's degree

Suppose a student has the following: physics major, psychology minor, 3.76 overall GPA, and a passing grade in 132 credits. Since this student has fulfilled all four necessary requirements, she qualifies for a bachelor's degree. This combination of fulfilled requirements is also referred to as a *set of necessary and sufficient conditions* (in this example, to get a bachelor's degree).

Now suppose another student has the following: economics major, history minor, 2.87 overall GPA, and has a passing grade in 119 credits. Since this student has not yet fulfilled requirement 4, he does not yet qualify for a bachelor's degree. (The student needs 6 more credits with a passing grade to fulfill requirement 4.) Therefore, this is not a set of necessary and sufficient conditions to get a bachelor's degree.

Necessary and sufficient conditions play an important role in the analysis of cause-effect relationships and in scientific reasoning. This topic will be revisited in Chapter 14.

CHECK YOUR UNDERSTANDING 3D

I. Determine whether a *sufficient condition* exists in the following statements.

1. If Ed is a bachelor, then Ed is an adult male.

Answer: Sufficient condition. A bachelor is defined as being an unmarried adult male. Given this, if the antecedent is true (if Ed is a bachelor), then the consequent will be true as well (Ed is an adult male).

2. If Ed is an adult male, then Ed is a bachelor.

3. If there is oxygen in the room, then there is a fire in the room.

4. If there is a fire in the room, then there is oxygen in the room.

⭐ 5. If this is the month of June, then this month has exactly 30 days.

6. If this month has exactly 30 days, then this is the month of June.

7. If I live in the White House, then I am the president of the United States.

8. If I am the president of the United States, then I live in the White House.

⭐ 9. If I have exactly 100 pennies, then I have at least the equivalent of $1.

10. If I have at least the equivalent of $1, then I have exactly 100 pennies.

11. If I am over 21 years of age, then I am over 10 years of age.

12. If I am over 10 years of age, then I am over 21 years of age.

⭐ 13. If I am eating a banana, then I am eating a fruit.

14. If I am eating a fruit, then I am eating a banana.

15. If I hurt a human, then I hurt a mammal.

16. If I hurt a mammal, then I hurt a human.

II. Determine whether a *necessary condition* exists in the following statements.

1. If Ed is not an adult male, then Ed is not a bachelor.

Answer: Necessary condition. A bachelor is defined as being an unmarried adult male. Given this, if the antecedent is true (if Ed is not an adult male), then the consequent will be true as well (Ed is not a bachelor).

2. If Ed is a not a bachelor, then Ed is not an adult male.

3. If there is not a fire in the room, then there is not oxygen in the room.

4. If there is not oxygen in the room, then there is not a fire in the room.

⭐ 5. If this month does not have exactly 30 days, then this is not the month of June.

6. If this is not the month of June, then this month does not have exactly 30 days.

7. If I am not the president of the United States, then I do not live in the White House.

8. If I do not live in the White House, then I am not the president of the United States.

⭐ 9. If I do not have at least the equivalent of $1, then I do not have exactly 100 pennies.

10. If I do not have exactly 100 pennies, then I do not have at least the equivalent of $1.

11. If I am not over 10 years of age, then I am not over 21 years of age.

12. If I am not over 21 years of age, then I am not over 10 years of age.

⭐ 13. If I am not eating a fruit, then I am not eating a banana.

14. If I am not eating a banana, then I am not eating a fruit.

15. If I do not hurt a mammal, then I do not hurt a human.

16. If I do not hurt a human, then I do not hurt a mammal.

Summary

- Diagramming premises and conclusions displays the relationships between all the parts of an argument.
- The first step in diagramming an argument is to number the statements as they appear in the argument. The next step is to diagram the relationships by connecting the premises to the conclusion with an arrow.
- Premises are independent when the falsity of any one would not nullify the support the others give to the conclusion.
- Convergent diagram: Reveals the occurrence of independent premises.
- Premises are dependent when they act together to support a conclusion. In this case, the falsity of any one weakens the support the others would give to the conclusion.
- Linked diagram: Reveals the occurrence of dependent premises.
- Divergent diagram: Shows a single premise used to support independent conclusions.
- Serial diagram: Shows a conclusion from one argument that becomes a premise in a second argument.
- Enthymemes: Arguments with missing premises, missing conclusions, or both.
- Principle of charity: We should choose the reconstructed argument that gives the benefit of the doubt to the person presenting the argument.
- Rhetorical language: When we speak or write for dramatic or exaggerated effect. When the language we employ may be implying things that are not explicitly said.
- Rhetorical question: Occurs when a statement is disguised in the form of a question.

- Rhetorical conditional: A conditional statement that is used to imply an argument.
- Rhetorical disjunction: A disjunction that is used to disguise a statement or an implied argument.
- Sufficient condition: Occurs whenever one thing or event ensures that another thing or event will happen.
- Necessary condition: When one thing or event is essential, mandatory, or required in order for another thing or event to be realized.

KEY TERMS

LOGIC CHALLENGE: THE TRAIN TO VEGAS

You live in Los Angeles and decide to spend New Year's Eve in Las Vegas. You board the nonstop express train and consult the timetable for departures and arrivals. You read that it takes exactly 5 hours to get from Los Angeles to Las Vegas and the same length of time for the return trip. You also read that a train leaves each of the two cities every hour on the hour, and a train arrives in each of the two cities every hour on the hour. Now suppose for the sake of accuracy and precision of reasoning that every train runs perfectly on time. (Yes, this is a fantasy.)

The express trains have their own private set of tracks, so you will only pass those express trains that left Las Vegas. You decide to count the number of trains that you will pass on the trip. Your train leaves at 3:00 PM, and just as you are departing, sure enough a train from Las Vegas arrives. You begin counting with the train that just arrived, so it is train number 1.

How many express trains will you see by the end of your trip?

Chapter 4

Informal Fallacies

A. *Fallacies of Relevance*
B. *Fallacies of Unwarranted Assumption*
C. *Fallacies of Ambiguity or Diversion*
D. *Recognizing Fallacies in Ordinary Language*

We run into arguments everywhere—even when we are not looking for them. For example, you might be watching television, listening to the news, or watching a sporting event when you hear the following:

> For a number of years, seven-time Tour de France bicycle champion Lance Armstrong has been accused of using performance-enhancing drugs. An article in the French newspaper *L'Equipe* alleged that six of Armstrong's urine samples from the 1999 race were retested and found to contain the drug erythropoietin (EPO). If EPO is injected it can give an athlete a tremendous performance boost; however, it had already been banned by the Tour de France in 1999. Both the newspaper that published the report and the Tour de France race are owned by Amaury Sport Organization (ASO). In his response to the accusation by the newspaper, Armstrong said, "My question is how ASO can own the paper and the race."
>
> Adapted from Philip Hersh, "Armstrong, Defenders Not Forthright," *Chicago Tribune*

Armstrong's response avoided the question of his possible use of the drug, and shifted any potential wrongdoing to ASO. He deflected our attention away by implying that since the newspaper and the race have the same owner, they have formed a conspiracy against him. Of course, Armstrong may be innocent of the drug charge, but his defense did nothing to clarify the issue or advance his cause.

We often encounter arguments that appear to be correct, but on close inspection they lack real merit. Trying to pin down why can be a challenge—or part of the game. Here is an example from a popular television show:

> *Homer*: Not a bear in sight. The Bear Patrol must be working like a charm!
> *Lisa*: That's specious reasoning, Dad.
> *Homer*: Thank you, dear.
> *Lisa*: By your logic I could claim that this rock keeps tigers away.
> *Homer*: Oh, how does it work?
> *Lisa*: It doesn't work.
> *Homer*: Uh-huh.

Lisa: It's just a stupid rock.
Homer: Uh-huh.
Lisa: But I don't see any tigers around, do you?
Homer: Lisa, I want to buy your rock.

From "Much Apu About Nothing," *The Simpsons*

Homer has committed a fallacy, and he is not going to give it up without a fight.

The term "fallacy" derives from a Latin word meaning *to deceive*. (Another label for fallacies is revealing—*non sequitur*, which literally means "it does not follow.") Fallacious arguments are often misleading or deceptive, but they can also be unintentional. They can also be intentionally comic, like in *The Simpsons*. Clearly fallacious reasoning is often used in literature, movies, and jokes to point out the irrelevancy or absurdity of a statement or an argument.

Arguments purport to offer evidence for a conclusion, but they can fail, and some special cases of failure are classified as fallacies. A **formal fallacy** is a logical error that occurs in the form or structure of an argument. Formal fallacies are restricted to deductive arguments, and an understanding of deductive analysis and logical form makes it possible to recognize and understand them. (Formal fallacies are discussed in Chapters 7 and 8.) An **informal fallacy** is a mistake in reasoning that occurs in ordinary language. Rather than an error in the form or structure of an argument, informal fallacies include mistakes of *relevance, unwarranted assumption*, and *ambiguity* or *diversion*. We shall meet them all in this chapter. These classifications are simply aids in recognizing similarities among informal fallacies ("family resemblance"), not a rigid method of categorization.

The mistakes that occur in informal fallacies are not always easy to spot. A subtle change in the meaning of words, a shift in the reference of names, or a hidden irrelevancy are just a few of the many ways we can be fooled. In addition, fallacies are sometimes so persuasive because they involve fear, anger, pity, or even admiration. We start by looking at fallacies of relevance.

A. FALLACIES OF RELEVANCE

In **fallacies of relevance**, irrelevant premises are offered in support of a conclusion. Arguments that use irrelevant premises in support of a conclusion suffer from serious flaws in reasoning. Premises must be relevant; they must establish logical, reasonable ties to the conclusion. In addition, many irrelevant premises rely on psychological or emotional appeal for their persuasive force. We can distinguish eight kinds of fallacies of relevance.

1. Argument Against the Person

(ARGUMENTUM AD HOMINEM—"TO THE PERSON")

The truth of a statement and the strength of an argument should be judged on objective grounds. In an **argument against the person**, a claim is rejected or judged to be false based on alleged character flaws of the person making the claim. This would

---

Formal fallacy A logical error that occurs in the form or structure of an argument; it is restricted to deductive arguments.

Informal fallacy A mistake in reasoning that occurs in ordinary language and is different from an error in the form or structure of arguments.

Fallacies of relevance Fallacies that occur whenever irrelevant premises are offered in support of a conclusion.

Argument against the person When a claim is rejected or judged to be false based on alleged character flaws of the person making the claim. A second common form occurs whenever someone's statement or reasoning is attacked by way of a stereotype, such as a racial, sexual, or religious stereotype. A third form involves the use of the circumstances of a person's life to reject his claims.

be attacking the person, not the person's assertions or arguments, and is commonly referred to by the Latin term *ad hominem*. Generally speaking, people's characters are irrelevant to the determination of the truth or falsity of their claims. An important exception to this rule occurs in sworn testimony. If someone has previously been exposed as a liar based on contradictions in statements given under oath, then there are objective grounds for suspicion about any current or future statements.

Clear cases of *ad hominem* are not difficult to recognize. They divert attention away from the objective truth or falsity of a claim and instead denigrate the character of the person making the claim. Here are some examples:

- Why should I believe what he says about our economy? He is not even a citizen.
- You can't accept her advice. She is so old she has no idea what goes on in today's world.
- Why would you listen to him? He's too young to have any wisdom about life.

In all these cases, the reason to reject someone's statement or position is based on irrelevant information. Another common form of *ad hominem* occurs whenever someone's statement or reasoning is attacked by way of a stereotype, such as a racial, sexual, or religious stereotype. It can be subtle rather than overtly dismissive. But it will not advance your cause. A reference to any kind of stereotype is irrelevant to the determination of the truth or falsity of a person's claim or argument.

Another form of the *ad hominem* fallacy involves the use of the circumstances of a person's life to reject his claims. Circumstances are different from character. For example, political affiliation, educational institution, place of birth, religious affiliation, and income are circumstances connected to people's lives. When we insinuate that someone's circumstances dictate the truth or falsity of the claim, then we are once again attacking the person rather than the claim. Here is an example:

Of course Senator Hilltop thinks my administration's tax proposals are bad for the country. After all, his political party lost the last election, and everyone knows that losers are jealous.

Paraphrasing the argument can help with the analysis:

Senator Hilltop thinks my administration's tax proposals are bad for the country. His political party lost the last election. Members of the losing party are always jealous of the winning party.

Now suppose that Senator Hilltop has provided reasons for why he is against the tax proposals. If so, then the foregoing argument is an instance of *ad hominem*, because it attacks the person and not the person's reasons. The premises attack Senator Hilltop's party affiliation and negatively stereotype the senator and his party.

The following two arguments illustrate the same point:

- You don't want cars to get better gas mileage because you are a stockholder in the three major gasoline companies. If cars get better gas mileage, then your stock dividends will go down.

- You are against euthanasia because you are a physician. You make money only if terminally ill people are kept alive as long as possible.

A special kind of *ad hominem* argument is called "poisoning the well." In these instances, the attack against the person occurs before opponents have a chance to present their case. The attacker mentions something about the opponent's character or life and uses that information to warn the audience not to believe anything they hear or read. For example:

> Before you read her article "Stop All Wars," you should know that she was arrested six times for protesting in front of the Pentagon and White House. She also has been investigated by the FBI for possible ties to peace movements in other countries, some of which resulted in violence. It is crystal clear that these kinds of people are dangerous and want to destroy our Constitution and take away our basic freedoms. We must not let them.

Once again, it is important to recognize that any criticism of a person's argument should be restricted to their argument and should not be based on *ad hominem* attacks. All *ad hominem* fallacies rest on the same kind of reasoning error—the rejection of a statement or argument by criticizing a person's character or circumstances. In all cases, neither the truth of the claim nor the strength of the argument is ever considered on logical or factual grounds.

2. *Tu Quoque*

A variety of the *ad hominem* fallacy known as **tu quoque** (meaning "you, too" or "look who's talking") is distinguished by the specific attempt of one person to avoid the issue at hand by claiming the other person is a hypocrite. For example:

> You have been lecturing me about not joining a gang. But Dad, you were a gang member, and you never went to jail. So, I'll make my own decision about joining a gang.

Tu quoque A variety of the *ad hominem* fallacy that is distinguished by the specific attempt of one person to avoid the issue at hand by claiming the other person is a hypocrite.

The premises are used to imply the following: *Dad, you are a hypocrite*. This result is then used to reject Dad's arguments: *I can disregard your lectures*. As we can see from the reconstructed argument, the conclusion is the result of a *tu quoque* fallacy. The fallacy occurs because the argument attacks Dad; therefore it fails to address Dad's arguments.

Another example comes from the political world. If a U.S. senator criticizes the human rights failings of China by offering a detailed description of recorded UN inquiries, a Chinese representative might say the following:

> The senator should look in his own backyard. What about the complete disregard of the universal rights of people who the U.S. government incarcerates without any recourse to courts or even to a lawyer? What about the U.S. policy of spying on its own citizens without a court order? The senator should not throw stones when he lives in a glass house. The senator quotes many of his pronouncements from the Bible, so let me remind him that "whoever is without sin let him cast the first stone."

Other than stringing together a number of clichés, this response offers no rational rebuttal of the assertions of human rights violations. Of course, the senator might respond with his own cliché: Two wrongs don't make a right.

Instances of *tu quoque* fallacies occur quite often in personal arguments within families. For example, a child might say the following:

> Dad, I don't know why you keep pressuring me to give up smoking. You keep showing me statistics proving that smoking is bad for my health, that it will shorten my life, that it costs too much money. But you started smoking at my age and only recently quit. How can you honestly tell me to stop?

Since there are many good reasons to support the conclusion that someone should stop smoking, these reasons must be rationally argued against. To attack the person making the argument rather than the argument is to commit the fallacy.

3. Appeal to the People
(ARGUMENTUM AD POPULUM)

Appeal to the people
The avoidance of objective evidence in favor of an emotional response defeats the goal of a rational investigation of truth. The tactic appeals to people's desire to belong to a group.

Some arguments or claims rely on the arousal of a strong emotional state or psychological reaction. In an **appeal to the people**, the avoidance of objective evidence in favor of an emotional response defeats the goal of a rational investigation of truth. This fallacious tactic has been used by tyrants and bigots throughout history, with devastating social effects. It often appeals to a mob mentality, to an "us against them" attitude, with a fixation on fear or hate. Exposing the fallacy can sometimes be the first step in defeating this potentially harmful social ill. Another term that has come to be associated with this fallacy is the "bandwagon effect," which derives its name from the emotions involved in joining a movement merely because it is popular (to "jump on the bandwagon").

The fallacy of appealing to the people is a common thread that also runs through much of today's advertising campaigns. Slick ads are created in order to arouse a desire to attain the product. Such products are often displayed being used by beautiful, successful, and happy people. The obvious implication is that if you use this product, you will be transformed into one of the lucky ones, the ones living life to the fullest. The ads push psychological buttons: the need to belong to a group, the desire to be respected, the desire to be successful, and so on. The emotional reasons for buying products are powerful tools that are understood and effectively used by corporations to sell their products.

Pollsters for political groups also use this tactic. They can manipulate poll questions so that the appeal to an emotional response overrides the rational grounds for a person's belief. Here is an example of a rhetorical, or loaded, question:

> Public schoolteachers are demanding a pay raise and threaten to strike if they don't get it. A prolonged strike will jeopardize our children's future. In addition, some economists predict that any substantial pay raise will result in an unbalanced budget, which in turn will lead to an increase in taxes. Although the school year lasts only 180 days, the teachers get paid 12 months a year, whether or not school is in session. So are you for or against a pay raise for public school teachers?

Since the final sentence is a rhetorical question, it needs to be rewritten as a statement: *You should be against a pay raise for public school teachers.* The language employed is meant to appeal to the emotions of taxpayers and voters. The terms "demanding," "threaten," "prolonged strike," and "jeopardize" are used to evoke a sense of dire consequences and to provoke anger. The argument offers only several negative consequences of a teachers' pay raise, but only as possibilities, not as facts. Also, the mention of higher taxes fuels the emotions of many voters.

4. Appeal to Pity

(ARGUMENTUM AD MISERICORDIAM—"FROM PITY OR GUILT")

A specific kind of emotional plea is the **appeal to pity**. For example, a defense attorney may attempt to get the jury to sympathize with the defendant prior to deliberation. If the defendant is found guilty, then the appeal may be addressed to the judge, asking for a light sentence based on the effects that a harsh sentence would have on the defendant's family. On the other side, the prosecution may appeal to the jury to sympathize with the victim, not the defendant. The prosecutor may appeal to the judge to consider the emotional devastation inflicted on the victim's family. In this way, he may persuade the judge to sentence the defendant to the maximum penalty allowed by law. However, trials are, ideally, rational decision-making processes. The image of justice as a blindfolded person holding a set of scales emphasizes the goal of an objective weighing of the evidence. If pity is substituted for evidence and the rule of law, then the judgment is fallacious.

> **Appeal to pity** A specific kind of emotional plea that relies solely on a sense of pity for support.

Here is a classic example:

> Your honor, before you sentence my client for the murder of his parents, I ask you to consider his situation. He is an orphan. Perhaps you can give him the lightest punishment possible.

The premises provide no objective evidence for a light punishment. The argument is ironic since the premises ask the judge to pity the defendant because he is a self-caused orphan.

Many charities arouse a sense of pity, and perhaps even guilt, when they solicit pledges of support. These charities know that people do not always act rationally and in their own long-term best interests. Nevertheless, any cause worthy of support should have rational, legitimate reasons, which, when understood, should be sufficient to get people to give. In addition to evoking our human sense of compassion for those who are suffering, a *legitimate* argument will not have to rely solely on pity to support its conclusion.

5. Appeal to Force

(ARGUMENTUM AD BACULUM—"APPEAL TO THE STICK")

The threat of physical harm, an **appeal to force**, can sometimes cause us to accept a course of action which otherwise would be unacceptable. There are cases where witnesses and jurors have been threatened with physical harm to themselves or to their families if they go against the defendant. Voters have been pressured into changing their vote by the threat of violence.

> **Appeal to force** A threat of harmful consequences (physical and otherwise) used to force acceptance of a course of action that would otherwise be unacceptable.

However, the threat need not be so overt and directly physical. For example, a large company may send out the following memo to its employees:

> If the workers of this company do not agree to a 25% cut in salary, then the company may have to shut its doors. Therefore, the workers of this company must agree to a 25% cut in salary.

The premise is an obvious threat. As such, it does not, by itself, provide objective evidence for the conclusion. If the company is in bad financial shape, then there should be objective evidence to present to the workers. The evidence would have to show that without the pay cut the company would be forced to close. However, without this evidence, the threat by the company to close its doors unless its employees vote to take a pay cut results in an instance of the fallacy of appeal to force.

Another example illustrates the same point. A parent may threaten a child with loss of privileges or being grounded in order to achieve desired results:

> You had better get straight A's on your next report card. If you don't, then we will have to punish you. You will be not allowed to go out with your friends for an entire month.

It is not difficult to imagine perfectly legitimate reasons why students should get good grades. Rational, objective evidence can be used as support for why students should do well in school. Anytime an overt or implied threat is used to convince someone to make a decision, in the absence of supporting evidence for the conclusion, the rational decision-making process is subverted.

6. Appeal to Ignorance

(ARGUMENTUM AD IGNORANTIAM—"ARGUING FROM IGNORANCE")

Appeal to ignorance
An argument built on a position of ignorance claims either that (1) a statement must be true because it has not been proven to be false or (2) a statement must be false because it has not been proven to be true.

An **appeal to ignorance** (lack of knowledge) makes one of two possible mistakes: (1) a claim is made that a statement must be true because it has not been proven to be false, or (2) a claim is made that a statement must be false because it has not been proven to be true. Both claims are unjustified. An example of the first kind of mistake is this:

> UFOs exist because nobody has proven that they don't exist.

Here is an example of the second kind of mistake:

> There is no life anywhere else in the universe. We have never received signals from any part of space.

The conclusion is based on a single factor—the lack of signals from outer space. But our failure to have detected any signals may signify our ignorance of sophisticated methods of detection. Also, the ability to send signals is not a necessary requirement for life to exist.

If substantial evidence is available to decide an issue, then the fallacy does not arise. For example, after thorough investigation, if no credible evidence is found linking a suspect to a crime, then we are justified in claiming the suspect is not guilty precisely because no evidence exists to prove guilt.

7. Missing the Point

(*IGNORATIO ELENCHI*—"IRRELEVANT PROOF")

The fallacy of **missing the point** occurs when premises that seem to lead logically to one conclusion are used instead to support an unexpected conclusion. A conclusion "misses the point" or "comes out of left field" when the premises do not adequately prepare us for it. For example:

> Hey Mom, guess what I found out? If we buy a second car, the insurance will only be an additional $400 a year! Let's go get one before the insurance company changes the rate.

The first sentence (the question) is not part of the argument, so we can disregard it for our analysis. The evidence regarding the cost of the insurance may not be in dispute, but the gap between the premises and conclusion is so great that the conclusion becomes, in a sense, irrelevant. The need for a second car has not been adequately established; nor has the family's financial situation been determined.

Missing the point
When premises that seem to lead logically to one conclusion are used instead to support an unexpected conclusion.

8. Appeal to an Unqualified Authority

(*ARGUMENTUM AD VERECUNDIAM*—"APPEAL TO REVERENCE OR RESPECT")

Arguments often rely on the opinions of experts, specialists whose education, experience, and knowledge provide relevant support for a claim. The appeal to expert testimony strengthens the probability that the conclusion is correct, as long as the opinion falls within the realm of the expert's field. On the other hand, arguments that rely on the opinions of people who have no expertise, training, or knowledge relevant to the issue at hand **appeal to an unqualified authority**.

The most prevalent fallacious use of inappropriate authority is in advertisements and commercials. Athletes, movie and television stars, and former politicians endorse products to boost sales. The consumer is expected to respect the famous personalities and trust their opinion.

Here is an example:

> I'm Nick Panning, quarterback of the Los Angeles Seals. I've been eating *Oaties* for breakfast since I was a kid. *Oaties* provides nutrition and vitamins and helps build strong bones. *Oaties* tastes great. You should get some for your kids today.

Appeal to an unqualified authority
An argument that relies on the opinions of people who have no expertise, training, or knowledge relevant to the issue at hand.

Merely being famous does not qualify someone to pronounce the merits of a product. An athlete generally has no expertise of the nutritional value of a breakfast cereal. On the other hand, a person with a Ph.D. in nutrition would presumably be in a good position to offer a fair assessment of the breakfast cereal (provided the opinion is not based on monetary compensation).

Albert Einstein, the famous physicist, was asked to be the first president of Israel. He humbly declined, stating that he had no idea how to run a country. Such modesty is rare.

Summary of Fallacies of Relevance

1. Argument against the person (*ad hominem*)
When a claim is rejected or judged to be false based on alleged character flaws of the person making the claim. A second common form occurs whenever someone's statement or reasoning is attacked by way of a stereotype, such as a racial, sexual, or religious stereotype. A third form involves the use of the circumstances of a person's life to reject his claims.

2. *Tu quoque*
A variety of the *ad hominem* fallacy in which one person attempts to avoid the issue at hand by claiming the other person is a hypocrite.

3. Appeal to the people
The avoidance of objective evidence in favor of an emotional response defeats the goal of a rational investigation of truth. The tactic appeals to people's desire to belong to a group.

4. Appeal to pity
A specific kind of emotional plea that relies solely on a sense of pity for support.

5. Appeal to force
A threat of harmful consequences (physical and otherwise) used to force acceptance of a course of action that would otherwise be unacceptable.

6. Appeal to ignorance
An argument claiming either that (1) a statement must be true because it has not been proven to be false or (2) a statement must be false because it has not been proven to be true.

7. Missing the point
When premises that seem to lead logically to one conclusion are used instead to support an unexpected conclusion.

8. Appeal to an unqualified authority
An argument that relies on the opinions of people who have no expertise, training, or knowledge relevant to the issue at hand.

CHECK YOUR UNDERSTANDING 4A

I. Determine whether each statement is true or false.

1. The appeal to an unqualified authority occurs when an argument relies on the experience, training, or knowledge of people who are experts relevant to the issue at hand.

Answer: False. The fallacy occurs when an argument relies on the opinions of people who have *no* expertise, training, or knowledge relevant to the issue at hand.

2. The appeal to pity is a specific kind of *ad hominem* fallacy.

3. An appeal to ignorance occurs when a person's character or circumstances are used to reject their claims.

4. The appeal to force uses rational reasons in support of a controversial position.

★ 5. *Tu quoque* is a variety of the *ad hominem* fallacy distinguished by the specific attempt of one person to avoid the issue at hand by claiming the other person is a hypocrite.

6. The fallacy of missing the point occurs in an argument where premises that seem to lead logically to one conclusion are used instead to support an unexpected conclusion.

7. An appeal to the people is not considered a specific kind of *ad hominem* fallacy.

8. An argument that claims either (1) a statement must be true because it has not been proven to be false or (2) a statement must be false because it has not been proven to be true is called *ad hominem*.

★ 9. A threat of harmful consequences (physical and otherwise) used to force acceptance of a course of action that would otherwise be unacceptable is called an appeal to an unqualified authority.

10. *Ad hominem* fallacies occur when an argument uses character flaws or circumstances of people's lives to reject their claims.

II. Each of the following passages contains a fallacy of relevance. Determine the fallacy that best fits each case. Explain your answer.

1. Biology 1 was easy for me. Physics 1 was no problem. I think I'm going to change my major to social work.

Answer: Missing the point. This is an example of an argument that does not work because the premises seem to head in one direction (the person does well in natural science courses), but the conclusion heads in another direction (changing to a social work major).

2. This team beat us 64-0 last year. So we need to go out and give them a taste of their own medicine and see how they like it. Are you ready to fight?

3. If we don't raise gasoline prices, then we can't afford to explore for new oil reserves. In that case our dependency on foreign oil will bankrupt the major gasoline companies. The price will skyrocket and will be out of the reach of most people.

4. Maybe you didn't know that she is an orphan. Her outrageous behavior should be excused because of her background.

★ 5. I saw him play football, and he is ferocious on the field; he tackles everything in sight. Don't hire him to tutor young kids; he's too violent.

6. That must be a great product for men since a former senator and presidential candidate endorsed it.

7. I believe that we are reincarnated. No one has ever been able to prove that after death our spirits don't move on to another baby.

8. He is an atheist. He cannot possibly have anything relevant to say on ethical issues.

★ 9. That guy plays a doctor on my favorite TV show. I saw him in a commercial where he said that Asperalinol was great for migraine headaches. It must really work, so the next time you go to a drugstore pick me up a bottle.

10. I know that Senator Wickhaven has been found guilty of harassment, but did you know that he was twice wounded in the Korean War? Since he has suffered so much for our country, he should not be punished for this crime.

11. If you don't break off your relationship with him, your mother and I will disinherit you.

12. She did not vote in the last election. Anything she suggests about how our country should be run cannot possibly be of any concern to us.

★ 13. Mr. Crabhouse is a hard grader. Not only that, he forces you to attend class, participate in discussions, and do homework. He actually expects us to think about the material outside of class. So you can believe that his class teaches students nothing about real life.

14. My uncle drinks a six-pack of beer a day, so I couldn't believe it when he lectured me on the dangers of alcohol. He's one to talk! Nothing he says about drinking can be true because he cannot stop drinking himself.

15. I know that we haven't looked for the missing money in the attic, but I'm sure that it is there.

16. I know that he did not do well on the exams; nevertheless, you should give him an A for the course. After all, he is taking 18 credits and is holding down a full-time job.

★ 17. Of course you should pay us for protection. After all, if you don't, we will have to break your arms, wreck your business, and harass your customers.

18. I would not believe anything he says in his book. He is constantly on TV, on the radio, and in magazines trying to promote it so it will become a best seller.

19. Aliens from another planet must have built the great pyramids of Egypt because there is no record of how they were actually constructed.

20. He has taken one psychology course, so he must be wrong when he claims that gambling is addictive.

★ 21. That physician is a male. He couldn't possibly know anything about female health problems.

22. I know that deep inside you love her. Draw on that undying love, and forget that she spent all the money on losing lottery tickets.

23. Statistics show that people with a college degree earn 50% more during their lifetime than those without a degree. So, you should begin investing in blue chip stocks.

24. I am going to vote for the incumbent, Senator Loweman, because my chemistry teacher said he is the best candidate.

⭐ 25. Since that sports reporter is a female, her analysis of what caused our team to lose the game is irrelevant.

26. Even though neither of us was at home when it happened, the dog must have broken the window by jumping on it. You have not shown me any other way that it could have happened.

27. He is a college student. That is enough to convince me that he drinks alcohol excessively.

28. The advertisement showed the latest Nobel Prize winner in literature drinking that new wine, Chateau Rouge. It must taste divine.

⭐ 29. I know you don't want to become a lawyer. However, your mother and I would be so proud to finally have a professional in the family. We would die happy if you go to law school.

30. I know your cousin recommends taking vitamins every day. After all, she's a pharmacist; what do you expect her to tell you?

31. He failed his final exam, so don't blame him for getting drunk and destroying his dorm room.

32. She is a chess grand master, so she can't be very beautiful.

⭐ 33. Look, the picture of the Olympic basketball team is on this cereal. It must be good for athletes.

34. Scientific experiments have never proved conclusively that there are not any ghosts; therefore, I firmly believe that they do exist.

35. He eats meat, so we should not invite him to speak at our seminar on animal rights.

36. I like chocolate. I like ice cream. Therefore, I'll take a hot dog for lunch.

⭐ 37. Your next-door neighbor works on his car day and night. You said you can't get any rest from the noise, so if you want him to stop, then let's steal his car and trash it out of town.

38. I have not decided if you can go to the concert tonight. I would like to see how much you contribute to this household. We will see what happens if you clean the house, wash the car, and do the grocery shopping today.

39. You can't give me an F on the exam. If you do, my mother and father will be so upset they will have to be hospitalized.

40. You tell me to wear a seat belt when I drive because it will protect me in case I get in an accident. I never saw you wear one when you drive, so why should I wear one?

B. FALLACIES OF UNWARRANTED ASSUMPTION

Fallacies of unwarranted assumption exhibit a special kind of reasoning error: they assume the truth of some unproved or questionable claim. The fallacies become apparent when the assumptions and lack of support are exposed. We can distinguish twelve kinds of fallacies of unwarranted assumption. (We continue our numbering of fallacies from the previous section.)

9. Begging the Question
(PETITIO PRINCIPII—"ASSUMPTION AT THE BEGINNING")

One type of the fallacy of **begging the question** assumes as evidence the very thing that it attempts to prove in a conclusion. In other words, the conclusion of an argument is smuggled into the premises. This can occur if the premises are confusing, complex, or obscure. It can occur even if the conclusion is assumed as an undeclared premise. Cases of begging the question can go unnoticed because they often sound so convincing. This should not be surprising; in many cases, the conclusion is already assumed in the premises, so on the surface it might appear to be a strong argument. However, premises can legitimately support conclusions only by providing reasons that are independent of the claim in the conclusion. No one would be fooled by the following argument:

> My brother has difficulty sleeping. Therefore, my brother has difficulty sleeping.

Since the conclusion merely restates the information in the premise, the argument is valid. However, the premise offers no independent or "new" information that would allow us to see that the conclusion has been well supported. Is the following argument any better?

> My brother suffers from insomnia. Therefore, my brother has difficulty sleeping.

At first sight it might appear that the information about insomnia offers an independent, good reason to accept the conclusion. However, close analysis reveals that the word "insomnia" means "having difficulty sleeping." In other words, the premise contains the same information as the conclusion, so the argument begs the question.

Now let's consider this argument:

> Jane has the highest GPA among all the seniors in my school. There are 300 graduating seniors in my class. Therefore, no senior has a higher GPA than she.

The conclusion is already assumed in the premises; it is merely worded differently. Both statements assert that Jane has the highest GPA among seniors. Obviously, if the claim is true in the premise, it will be true in the conclusion. In fact, the second premise becomes irrelevant; the number of graduating seniors has no bearing on the conclusion. The argument begs the question because it assumes what it intends to prove.

A different kind of fallacy of begging the question occurs when a premise needs independent support for its acceptance. For example, if your argument relies on a controversial or unsubstantiated premise, then you are assuming information that is by itself unwarranted and that could be unacceptable to those you are trying to convince. Consider this argument:

> The murder of a human being is always wrong. Abortion is the murdering of an embryo or fetus, both of which are human beings. Therefore, abortion is always wrong.

Most people would probably accept the first premise. If clarity is needed, we could offer a definition of "murder" as "the unjustified taking of the life of a human being." Our discussion might exempt cases of self-defense, legitimate police activity while protecting the citizenry, and certain military engagements. However, the second premise presents a greater challenge. The assertion that an embryo or fetus is a human being is often the central point on which opposing positions regarding abortion rest. Someone who disagrees with the conclusion of the argument can point out that the second premise "begs the question," in that it presents as a good reason what is in fact an unwarranted assumption: an embryo or fetus is a human being. The fallacious nature of the argument is not based on the underlying logic, because if both premises are true, then the argument is valid. The fallacy occurs because the truth of the second, controversial, premise has been assumed. The argument lacks sufficient additional, independent reasons to make the second premise acceptable and warranted.

Another type of begging the question is *circular reasoning*. Here is an example:

> You can believe him because he never lies. Furthermore, since he always tells the truth, he is someone that you can believe.

Paraphrasing the argument reveals the problem:

> You can believe him. He never lies. He always tells the truth. He is someone that you can believe.

If you look closely, you can see that the second and third statements say the same thing: Saying that someone never lies is the same thing as saying that he or she always tells the truth. Also, the first and fourth statements say the same thing; they both say that you can believe him. In other words, ultimately, the first statement is used to support the second statement, which in turn, is then used to support the first statement. The argument goes in a circle.

10. Complex Question

The fallacy of **complex question** occurs when a single question actually contains multiple, hidden parts. The questioner tries to force a single answer that, in turn, is used against the respondent. For example, suppose you are asked the following question:

> Do you still cheat on your taxes?

Complex question
A single question that actually contains multiple, hidden parts.

Answering either *yes* or *no* is an admission that you did, in fact, cheat on your taxes. The key words that create the complex question are "still cheat." If you answer "Yes," then the questioner can conclude that you currently cheat on your taxes and you have done so in the past. On the other hand, even if you never cheated on your taxes, answering "No," is an admission that you once did cheat on your taxes, but you no longer do. Therefore, the questioner can use this as evidence to support the conclusion that you cheated on your taxes. Here is how the questioner's argument would look:

> I asked you if you still cheated on your taxes. You said "No." Therefore, by your own admission you did cheat on your taxes.

The premises rely on the fact that the complex question contained two distinct questions that should have been asked separately: A. Did you ever cheat on your taxes? B. Do you now cheat on your taxes?

The ability to recognize that there are actually two questions at work here allows us to avoid the trap of the complex question. Once the questions are separated an innocent person can answer "No" to question A (Did you ever cheat on your taxes?) and "No" to question B (Do you now cheat on your taxes?). This prevents the questioner from drawing an unjustified conclusion.

Complex questions can be used to trap us in unacceptable situations. For example, suppose someone asks,

> Aren't you going to do something about your child's terrible behavior?

This complex question presupposes the following: (1) you agree that your child's behavior needs correcting and (2) you are going to correct it. Therefore, if you answer "Yes" to the complex question, you have admitted the child's behavior needs correcting. However, if you answer "No" to the complex question, then you have,

---

PROFILES IN LOGIC

Arthur Schopenhauer

Arthur Schopenhauer (1788–1860) is not generally regarded as a logician or a mathematician, but rather as a philosopher who devoted his life to, as he tells us, "debunking charlatans, windbags, and claptrap." Schopenhauer firmly believed that fallacies should be exposed whenever they appear. In *The Art of Controversy*, he remarks that "it would be a very good thing if every trick could receive some short and obviously appropriate name, so that when a man used this or that particular trick, he could be at once reproached for it." Indeed, hundreds of fallacies have been recognized, described, and named.

Schopenhauer is often called the philosopher of pessimism because he thought that human experience is filled with all manner of brutality, pain, and suffering. Humans are compelled to hate, love, and desire, with only temporary escapes—philosophic contemplation, art (especially music), and sympathy for the plight of others.

In addition, Schopenhauer was one of the first Western philosophers to recognize and incorporate ideas from Eastern religions, such as Buddhism. In his system of thought, we are asked to "see ourselves in all existence."

once again, admitted the behavior needs correcting. You simply are not going to do anything about it.

11. Biased Sample

In the fallacy of **biased sample**, an argument uses a nonrepresentative sample as support for a statistical claim about an entire population. A representative sample occurs when the characteristics of a sample are correctly identified and matched to the population under investigation. For example, consider this argument:

> Evidence shows that approximately 85% of all Americans believe that abortion is morally wrong. Recently, a sample of Catholics revealed that 85% believe that abortion is morally wrong.

The sample surveyed only Catholics, but the conclusion generalizes to all Americans. This illustrates how a sample may intentionally or unintentionally exclude segments of the entire population. This results in a nonrepresentative sample, and the argument commits the fallacy of biased sample.

Here is another example:

> A survey of 100 seniors at our university showed that 90% do not oppose a parking fee increase that will go into effect next year. Therefore, we can report that nearly all the students do not oppose a parking fee increase.

The sample surveyed only seniors at the university, but the conclusion generalizes to all students. Since seniors are unlikely to be affected by an increase in parking fees next year, the sample intentionally or unintentionally excluded segments of the entire population. The resulting biased sample does not provide good evidence for the conclusion. (Chapter 13 returns to statistical arguments.)

12. Accident

(RIGID APPLICATION OF A GENERALIZATION)

The fallacy of **accident** arises when a generalization is inappropriately applied to the case at hand. In fact, many generalizations have exceptions—a special case that does not fall under the general rule. We often make allowances for circumstances that permit breaking a rule. Therefore, to rigidly apply an otherwise acceptable generalization, even in the face of known exceptions, is to commit the fallacy of accident. For example, suppose someone says the following:

> I can't believe that the police didn't give the driver of that ambulance any citations. The driver was speeding. The driver went through a red light. The ambulance swerved from lane to lane without using any turn signals.

It is true that under nonemergency circumstances the driver's behavior would be subject to penalties. However, exceptions apply to ambulance drivers, firefighters, and to the police when they are responding to emergencies. Similarly, you probably would

Biased sample An argument that uses a nonrepresentative sample as support for a statistical claim about an entire population.

Accident When a generalization is inappropriately applied to the case at hand.

be excused if you had to rush a seriously injured person to the hospital. Therefore, the speaker in the foregoing example has rigidly applied an otherwise acceptable generalization in the face of known exceptions. The unwarranted assumption in this case is that there are no exceptions to the rule.

13. Hasty Generalization
(CONVERSE ACCIDENT)

Fallacies can occur from the mistaken application of generalizations. For example, it is not unusual for someone to have a few negative experiences with members of a group and then quickly stereotype that group by assigning derogatory characteristics to the entire group. However, it is improbable that such a small sample will be representative of an entire group of humans. Any argument that concludes with a generalization based on a few instances would be terribly weak, and it is an example of the fallacy of **hasty generalization**. For example, consider this argument:

Hasty generalization
A generalization created on the basis of a few instances.

> I saw a fraternity guy act rudely to a fast-food employee in the food court at lunch today. Probably most fraternity and sorority members are rude and arrogant.

The premise reports the observation of a single instance. However, the conclusion generalizes the observed behavior to most fraternity and sorority members. We are not justified in saying that all or most members of a class of people have a certain characteristic simply because the characteristic was observed in one or a few members of the class. The evidence is not adequate to make such a generalization, so the premise cannot provide a good reason to support the conclusion.

Here is another example:

> The first two students whose exams I graded each got an A. Thus, I expect all 50 students in the class to get A's on the exam.

The teacher is probably being overly optimistic. Although it is possible that all 50 students will get an A on the exam, the fallacy of hasty generalization is apparent in this case. The conclusion follows from the unwarranted assumption that the grades of 2 students are a representative sample and can therefore be generalized to all 50 students in the class.

14. Misleading Precision

Misleading precision A claim that appears to be statistically significant but is not.

A fallacy of **misleading precision** occurs when a claim appears to be statistically significant but is not. Often statistics are used misleadingly. The following is an example that we might find in an advertisement:

> Our cookies contain 30% less fat, so you should start eating them if you want to lose weight.

The argument does not stand up to scrutiny. It is fair to ask, "30% less fat than what?" The asserted percentage is relative to some other item, and we need to know what that is in order to know if this product is really significantly lower in fat than competing products of the same type. It might also be the case that the cookies have 30% less fat than they did before, but they still might contain much more fat than is allowed for someone trying to lose weight.

Here is another example of the kind of claim we might find in an advertisement:

> In order to clear out our inventory, we have reduced our used car prices by 20%. These prices won't last forever, so you better hurry in and buy one of these cars before the sale ends.

In this example we need to ask, "Reduced by 20% from what?" The car dealership might have used an outdated markup price no longer in effect in order to get an artificial reduction. Another possibility is that the dealer might have recently tried raising the cost of used cars and, if sales were slow, simply returned the car prices to their previous level.

The fallacy of misleading precision can even occur in a seemingly straightforward scientific claim. For example, consider the following:

> The full moon affects people in strange ways. We have found that you have a 100% greater chance of being physically assaulted during a full moon than at any other time of the month.

In order to evaluate the argument, we need to know the average rate of physical assault over an extended period of time. For example, suppose we find that the average physical assault rate per month is 1 out of every 10,000 persons. According to the argument, the full moon rate would then be 2 out of every 10,000 persons. Although the statistics do show that you have a 100% greater chance of being physically assaulted during a full moon, nevertheless the greater chance is not statistically significant. Whenever statistics are used without a reference or comparison group, you should try to determine if this is an instance of misleading precision.

15. False Dichotomy

The fallacy of **false dichotomy** (*dichotomy* means "to cut in two parts") occurs when it is assumed that only two choices are possible, when in fact others exist. Examples can often be found in television programs where two or more self-proclaimed intellectuals shout insults at each other for a half hour at a time. At some point, we might hear the following:

> Either you agree with me or you are an idiot.

The arguer assumes that we will flesh out the appropriate conclusion. Let's look at two possible argument reconstruction scenarios:

Either you agree with me or you are an idiot.	Either you agree with me or you are an idiot.
<u>You are not an idiot.</u>	<u>You do not agree with me.</u>
You agree with me.	You are an idiot.

False dichotomy A fallacy that occurs when it is assumed that only two choices are possible, when in fact others exist.

The two reconstructions create deductive arguments. In fact, both arguments are valid. Let's look at the argument form for the first reconstruction. If we let A = *you agree with me*, and I = *you are an idiot*, then we get this result:

A or I
Not I
A

If we assume that the first premise is true, then there are only two options, A or I. Next, if we assume that the second premise is true, then option I is eliminated. Therefore, A follows necessarily.

However, the question of soundness yields interesting results. An evaluation of the truth content of the first premise reveals a major problem. The first premise offers only two alternatives, but surely there are more than these two possibilities. The first premise provides the necessary ingredient for an instance of the fallacy of false dichotomy because the asserted disjunction assumes that only two choices are possible, when, in fact, others exist. If we add even one more possibility, we can reconstruct a new argument:

Either you agree with me, or you are an idiot, or your position is correct.
You do not agree with me.
You are not an idiot.
Your position is correct.

In the original argument the speaker used a false dichotomy to try to trap us into agreeing with his position. Revealing the fallacy allows us to analyze and evaluate the argument in a comprehensive manner. Of course, the opponent might have tried to turn the tables on the speaker by responding rhetorically, "If I have to agree with you, then I really am an idiot."

16. False Dilemma

A special kind of false dichotomy is the fallacy of false dilemma (*dilemma* means "double proposition"). When we are confronted with a choice between two alternatives, both of which will lead to unwanted results, then we are facing a dilemma. For example, suppose you promise to help someone at a certain time and date, and later you realize that you had already made a promise to another person for that same time. If it is not possible to fulfill both promises, then your dilemma is choosing which person to hurt, that is, which promise you will break. Situations like these are sometimes referred to as "being between a rock and a hard place." In these instances someone is likely to advise you to "choose the lesser of two evils." (For a powerful example of a dilemma, you should read *Sophie's Choice*, by William Styron.)

However, the term "dilemma" is often misapplied, as in these examples:

A. I just won the lottery, but now I have a dilemma. Should I take the five million in one lump sum or spread it out over 20 years?

B. My parents are buying me a car for graduation, so now my dilemma is whether to choose a BMW or a Porsche.

Since neither of these cases contains a choice that would lead to an unwanted result, these are clearly not dilemmas.

The fallacy of **false dilemma** occurs when two choices are asserted, each leading to an unwanted result, but there is a failure to acknowledge that other possibilities exist. For example, a person defending the Patriot Act and its potential infringement on certain basic freedoms might say the following:

> Either we give up some traditional basic freedoms or we lose the war on terror.

The argument is missing a premise and the conclusion. Since the person is defending the Patriot Act, the missing premise is "No one wants to lose the war on terror," and the missing conclusion is "We must give up some traditional basic freedoms."

Let's reveal the argument form. If we let G = *we give up some traditional basic freedoms*, and L = *we lose the war on terror*, then we get this result:

G or L
Not L
G

Premise 1 fails to acknowledge that other possibilities exist; thus it sets up a false dilemma. If we are captured by the passionate nature of the assertion and its implications, then we seem to be facing a dilemma. According to the assertion there are only two choices. If we don't want to lose the war on terror, then we must conclude that we are willing to give up some traditional basic freedoms. On the other hand, if we are not willing to give up some traditional basic freedoms, then we must conclude that we will lose the war on terror. However, once we see that this is really an instance of the fallacy of false dilemma, we can reject the entire notion of having only two choices in the matter. We can argue that it is possible to win the war on terror without giving up traditional basic freedoms.

FALSE CAUSE FALLACIES

Fallacies of false cause are a special subset of fallacies of unwarranted assumption. These fallacies include *coincidence,* post hoc *fallacy, common cause fallacy,* and *slippery slope.* As we will see in Chapter 14, cause-effect patterns help us to understand the world and to predict future events. However, fallacies of **false cause** occur when a causal connection is assumed to exist between two events when none actually exists. Since causal claims require strong evidence, a cause-effect claim based on insufficient evidence commits the fallacy of false cause.

Consider the following argument:

> I told you not to trust him. After all, he was born under the sign of Aquarius in the year of the Rabbit. He can't help himself; the stars dictate his behavior.

Astrology places human behavior under the influence of the planets and stars. It claims that we are causally connected to astral influences that occurred at the time of our birth and continue throughout our lives. Of course, these causal claims do not have any credible scientific evidence in their support; they are based mostly on anecdotal evidence. In addition, the general personality traits associated with astrology can be applied to anyone.

False dilemma A fallacy that occurs when two choices are asserted, each leading to an unwanted result, but there is a failure to acknowledge that other possibilities exist.

False cause A fallacy that occurs when a causal connection is assumed to exist between two events when none actually exists.

17. Coincidence

Coincidence A fallacy that results from the accidental or chance connection between two events.

A fallacy of **coincidence** results from the accidental or chance connection between two events. For example, suppose someone says the following:

> I can prove that some dreams let us see into the future. Last week, I dreamed that my cousin Charlie was in a terrible car wreck. Just now, I got a phone call from my cousin Charlie's wife saying that he is in the hospital because he was in a car accident.

If someone dreams that a relative or friend is injured or dies and a similar event actually happens, then the dream might be interpreted as being *caused* by the future event. However, a belief in "backward causality" (a future event causing the present dream) violates a fundamental principle of science: causes must precede effects.

The coincidence can be explained by recognizing that we have thousands of dreams a year, a few of which are likely to resemble real events. Also, the vast majority of dreams do not connect to real events, but we tend to forget that important fact.

It is normal and helpful for us to look for connections between events; that's how we learn about the world. Scientific results are achieved by correctly identifying cause-effect connections. This is how we are able to discover the cause of diseases, how and why things deteriorate over time, how to develop helpful drugs, how certain genes are connected to risk factors, and many other types of knowledge. However, not every connection that we happen to notice reveals a true cause-effect relationship. When unwanted things happen to us, it is reasonable to seek out the cause, but we must recognize that many things we connect in our day-to-day life are just coincidences.

Superstitions develop over time when instances of individual coincidences get passed from one person to another. After a few instances are noticed, it often becomes accepted that a cause-effect relationship exists. However, this is a self-sustaining result: only positive connections are recognized; negative instances are overlooked. A scientific approach would record the number of positive and negative instances to see if there is truly a causal connection. Instead of this, anecdotal evidence that recognizes only positive instances gets passed on, thus reinforcing the superstition. The type of fallacious reasoning that develops over time from a few coincidences is related to the *post hoc* fallacy, our next topic.

18. Post Hoc Fallacy

***Post hoc* fallacy** A fallacy involving either a short-term or long-term pattern that is noticed after the fact.

Another type of false cause fallacy, the ***post hoc* fallacy**, concerns a pattern that is noticed "after the fact." (The full name of this type of fallacy is called *post hoc, ergo propter hoc*, which means "after the fact, therefore because of the fact.") It is not unusual for someone to find either a short-term or long-term pattern and to make a causal connection between two things. The fallacy lies in mistaking the statistical pattern, or *correlation*, for cause and effect.

For example, we might read the following:

> Researchers have discovered that, for over 30 years, there has been a definite pattern connecting the party affiliation of the U.S. president and specific soft

drink sales. During the years when a Democrat was president, Morphiacola topped all soft drink sales. When a Republican was president, Opiacola was number one in sales. If you are an investor, we advise you to put your money on the soft drink company based on who is in the White House.

The premises fail to provide the necessary support for a true causal claim. Arguments that use *post hoc* reasoning fall prey to the mistake of confusing a correlation with a cause. Fallacies of this type can be persuasive, because unlike a mere coincidence, a regular pattern seems to have emerged. Although every cause-effect relationship reveals a strong correlation, not all strong correlations reveal cause-effect relationships. For example, there is a strong correlation between wearing bathing suits and getting wet, but wearing a bathing suit does not cause us to get wet. (For more details on the difference between a *correlation* and a *cause*, see Chapter 14.)

The pattern in the cola argument was between the party in the White House and the type of cola having the most sales. Patterns like these are also referred to as *trends* and are often the basis for gambling purposes. For example, in baseball, the National League may win four straight All-Star games. In football, the American Conference might win three consecutive Super Bowls. In roulette, a red number may come up six times in a row. However, trends are temporary, and unless some definite cause-effect relationship is independently discovered that would *explain* the trend, we should not expect the trend to continue indefinitely.

19. Common Cause Fallacy

The **common cause fallacy** occurs when one event is believed to cause a second event, when in fact both events are the result of a common cause. For example, someone might claim that the falling barometer is the cause of a storm, when in fact both events are caused by a change in atmospheric pressure. The following illustration reveals the common cause fallacy:

Common cause fallacy
A mistake that occurs when someone thinks that one event causes another, when in fact both events are the result of a common cause.

Atmospheric Pressure

Falling Barometer ◄——✕——► Storm

The two downward arrows indicate that the atmospheric pressure is the common cause of both the falling barometer and the storm. The arrow with the large X through it shows the fallacious cause-effect claim.

Another example of the fallacy occurs when someone mistakenly thinks that a rash is causing a fever. It is quite possible that both the rash and the fever have a common cause: a virus.

20. Slippery Slope

Some complex arguments attempt to link events in such a way as to create a chain reaction. The idea is to create a series of occurrences whereby the first link in a chain leads directly to the next, and so on, until the final result is achieved. A **slippery slope** fallacy attempts to make a final event the inevitable outcome of an initial act. We are

Slippery slope An argument that attempts to make a final event the inevitable outcome of an initial act.

then urged to stop the chain reaction before it has a chance to begin, by preventing the first act from ever happening. For example, consider the following argument:

> If you start smoking marijuana for pleasure, then you will need more and more to achieve the expected high. You will begin to rely on it whenever you feel depressed. Eventually you will experiment with more powerful drugs that act faster and last longer. Of course, the amount of drug intake will have to increase to achieve the desired results. At this point, the addiction will take hold and will lead to a loss of ambition, a loss of self-esteem, the destruction of your health, and the dissolution of all social ties. Therefore, you should not start smoking marijuana.

Slippery slope arguments rely on a kind of causal network where each step in the chain causes the next step. However, the alleged inevitability of the final act needs to be supported by providing specific objective evidence for the supposed causal network. Each link in the chain of arguments requires relevant evidence for its connection to the next link in the chain. Until this is objectively established, the argument need not be accepted.

Summary of Fallacies of Unwarranted Assumption

9. Begging the question
An argument that assumes as evidence in the premises the very thing that it attempts to prove in the conclusion.

10. Complex question
A single question that actually contains multiple, hidden parts.

11. Biased sample
An argument that uses a nonrepresentative sample as support for a statistical claim about an entire population.

12. Accident
When a generalization is inappropriately applied to the case at hand.

13. Hasty generalization
A generalization created on the basis of a few instances.

14. Misleading precision
A claim that appears to be statistically significant, but is not.

15. False dichotomy
A fallacy that occurs when it is assumed that only two choices are possible, when in fact others exist.

16. False dilemma
A fallacy that occurs when two choices are asserted, each leading to an unwanted result, but there is a failure to acknowledge that other possibilities exist.

17. Coincidence
A fallacy that results from the accidental or chance connection between two events.

18. Post hoc fallacy

A fallacy involving either a short-term or long-term pattern that is noticed after the fact. This type of false cause fallacy is also called *post hoc, ergo propter hoc* ("after the fact, therefore because of the fact").

19. Common cause fallacy

The assumption that one event causes another, when in fact both events are the result of a common cause.

20. Slippery slope

An argument that attempts to make a final event the inevitable outcome of an initial act.

CHECK YOUR UNDERSTANDING 4B

I. Determine whether each statement is true or false.

1. A complex question is a single question that actually contains multiple, hidden parts.

Answer: True.

2. A hasty generalization occurs whenever a generalization leaves out members of a subset of the population that is referred to in the conclusion.

3. When a claim is made that appears to be statistically significant but which, upon analysis, is not, is an example of the fallacy of misleading precision.

4. A coincidence is a special type of false cause fallacy concerning a short-term pattern that is noticed after the fact.

5. A biased sample leaves out members of a subset of the population that is referred to in the conclusion.

6. An argument that attempts to make a final event the inevitable outcome of an initial act is called *post hoc*.

7. To rigidly apply an otherwise acceptable generalization, even in the face of known and understood exceptions, is to commit the fallacy of common cause.

8. An argument that offers only two alternatives when in fact more exist is an example of a biased sample.

9. An argument that assumes as evidence the very thing that it attempts to prove in the conclusion begs the question.

10. A slippery slope fallacy concerns a short-term pattern that is noticed after the fact.

11. An argument that offers two choices each of which leads to an undesirable outcome is an example of false dilemma.

12. A claim that appears to be statistically significant, but which upon analysis is not, is the fallacy of accident.

II. Each of the following passages contains a fallacy of unwarranted assumption. Determine the fallacy that best fits each case. Explain your answer.

1. Do you still plagiarize your research papers from the Internet?

Answer: Complex question: A single question that actually contains multiple, hidden parts.

2. This car gets the highest gas mileage of any car on the market. So, you can't buy a more fuel efficient car at any cost.

3. That ambulance didn't even stop for the red light. It went zooming right through! If I did that, I would get a citation. Life just isn't fair.

4. All the people in my fraternity think that hazing is not a problem. So, I'm sure that the entire student population agrees with us on this issue.

5. Last week's poll showed the incumbent senator had 52% of the votes and the challenger had 48%. This week's poll shows the incumbent ahead 54% to 46%. So, we can safely say that the incumbent will get at least 53% of the votes on Election Day.

6. I met two people from that state, and they both were rude. There must be something in the drinking water of that state that makes all the people from there so rude.

7. Have you stopped stealing money from your parents' wallets?

8. The label on that cheesecake says that it has 40% fewer calories. If I eat that cheesecake regularly, then I should lose some weight.

9. I don't recommend that you eat at that restaurant. I did not like the breakfast I had there last week. I'm sure that all of their meals are of poor quality.

10. That is the type of movie you hate; lots of jokes and slapstick. So, you will hate it.

11. Ninety-five percent of a sample of registered Republicans in this state said that they will vote for the Republican nominee for Congress from their district. I predict that the Republican nominee will definitely get around 95% of the total vote this fall.

12. Everything written in that book is 100% accurate. It has to be, since nothing in it is false.

13. When I need to travel to another city I have to buy my own airplane ticket. The president of the United States has Air Force One to take him wherever he wants to go, and he doesn't have to pay a penny. Why can't I have a deal like that?

14. The advertisement for that DVD player claims that it has 50% fewer moving parts. You should buy it; it is less likely to break down in the future.

15. He is a very honest individual because he is not dishonest.

16. My horoscope said I would meet someone new. Today my company hired a really good-looking salesperson and we will be working closely together. Now do you see why I read my horoscope every day?

⭐ 17. If you don't clean your room, then the dirt and dust will build up. Before you know it, bacteria grow. Whatever you touch in your room will then spread bacteria, which will contaminate the entire house. We will all wind up in the hospital, terminally ill.

18. On seven different occasions it rained the day after I washed my car. I washed my car today, so take your umbrella with you tomorrow.

19. I had two station wagons, and they both were lemons. I'm sure that there is something in the design of station wagons that makes them all terrible vehicles.

20. Every football player at Crestfallen High School can run 2 miles in under 15 minutes. They have good physical education teachers, so the students at that school must be in great physical condition.

⭐ 21. She began making $100,000 the year after she graduated from college, and when she took an IQ test, she scored 20 points higher than when she was in high school. See, I told you: money makes people smarter.

22. My bill at the restaurant was $4.29. I played the number 429 on the lottery today, and it came up. Therefore, it was my destiny to play that number today and win.

23. That politician never tells the truth because every time he tries to explain why he did something wrong, he fabricates a story.

24. Do you still look for discarded food in dumpsters?

⭐ 25. Every time the barometer drops below 30, it rains. It has some mysterious power over the weather, I guess.

26. Either we cut school funding or we raise taxes. Nobody wants to cut school funding, so we must raise taxes.

27. For the last 50 years, whenever the American League won the World Series, there was a recession that year, but when the National League won, stock prices went up. There must be some unknown economic force at work that we don't understand.

28. That fire engine was going over 60 mph in a 35-mph zone. The police should give the driver a ticket.

⭐ 29. I have certain inalienable rights because they have never been taken away from me.

30. If you drop out of one course this semester, you will have less than a full-time load. It will take you longer to graduate. It will delay your getting a job another year, meaning that you won't get promoted as fast as others who graduated on time. So, you can expect to lose approximately $100,000 during your lifetime.

31. Whenever I step in the shower, either my phone rings or someone knocks on the door. I'll have to change my bathing habits, I suppose.

32. Either you love your country or you are a traitor. I'm sure you are not a traitor. Therefore, you must love your country.

C. FALLACIES OF AMBIGUITY OR DIVERSION

Fallacy of ambiguity or diversion A fallacy that occurs when the meanings of terms or phrases are changed (intentionally or unintentionally) within the argument, or when our attention is purposely (or accidentally) diverted from the issue at hand.

A **fallacy of ambiguity or diversion** occurs when the meanings of terms or phrases are changed (intentionally or unintentionally) within the argument, or when our attention is purposely (or accidentally) diverted from the issue at hand. Fallacies of ambiguity depend on the fact that words or phrases can have many different meanings, and context is crucial. Ambiguity, vagueness, or any unclear use of a term can seriously affect the understanding, analysis, and evaluation of an argument. We can distinguish seven kinds of fallacies of ambiguity and diversion. (We will continue to number the fallacies starting from the previous section.)

21. Equivocation

Equivocation The intentional or unintentional use of different meanings of words or phrases in an argument.

To shift the meaning of a term during the course of an argument is to commit the fallacy of **equivocation**. For example, someone might say the following:

> My older brother tries hard to be cool. I told him he has the personality of a cucumber. Since a refrigerator is a good place to keep things cool, he should spend some time there.

The word "cool" obviously has numerous meanings that tend to sort themselves out in the context of particular sentences.

Equivocation can also occur when *relative terms* are misused, such as "big" and "small." For example:

> I was told that he is a big man on campus (BMOC). But look at him; he's no more than 5′7″ tall.

The equivocation is compounded by the fact that the term "big" in BMOC does not refer to height. Here are two other examples of the fallacy:

- Judy said she had a hot date last night. Therefore, the air conditioning in her apartment must not have been working.
- That looks like a hard outfit to get into. So maybe you should wash it in some fabric softener.

The world of politics offers numerous examples of equivocation. A major issue discussed quite often during presidential campaigns is employment. For example, a recent administration had to respond to a huge loss of manufacturing jobs during its time in office. To counteract the statistics showing a loss of jobs, the administration proposed that some fast-food workers should be reclassified from service workers to manufacturing workers. Under the new definition, anyone who cooked a burger, placed it on a bun, added condiments, and put it in a wrapper was engaged in manufacturing a product. There would thus have been a gain in manufacturing jobs over the previous four years. Of course, once the opposing political party found out about the idea, it was quickly dropped.

An earlier administration hatched a similar idea. The federal government normally defines the "unemployed" as only those people who are actively collecting government unemployment checks. Under this definition, people who have either exhausted their checks or are on welfare are not unemployed. The unemployment rate is then calculated by finding the number of unemployed and comparing this with the total number of those employed. In addition, the entire military did not count toward the unemployment rate. In other words, the military was considered neither employed nor unemployed. Again, just before a presidential election, a scheme was considered. It was proposed that all active military personnel should be considered employed. This would have seriously reduced the unemployment rate, favoring the incumbent administration. Once again, the idea was exposed and abandoned.

22. Amphiboly

Amphiboly ("irregular speech") is ambiguity that arises when a poorly constructed statement muddles the intended meaning. Premises and a conclusion appear to be true, because two different interpretations are being used. If we retain one meaning throughout the argument, we can usually spot the mistake:

> **Amphiboly** Ambiguity that arises when a poorly constructed statement muddles the intended meaning.

- He was shot in the train in the back in the sleeping car.
- She watched the monkey eating a banana.
- Sipping on cold coffee, the corpse lay in front of the tired detective.
- Cursing his bad luck, the DVD player refused to work for Eddie.

In the first example, we can conclude either that (1) the bullet is lodged in the victim's back or (2) the shooting occurred in the sleeping car, which is in the back of the train. In the second example, we can conclude either that (1) the monkey was eating a banana or (2) the person watching the monkey was eating a banana. In the third example, either (1) the detective was sipping on cold coffee or (2) the corpse was sipping on coffee at the time of death. In the final example, either (1) Eddie was cursing his bad luck or (2) the DVD player was cursing its bad luck and refused to play.

Amphiboly relies on the confusion caused by grammatical errors. For example:

> *John*: In my backyard a bird did not see my cat hunched on all fours ready to pounce but suddenly he flew away.
> *Barb*: I didn't know cats could fly.

23. Composition

In the fallacy of **composition**, an attribute of the individual parts of an object is mistakenly transferred to the entire object. For example, suppose someone said the following of a 7-foot-tall basketball player:

> **Composition** The mistaken transfer of an attribute of the individual parts of an object to the object as a whole.

> All the cells in his body are tiny. Thus, he is tiny.

The mistake is taking an attribute that is true of the parts and erroneously applying it to the whole. The fallacy can also occur when the conclusion is not necessarily untrue, but merely in doubt:

> The bricks in this building are sturdy, so the building must be sturdy.

Even if the individual bricks are sturdy (the premise), the building may not be sturdy (the conclusion). Here are three other examples of the fallacy of composition:

- The thread you are using is easily torn, so the garment you are making will be easily torn.
- Each ingredient you are using tastes delicious. Therefore, the cake has to taste delicious.
- I understand every word in the poem, so I must understand what the poet is getting at.

We must be careful not to misapply this fallacy. Not every argument that reasons from parts to a whole is fallacious. For example:

> Every thread of material of which this shirt is composed is red, so the shirt is red.

This argument does not commit the fallacy of composition; in fact, it is a strong argument. Here is another legitimate use of composition:

> Since every piece of my sewing machine is made from steel, it follows that my sewing machine is steel.

Compare the fallacious examples with the legitimate ones. You can see that fallacies here are not mistakes in the structure of an argument. Rather, the context of an argument, together with our knowledge of the world, is often needed to distinguish fallacious from nonfallacious informal arguments.

All of the examples of the composition fallacy so far have concerned a possible mistaken identity—of parts of an object with the whole object (a body, a building, a garment, a cake, and a poem). However, another kind of composition fallacy occurs when the attributes of individual members of a class are mistakenly applied to the collection of objects itself. This mistake occurs when we confuse the *distributive* and *collective* use of terms. "Distributive" refers to the individual members of a group. In the statement "Motorcycles are noisy," the term "noisy" is being used distributively to refer to individual motorcycles. "Collective" refers to the group as a whole. In the statement "Motorcycles make up only 5% of all vehicles on U.S. roadways," the phrase "make up only 5% of all vehicles on U.S. roadways" is being used collectively to refer to the class of all motorcycles, not to individual motorcycles. This type of composition fallacy is revealed in the following argument:

> More noise is produced by a motorcycle than by a car. Therefore, more noise is produced on U.S. roadways by motorcycles than by cars.

24. Division

Division The mistaken transfer of an attribute of an object as a whole to its individual parts.

In the fallacy of **division**, an attribute of an object as a whole is mistakenly transferred to its individual parts. The fallacy of division is the opposite of the fallacy of composition. For example, suppose someone said the following of a 7-foot-tall basketball player:

> He is huge, so he must have huge cells.

The mistake is taking an attribute that is true of the whole object and erroneously applying it to the parts that make up the object. Here are three other examples of the fallacy:

- She is intelligent, so she must have smart brain cells.
- The garment is strong, so the individual threads must be strong.
- The cake tastes burnt, so you must have used burnt ingredients.

As with the fallacy of composition, we must be careful not to misapply the fallacy of division. Not every argument that reasons from the whole object to its parts is fallacious. For example:

> That is a wooden chair, so the legs are made of wood.

This argument does not commit the fallacy of division; in fact, it is a strong argument. Here is another example of a legitimate use of division:

> The book he is reading is made of paper. Therefore, the pages of the book are made of paper.

All the examples of the fallacy so far have concerned a possible mistaken identity of an object (a body, a person's intelligence, a garment, and a cake) with its parts. However, a second kind of division fallacy is similar to the second kind of composition fallacy. This occurs when attributes of a collection of objects are mistakenly applied to the individual members of that class. As before, the mistake occurs when the distributive and collective uses of terms are confused. In the statement "Bald eagles are disappearing," the term "disappearing" is being used collectively to refer to the class of bald eagles; individual members may still live full lives. The second type of division fallacy can be recognized in the following argument:

> My teacher said that bald eagles are disappearing. I remember seeing a bald eagle down at the zoo. Let's hurry down to see it before it disappears.

25. Emphasis

Fallacies of **emphasis** (also called *accent*) can occur when attention is purposely (or accidentally) diverted from the issue at hand. In other words, statements or arguments intending one thing are subtly distorted in order to shift the emphasis to another issue. The use of emphasis occurs in everyday conversation as well, as in this discussion:

> *Jenn*: He did win an Academy Award for best actor.
> *Jess*: You might think he did, but you're wrong.
> *Jenn*: I don't think. I know.
> *Jess*: I don't think you know either.

Emphasis A fallacy that occurs when attention is purposely (or accidentally) diverted from the issue at hand.

Jess twists the meaning of a key phrase by changing the emphasis of Jenn's claim. This emphasis seems to refute Jenn's claim of knowledge. The same kind of mistake occurs in the next passage:

> *Mary Lynn*: Lee Ann, you will wash the car this afternoon.
> *Lee Ann*: I will?
> *Mary Lynn*: I'm glad you agree.

Lee Ann's question is turned into an assertion by Mary Lynn's change of emphasis. Although these particular verbal changes are fairly easy to spot, they nevertheless reveal the possibility of altering meaning by shifting emphasis at a key point.

26. Straw Man Fallacy

Straw man A fallacy that occurs when someone's written or spoken words are taken out of context. It purposely distorts the original argument to create a new, weak argument that can be easily refuted (a straw man that is easily knocked down).

There are two major kinds of fallacies of emphasis. The first, called the **straw man** fallacy, often occurs when someone's written or spoken words are taken out of context. This effectively creates a new argument, which can be easily refuted. The new argument is so weak that it is "made of straw." This tactic is common in the political arena. Candidates distort the views of their opponents by clipping a small piece out of a speech or interview. Taken out of context, a word or phrase might give an impression directly opposite from that of the original. For example, a person running for public office might say the following:

> I oppose the law that requires teaching intelligent design as an alternative to evolutionary theory in public school biology classes. Evolution is an established scientific theory and deserves to be taught in a science class. Intelligent design is not a scientific theory, and it should not be taught in a science class.

An opponent of this candidate might criticize her position this way:

> She is against the new law that mandates teaching intelligent design alongside the theory of evolution. It should be obvious to anyone that she really wants to eliminate religious beliefs. She wants us to destroy one of the basic principles of the Constitution of the United States.

A straw man argument has been created by several steps. The opponent takes the original statement and adds an unjustified premise, "It should be obvious to anyone that what she really wants to do is to eliminate all religious beliefs." The fallacy concludes that "She wants us to destroy one of the basic principles of the Constitution of the United States."

Distortions of this kind are not limited to politics. It is not difficult to extract passages from an article to make it appear that the author is contradicting herself.

27. Red Herring Fallacy

Red herring A fallacy that occurs when someone completely ignores an opponent's position and changes the subject, diverting the discussion in a new direction.

The second type of fallacy of emphasis, the **red herring** fallacy, occurs when someone completely ignores an opponent's position. By changing the subject, the red herring "throws one off the scent," diverting the discussion in a new direction. For example:

Many people criticize TV as turning America into an illiterate society. How can we criticize the very medium that is the envy of countries all over the world? The entertainment quality and variety of TV programs today are greater than ever before, not to mention the enormous number of cable options available to members of the viewing audience.

Rather than presenting evidence, the passage shifts the emphasis to the entertainment value of TV. This diversion ignores the question of whether TV is causing America to become an illiterate society. The red herring argument has ignored the crucial issue at hand.

In 2003, a photograph purported to show that Jose Santos, the jockey of Kentucky Derby winner Funny Cide, was carrying an illegal object. The picture showed a dark spot in Santos's hand. Some concluded that a "battery" was used to provide an electrical shock through the whip, causing the horse to run faster. But those who emphasized the dark spot deemphasized or overlooked the film of the race. It clearly shows Santos switching hands with his whip more than once. As one commentator remarked, holding a battery while performing these tricky maneuvers would make Santos one of the world's best magicians. A thorough analysis of the available information exonerated the jockey.

Summary of Fallacies of Ambiguity or Diversion

21. Equivocation
The intentional or unintentional use of different meanings of words or phrases in an argument.

22. Amphiboly
Ambiguity that arises when a poorly constructed statement muddles the intended meaning.

23. Composition
The mistaken transfer of an attribute of the individual parts of an object to the object as a whole.

24. Division
The mistaken transfer of an attribute of an object as a whole to its individual parts.

25. Emphasis
A fallacy that occurs when attention is purposely (or accidentally) diverted from the issue at hand.

26. Straw man fallacy
A fallacy that occurs when someone's written or spoken words are taken out of context. It purposely distorts the original argument to create a new, weak argument that can be easily refuted (a straw man that is easily knocked down).

27. Red herring fallacy
A fallacy that occurs when someone completely ignores an opponent's position and changes the subject, diverting the discussion in a new direction.

CHECK YOUR UNDERSTANDING 4C

I. Determine whether each statement is true or false.

1. The fallacy of composition occurs when an attribute of the individual parts of an object are transferred to the entire object.

Answer: True.

2. The red herring fallacy occurs when someone's words are taken out of context to create an argument that distorts the person's position.

3. A mistake of interpretation that occurs because of the grammar or syntax of a statement is called the fallacy of emphasis.

4. A fallacy of equivocation can happen only if the argument intentionally uses different meanings of words or phrases.

⭐ 5. A straw man fallacy is a mistake in grammar.

6. To mistakenly transfer an attribute of the individual parts of an object to the entire object is to commit the fallacy of division.

7. A fallacy of emphasis occurs when a word has a different meaning in the premises than it has in the conclusion.

8. A fallacy of equivocation mistakenly transfers an attribute of the individual parts of an object to the entire object.

II. Each of the following passages contains a fallacy of ambiguity or diversion. Determine the fallacy that best fits each case. Explain your answer.

1. Each grain of sand is hard, so your sand castle will be hard.

Answer: Composition: The mistaken transfer of an attribute of the individual parts of an object to the object as a whole.

2. *Sam:* I think you broke my watch.
   Joe: I did?
   Sam: Well since you admit it, now I know you did it.

3. He's a real pain the neck. Cortisone shots help relieve neck pain. Maybe a good dose of cortisone will change his attitude.

4. She is very beautiful. I bet even her appendix is lovely.

⭐ 5. Just waiting to be eaten, he noticed the cake in the corner.

6. My father said that the Super Bowl halftime show was a real disaster. That's interesting because I read in the newspaper that the federal government has relief funds available for victims of disasters. Maybe my dad can apply for some relief funds.

7. If you are going to have that fruit juice tomorrow morning, then you better start shaking the bottle right now. I read the label, and it recommends that you shake the contents well before using.

8. I read that cars in the United States consume more gasoline each year than trucks. I guess that means that my car uses more gasoline each year than that tractor trailer over there.

9. I know for a fact that the acrylic paints that Vincent van Gogh used to create this portrait were very inexpensive. So even though his painting is hanging in a museum, it can't be very expensive.

10. I heard that he got injured in that building in the rear.

11. My mother, a professional poker player, always told me that having one pair is better than nothing. Of course, in the game of poker nothing beats a royal flush. It follows that my one pair beats your royal flush.

12. He said that walking around the corner the Eiffel Tower suddenly took his breath away. I didn't know those famous Parisian landmarks roamed the streets.

13. According to the census data, the population of that city is 10% atheists. My Uncle Sam lives there, so he must be 10% atheist.

14. In physics class we learned that elementary particles have little or no mass. My $150 physics textbook is made up of elementary particles, thus it has little or no mass.

15. I hear that Walter is handling some hot stocks right now. The new asbestos gloves I bought protect your hands from hot objects. Maybe I should give them to Walter for protection.

16. Sitting in the front seat of the car, the cow stared intently into Jim's eyes. Of course, from this we can conclude that it was a very large car indeed.

17. My mother wants me to take piano lessons because studies show that early music training helps students in math. But pianos cost a lot of money, and even if we could afford one, our apartment is too small.

18. Evolution is a biological law of nature. All civilized people should obey the law. Therefore, all civilized people should obey the law of evolution.

19. Chicken eggs do not weigh very much. So if I eat an omelet made from fifty eggs, it will not weigh very much.

20. My boss caught me playing video games on my office computer during work hours. He said that it was a violation of office policies, and he warned me to stop or I would be fired. Pretty soon he will try to eliminate coffee breaks or even going to the bathroom. He doesn't have the right to take away all my benefits.

21. The sign says that there is no mass on Sunday. But my science teacher said that mass is the same as energy. So I guess there is no energy on Sunday either.

22. Sitting in front of the open window, the freshly mowed grass satisfied Robert.

23. Each page of the encyclopedia weighs practically nothing, so the encyclopedia weighs practically nothing.

24. You have chosen great paint colors; therefore, your house will look great.

⭐ 25. *Walter:* You will help me with my homework.
Sandy: I will?
Walter: I knew you would cooperate.

26. That comedian is a real ham. Of course, ham and eggs are good for breakfast. So, if that comedian added some eggs to his act, it would make a good breakfast.

27. The house is poorly constructed, so the material it is made of must be poorly constructed as well.

28. The stone hit the window. The force broke it into a thousand pieces.

D. RECOGNIZING FALLACIES IN ORDINARY LANGUAGE

The examples of informal fallacies analyzed so far have been constructed to reveal clearly the mistake in reasoning. They were meant to be fairly easy to recognize—once you understand the underlying techniques. However, when you read something or hear someone talk, then detecting any informal fallacies may be a bit more challenging. A writer who has a fluid prose style can sometimes produce a persuasive passage merely by dazzling you with her brilliant writing style. A great speaker can mesmerize his audience with the mere sound of his voice, so much so that we overlook the substance of what it being said.

For example, the great actor Laurence Olivier gave an emotional acceptance speech at the Academy Awards:

> Mr. President and Governors of the Academy, Committee Members, fellows, my very noble and approved good masters, my colleagues, my friends, my fellow-students. In the great wealth, the great firmament of your nation's generosity, this particular choice may perhaps be found by future generations as a trifle eccentric, but the mere fact of it—the prodigal, pure, human kindness of it—must be seen as a beautiful star in that firmament which shines upon me at this moment, dazzling me a little, but filling me with warmth and the extraordinary elation, the euphoria that happens to so many of us at the first breath of the majestic glow of a new tomorrow. From the top of this moment, in the solace, in the kindly emotion that is charging my soul and my heart at this moment, I thank you for this great gift which lends me such a very splendid part in this, your glorious occasion.

This short speech left most of the audience in awe, in part because Olivier was considered perhaps the greatest Shakespearian actor and in part because of his dramatic delivery. Few people went back to read the words, which, although poetic and emotional, do not contain much of substance. The moral of the story is that we have to be careful when we encounter either impressive-sounding speech or beautifully crafted written material. This is especially true if the passages contain arguments.

Some fallacies occur because the emotional attachment to a belief overrides the demands of a clear, rational, well-supported argument. Here is one example:

> Our acceptance of abortion does not end with the killing of unborn human life; it continues on to affect our attitude toward all aspects of human life. This is most obvious in how quickly, once we accept abortion, then comes the acceptance of infanticide, the killing of babies who after birth do not come up to someone's standard of life worthy to be lived, and then on to euthanasia of the aged. If human life can be taken before birth, there is no logical reason why human life cannot be taken after birth.   Francis Schaeffer, *Who Is for Life?*

The author's position about abortion is clear. However, the attempt to discredit any acceptance of abortion leads the author to commit the slippery slope fallacy. No evidence is offered in the passage to support the (assumed) link in the chain of reasoning that "once we accept abortion, then comes the acceptance of infanticide." Similarly, the author provides no support for the next (assumed) link in the chain, namely the claim that "and then on to euthanasia of the aged." This example points out the importance of separating a belief from the possible reasons in support of a belief. It also illustrates the need to guard against the quick acceptance (or rejection) of a position based solely on our emotional attachment to a position.

Fallacies are not just the result of an emotional attachment to a moral question or to a controversial political viewpoint. In fact, they can occur in a scientific study:

> Winning the Nobel Prize adds nearly two years to your lifespan, and it's not because of the cash that goes with it. The status alone conferred on a scientist by the world's most famous prize is enough to prolong his life; in fact, the status seems to work a *health-giving magic*. The study compared Nobel Prize winners with scientists who were nominated, but did not win. The average lifespan for the winners was just over 76 years, while those who had merely been nominated lived on average for 75.8 years. The researchers found that since the amount of actual prize money won had no affect on longevity, therefore the sheer status of the award is the important factor in extending lifespan.
> Donald MacLeod, "Nobel Prize Winners Live Longer," *Education Guardian*

Quite often, a single piece of research gets widespread coverage because it seems to indicate some new and exciting discovery. However, advances in science occur through repeated and exhaustive trials in which many groups of researchers try to eliminate every possible explanation for an effect, leaving only one answer. Therefore, preliminary results, or studies with limited data need to be carefully weighed. In this example, a correlation has been found, but the difference in longevity between the two groups is small. The argument to support the claim that "status causes the Nobel Prize winners to live longer" could be an instance of the *post hoc* fallacy—or simple coincidence.

Although emotional appeals are a powerful way to sway public opinion, unfortunately some of those appeals are fallacious. Most of us try to balance our feelings with our reason, but it is not always easy. Strong emotions can sometimes override rational thinking and lead to disastrous results. This can be seen in the increase in political anger in the United States and the way it is broadcast over the airwaves. Incivility is on view almost daily, and rudeness, discourteous behavior, and disrespect can escalate into violence.

Many people have begun pleading for a less heated and less passionate climate in the public arena. The call is for a reduction in unhelpful rhetoric—in thinly veiled acts of retaliation, in blatant threats, in the exaggeration of apocalyptic social and political consequences, in direct insults, in misinformation and outright lies, and in an unhealthy disregard of intellectual thought and the role of reason. We can replace the negative and destructive tone with constructive and reasonable debate. Issues can be discussed based on facts and the merits of the arguments, without resorting to emotionally charged language that does nothing to advance the correctness of a position.

The call for a reduction in highly charged political discourse reached a high point following the shooting of a member of Congress in 2011. However, another member of Congress objected:

> We can't use this as a moment to try to stifle one side or the other. We can't use this as a moment to say, one side doesn't have a right to talk about the issues they are passionate about.

The response sets up a *straw man* by claiming that the advocates for a reduction in emotional rhetoric are saying that "one side doesn't have a right to talk about the issues they are passionate about." The speaker is arguing against a position that no one holds.

The principles of reason, intellectual honesty, and analysis that we applied to short examples can be adapted to longer passages as well. In fact, the next *Check Your Understanding* allows you to apply those principles to recent events and to historically important cases, many of which are examples of extended arguments.

CHECK YOUR UNDERSTANDING 4D

The following passages were taken from various sources. Use your understanding of all the fallacies that were presented in this chapter to determine which fallacy best fits the passage. In some cases a passage may contain more than one fallacy. Explain your answers.

1. You can't speak French. Petey Bellows can't speak French. I must therefore conclude that nobody at the University of Minnesota can speak French.

   Max Shulman, "Love Is a Fallacy"

Answer: Hasty generalization. The conclusion about the entire university is based on two instances.

2. It's a mistake because it is in error.

   William Safire, "On Language: Take My Question Please!"

3. Police authorities are finding the solution of murders more and more difficult because the victims are unwilling to cooperate with the police.

Radicalacademy.com

4. Either man was created just as the Bible tells us, or man evolved from inanimate chemicals and random chance.

Skeptic.org

⭐ 5. I always said the only failure is when you fail to try. I guess the other failure would not be giving your best effort. And I did both.

Martina Navratilova, quoted in Telegraph.co.uk

6. Do you favor the United States Army abolishing the affirmative-action program that produced Colin Powell?

Bill Clinton, quoted in the *New York Times*

7. It is the case that either the nobility of this country appear to be wealthy, in which case they can be taxed, or else they appear to be poor, in which case they are living frugally and must have immense savings, which can be taxed.

"Morton's Fork," *Encyclopedia Britannica*

8. I don't like spinach, and I'm glad I don't, because if I liked it I'd eat it, and I just hate it.

Clarence Darrow, in *Clarence Darrow: A One-Man Play*

⭐ 9. I often read the Mexico enablers justify the 800,000 Mexicans illegally crossing the U.S. border each year, rationalizing this with a statement such as, "well it is either they stay in Mexico and starve, or risk their lives crossing the border."

"The Fulano Files," at Fulanofiles.blogspot.com

10. To be an atheist, you have to believe with absolute certainty that there is no God. In order to convince yourself with absolute certainty, you must examine all the Universe and all the places where God could possibly be. Since you obviously haven't, your position is indefensible.

Infidels.org

11. Near-perfect correlations exist between the death rate in Hyderabad, India, from 1911 to 1919, and variations in the membership of the International Association of Machinists during the same period.

David Hackett Fischer, *Historians' Fallacies*

12. I hardly think that 58 is the right age at which to talk about a retirement home unless there are some serious health concerns. My 85-year-old mother power-walks two miles each day, drives her car safely, climbs stairs, does crosswords, and reads the daily paper.

Letter to the editor, *Time*

⭐ 13. For the natives, they are near all dead of the smallpox, so as the Lord hath cleared our title to what we possess.

John Winthrop, governor, Massachusetts Colony, 1634

14. He's not a moron at all, he's a friend. My personal relations with the president are extremely good.

Canadian prime minister Jean Chrétien, quoted in the *Canadian Press*

15. Why opium produces sleep: Because there is in it a dormitive power.

Molière, *The Imaginary Invalid*

16. My opponent wants to sever the Danish church from the state for his own personal sake. His motion is an attempt to take over the church and further his ecumenical theology by his usual mafia methods.

Charlotte Jorgensen, "Hostility in Public Debate"

17. I do not have much information on this case except the general statement of the agency that there is nothing in the files to disprove his Communist connections.

Richard H. Rovere, *Senator Joe McCarthy*

18. We took the Bible and prayer out of public schools, and now we're having weekly shootings practically. We had the '60s sexual revolution, and now people are dying of AIDS.

Christine O'Donnell, quoted in the *New Statesman*

19. How is education supposed to make me feel smarter? Besides, every time I learn something new, it pushes some old stuff out of my brain. Remember when I took that home winemaking course, and I forgot how to drive?

Homer Simpson, "Secrets of a Successful Marriage," *The Simpsons*

20. The community of Pacific Palisades is extremely wealthy. Therefore, every person living there is extremely wealthy.

Peter A. Angeles, *Dictionary of Philosophy*

21. Dear Friend, a man who has studied law to its highest degree is a brilliant lawyer, for a brilliant lawyer has studied law to its highest degree.

Oscar Wilde, *De Profundis*

22. The most stringent protection of free speech would not protect a man in falsely shouting fire in a theater and causing a panic.

Oliver Wendell Homes, Supreme Court Opinion, *Schenk v. United States*

23. Twenty seven years ago, Luis Alvarez first proposed that the Cretaceous–Tertiary extinction event was caused by an asteroid that struck the earth 65.5 million years earlier. This means the dinosaurs died out 65,500,027 years ago.

Worldlingo.com

24. Should we not assume that just as the eye, hand, the foot, and in general each part of the body clearly has its own proper function, so man too has some function over and above the function of his parts?

Aristotle, *Nicomachean Ethics*

25. We will starve terrorists of funding, turn them one against another, drive them from place to place, until there is no refuge or rest. And we will pursue nations that provide aid or safe haven to terrorism. Every nation, in every region, now has a decision to make. Either you are with us, or you are with the terrorists.

George W. Bush, Sept. 20, 2001, in an address to Congress

26. You may be interested to know that global warming, earthquakes, hurricanes, and other natural disasters are a direct effect of the shrinking numbers of Pirates since the 1800s. For your interest, I have included a graph of the approximate number of pirates versus the average global temperature over the last 200 years. As you can see, there is a statistically significant inverse relationship between pirates and global temperature.

Bobby Henderson, "Open Letter to Kansas School Board"

27. Following a tip-off from hospital administrators, investigators looked into a series of "suspicious" deaths or near deaths in hospital wards where a certain nurse had worked from 1999 to 2001, and they found that the nurse had been physically present when many of them took place. The nurse is serving a life sentence for seven murders and three attempted murders.

Mark Buchanan, *New York Times*

28. Gerda Reith is convinced that superstition can be a positive force. "It gives you a sense of control by making you think you can work out what's going to happen next," she says. "And it also makes you feel lucky. And to take a risk or to enter into a chancy situation, you really have to believe in your own luck. In that sense, it's a very useful way of thinking, because the alternative is fatalism, which is to say, 'Oh, there's nothing I can do.' At least superstition makes people do things."

David Newnham, "Hostages to Fortune"

★ 29. *Doctor:* I can't find the cause of your illness, but frankly I think it's due to drinking.
Patient: Then I'll come back when you are sober.

Anonymous—used by many comedians

30. Morality in this nation has worsened at the same time that adherence to traditional Christian beliefs has declined. Obviously, the latter has caused the former, so encouraging Christianity will ensure a return to traditional moral standards.

About.com

31. Whether deconstruction is an art or a science, a malady or a Catch-22, it would seem to belong at honours level in university degrees. School is for basics and knowledge, certainly accompanied by critical thinking, but not in a milieu where all is relative and there are no absolutes for young people who do not have the intellectual maturity to cope with the somewhat morbid rigour of constant criticism and questioning of motives. If you go on deconstructing for long enough you will become a marshmallow or a jelly.

Kenneth Wiltshire, "In Defense of the True Values of Learning"

32. *Dan Quayle:* I have far more experience than many others that sought the office of vice president of this country. I have as much experience in Congress as Jack Kennedy did when he sought the presidency. I will be prepared to deal with the people in the Bush administration, if that unfortunate event would ever occur.
Lloyd Bentsen: I served with Jack Kennedy; I knew Jack Kennedy; Jack Kennedy was a friend of mine. Senator, you're no Jack Kennedy.

The 1988 U.S. vice presidential debates

★ 33. I call this the "Advertiser's Fallacy" because it's so prevalent in commercials, such as the one where a famous baseball slugger gives medical advice on erectile dysfunction (that should pick up the hit count!). No. See a properly qualified doctor for ED, see Rafael Palmiero only if you want to improve your baseball swing.

Joe McFaul, "Law, Evolution, Science, and Junk Science"

34. Recently, we highlighted a British journalist's story about the underside of Dubai's startling ascent. Some in Dubai called foul, including one writer who wants to remind Britons that their own country has a dark side. After all, what to think of a country in which one fifth of the population lives in poverty?

Freakonomics.com, "Dubai's Rebuttal"

35. The anti-stem-cell argument goes like this: If you permit scientists to destroy human embryos for the purpose of research, [then it goes] from there to killing human fetuses in order to harvest tissue, and from there to euthanizing disabled or terminally ill people to harvest their organs, and from there to human cloning and human-animal hybrids, and if making chimeras is okay, well then Dr. Frankenstein must also be okay, and Dr. Mengele, too, and before you know it, it's one long hapless inevitable slide from high-minded medicine to the Nazis.

Marty Kaplan, in an article at Huffingtonpost.com

36. The first mate on a ship decided to celebrate an occasion with some rum. Unfortunately he got drunk. The captain saw him drunk and when the first mate was sober, showed him the following entry in the ship's log: *The first mate was drunk today.*

"Captain please don't let that stay in the log," the mate said. "This could add months or years to my becoming a captain myself."
"Is it true?" asked the captain, already knowing the answer.
"Yes, it's true" the mate said.
"Then if it is true it has to go in the log. That's the rule. If it's true it goes into the log. End of discussion," said the captain sternly.
Weeks later, it was the first mate's turn to make the log entries. The first mate wrote: *The ship seems in good shape. The captain was sober today.*

Adapted from "The Captain Was Sober Today," at Blogs.rassak.com

37. These are the times that try men's souls. The summer soldier and the sunshine patriot will in this crisis shrink from the service of his country; but he that stands it now deserves the love and thanks for man and woman. Tyranny, like hell, is not easily conquered; yet we have this consolation with us, that the harder the conflict, the more glorious the triumph. What we obtain too cheap, we esteem too lightly; 'tis dearness only that gives everything its value. Heaven knows how to put a proper price upon its goods; and it would be strange indeed, if so celestial an article as freedom should not be highly rated. Britain, with an army to enforce her tyranny, has declared that she has a right (not only to tax) but "to bind us in all cases whatsoever," and if being bound in that manner is not slavery, then there is no such thing as slavery upon earth.   Thomas Paine, *The Crisis*

38. It is argued that in these tragic cases the great value of the mental health of a woman who becomes pregnant as a result of rape or incest can best be safeguarded by abortion. It is also said that a pregnancy caused by rape or incest is the result of a grave injustice and that the victim should not be obliged to carry

the fetus to viability. This would keep reminding her for nine months of the violence committed against her and would just increase her mental anguish. It is reasoned that the value of the woman's mental health is greater than the value of the fetus. In addition, it is maintained that the fetus is an aggressor against the woman's integrity and personal life; it is only just and morally defensible to repel an aggressor even by killing him if that is the only way to defend personal and human values. It is concluded, then, that abortion is justified in these cases.

Andrew Varga, The Main Issues in Bioethics

39. If the Iraqi regime is able to produce, buy, or steal an amount of highly-enriched uranium a little larger than a single softball, it could have a nuclear weapon in less than a year. And if we allow that to happen, a terrible line would be crossed. Saddam Hussein would be in a position to blackmail anyone who opposes his aggression. He would be in a position to dominate the Middle East. He would be in a position to threaten America. And Saddam Hussein would be in a position to pass nuclear technology to terrorists. Knowing these realities, America must not ignore the threat gathering against us. Facing clear evidence of peril, we cannot wait for the final proof—the smoking gun—that could come in the form of a mushroom cloud.   President George W. Bush, October 8, 2002

40. A person apparently hopelessly ill may be allowed to take his own life. Then he may be permitted to deputize others to do it for him should he no longer be able to act. The judgment of others then becomes the ruling factor. Already at this point euthanasia is not personal and voluntary, for others are acting on behalf of the patient as they see fit. This may well incline them to act on behalf of other patients who have not authorized them to exercise their judgment. It is only a short step, then, from voluntary euthanasia (self-inflicted or authorized), to directed euthanasia administered to a patient who has given no authorization, to involuntary euthanasia conducted as a part of a social policy.

J. Gay Williams, "The Wrongfulness of Euthanasia"

⭐ 41. Once, many National Football League (NFL) teams played on Thanksgiving; to this day, high school teams play championship or rivalry games on Thanksgiving. In the 1950s, the old NFL began a tradition of having only one game on turkey day, always at Detroit. In the 1960s, a Cowboys' home date was added on Thanksgiving, to help the Dallas expansion franchise become established. Detroit and Dallas have been the traditional hosts since. There's no larger reason—the reason is, "We do it that way because that's the way we do it."

Gregg Easterbrook, ESPN.com's Page 2

42. If I were to suggest that between the Earth and Mars there is a china teapot revolving about the sun in an elliptical orbit, nobody would be able to disprove my assertion provided I were careful to add that the teapot is too small to be revealed even by our most powerful telescopes. But if I were to go on to say that, since my assertion cannot be disproved, it is an intolerable presumption on the part of human reason to doubt it, I should rightly be thought to be talking

nonsense. If, however, the existence of such a teapot were affirmed in ancient books, taught as the sacred truth every Sunday, and instilled into the minds of children at school, hesitation to believe in its existence would become a mark of eccentricity and entitle the doubter to the attentions of the psychiatrist in an enlightened age or of the Inquisitor in an earlier time.

Bertrand Russell, "Is There a God?"

43. *Dorothy:* Are you doing that on purpose, or can't you make up your mind?
Scarecrow: That's the trouble. I can't make up my mind. I haven't got a brain—just straw.
Dorothy: How can you talk if you haven't got a brain?
Scarecrow: I don't know. But some people without brains do an awful lot of talking, don't they?
Dorothy: I guess you're right.

From the movie *The Wizard of Oz*

44. To cast abortion as a solely private moral question is to lose touch with common sense. How human beings treat one another is practically the definition of a public moral matter. Of course, there are many private aspects of human relations, but the question whether one human being should be allowed fatally to harm another is not one of them. Abortion is an inescapably public matter.

Helen M. Alvaré, *The Abortion Controversy*

★ 45. Consider a precise number that is well known to generations of parents and doctors: the normal human body temperature of 98.6 degrees Fahrenheit. Recent investigations involving millions of measurements have revealed that this number is wrong; normal human body temperature is actually 98.2 degrees Fahrenheit. The fault, however, lies not with Dr. Wunderlich's original measurements—they were averaged and sensibly rounded to the nearest degree: 37 degrees Celsius. When this temperature was converted to Fahrenheit, however, the rounding was forgotten, and 98.6 was taken to be accurate to the nearest tenth of a degree. Had the original interval between 36.5 degrees Celsius and 37.5 degrees Celsius been translated, the equivalent Fahrenheit temperatures would have ranged from 97.7 degrees to 99.5 degrees.

John Allen Paulos, *A Mathematician Reads the Newspaper*

Summary

- Formal fallacy: A logical error that occurs in the form or structure of an argument and is restricted to deductive arguments.
- Informal fallacy: A mistake in reasoning that occurs in ordinary language and is different from an error in the form or structure of arguments.
- Fallacies of relevance: Occur whenever irrelevant premises are offered in support of a conclusion.
- Argument against the person (*ad hominem*): Occurs when a claim is rejected or judged to be false based on alleged character flaws of the person making

the claim. A second common form occurs whenever someone's statement or reasoning is attacked by way of a stereotype, such as a racial, sexual, or religious stereotype. A third form involves the use of the circumstances of a person's life to reject his claims.

- *Tu quoque*: A variety of the *ad hominem* fallacy that is distinguished by the specific attempt of one person to avoid the issue at hand by claiming the other person is a hypocrite ("you, too" or "look who's talking").
- Appeal to the people: The avoidance of objective evidence in favor of an emotional response defeats the goal of a rational investigation of truth. The tactic appeals to people's desire to belong to a group.
- Appeal to pity: A specific kind of emotional plea that relies solely on a sense of pity for support.
- Appeal to force: A threat of harmful consequences (physical and otherwise) used to force acceptance of a course of action that would otherwise be unacceptable.
- An argument built on a position of ignorance claims either that (1) a statement must be true because it has not been proven to be false or (2) a statement must be false because it has not been proven to be true.
- Missing the point: Occurs when premises that seem to lead logically to one conclusion are used instead to support an unexpected conclusion.
- Appeal to an unqualified authority: Occurs when an argument that relies on the opinions of people who have no expertise, training, or knowledge relevant to the issue at hand.
- Fallacies of unwarranted assumption: Assume the truth of some unproved or questionable claim.
- Begging the question: Occurs when an argument assumes as evidence in the premises the very thing that it attempts to prove in the conclusion.
- Complex question: A single question that actually contains multiple, hidden parts.
- Biased sample: An argument that uses a nonrepresentative sample as support for a statistical claim about an entire population.
- Accident: The fallacy that arises when a generalization is inappropriately applied to the case at hand.
- Hasty generalization: A generalization created on the basis of a few instances.
- Misleading precision: Occurs when a claim appears to be statistically significant but is not.
- False dichotomy: Occurs when it is assumed that only two choices are possible, when in fact others exist.
- False dilemma: Occurs when two choices are asserted, each leading to an unwanted result, but there is a failure to acknowledge that other possibilities exist.
- False cause: Occurs when a causal connection is assumed to exist between two events when none actually exists.
- Coincidence: A fallacy that results from the accidental or chance connection between two events.

- *Post hoc* fallacy: A fallacy involving either a short-term or long-term pattern that is noticed after the fact.
- Common cause fallacy: A mistake that occurs when someone thinks that one event causes another when in fact both events are the result of a common cause.
- Slippery slope: The attempt to make a final event the inevitable outcome of an initial act.
- Fallacy of ambiguity or diversion: Occurs when the meanings of terms or phrases are changed (intentionally or unintentionally) within the argument, or when our attention is purposely (or accidentally) diverted from the issue at hand.
- Equivocation: The intentional or unintentional use of different meanings of words or phrases in an argument.
- Amphiboly: Ambiguity that arises when a poorly constructed statement muddles the intended meaning ("irregular speech").
- Composition: When an attribute of the individual parts of an object is mistakenly transferred to the entire object.
- Division: When an attribute of an object as a whole is mistakenly transferred to its individual parts.
- Emphasis: Occurs when attention is purposely (or accidentally) diverted from the issue at hand.
- Straw man: A fallacy that occurs when someone's written or spoken words are taken out of context. It purposely distorts the original argument to create a new, weak argument that can be easily refuted (a straw man that is easily knocked down).
- Red herring: When someone completely ignores an opponent's position and changes the subject, diverting the discussion in a new direction.

KEY TERMS

LOGIC CHALLENGE: A CLEVER PROBLEM

In a certain faraway country (long, long, ago), prisoners to be executed were either shot or hanged. Prisoners were allowed to make one statement. If their statement turned out to be true, then they were hanged. If their statement turned out to be false, then they were shot. That is, until one clever prisoner put an end to the practice of execution. The prisoner made her one statement, upon which the judge was forced to set her free. What statement did she make?

Part III

FORMAL LOGIC

Chapter 5

Categorical Propositions

What if you saw a sign in a store: "No discounted items are returnable." You have just bought those new running shoes you needed—and paid full price. Are they returnable? Based on this single sign, can you conclude that *all* (or at least *some*) nondiscounted items are returnable? Is it possible that *none* of the items in the store are returnable?

Now you get an e-mail: "All graduating seniors are expected to pay their outstanding debts in full." Can you conclude that, if you are a sophomore, then you are *not* expected to pay your outstanding debts in full? Are graduating seniors the only students expected to pay their debts?

On another occasion, you happen to overhear someone talking about a restaurant: "Some of the food they serve is absolutely horrible." Can you conclude that, according to the speaker, some of the food the restaurant serves is *not* absolutely horrible?

These examples all refer to groups of objects: "discounted items," "graduating seniors," and "food the restaurant serves." Statements about groups like these are the subject of *categorical logic*. They are part of the generalizations we make every day about our experiences, about other people, and about ourselves. In fact, when it comes to politics or our futures, it is hard to resist making generalizations—but how valid are they, and what can we safely conclude when it comes to particulars? This chapter explores the foundations of categorical logic, which go back to Aristotle's fundamental work in the 4th century BC. A thorough exploration will take us to two modern thinkers, George Boole and John Venn, whose work led to an alternative system to Aristotle's interpretations. As we saw in Chapter 3, diagrams can guide us through arguments. In much the same way, Venn showed how to picture categorical logic.

A. CATEGORICAL PROPOSITIONS

We begin with a discussion of classes, or *categories*. A **class** is a group of objects, and a **categorical proposition** relates two classes of objects. For example:

> All stand-up comedians are witty persons.

This categorical proposition refers to two classes of objects—*stand-up comedians* and *witty persons*. In this proposition, "stand-up comedians" is the **subject term**, and "witty persons" is the **predicate term**. In addition to claiming that *all* stand-up comedians are witty persons we might instead say that *some* of them are:

> Some stand-up comedians are witty persons.

In contrast, we might say that *none* of them are:

> No stand-up comedians are witty persons.

Finally, we might say that *some* of them *are not*:

> Some stand-up comedians are not witty persons.

If we let S stand for the subject term and P stand for the predicate term in a categorical proposition, then we can say any of the following regarding S and P:

All S are P.   **Some S are P.**   **No S are P.**   **Some S are not P.**

As these examples illustrate, categorical propositions are about *class inclusion*, or what objects belong to a class. They either affirm or deny total class inclusion, or else they affirm or deny partial class inclusion. Centuries ago, logicians took the vowels from the Latin words *affirmo* (meaning "I affirm") and *nego* (meaning "I deny") and used them to designate the four types of categorical propositions:

- **A-propositions** assert that the entire subject class is included in the predicate class:
  A: All S are P.
- **I-propositions** assert that part of the subject class is included in the predicate class:
  I: Some S are P.
- **E-propositions** assert that the entire subject class is excluded from the predicate class:
  E: No S are P.
- **O-propositions** assert that part of the subject class is excluded from the predicate class:
  O: Some S are not P.

The letters **A, E, I,** and **O** designate the four *standard forms* of categorical propositions. Since these are forms of propositions rather than actual propositions, they are neither true nor false. Replacing the S and P in a standard form with terms denoting classes of objects—the subject and predicate terms—results in a **standard-form categorical proposition** that is either true or false. For example, "All cell phones are expensive toys"

Class A group of objects.

Categorical proposition A categorical proposition relates two classes of objects.

Subject term The term that comes first in a standard-form categorical proposition.

Predicate term The term that comes second in a standard-form categorical proposition.

A-proposition A categorical proposition having the form "All S are P."

I-proposition A categorical proposition having the form "Some S are P."

E-proposition A categorical proposition having the form "No S are P."

O-proposition A categorical proposition having the form "Some S are not P."

Standard-form categorical proposition
A proposition that has one of the following forms: "All S are P," "Some S are P," "No S are P," "Some S are not P."

Universal affirmative
An **A**-proposition. It affirms that every member of the subject class is a member of the predicate class.

Universal negative An **E**-proposition. It asserts that no members of the subject class are members of the predicate class.

Particular affirmative
An **I**-proposition. It asserts that at least one member of the subject class is a member of the predicate class.

is an **A**-proposition; the class terms "cell phones" and "expensive toys" replace the S and P in the standard form "All S are P." If you were to utter this proposition, then you would be claiming that *every* member of the subject class (cell phones) is a member of the predicate class (expensive toys). Since **A**-propositions affirm that every member of the subject class is a member of the predicate class, they are also called **universal affirmative** propositions.

We can substitute the terms "cell phones" and "expensive toys" for the subject and predicate of the three remaining standard forms as well. The first, "No cell phones are expensive toys" is an **E**-proposition. If you make this claim, then you are asserting that *no* members of the subject class (cell phones) are members of the predicate class (expensive toys). Since **E**-propositions assert that no members of the subject class are members of the predicate class, they are called **universal negative** propositions.

The next example, "Some cell phones are expensive toys," is an **I**-proposition. If you make this claim, then you are asserting that *at least one* member of the subject class (cell phones) is a member of the predicate class (expensive toys). Since **I**-propositions assert that *at least one* member of the subject class is a member of the predicate class, they are called **particular affirmative** propositions.

The final example, "Some cell phones are not expensive toys," is an **O**-proposition. If you make this claim, then you are asserting that *at least one* member of the subject class (cell phones) is *not* a member of the predicate class (expensive toys). Since

PROFILES IN LOGIC

Aristotle

Aristotle (384–322 BC) is often said to have originated the study of logic, and his ideas dominated Western thought for 2000 years. His writings influenced every aspect of European culture—from politics and art to ethics and philosophy.

Aristotle wanted logic and science to complement each other, and he developed his logic, in no small part, to make scientific reasoning more solid. Aristotle's science relied on the idea of classification: To understand the things around us, we look at what they share and we rely on what we know. We therefore group them together, as a subclass of a class that is already well understood. In much the same way, Aristotle's system of logic is based on relationships between classes. For example, the statement "All humans are mortal" contains a subject term ("humans") and a predicate term ("mortal"). It asserts that the class of humans is included in the class of mortals.

"All humans are mortal" is a *universal statement*—it applies to every one of us. But Aristotle went a step further. Because it applies to all of us, he reasoned, it is a statement about the world: The class of humans or mortals has members that actually exist. When we analyze an argument, he assumed, we are also investigating whether the statements are true. In contrast, modern logic separates of the *truth of statements* from the *validity of arguments*.

O-propositions assert that *at least one* member of the subject class is not a member of the predicate class, they are called **particular negative** propositions.

Since Aristotle is credited with doing substantial work on the subject of categorical logic, it seems appropriate to use his name as a tool for remembering the different designations. The four vowels in "Aristotle" match the ones used in our discussion.

> **Particular negative** An **O**-proposition. It asserts that at least one member of the subject class is not a member of the predicate class.

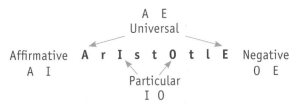

When people speak or write in ordinary language, they might not use standard-form categorical propositions. Later in this chapter you will see how ordinary language statements can be translated into standard-form categorical propositions. Since some ordinary language statements are ambiguous, translations (where appropriate) into standard-form categorical propositions can reduce the ambiguity. For now, though, we will continue exploring standard-form categorical propositions.

CHECK YOUR UNDERSTANDING 5A

Analyze each categorical proposition by doing the following: (1) Identify the subject and predicate of each proposition; (2) identify the categorical proposition as either **A** (All S are P), **E** (No S are P), **I** (Some S are P), or **O** (Some S are not P).

1. All senior citizens are people eligible for subsidized drug prescriptions.
Answer: Subject: *senior citizens.* Predicate: *people eligible for subsidized drug prescriptions.* This is an example of an **A**-proposition.

2. Some public schools are not schools meeting national standards for excellence.

3. Some family incomes are incomes below the poverty line.

4. No national health-care plans are ideas worth implementing.

⭐ 5. All malicious murderers are evil people.

6. All X-rated movies are intellectually stimulating events.

7. Some video games are not violent activities.

8. Some petty bureaucrats are tyrannical people.

⭐ 9. No lottery winners are lucky people.

10. Some diet fads are not healthy lifestyles.

11. All sporting events are television shows worth watching.

12. Some philosophy books are important contributions to literature.

⭐ 13. No amendments to the U.S. Constitution are unconstitutional acts.

14. All gamblers are superstitious people.

15. Some psychics are frauds.

B. QUANTITY, QUALITY, AND DISTRIBUTION

Quantity When we classify a categorical proposition as either universal or particular we are referring to its quantity.

Quality When we classify a categorical proposition as either affirmative or negative we are referring to its quality.

When we classify a categorical proposition as either *universal* or *particular,* we are referring to its **quantity**. Universal categorical propositions (**A** or **E**) refer to *every* member of the subject class, while particular categorical propositions (**I** or **O**) refer to *at least one* member of the subject class. When we classify a categorical proposition as either *affirmative* or *negative* we are referring to its **quality**, which deals with class inclusion or exclusion. The affirmative categorical propositions are **A** and **I**. In **A**-propositions, the subject class is completely included in the predicate class; in **I**-propositions, the subject class is only partially included in the predicate class. The negative categorical propositions are **E** and **O**. In **E**-propositions, the subject class is completely excluded from the predicate class; in **O**-propositions, the subject class is only partially excluded from the predicate class. Once again, it is important to separate these logical issues from any determination of the actual truth value of a categorical proposition.

		Subject		Predicate	Quantity	Quality
A:	All	S	are	P.	*universal*	*affirmative*
E:	No	S	are	P.	*universal*	*negative*
I:	Some	S	are	P.	*particular*	*affirmative*
O:	Some	S	are not	P.	*particular*	*negative*

Quantifier The words "all," "no," and "some" are quantifiers. They tell us the extent of the class inclusion or exclusion.

Copula The words "are" and "are not" are forms of "to be" and serve to link (to "couple") the subject class with the predicate class.

In categorical propositions, the words "all," "no," and "some" are called **quantifiers** because they tell us the extent of the class inclusion or exclusion. The words "are" and "are not" are referred to as **copula**. They are simply forms of "to be" and serve to link (to "couple") the subject class with the predicate class.

It is important to recognize that quantifiers refer to the subject class and not to the predicate class. For example, if I say "All romantic movies are good places to go on a first date," then I am asserting something definite about the subject class (romantic movies)—namely, that it is completely included in the predicate class (good places to go on a first date). But my assertion leaves open the extent of the predicate class.

If a categorical proposition asserts something definite about every member of a class, then the term designating that class is said to be **distributed**. For example, anyone uttering the proposition "All cats are mammals" makes an assertion about every member of the class of cats. Since the assertion is that *every cat* is a mammal, the subject term is distributed. On the other hand, if the proposition does not assert something definite about every member of a class, then the term designating that class is said to be **undistributed**. In "All cats are mammals," the predicate term is not distributed, since the word "all" does not extend its reference to mammals. In the same way, in the categorical proposition "All cats are diplomats," the subject term is distributed and the predicate term is undistributed. (Remember that this is a logical discussion. It does not address the question of truth value.)

The distinction between distributed and undistributed terms does not just apply to **A**-propositions. Take "No public universities are adequately funded institutions." Since this is an **E**-proposition, the quantifier makes an assertion regarding every member of the subject class: it claims that *not even one* is a member of the predicate class. Thus, the subject term is distributed. However, unlike the results for **A**-propositions, **E**-propositions result in the predicate term being distributed. This follows because if no member of the subject class is a member of the predicate class, then the reverse must be true, too. Therefore, in **E**-propositions both the subject term and predicate term are distributed.

The next example concerns **I**-propositions. If you say "Some students in this class are sophomores," then we know that the quantifier "some" refers to the subject class. Since your assertion is only that *at least one* of the students in this class is a sophomore, the subject term is not distributed. In addition, the predicate term is not distributed. Bear in mind that it is easy to misinterpret **I**-propositions. In the categorical proposition "Some students in this class are sophomores," it is *possible* for every member of the subject class to be included in the predicate class. In other words, it is possible that every student in this class is a sophomore. Recognizing this possibility eliminates a potential misunderstanding. It is incorrect to conclude that "Some students in this class are *not* sophomores."

The proposition "Some cars are not fuel-efficient vehicles" is an **O**-proposition. Here again, the quantifier word "some" refers only to the subject class. If you utter this proposition, then you are asserting that *at least one* car is not a fuel-efficient vehicle. Since nothing definite is asserted about every member of the subject class, the subject term is not distributed. But in an interesting twist, something definite about the predicate class is revealed. The predicate class is completely distinguished from the single member of the subject class referred to by the proposition. And because of this curious twist, the predicate term is distributed. Whenever a categorical proposition says something definite about *every member* of a class, then the term designating that class is distributed. In our example, since at least one member of the subject class is excluded from every member of the predicate class, then the predicate term is distributed.

Once again, we must be careful not to misinterpret these results. The quantifier "some" in the **O**-proposition allows the *possibility* that every member of the subject class is excluded from the predicate class. It is, therefore, incorrect to think that the proposition "Some cars are not fuel-efficient vehicles" allows you to logically conclude that as also claiming that "Some cars are fuel-efficient vehicles." In other words, the proposition does not rule out the possibility that every member of the subject class is excluded from the predicate class.

Distributed If a categorical proposition asserts something definite about every member of a class, then the term designating that class is said to be distributed.

Undistributed If a proposition does not assert something definite about every member of a class, then the term designating that class is said to be undistributed.

QUANTITY, QUALITY, AND DISTRIBUTION APPLIED TO A, E, I, AND O			
Proposition	*Quantity*	*Quality*	*Term Distributed*
A: All S are P.	universal	affirmative	subject
E: No S are P.	universal	negative	subject and predicate
I: Some S are P.	particular	affirmative	no distribution
O: Some S are not P.	particular	negative	predicate

A *mnemonic* is something that can be used to assist the memory. (The movie *Johnny Mnemonic* was about a person who had a cybernetic brain implant to store information.) For example, many people refer to the National Collegiate Athletic Association by the acronym NCAA. If you have studied a musical instrument you probably used the phrase "Every Good Boy Deserves Favor" to remember the notes on the treble clef—EGBDF. If it helps, you can use the following mnemonic device to remember that *subjects get distributed by universals, and predicates get distributed by negatives.*

S U P N	Subjects—Universals	Predicates—Negatives

CHECK YOUR UNDERSTANDING 5B

The categorical propositions below are to be analyzed in the following three ways: (1) the correct *quantity* (*universal* or *particular*); (2) the correct *quality* (*affirmative* or *negative*); (3) the correct *distribution* (subject term distributed; predicate term distributed; both terms distributed; or neither term distributed).

1. All ice-cold soft drinks are thirst-quenching beverages.
Answer: Universal affirmative; subject term distributed; predicate term undistributed.

2. Some popular music pieces are not addictive products.

3. No computer software programs are easily installed items.

4. Some DVDs are overpriced consumer goods.

★ 5. No cannibals are vegetarians.

6. No fast-food franchises are benevolent employers.

7. Some universities are intellectual gardens.

8. Some tattoos are not acceptable fashions for parents.

★ 9. All body-piercing rituals are beliefs based on ancient religions.

10. No winning gamblers are probability deficient people.

11. All sugar-free pastries are foods pleasing to the palate.

12. Some gymnasium locker rooms are not aromatically pleasant places.

★ 13. No reality television shows are scripted programs.

14. Some tropical islands are wonderful vacation getaways.

15. No green vegetables are vitamin-deficient foods.

C. THE SQUARE OF OPPOSITION

We have seen that the four types of categorical proposition forms differ in quality, quantity, or both. **Opposition** occurs whenever two categorical proposition forms have the same subject and predicate classes but differ in quality, quantity, or both. And so far, we have been concerned only with understanding the structure of these propositions. We have not considered their logical consequences. If they are taken as true or false, what can we conclude?

The first relationship we will look at is called **contradictories**, which is a pair of propositions in which one is the negation of the other (they have opposite truth values). This occurs when we recognize that it is impossible for both propositions to be true or both to be false at the same time. Contradictory categorical statements differ from each other in both quantity and quality. For example,

(1) All interstate highways are projects built with taxpayers' money. (**A**-proposition)

(2) Some interstate highways are not projects built with taxpayers' money. (**O**-proposition)

Can both of these propositions be true (or false) at the same time? Think about it. The answer is *No*. If the first proposition is true, then the second must be false. If all (every) interstate highways are projects built with taxpayers' money, then there cannot be even one that is *not* built with taxpayers' money. Likewise, if the second proposition is true, then the first must be false. If there is at least one interstate highway that is *not* built with taxpayers' money, then it cannot be true that all of them are built with taxpayers' money.

What happens if the first proposition is false? Well, then the second proposition would have to be true. If not every interstate highway is built with taxpayers' money, then there must be at least one that is *not* built with taxpayers' money. Likewise, if the second proposition is false, then the first must be true. If there is not even one interstate highway that is *not* built with taxpayers' money, then it must be true that all of them are built with taxpayers' money.

For any two propositions to be truly contradictories, one of them has to be true and the other has to be false. As we saw for propositions (1) and (2), **A**- and **O**-propositions are contradictories.

E- and **I**-propositions are contradictories, too:

(3) No interstate highways are projects built with taxpayers' money. (**E**-proposition)

(4) Some interstate highways are projects built with taxpayers' money. (**I**-proposition)

Opposition When two standard-form categorical propositions refer to the same subject and predicate classes, but differ in quality, quantity, or both.

Contradictories In categorical logic, pairs of propositions in which one is the negation of the other.

If the first proposition is true then the second must be false, and vice versa. Also, if the first proposition is false then the second must be true, and vice versa.

We can display the results discussed so far as a bare-bones square. It is our first step in building what we shall call the *square of opposition*:

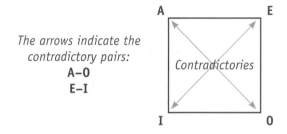

The arrows indicate the contradictory pairs:
A–O
E–I

Figure 5.1 spells out what that means. Since **A**- and **O**-propositions are contradictory, they should have opposite values for quantity, quality, and distribution. So should the contradictory propositions **E** and **I**.

Figure 5.1

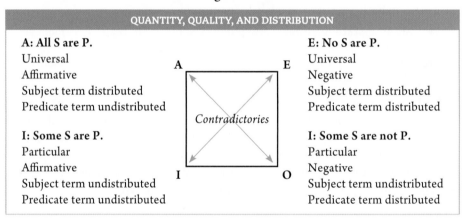

QUANTITY, QUALITY, AND DISTRIBUTION	
A: All S are P.	**E: No S are P.**
Universal	Universal
Affirmative	Negative
Subject term distributed	Subject term distributed
Predicate term undistributed	Predicate term distributed
I: Some S are P.	**I: Some S are not P.**
Particular	Particular
Affirmative	Negative
Subject term undistributed	Subject term undistributed
Predicate term undistributed	Predicate term distributed

Let's see if you have grasped the idea of contradictories. Are the following two propositions contradictories?

(5) All zoos are places where animals are treated humanely. (**A**-proposition)
(6) No zoos are places where animals are treated humanely. (**E**-proposition)

If the first proposition is true, then the second must, of course, be false. Likewise, if the second is true, then the first must be false. However, if you guessed that they are contradictories, you would be wrong. To see this, consider what would happen if the first proposition were false. In that case, must the second proposition be true? Again, think about it. If it is false that "All zoos are places where animals are treated humanely," must it be true that "No zoos are places where animals are treated humanely"? The answer is *No* because there might be *one or more* zoos where animals are treated humanely. Since this is possible, it would make the second proposition false, too. Since contradictory propositions cannot both be false at the same time, we have shown that propositions (5) and (6) are not contradictories. Therefore, **A**- and **E**-propositions are not contradictories.

This example reveals a new type of logical relationship. Propositions (5) and (6) cannot both be true at the same time, but they can both be *false* at the same time. Pairs of propositions showing this particular relationship are called **contraries**. Here is another example of contraries:

> **Contraries** Pairs of propositions that cannot both be true at the same time, but can both be false at the same time.

(7) All hurricanes are storms formed in the Atlantic Ocean. (**A**-proposition)
(8) No hurricanes are storms formed in the Atlantic Ocean. (**E**-proposition)

If the first proposition is true, then the second must be false, and vice versa. However, they both can be false at the same time, because it is possible that just some hurricanes are formed in the Atlantic Ocean. This analysis reveals that **A**- and **E**-propositions are contraries. We can add this information to our square of opposition:

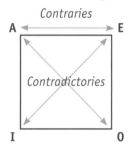

The flip side of contraries are **subcontraries,** which cannot both be false at the same time, but can both be true at the same time. Also, if one is false, then the other must be true. The next two propositions are subcontraries:

> **Subcontraries** Pairs of propositions that cannot both be false at the same time, but can both be true; also, if one is false, then the other must be true.

(9) Some hurricanes are storms formed in the Atlantic Ocean. (**I**-proposition)
(10) Some hurricanes are not storms formed in the Atlantic Ocean. (**O**-proposition)

It is possible for both of these propositions to be true at the same time. All that would be needed would be to find one hurricane that formed in the Atlantic Ocean and one that was not formed in the Atlantic Ocean. However, both propositions cannot be false at the same time. Why not? If proposition (9) is false, then not even one hurricane was formed in the Atlantic Ocean. If that is so, then proposition (10) must be true, because it asserts that at least one hurricane is not formed in the Atlantic Ocean. The same result is attained if we start by making proposition (10) false. Doing this would logically make proposition (9) true. We have shown that **I**- and **O**-propositions are subcontraries, and we can now add these results to the square of opposition:

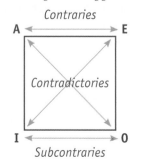

Subalternation The relationship between a universal proposition (referred to as the *superaltern*) and its corresponding particular proposition (referred to as the *subaltern*).

We need one final relationship in order to complete the square of opposition. **Subalternation** is the relationship between a universal proposition (referred to as the *superaltern*) and its corresponding particular proposition (referred to as the *subaltern*). There are two kinds of corresponding propositions:

A: All S are P	*corresponds to*	**I:** Some S are P.
E: No S are P	*corresponds to*	**O:** Some S are not P.

If the universal proposition of a pair is true, then its corresponding particular will also be true. For example, if it is true that "All modern holidays are greeting-card company creations," then it is also true that "Some modern holidays are greeting-card company creations." Likewise, if it is true that "No modern holidays are greeting-card company creations," then it is also true that "Some modern holidays are not greeting-card company creations." However, the reverse does not hold. That is, if the particular proposition of a pair is true, then its corresponding universal might be true—or it might be false.

Here is an example of subalternation:

(11) All musical instruments are difficult things to master. (**A**-proposition)
(12) Some musical instruments are difficult things to master. (**I**-proposition)

If the universal affirmative categorical proposition (**A**) is true, then its corresponding particular (**I**) will be true, too. However, we can see that even if proposition (12), the particular affirmative (**I**) is true, then its corresponding universal (**A**) might be true or false. These same results hold for the categorical propositions **E** and **O**. For example:

(13) No musical instruments are difficult things to master. (**E**-proposition)
(14) Some musical instruments are not difficult things to master. (**O**-proposition)

As before, if proposition (13), a universal negative (**E**) is true, then its corresponding particular (**O**) will be true, too. However, we can see that even if proposition (14), the particular negative (**O**) is true, then its corresponding universal (**E**) might be true or false.

Subalternation gets more interesting if we ask what happens when one member of a corresponding pair is false. On the one hand, if the universal proposition of a pair is false, then its corresponding particular partner could be true or false. For example, if it is false that "All honor students are hard workers" (**A**), then the proposition "Some honor students are hard workers" (**I**) could be either true or false. Similarly, if it is false that "No honor students are hard workers" (**E**), then the proposition "Some honor students are not hard workers" (**O**) could be either true or false. However, the reverse does not hold. That is, if the particular proposition of a pair of corresponding propositions is false, then its corresponding universal must be false as well. Here is an example:

(15) All musical instruments are difficult things to master. (**A**-proposition)
(16) Some musical instruments are difficult things to master. (**I**-proposition)

If proposition (15), a universal affirmative (**A**) is false, then its corresponding particular (**I**) could be either true or false. However, we can see that if proposition (16), the particular affirmative (**I**), is false, then its corresponding universal (**A**) must be false, too. These same results hold for **E**- and **O**-propositions. Here is an example:

(17) No musical instruments are difficult things to master. (**E**-proposition)
(18) Some musical instruments are not difficult things to master. (**O**-proposition)

As before, if proposition (17), a universal negative (**E**) is false, then its corresponding particular (**O**) could be either true or false. But, once again, we can see that if proposition (18), the particular negative (**O**) is false, then its corresponding universal (**E**) must be false, too.

We can now complete the *square of opposition*:

Figure 5.2

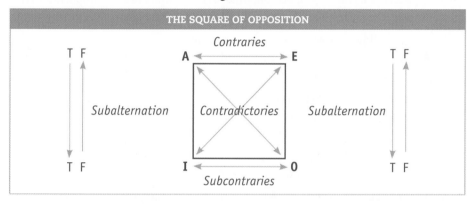

Let's try it out and see where it takes us. Our discussion has included the creation and analysis of **immediate arguments**, which are arguments that contain only one premise. (Arguments that have more than one premise are called **mediate arguments**.) Now suppose the following proposition is true: "All clowns are scary people" (**A**). If so, can we go around the square of opposition and say something about each of the remaining three categorical proposition forms? We can. The proposition, "No clowns are scary people" (**E**), is the contrary of the original proposition (**A**). Since contraries cannot both be true at the same time, the proposition, "No clowns are scary people" (**E**), is false. Also, since the proposition, "Some clowns are not scary people" (**O**), is the contradictory of the original proposition (**A**), it, too, is false. The remaining proposition, "Some clowns are scary people" (**I**), is the subaltern of the original proposition (**A**), and so it is true.

Now let's try the opposite truth value. What if the proposition "All clowns are scary people" (**A**) is false? The contrary of this proposition is "No clowns are scary people" (**E**). And going around the square, we determine that it could be true or false, so its truth value is *undetermined*. However, the proposition "Some clowns are not scary people" (**O**), the contradictory of the original proposition (**A**), must then be true. The remaining proposition, "Some clowns are scary people" (**I**), the subaltern of the original proposition (**A**), might be true or false, so its truth value is therefore undetermined.

Immediate argument An argument that has only one premise.

Mediate argument An argument that has more than one premise.

CHECK YOUR UNDERSTANDING 5C

I. Use your understanding of the square of opposition to determine the correct answer.

1. The *contradictory* of "No football players are opera singers" is:

   (a) All football players are opera singers.
   (b) Some football players are opera singers.
   (c) Some football players are not opera singers.

Answer: (b) is correct. Since "No football players are opera singers" is an **E**-proposition its contradictory must be an **I**-proposition, which is answer (b). The correct answer cannot be (a) because it is an **A**-proposition, which is the *contrary* of an **E**-proposition. Also, (c) is not correct because it is an **O**-proposition, which is the subaltern of an **E**-proposition.

2. Are the following two propositions *contraries*?
   All yo-yos are toys better left untouched.
   No yo-yos are toys better left untouched.

3. Are the following two propositions *subcontraries*?
   Some contact lenses are gas-permeable objects.
   Some contact lenses are not gas-permeable objects.

4. True or False: In the square of opposition, two contradictory categorical propositions can both be false at the same time.

5. True or False: In the square of opposition, two contrary categorical propositions can both be false at the same time.

II. Use your understanding of the square of opposition to determine the correct answer: a. True, b. False, or c. Undetermined.

1. If it is false that "Some implants are easily detectable objects," then the proposition "No implants are easily detectable objects" must be:

Answer: a. True. The first is an **I**-proposition, and if it is false, its contradictory **E**-proposition must be true.

2. If it is false that "Some implants are easily detectable objects," then the proposition "No implants are easily detectable objects" must be:

3. If it is false that "Some games are crazy inventions," then the proposition "All games are crazy inventions" must be:

4. If it is true that "Some games are crazy inventions," then the proposition "All games are crazy inventions" must be:

5. If it is true that "No games are crazy inventions," then the proposition "Some games are not crazy inventions" must be:

6. If it is false that "No games are crazy inventions," then the proposition "Some games are not crazy inventions" must be:

III. Use your understanding of the square of opposition to determine the correct answer.

1. Write the contradictory of "All sports cars are gas-guzzling machines."

Answer: Some sports cars are not gas-guzzling machines. Since the first sentence is an **A**-proposition, its contradictory must be an **O**-proposition.

2. Write the contrary of "All diamond rings are expensive items."

3. What is the relationship of opposition, if any, between these two propositions?

   (a) Some foreign movies are dramas.
   (b) Some foreign movies are comedies.

4. If it is true that "Some theoretical scientists are humanists," then what can be said about the proposition "No theoretical scientists are humanists"?

⭐ 5. If it is false that "All theoretical scientists are humanists," then what can be said about the proposition "Some theoretical scientists are humanists"?

IV. For each of the following questions, you will be told the truth value of one of the four types of categorical propositions. From this information you are to determine the truth values of the other three types of categorical propositions as you go around the square of opposition. Choose the correct answer: a. True, b. False, or c. Undetermined.

1. If an **A**-proposition is true, then you can conclude that the **E**-proposition would be:

Answer: b. False. Since they are *contraries*, they cannot both be true at the same time.

2. If an **A**-proposition is *true*, then you can conclude that the **I**-proposition would be:

3. If an **A**-proposition is *true*, then you can conclude that the **O**-proposition would be:

4. If an **A**-proposition is *false*, then you can conclude that the **E**-proposition would be:

⭐ 5. If an **A**-proposition is *false*, then you can conclude that the **I**-proposition would be:

6. If an **A**-proposition is *false*, then you can conclude that the **O**-proposition would be:

7. If an **E**-proposition is *true*, then you can conclude that the **A**-proposition would be:

8. If an **E**-proposition is *true*, then you can conclude that the **I**-proposition would be:

⭐ 9. If an **E**-proposition is *true*, then you can conclude that the **O**-proposition would be:

10. If an **E**-proposition is *false*, then you can conclude that the **A**-proposition would be:

11. If an **E**-proposition is *false*, then you can conclude that the **I**-proposition would be:

12. If an **E**-proposition is *false*, then you can conclude that the **O**-proposition would be:

⭐ 13. If an **I**-proposition is *true*, then you can conclude that the **A**-proposition would be:

14. If an **I**-proposition is *true*, then you can conclude that the **E**-proposition would be:

15. If an **I**-proposition is *true*, then you can conclude that the **O**-proposition would be:

16. If an **I**-proposition is *false*, then you can conclude that the **A**-proposition would be:

⭐ 17. If an **I**-proposition is *false*, then you can conclude that the **E**-proposition would be:

18. If an **I**-proposition is *false*, then you can conclude that the **O**-proposition would be:

19. If an **O**-proposition is *true*, then you can conclude that the **A**-proposition would be:

20. If an **O**-proposition is *true*, then you can conclude that the **E**-proposition would be:

⭐ 21. If an **O**-proposition is *true*, then you can conclude that the **I**-proposition would be:

22. If an **O**-proposition is *false*, then you can conclude that the **A**-proposition would be:

23. If an **O**-proposition is *false*, then you can conclude that the **E**-proposition would be:

24. If an **O**-proposition is *false*, then you can conclude that the **I**-proposition would be:

D. CONVERSION, OBVERSION, AND CONTRAPOSITION

The square of opposition is a surprisingly powerful tool. Consider next some special cases of immediate argument—and how we get from one to another.

Conversion

Conversion An immediate argument created by interchanging the subject and predicate terms of a given categorical proposition.

An immediate argument can be created by interchanging the subject and predicate terms of a given categorical proposition, a process called **conversion**. The proposition we start with is called the *convertend,* and it becomes the premise of the argument. The proposition we end up with after applying the process of conversion is called the *converse,* and it becomes the conclusion of the argument. For example, consider these two propositions:

Convertend:	**E**-proposition:	No beer commercials are subtle advertisements.
Converse:	**E**-proposition:	No subtle advertisements are beer commercials.

The second proposition can be validly inferred from the first. This can be understood if you recall that **E**-propositions completely separate the subject and predicate classes. So if no beer commercials are subtle advertisements, then of course no subtle advertisements can be beer commercials. The conversion works for **E**-propositions. The same idea holds true for **I**-propositions:

Convertend:	I-proposition:	Some textbooks are entertaining diversions.
Converse:	I-proposition:	Some entertaining diversions are textbooks.

Recall that **I**-propositions make the subject and predicate classes overlap to some degree; this means that if some textbooks are entertaining diversions, then, of course, some entertaining diversions must be textbooks. Therefore, conversion works for **I**-propositions.

Strictly speaking, conversion does not work for **A**-propositions. We can see this in the following example:

| Convertend: | **A**-proposition: | All spam e-mailings are invasions of your home. |
| Converse: | **A**-proposition: | All invasions of your home are spam e-mailings. |

Clearly, **A**-propositions cannot be directly converted. However, we can use what we know to make conversion work in a limited way. The idea of subalternation tells us that if an **A**-proposition is true, then its corresponding particular **I**-proposition is true, too. And since we already saw that conversion works for **I**-propositions, we can do something called **conversion by limitation.** Here we first change a universal **A**-proposition into its corresponding particular **I**-proposition, and then we use the process of conversion on the **I**-proposition. The process looks like this:

Convertend:	**A**-proposition:	All spam e-mailings are invasions of your home.
Corresponding particular:	**I**-proposition:	Some spam e-mailings are invasions of your home.
Converse:	**I**-proposition:	Some invasions of your home are spam e-mailings.

Conversion by limitation We first change a universal **A**-proposition into its corresponding particular **I**-proposition, and then we use the process of conversion on the **I**-proposition.

We have created a valid argument. The square of opposition enabled us to use subalternation to make conversion work for **A**-propositions.

The final type of proposition to consider for conversion is **O**-propositions. Let's look at this set of propositions.

| Convertend: | **O**-proposition: | Some vegetables are not carrots. |
| Converse: | **O**-proposition: | Some carrots are not vegetables. |

As we can plainly see, the conversion does not work for **O**-propositions. The premise is, of course, true because many vegetables, such as potatoes, celery, spinach, and so forth are certainly not carrots; but the conclusion is false: every carrot is indeed a vegetable.

THE METHOD OF CONVERSION	
Interchange the subject and predicate.	
Subject ◄————————► Predicate	
Convertend	**Converse**
A: All S are P.	**I:** Some P are S. *(by limiation)*
E: No S are P.	**E:** No P are S.
I: Some S are P.	**I:** Some P are S.
O: Some S are not P.	*(Conversion is not valid)*

Obversion

A second type of immediate argument is formed by (1) changing the quality of the given proposition and (2) by replacing the predicate term with its *complement*. The

Complement The set of objects that do not belong to a given class.

Obversion An immediate argument formed by changing the quality of the given proposition, and then replacing the predicate term with its complement.

complement is defined as the set of objects that do not belong to a given class. The complement of a given class is everything outside that given class, and, in this case, the complement is formed by attaching the prefix *non-* to the predicate term. This complete process is called **obversion**. The *obvertend* is the proposition we start with, so it becomes the premise of an immediate argument. The *obverse* is the proposition we wind up with, so it becomes the conclusion. Consider this pair of propositions:

| Obvertend: | **A**-proposition: | All jackhammers are weapons. |
| Obverse: | **E**-proposition: | No jackhammers are non-weapons. |

To get the obverse, we first had to change the quality, so we go from affirmative to negative (from **A** to **E**). Second, we had to replace the predicate term in the obverse with its complement ("weapons" becomes "non-weapons"). Although it may be difficult to see at first, you should agree that this is a valid immediate argument. If every jackhammer *is* a weapon, then it must be true that no jackhammer is a non-weapon.

The process of obversion is straightforward in that it is applicable to all four standard-form categorical propositions. The following immediate arguments are therefore valid:

Obvertend:	**E**-proposition:	No comedians are brain surgeons.
Obverse:	**A**-proposition:	All comedians are non-brain surgeons.
Obvertend:	**I**-proposition:	Some athletes are overpaid egoists.
Obverse:	**O**-proposition:	Some athletes are not non-overpaid egoists.
Obvertend:	**O**-proposition:	Some pets are not lovable animals.
Obverse:	**I**-proposition:	Some pets are non-lovable animals.

THE METHOD OF OBVERSION
Step 1: Change the *quality* of the given proposition.
Step 2: Replace the *predicate term* with its *complement*.

Obvertend	Obverse
A: All S are P.	**E**: No S are non-P.
E: No S are P.	**A**: All S are non-P.
I: Some S are P.	**O**: Some S are not non-P.
O: Some S are not P.	**I**: Some S are non-P.

Contraposition

Contraposition We replace the subject term of a given proposition with the complement of its predicate term, and then replace the predicate term of the given proposition with the complement of its subject term.

The final type of immediate argument to consider, **contraposition**, is formed by applying two steps: (1) switch the subject and predicate terms, and (2) replace both the subject and predicate terms with their term complements. This is illustrated in the next pair of propositions:

| Given proposition: | **A**-proposition: | All pencils are ink-free writing tools. |
| Contrapositive: | **A**-proposition: | All non-ink-free writing tools are non-pencils. |

The first proposition places every pencil in the class of ink-free writing tools. The *contrapositive* of this proposition claims that anything that is a non-ink-free writing tool is also a non-pencil, and surely this must be correct. So contraposition works for **A**-propositions.

Let's try a different pair of propositions:

Given proposition:	**O**-proposition:	Some hairy creatures are not cuddly things.
Contrapositive:	**O**-proposition:	Some non-cuddly things are not non-hairy creatures.

This may seem confusing, but let's take it apart very slowly. The first proposition says that at least one member of the class of hairy creatures is *not* in the class of cuddly things. The second proposition claims that at least one non-cuddly thing (something not in the class of cuddly things) is also *not* a non-hairy creature. But since, by definition, the class of non-hairy creatures is everything outside the class of hairy creatures, we can see that the phrase "are not non-hairy creatures" places us back within the class of hairy creatures. The argument is valid.

E-propositions are more problematic:

Given proposition:	**E**-proposition:	No gorillas are lions.
Contrapositive:	**E**-proposition:	No non-lions are non-gorillas.

Even if the first proposition is true, the second can still be false. This may be hard to see at first, but close analysis reveals the problem. The first proposition, if true, clearly separates the two classes, allowing no overlap between them. However, it does not tell us anything specific about what is *outside* those respective classes. And the second proposition specifically refers to the area outside the given classes—and what it says might be false. It claims that there is not even one thing outside the class of lions (non-lions) that is, at the same time, outside the class of gorillas (non-gorillas). But surely a banana is not a lion, and it is also not a gorilla. So clearly the contrapositive doesn't work here.

However, we can do something similar to what we did for **A**-propositions, and once again we rely on the square of opposition. Contraposition of **E**-propositions can be understood as valid if we use **contraposition by limitation**: subalternation is used to change the universal **E**-proposition into its corresponding particular **O**-proposition. We then apply the regular process of forming a contrapositive to this **O**-proposition. (We have already shown that this process works on **O**-propositions.) The completed process looks like this:

Contraposition by limitation
Subalternation is used to change a universal **E**-proposition into its corresponding particular **O**-proposition. We then apply the regular process of forming a contrapositive to this **O**-proposition.

Given proposition:	**E**-proposition:	No gorillas are lions.
Corresponding particular:	**O**-proposition:	Some gorillas are not lions.
Contrapositive:	**O**-proposition:	Some non-lions are not non-gorillas.

The square of opposition has thus enabled us to make contraposition work for **E**-propositions by again using subalternation.

The process involved in contraposition does not work for **I**-propositions (for reasons similar to why conversion did not work for **O**-propositions). Let's look at this set of propositions:

Given proposition:	**I**-proposition:	Some humans are non-registered voters.
Contrapositive:	**I**-proposition:	Some registered voters are non-humans.

The first proposition is true (some people fail to register to vote), but the second is clearly false. (We have reduced the phrase "*non-non*-registered voters" to simply "registered voters.") So contraposition does not yield valid immediate arguments for **I**-propositions.

THE METHOD OF CONTRAPOSITION	
Step 1: Switch the subject and predicate terms.	
Step 2: Replace both the subject and predicate terms with their term complements.	
Given Proposition	**Contrapositive**
A: All S are P.	**A**: All non-P are non-S.
E: No S are P.	**O**: Some non-P are not non-S. (*by limitation*)
I: Some S are P.	(*Contraposition is not valid*)
O: Some S are not P.	**O**: Some non-P are not non-S.

CHECK YOUR UNDERSTANDING 5D

For each of the following, provide the converse, obverse, and contrapositive of the given proposition. Also state whether any of the subsequent immediate arguments are not valid.

1. Some games of chance are sucker bets.
   A. Converse:
   B. Obverse:
   C. Contrapositive:

Answers:
   A. Converse: Some sucker bets are games of chance.
   B. Obverse: Some games of chance are not non-sucker bets.
   C. Contrapositive: Some non-sucker bets are non-games of chance. (Contraposition is not valid for **I**-propositions.)

2. Some sandwiches are not meaty things.
   A. Converse:
   B. Obverse:
   C. Contrapositive:

3. No bats are vegetarians.
   A. Converse:
   B. Obverse:
   C. Contrapositive:

4. All designer jeans are genetically engineered objects.
   A. Converse:
   B. Obverse:
   C. Contrapositive:

⭐ 5. No greedy politicians are people likely to go to prison.
   A. Converse:
   B. Obverse:
   C. Contrapositive:

6. Some fruitcakes are not regifted presents.
   A. Converse:
   B. Obverse:
   C. Contrapositive:

7. All embezzlers are social deviants.
   A. Converse:
   B. Obverse:
   C. Contrapositive:

8. Some traffic accidents are speeding incidents.
   A. Converse:
   B. Obverse:
   C. Contrapositive:

⭐ 9. All public holidays are days when banks close.
   A. Converse:
   B. Obverse:
   C. Contrapositive:

10. Some music videos are not tragedies.
   A. Converse:
   B. Obverse:
   C. Contrapositive:

11. Some T-bone steaks are juicy items.
   A. Converse:
   B. Obverse:
   C. Contrapositive:

12. Some fajitas are mouth-watering morsels.
   A. Converse:
   B. Obverse:
   C. Contrapositive:

⭐ 13. No ice cream toppings are diet-busters.
   A. Converse:
   B. Obverse:
   C. Contrapositive:

14. All yogurt products are healthy foods.
    A. Converse:
    B. Obverse:
    C. Contrapositive:

15. No vegetables are vitamin-deficient foods.
    A. Converse:
    B. Obverse:
    C. Contrapositive:

16. Some barbeque wings are spicy meals.
    A. Converse:
    B. Obverse:
    C. Contrapositive:

⭐ 17. All French fries are grease-laden products.
    A. Converse:
    B. Obverse:
    C. Contrapositive:

18. Some cheesecakes are sugar-free products.
    A. Converse:
    B. Obverse:
    C. Contrapositive:

19. All bananas are foods best eaten when ripe.
    A. Converse:
    B. Obverse:
    C. Contrapositive:

20. Some tofu products are delicious snacks.
    A. Converse:
    B. Obverse:
    C. Contrapositive:

⭐ 21. Some tattoos are great works of art.
    A. Converse:
    B. Obverse:
    C. Contrapositive:

22. Some modern clothes are not warm garments.
    A. Converse:
    B. Obverse:
    C. Contrapositive:

23. No swimming pools are easy-to-clean objects.
    A. Converse:
    B. Obverse:
    C. Contrapositive:

24. All movie theater drinks are artificially sweetened products.
    A. Converse:
    B. Obverse:
    C. Contrapositive:

⭐ 25. No good deeds are acts left unrewarded.
    A. Converse:
    B. Obverse:
    C. Contrapositive:

E. EXISTENTIAL IMPORT

When a categorical proposition refers to objects that actually exist, such as horses, it seems only natural to look at its truth value. But consider this proposition: "All unicorns are mammals." We can say the proposition is false because no unicorns actually exist. A proposition is said to have **existential import** if it presupposes the existence of certain kinds of objects. Its truth value therefore depends on whether a class is empty. Should it be assumed that *every* universal proposition has existential import? If the answer is *yes*, then the proposition "All unicorns are mammals" is false since no unicorns exist. Yet the stories we tell may say quite a bit about unicorns. At the very least, we are probably pretty sure that they are more like horses than toadstools or reptiles.

In an alternative way of interpreting universal categorical propositions, the **A**-proposition, "All scientists are people trained in mathematics," can be translated as "*If* a person is a scientist, *then* that person is trained in mathematics." The proposition "All unicorns are mammals" can then be translated as "*If* something is a unicorn, *then* that thing is a mammal."

Given this *modern* interpretation, the universal **E**-proposition "No slackers are reliable workers" can be translated as "*If* a person is a slacker, *then* that person is not a reliable worker." The modern interpretation sets aside questions concerning the existence of the objects referred to by the proposition. Therefore, no decision has to be made concerning the existence of members of a class (whether or not the class is empty). As we will soon see, the modern interpretation affects the square of opposition.

Unlike universal propositions, particular categorical propositions (**I** and **O**) are always understood as having existential import. Under the traditional system, we accept that **I**-propositions and **O**-propositions both assert that their respective classes are not empty: they have at least one member that exists. According to the traditional square of opposition, particular propositions follow validly from their corresponding universal propositions by subalternation. However, if this is correct, then the universal propositions must themselves have existential import, because a proposition with existential import cannot be derived from one that does not have it. For example, under the traditional square, the proposition "Some whales are mammals" follows validly from "All whales are mammals" by subalternation. This result requires that

Existential import
A proposition has existential import if it presupposes the existence of certain kinds of objects.

the universal proposition asserts the existence of whales—and that the *subject class is not empty*. This is precisely where the modern interpretation shifts the analysis. Under the traditional interpretation of universal propositions, we are required to determine whether or not the subject class denotes actually existing things. Adopting the modern view eliminates this requirement.

Let's explore some of the results of the modern interpretation. As you know, **A**-propositions and **O**-propositions are contradictories, which means that one must be true and the other false. Consider these two propositions:

A-proposition: All dragons are birds.
O-proposition: Some dragons are not birds.

We recognize that they are contradictories. But if they both are understood as asserting existential import (if they both assert that there are dragons), *then both propositions are false, if no dragons exist*. But if they could both be false, then they cannot be contradictories.

The traditional interpretation might be understood as requiring that all universal propositions must refer to classes that are not empty. But adopting this requirement has some unwanted consequences; we would have to eliminate many potentially good propositions from our vocabulary. For example, in the proposition "All future murderers will be executed," the subject class (*future murderers*) has no members; nevertheless, we think it is a perfectly good proposition. However, it would be eliminated from our vocabulary, if we adopt the new requirement. In addition, we often reason about *What if?* questions; in fact, as we'll see in Chapter 14, they are essential to science. Hypothetical reasoning and conjectures are acceptable ways of reasoning, and they work without necessarily presupposing the existence of anything. But again, these would be banned from discussion.

In line with what we learned earlier, if we have to decide an existence question, then we are not asking logical questions, but rather questions concerning truth value. The truth value of a proposition would then become part of the *logical* discussion, but this is what we took great pains to avoid. We have tried to maintain the idea that validity is a purely logical question.

Drawing on some ideas of George Boole, we can lay the groundwork for the modern square of opposition. First, we stipulate that both **I**-propositions and **O**-propositions have existential import, because both assert the existence of at least one entity. On the other hand, both **A**-propositions and **E**-propositions do not have existential import. As a direct consequence, we now have to eliminate the idea of subalternation, the cause of one of our early problems. If you recall, we had to do some fancy footwork to make conversion by limitation and contraposition by limitation work. That's because they relied on subalternation to make the arguments valid.

In the new square of opposition, **A-O** and **E-I** combinations will still be contradictories. However, the idea of subcontraries has to go. This is necessitated by the acknowledgment that both an **I**-proposition and an **O**-proposition could be false at the same time, provided the subject class is empty. In that case, both **E** and **A** would be true at the same time, since they are the contradictories of **I** and **O.** Therefore, the idea of contraries has to go, too.

F. THE MODERN SQUARE OF OPPOSITION

In order to flesh out the details of the new square of opposition, we have to introduce some symbolic notation. Since we are allowing a class to have no members, we will use a zero (0) to designate this possibility (this is sometimes referred to as an *empty set*). So, a class S that has no members is shown by the equation $S = 0$. On the other hand, a class S with at least one member is shown by the equation $S \neq 0$.

Since categorical propositions refer to two classes, we will need special notation to deal with the various combinations. If two classes, S and P, have some members in common, then this common membership will be called the *product*, or intersection, of the two classes; it is symbolized as SP. **E**-propositions claim that the product is empty, and thus are symbolized as $SP = 0$. Since our new square of opposition retains the idea of contradictories, **I**-propositions will be symbolized as $SP \neq 0$. In order to capture the intent of **A**- and **O**-propositions, we need to use a concept defined before, namely class complement, which is the class of all things *not* belonging to the original class. If the class of all milkshakes is designated by M, then its complement class would be everything that is *not* a milkshake, the class of all non-milkshakes, symbolized as $\overline{M}$.

A-propositions make the claim that every S is a P and are symbolized as $S\overline{P} = 0$. This notation is interpreted as claiming that there is no S outside the class of P. Since **A**-propositions and **O**-propositions are contradictories, **O**-propositions can be

symbolized as $S\overline{P} \neq 0$. This asserts that there is at least one member of S outside the class of P. Our new square reflects these additions:

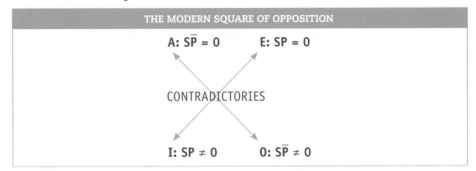

THE MODERN SQUARE OF OPPOSITION

A: $S\overline{P} = 0$ E: $SP = 0$

CONTRADICTORIES

I: $SP \neq 0$ O: $S\overline{P} \neq 0$

The square is now complete, but we still need to learn how to diagram our results. The idea is based on the work of John Venn, and representations of categorical proposition forms are called **Venn diagrams**. To begin, we can use a circle to represent a class:

Venn diagram Diagram that uses circles to represent categorical proposition forms.

The area inside the circle contains every member of a class of objects, such as the class of video games. Continuing with this example, the area outside the circle would contain everything that is not a video game. Since categorical propositions refer to the relationship between two classes, we will start by drawing two intersecting circles. The starting point for creating Venn diagrams for a categorical proposition looks like this:

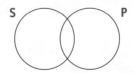

The area designating those members of S that are *not* members of P is the area symbolized by $S\overline{P}$:

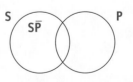

The area designating those members of P that are *not* members of S is the area symbolized by $\overline{S}P$:

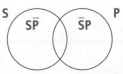

The area designating members of S that are at the same time members of P is symbolized as SP:

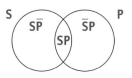

Finally, the area that designates where *no* members of either S or P can be found is symbolized as $\overline{SP}$:

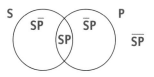

We are now ready to complete the diagrams for our four categorical propositions. First, to show that a class is empty (S = 0), we shade the circle completely, which indicates that it has no members:

Let's see how this works for a specific case. To diagram *All S are P*, we start with the basic diagram:

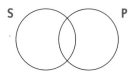

As discussed earlier, an **A**-proposition is to be understood as asserting "*If* something is an S, then it is also a P." Therefore, we need to shade any area of S that is outside of P. We do this by shading in the area designated $S\overline{P} = 0$:

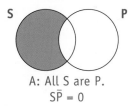

A: All S are P.
$S\overline{P} = 0$

At this point, we must be careful not to misinterpret the diagram. Although the area where S and P overlap is not shaded, this does not allow us to assert that the area has members. If you recall, universal categorical propositions are to be interpreted as not having existential import, so we must remain neutral about whether there are individuals in unshaded areas. Therefore, the diagram correctly represents the proposition *"If* something is an S, then it is also a P."

We can compare this result with a diagram for a particular categorical proposition. In order to show that a class has at least one member, we can place an X anywhere inside the circle:

To diagram *Some S are P*, we start with the basic Venn diagram:

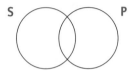

Since an **I**-proposition makes the claim that at least one member of S is a member of P, we need to place the X in the area where S and P overlap. The completed diagram will show that $SP \neq 0$:

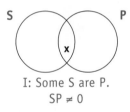

I: Some S are P.
$SP \neq 0$

Our two examples of Venn diagrams illustrate how universal and particular categorical propositions differ when it comes to existential import. Since we are interpreting universal propositions as not having existential import, we must remain neutral about whether there are individuals in the unshaded areas. On the other hand, since particular categorical propositions have existential import, an X indicates that at least one individual is in that area.

Here are the Venn diagrams of the four standard-form categorical propositions:

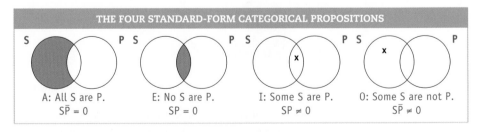

THE FOUR STANDARD-FORM CATEGORICAL PROPOSITIONS			
A: All S are P.	E: No S are P.	I: Some S are P.	O: Some S are not P.
$S\bar{P} = 0$	$SP = 0$	$SP \neq 0$	$S\bar{P} \neq 0$

G. CONVERSION, OBVERSION, AND CONTRAPOSITION REVISITED

Under Aristotle's system, it took some effort to properly grasp conversion, obversion, and contraposition. It was necessary to rely on an intuitive feel for the underlying complex logical apparatus at work. This new method makes the results more accessible, thanks to a diagram that anyone can inspect. Take the immediate arguments for conversion:

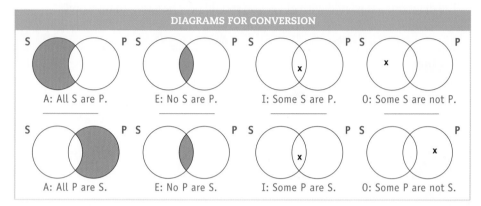

The lines separating the top and bottom diagrams can be understood as dividing the premise (above) from the conclusion (below) for the four immediate arguments. The diagrams for **E** and **I** verify that these two are valid arguments. Their validity rests on the visual equivalence of the two diagrams (the premise and conclusion of the **E** and **I** conversions). Since we can see that the premise and conclusion of both **E** and **I** conversions are logically equivalent propositions, it is easy to understand why these are valid arguments. After all, if the premise is true, the conclusion must be true, too.

The conversion for **O**-propositions does not work because the diagrams are not identical. Therefore, if the premise is true, the conclusion might be false. This also helps us to understand why conversion for **A**-propositions does not work.

We have one last major hurdle to overcome when trying to understand obversion and contraposition—the prefix *non*. Let's learn how to diagram the logic behind this prefix. Since we diagram the class designated by S as a circle, we can stipulate that everything outside that circle is non-S.

With two overlapping circles, S and P, there is more to annotate. We will number each area in order to make our references clear. In the diagram below,

- If something is in Area 1, then it is an S and a non-P.
- If something is in Area 2, then it is both an S and a P.

- If something is in Area 3, then it is a P and a non-S.
- If something is in Area 4, then it is both a non-S and a non-P.

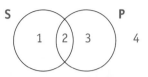

The diagrams associated with obversion should now be easier to interpret:

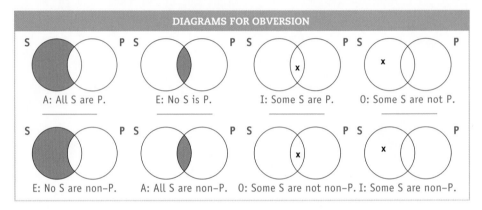

Visual inspection verifies that the premise and conclusion of each of the four immediate arguments are logically equivalent. Thus, obversion is valid for all four standard-form categorical propositions.

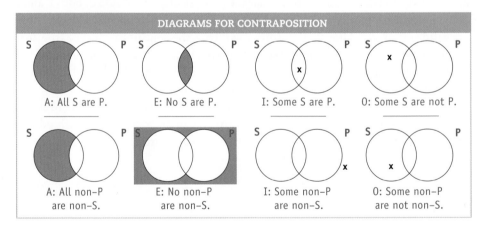

The diagrams illustrate why contraposition for **A**- and **O**-propositions produces valid immediate arguments. We can see right away the logical equivalence. We also see that contraposition produces invalid immediate arguments for both **E**- and **I**-propositions. At this point, it should be clear that contraposition by limitation for **E**-propositions cannot be justified: The two diagrams for **E**-propositions are not equivalent.

The need for a new square of opposition was fueled by the consequences of existential import. The modern square of opposition, along with the diagram technique, provides an alternative method of analysis of categorical propositions and categorical arguments.

CHECK YOUR UNDERSTANDING 5G

Reveal the form of the following categorical propositions, and draw Venn diagrams to represent the relationship.

1. Some snowmen are permanent lawn fixtures.

Answer: Let S = *snowmen*, and P = *permanent lawn fixtures*. Some S are P.

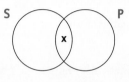

2. No leeches are lawyers.

3. Some television newscasters are good actors.

4. All donuts are fat-free snacks.

⭐ 5. All psychics are frauds.

6. Some children are not offspring following in their parents' footsteps.

7. No volcanoes are currently active geologic structures.

8. Some wrestling shows are scripted events.

⭐ 9. All teachers are miserable wretches.

10. Some poems are beautifully written works of literature.

11. Some viruses are not lethal organisms.

12. No Nobel laureates are Olympic champions.

⭐ 13. All sea creatures are bivalves.

14. Some rock stars are good parents.

15. All condiments are free items.

16. Some exotic vegetables are not edible products.

⭐ 17. Some scientific researchers are people with impeccable credentials.

18. No television commercials are events worthy of our attention.

19. All finely tuned instruments are noise emitters.

20. Some floppy disks are defective products.

⭐ 21. All French pastries are baked items.

22. Some cows are not flatulent animals.

23. No Nobel Prize winners are illiterate people.

24. Some swimmers are healthy athletes.

⭐ 25. All dogs are faithful pets.

26. No spiders are nocturnal creatures.

27. Some race car drivers are fearless competitors.

28. Some college textbooks are works of art.

⭐ 29. All teachers are inspired orators.

30. Some games of chance are sucker bets.

31. Some sandwiches are meatless foods.

32. No bats are vegetarians.

⭐ 33. All designer jeans are genetically engineered objects.

34. No greedy politicians are people likely to go to prison.

35. Some fruitcakes are not regifted presents.

36. All embezzlers are social deviants.

⭐ 37. Some traffic accidents are speeding incidents.

38. All public holidays are days when banks close.

39. Some music videos are not tragedies.

40. Some fajitas are mouth-watering morsels.

⭐ 41. No ice cream toppings are diet-friendly products.

42. All yogurt products are healthy foods.

43. No vegetables are vitamin-deficient produce.

44. Some barbeque wings are undercooked meat.

⭐ 45. All French fries are grease-laden spuds.

H. VENN DIAGRAMS AND THE TRADITIONAL SQUARE

We can modify the way we have been drawing Venn diagrams to accommodate the traditional interpretation of universal categorical propositions as well. A full analysis of an immediate argument under the traditional interpretation requires determining whether the subject class denotes actually existing objects. Therefore, we need to introduce a new symbol to represent what we will call the "Assumption of Existence." This term is appropriate because this new symbol will be used for diagramming **A**- and **E**-propositions. The symbol will be a red X surrounded by a red circle. Here are the new diagrams:

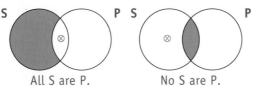

All S are P.   No S are P.

Remember that the new symbol is used to indicate the *assumption of existence*. It therefore functions differently from the X in particular **I**- and **O**-propositions. For an **A**-proposition, if there are any members of S, then they will be in the area where S and P overlap. For an **E**-proposition, if there are any members of S, then they will be in the area of S that is unshaded.

The diagrams for the particular categorical propositions (**I** and **O**) do not need to be changed.

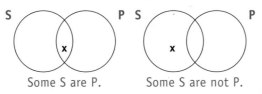

Some S are P.   Some S are not P.

Now let's look at an immediate argument and see how the two interpretations proceed.

> All perpetual motion machines are patented inventions. Therefore, some perpetual motion machines are patented inventions.

Using the modern interpretation we start by drawing a Venn diagram of the premise.

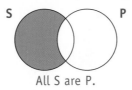

All S are P.

Next, we check to see if the conclusion is necessarily true. Since the conclusion is an **I**-proposition, in order for it to be true there would have to be an X in the area where S and P overlap. But as we can see, there is none. Since the truth of the premise does not guarantee the truth of the conclusion, this is an invalid argument under the modern interpretation.

Now we will use the traditional interpretation. We once again start by drawing a Venn diagram of the premise.

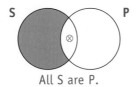

All S are P.

Next, we check to see if the conclusion is necessarily true. Since the conclusion is an **I**-proposition, in order for it to be true there would have to be an X in the area where S and P overlap. As we can see, the assumption of existence symbol (the red circled X) is in the area. This is where we need to go one further step. We need to see if the red circled X represents something that actually exists. Since the "S" stands for *perpetual motion machines*, we need to determine if any actually exist. In fact, a perpetual motion machine is a purely hypothetical concept. The machine would have to produce more work or energy than it consumes, and this violates the laws of physics. Therefore, the assumption of existence symbol does not represent anything that actually exists, and the argument is invalid under the traditional interpretation.

Let's examine another argument:

> All improvised explosive devices are unconventional military weapons. Therefore, some improvised explosive devices are unconventional military weapons.

Using the modern interpretation we start by drawing a Venn diagram of the premise:

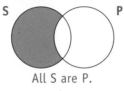

All S are P.

Next, we check to see if the conclusion is necessarily true. Since the conclusion is an **I**-proposition, in order for it to be true there would have to be an X in the area where S and P overlap. But as we can see, there is none. Since the truth of the premise does not guarantee the truth of the conclusion, this is an invalid argument under the modern interpretation.

Now we will use the traditional interpretation. We once again start by drawing a Venn diagram of the premise:

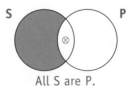

All S are P.

Next, we check to see if the conclusion is necessarily true. Since the conclusion is an **I**-proposition, in order for it to be true there would have to be an X in the area where S and P overlap. As we can see, the red circled X is in the area. Once again, we now need to go one further step. We need to see if the symbol represents something that actually exists. Since the "S" stands for *improvised explosive devices*, we need to determine if any actually exist. In fact, they are a large part of modern warfare. Given this determination, the assumption of existence symbol does represent something that actually exists. Therefore, the argument is valid under the traditional interpretation.

As we can see, the major difference between the traditional and modern interpretations of universal categorical propositions is in the area of existential import. For some logicians, determining whether or not a class is empty allows some useful arguments to be valid that would otherwise be invalid under the modern interpretation. (The foregoing argument regarding improvised explosive devices is just one example.) However, other logicians regard validity as a purely formal question. To this way of thinking, the need to determine whether members of a class of objects exist adds another layer of analysis to an argument. This topic will come up again in the next chapter, when we explore categorical syllogisms, and we will have more opportunity to see how the two interpretations differ.

CHECK YOUR UNDERSTANDING 5H

Draw Venn diagrams for the following immediate arguments. Determine whether the arguments are valid or invalid using both the modern and traditional interpretations.

1. No fashion models are camera-shy people. Therefore, some fashion models are not camera-shy people.

Answer: The premise is an **E**-proposition. First, we draw the Venn diagram under the modern interpretation:

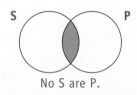

No S are P.

Next, we check to see if the conclusion is necessarily true. Since the conclusion is an **O**-proposition, in order for it to be true there would have to be an X in the unshaded area of S. But as we can see, there is none. Since the truth of the premise does not guarantee the truth of the conclusion, this is an invalid argument under the modern interpretation.

Now we will use the traditional interpretation. We once again start by drawing a Venn diagram of the premise:

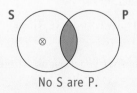

No S are P.

Next, we check to see if the conclusion is necessarily true. Since the conclusion is an **O**-proposition, in order for it to be true there would have to be an X in the unshaded area of S. As we can see, the assumption of existence symbol (the red circled X) is in the area. Now we need to see if the red circled X represents something that actually exists. Since the "S" stands for *fashion models*, and they surely exist, the assumption of existence symbol does represent something that actually exists. Therefore, the argument is valid under the traditional interpretation.

2. All cruise ships are romantic locations. Therefore, some cruise ships are romantic locations.

3. No centaurs are gentle creatures. Therefore, all centaurs are gentle creatures.

4. Some leprechauns are mischievous people. Therefore, no leprechauns are mischievous people.

★ 5. No former presidents of the United States are great-grandfathers. Therefore, some former presidents of the United States are great-grandfathers.

6. All former Soviet premiers are members of the KGB. Therefore, some former Soviet premiers are not members of the KGB.

7. Some used-car salespersons are honest people. Therefore, all used-car salespersons are honest people.

8. Some bank loans are low-interest loans. Therefore, some bank loans are not low-interest loans.

★ 9. Some used books are not high-priced items. Therefore, some used books are high-priced items.

10. All credit card billing statements are complex items. Therefore, some credit card billing statements are complex items.

11. Some text messages are not interesting pieces of writing. Therefore, some text messages are interesting pieces of writing.

12. All dogs are social animals. Therefore, some dogs are social animals.

★ 13. All soft drinks are acid-based beverages. Therefore, no soft drinks are acid-based beverages.

14. No batteries are perfectly efficient devices. Therefore, some batteries are perfectly efficient devices.

15. All patented inventions are physical machines. Therefore, some patented inventions are not physical machines.

16. Some sales items are defective products. Therefore, all sales items are defective products.

★ 17. All abominable snowmen are vegetarians. Therefore, some abominable snowmen are vegetarians.

18. Some canaries are not yellow birds. Therefore, all canaries are yellow birds.

19. All bathing suits are lightweight clothes. Therefore, some bathing suits are lightweight clothes.

20. Some phone apps are not expensive items. Therefore, some phone apps are expensive items.

I. TRANSLATING ORDINARY LANGUAGE INTO CATEGORICAL PROPOSITIONS

Categorical propositions can be found in everyday life. Here is one example:

> Some football coaches are persons of character who always put their players' health first.   Gregg Easterbrook, "Concussion Hazards Must Be Addressed"

We have already seen how logic can help us make sense of the claims all around us—but first we need to be able to paraphrase statements in ordinary language. As we are all aware, ordinary language statements can be subject to differing interpretations. If you recall from Chapter 3, sometimes missing information requires us to reconstruct arguments based on our understanding of the context. If we can translate an ordinary language statement into a standard-form categorical proposition, then we can reduce the possibility of ambiguity. A correct translation does this by clearly formulating the subject and predicate terms, the quantity (universal or particular), and the quality (affirmative or negative).

Any translation starts with an analysis of the meaning of the ordinary language. Once we are satisfied that we understand the statement, we then construct the appropriate categorical proposition. This requires deciding on the correct quantifier (*all, no, some*), the subject term, the copula (*are, are not*), and the predicate term. Since ordinary language contains an unlimited number of possible statements, we will concentrate on a few of the types that you are most likely to encounter.

Missing Plural Nouns

Consider the following statement:

> Some alcoholics are convicts.

This is a standard-form categorical proposition and contains the terms "alcoholics" and "convicts." Each of these terms is a plural noun, and each denotes a class of objects. (A *noun* is a word or group of words that refers to a person, place, or thing.) If we switch the position of the two terms, the result is again a perfectly acceptable standard-form categorical proposition:

> Some convicts are alcoholics.

Now consider a second statement:

> Some political parties are disorganized.

Most people would have little difficulty understanding this example. On the surface, it appears to be a standard-form categorical proposition. But this is deceiving. Let's see what happens if we switch the position of the two terms:

> Some disorganized are political parties.

We no longer have an acceptable statement. The problem is that the word "disorganized" is an *adjective*, not a noun. Adjectives are used to modify nouns, and they cannot normally stand alone. Although the original statement is acceptable as far as ordinary language is concerned, in order to translate it into a standard-form categorical proposition, we have to add a plural noun, so that the resulting term will denote a class. For example:

> Some political parties are disorganized groups.

The term "disorganized groups" denotes a class of objects. If we now switch the terms, we get this result:

> Some disorganized groups are political parties.

When you translate ordinary language statements into standard-form categorical propositions, always make sure that the subject and predicate terms contain plural nouns.

Nonstandard Verbs

As we have seen in this chapter, standard-form categorical propositions use two forms of the verb "to be"—"are" and "are not." The copula is needed to connect the subject and predicate terms; it is a linking verb. However, many ordinary language statements use other forms of the verb "to be." For a regular verb, the past tense is typically formed by adding an "-ed" ending (e.g., "talk," "talked"). But the verb "to be" is an irregular verb, which means that different tenses do not follow general rules. In fact, "to be" is considered by many language experts to be the most irregular verb in the English language. Here are a few of the forms that it takes: *is, are, was, being, been, be, will (be), would (be),* and *were.* This means that many everyday examples of ordinary language statements contain verbs that must be translated into either "are" or "are not."

Here are some examples:

Ordinary Language Statement:
All the protesters at the convention were arrested.

Standard-Form Translation:
All the protesters at the convention are people who were arrested.

Ordinary Language Statement:
Some students would prefer to cheat rather than learn the material.

Standard-Form Translation:
Some students are people who would prefer to cheat rather than learn the material.

Ordinary Language Statement:
Trespassers will be prosecuted.

Standard-Form Translation:
All trespassers are people who will face prosecution.

As these examples illustrate, you must be careful to translate the verb into either "are" or "are not," and you must make sure that translation contains terms that denote classes.

Many ordinary language statements do not use any form of the verb "to be." In these cases you have to look closely to grasp the meaning of the statement. Here are some examples:

Ordinary Language Statement:
Some assembly required.

Standard-Form Translation:
Some parts of this item are parts that need assembling.

Ordinary Language Statement:
No pain, no gain.

Standard-Form Translation:
No exercise routines without physical pain are exercise routines offering physical gain.

Even short sentences in ordinary language can be misunderstood. The tradeoff of creating translations that are lengthy and repetitive is that they offer clarity, as we shall see again in the next chapter.

Singular Propositions

The examples so far have contained plural nouns denoting classes, but it is possible that a class has only one object. These cases occur in ordinary language when the proposition is **singular** in nature; that is, something is asserted about a specific person, place, or thing. A singular proposition can normally be translated into a universal proposition. Here is one example:

> **Singular proposition** A proposition that asserts something about a specific person, place, or thing.

Ordinary Language Statement:
Al Gore is a Nobel Prize winner.

Standard-Form Translation:
All persons identical to Al Gore are persons who have won a Nobel Prize.

The phrase "persons identical to Al Gore" may seem odd, but there is a reason for it. Since the subject is a single individual (Al Gore), the subject term of the translation must designate a class of objects which happens to have exactly one member. There is only one person identical to Al Gore, and that is Al Gore himself. So, the phrase "persons identical to Al Gore" refers to a class of objects that has exactly one member.

The phrase "persons identical to" is called a *parameter*. A parameter must accurately represent the intended meaning of an ordinary language statement, while at the same time transforming it into a standard-form categorical proposition. Here are some parameters that you can use to translate singular propositions:

persons identical to	places identical to
things identical to	events identical to
times identical to	cases identical to

Always remember that a singular proposition refers to a *specific* person (place, thing, etc). Given this, the phrase "identical to" is to be taken literally. There is only one Eiffel

Tower, and it is in Paris. If you go to Las Vegas, you will see a structure that looks *very much like* the Eiffel Tower (at one-third the size), but there is only one tower *identical* to the Eiffel Tower.

Here are some more singular propositions in ordinary language and their translations:

Ordinary Language Statement:
Shane is good at DDR (*DanceDanceRevolution*).

Standard-Form Translation:
All persons identical to Shane are persons good at DDR (*DanceDanceRevolution*).

Ordinary Language Statement:
Hugo did not go to Hawaii last spring break.

Standard-Form Translation:
No persons identical to Hugo are persons who went to Hawaii last spring break.

Ordinary Language Statement:
My car is in Joe's garage for repairs.

Standard-Form Translation:
All things identical to my car are things in Joe's garage for repairs.

Ordinary Language Statement:
Leo was ill last night.

Standard-Form Translation:
All times identical to last night are times that Leo was ill.

Parameters are used when translating singular propositions. They are not needed when the ordinary language statement has plural nouns.

Adverbs and Pronouns

Some ordinary language statements contain adverbs that describe places or times. For example, in the statement "Wherever there is smoke there is fire," the word "wherever" is a *spatial* adverb. Spatial adverbs describe where something happens. Here are some spatial adverbs: *wherever, everywhere, anywhere, somewhere, nowhere, upstairs,* and *underground.*

In the statement "Whenever you are audited by the IRS, you had better get legal help," the word "whenever" is a *temporal* adverb. Temporal adverbs describe when something happens. Here are some temporal adverbs: *whenever, never, always, anytime, yesterday,* and *tomorrow.*

Translating ordinary language statements into standard-form categorical propositions using these kinds of adverbs is relatively straightforward:

Ordinary Language Statement:
Wherever there is smoke, there is fire.

Standard-Form Translation:
All places that have smoke are places that have fire.

Ordinary Language Statement:
Whenever you are audited by the IRS, you should get legal help.

Standard-Form Translation:
All times you are audited by the IRS are times that you should get legal help.

Pronouns are often used to replace nouns that are unspecified. Some ordinary language statements contain pronouns that describe unspecified persons. For example, in the statement "Whoever took my laptop is in big trouble," the pronoun "whoever" refers to an unspecified person (or persons). Here are some pronouns referring to persons: *whoever, anyone, anybody, everyone, no one,* and *someone.* In the statement "What goes around comes around," the pronoun "what" refers to an unspecified thing (or things). Here are some pronouns referring to things: *what, whatever, anything, something,* and *everything.*

Here are translations of the last two examples:

Ordinary Language Statement:
Whoever took my laptop is in big trouble.

Standard-Form Translation:
All persons who took my laptop are persons in big trouble.

Ordinary Language Statement:
What goes around comes around.

Standard-Form Translation:
All things that go around are things that come around.

"It Is False That . . ."

Suppose you hear the following statement: "Every professional athlete uses steroids." This can be translated as the **A**-proposition "All professional athletes are people who use steroids." Now if you happen to believe that the proposition is false, you can say, "It is false that every professional athlete uses steroids." What your statement does is to *negate* (or deny) the original statement. Since your statement is the contradictory of an **A**-proposition, it gets translated as an **O**-proposition: "Some professional athletes are not people who use steroids."

Since **E**- and **I**-propositions are contradictory, creating a negation works much the same way. For example, the statement "It is not the case that some rapes are forgivable" gets translated as an **E**-proposition: "No rapes are forgivable acts." The phrase "It is not the case" negates the translated **I**-proposition "Some rapes are forgivable acts."

Here are some useful negation phrases:

It is false that . . .
It is not the case that . . .
It is not true that . . .

Remember that all three of these phrases negate the statement following it. If what follows the negation phrase is an **A**-proposition, then the translation results in an **O**-proposition, and vice versa. On the other hand, if what follows the negation phrase is an **E**-proposition, then the translation results in an **I**-proposition, and vice versa.

Implied Quantifiers

As we saw in Chapter 3, some statements in ordinary language imply something without actually saying it. Important terms are either left out on purpose or simply overlooked. In these cases we have to supply the missing terms. If the missing term is a quantifier word (*all*, *no*, *some*), then our translation into a standard-form categorical proposition must rely on a close reading of the intended meaning. Here is one example:

Sharks are predators.

The statement connects a species of animals (*sharks*) with a specific characteristic (*being a predator*). As such, it refers to the entire subject class and can be translated as follows:

All sharks are predators.

Now let's look at another example that uses the same subject (sharks):

There are sharks in the local aquarium.

It is unlikely that the person making the assertion is claiming that the entire class of sharks is in the local aquarium. Therefore, our translation will have to use the quantifier "some":

Some sharks are animals in the local aquarium.

We had to add the word "animals" because the phrase "in the local aquarium" would not by itself designate a class of objects.

How would you translate the next statement?

A professor is a human being.

Although the statement contains the phrase "a professor," it appears likely that the assertion is about every professor. It can therefore be translated as follows:

All professors are human beings.

What about this example?

A professor is not a machine.

This statement also refers to every professor, but it contains the word "not." It is tempting to translate the statement as follows:

All professors are not machines.   *Incorrect*

The correct form of a universal affirmative categorical proposition is *All S are P*, so we cannot add the word "not" using this form. The universal negative form solves our problem:

No professors are machines.   *Correct*

Here is one more example to consider:

A professor won the Nobel Prize.

This statement also contains the phrase "a professor" but it is unlikely that it is meant to refer to every professor. It can be translated as follows:

Some professors are winners of the Nobel Prize.

Earlier we had to make the subject term a plural noun in order for it to designate a class. Of course, if a specific professor had been named (e.g., Professor Blake), then we would have used the information regarding singular propositions to get the correct translation.

Now try a more complex example:

We will not be able to finish all the costumes by 5:00.

A quick reading might suggest that the quantifier word "all" means that this should be translated as a universal affirmative proposition. However, the word "not" indicates negation. Combining these two words gives us the phrase "not all." It is unlikely that the speaker is claiming that no costumes will be finished by 5:00. (If this had been intended, then we would expect the statement to be "We will not be able to finish *any* costume by 5:00.") Therefore, the correct quantifier is "some," and the translated statement must include the word "not":

Some costumes are not costumes that will be finished by 5:00.

This example illustrates why ordinary language statements often require a careful reading in order to understand the meaning and to arrive at a correct translation.

Nonstandard Quantifiers

Ordinary language statements might contain quantifiers that are nonstandard, because they are not one of the following: *all*, *no*, or *some*. Here is an example:

Not every investment banker is a crook.

In this statement the nonstandard quantifier "not every" probably means at least one investment banker is not a crook. Given this interpretation, the translation would be the following:

Some investment bankers are not crooks.

Notice that we once again had to change the subject and predicate terms into plural nouns.

Here are some nonstandard quantifiers: *any, many, most, a few, one, several,* and *not every.* Let's take one from the list and look at another example:

Not every novel about romance is interesting.

In this statement the nonstandard quantifier "not every" means that there are some novels about romance that are not interesting. Given this interpretation, the translation would be the following:

Some novels about romance are not interesting novels.

Here is another statement in ordinary language that uses a nonstandard quantifier:

A few movies at the mall are worth watching.

Here the quantifier "a few" is likely to mean that at least one movie at the mall is worth watching. The translation would be the following:

Some movies at the mall are movies worth watching.

Since the phrase "worth watching" does not by itself designate a class, we had to add the term "movies" to it.

Conditional Statements

We have already encountered conditional statements when we looked at existential import. The **A**-proposition "All scientists are people trained in mathematics" can be translated as "*If* a person is a scientist, *then* that person is trained in mathematics." The **E**-proposition "No slackers are reliable workers" can be translated as "*If* a person is a slacker, *then* that person is not a reliable worker." These translations are a result of the Boolean interpretation of universal categorical propositions.

As you might know from Chapter 3, the part of the conditional statement that follows the word "if" is called the *antecedent*, and the part that follows the word "then" is called the *consequent*. Here are some simple examples:

Ordinary Language Statement:
If a person has $10 in her checking account, then she is not rich.

Standard-Form Translation:
No persons having $10 in their checking account are rich persons.

Ordinary Language Statement:
If a salesperson calls on the phone, then I just hang up.

Standard-Form Translation:
All calls from salespersons are calls where I hang up.

Sometimes ordinary language statements do not have the word "if" at the beginning. When this occurs, we simply reposition the appropriate part so the antecedent comes first:

Ordinary Language Statement:
Pizza is a healthy meal if it has vegetable toppings.

Standard-Form Translation:
All pizzas with vegetable toppings are healthy meals.

Ordinary Language Statement:
A dog is not dangerous if it has been well-trained.

Standard-Form Translation:
No well-trained dogs are dangerous animals.

The conditional statement "If your cup of coffee is not perfect, then you are not drinking a cup of Bigbucks coffee" poses a new kind of problem for translation. To assist us, we need to introduce *transposition*. This rule is a two-step procedure. First, we switch the positions of the antecedent and the consequent, and second, we negate both of them. Let's work through it step by step and make any additional changes in wording as we go to capture the meaning of the statement:

First Step:
If you are not drinking a cup of Bigbucks coffee, then your cup of coffee is not perfect.

Second Step:
If you are drinking a cup of Bigbucks coffee, then your cup of coffee is perfect.

Final Translation:
All cups of Bigbucks coffee are perfect cups of coffee.

Now let's look at an example that is a little more challenging. The conditional statement "If murderers do not get punished, then they do not stop their behavior" requires a bit of rewriting to capture the meaning in standard-form categorical proposition. As before, we will take it step by step and apply the rule of transposition:

First Step:
If murderers do not stop their behavior, then murderers do not get punished.

Second Step:
If murderers stop their behavior, then murderers get punished.

Final Translation:
All murderers who have stopped their behavior are murderers who have been punished.

In order to translate the statement "A citizen cannot be president unless the citizen is at least 35 years old," we need to understand how the word "unless" gets translated. In most statements, the word "unless" means "if not." Substituting this into the original statement gives us this result: "A citizen cannot be president if the citizen is not at least 35 years old." Next, we can place the antecedent at the beginning of the statement: "If the citizen is not at least 35 years old, then a citizen cannot be president." We are now in a position to apply the two-step rule of transposition:

If a citizen can be president, then the citizen is at least 35 years old.

The last step completes the translation into a standard-form categorical proposition:

All citizens that can be president are citizens at least 35 years old.

Exclusive Propositions

Suppose you hear this announcement over a loudspeaker:

Only persons with tickets can enter the arena.

The announcement means that admission into the arena is limited to those holding tickets. Therefore, anyone who does not have a ticket is *excluded* from entering the arena, and we call this an *exclusive proposition*. Another way of saying this is "If a person does not have a ticket, then that person cannot enter the arena." Applying transposition to this statement, we get:

> If a person can enter the arena, then that person has a ticket.

This statement can now be translated into a standard-form categorical proposition:

> All persons who can enter the arena are persons that have tickets.

Here are some other words that indicate an exclusive proposition: *none but, solely, alone,* and *none except.* Let's take the first one from the list and analyze a statement that contains the words "none but":

> None but students can see the movie for free.

According to the statement, anyone who is not a student is excluded from seeing the movie for free. This can be rewritten as "If a person is not a student, then that person cannot see the movie for free." Applying transposition to this statement we get:

> If a person can see the movie for free, then that person is a student.

This statement can now be translated into a standard-form categorical proposition:

> All persons who can see the movie for free are students.

Some ordinary language statements do not have the exclusive term at the beginning. For example, "Lottery winners get lucky only once in their lives." In these cases, we have to rewrite the terms in order to designate the correct classes:

> All lottery winners are persons who get lucky once in their lives.

"The Only"

Although the words "only" and "the only" seem very much alike, they sometimes require different kinds of translations. For example, the statement "The only true friends are people who want nothing from you" can be directly translated as "All true friends are people who want nothing from you." However, if the words "the only" occurs in a different part of a statement, then you rewrite the statement by placing it and the phrase following it at the beginning. Here is an example:

> Android phones are the only phones imported by her company.

The first step is to put "the only" phrase at the beginning: "The only phones imported by her company are Android phones." The final step is the translation into a standard-form categorical proposition:

> All phones imported by her company are Android phones.

Propositions Requiring Two Translations

The examples so far could be translated as single statements. However, some statements need to be translated into *compound* statements, containing the word "and." For example, propositions that take the form "All except S are P" and "All but S are P" are called *exceptive propositions.* Here is one exceptive proposition: "All except those under

21 are allowed to gamble in Las Vegas." The meaning of the statement is quite clear: If you are under 21 you cannot gamble, and if you are 21 or older you can. In other words, the statement relates the predicate to both the class designated by subject term *and* to its complement. Hence the complete translation will result in a compound statement:

> No under-21 persons are persons allowed to gamble in Las Vegas, and all non-under-21 persons are persons allowed to gamble in Las Vegas.

Here is another example:

> Everyone but gamblers sleep well at night.

Translation:

> No gamblers are people who sleep well at night, and all non-gamblers are people who sleep well at night.

Knowing the context in which ordinary language statements occur can help in making correct translations. When we have a conversation, we can ask questions to clear up any ambiguity. This option is obviously not available when we are reading something and the author is not present. When in doubt, it is better to do more than less. In other words, if there are two reasonable interpretations of the meaning of a statement, then you had best work out the details of both. For example, suppose you read the following: "The heavy snowfall affected the turnout. Few registered voters went to the polls today." Clearly, some registered voters went to the polls and some didn't. This can be translated as a compound statement:

> Some registered voters are persons who went to the polls today, and some registered voters are not persons who went to the polls today.

Earlier, the nonstandard quantifier "a few" was translated as a single **I**-proposition. ("A few movies at the mall are worth watching" was translated as "Some movies at the mall are movies worth watching.") However, sometimes "a few" should be translated as a compound statement. Again, the context is your best guide to which translation is appropriate.

Sometimes we should translate an exclusive proposition containing "only" as a compound statement. For example, the statement "Only Carly designed the wedding gown" makes two assertions. First, Carly designed the wedding gown, and second, no one else did. Also, since the statement asserts something about a specific person (an individual), our translation has to take that into account:

> All persons identical to Carly are persons who designed the wedding gown, and all persons who designed the wedding gown are persons identical to Carly.

We get the same results for the statement "The only person who designed the wedding gown is Carly." In this case, the statement is equivalent to "Only Carly designed the wedding gown," and therefore, it gets the same translation.

Here is one more example:

> Barack Obama alone is the forty-fourth president of the United States.

This example contains two references. The first is to an individual (Barack Obama), and the second is to an elected office. We can translate the statement as follows:

> All persons identical to Barack Obama are persons identical to the forty-fourth president of the United States, and all persons identical to the forty-fourth president of the United States are persons identical to Barack Obama.

Translations into standard-form categorical propositions often require close and careful reading, but the effort pays off by reducing the chance of misunderstanding. It makes us aware of the many possible ambiguities in ordinary language, and it makes our spoken and written communication more precise.

CHECK YOUR UNDERSTANDING 5I

Translate the following ordinary language statements into standard-form categorical propositions.

1. An apple is in the refrigerator.

Answer: Some apples are items in the refrigerator.

Although the statement is referring to a particular apple, the use of "some" is appropriate in this translation because it has been stipulated that it means "at least one."

2. Any medical doctor is well-educated.

3. No insects sing.

4. A flower is a plant.

★ 5. All happy people dance.

6. Some bears hibernate.

7. Some cars don't pollute.

8. A mango is not a vegetable.

★ 9. It is not the case that every novel is a satire.

10. Every office worker is under pressure to perform.

11. A tsunami is dangerous.

12. Some people don't jaywalk.

★ 13. Not every final exam in calculus is a challenging test.

14. Every opera is easy to understand.

15. Not every dog is friendly.

16. Any company that introduces green technology will succeed.

★ 17. Young children are not protected from the dangers of war.

18. Ocean levels rise whenever glaciers melt.

19. Styrofoam is 98% air.

20. Not all accidents are preventable.

⭐ 21. Every video game company hires game-testers.

22. If it's all right with you, then it's all right with me.

23. A movie that depicts courage will inspire courage.

24. No good deed goes unpunished.

⭐ 25. Those who laugh last, laugh best.

26. Underpaid workers do not expect promotions.

27. None but novelists are wordsmiths.

28. A full house always beats a flush.

⭐ 29. Marie Curie is the only person to win Nobel Prizes in two different sciences.

30. A few spices are imported.

31. The people on the FBI's ten most wanted list are dangerous criminals.

32. Asteroids are the only threats to our existence on Earth.

⭐ 33. There is a diamond mine in California.

34. If you play with fire, you will get burned.

35. It is not true that all aerobic exercises are strenuous activities.

36. Barometers are devices for measuring atmospheric pressure.

⭐ 37. The best intentions are not defeated.

38. The Super Bowl is always the highest rated sporting event.

39. You cannot master a skill unless you practice for 10,000 hours.

40. People get depressed whenever tragedy strikes.

⭐ 41. If a religion isn't certified by the government, then it isn't legitimate.

42. All but the most loyal left the stadium.

43. A speeding violation is serious if the fine is more than $100.

44. Katharine Hepburn alone has four Academy Award best actress wins.

⭐ 45. Unless you pay your electric bill, you cannot get electricity in your apartment.

46. Whoever leaves a child in a car unattended will be arrested.

47. All vegetables except onions taste sweet.

48. Few cast members showed up for rehearsal today.

⭐ 49. Orangutans are native to Borneo.

50. If you are a credit card holder, then you are subjected to hidden charges.

51. Not all soap operas are boring.

52. Magicians are the only people capable of keeping a secret.

★ 53. Whatever improvement is made to the gas engine decreases our need for oil.

54. Beauty is not skin deep.

55. A practical joke is not funny if it harms someone.

56. All sharks hunt.

★ 57. Some people don't bowl.

58. Not every computer is expensive.

59. Most smokers wish they could quit.

60. All good things must come to an end.

★ 61. Beliefs worth having must withstand doubt.

62. If something is worth having, then it's worth struggling for.

63. Fair-weather friends are not trustworthy.

64. Not all that glitters is gold.

★ 65. Every ending is a new beginning.

66. Whoever saves even one life saves the entire world.

67. The enemy of my enemy is my friend.

68. Everything old is new again.

★ 69. It is false that people over 30 years of age are not to be trusted.

70. Two snowflakes are never the same.

71. Whoever controls the media, controls the mind.
    Jim Morrison, quoted in *Telling It Like It Is* by Paul Bowden

72. Every unhappy family is unhappy in its own way.   Leo Tolstoy, *Anna Karenina*

★ 73. Whoever is winning at the moment will always seem to be invincible.
    George Orwell, *The Orwell Reader*

74. If you tell the truth, you don't have to remember anything.
    Mark Twain, *Notebook*

75. Whoever undertakes to set himself up as a judge in Truth and Knowledge is shipwrecked by the laughter of the gods.
    Albert Einstein, quoted in *The Princeton Companion to Mathematics*

Summary

- Class: A group of objects.
- Categorical proposition: Relates two classes of objects.
- Subject term: The term that comes first in a standard-form categorical proposition.
- Predicate term: The term that comes second in a standard-form categorical proposition.
- **A**-proposition: Asserts that the entire subject class is included in the predicate class ("All S are P").
- **I**-proposition: Asserts that part of the subject class is included in the predicate class ("Some S are P").
- **E**-proposition: Asserts that the entire subject class is excluded from the predicate class ("No S are P").
- **O**-proposition: Asserts that part of the subject class is excluded from the predicate class ("Some S are not P").
- "Universal" and "particular" refer to the quantity of a categorical proposition.
- "Affirmative" and "negative" refer to the quality of a categorical proposition.
- The words "all," "no," and "some" are called "quantifiers." They tell us the extent of the class inclusion or exclusion.
- The words "are" and "are not" are referred to as "copula." They are simply forms of "to be" and serve to link (to "couple") the subject class with the predicate class.
- If a categorical proposition asserts something definite about every member of a class, then the term designating that class is said to be *distributed*. On the other hand, if the proposition does not assert something definite about every member of a class, then the term designating that class is said to be *undistributed*.
- Opposition: Occurs when two standard-form categorical propositions refer to the same subject and predicate classes, but differ in quality, quantity, or both.
- Contradictories: Pairs of propositions in which one is the negation of the other. **A**- and **O**-propositions are contradictories, as are **E**- and **I**-propositions.
- Contraries: Pairs of propositions that cannot both be true at the same time, but can both be false at the same time. **A**- and **E**-propositions are contraries.
- Subcontraries: Pairs of propositions that cannot both be false at the same time, but can both be true; also, if one is false then the other must be true. **I**- and **O**-propositions are subcontraries.
- Subalternation: The relationship between a universal proposition (the *superaltern*) and its corresponding particular proposition (the *subaltern*).
- Immediate argument: An argument that has only one premise.
- Mediate argument: An argument that has more than one premise.
- Conversion: An immediate argument created by interchanging the subject and predicate terms of a given categorical proposition.
- Conversion by limitation: When we first change a universal **A**-proposition into its corresponding particular **I**-proposition, and then we use the process of conversion on the **I**-proposition.

- Obversion: An immediate argument formed by changing the quality of the given proposition, and then replacing the predicate term with its complement.
- Complement: The set of objects that do not belong to a given class.
- Contraposition: Formed by replacing the subject term of a given proposition with the complement of its predicate term and then replacing the predicate term of the given proposition with the complement of its subject term.
- Contraposition by limitation: When subalternation is used to change the universal **E**-proposition into its corresponding particular **O**-proposition. We then apply the regular process of forming a contrapositive to this **O**-proposition.
- Existential import: When a proposition presupposes the existence of certain kinds of objects.
- The modern square of opposition offers a new interpretation of the various relationships between the four standard-form categorical propositions.
- Venn diagrams use circles to represent categorical proposition forms.
- Singular proposition: Asserts something about a specific person, place, or thing.
- Exceptive propositions: Statements that need to be translated into compound statements containing the word "and." (For example, propositions that take the form "All except S are P" and "All but S are P.")

KEY TERMS

LOGIC CHALLENGE: GROUP RELATIONSHIP

The Masons are a somewhat secretive group. Based on the following information, draw a diagram using four interlocking circles that correctly captures the relationship between Masons and three other groups:

1. Every member of the *Scottish Rite* must be a *Mason*.
2. Every member of the *York Rite* must be a *Mason*.
3. It is possible to be a member of both the *Scottish Rite* and the *York Rite*.
4. Every *Shriner* must be a member of the *Scottish Rite*, the *York Rite*, or both.
5. *Masons* do not have to be members of the *Shriners*, or the *Scottish Rite*, or the *York Rite*.

Chapter 6

Categorical Syllogisms

Our effort to understand the logic of categorical statements gave us the ability to clarify ordinary language so that we could investigate some immediate inferences for validity. We can build on this foundation to explore complex arguments that are constructed from categorical statements. Take this, for example:

> All comedians are shy people.
> <u>Some comedians are good actors.</u>
> Some good actors are shy people.

We already saw one valuable tool, Venn diagrams, for making sense of generalizations like these—outrageous or not. But can we logically connect them? Can we make our way from the premises to the conclusion?

In addition to advancing the use of Venn diagrams, we will expand the discussion of existential import and how it affects the analysis of some arguments. We will also introduce a new set of rules that complements the use of Venn diagrams for determining validity. Finally, translating ordinary language arguments will round out the discussion of categorical logic.

A. STANDARD-FORM CATEGORICAL SYLLOGISMS

Syllogism A deductive argument that has exactly two premises and a conclusion.

Categorical syllogism A syllogism constructed entirely of categorical propositions.

A **syllogism** is a deductive argument that has exactly two premises and a conclusion. A **categorical syllogism** is a syllogism constructed entirely of categorical propositions. It contains three different terms, each of which is used two times. Consider the same example:

> All comedians are shy people.
> <u>Some comedians are good actors.</u>
> Some good actors are shy people.

Each of the three terms—*comedians, shy people,* and *good actors*—occurs twice in the categorical syllogism. By definition, the **minor term** is the subject of the conclusion (*good actors*), and the **major term** is the predicate of the conclusion (*shy people*). The term that occurs only in the premises (*comedians*) is called the **middle term**. Also, by definition, the first premise of a categorical syllogism contains the major term and it is called the **major premise**. The second premise contains the minor term, and it is called the **minor premise**.

In order to be a **standard-form categorical syllogism**, a syllogism must meet three requirements:

1. All three statements (the two premises and the conclusion) must be standard-form categorical propositions. (Any statement that is not in standard-form would have to be rewritten, as illustrated in Chapter 5.)
2. The two occurrences of each term must be identical and have the same sense. (This requirement eliminates instances of equivocation.)
3. The major premise must occur first, the minor premise second, and the conclusion last.

Since the syllogism at the beginning of this section meets all three requirements, it is a standard-form categorical syllogism. However, the next example fails to meet each of the three requirements.

> All superstitions are religious beliefs.
> <u>Some false beliefs are old superstitions.</u>
> Many religious beliefs are false beliefs.

The first requirement is not met because the conclusion begins with the word "Many" (it would have to be rewritten as a standard-form proposition). The second requirement is not met because the terms "superstitions" and "old superstitions" are not identical. Finally, the third requirement is not met because the major premise occurs second, so the order of the two premises would have to be switched.

THE STRUCTURE OF STANDARD-FORM CATEGORICAL SYLLOGISMS
First premise: The *major premise.*   Second premise: The *minor premise.*   Conclusion: The *minor term* is the subject, and the *major term* is the predicate.

We will look at two methods of determining whether a standard-form categorical syllogism is valid or invalid. The first method relies on the basic ideas of Venn diagrams introduced in Chapter 5. The second method uses a small set of rules to determine whether a standard-form categorical syllogism is valid or invalid.

B. DIAGRAMMING IN THE MODERN INTERPRETATION

We will start by using the Boolean interpretation of categorical propositions. The diagrams in this first part will rely on the techniques introduced in Chapter 5. If you

Minor term The subject of the conclusion of a categorical syllogism.

Major term The predicate of the conclusion of a categorical syllogism.

Middle term The term that occurs only in the premises of a categorical syllogism.

Major premise The first premise of a categorical syllogism (it contains the major term).

Minor premise The second premise of a categorical syllogism (it contains the minor term).

Standard-form categorical syllogism A categorical syllogism that meets three requirements: (1) All three statements must be standard-form categorical propositions. (2) The two occurrences of each term must be identical and have the same sense. (3) The major premise must occur first, the minor premise second, and the conclusion last.

recall, categorical propositions contain two terms and are diagrammed using a pair
of overlapping circles:

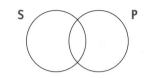

Universal propositions refer to class inclusion or exclusion. If one class is entirely
included in another class (**A**-proposition) or entirely excluded from another class (**E**-
proposition), then our diagrams must shade out the appropriate areas.

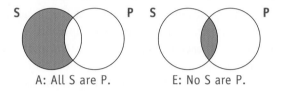

A: All S are P.   E: No S are P.

We also learned how to diagram the particular propositions **I** and **O**. Unlike universal propositions, particular propositions refer to individual members of a class. The
diagrams for **I** and **O** propositions used an X to denote a specific member of a class.

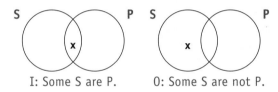

I: Some S are P.   O: Some S are not P.

If you recall, we were also able to refer to the different areas in the diagram:

- If something is in Area 1, then it is an S and a non-P.
- If something is in Area 2, then it is both an S and a P.
- If something is in Area 3, then it is a P and a non-S.
- If something is in Area 4, then it is both a non-S and a non-P.

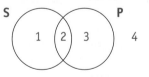

Since standard-form categorical syllogisms have three terms (major, minor, and
middle), we have to add a circle to our diagram:

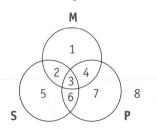

Here "**S**" stands for the class referred to by the minor term, "**P**" for the class referred to by the major term, and "**M**" for the class referred to by the middle term:

- If something is in Area 1, then it is an M, a non-S, and a non-P.
- If something is in Area 2, then it is an M, an S, and a non-P.
- If something is in Area 3, then it is an M, an S, and a P.
- If something is in Area 4, then it is an M, a P, and a non-S.
- If something is in Area 5, then it is an S, a non-M, and a non-P.
- If something is in Area 6, then it is an S, a P, and a non-M.
- If something is in Area 7, then it is a P, a non-S, and a non-M.
- If something is in Area 8, then it is a non-M, a non-S, and a non-P.

The three interlocking circles might look complicated, but just a few simple tools are needed to complete the Venn diagram. As we will soon learn, the results will allow us to determine whether a standard-form categorical syllogism is valid or invalid. And that means we can answer a crucial question: Does the conclusion follow necessarily from the premises?

To answer this question, all we need to do is diagram the two premises (major and minor); we do not need to diagram the conclusion. The reason is this: a valid syllogism's conclusion is automatically diagrammed once all the premises are diagrammed. In other words, in a valid syllogism, true premises guarantee a true conclusion. In contrast, the conclusion of an invalid syllogism does not necessarily follow from the premises. As we shall see, a correctly drawn Venn diagram will reveal just that.

Diagramming A-propositions

We can start by diagramming **A**-propositions. Suppose the major premise is "All P are M." Following Chapter 5, we need to shade the areas of P that are outside of M:

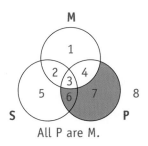

All P are M.

The S circle makes things look more complicated, but it does not change the basic principle. Since all the areas of P outside M must be shaded, we just need to shade both Areas 6 and 7.

Since the major premise must contain the major term and the middle term, the only other possible **A**-proposition for it is "All M are P." To diagram this, we need to shade all the areas of M that are outside of P:

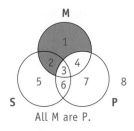

All M are P.

Since all the areas of M outside P must be shaded, we need to shade both Areas 1 and 2. The same principle applies to the minor premise. In fact, there are only two more possible diagrams to consider for **A**-propositions. The minor premise can be either "All S are M" or "All M are S."

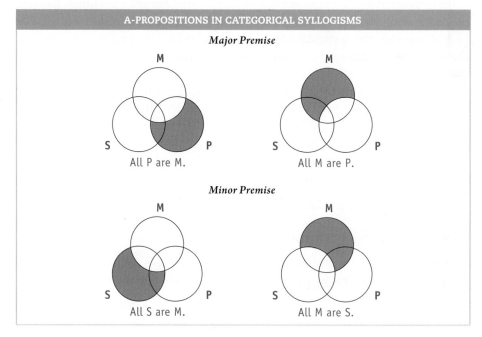

Diagramming E-propositions

The next step is to learn how to diagram **E**-propositions. This time we will do a diagram for a possible minor premise. For example, suppose the minor premise is "No S are M." Following our basic method, we need to shade the areas of S that overlap M:

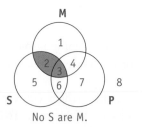

No S are M.

Since all the areas of S that overlap with M must be shaded, we need to shade Areas 2 and 3. We know that the minor premise must contain the minor term and the middle term, so the only other possible **E**-proposition for the minor premise is "No M are S." If you recall the basic principle from Chapter 5 regarding **E**-propositions, we can state that the diagram for "No M are S" is identical to the diagram for "No S are M." Given this, we need to consider only two possible diagrams.

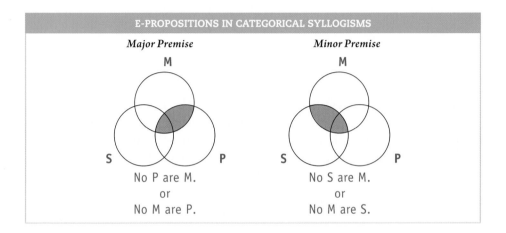

E-PROPOSITIONS IN CATEGORICAL SYLLOGISMS

Major Premise

No P are M.
or
No M are P.

Minor Premise

No S are M.
or
No M are S.

Diagramming I-propositions

We now turn to **I**-propositions. This time, we will do a diagram for a possible major premise. For example, suppose the major premise is "Some P are M." Following our basic method, we need to place an X in the area where P and M overlap. The fact that we have three interlocking circles now complicates the process a bit, but it is easily overcome. Let's consider three possible locations:

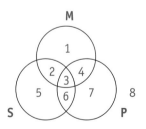

We know that the X is located somewhere in Area 3 or Area 4 (where P and M overlap). But the objects in these two areas are not the same. For example, an object in Area 3 is a P, and it is both an M and an S. However, an object in Area 4 is a P and an M, but it is *not* an S. Our problem is that the single premise "Some P are M" does not provide by itself enough information to place the X in either of these areas. Also, we cannot place an X in both areas, because we can use only one X for each particular statement in our diagram. We solve this problem by placing the X on the line separating the two areas where the object might exist:

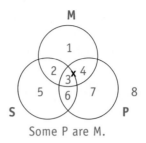

Some P are M.

The placement of X tells us that P is either in Area 3 or in Area 4. What additional information would we need in order to place the X directly in Area 3 or Area 4—and not on the line separating the two? Since we are examining the possible major premise "Some P are M," the minor premise would have to be a universal proposition. There are only four possibilities to consider: "All S are M," "All M are S," "No S are M," and "No M are S." And since we know that the diagrams for the two E-propositions are identical, we need to draw only three diagrams.

Figure 1

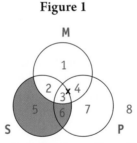

Major Premise: Some P are M.
Minor Premise: All S are M.

Figure 2

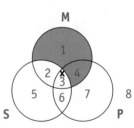

Major Premise: Some P are M.
Minor Premise: All M are S.

Figure 3

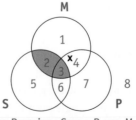

Major Premise: Some P are M.
Minor Premise: No S are M.

In Figure 1 the diagram for the minor premise "All S are M" did not shade either Area 3 or Area 4, and therefore the X remains on the line. However, in Figure 2 the diagram for the minor premise "All M are S" did shade Area 4. Since the shading indicates that Area 4 is empty (it has no members), we can now position the X in Area 3. Figure 3 reveals a third possibility. Here the diagram for the minor premise "No S are M" did shade Area 3. And since the shading indicates that Area 3 is empty (it has no members), we can position the X directly in Area 4.

We can already see a strategy emerging. If one of the premises of a categorical syllogism is a particular proposition (**I** or **O**) and one is a universal proposition (**A** or **E**), then diagram the universal one first. Although, as we saw in Figure 1, you cannot always position the X directly in an area, the strategy will help in many cases.

Since conversion works for **I**-propositions, we need to consider only two possible diagrams:

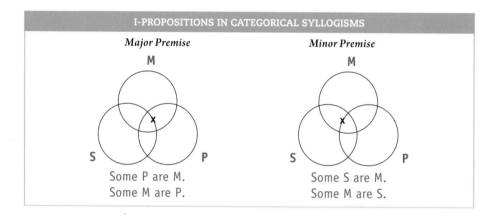

I-PROPOSITIONS IN CATEGORICAL SYLLOGISMS

Major Premise

Some P are M.
Some M are P.

Minor Premise

Some S are M.
Some M are S.

Diagramming O-propositions

We now turn to **O**-propositions. This time we will do a diagram for a possible minor premise. For example, suppose the minor premise is "Some S are not M." Following our basic method we need to place an X in the area of S that is outside of M. Once again, we need to deal with the three interlocking circles. Let's consider three possible locations.

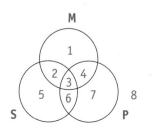

We know that the X is located somewhere in Area 5 or Area 6 (where S is outside M). But the objects in these two areas are not the same. For example, an object in Area 5 is an S, but it is not a P, and it is not an M. However, an object in Area 6 is an S, and it is a P, but it is not an M. The single premise "Some S are not M" by itself does not provide enough information to definitively allow us to place the X in either of these areas. Also, we cannot place an X in both areas; for although it is possible that there is more than one S that is not an M, we can use only one X for each particular statement in our diagram. We again solve this problem by placing the X on the line separating the two possible areas where the object might exist:

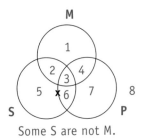

Some S are not M.

This placement of X informs us that the S is either in Area 5 or in Area 6. However, without further information we cannot yet place it in either one.

We know that the minor premise must contain the minor term and the middle term, so the only other possible **O**-proposition for the minor premise is "Some M are not S." We need to draw a new diagram, applying what we have learned so far:

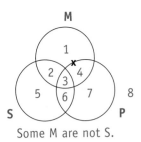

Some M are not S.

This placement of X informs us that the M referred to is either in Area 1 or in Area 4. However, again, without further information we cannot yet place it in either one.

The same principle applies to the major premise for **O**-propositions. In fact, there are only two more possible diagrams to consider. The major premise can be either "Some P are not M" or "Some M are not P":

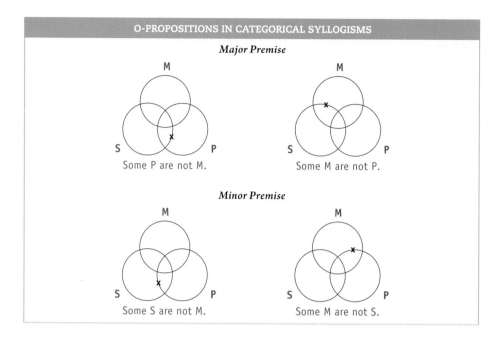

O-PROPOSITIONS IN CATEGORICAL SYLLOGISMS

Major Premise

Some P are not M.

Some M are not P.

Minor Premise

Some S are not M.

Some M are not S.

Wrapping Up the X

There is one more item to clarify. The placement of the X in a Venn diagram is restricted to certain locations. Since a particular categorical proposition refers to two classes, we must make sure the position of the X retains the reference. Let's examine a correct and incorrect Venn diagram of an **O**-proposition: "Some S are not M."

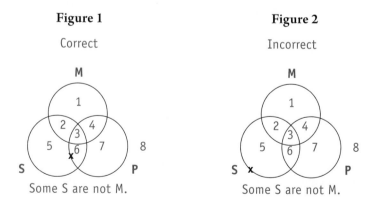

Figure 1

Correct

Some S are not M.

Figure 2

Incorrect

Some S are not M.

In Figure 1 the X is correctly placed on the line separating Area 5 and Area 6. This position of the X indicates that an object exists in at least one of those two areas. The important thing for us is that both Area 5 and Area 6 are outside the M circle, but they are within the S circle. However, this is not the case in the Figure 2. The X is incorrectly placed on the line separating Area 5 and Area 8. This position of the X indicates that an object exists in at least one of those two areas. But since the X has to be located within the S circle, this position of the X violates our requirement.

Let's examine a correct and an incorrect Venn diagram of an I-proposition: "Some M are P."

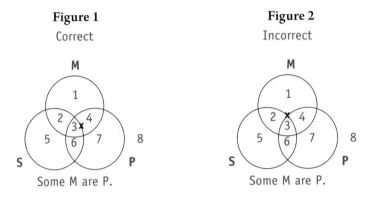

In Figure 1 the X is correctly placed on the line separating Area 3 and Area 4. This position of the X indicates that an object exists in at least one of those two areas. The important thing for us is that both Area 3 and Area 4 are both within the M circle and the P circle. However, this is not the case in the Figure 2. The X is incorrectly placed at the intersection of two lines. This position would mean that the X could be in any of four areas—Area 1, Area 2, Area 3, or Area 4. However, Area 1 and Area 2 are both outside the P circle, while the X has to be located within the P circle.

We can now summarize the results:

1. The position of the X cannot be on an outside line of a circle.
2. The position of the X cannot be at the intersection of two lines.

Is the Syllogism Valid?

We are now in position to determine if a standard-form categorical syllogism is valid or invalid. Let's analyze this example:

> All censored news reports are biased information.
> All network news shows are censored news reports.
> All network news shows are biased information.

The first step is to replace the three terms with single letters. For example, we can let C = *censored news reports* (the middle term), B = *biased information* (the major term), and N = *network news shows* (the minor term):

> All C are B.
> All N are C.
> All N are B.

We diagram the premises by assuming they are true. (Remember: we are not yet concerned with truth values, only for a valid deduction.) Since both premises are universal propositions, we can diagram either one first. (If one of the premises were a particular proposition, then we would diagram it after the universal one.) Let's diagram the first premise (All C are B):

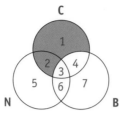

Based on the assumption of the truth of the major premise, Area 1 and Area 2 were both shaded (any area of C outside B is empty). What our diagram illustrates so far is that if anything is a C it is a member of B (Areas 3 and 4).

The next step is to diagram the information in the second premise (All N are C).

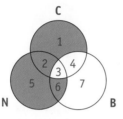

Based on the assumption of the truth of the minor premise, Area 5 and Area 6 were both shaded (any area of N outside C is empty).

The diagram is finished. In order to determine whether the syllogism is valid or invalid, we check to see if diagramming the premises created a diagram of the conclusion. In other words, does the conclusion follow necessarily from the premises? In our example, the conclusion is "All N are B." The only part of the N circle left unshaded is Area 3, and it is located within the B circle. We interpret the universal proposition "All N are B" as meaning that if something is an N, then it is a B. The Venn diagram shows that if the premises are true, then the conclusion follows necessarily; therefore, the form of the syllogism is valid. The original categorical syllogism regarding "censored new reports" is valid as well.

Let's diagram another example to see how to determine that a standard-form categorical syllogism is invalid. Consider this argument:

> No members of the U.S. Congress are unemployed workers.
> All unemployed workers are people searching for jobs.
> No people searching for jobs are members of the U.S. Congress.

The first step is to replace the three terms with single letters. We can let C = *members of the U.S. Congress* (the major term), U = *unemployed workers* (the middle term), and J = *people searching for jobs* (the minor term):

> No C are U.
> All U are J.
> No J are C.

Since the syllogism has two universal premises, we can start with either one. Let's diagram the major premise (No C are U):

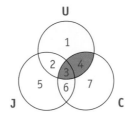

Based on the assumption of the truth of the major premise, Area 3 and Area 4 were both shaded (and both areas are empty). Now we can diagram the minor premise (All U are J):

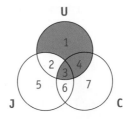

Based on the assumption of the truth of the minor premise, Area 1 and Area 4 need to be shaded. But since Area 4 was already shaded, we had only to shade Area 1.

The diagram is complete. Once again, to determine whether the syllogism is valid or invalid, we check to see if diagramming the premises created a diagram of the conclusion. In this example, the conclusion is "No J are C." In order for the conclusion to follow necessarily from the premises, both Area 3 and Area 6 would have to be shaded. (They would both have to be empty.) Although Area 3 is indeed shaded, Area 6 is not. Therefore, the premises have not ruled out the possibility that Area 6 has members. Since the Venn diagram has shown that it is possible for the premises to be true and the conclusion false, the syllogism form is invalid. Given this, the original categorical syllogism regarding "members of the U.S. Congress" is invalid as well.

Now let's analyze a standard-form categorical syllogism that has one universal and one particular proposition as premises.

> Some birthday gifts are expensive presents.
> <u>All expensive presents are luxury items.</u>
> Some luxury items are birthday gifts.

The first step is to replace the three terms with single letters. We can let B = *birthday gifts* (the major term), E = *expensive presents* (the middle term), and L = *luxury items* (the minor term):

> Some B are E.
> <u>All E are L.</u>
> Some L are B.

Recall that our strategy is to diagram the universal (minor) premise first (All E are L):

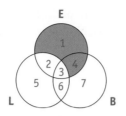

Based on the assumption of the truth of the minor premise, Area 1 and Area 4 were both shaded (and both areas are empty). Now we can diagram the particular (major) premise (Some B are E):

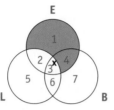

If Area 4 were not shaded, then we would have to place the X on the line separating Area 3 and Area 4. But since we applied the strategy of diagramming the universal premise first, Area 4 is already shaded. Therefore, we place the X directly into Area 3.

The diagram is finished, so we can now check for validity. In this example, the conclusion "Some L are B" is true if an X is in either Area 3 or Area 6. Since an X is located in Area 3, the Venn diagram shows that if the premises are true, then the conclusion follows necessarily. Therefore the form of the syllogism is valid. The original categorical syllogism regarding "birthday gifts" is valid as well.

Let's do one last case. We can now analyze a standard-form categorical syllogism in which both premises are particular propositions:

> Some designer drugs are addictive chemical substances.
> <u>Some illegal drugs are not designer drugs.</u>
> Some illegal drugs are not addictive chemical substances.

The first step is to replace the three terms with single letters. We can let D = *designer drugs* (the middle term), A = *addictive chemical substances* (the major term), and I = *illegal drugs* (the minor term):

> Some D are A.
> <u>Some I are not D.</u>
> Some I are not A.

Since both premises are particular propositions, we can diagram either one first. Let's do the major premise (Some D are A):

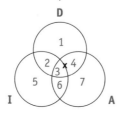

Based on the assumption of the truth of the major premise, we must place an X on the line separating Area 3 and Area 4. Now we can diagram the minor premise (Some I are not D):

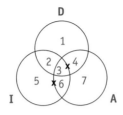

Based on the assumption of the truth of the minor premise, we must place an X on the line separating Area 5 and Area 6.

The diagram is complete. In order to determine whether the syllogism is valid or invalid, we check to see if diagramming the premises created a diagram of the conclusion. In this example, the conclusion is "Some I are not A." In order for the conclusion to follow necessarily from the premises, an X would have to be directly in either Area 2 or Area 5. However, the premises have not ruled out the possibility that no X exists in either Area 2 or Area 5. Since the Venn diagram has shown that it is possible for the premises to be true and the conclusion false, the syllogism is invalid. The original categorical syllogism regarding "designer drugs" is invalid as well.

CHECK YOUR UNDERSTANDING 6B

I. Use Venn diagrams to determine whether the following categorical syllogism forms are valid or invalid under the modern (Boolean) interpretation.

1. All M are P.
   <u>Some M are S.</u>
   Some S are P.

Answer: Valid

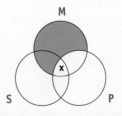

2. No M are P.
   <u>Some S are not M.</u>
   Some S are not P.

3. All P are M.
   <u>All S are M.</u>
   All S are P.

4. Some P are M.
   Some S are M.
   Some S are P.

★ 5. Some M are not P.
   Some M are not S.
   Some S are not P.

6. No P are M.
   No M are S.
   No S are P.

7. All P are M.
   Some S are M.
   All S are P.

8. Some P are M.
   Some M are not S.
   Some S are not P.

★ 9. All M are P.
   No S are M.
   Some S are not P.

10. No M are P.
   Some S are M.
   Some S are P.

11. All M are P.
   No S are M.
   No S are P.

12. No P are M.
   Some S are M.
   Some S are not P.

★ 13. All M are P.
   All S are M.
   All S are P.

14. All M are P.
   Some S are not M.
   Some S are not P.

II. Translate the following arguments into standard-form categorical syllogism forms. Then use Venn diagrams to determine whether they are valid or invalid under the modern interpretation.

1. All fast-food items are overpriced objects. No overpriced objects are nutritious products. Therefore, no nutritious products are fast-food items.

Answer: Valid. Let F = *fast-food items*, O = *overpriced objects*, and N = *nutritious products.*

All F are O.
No O are N.
No N are F.

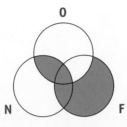

2. Some vegetables are not tasty foods. Therefore some tasty foods are not green foods, because some vegetables are not green foods.

3. All mechanical objects are noisy objects. All airplanes are noisy objects. Thus, all airplanes are mechanical objects.

4. Some pens are not useful tools. This is because some pens are leaky writing implements, and no leaky writing implements are useful tools.

★ 5. No septic tanks are swimming pools. No sewers are swimming pools. Therefore, no septic tanks are sewers.

6. All voice messages are distracting information. Some games people play are distracting information. So some voice messages are games people play.

7. Some universities are not expensive places to attend. Some universities are conveniently located complexes. Thus, some expensive places to attend are not conveniently located complexes.

8. No sports fanatics are rational creatures. Therefore, no sports fanatics are benevolent people, since all rational creatures are benevolent people.

★ 9. Some buildings are poorly constructed domiciles. Some buildings are architectural nightmares. So some architectural nightmares are poorly constructed domiciles.

10. All sea creatures are intelligent animals. Some sea creatures are predators. So, some intelligent animals are predators.

C. DIAGRAMMING IN THE TRADITIONAL INTERPRETATION

We can modify the way we have been drawing Venn diagrams to accommodate the traditional Aristotelian interpretation of universal categorical propositions. The major difference is that we must take into account existential import (Chapter 5). Determining whether a class has actually existing members allows some syllogisms to be valid under the traditional interpretation that would be invalid under the modern interpretation. However, we will need to investigate the assumption of existence *only* when a syllogism has a particular proposition (either **I** or **O**) as the conclusion and at least one universal premise.

A-propositions

In Chapter 5 the circled red X was introduced to represent the "**A**ssumption of Existence," as illustrated in the next two diagrams:

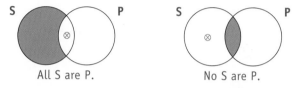

All S are P.   No S are P.

   Once again, we start by learning how to diagram **A**-propositions under the traditional interpretation. For example, suppose the major premise is "All P are M." Adapting our method of shading to the introduction of the assumption of existence, we get the following diagram:

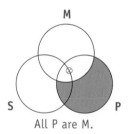

All P are M.

   The areas of P outside M are shaded, and we had to place the circled red X in the appropriate location. Here we need to draw on some additional information from Chapter 5. If you recall, when a categorical proposition asserts something definite about every member of a class, then the term designating that class is said to be *distributed*. For **A**-propositions, the subject term is distributed, but the predicate term is undistributed. In this case, the assumption of existence concerns the class of objects referred to by P. Therefore, we place the circled red X on the line that separates the two areas where P and M overlap. The assumption of existence regarding the proposition "All P are M" refers to these two areas.

   Since the major premise must contain the major term and the middle term, the only other possible **A**-proposition for the major premise is "All M are P":

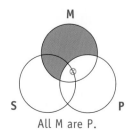

All M are P.

Once again, for **A**-propositions, the subject term is distributed, but the predicate term is undistributed. Therefore, we place the circled red X on the line that separates the two areas where M and P overlap. The assumption of existence regarding the proposition, "All M are P," refers to these two areas.

The same principles apply to the minor premise, but there are only two more possible diagrams to consider. The minor premise can be either "All S are M" or "All M are S":

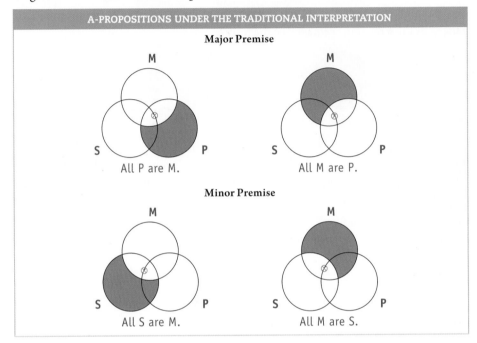

A-PROPOSITIONS UNDER THE TRADITIONAL INTERPRETATION

Major Premise

All P are M.

All M are P.

Minor Premise

All S are M.

All M are S.

E-propositions

The next step is to learn how to diagram **E**-propositions. This time we will do a diagram for a possible minor premise. For example, suppose the minor premise is "No S are M." Following our basic method, we know that we need to shade the areas of S that overlap M. But we also need to add the symbol for the assumption of existence. Once again, we have to rely on information regarding distribution. Unlike **A**-propositions, **E**-propositions result in both the subject term and predicate term being distributed:

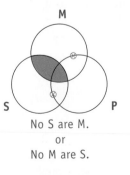

No S are M.
or
No M are S.

Since both the subject term and predicate term are distributed in "No S are M," we must use two symbols for the assumption of existence: one for the subject and one for the predicate. For the subject, S, we place a circled red X on the line that separates the two areas belonging to S that are outside M. For the predicate, M, we place another circled red X on the line that separates the two areas belonging to M that are outside S. Since the diagram for "No M are S" is identical to the diagram for "No S are M," the two possibilities are listed together.

These same principles apply to the major premise, but there are only two possible diagrams to consider:

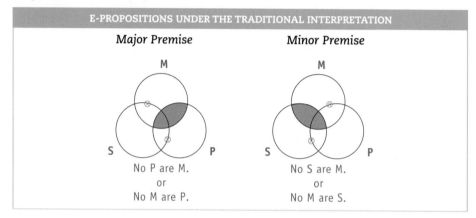

E-PROPOSITIONS UNDER THE TRADITIONAL INTERPRETATION

Major Premise

No P are M.
or
No M are P.

Minor Premise

No S are M.
or
No M are S.

We can take what we have learned and apply it to a standard-form categorical syllogism. Let's examine the following argument:

All college fraternities are environmentally conscious groups.
All environmentally conscious groups are tax-exempt organizations.
Some tax-exempt organizations are college fraternities.

If we let C = *college fraternities*, E = *environmentally conscious groups*, and T = *tax-exempt organizations*, we can reveal the argument form:

All C are E.
All E are T.
Some T are C.

We already know how to diagram this using the modern interpretation, so we can do that first (Figure 1):

Figure 1

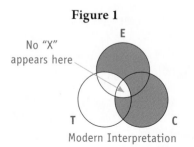

No "X" appears here

Modern Interpretation

Under the modern interpretation the syllogism is invalid. This should not be surprising. Under the modern interpretation, universal propositions do not assume existential import. Since both premises of the syllogism are universal propositions, diagramming them will produce only shading; therefore, no X will appear. However, the conclusion is an **I**-proposition, and for it to be true an X would have to appear in the area indicated by the arrow. Since no X appears in this area, the syllogism is invalid.

Now we will draw a Venn diagram using the traditional interpretation (Figure 2). This time we will diagram one premise at a time in order to get familiar with the procedure. Let's start by diagramming the major premise "All C are E":

Figure 2

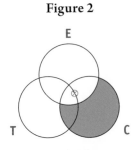

We place the circled red X much as we did for **A**-propositions under the traditional interpretation. In this case, the assumption of existence concerns the class of objects referred to by C. Therefore, we place the circled red X on the line that separates the two areas where C and E overlap.

The next step is to add the diagram for the minor premise "All E are T":

Figure 3

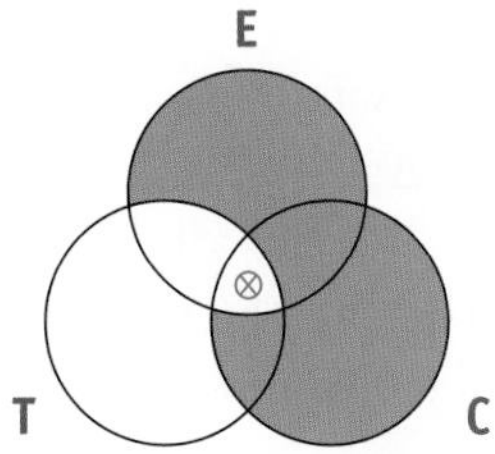

Since one of the areas where the circled red X might have gone has now been shaded, we are justified in moving it into the only remaining area. Since a circled red X appears in the nonempty area where T and C overlap, the conclusion "Some T are C" is true. However, the syllogism is at this point only "provisionally valid," because there is one more step to complete. Under the traditional interpretation, we now have to consider the assumption of existence. We must therefore investigate whether the circled red X refers to something that actually exists.

In our example, the assumption of existence concerns the class of objects referred to by C (which is why we placed the circled red X on the line that separated the two areas where C and E overlapped). Since "C" stands for *college fraternities*, which exist, the circled red X represents an actually existing object. Therefore, under the traditional interpretation the syllogism is valid.

To illustrate the idea behind provisionally valid syllogisms under the traditional interpretation, we can examine the following argument:

All centaurs are egoists.
All egoists are talented people.
Some talented people are centaurs.

If we let C = *centaurs*, E = *egoists*, and T = *talented people*, we can reveal the argument form:

All C are E.
All E are T.
Some T are C.

This form is identical to the one we previously examined. Under the modern interpretation, we already know that it is invalid. However, under the traditional interpretation it is provisionally valid. Therefore, we now have to consider the assumption of existence. In this new example, "C" stands for centaurs, which do not exist. Since "C" refers to something that does not exist, the circled red X does not represent an actually existing object. Therefore, under the traditional interpretation the syllogism is invalid.

In sum, the provisionally valid nature of some syllogisms under the traditional interpretation means that some forms can have both valid and invalid instances. Final determination then rests on the assumption of existence. The modern interpretation does not require this additional investigation.

When Both Interpretations Give the Same Results

Let's look at an example in which the syllogism is invalid under *both* the traditional and modern interpretations:

> No vaccinations are completely safe medical procedures.
> All completely safe medical procedures are laboratory certified methods.
> Some laboratory certified methods are vaccinations.

On the surface, it is difficult to see that the argument is invalid. If we let V = *vaccinations*, C = *completely safe medical procedures*, and L = *laboratory certified methods*, we can reveal the argument form:

> No V are C.
> All C are L.
> Some L are V.

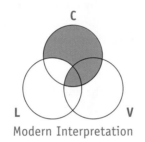
Modern Interpretation

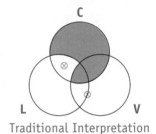
Traditional Interpretation

Since both premises of the syllogism are universal propositions, under the modern interpretation diagramming the premises will only produce shading; therefore, no X will appear in the diagram. However, the conclusion is an **I**-proposition, and for it to be true an X would have to appear in the area of L that overlaps with V. Since no X appears in this area, the syllogism is invalid under the modern interpretation.

Under the traditional interpretation, diagramming the two universal premises will produce both shading and a circled red X. The diagram of the major premise places one circled red X on the line separating the two areas of the V circle that are outside the C circle, and it places another circled red X on the line separating the two areas of the C circle that are outside the V circle. But when we diagram the minor premise, one of the two possible areas in C now gets shaded in, so we move the circled red X to the remaining area in C. Since the conclusion is an **I**-proposition, for it to be true a circled red X would have to appear directly in the area of L that overlaps with V. However, the circled red X is on a line that separates two areas. Since this means that it is possible for the conclusion to be false while the premises are true, the syllogism is invalid under the traditional interpretation as well. Also, since it is invalid, we do not need to investigate the assumption of existence.

We can also produce a simple counterexample (using the syllogism form as our guide) in which the premises are true and the conclusion false:

> No watermelons are pigs.
> All pigs are mammals.
> Some mammals are watermelons.

Now let's look at an example where both the traditional and modern interpretations show the syllogism is valid:

All cases of euthanasia are legally prosecuted acts.
<u>Some cases of euthanasia are ethically justified behaviors.</u>
Some ethically justified behaviors are legally prosecuted acts.

It might be difficult to see that the argument is valid at this point. If we let C = *cases of euthanasia*, L = *legally prosecuted acts*, and E = *ethically justified behaviors*, we can reveal the argument form.

All C are L.
<u>Some C are E.</u>
Some E are L.

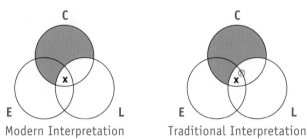

Modern Interpretation   Traditional Interpretation

Under the modern interpretation, diagramming the major (universal) premise produces shading. However, the minor premise is a particular **I**-proposition, so an X appears in the diagram. Since diagramming the premises has automatically diagrammed the conclusion ("Some E are L"), the syllogism is valid under the modern interpretation.

Under the traditional interpretation, diagramming the premises added a circled red X (from the major premise). However, the placement of the X (from the minor premise) is enough to show the syllogism is valid, so the circled red X does not factor into our determination. The syllogism is valid under the traditional interpretation, and we do not need to investigate the assumption of existence.

Since we have shown that the syllogism form is valid, that means that the original argument regarding cases of euthanasia is valid as well. No counterexample can be produced.

CHECK YOUR UNDERSTANDING 6C

I. Use Venn diagrams to determine whether the following categorical syllogism forms are *valid, provisionally valid* or *invalid* under the traditional (Aristotelian) interpretation.

1. No M are P.
   <u>Some S are not M.</u>
   Some S are not P.
Answer: Invalid.

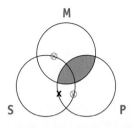

When we diagram the major (universal) premise, we shade the areas where M and P overlap, and we place one circled red X on the line in the M circle and one circled red X on the line in the P circle. When we diagram the minor (particular) premise, we place an X on the line in the S circle. In order for the conclusion to be true, either the X or the circled red X that is on the line separating S and M would have to be directly in one of the areas of S that is outside P. However, it is possible that the X is in the area of S that is also P. It is also possible that the circled red X is in the area of M that is outside S. Since this means that it is possible for the conclusion to be false while the premises are true, the syllogism is invalid. And since it is invalid, we do not need to investigate the assumption of existence.

2. All M are P.
   <u>Some M are S.</u>
   Some S are P.

3. All P are M.
   <u>All S are M.</u>
   Some S are P.

4. Some P are M.
   <u>All S are M.</u>
   Some S are P.

★ 5. Some M are not P.
   <u>No M are S.</u>
   Some S are not P.

6. No P are M.
   <u>No M are S.</u>
   Some S are not P.

7. All P are M.
   <u>Some S are M.</u>
   Some S are P.

8. All P are M.
   <u>Some M are not S.</u>
   Some S are not P.

⭐ 9. All M are P.
    <u>No S are M.</u>
    Some S are not P.

10. No M are P.
    <u>Some S are M.</u>
    Some S are P.

11. All M are P.
    <u>No S are M.</u>
    Some S are not P.

12. No P are M.
    <u>Some S are M.</u>
    Some S are not P.

⭐ 13. All M are P.
    <u>All S are M.</u>
    Some S are not P.

14. All M are P.
    <u>Some S are not M.</u>
    Some S are not P.

II. Translate the following arguments into standard-form categorical syllogism forms. Then use Venn diagrams to determine whether they are valid or invalid under the traditional (Aristotelian) interpretation.

1. All fast-food items are overpriced objects. No overpriced objects are nutritious products. Therefore, some nutritious products are not fast-food items.

Answer: Let F = *fast-food items*, O = *overpriced objects*, and N = *nutritious products*.

All F are O.
<u>No O are N.</u>
Some N are not F.

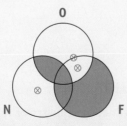

When we diagram the major premise, we shade the areas of F outside O, and place one circled red X on the line in the area where F and O overlap. However, when we diagram the minor premise, we shade the areas where N and O overlap. This requires moving the first circled red X from the line where F and O overlap to the unshaded area where F and O overlap. The next step is to complete the diagram for the minor premise. We place one circled red X on the line where F and O overlap, and another circled red X in the unshaded area of N. In order for the conclusion to be true, either an X or a circled red X would have to be directly in one of the areas of N that is outside F. Since there is a circled red X in this area, the argument is *provisionally valid*.

The final step of the analysis is the investigation of the assumption of existence. Since "N" stands for *nutritious products*, which exist, the circled red X represents an actually existing object. Therefore, under the traditional interpretation the syllogism is valid.

2. Some vegetables are not tasty foods. So some tasty foods are not green foods, because no vegetables are green foods.

3. All mechanical objects are noisy objects. All airplanes are noisy objects. Thus, some airplanes are mechanical objects.

4. Some pens are not useful tools. This is because some pens are leaky writing implements, and no leaky writing implements are useful tools.

5. No septic tanks are swimming pools. No sewers are swimming pools. Therefore, some septic tanks are not sewers.

6. All voice messages are distracting information. Some games people play are distracting information. So, some voice messages are games people play.

7. Some universities are not expensive places to attend. No universities are conveniently located complexes. Thus, some expensive places to attend are not conveniently located complexes.

8. Some sports fanatics are rational creatures. Therefore, some sports fanatics are benevolent people, since all rational creatures are benevolent people.

9. Some buildings are poorly constructed domiciles. No buildings are architectural nightmares. So, some architectural nightmares are poorly constructed domiciles.

10. All sea creatures are intelligent animals. Some sea creatures are predators. So, some intelligent animals are predators.

D. MOOD AND FIGURE

Mood The mood of a categorical syllogism consists of the type of categorical propositions involved (**A**, **E**, **I**, or **O**) and the order in which they occur.

The **mood** of a categorical syllogism consists of the type of categorical propositions involved (**A**, **E**, **I**, or **O**) and the order in which they occur. Here are some examples:

All P are M.	All P are M.	Some P are not M.	No P are M.
All S are M.	Some S are M.	No S are M.	No S are M.
All S are P.	Some S are P.	Some S are not P.	Some S are not P.
Mood: AAA	**Mood: AII**	**Mood: OEO**	**Mood: EEO**

The middle term in the two premises can be arranged in any one of four different ways, called the **figure** of the categorical syllogism:

THE FOUR FIGURES OF CATEGORICAL SYLLOGISMS			
M P S M S P	P M S M S P	M P M S S P	P M M S S P
Figure 1	**Figure 2**	**Figure 3**	**Figure 4**

Here are some examples:

All P are M.	All M are P.	Some P are not M.	No M are P.
All S are M.	Some S are M.	No M are S.	No M are S.
All S are P.	Some S are P.	Some S are not P.	Some S are not P.
AAA-2	**AII-1**	**OEO-4**	**EEO-3**

Since there are only four categorical propositions (**A, E, I,** and **O**), and since each standard-form categorical syllogism contains exactly three propositions (two premises and a conclusion), we get $4 \times 4 \times 4 = 64$ combinations for the mood. But we also know that there are four figures to consider. Therefore, we get $64 \times 4 = 256$ possible standard-form categorical syllogisms.

Figure The middle term can be arranged in the two premises in four different ways. These placements determine the figure of the categorical syllogism.

PROFILES IN LOGIC

Christine Ladd-Franklin

Christine Ladd-Franklin (1847–1930) did substantial work in symbolic logic, mathematics, physiological optics, and the theory of color vision. While at Johns Hopkins she attended the lectures of Charles S. Peirce, whose ideas on symbolic logic helped Ladd-Franklin develop her ideas. In fact, Peirce thought so much of her dissertation that he had it published in *Studies in Logic by Members of the Johns Hopkins University*. In this work, Ladd-Franklin tried to solve a problem that began with Aristotle, to find a single test that would capture all valid syllogisms. The solution requires that they all share something in common—and some general test would reveal just what.

Ladd-Franklin proposed that the premises of any valid syllogism will be inconsistent with the *negation* of the conclusion. As Josiah Royce of Harvard University said of Ladd-Franklin's test, "There is no reason why this should not be accepted as the definite solution to the problem of the reduction of syllogisms."

Although her dissertation "The Algebra of Logic" was published in 1883, she was not able to receive a Ph.D. because technically she was not even enrolled at Johns Hopkins University, which at the time was all male. Only after a lifetime of important work was she finally awarded a doctorate degree in 1926.

When we apply the Venn diagram method to each of these, we find that fifteen categorical syllogisms are valid in both the modern and the traditional interpretation:

CATEGORICAL SYLLOGISMS VALID UNDER BOTH INTERPRETATIONS			
AAA-1	AEE-2	AII-3	AEE-4
AII-1	AOO-2	EIO-3	EIO-4
EAE-1	EAE-2	IAI-3	IAI-4
EIO-1	EIO-2	OAO-3	

However, under the traditional or Aristotelian interpretation, an additional nine categorical syllogisms are valid:

CATEGORICAL SYLLOGISMS VALID UNDER THE TRADITIONAL INTERPRETATION ALONE			
AAI-1	AEO-2	AAI-3	AAI-4
EAO-1	EAO-2	EAO-3	AEO-4
EAO-4			

Remember that if the terms needed to make the conclusion true denote actually existing objects, then the syllogism is valid under the traditional interpretation.

Under the modern or Boolean interpretation, these nine syllogisms are all invalid. You can recognize this immediately if you notice that in each case a particular conclusion follows from two universal premises. It would be logically impossible to get an X anywhere in the Venn diagram.

CHECK YOUR UNDERSTANDING 6D

I. Identify the major, minor, and middle terms, and the mood and figure of the following categorical syllogisms:

1. No animals are vegetarians.
   <u>All bears are animals.</u>
   No bears are vegetarians.
   A. Major term:
   B. Minor term:
   C. Middle term:
   D. Mood:
   E. Figure:

Answers::

1. A. Major term: vegetarians
   B. Minor term: bears
   C. Middle term: animals
   D. Mood: **EAE**
   E. Figure: **1**

2. Some parents are college students.
   <u>Some politicians are not college students.</u>
   Some politicians are not parents.
   A. Major term:
   B. Minor term:
   C. Middle term:
   D. Mood:
   E. Figure:

3. No jet airplanes are quiet vehicles.
   <u>All jet airplanes are fast machines.</u>
   No fast machines are quiet vehicles.
   A. Major term:
   B. Minor term:
   C. Middle term:
   D. Mood:
   E. Figure:

4. No hot dogs are cholesterol-free food.
   <u>Some beef products are hot dogs.</u>
   Some beef products are not cholesterol-free food.
   A. Major term:
   B. Minor term:
   C. Middle term:
   D. Mood:
   E. Figure:

★ 5. Some cats are not independent creatures.
   <u>Some cats are not lovable pets.</u>
   Some lovable pets are not independent creatures.
   A. Major term:
   B. Minor term:
   C. Middle term:
   D. Mood:
   E. Figure:

II. Use Venn diagrams to verify that the correct fifteen standard-form categorical syllogisms are valid under both the modern and traditional interpretations.

1. **AAA-1**
Answer: Valid under both interpretations.

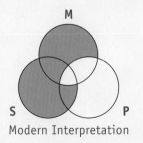

Modern Interpretation

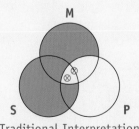

Traditional Interpretation

2. **AII-1**

3. **EAE-1**

4. **EIO-1**

⭐ 5. **AEE-2**

6. **AOO-2**

7. **EAE-2**

8. **EIO-2**

⭐ 9. **AII-3**

10. **EIO-3**

11. **IAI-3**

12. **OAO-3**

⭐ 13. **AEE-4**

14. **EIO-4**

15. **IAI-4**

III. Use Venn diagrams to verify that the nine additional standard-form categorical syllogisms listed are *provisionally valid* under the traditional interpretation, but *invalid* under the modern interpretation.

1. **AAI-1**

Answer: Invalid under the modern interpretation, but provisionally valid under the traditional interpretation.

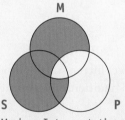
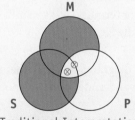

Modern Interpretation   Traditional Interpretation

2. **EAO-1**

3. **AEO-2**

4. **EAO-2**

⭐ 5. **AAI-3**

6. **EAO-3**

7. **AAI-4**

8. **AEO-4**

⭐ 9. **EAO-4**

E. RULES AND FALLACIES

Of course, we could use Venn diagrams to test the validity of all 256 categorical syllogisms and apply them to each example. Fortunately, six rules form a handy checklist. If the syllogism does not violate any rule, then it is valid; but if it violates any of the six rules, then it is invalid. As we shall see, every violation of a rule is associated with a fallacy—a mistake in reasoning.

Rule 1: The middle term must be distributed in at least one premise.

ASSOCIATED FALLACY: UNDISTRIBUTED MIDDLE

The conclusion of a categorical syllogism asserts a relationship between the classes designated by the minor and major terms. And the premises must lay the foundation for that relationship. This can be achieved only if the premises distribute the class designated by the middle term *at least once*. Either the subject or predicate of the conclusion, or both, must be related to the entire class designated by the middle term. Otherwise the fallacy of the **undistributed middle** occurs. For example:

> All poets are creative people.
> <u>All engineers are creative people.</u>
> All engineers are poets.

The major and minor premises are both **A**-propositions. Since the middle term "creative people" occurs as the predicate in each premise, it is undistributed in the syllogism. (Recall that **A**-propositions distribute only the subject term.) This means that the major and minor terms (which are distributed in the premises) may be related to different parts of M and not to each other. This possibility renders the syllogism invalid.

We can use Venn diagrams to verify Rule 1, letting P = *poets*, C = *creative people*, and E = *engineers*.

> All P are C.
> <u>All E are C.</u>
> All E are P.

Undistributed middle A formal fallacy that occurs when the middle term in a categorical syllogism is undistributed in both premises of a categorical syllogism.

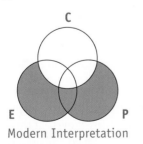
Modern Interpretation

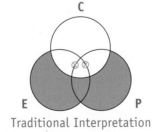
Traditional Interpretation

The syllogism is invalid under both the modern and traditional interpretations. For the conclusion ("All E are P") to be true, the unshaded area of E outside P would have to be shaded and empty. As it stands, the diagrams show this area could have members. We can see why the middle term must be distributed in at least one premise.

Rule 2: If a term is distributed in the conclusion, then it must be distributed in a premise.

ASSOCIATED FALLACIES: ILLICIT MAJOR/ILLICIT MINOR

If a categorical proposition says something definite about every member of the class designated by a term, then the term is said to be distributed. In contrast, if the proposition does not say something definite about every member of the class designated by a term, then the term is undistributed. If neither the major term nor the minor term in the conclusion is distributed, then Rule 2 does not come into play. However, if the major term is distributed in the conclusion but not in the major premise, then the conclusion goes beyond what was asserted in the premise. This is the fallacy of an **illicit major**.

The reasoning behind the rule is clear. If the major term is distributed in the conclusion, then the conclusion makes an assertion regarding *every* member of the class designated by the major term. Hence, if the major term is not distributed in the major premise, then the premise makes an assertion regarding only *some* members of the class designated by the major term. Therefore, the conclusion goes beyond the information provided in the premises.

Illicit major A formal fallacy that occurs when the major term in a categorical syllogism is distributed in the conclusion but not in the major premise.

Let's look at an example.

All bananas are fruit.
No strawberries are bananas.
No strawberries are fruit.

Once again, Venn diagrams can help verify the rule, letting B = *bananas*, F = *fruit*, and S = *strawberries*:

All B are F.
No S are B.
No S are F.

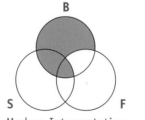
Modern Interpretation

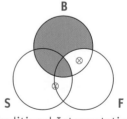
Traditional Interpretation

The syllogism is invalid under both the modern and traditional interpretations. For the conclusion ("No S are F") to be true, the area of S that overlaps with F would have to be shaded and empty. As it stands, the diagrams show that this area may have members. Hence, if the major term is distributed in the conclusion, then it must be distributed in the premises.

If the minor term is distributed in the conclusion but not in the minor premise, then the conclusion goes beyond what was asserted in the premises. This is the fallacy of **illicit minor**. For example:

Illicit minor A formal fallacy that occurs when the minor term in a categorical syllogism is distributed in the conclusion but not in the minor premise.

```
All bananas are fruit.
All bananas are yellow things.
All yellow things are fruit.
```

The fallacy of illicit minor occurs for the same reason as the fallacy of illicit major. Both fallacies fail to observe the rule that any term that is distributed in the conclusion must be distributed in the premises.

We can diagram the syllogism by letting B = *bananas*, F = *fruit*, and Y = *yellow things*.

```
All B are F.
All B are Y.
All Y are F.
```

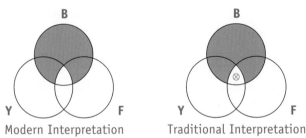

The syllogism is invalid under both the modern and traditional interpretations. For the conclusion ("All Y are F") to be true, the area of Y outside F would have to be shaded and empty. As it stands, the diagrams show that this area may have members. Hence, if the minor term is distributed in the conclusion, then it must be distributed in the premises.

Rule 3: A categorical syllogism cannot have two negative premises.

ASSOCIATED FALLACY: EXCLUSIVE PREMISES

The fallacy of **exclusive premises** rests on the principle that two negative premises will always result in an invalid syllogism. The major (negative) premise will exclude part or all of the class designated by the major term from the class designated by the middle term. The minor (negative) premise will exclude part or all of the class designated by the minor term from the class designated by the middle term. It is then impossible to deduce any kind of relationship between the classes designated by the major and minor terms, whether positive or negative. For example:

Exclusive premises A formal fallacy that occurs when both premises in a categorical syllogism are negative.

```
No Facebook entries are interesting topics.
Some blogs are not Facebook entries.
Some blogs are not interesting topics.
```

Venn diagrams can help verify Rule 3, where we let F = *Facebook entries*, I = *interesting topics*, and B = *blogs*:

```
No F are I.
Some B are not F.
Some B are not I.
```

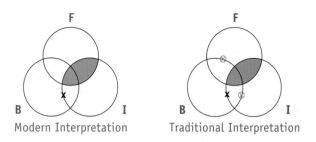

Modern Interpretation   Traditional Interpretation

The syllogism is invalid under both the modern and traditional interpretations. For the conclusion ("Some B are not I") to be true, there would have to be an X (or a circled red X) directly in one of the two unshaded areas of B that are outside I. As it stands, the diagrams show that it is possible that these areas have no members. Hence, a syllogism cannot have two negative premises.

Rule 4: A negative premise must have a negative conclusion.

ASSOCIATED FALLACY: AFFIRMATIVE CONCLUSION/NEGATIVE PREMISE

Since class inclusion requires an affirmative proposition, a categorical syllogism with an affirmative conclusion can validly follow only from two affirmative premises. In other words, an affirmative conclusion asserts that S is either completely or partially included in P. If one of the premises is negative, then either S or P will be excluded from the class designated by the middle term M. Since the middle term cannot connect the S and P, an affirmative conclusion cannot follow by necessity. A negative premise thus results in the fallacy of **affirmative conclusion/negative premise**.

Affirmative conclusion/ negative premise A formal fallacy that occurs when a categorical syllogism has a negative premise and an affirmative conclusion.

Let's look at an example:

No happy people are underpaid employees.
All teachers are happy people.
All teachers are underpaid employees.

The conclusion is a universal affirmative proposition, but one of the premises is negative. We can diagram the syllogism by letting H = *happy people*, U = *underpaid employees*, and T = *teachers*:

No H are U.
All T are H.
All T are U.

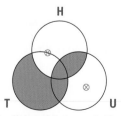

Modern Interpretation   Traditional Interpretation

The syllogism is invalid under both the modern and traditional interpretations. For the conclusion ("All T are U") to be true, there would have to be at least one area where T and U overlap that is unshaded. But as we can see, the two areas where T and U overlap are both shaded and empty. Hence, an affirmative conclusion cannot have a negative premise.

Rule 5: A negative conclusion must have a negative premise.

ASSOCIATED FALLACY: NEGATIVE CONCLUSION/AFFIRMATIVE PREMISES

Since class exclusion requires a negative proposition, a categorical syllogism with a negative conclusion cannot validly follow from two affirmative premises that assert class inclusion. A syllogism that violates this rule commits the fallacy of **negative conclusion/affirmative premises**. In other words, a negative conclusion asserts that S is either completely or partially excluded from P. However, if both premises are affirmative, then they both assert class inclusion instead of exclusion. Therefore, the information in the premises will not be adequate for the conclusion to follow by necessity.

Let's look at an example:

All carbonated drinks are bubbly beverages.
All soft drinks are carbonated drinks.
No soft drinks are bubbly beverages.

We can diagram the syllogism by letting C = *carbonated drinks*, B = *bubbly beverages*, and S = *soft drinks*:

All C are B.
All S are C.
No S are B.

> **Negative conclusion/ affirmative premises**
> A formal fallacy that occurs when a categorical syllogism has a negative conclusion and two affirmative premises.

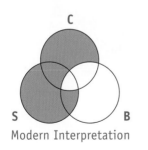

Modern Interpretation

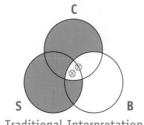

Traditional Interpretation

The syllogism is invalid under both the modern and traditional interpretations. For the conclusion ("No S are B") to be true, both areas where S and B overlap would have to be shaded and empty. But as we can see, one of the areas is unshaded. As it stands, the diagrams show that this area may have members. Hence, a negative conclusion cannot have all affirmative premises.

Rule 6: Two universal premises cannot have a particular conclusion.

ASSOCIATED FALLACY: EXISTENTIAL FALLACY

Existential fallacy
A formal fallacy that occurs when a categorical syllogism has a particular conclusion and two universal premises.

As we already know, under the modern or Boolean interpretation, universal propositions do not have existential import, but particular propositions do. Therefore, under the modern interpretation, any categorical syllogism that has two universal premises and a particular conclusion will be invalid. It is logically impossible to get an X anywhere in a Venn diagram if both premises are universal propositions. But since neither premise makes an existential assertion, but the particular conclusion does, an **existential fallacy** is committed. Under the modern interpretation, the additional nine syllogisms that were valid under the traditional interpretation all commit an existential fallacy.

Under the traditional interpretation, a syllogism can be provisionally valid, meaning that the assumption of existence requirement has to be met. As long as the term needed to make the conclusion true denotes actually existing objects, then the syllogism is valid under the traditional interpretation.

Let's look at an example:

All disgruntled creatures are nihilists.
All pterodactyls are disgruntled creatures.
Some pterodactyls are nihilists.

We can diagram the syllogism by letting D = *disgruntled creatures*, N = *nihilists*, and P = *pterodactyls*:

All D are N.
All P are D.
Some P are N.

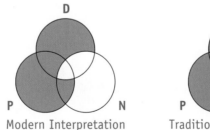
Modern Interpretation

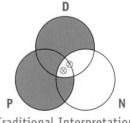
Traditional Interpretation

Under the modern interpretation, the syllogism is invalid and it commits the existential fallacy. For the conclusion ("Some P are N") to be true, the unshaded area of P would have to contain an X. But, as we can see in the diagram for the modern interpretation, no X appears in that area.

However, under the traditional interpretation, the syllogism is provisionally valid. As the diagram for the traditional interpretation shows, a circled red X appears directly in the unshaded area of P that is required to make the conclusion ("Some P are N") true. Therefore, the next step is to see if the assumption of existence requirement is met. Since the subject term of the conclusion ("pterodactyls") does not denote actually existing objects, the syllogism is invalid under the traditional interpretation, and it commits the existential fallacy.

SUMMARY OF RULES

Rule 1: The middle term must be distributed in at least one premise.
Rule 2: If a term is distributed in the conclusion, then it must be distributed in a premise.
Rule 3: A categorical syllogism cannot have two negative premises.
Rule 4: A negative premise must have a negative conclusion.
Rule 5: A negative conclusion must have a negative premise.
Rule 6: Two universal premises cannot have a particular conclusion.

CHECK YOUR UNDERSTANDING 6E

I. Determine the mood and figure of each of the following:

1. All M are P.
   <u>Some M are S.</u>
   Some S are P.

Answer: **AII-3**

2. No M are P.
   <u>Some S are not M.</u>
   Some S are not P.

3. All P are M.
   <u>All S are M.</u>
   All S are P.

4. Some P are M.
   <u>Some S are M.</u>
   Some S are P.

★ 5. Some M are not P.
   <u>Some M are not S.</u>
   Some S are not P.

6. No P are M.
   <u>No M are S.</u>
   No S are P.

7. All P are M.
   <u>Some S are M.</u>
   All S are P.

8. Some P are M.
   <u>Some M are not S.</u>
   Some S are not P.

☆ 9. All M are P.
   <u>No S are M.</u>
   Some S are not P.

10. No M are P.
   <u>Some S are M.</u>
   Some S are P.

II. Use the six rules to discuss why the fifteen standard-form categorical syllogisms are valid under both the modern and traditional interpretations.

1. **AAA-1**

Answer: All six rules are met.

Rule 1: The middle term is distributed in the first premise.

Rule 2: The major term is not distributed in the conclusion.

Rule 3: **AAA-1** does not have two negative premises.

Rule 4: **AAA-1** does not have a negative premise.

Rule 5: **AAA-1** does not have a negative conclusion.

Rule 6: **AAA-1** does not have universal premises and a particular conclusion.

2. **AII-1**

3. **EAE-1**

4. **EIO-1**

☆ 5. **AEE-2**

6. **AOO-2**

7. **EAE-2**

8. **EIO-2**

☆ 9. **AII-3**

10. **EIO-3**

11. **IAI-3**

12. **OAO-3**

☆ 13. **AEE-4**

14. **EIO-4**

15. **IAI-4**

III. First, translate the following arguments into standard-form categorical syllogisms. Second, name the mood and figure of each. Third, use Venn diagrams and the six rules to determine whether the arguments are valid or invalid.

1. All cultures that venerate senior citizens are systems built on a strong tradition of philosophical inquiry. Some recently developed cultures are not systems built on a strong tradition of philosophical inquiry. Therefore, some recently developed cultures are not cultures that venerate senior citizens.

Answer: Let C = *cultures that venerate senior citizens*, S = *systems built on a strong tradition of philosophical inquiry*, and R = *recently developed cultures*.

All C are S.
Some R are not S.
Some R are not C.

AOO-2. Valid under both interpretations. No rules are broken.

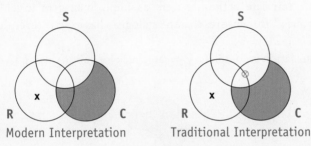

Modern Interpretation   Traditional Interpretation

2. Some planets with oxygen are planets capable of sustaining life. Some planets outside our solar system are planets with oxygen. So, some planets outside our solar system are planets capable of sustaining life.

3. All great works of literature are creative illuminations of the human predicament. Thus, no pulp fiction novels are great works of literature, because no pulp fiction novels are creative illuminations of the human predicament.

4. All natural disasters are scientifically explainable phenomena. Some human maladies are scientifically explainable phenomena. Thus, some human maladies are natural disasters.

★ 5. Some furry creatures are lovable pets. Some eccentric people are lovable pets. So, some eccentric people are furry creatures.

F. ORDINARY LANGUAGE ARGUMENTS

As we saw in Chapter 5, ordinary language often contains statements that need to be translated into standard-form categorical propositions. They can then be analyzed using either Venn diagrams or the six rules.

Reducing the Number of Terms in an Argument

A standard-form categorical syllogism must contain exactly three different terms, and each term must occur twice in the syllogism. If an ordinary language argument contains more than three different terms, it can often be translated into a standard-form categorical syllogism. We will explore five ways to reduce the number of terms: (1) eliminating superfluous words; (2) using synonyms; (3) using class complements; (4) using conversion, obversion, and contraposition; and (5) eliminating certain prefixes.

Sometimes all that is needed is to eliminate needless words. Suppose you encounter the following:

> All managers are college graduates.
> <u>Some of the managers are workaholics.</u>
> Some workaholics are college graduates.

We can usually translate "of the managers" as simply "managers" to get "Some managers are workaholics." This ensures that the syllogism has exactly three different terms, and each term is used twice.

Once the translation is complete, you can check for validity using a Venn diagram:

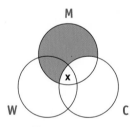

Since the syllogism does not violate any of the six rules, we have additional confirmation that it is valid.

If two of the terms in a syllogism are synonyms, then we can choose one and substitute it for the other term. For example:

> All rich people are materialistic individuals.
> <u>No materialistic individuals are altruists.</u>
> No altruists are wealthy people.

The syllogism has four terms: "rich people," "materialistic individuals," "altruists," and "wealthy people." Since the terms "rich people" and "wealthy people" are synonyms, you can choose either "rich people" or "wealthy people" and substitute it for the other:

> All rich people are materialistic individuals.
> <u>No materialistic individuals are altruists.</u>
> No altruists are rich people.

A Venn diagram shows the syllogism to be valid:

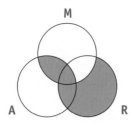

Since the syllogism does not violate any of the six rules, we have additional confirmation that it is valid.

Next, we can substitute complements for terms. As we saw in Chapter 5, the complement is the set of objects that do not belong to a given class. For example, the complements of the terms "sharp objects" and "dull objects" are "non-sharp objects" and "non-dull objects." Here is an example:

> All knives are sharp objects.
> Some knives are illegal items.
> Some legal items are dull objects.

There are five terms in the argument: "knives," "sharp objects," "illegal items," "legal items," and "dull objects." The pair of terms "sharp objects" and "dull objects" are complements, as is the pair "illegal items" and "legal items." The first step is to translate the term "dull objects" into "non-sharp objects" and the term "illegal items" into "non-legal items":

> All knives are sharp objects.
> Some knives are non-legal items.
> Some legal items are non-sharp objects.

There are still too many terms, so we have to use other methods to reduce the number to three. The major premise seems to be in order, so let's eliminate the two instances of "non-" in the minor premise and the conclusion. Since the minor premise is an I-proposition, we can use either conversion or obversion. If you recall, conversion is allowed on only E- and I-propositions, obversion is allowed on all four categorical propositions, and contraposition is allowed on only A- and O-propositions:

Conversion	
E: No S are P.	No P are S.
I: Some S are P.	Some P are S.
Obversion	
A: All S are P.	No S are non-P.
E: No S are P.	All S are non-P.
I: Some S are P.	Some S are not non-P.
O: Some S are not P.	Some S are non-P.
Contraposition	
A: All S are P.	All non-P are non-S.
O: Some S are not P.	Some non-P are not non-S.

Applying obversion results in "Some weapons are not non-non-legal items," which can be reduced to "Some weapons are not legal items." The translated term ("legal items") is now identical to the minor term in the conclusion.

The conclusion is also an **I**-proposition; therefore we can apply obversion to it. The result is "Some legal items are not non-non-sharp objects," which can be reduced to "Some legal items are not sharp objects." The translated term ("sharp objects") is now identical to the major term in the premise. The final translation looks like this:

> All knives are sharp objects.
> Some knives are not legal items.
> Some legal items are not sharp objects.

We can let K = *knives*, S = *sharp objects*, and L = *legal items*:

> All K are S.
> Some K are not L.
> Some L are not S.

A Venn diagram then shows the syllogism to be invalid:

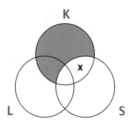

We can also find that the syllogism violates Rule 2: If a term is distributed in the conclusion, then it must be distributed in a premise. Since the major term is distributed in the conclusion, but not in the major premise, this is an instance of the fallacy of illicit major.

If an ordinary language argument contains the prefixes "in," "un," or "dis," they can often be eliminated by substituting "non-" for each prefix. Here is an example:

> All inconsiderate people are dishonorable people.
> Some interesting people are considerate people.
> No uninteresting people are honorable people.

The first step is to translate the prefixes using "non-":

> All non-considerate people are non-honorable people.
> Some interesting people are considerate people.
> No non-interesting people are honorable people.

The next steps rely on our understanding of conversion, obversion, and contraposition. Since the major premise is an **A**-proposition, we can use either conversion or contraposition. If we apply contraposition, the result is "All non-non-honorable people are non-non-considerate people." This can be reduced to "All honorable people are considerate people."

The minor premise seems fine as it stands, so we can move on to the conclusion. Since the conclusion is an E-proposition, we can use either conversion or obversion. If we apply obversion, the result is "All non-interesting people are non-honorable people." We now have an A-proposition, so we can use contraposition. The result is "All honorable people are interesting people."

Let's reconstruct the argument based on these results:

> All honorable people are considerate people.
> <u>Some interesting people are considerate people.</u>
> All honorable people are interesting people.

We have successfully reduced the terms down to three, and they each occur twice. However, the application of obversion and contraposition to the conclusion has resulted in the major term occurring in the minor premise and the minor term occurring in the major premise. We need to change the order of the premises to make it a standard-form categorical syllogism. This does not affect its validity or invalidity (which is why we can diagram either the major or the minor premise first). Here is the final result:

> Some interesting people are considerate people.
> <u>All honorable people are considerate people.</u>
> All honorable people are interesting people.

We can let I = *interesting people*, C = *considerate people*, and H = *honorable people*:

> Some I are C.
> <u>All H are C.</u>
> All H are I.

A Venn diagram then reveals that the syllogism is invalid:

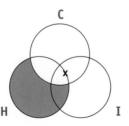

We can also find that the syllogism violates Rule 1: The middle term must be distributed in at least one premise. Since the middle term is not distributed in either premise, this is an instance of the fallacy of undistributed middle.

Let's consider another argument:

> Some non-citizens pay taxes.
> <u>All taxpayers can collect Social Security.</u>
> Some non-citizens can collect Social Security.

So far, the phrases "pay taxes" and "collect Social Security" are not class terms. However, first, we can translate "pay taxes" into "taxpayers" so it matches the term in the minor premise. And second, we can translate "collect Social Security" into "people who collect Social Security" in both the minor premise and the conclusion.

The copula is missing in each statement as well, so we need to add them:

> Some non-citizens are taxpayers.
> All taxpayers are people who can collect Social Security.
> Some non-citizens are people who can collect Social Security.

Since there are three different terms and each occurs twice, it is not necessary to eliminate the two instances of "non-." We can let non-C = *non-citizens*, T = *taxpayers*, and P = *people who can collect Social Security*:

> Some non-C are T.
> All T are P.
> Some non-C are P.

A Venn diagram then shows the syllogism to be valid:

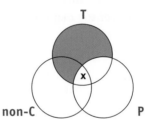

Since the syllogism does not violate any of the six rules, we have additional confirmation that it is valid.

CHECK YOUR UNDERSTANDING 6F.1

I. The following syllogisms need to be rewritten into standard form. Use the tools discussed in this section to reduce the number of terms. Then use Venn diagrams and the six rules to determine whether the syllogisms are valid or invalid under the modern interpretation.

1. Some C are not B.
   Some non-A are B.
   Some non-C are not A.

Answer: First, use contraposition on the conclusion to obtain the following: *Some non-A are not non-non-C.* Next, rewrite to eliminate the "non-non": *Some non-A are not C.* Finally, reconstruct the syllogism:

> Some C are not B.
> Some non-A are B.
> Some non-A are not C.

The following Venn diagram shows that the syllogism is invalid.

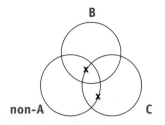

The syllogism violates one of the six rules: ***Rule 2 is violated:*** The major term is distributed in the conclusion but not in the first premise.

2. No A are B.
    <u>All non-A are C.</u>
    Some C are not B.

3. No non-A are B.
    <u>Some non-B are non-C.</u>
    Some C are not A.

4. No A are B.
    <u>Some non-C are A.</u>
    Some B are not C.

★ 5. Some A are non-B.
    <u>All B are non-C.</u>
    Some C are not A.

6. All A are B.
    <u>Some B are not C.</u>
    Some C are not non-A.

7. Some non-A are non-C.
    <u>All A are B.</u>
    Some C are non-B.

8. All non-C are B.
    <u>No A are B.</u>
    All C are A.

★ 9. All non-A are non-C.
    <u>No A are B.</u>
    All C are B.

10. No B are non-C.
    <u>Some A are non-B.</u>
    Some C are A.

11. All A are non-B.
    <u>Some C are not B.</u>
    Some non-C are A.

12. All A are B.
 <u>Some non-B are C.</u>
 Some C are not non-A.

★ 13. All C are A.
 <u>All A are B.</u>
 All non-C are non-B.

14. All non-A are non-C.
 <u>No non-A are non-B.</u>
 All C are non-B.

15. Some A are non-B.
 <u>No C are non-A.</u>
 Some C are not B.

II. The following arguments need to be translated and rewritten into standard form. Use the tools discussed in this section to reduce the number of terms. Then use Venn diagrams and the six rules to determine whether the syllogisms are valid or invalid under the modern interpretation.

1. Some TV ads are things meant to make us laugh. Therefore, some things meant to make us laugh are silly entertainment, because all television ads are foolish entertainment.

Answer: There are four terms: "TV ads," "things meant to make us laugh," "silly entertainment," and "foolish entertainment." Since "silly" and "foolish" are synonyms, we can replace one with the other. Let T = *TV ads*, L = *things meant to make us laugh*, and F = *foolish entertainment*. Here is the rewritten syllogism:

All T are F.
<u>Some T are L.</u>
Some L are F.

The following Venn diagram shows that the syllogism is valid.

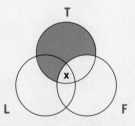

The syllogism does not violate any of the six rules.

2. All colleges without philosophy courses are institutions lacking in liberal arts programs. Every institution lacking a liberal arts program is an institution graduating students who miss out on the best ideas ever written. Thus, some colleges with philosophy courses are not institutions graduating students who miss out on the best ideas ever written.

3. Some over-the-counter drugs are unsafe for children. It follows that no non-prescription drugs are safe for children, because all over-the-counter drugs are not prescription drugs.

4. Some gangs are dangerous groups. That's because all gangs are mindless mobs, and some safe groups are not mindless mobs.

★ 5. All self-motivated students are using their intellectual capabilities. But no disinterested students are using their intellectual capabilities. Therefore, all self-motivated students are interested students.

6. No poorly paying jobs are sufficient to sustain a family's needs. Some well-paying jobs are not mindless careers. Thus, no jobs sufficient to sustain a family's needs are mindless careers.

7. Some managers are irresponsible employees. So, all non-managers are burdened with too much work, because all people burdened with too much work are responsible employees.

8. Some politicians are public representatives without ethical values. No public representatives with ethical values are corrupt. Therefore, some incorrupt people are politicians.

★ 9. Some preschool children are severely overweight. Some obese students are susceptible to diabetes. Therefore, some preschool children are not susceptible to diabetes.

10. Every pork-belly legislation is a waste of taxpayers' money. No reasonable law is a waste of taxpayers' money. So, no pork-belly legislation is a reasonable law.

Paraphrasing Ordinary Language Arguments

Sometimes we need to paraphrase an ordinary language argument in order to produce a standard-form categorical syllogism. Consider this argument:

> Drug tests shouldn't be used. Of course, if something is reliable, then it should be used. But unfortunately, drug tests aren't reliable.

The conclusion is "Drug tests shouldn't be used," and the other two statements are the premises. We could simply start translating any statement we wish, but it is better to have a strategy. Our aim is to translate statements so the terms match those in the other statements, if possible. Given this goal, a translation of the statement "If something is reliable, then it should be used" seems fairly straightforward. The translation is "All reliable things are things that should be used." The translation incorporated two key moves. First, since the word "reliable" does not designate a class, it was translated as "reliable things." Second, although the phrase "Of course" is often a premise indicator, it is superfluous in this context, so we eliminated it from the translation.

Now we can try to translate the other two statements to match the two available terms, "reliable things" and "things that should be used." The conclusion seems to be making a blanket statement about drug testing, so we can translate it as a universal proposition. If we try an **A**-proposition, we get "All drug tests are things that should not be used." The problem with this translation is that "things that should not be used" does not match the term "things that should be used," so we should look for an alternative. If we translate the conclusion as an **E**-proposition, the result is "No drug tests are things that should be used." Ah, just what we want.

The remaining statement to translate is "Drug tests aren't reliable." Although the word "but" is often a premise indicator, the phrase "But unfortunately" is superfluous in this context, so we can eliminate it. Once again, we translate the statement as a universal proposition. If we translate the statement as an **E**-proposition, we get "No drug tests are reliable things." This translation results in terms that match already existing ones:

> All reliable things are things that should be used.
> No drug tests are reliable things.
> No drug tests are things that should be used.

We can let R = *reliable things*, T = *things that should be used*, and D = *drug tests*:

> All R are T.
> No D are R.
> No D are T.

A Venn diagram then shows that the syllogism is invalid:

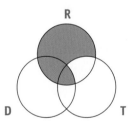

As confirmation, the syllogism violates Rule 2: If a term is distributed in the conclusion, then it must be distributed in a premise. Since the major term is distributed in the conclusion but not in the major premise, the syllogism commits the fallacy of illicit major.

Categorical Propositions and Multiple Arguments

In Chapter 5 we saw that propositions that take the form "All *except* S are P" and "All *but* S are P" are *exceptive* propositions. These propositions relate the predicate to both the class designated by the subject term and its complement. Hence, a translation results in a compound statement, containing the word "and." When an exceptive proposition occurs as a premise in a categorical syllogism, then we need to create two translations and two syllogisms. Let's look at the following argument:

> Everyone except those under 18 years of age is eligible to vote. My brother John is older than 18, so he can vote.

The conclusion of the argument is "he can vote." Based on the information in the passage, this can be translated as "All persons identical to my brother John are persons eligible to vote." The next step is to translate the exceptive proposition "Everyone except those under 18 years of age is eligible to vote." The word "Everyone" indicates that both translations will have to be universal statements. Paraphrasing the original statement gives us: "No under-18 years of age persons are persons eligible to vote" and "All non-under-18 years of age persons are persons eligible to vote." There is one more statement to translate. However, we should keep in mind that, if possible, the translation will match terms already used. Hence, the statement "My brother John is older than 18" can be translated as "No persons identical to my brother John are under-18 years of age persons." We can now put the pieces together to form two syllogisms.

A. No under-18 years of age persons are persons eligible to vote.
No persons identical to my brother John are under-18 years of age persons.
All persons identical to my brother John are persons eligible to vote.

This syllogism has exactly three different terms and each term is used twice. Also, the major and minor premises are in the correct location, so we do not need to change anything. We can let U = *under-18 years of age persons*, E = *persons eligible to vote*, and J = *persons identical to my brother John*:

No U are E.
No J are U.
All J are E.

A Venn diagram shows that the syllogism is invalid:

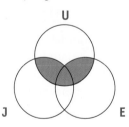

As confirmation, the syllogism violates Rule 3: A categorical syllogism cannot have two negative premises. Since this syllogism has two negative premises, it commits the fallacy of exclusive premises.

However, our analysis is not finished. Since we are dealing with an exceptive proposition, we have one more syllogism to analyze. The basic rule is that if *either* of the two syllogisms formed by translating an exceptive proposition is valid, then the original argument is valid. Here is the second syllogism:

B. All non-under-18 years of age persons are persons eligible to vote.
No persons identical to my brother John are under-18 years of age persons.
All persons identical to my brother John are persons eligible to vote.

Although the major and minor premises are in the correct location, there is a problem. This syllogism has four different terms, since "non-under-18 years of age persons" and "under-18 years of age persons" are not the same. We can, however, use obversion on the minor premise. The result is "All persons identical to my brother John are non-under-18 years of age persons." Now the syllogism has exactly three different terms, and each term is used twice:

> All non-under-18 years of age persons are persons eligible to vote.
> <u>All persons identical to my brother John are non-under-18 years of age persons.</u>
> All persons identical to my brother John are persons eligible to vote.

We can let non-U = *non-under-18 years of age persons*, E = *persons eligible to vote*, and J = *persons identical to my brother John*:

> All non-U are E.
> <u>All J are non-U.</u>
> All J are E.

The Venn diagram shows that the syllogism is valid:

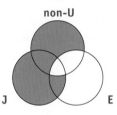

As confirmation, the syllogism does not violate any of the six rules.

CHECK YOUR UNDERSTANDING 6F.2

The following arguments need to be translated into standard form. Use all the tools discussed so far—including reducing the number of terms, paraphrasing, and the techniques in Chapter 5. Then use Venn diagrams and the six rules to determine whether the syllogisms are valid or invalid under the modern interpretation.

1. Not all nuclear power plants are dangerous to humans. Haskerville NP is a nuclear power plant, so it is not dangerous.

Answer: Rewrite the syllogism. Let N = *nuclear power plants*, D = *places dangerous to humans*, and H = *places identical to Haskerville NP*.

> Some N are not D.
> <u>All H are N.</u>
> No H are D.

The following Venn diagram shows that the syllogism is invalid:

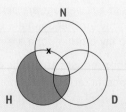

The syllogism violates Rule 1: The middle term is not distributed in at least one premise.

2. No religion can be taught in public schools. Since creationism is a religion, it cannot be taught in public schools.

3. Whenever comets appear in the sky, the stock market falls. Today, there are no comets appearing in the sky; so today the stock market will rise.

4. Shane's vehicle is not a Hummer; therefore, it gets good gas mileage, because all vehicles except Hummers get good gas mileage.

★ 5. Refurbished computers are not expensive, because every computer my uncle buys is refurbished, and every computer he buys is inexpensive.

6. I am not a genius, because my I.Q. is 115, and anyone who has an I.Q. over 140 is a genius.

7. Chimpanzees are conscious. That's because chimpanzees make tools, and any animal that makes tools is conscious.

8. Whoever killed Mr. Boddy had a dagger. Col. Mustard has a dagger, so he killed Mr. Boddy.

★ 9. Some starvation diets are effective ways to lose weight. However, starving yourself is bad for your heart. Thus, some effective ways to lose weight are bad for your heart.

10. If you have a credit card, you can buy a new television. If you can buy a new television, you can watch mind-numbing TV programs. It follows that if you have a credit card, you can watch mind-numbing TV programs.

11. Whenever the underdog wins the Super Bowl, beer sales rise. The underdog lost the Super Bowl this year, so this year beer sales will fall.

12. Most philosophy majors score high on the LSAT. Therefore, most get into the law school of their choice, because many people who score high on the LSAT get into the law school of their choice.

★ 13. Traditional Western philosophy is a series of footnotes to Plato. However, since Asian philosophy is not part of traditional Western philosophy, we can conclude that Asian philosophy is not a series of footnotes to Plato.

14. Only those who have the numbers 4, 10, 14, 24, 27, and 36 have won this week's lottery. I do not have those numbers, so I did not win the lottery.

15. Every college student is interested in finding their place in life. Every college student is anxious to impress their parents. So everyone interested in finding their place in life is anxious to impress their parents.

G. ENTHYMEMES

Some ordinary language arguments leave out important information. Chapter 3 introduced *enthymemes*, arguments with missing premises, missing conclusions, or both. The missing information is usually implied, so the arguments are usually best reconstructed based on knowledge of the context in which they appear. However, sometimes we do not have access to the context, so we should reconstruct the argument that gives the benefit of the doubt to the person presenting the argument (the principle of charity). For example, suppose someone says:

> There is no good scientific evidence to support a belief in ghosts; so anyone who believes in ghosts is superstitious.

Since the word "so" is a good conclusion indicator, the missing information is a second premise. We add the missing premise (along with paraphrasing the existing information):

> Whenever there is no good scientific evidence for something, then it is a superstitious belief. There is no good scientific evidence to support anyone's belief in ghosts. So everyone's belief in ghosts is superstitious.

It is not difficult to translate the argument into a standard-form categorical syllogism:

> All beliefs that lack good scientific evidence are superstitious beliefs.
> <u>All people's beliefs about ghosts are beliefs that lack good scientific evidence.</u>
> All people's beliefs about ghosts are superstitious beliefs.

We can let B = *beliefs that lack good scientific evidence*, S = *superstitious beliefs*, and G = *people's beliefs about ghosts*:

> All B are S.
> <u>All G are B.</u>
> All G are S.

A Venn diagram shows that the syllogism is valid:

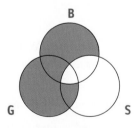

As confirmation, the syllogism does not violate any of the six rules.

An ordinary language argument might be missing both a premise and a conclusion. For example, in his inaugural address of 1933 during the Great Depression, President Franklin D. Roosevelt wanted to relieve people's worries about the ongoing economic crisis. He told the American public:

> The only thing we have to fear is fear itself.

We can fill in the missing information in the following manner:

The only thing we have to fear is fear itself.
The economic crisis is not fear itself. *(Missing premise)*
The economic crisis is not something to be feared. *(Missing conclusion)*

As we saw in Chapter 5, "the only" can be translated as a universal affirmative proposition. Therefore, we can paraphrase the major premise, "The only thing we have to fear is fear itself," as "All things that we have to fear are things identical to fear itself." The minor premise and the conclusion should be paraphrased using the terms "things that we have to fear" and "things identical to fear itself." Hence, the minor premise can be translated as "No things identical to the economic crisis are things identical to fear itself." The conclusion can be translated as "No things identical to the economic crisis are things that we have to fear." Putting the pieces together produces the syllogism:

All things that we have to fear are things identical to fear itself.
No things identical to the economic crisis are things identical to fear itself.
No things identical to the economic crisis are things that we have to fear.

We can let H = *things that we have to fear*, F = *things identical to fear itself*, and E = *things identical to the economic crisis*:

All H are F.
No E are F.
No E are H.

A Venn diagram shows that the syllogism is valid:

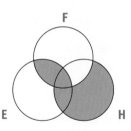

As confirmation, the syllogism does not violate any of the six rules.

We need to be careful in supplying a missing premise or conclusion, because our decisions can affect our evaluation of the argument. The next example illustrates why:

You won't be able to finish the assigned material by tomorrow morning; therefore, you will fail the exam.

The word "therefore" is a good conclusion indicator, so the statement "You will fail the exam" can be translated as "All persons identical to you are persons who will fail the exam." Both the existing premise and the missing premise should be written, if possible, to include the terms "persons identical to you" and "persons who will fail the exam." The statement "You won't be able to finish the assigned material by tomorrow morning" can be paraphrased as "All persons identical to you are persons unable to finish the assigned material by tomorrow morning." This premise contains the minor term, "persons identical to you," so it becomes the minor premise.

The missing major premise needs to tie the information together. However, at this point we have to consider a few different possibilities. The speaker might be implying that "All persons unable to finish the assigned material by tomorrow morning are persons who will fail the exam." Another possibility is that the speaker might be implying that "Most persons unable to finish the assigned material by tomorrow morning are persons who will fail the exam." Let's examine both possibilities. The first option results in the following syllogism:

> All persons unable to finish the assigned material by tomorrow morning are persons who will fail the exam.
> All persons identical to you are persons unable to finish the assigned material by tomorrow morning.
> All persons identical to you are persons who will fail the exam.

We let A = *persons unable to finish the assigned material by tomorrow morning*, F = *persons who will fail the exam*, and Y = *persons identical to you*:

> All A are F.
> All Y are A.
> All Y are F.

A Venn diagram shows that the syllogism is valid:

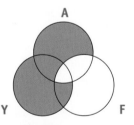

As confirmation, the syllogism does not violate any of the six rules.

Although the syllogism is valid, it may be unsound—because the major premise is likely to be false. It is possible that someone who does not finish the assigned material can still pass the exam.

Let's now try the second alternative. We will have to translate the statement "Most persons unable to finish the assigned material by tomorrow morning are persons who will fail the exam." Using the tools in Chapter 5, we can translate "most" to "some." This second option results in the following syllogism:

> Some persons unable to finish the assigned material by tomorrow morning are persons who will fail the exam.
> All persons identical to you are persons unable to finish the assigned material by tomorrow morning.
> All persons identical to you are persons who will fail the exam.

We let A = *persons unable to finish the assigned material by tomorrow morning*, F = *persons who will fail the exam*, and Y = *persons identical to you*:

Some A are F.
<u>All Y are A.</u>
All Y are F.

A Venn diagram shows that the syllogism is invalid:

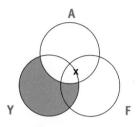

As confirmation, the syllogism violates Rule 1: The middle term must be distributed in at least one premise. Since the middle term is not distributed, the syllogism commits the fallacy of undistributed middle. The syllogism cannot be sound, even though the major premise is probably true. All that would be needed is for one person who did not finish the assigned material to fail the exam. Let's bring together the results of the two options:

1. The first syllogism is valid, but probably not sound, because the major premise is likely to be false.
2. The second syllogism is invalid and unsound, but the major premise is likely to be true.

As we saw in Chapter 3, not all uses of language are transparent. Sometimes language is used *rhetorically*—to imply things that are not explicitly said. A premise or conclusion can be disguised as a question. For example, someone might say, "Do you think I'm that stupid?" Although the sentence poses a question, it should be clear that the speaker's intention is to make an assertion: "I'm not stupid."

A rhetorical question can be used effectively in an enthymeme because it forces the audience to supply an obvious answer. For example, you might hear the following:

We shouldn't cut taxes for the big corporations. Do you really think they care about sharing their wealth will the rest of us?

The conclusion is the first sentence, and it can be translated into a categorical proposition: "No big corporations are organizations for which we should cut taxes." The term "big corporations" will have to occur in the minor premise, and the term "organizations for which we should cut taxes" will occur in the major premise. The rhetorical question gets rewritten as "No big corporations are groups interested in sharing their wealth." This is the minor premise, and the term "organizations interested in sharing their wealth" is the middle term. The major (missing) premise can be written as "All organizations for which we should cut taxes are groups interested in sharing their wealth." We can now reconstruct the argument.

All organizations for which we should cut taxes are groups interested in sharing their wealth.
<u>No big corporations are groups interested in sharing their wealth.</u>
No big corporations are organizations for which we should cut taxes.

We let O = *organizations for which we should cut taxes*, G = *groups interested in sharing their wealth*, and B = *big corporations*:

All O are G.
<u>No B are G.</u>
No B are O.

A Venn diagram shows that the syllogism is valid:

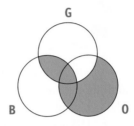

As confirmation, the syllogism does not violate any of the six rules. We leave it to you to decide on the truth value of the premises.

Leonhard Euler

Leonhard Euler (1707–83), who wrote over 800 mathematical treatises, is the most prolific mathematician in history. His abilities and memory were so remarkable that he was still able to offer original contributions to nearly every area of mathematics even after he went blind.

Euler applied special diagrams, today called *Euler diagrams*, to represent logical relations. Aristotelian syllogisms deal with classes by asking what each class includes and excludes—two ideas that can be captured visually. By providing the first steps toward a rigorous proof, Euler diagrams offer an alternative to Venn diagrams and can be used as a foundation for logical analysis. Although Euler's system is perfectly suited to mathematical and logical reasoning, its flexibility allows for many other applications as well.

Euler also studied matrices—numbers or symbols arranged in rows and columns. In what he called *Latin squares*, symbols never appear twice in the same row or column. A special version of those squares is a popular pastime today. It is called Sudoku.

CHECK YOUR UNDERSTANDING 6G

I. First, supply the missing premise or conclusion for the following enthymemes such that each one results in a valid argument. Second, translate the results into standard-form categorical syllogisms. Third, test your answers by using Venn diagrams and the six rules under the modern interpretation.

1. Anything that lacks credible evidence does not exist. Therefore, UFOs do not exist.

Answer: Rewrite the syllogism. Let L = *things that lack credible evidence*, E = *things that exist*, and U = *UFOs*.

No L are E.
<u>All U are L.</u>   *Missing premise:* All UFOs are things that lack credible evidence.
No U are E.

The following Venn diagram shows that the syllogism is valid:

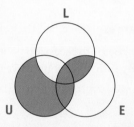

Applying the six rules verifies that the syllogism is valid:

Rule 1: The middle term is distributed in the first premise.
Rule 2: The subject term is distributed in the conclusion and in the second premise;
the predicate term is distributed in the conclusion and in the first premise.
Rule 3: The syllogism does not have two negative premises.
Rule 4: The syllogism has a negative premise and a negative conclusion.
Rule 5: The syllogism has a negative conclusion and a negative premise.
Rule 6: The syllogism does not have two universal premises and a particular conclusion.

2. Religious fanatics do not believe in freedom of thought, because they think that their belief is absolutely correct.

3. The people in Congress do not deserve a raise. Don't they get enough money now?

4. Talkative students disrupt a class, so these people are unfair to the other students.

⭐ 5. A broken cell phone will be replaced only if it is accompanied by a sales slip. I do not have the sales slip for my broken cell phone.

6. All of the games in my room are missing pieces. Monopoly is not missing any pieces.

7. My child has experienced a substantial change in body temperature. Any substantial change in body temperature is an indication of illness.

8. Only bacterial infections are effectively treated with antibiotics, so my infection will not be effectively treated with antibiotics.

★ 9. Anyone who can successfully find their way home can learn logic. All the students in this class can successfully find their way home.

10. Capital punishment should be abolished. Why do something that fails to reduce crime?

11. Coal furnaces are being phased out, because they are a major source of air pollution.

12. The only animal with a brain the same size as humans is the dolphin. Dolphins are not fish.

★ 13. A few state laws are unconstitutional. They will be overturned by the Supreme Court.

14. Not all cultured pearls are expensive, but they all are beautiful.

15. Whenever the economy goes into recession people will blame the non-citizens, and the economy is going into recession this year.

16. A conscious person has certain rights, so it follows that any living person has certain rights.

★ 17. Some airline companies take their customers for granted, because any company that refuses to give a refund on a purchase takes their customers for granted.

18. Shouldn't all citizens fulfill mandatory duties? Then all citizens should fulfill public service.

19. I didn't ask to be born. Therefore, I don't owe anything to anyone.

20. Dancing is exercise. Therefore, dancing is good for your health.

II. The following enthymemes were adapted from newspapers, websites, and other sources. First, supply the missing premise or conclusion for the following enthymemes. Second, translate the results into standard-form categorical syllogisms. Third, test your answers by using Venn diagrams and the six rules under the modern interpretation. Fourth, try to make the syllogism valid. If it cannot be made valid, then explain why.

1. It is almost impossible to stop the spread of these cases (cholera), because it is so contagious.   Patrick Worsnip, "Haiti Cholera Spreading Faster Than Predicted," Reuters

Answer: Missing premise: All contagious diseases are diseases in which the spread is almost impossible to stop.

Rewritten syllogism: All contagious diseases are diseases in which the spread is almost impossible to stop. All cholera cases are contagious diseases. Therefore, all cholera cases are diseases in which the spread is almost impossible to stop.

Let T = *contagious diseases*, I = *diseases in which the spread is almost impossible to stop*, and C = *cholera cases*.

> All T are I.
> <u>All C are T.</u>
> All C are I.

The following Venn diagram shows that the syllogism is valid:

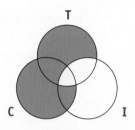

Applying the six rules verifies that the syllogism is valid:

Rule 1: The middle term is distributed in the first premise.
Rule 2: The subject term is distributed in the conclusion and in the second premise.
Rule 3: The syllogism does not have two negative premises.
Rule 4: The syllogism has a negative premise and a negative conclusion.
Rule 5: The syllogism has a negative conclusion and a negative premise.
Rule 6: The syllogism does not have two universal premises and a particular
    conclusion.

2. Henry David Thoreau said, "What is once well done is done forever." To which someone once added, "Nothing done forever is done easily."

3. Most Americans who cast their ballot in the recent midterm elections are preoccupied with the United States' economic problems. Also, most voters concerned with the country's economic problems are not people who voted on the basis of foreign policy.
    Richard N. Haass, "American Foreign Policy After the Mid-Term Elections," Project-Syndicate.org

4. Keir Dillon, professional snowboarder, said, "I respect that everyone should wear a helmet. But I don't think it should be mandated."
    Matt Higgins, "Head Games," ESPN.com

5. The two Koreas are still technically at war—the Korean War ended only with a truce.
    Peter Beck, "Obama and South Korea Leader Agree to Hold Joint Military Exercise," MSNBC.com

6. Of the 43 horses that started in synthetic track races at Santa Anita off of prep races on dirt, not one of them won, and not every one of them was hopelessly overmatched.   Mike Watchmaker, "Beware of Breeders' Cup Generalizations," Drf.com

7. Perfection is achieved, not when there is nothing more to add, but when there is nothing left to take away.   Antoine De Saint Exupery, *Wind, Sand, and Stars*

8. An immigrant who uses a false Social Security number to get a job doesn't intend to harm anyone. It makes no sense to spend our tax dollars to imprison them for two years.   Chuck Roth, in a statement to the *New York Times*

★ 9. All of us failed to match our dreams of perfection. So I rate us on the basis of our splendid failure to do the impossible.

William Faulkner, *Writers at Work, First Series*, ed. Malcolm Cowley

10. If you don't dream, you're living in a memory. Who wants to live in a memory?

Chris Del Conte, quoted at Sports.espn.go.com

H. SORITES

Sorites A special type of enthymeme that is a chain of arguments. The missing parts are intermediate conclusions, each of which, in turn, becomes a premise in the next link in the chain.

A special type of enthymeme is a chain of arguments called a **sorites**. These arguments typically have many premises. The missing parts are intermediate conclusions each of which, in turn, becomes a premise in the next link in the chain. And if one of the links fails, so does the chain: If any syllogism in the chain is invalid, then the sorites is invalid. Let's look at an example:

All drunk drivers are criminals.
All drivers with blood alcohol concentration above 0.08% are drunk drivers.
<u>All drivers who have had the equivalent of six 12-oz. beers are drivers with blood alcohol concentrations above 0.08%.</u>
All drivers who have the equivalent of six 12-oz. beers are criminals.

We can let D = *drunk drivers*, C = *criminals*, A = *drivers with blood alcohol concentration above 0.08%*, and S = *drivers who have the equivalent of six 12-oz. beers*:

All D are C.
All A are D.
<u>All S are A.</u>
All S are C.

If the first two premises, "All D are C" and "All A are D," are used as the major and minor premises of a categorical syllogism, then we can supply the intermediate conclusion: "All A are C" (for "All drivers with blood alcohol concentration above .08% are criminals"):

All D are C.
<u>All A are D.</u>
All A are C. (*Intermediate conclusion*)

A Venn diagram shows that the syllogism is valid:

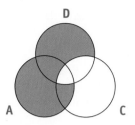

Since the syllogism does not violate any of the six rules, we have additional confirmation that it is valid.

The intermediate conclusion, "All A are C," now becomes the major premise of the next syllogism. The remaining premise of the original argument, "All S are A," becomes the minor premise, and the final conclusion is "All S are C" (which stands for "All drivers who have the equivalent of six 12-oz. beers are criminals"):

All A are C.
All S are A.
All S are C.

A Venn diagram shows that the syllogism is valid:

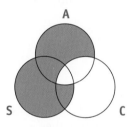

Since the syllogism does not violate any of the six rules, we have additional confirmation that it is valid.

As we already know, ordinary language arguments often require paraphrasing and reordering. Here is an example of a sorites:

Every agreement to lift embargoes is a program designed to reduce a country's international debt. It is obvious that no weapons of mass destruction are humanitarian assistance programs. It is just as clear that some chemical weapons are not agreements to lift embargoes. Also, every program designed to reduce a country's international debt is a humanitarian assistance program. Thus, some chemical weapons are not weapons of mass destruction.

The first step is to translate the statements into standard-form categorical propositions (using paraphrasing when appropriate):

All agreements to lift embargoes are programs designed to reduce a country's international debt.
No weapons of mass destruction are humanitarian assistance programs.
Some chemical weapons are not agreements to lift embargoes.

<u>All programs designed to reduce a country's international debt are humanitarian assistance programs.</u>
Some chemical weapons are not weapons of mass destruction.

The next step is to reveal the form of the argument. We let A = *agreements to lift embargoes*, P = *programs designed to reduce a country's international debt*, W = *weapons of mass destruction*, H = *humanitarian assistance programs*, and C = *chemical weapons*:

All A are P.
No W are H.
Some C are not A.
<u>All P are H.</u>
Some C are not W.

The next step is very important: We have to arrange the premises in the correct order. A simple method will ensure the correct outcome. First, locate the predicate in the conclusion (W); second, find the premise that contains the same letter (i.e., "No W are H"); and third, make that the first premise. The other term in this premise then becomes the next term, and its matching pair ("All P are H") becomes the next premise. We simply repeat the process until all premises are accounted for:

No W are H.
All P are H.
All A are P.
<u>Some C are not A.</u>
Some C are not W.

If the first two premises ("No W are H" and "All P are H") are used as the major and minor premises of a categorical syllogism, then we can supply the missing intermediate conclusion ("No P are W"):

No W are H.
<u>All P are H.</u>
No P are W. (*Intermediate conclusion*)

A Venn diagram shows that the syllogism is valid:

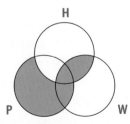

Since the syllogism does not violate any of the six rules, we have an additional confirmation that it is valid. The intermediate conclusion ("No P are W") now becomes the major premise of the next syllogism. The next premise of the argument ("All A are P") becomes the minor premise, and the next intermediate conclusion is "No A are W":

No P are W.
All A are P.
No A are W. (*Intermediate conclusion*)

A Venn diagram shows that the syllogism is valid:

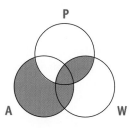

Since the syllogism does not violate any of the six rules, we have an additional confirmation. The intermediate conclusion ("No A are W") now becomes the major premise of the final syllogism. The last premise of the argument ("Some C are not A") becomes the minor premise, and the final conclusion is "Some C are not W":

No A are W.
Some C are not A.
Some C are not W.

Here a Venn diagram shows that the syllogism is invalid:

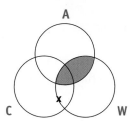

As confirmation, the syllogism violates Rule 3: A categorical syllogism cannot have two negative premises. Since the syllogism has two negative premises, it commits the fallacy of exclusive premises.

CHECK YOUR UNDERSTANDING 6H

I. First, put the following sorites into standard form and reduce the number of terms whenever necessary. Second, determine the intermediate conclusions. Third, use Venn diagrams and the six rules to determine whether the syllogisms are valid or invalid under the modern interpretation.

1. No A are C.
   All non-D are non-B.
   No D are non-C.
   No B are A.

Answer: Rewrite the syllogism. First, apply contraposition to "All non-D are non-B" to obtain "All B are D." Second, apply obversion to "No D are non-C" to obtain "All D are C."

No A are C.
All B are D.
<u>All D are C.</u>
No B are A.

Next, locate the predicate in the conclusion; the premise that contains the same letter is the first premise of our constructed syllogism. The other term in this premise then becomes the next term, and its matching pair becomes the next premise.

No A are C.
<u>All D are C.</u>
No D are A. (*Intermediate conclusion*)

The syllogism does not violate any of the six rules.
The following Venn diagram shows that the syllogism is valid:

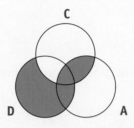

The intermediate conclusion now becomes the major premise of the final syllogism, and the remaining premise becomes the minor premise:

No D are A.
<u>All B are D.</u>
No B are A.

The syllogism does not violate any of the six rules.
The following Venn diagram shows that the syllogism is valid:

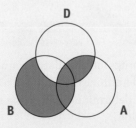

2. Some A are not C.
   No A are B.
   <u>All D are C.</u>
   Some B are not D.

3. Some A are C.
    All A are non-B.
    <u>All D are B.</u>
    Some non-D are not non-C.

4. No C are A.
    All D are C.
    <u>Some B are A.</u>
    Some B are not D.

★ 5. All B are D.
    No E are C.
    No A are non-C.
    <u>All non-A are non-B.</u>
    All D are non-E.

6. No B are C.
    All A are D.
    Some A are B.
    <u>Some D are E.</u>
    Some E are not C.

7. All non-C are non-E.
    All C are B.
    All A are non-B.
    <u>Some D are A.</u>
    Some non-E are not non-D.

8. No E are non-A.
    All D are non-B.
    All A are B.
    No E are F.
    <u>No non-C are D.</u>
    All C are non-F.

★ 9. Some B are E.
    All C are A.
    All D are C.
    <u>No A are B.</u>
    Some E are not D.

10. No non-F are C.
    All non-A are non-B.
    All E are non-D.
    Some B are C.
    <u>All D are non-A.</u>
    Some F are not E.

II. Rewrite each of the following sorites in standard form and reduce the number of terms whenever necessary. Second, determine the intermediate conclusions. Third, use Venn diagrams and the six rules under the modern interpretation to determine whether the syllogisms are valid or invalid.

1. All the clothes in my closet are old.
   No popular clothes are old.
   <u>All expensive clothes are popular.</u>
   Not a single item of clothing in my closet is expensive.

Answer: Rewrite the conclusion as follows: "No clothes in my closet are expensive."
Let C = *clothes in my closet*, O = *old things*, P = *popular clothes*, and E = *expensive clothes*.

> All C are O.
> No P are O.
> <u>All E are P.</u>
> No C are E.

Next, we locate the predicate in the conclusion and construct a syllogism:

> All E are P.
> <u>No P are O.</u>
> No O are E. (*Intermediate conclusion*)

The syllogism does not violate any of the six rules.
The following Venn diagram shows that the syllogism is valid:

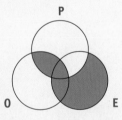

The intermediate conclusion now becomes the major premise of the final syllogism, and the remaining premise becomes the minor premise:

> No O are E.
> <u>All C are O.</u>
> No C are E.

The syllogism does not violate any of the six rules.
The following Venn diagram shows that the syllogism is valid:

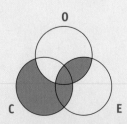

2. No one but an artist has an adoring public.
   No artists wonder whether they will be famous.
   <u>No one who wonders whether he will be famous is a logic instructor.</u>
   No logic instructor has an adoring public.

3. Fake diamonds turn dull over time.
   No polished jewelry turns dull over time.
   <u>No expensive jewelry is unpolished jewelry.</u>
   Fake diamonds are inexpensive jewelry.

4. All my mom's books are classics.
   No classic books have a copyright.
   <u>All popular books are copyrighted.</u>
   None of my mom's books are popular.

⭐ 5. No famous sitcoms are controversial shows.
   All famous sitcoms are written for mass audiences.
   <u>All X-rated movies are written for small audiences.</u>
   All X-rated movies are controversial programs.

6. None of my dogs are overweight.
   All of my cats sleep 18 hours a day.
   All of my pets who chase other animals are cats.
   <u>None of my pets who chase other animals are overweight.</u>
   None of my dogs sleep 18 hours a day.

7. All reasoning that uses the principles of logic are well-grounded ideas.
   Irrational thinking does not use the principles of logic.
   Rational thinking is more likely to achieve correct decisions.
   <u>All decisions based on probabilities are more likely to achieve correct decisions.</u>
   All decisions based on probabilities are well-grounded ideas.

8. All satisfied restaurant customers will recommend the food to their friends.
   All dirty restaurants are health hazards.
   All satisfied restaurant customers are people who ate well-cooked food.
   No people who ate well-cooked food are health hazards.
   <u>All people who will recommend the food to their friends are repeat customers.</u>
   No dirty restaurants have repeat customers.

⭐ 9. My neighbor plays loud music.
   Drum sounds are the heart of song.
   My neighbor plays music that has a melody.
   The music that you can hear is from people who play loud music.
   <u>Music that has a melody uses drum sounds.</u>
   The only music that you can hear is the heart of song.

10. All industrial strength cleaners are toxic.
   All products that can be sold in grocery stores are tested in a public consumer's laboratory.
   Crudex is a salad dressing.
   Some industrial strength cleaners are tested in a public consumer's laboratory.
   <u>Only products that can be sold in grocery stores are salad dressings.</u>
   Crudex is not toxic.

Summary

- Syllogism: A deductive argument that has exactly two premises and a conclusion.
- Categorical syllogism: A syllogism constructed entirely of categorical propositions. It contains three different terms, each of which is used two times.
- Minor term: The subject of the conclusion of a categorical syllogism.
- Major term: The predicate of the conclusion of a categorical syllogism.
- Middle term: The term that occurs only in the premises of a categorical syllogism.
- Major premise: The first premise of a categorical syllogism contains the major term.
- Minor premise: The second premise of a categorical syllogism contains the minor term.
- In order to be a standard-form categorical syllogism, three requirements must be met: (1) All three statements must be standard-form categorical propositions. (2) The two occurrences of each term must be identical and have the same sense. (3) The major premise must occur first, the minor premise second, and the conclusion last.
- The mood of a categorical syllogism consists of the type of categorical propositions involved (**A**, **E**, **I**, or **O**) and the order in which they occur.
- The middle term can be arranged in the two premises in four different ways. These placements determine the figure of the categorical syllogism.
- There are six rules for standard-form categorical syllogisms: (1) The middle term must be distributed in at least one premise. (2) If a term is distributed in the conclusion, then it must be distributed in a premise. (3) A categorical syllogism cannot have two negative premises. (4) A negative premise must have a negative conclusion. (5) A negative conclusion must have a negative premise. (6) Two universal premises cannot have a particular conclusion.
- Sorites: A special type of enthymeme in which the missing parts are intermediate conclusions each of which, in turn becomes a premise in the next link in the chain.

KEY TERMS

syllogism   218
categorical
  syllogism   218
minor term   219
major term   219
middle term   219
major premise   219
minor premise   219

standard-form categorical
  syllogism   219
mood   244
figure   245
undistributed middle   249
illicit major   250
illicit minor   250
exclusive premises   251

affirmative conclusion/
  negative premise   252
negative conclusion/
  affirmative
  premises   253
existential fallacy   254
sorites   278

LOGIC CHALLENGE: THE FOUR CIRCLES

Suppose you are told that there are three interesting relationships among four distinct groups of objects (which we will refer to as A, B, C, and D). Here are the relationships:

- All A are B.
- All C are D.
- Some B are C.

If all three relationships are true, then which one of the five following relationships would also be true?

1. All C are B.
2. All D are A.
3. Some C are A.
4. Some D are B.
5. Some A are D.

Note: Since there are four distinct groups (referred to as A, B, C, and D), you can construct a diagram that has four interlocking circles. That's a big part of the challenge.

Chapter 7

Propositional Logic

Sports championships offer a chance for a city to celebrate, but they can also result in violence, looting, and even death. News coverage often shows burning cars, smashed store windows, and struggles between police and rioters. Here is one recent account:

> Fans wandered amid the chaos, some with bandanas or T-shirts pulled over their faces—either to hide their faces from police and TV cameras or to guard against the smoke, or both.
>
> "Rioters Run Wild in Vancouver After Cup Loss," Associated Press

This brief description is actually quite complex. Several simple statements are connected by a few key words. The reporter makes all of the following claims: Some fans hid their faces with bandanas *or* T-shirts pulled over their faces in order to hide from police *and* TV cameras *or* guard against smoke, *or* both. The italicized words indicate the presence of multiple statements at work. When we read the passage, we barely notice the simple words "and" and "or," and yet their role in helping us understand the reporter's claims are crucial. In fact, the words express a logical function that guides us in understanding the connection between the several claims.

Complex statements that contain words like "and" and "or" are common in ordinary language and are used in almost every form of communication—in business, in law, in politics, in academics, and in everyday conversations.

Here is another example about a contemporary topic:

> The proposition that Muslims are welcome in Britain if, and only if, they stop behaving like Muslims is a doctrine which is incompatible with the principles that guide a free society.
>
> Roy Hattersley (former deputy leader of the British Labour Party, quoted in the *Independent*)

The passage contains another complex statement. The key logical part is the phrase "if, and only if," which indicates that multiple claims are being made. To fully understand Mr. Hattersley's claims, and to offer an analysis of them, requires knowing that the word "if" has a different logical function than "only if."

Words such as "and," "or," "if," and "only if" are sometimes used imprecisely or ambiguously in ordinary language. However, propositional logic provides precise definitions. The clarity and precision of the basic language of propositional logic guides us through the analysis of many kinds of deductive arguments. This chapter explores the foundations of propositional logic and explains how it captures much of what is expressed in ordinary language. It also provides the foundation for the next two chapters.

A. LOGICAL OPERATORS AND TRANSLATIONS

As we saw in Chapters 5 and 6, ordinary language can often be translated by using letters to represent class terms. The symbolic translations reduced the vagueness or obscurity of everyday linguistic usage. In this chapter we learn to translate ordinary language statements using special symbols called **logical operators**, or *connectives*. In categorical logic the basic elements are class terms (which by themselves are neither true nor false). However, in **propositional logic** the basic elements are statements (which are either true or false). The statements are represented by letters and, unlike the four categorical statements (**A, E, I, O**), propositional logic contains an unlimited number of complex statements.

Logical operators Special symbols that can be used as part of ordinary language statement translations.

Propositional logic The basic components in propositional logic are statements.

Simple and Compound Statements

In order to see how these complex statements are formed, we must first distinguish between simple and compound statements. A **simple statement** is one that does not have any other statement as a component. Here are some examples:

- Harrisburg is the capital of Pennsylvania.
- Wednesday is hump day.
- Grilled hamburgers taste delicious.
- Detective novels make great movies.

Simple statement One that does not have any other statement as a component.

Simple statements are translated by using any uppercase letter. For example, the letter "H" can be used to represent the statement "Harrisburg is the capital of Pennsylvania." Although we typically pick a letter that easily identifies the statement (in this case "H"), any other letter would be fine. The remaining simple statements can be translated similarly. For example, the letter "W" can be used to represent the statement "Wednesday is hump day"; the letter "G" can be used to represent the statement "Grilled hamburgers taste delicious"; and finally, the letter "D" can be used to represent the statement "Detective novels make great movies."

A **compound statement** is a statement that has at least one simple statement as a component. Here are some examples:

Compound statement A statement that has at least one simple statement as a component.

1. It is not the case that drinking hot coffee reduces sweating.
2. *Hamlet* is a tragedy and *Kung Fu Panda* is a comedy.
3. Either we reduce carbon emissions or global warming will get worse.
4. If the IRS processed my return, then I should get my refund this week.
5. You will graduate if and only if you meet all university requirements.

These compound statements can be represented by using uppercase letters to stand for the simple statements:

1. It is not the case that *D*.
2. *H* and *K*.
3. Either *C* or *G*.
4. If *I*, then *R*.
5. *G* if and only if *U*.

The translation of example 4 illustrates an important point. Notice that we did the following: We let *I* = *the IRS processed my return*, and *R* = *I should get my refund this week*. Once we designate the meaning of the letter "I" in a compound statement, we cannot use that letter again. In other words, we can use the letter "I" for either "the IRS processed my return" or "I should get my refund this week," but not both. This restriction holds for arguments as well—a particular letter can stand for at most one statement.

Now it may seem odd that the first statement is considered compound. After all, it has only the single simple statement *D*, whereas the other four statements each have two simple statements. It consists of an affirmative statement ("drinking hot coffee reduces sweating") and the phrase "it is not the case that," which is translated by a logical operator. In fact, the expressions "and," "or," "if . . . then," and "if and only if" are all translated by logical operators. Here are the translations:

Operator	Name	Compound Type	Used to Translate
~	tilde	negation	not; it is not the case that
·	dot	conjunction	and; also; moreover
v	wedge	disjunction	or; unless
⊃	horseshoe	conditional	if . . . then . . . ; only if
≡	triple bar	biconditional	if and only if

We can now use the operators to translate our five examples of compound statements:

1. ~ *D*
2. *H* · *K*
3. *C* v *G*
4. *I* ⊃ *R*
5. *G* ≡ *U*

A word of caution: Although the logical operators are used to translate the statements, the symbolic translations are not synonymous with the original English expressions. For example, in ordinary language the expressions "and," "or," and "if" are often vague or ambiguous. However, as we shall soon see, the meaning of the logical operators is precise and unambiguous. For now, we will continue to concentrate on learning how to translate English statements using the logical operators. We will start by using the operators to translate simple statements. You will then learn how to translate more complex statements.

Negation

The tilde symbol (~) is used to translate any ordinary language negated proposition. Some of the words and phrases that you might find in ordinary language statements are "not," "it is not the case that," "it is false that," and "it is not true that." For example, the statement "Today is not Monday" is the negation of the simple statement "Today is Monday." The word "not" and the phrase "it is not the case that" are used to deny the statement that follows them, and we refer to their use as **negation**.

Here are some examples of English statements and their translations:

- Barack Obama is not a member of the Republican Party.   ~ B
- It is false that gold is currently selling at $1000 an ounce.   ~ G
- It is not the case that home foreclosures have peaked.   ~ H

As the examples illustrate, the tilde is positioned directly in front of the proposition that it negates. (This is not a problem for simple statements, but, as we shall soon see, some complex statements require a bit more apparatus for the correct placement of the tilde.)

Negation The word "not" and the phrase "it is not the case that" are used to deny the statement that follows them, and we refer to their use as negation.

Conjunction

The dot symbol (·) is used to translate propositions in ordinary language that use any of the following words: "and," "but," "still," "moreover," "while," "however," "also," "moreover," "although," "yet," "nevertheless," and "whereas." A **conjunction** is a compound statement that has two distinct statements (called *conjuncts*) connected by the dot symbol. Here are some examples of English statements and their translations:

- Facebook is selling stock, and Twitter is a global phenomenon.   F · T
- Music videos are dying out, and cloud computing is growing.   M · C
- Honesty is the best policy, and lying is for scoundrels.   H · L

Conjunction A compound statement that has two distinct statements (called conjuncts) connected by the dot symbol.

Now consider this statement:

Frank and Ernest teach music.

The statement is a shorthand way of writing "Frank teaches music, and Ernest teaches music." Therefore, it can be easily translated as "F · E." As we learned in the previous chapters, whenever there is ambiguity in ordinary language, we must do our best to capture its meaning. We can typically understand the common use of phrases and terms based on their context.

Disjunction

The wedge symbol (v) is used to translate ordinary language statements containing the words "or," "unless," and "otherwise," and the phrase "either … or." Sometimes the word "unless" functions like the word "or." For example, the statement "You can't go to the party unless you clean your room," can be rewritten as "Either you clean your room or you can't go to the party."

Disjunction A compound statement that has two distinct statements (called disjuncts) connected by the wedge symbol.

A **disjunction** is a compound statement that has two distinct statements (called *disjuncts*) connected by the wedge symbol. (Disjunctions were first introduced in Chapter 3.) Here are some examples of English statements and their translations:

- You can have steak or chicken. $S \vee C$
- She is either a Pisces or a Scorpio. $P \vee S$
- Paris is the city of lights, or Big Ben is in London. $P \vee B$
- Unless it rains today, we will go swimming. $R \vee S$

Conditional

Conditional In ordinary language, the word "if" typically precedes the antecedent of a conditional. The horseshoe symbol is used to translate a conditional statement.

The horseshoe symbol ($\supset$) is used to translate a **conditional** statement. (Chapter 3 introduced conditional statements and its application to necessary and sufficient conditions. Additional discussion of necessary and sufficient conditions occurs later in this chapter.) For example, the ordinary language statement "If you smoke two packs of cigarettes a day, then you have a high risk of getting lung cancer" can be translated as "$S \supset L$." The statement that follows the "if" is the *antecedent*, and the statement that follows the "then" is the *consequent*. Therefore, whatever phrase follows "if" must be placed first in the translation. Here are two examples to illustrate this point:

- If you wash the car, then you can go to the movies. $W \supset M$
- You can go to the movies, if you wash the car. $W \supset M$

The word "if" is a clear indicator word, one that immediately reveals the existence of a conditional statement. There are additional English words and phrases that can indicate a conditional statement. For example, consider this statement: "Whenever it snows, my water pipes freeze." This statement can be translated as "$S \supset F$." Here are more words and phrases that indicate conditionals:

Every time P, then Q.	Given that P, then Q.
Each time P, then Q.	Provided that P, then Q.
All cases where P, then Q.	In any case where P, then Q.
Anytime P, then Q.	P implies Q.
In the event of P, then Q.	On any occurrence of P, then Q.
On condition that P, then Q.	For every instance of P, then Q.

Each of these can be translated as "$P \supset Q$." Learning to recognize conditional statements makes the task of translation easier.

Distinguishing "If" from "Only If"

We already stipulated that "if" precedes the antecedent of a conditional. We can now stipulate that "only if" precedes the consequent of a conditional. Here are some examples:

- You will get the bonus only if you finish by noon. $B \supset F$
  (B = *You will get the bonus*, and F = *you finish by noon*.)
- Only if she has a 10% down payment will she get a mortgage. $M \supset P$
  (M = *she will get a mortgage*, and P = *she has a 10% down payment*.)

Here are some more examples to illustrate the many different uses of "if" and "only if":

1. *If* you manage to win the lottery, then you will be contacted by relatives you never knew existed. $M \supset C$
   (M = *you manage to win the lottery*, and P = *you will be contacted by relatives you never knew existed*.)
2. *Only if* you manage to win the lottery, you will be contacted by relatives you never knew existed. $C \supset M$
3. You will be contacted by relatives you never knew existed, *if* you manage to win the lottery. $M \supset C$
4. You will be contacted by relatives you never knew existed, *only if* you manage to win the lottery. $C \supset M$

Biconditional

The triple bar symbol ($\equiv$) is used to translate a **biconditional** statement. For example, the ordinary language statement "You will get ice cream if and only if you eat your spinach" can be translated as "$I \equiv S$." This compound statement is made up of two conditionals: one is indicated by the word "if" and the other by the phrase "only if." We can reveal the two conditionals as follows:

> If you eat your spinach, then you get ice cream, and you get ice cream only if you eat your spinach.

Notice that this complex statement is a conjunction. However, both components of the conjunction are conditionals. The first component can be translated as "$S \supset I$"; the second component can be translated as "$I \supset S$." The complete translation of this complex statement can now be given:

$$(S \supset I) \cdot (I \supset S)$$

The triple bar reduces the complexity: "$I \equiv S$." (We placed the letter "I" first in the biconditional because it occurred first in the original English statement.)

Biconditional A compound statement consisting of two conditionals—one indicated by the word "if" and the other indicated by the phrase "only if." The triple bar symbol is used to translate a biconditional statement.

SUMMARY OF OPERATORS AND ORDINARY LANGUAGE	
Operator	**Words and Phrases in Ordinary Language**
~	*not; it is not the case that; it is false that; it is not true that*
·	*and; but; still; moreover; while; however; also; moreover; although; yet; nevertheless; whereas*
v	*or; unless; otherwise; either . . . or*
⊃	*if; only if; every time; given that; each time; provided that; all cases where; in any case where; any time; supposing that; in the event of; on any occurrence of; on condition that; for every instance of*
≡	*if and only if*

CHECK YOUR UNDERSTANDING 7A

Translate the following statements into symbolic form by using logical operators and uppercase letters to represent the English statements. Specify the meaning of the letters you choose in the symbolizations.

1. Either it will rain tomorrow or it will be sunny.

Answer: $R \lor S$. Let $R =$ *it will rain tomorrow,* and $S =$ it will be sunny.

2. The food in that restaurant stinks, and the portions are too small.

3. Your ice is not cold.

4. If my stock portfolio is weak, then I am losing money.

⭐ 5. My car does not look great, but it gets great gas mileage.

6. If you feel great, then you look great.

7. My test score was high or I am mistaken.

8. You passed the exam only if you got at least a C.

⭐ 9. Either candy or tobacco is bad for your teeth.

10. Bill is cold and Mary is late.

11. Today is Monday or today is Tuesday.

12. He is not a U.S. senator.

⭐ 13. Toothpaste is good for your teeth, but tobacco is not.

14. Driving too fast is hazardous to your health; also driving without buckling up.

15. Pizza contains all the basic food groups if, and only if, you get it with anchovies.

16. Lava lamps are distracting, while music in the background is soothing.

⭐ 17. My room could use a good cleaning, but I am too lazy to do anything about it.

18. You must get a passing grade on the next exam; otherwise you will fail.

19. If Carly agrees to do a job, then she will make sure it is done right.

20. It is not true that *Titanic* is the highest grossing film of all time.

⭐ 21. I will leave a big tip only if the dinner is excellent.

22. Your paper was turned in late; however, I am willing to grant you an extension.

23. Unless you stop eating too much pepperoni, you will develop a stomach ulcer.

24. Only if your paper was turned in late, I will deduct a letter grade.

⭐ 25. It is false that Grover Cleveland was the greatest U.S. president.

26. She is happy with her box of candy; however, she would have preferred a new car.

27. Only if my car has a turbocharger, it is fast.

28. *Citizen Kane* did not win the Academy Award for best picture, but it is still the greatest movie ever made.

⭐ 29. Barbara is going to lose her football bet and Johnny will get a night at the ballet.

30. My father is wise only if he is honest.

31. Either my stock portfolio is strong or I am losing money.

32. If I am lazy, then my room is not clean.

⭐ 33. If driving too fast is hazardous to your health, then so is driving without buckling up.

34. My father is wise and he is honest.

35. My stock portfolio is weak only if I am losing money.

36. There are not too many circus acts in Las Vegas.

⭐ 37. Only if my room could use a good cleaning, I am too lazy to do anything about it.

38. Watching circus acts is hazardous to your health and so is falling into deep holes.

39. If my father is wise, then he is honest.

40. My car is fast, if it has a turbocharger.

⭐ 41. If it rains tomorrow, then I will not have to water my plants.

42. Reading is relaxing and thinking is productive.

43. Cats and dogs make great pets.

44. The decathlon is a difficult Olympic event.

⭐ 45. My car is old, but it is still reliable.

46. Only if you are registered can you vote.

47. Either coffee or tea contains caffeine.

48. Today is Monday unless today is Tuesday.

⭐ 49. Teaching is a challenging profession.

50. It is not the case that Halley's Comet returned in 2008.

B. COMPLEX STATEMENTS

In the translation of any compound statement, we must make sure to use the logical operator symbols correctly. Just as there are rules of grammar in English, there are grammatical (syntactical) rules for using symbols as well. For example, we immediately recognize that the English sentence "Carly is an excellent costume designer and a gifted pattern-maker" is grammatically correct. We also know that a different arrangement of the same words may violate rules of grammar. For example, "And excellent costume designer is an Carly gifted pattern-maker a."

Well-Formed Formulas

Well-formed formulas
Compound statement forms that are grammatically correct.

A few simple rules for using operator symbols ensure that the compound statement forms are grammatically correct. Such statements are also called **well-formed formulas**, or *WFFs*.

Rule 1:
The dot, wedge, horseshoe, and *triple bar* symbols must go between two statements (either simple or compound).

Applying the rule ensures that "$P \cdot Q$," "$P \vee Q$," "$P \supset Q$," and "$P \equiv Q$" are all *WFFs*, where the four operators go between simple statements. Here are some examples of *WFFs* where the operators go between compound statements:

$$(P \vee Q) \supset\, \sim R \qquad\qquad (S \cdot P) \vee (Q \cdot S)$$

However, "$\cdot P$," "$P \cdot$," "$P\,Q\,v$," "$\supset P$," and "$P\,Q \equiv$" are not *WFFs* because in each case an operator is not between two statements.

Rule 2:
The tilde (~) goes in front of the statement it is meant to negate.

Applying the rule ensures that "~ P" is a *WFF*. Here are some more examples of *WFFs* using the tilde:

$$\sim (P \vee Q) \supset \sim R \qquad\qquad (S \cdot P) \vee \sim (\sim Q \cdot S)$$

However, "*P* ~," "(*P* ∨ *Q*) ~," and "~ (*S* · *P*) ~" are not *WFFs*.

Rule 3:

The tilde (~) cannot, *by itself*, go between two statements.
   For example, "*P* ~ *Q*" is not a *WFF*. However, "*P* ∨ ~ *Q*" is a *WFF*.

Rule 4:

Parentheses, brackets, and braces are required in order to eliminate ambiguity in a complex statement.
   The following three examples show how parentheses, brackets, and braces are used:

1. Both "*P* ∨ (*Q* · *R*)" and "(*P* ∨ *Q*) · *R*" are *WFFs*. However, "*P* ∨ *Q* (· *R*)" is not a *WFF* because the dot does not have either a simple or compound statement directly to its left. Since the *dot* is not between two statements, Rule 1 is broken.
2. "[(*P* ∨ *Q*) · (~ *R* ⊃ *S*)] ∨ *Q*" uses both parentheses and brackets. Since no rules are broken, it is a *WFF*.
3. "{ [(*P* ∨ ~ *Q*) · (*R* ⊃ *S*)] ∨ ~ *P* } ⊃ ~ (*R* · *M*) uses parentheses, brackets, and braces. Since no rules are broken, it is a *WFF*.

CHECK YOUR UNDERSTANDING 7B.1

Determine whether the following arrangements of operator symbols and letters are *WFFs*. If any are not *WFFs*, point out the mistake and the rule that is violated. (Some examples may contain more than one mistake.)

1. $P \vee \sim Q$

Answer: This is a *WFF*.

2. $R \sim \vee T$

3. K

4. $K \cdot (P \sim Q)$

★ 5. $L \supset \sim P$

6. $L \supset \sim (P \vee \supset Q)$

7. $M (\supset P \supset Q)$

8. $(P \vee Q \supset R)$

★ 9. $[(P Q)] \vee \sim R$

10. $\sim P (v \sim R) \cdot \sim S$

11. $P \cdot \vee Q$

12. $R \vee T \sim$

★ 13. $P Q$

14. $K \cdot (P \vee \sim Q)$

15. $L \sim P$

Main Operator

In order to fine-tune your knowledge of the rules for *WFFs* and to understand how to translate complex statements, we need to discuss the *main operator*. This discussion will also add to your understanding of the necessity of using parentheses, brackets, and braces to eliminate ambiguity. We start by specifying three important factors concerning the main operator:

Main operator
The operator that has in its range the largest component or components in a compound statement.

A. The **main operator** is the operator that has in its range the largest component or components in a compound statement.
B. The *main operator* is either one of the four operators that go between statements or else it is the negation operator.
C. There can be only one main operator in a compound statement.

Let's put these stipulations to work by looking at examples of compound statements:

1. $\sim R$
2. $\sim (P \vee Q)$
3. $\sim [(P \vee Q) \cdot (R \cdot S)]$

The main operator for all three examples is the tilde. The only component in example 1 is the simple statement R, and it is in the range of the tilde. In example 2, the largest component is the compound statement contained within the parentheses, and it is in the range of the tilde. In example 3, the largest component is the compound statement contained within the brackets, and it is in the range of the tilde.

4. $\sim R \cdot S$
5. $(P \vee Q) \cdot R$
6. $[(P \vee \sim Q) \cdot (R \cdot S)] \cdot \sim (M \supset N)$

The main operator for examples 4–6 is the dot. In example 4, the component $\sim R$ and the component S are both in the range of the dot. In example 5, the large component to the left of the dot and the simple statement to its right are both in its range. In example 6, both the larger component within brackets and the smaller component within parenthesis are in the range of the dot.

7. $R \vee S$
8. $(P \vee Q) \supset \sim R$
9. $\{ [(\sim P \vee Q) \cdot (R \cdot S)] \cdot (M \supset N) \} \equiv \sim (P \vee M)$

The main operator for example 7 is the wedge; the two simple statements, R and S are both within its range. In example 8, the component in parentheses and the

component ~ R are both in the range of the horseshoe; therefore, it is the main operator. Finally, in example 9, the larger component within braces to the left of the triple
bar and the smaller component to its right are both within the range of the triple bar;
therefore, it is the main operator.

There is one further point to illustrate. As mentioned earlier, there can be only one
main operator in a compound statement. To see why this is necessary, consider this
example:

$$P \vee Q \cdot R$$

As it stands, the compound statement is ambiguous. This is where Rule 4 comes in
handy. To fully understand this, let's suppose that we are discussing the possibility that
three people—Paul, Quincy, and Rita—are going to a party. Let *P = Paul will go to the
party, Q = Quincy will go to the party*, and *R = Rita will go to the party*. If we follow Rule
1, the operators "v" and "·" in "*P* v *Q* · *R*" are *each* supposed to connect two statements
(simple or compound). However, without parentheses, the *Q* gets dragged in two directions at once. Therefore, we do not know whether to connect the *Q* to the *P* or to the *R*.

There are two choices we can make: either "*P* v (*Q* · *R*)" or "(*P* v *Q*) · *R*." In either
case, the ambiguity has been eliminated by the proper use of parentheses. But which is
meant? The parentheses can help to explain why these are *not* identical statements. In
the first choice, "*P* v (*Q* · *R*)" the wedge is the main operator. If we replace the letters
with the corresponding English statements, we get this:

A. *Either* Paul will go to the party, *or both* Quincy *and* Rita will go to the
party.

On the other hand, in the second choice, "(*P* v *Q*) · *R*" the dot is the main operator.
Once again, if we replace the letters with the corresponding English statements we
get this:

B. *Either* Paul *or* Quincy will go to the party, *and* Rita will go to the party.

A comparison of A and B shows that they are not identical statements; they do not
express the same proposition.

We will add one more example. When negation is the main operator, the tilde
completely governs the compound statement. For example, " ~ *K*," " ~ (*P* v *Q*),"
and "~ [(*K* · ~ *L*) ⊃ (~ *P* v *Q*)]," all have the *leftmost* negation symbol as the main
operator. Now let's compare the statement "~ (*P* v *Q*)" with the statement "~ *P* v *Q*."
We can use the same English substitutions for the letters that we used earlier: Let *P =
Paul will go to the party*, and *Q = Quincy will go to the party*. In the first choice, the tilde
is the main operator. Since the negation governs everything inside the parentheses,
the statement becomes this:

C. *Neither* Paul *nor* Quincy will go to the party.

However, in the second statement the wedge is the main operator. In this case, the
tilde negates only the simple statement *P*. The result is the following:

D. *Either* Paul will *not* go to the party, *or* Quincy will go to the party.

Once again we can see how the main operator ranges over the entire compound statement. These examples illustrate why there can be only one main operator in a complex statement. This also shows why we need to reduce the ambiguity in complex statements—and why the rules for *WFFs* can help.

CHECK YOUR UNDERSTANDING 7B.2

Identify and draw a circle around the main operator in each of the following *WFFs*.

1. ~ Q ∨ P

Answer:: The wedge is the main operator. ~ Q Ⓥ P

2. R · (~ T ∨ K)

3. ~ K

4. (P · ~ Q) ∨ K

★ 5. L ⊃ ~ P

6. (L ⊃ ~ P) ⊃ Q

7. (M ∨ P) ⊃ (Q ∨ R)

8. [P ∨ (Q ⊃ R)] · (~ R ∨ S)

★ 9. (P · Q) ∨ ~ R

10. ~ [(P ∨ ~ R) · ~ S]

11. (~ Q ∨ P) ⊃ R

12. [R · (~ T ∨ K)] ∨ S

★ 13. ~ K ⊃ ~ P

14. (P · ~ Q) ∨ (K ⊃ R)

15. (L ⊃ ~ P) · ~ R

16. [(L ⊃ ~ P) ⊃ Q] ⊃ ~ S

★ 17. [(M ∨ P) ⊃ (Q ∨ R)] ∨ (S · ~ P)

18. [P ∨ (Q ⊃ R)] ⊃ ~ (~ R ∨ S)

19. (P · Q) ∨ (~ R ∨ S)

20. ~ [(P ⊃ ~ R) ⊃ (~ S ∨ Q)]

★ 21. ~ Q · P

22. (R · Q) ∨ (~ T ∨ K)

23. P

24. (P · ~ Q) · K

★ 25. L ⊃ (~ P ⊃ Q)

Translations and the Main Operator

As mentioned earlier, whenever we translate sentences from ordinary language we must try our best to use logical operators to reduce or eliminate ambiguity. Translating complex statements from English often requires the correct placement of parentheses. One strategy to apply is to look for the main operator. Once you locate the main operator, then you can apply parentheses as needed to ensure that the largest components in the statement are within the range of the main operator. Here is an example:

Either Tracy or Becky owns a DVD player, but Sophie owns one for sure.

In this example the comma helps us to locate the main operator. The word "but" indicates that the main operator is a conjunction. To the left of the comma, the statement "Either Tracy or Becky owns a DVD player" is a disjunction. To the right of the comma is the simple statement "Sophie owns one (DVD player) for sure."

We are now in position to translate the complex statement. If we let $T = Tracy\ owns$ $a\ DVD\ player$, $B = Becky\ owns\ a\ DVD\ player$, and $S = Sophie\ owns\ one\ (DVD\ player)\ for$ $sure$, then we can translate the statement as follows:

$$(T \lor B) \cdot S$$

The parentheses clearly separate the compound statement about Tracy and Becky from the simple statement about Sophie. Once we saw that the main operator was a *conjunction*, we then needed to place the disjunction about Tracy and Becky in parentheses. This ensured that the main operator would be the dot, and it eliminated any potential ambiguity.

The statement "Both Suzuki and Honda are Japanese-owned companies" can be translated without using parentheses, as "$S \cdot H$". Now let's compare this to a slightly different statement:

Not both Suzuki and Honda are Japanese-owned companies.

This is a more complex statement, and it will require the use of parentheses to translate it accurately. The two statements about Suzuki and Honda are clearly joined by the conjunction word "and." However, notice that the placement of the word "not" is intended to *deny the conjunction*. In other words, since the negation is the main operator in this sentence, we must place parentheses around the conjunction. This results in the following translation:

$$\sim (S \cdot H)$$

If this seems confusing, then consider another similar example. Suppose my neighbor claims that both my cat and my dog have fleas. This can be translated as the conjunction of two simple statements: "$C \cdot D$."

Now I can *negate* my neighbor's claim by saying, "It is not the case that both my cat and my dog have fleas." Here, I am merely claiming that *at least one* of the simple statements is false. When I negate the conjunction, I am *not* necessarily saying that both the simple statements are false. Therefore, my statement gets translated by making sure the negation is the main operator: "$\sim (C \cdot D)$."

Here is another example of a complex ordinary language statement: "Neither Ford nor Chevrolet is a Japanese-owned company." Translating this statement also requires the careful placement of parentheses. One strategy to get started is to recognize that if we eliminate the letter "n" from *"neither . . . nor"* we get *"either . . . or."* The *n*'s act as a negation device in this sentence. In other words, the statement can be rewritten as follows:

> *It is not the case* that either Ford or Chevrolet is a Japanese-owned company.

The main operator is the negation; therefore we must place parentheses around the disjunction. The translation is this: "$\sim (F \lor C)$."

CHECK YOUR UNDERSTANDING 7B.3

I. Translate the following statements into symbolic form by using logical operators and uppercase letters to represent the English statements

1. It is not the case that Shane and Carly are hungry.
Answer: $\sim (S \cdot C)$. Let S = *Shane is hungry,* and C = *Carly is hungry.*

> The conjunction "Shane and Carly are hungry" contains two simple statements: "Shane is hungry," and "Carly is hungry." However, the main operator is a negation ("It is not the case that"); therefore the tilde must be placed outside the parentheses that contain the conjunction.

2. I am not mistaken and my test score was high, and I am happy about the result.

3. He neither attended a remedial driver's education course nor did he lose his license.

4. Not both Mike and Jane wear braces on their teeth.

⭐ 5. If you can save $100 a month, then if you can afford the insurance, then you can buy a motorcycle.

6. If you exercise for 20 minutes a day and you cut out 1000 calories a day, then you will be in top physical condition in 6 months.

7. It is not the case that if you stop studying, then you will both pass the course and keep your scholarship.

8. We will reinstitute a military draft, only if either we are attacked on our soil or too few people sign up voluntarily.

⭐ 9. If neither Walter nor Sandy can drive to Pittsburgh next weekend, then Jessica will not come home, unless Jennifer is able to arrive on time.

10. It is not the case that his business is fair or reputable.

11. If we are not careful and we don't change the oil often enough, then the engine will be ruined.

12. Either he is not allowed to go to the concert or if he finishes work on time, then he can meet us at the coffee shop.

⭐ 13. If your disc player breaks, then I will get you a new one for your birthday, or you can see about getting it fixed.

14. He did not admit to taking the camera, but if he is lying, then either he pawned it for the money or he has it in his apartment.

15. Her painting is valuable, and either she can keep it or sell it for a lot of money.

16. If soccer is the world's most popular sport, then if it catches on in the United States, then football and basketball will lose fans.

⭐ 17. It is not the case that if you eat a lot of salads, then you will get a lot of vitamins, and it is not the case that if you take a lot of vitamins, then you will eat a lot of salads.

18. She is athletic and creative, unless I am mistaken.

19. Johnny and Barbara will visit Las Vegas, only if Mary Lynn and Lee Ann can get a seat on the same flight.

20. Joyce has visited Hawaii, but neither Judy nor Eddie has been there.

II. Translate the following quotes into symbolic form.

1. Give me liberty or give me death.

> Patrick Henry, in a March 23, 1775, speech to the Virginia House of Delegates

Answer:: Let L = Give me liberty, and D = give me death: $L \lor D$

2. A house is not a home unless it contains food and fire for the mind as well as the body.

> Margaret Fuller, quoted in *Roots of Wisdom* by Helen Buss Mitchell

3. If you wish to make an apple pie truly from scratch, you must first invent the universe.

> Carl Sagan, quoted in *Seven Wonders of the Universe That You Probably Took for Granted* by C. Renée James and Lee Jamison

4. I disapprove of what you say, but I will defend to the death your right to say it.

> Voltaire, quoted in *The Second Sin* by Thomas Stephen Szasz

⭐ 5. But a spirit of harmony will survive in America only if each of us remembers that we share a common destiny.

> Barbara Jordan, quoted in *Encyclopedia of Women and American Politics* by Lynne E. Ford

6. Life shrinks or expands in proportion to one's courage.

> Anaïs Nin, quoted in *A Divine Ecology* by Ian Mills

7. I hear and I forget. I see and I remember. I do and I understand.

> Chinese proverb; often attributed to Confucius

8. If one man offers you democracy and another offers you a bag of grain, at what stage of starvation will you prefer the grain to the vote?

> Bertrand Russell, *The Basic Writings of Bertrand Russell*

⭐ 9. I have not failed. I've just found 10,000 ways that won't work.

Thomas A. Edison, quoted in *Dictionary of Proverbs* by Grenville Kleiser

10. America is not anything if it consists of each of us. It is something only if it consists of all of us.   Woodrow Wilson, in a January 29, 1916, speech

11. Either he's dead or my watch has stopped.

Groucho Marx, in the movie *A Day at the Races*

12. It is not from the benevolence of the butcher, the brewer, or the baker that we expect our dinner, but from their regard to their own interest.

Adam Smith, *The Wealth of Nations*

⭐ 13. If the only tool you have is a hammer, you tend to see every problem as a nail.

Abraham Maslow, quoted at Abraham-maslow.com

14. An insincere and evil friend is more to be feared than a wild beast; a wild beast may wound your body, but an evil friend will wound your mind.

Buddha, quoted in *Buddha, Truth and Brotherhood* by Dwight Goddard

15. The average man will bristle if you say his father was dishonest, but he will brag a little if he discovers that his great-grandfather was a pirate.

Emil Ahangarzadeh, *The Secret at Mahone Bay*

16. Knowledge is a great and very useful quality.   Michel de Montaigne, *The Essays*

⭐ 17. The fight is won or lost far away from witnesses—behind the lines, in the gym, and out there on the road, long before I dance under those lights.

Muhammad Ali, quoted in *My View from the Corner: A Life in Boxing* by Angelo Dundee and Bert Sugar

18. A bill of rights is what the people are entitled to against every government on earth, general or particular, and what no just government should refuse, or rest on inference.   Thomas Jefferson, *The Papers of Thomas Jefferson*

19. Fundamentally an organism has conscious mental states if and only if there is something that it is like to *be* that organism—something it is like *for* the organism.   Thomas Nagel, "What Is It Like to Be a Bat?"

20. Education is not the filling of a pail, but the lighting of a fire.

William Butler Yeats, quoted in *Handbook of Reflection and Reflective Inquiry* by Nona Lyons

C. TRUTH FUNCTIONS

The truth value of a truth-functional compound proposition is determined by the truth values of its components and by the logical operators involved. Any truth-functional compound proposition that can be determined in this manner is said to be a **truth function**.

We begin by defining the operators that we met earlier in this chapter. Along the way we will ask how well symbolic expressions using the five operators match the meaning of ordinary language expressions.

Defining the Five Logical Operators

In the first part of the chapter, we used uppercase letters to stand for simple statements. We were then able to create compound statements by using the five operators. In order to define the logical operators, however, we need to know how to apply them to any statement—and how they determine the statement's truth value. A **statement variable** can stand for any statement, simple or complex. We use lowercase letters such as *p, q, r,* and *s.* For example, the statement variable *r* can stand for any of the following:

$$S$$
$$\sim P \lor Q$$
$$(R \supset P) \cdot S$$

A **statement form** is a pattern of statement variables and logical operators. Any uniform substitution of statements for the variables in a statement form results in a statement. For example, we know from earlier that we can substitute the simple statement *S* for the statement variable *r.* We can also substitute the complex statement $(R \lor P) \cdot S$ for the statement variable *r.* In other words, any substitution of statements for statement variables can result in a statement, as long as the substitution is uniform and it is a *WFF.*

The same principle holds for statement forms that have logical operators. For example, the statement form $\sim p$ can have any of the following substitutions:

$$\sim P$$
$$\sim (M \lor N)$$
$$\sim [(R \equiv S) \cdot (P \lor Q)]$$

Each example substitutes a statement, either simple or complex, for the statement variable *p.* Also, each substitution results in a negation because the logical form that we start with, $\sim p$, is a negation.

We can now start defining the five logical operators. Each definition is given by a *truth table.* A **truth table** is an arrangement of truth values for a truth-functional compound proposition. It shows for every possible case how the truth value of the proposition is determined by the truth values of its simple components.

Negation

Since negation simply changes the truth value of the statement that follows it, the truth table definition is easy to construct:

NEGATION

p	$\sim p$
T	F
F	T

The leftmost *p* is the guide for the truth table. It lists the truth values for a statement variable. In this example, *p* stands for any statement that can be either true or false. The tilde *changes the value of the statement that follows it.* Therefore, if *p* is true, then its

Truth function The truth value of a truth-functional compound proposition is determined by the truth values of its components and the definitions of the logical operators involved. Any truth-functional compound proposition that can be determined in this manner is said to be a truth function.

Statement variable A statement variable can stand for any statement, simple or complex.

Statement form A pattern of statement variables and logical operators.

Truth table An arrangement of truth values for a truth-functional compound proposition that displays for every possible case how the truth value of the proposition is determined by the truth values of its simple components.

negation, ~ p, is false, which is what the truth table indicates. (You can think of negation as somewhat like the minus sign in arithmetic; it changes the value of what follows.)

Here are two examples from ordinary language:

- Kentucky is not called the *Sunshine State*. ~ K
- It is not the case that Albany is the capital of New York.   ~ A

The first compound statement is true because the simple statement K (Kentucky is called the *Sunshine State*) is false. Therefore, the negation of K is true. The second compound statement is false because the simple statement A (Albany is the capital of New York) is true. Therefore, the negation of A is false.

Conjunction

The construction of truth tables for the four remaining logical operators will be a little different than for negation, because each of them has two components. For example, the logical form for conjunction, $p \cdot q$, has two statement variables (p and q), each of which can be either true or false (two truth values). This means that the truth table will have to display four lines ($2 \times 2 = 4$):

CONJUNCTION

p	q	$p \cdot q$
T	T	T
T	F	F
F	T	F
F	F	F

An easy way to ensure that you have all the correct arrangements of truth values is to begin with the leftmost guide column (in this case, p) and divide the number of lines in half. Since we calculated that the truth table will have four lines, the first two lines under the p will have T and the last two lines F. For the next column in the guide, q, we alternate one T and one F.

A general rule to follow is this: The leftmost column has the first half of the lines as T and the second half as F. The next column to the right then cuts this in half, again alternating T and F. This continues until the final column to the left of the vertical line has one T and one F alternating with each other. This procedure will be followed when we get to more complex truth tables.

The truth table definition for conjunction (the dot) shows that a conjunction is true when both conjuncts are true; otherwise it is false. Therefore, if either one or both conjuncts are false, then the conjunction is false. A simple rule for conjunction holds for all cases: *For any compound statement containing the dot as the main logical operator to be true, both conjuncts must be true.*

Let's apply this to a simple example using ordinary language:

Today is Monday and it is raining outside.

If we let $p = today is Monday$, and $q = it is raining outside$, then the logical form of the statement is $p \cdot q$. Now, suppose that it is true that today is Monday, and it is also true that it is raining outside. Clearly, the compound statement is true. On the other hand, suppose that it is raining but today is not Monday. In that case, the *compound statement* is false even though one of its components is true. Of course, if both components are false, then the conjunction is false.

Disjunction

The truth table definition for disjunction also has four lines:

DISJUNCTION

p	q	$p \vee q$
T	T	T
T	F	T
F	T	T
F	F	F

The truth table definition for disjunction (the wedge) shows that a disjunction is false when both disjuncts are false; otherwise it is true. Therefore, a disjunction is true when one disjunct is true or when both are true. This interpretation of the word "or" and the definition of the logical operator for disjunction are referred to as *inclusive disjunction*. In other words, **inclusive disjunction** includes those cases where both disjuncts can be true at the same time, and it is used in many instances of ordinary language. Here are a few examples:

1. Memorial Day is the last Monday of May or Mount Rushmore is in South Dakota.
2. Either June or August has 31 days.
3. Either George W. Bush is a Democrat or Bill Clinton is a Republican.

Inclusive disjunction
An inclusive disjunction is where both disjuncts can be true at the same time.

In example 1, the compound statement is true because both disjuncts are true. In example 2, the first disjunct is false, but the compound statement is true because the second disjunct is true. In example 3, since both disjuncts are false the compound statement is false.

In contrast to this, in an **exclusive disjunction** both disjuncts cannot be true at the same time. In other words, the truth of one *excludes* the truth of the other. Here are some examples:

1. The Lincoln Memorial is either in Washington, D.C., or it is in Seattle.
2. Today is Monday or today is Wednesday.
3. You can have spaghetti or fish for dinner.

Exclusive disjunction
An exclusive disjunction is where both disjuncts cannot be true at the same time.

In example 1, it is clear that the normal sense of the statement excludes the possibility that both disjuncts are true. In example 2, at most one of the disjuncts can be true; however, both can be false. Example 3 is a bit more complicated because it is ambiguous. More information is needed to eliminate the ambiguity. For example, if you are really hungry you might ask if you can have both spaghetti and fish. If the answer is *Yes*, then this is a case of inclusive disjunction. However, if the answer is *No*, then this is a case of exclusive disjunction.

In most circumstances, the context reveals which kind of disjunction we are dealing with, if it is not obvious from the statement alone. If there is a possibility of misunderstanding through ambiguity, then it is better to spell out the exclusive disjunction. For example, the statement "You can have spaghetti or fish for dinner, *but not both*" identifies it as an exclusive disjunction. If we let S = *You can have spaghetti for dinner*, and F = *You can have fish for dinner*, then it can be translated as follows:

$$(S \vee F) \cdot \sim (S \cdot F)$$

Conditional

The truth table definition for the conditional also has four lines:

CONDITIONAL

p	q	$p \supset q$
T	T	T
T	F	F
F	T	T
F	F	T

The truth table definition for the conditional (the horseshoe) shows that a conditional is false when the antecedent is true and the consequent is false; otherwise it is true. The first two lines of the truth table seem to fit our normal expectations. For example, suppose a friend is giving you directions to Los Angeles. She tells you the following:

If you drive south on I-15, then you will get to Los Angeles.

Now suppose you drive south on I-15 and you do get to Los Angeles. In this case, since both the antecedent and consequent are true you would say that your friend's statement was true. This corresponds to the first line of the truth table. However, suppose you drive south on I-15 and you do *not* get to Los Angeles. In this case, since the antecedent is true and the consequent is false, you would say that your friend's statement was false. This corresponds to the second line of the truth table. So far the truth table matches our expectations.

Now suppose that you decide not to drive south on I-15. Perhaps you want to avoid highway driving or you just want to use back roads to see more of the countryside. Two outcomes are possible: Either you get to Los Angeles or you don't. The first of these corresponds to the third line of the truth table: false antecedent, true consequent. The second corresponds to the fourth line of the truth table: false antecedent, false consequent. According to the truth table, in both of these cases the conditional statement is true. For many people, this result is not intuitive. Let's try to clear things up.

We can start by reexamining your friend's conditional statement. For convenience, let D = *you drive south on I-15*, and L = *you will get to Los Angeles*. Your friend claims that whenever D is true, L will be true. However, it would be incorrect to assume that her statement makes the additional claim that whenever L is true, then D is true. In other words, your friend did *not* say that the *only way* to get to Los Angeles is to drive south on I-15. Therefore, if you do not drive south on I-15 (the antecedent is false), then in neither case does that make your friend's statement false. And this is just what the truth table shows.

Biconditional

The truth table definition for the biconditional also has four lines:

BICONDITIONAL

p	q	$p \equiv q$
T	T	T
T	F	F
F	T	F
F	F	T

According to the truth table, a biconditional as the main operator is true when both components have the same truth value (either both true or both false); otherwise it is false. This result can be understood if we recall that the triple bar symbol for the biconditional is a shorthand way of writing the conjunction of two conditionals:

$$(p \supset q) \cdot (q \supset p)$$

Let's see what would happen if both p and q are true. First, we need to rely on our knowledge of the truth table for conditionals, and then we need to refer to the truth table for a conjunction. The truth table for conditionals reveals that, in this instance, both conjuncts are true, and therefore the conjunction is true. This result corresponds to the first line of the biconditional truth table.

Next, let's see what would happen if both p and q are false. The truth table for conditionals reveals that in this instance both conjuncts are true, and therefore the conjunction is true. This result corresponds to the fourth line of the biconditional truth table.

What happens when p is true and q is false? The truth table for conditionals reveals that in that case the first conjunct "$p \supset q$" is false. This result, by itself, is sufficient to make the conjunction false. This result corresponds to the second line of the biconditional truth table.

Finally, what happens when p is false and q is true? The truth table for conditionals reveals that the first conjunct "$p \supset q$" is true, but the second conjunct "$q \supset p$" is false. Therefore, the conjunction is false. This result corresponds to the third line of the biconditional truth table.

Our analysis of a biconditional as the conjunction of two conditionals has provided another way to understand the truth table results. It also offered the opportunity to use the truth tables for several logical operators.

CHECK YOUR UNDERSTANDING 7C

Choose the correct answer.

1. If "X · Y" is true, then which of the following is correct?
    (a) X must be true.
    (b) X must be false.
    (c) X could be true or false.

Answer: (a) X must be true. The only way for a conjunction to be true is if both conjuncts are true.

2. If "X · Y" is false, then which of the following is correct?
    (a) X must be true.
    (b) X must be false.
    (c) X could be true or false.

3. If "X ∨ Y" is true, then which of the following is correct?
    (a) X must be true.
    (b) X must be false.
    (c) X could be true or false.

4. If "X ∨ Y" is false, then which of the following is correct?
    (a) X must be true.
    (b) X must be false.
    (c) X could be true or false.

★ 5. If "~ X" is false, then what must X be?
    (a) X must be true.
    (b) X must be false.
    (c) X could be true or false.

6. If "~ X" is true, then what must X be?
    (a) X must be true.
    (b) X must be false.
    (c) X could be true or false.

7. If "X ∨ Y" is true, but X is false, then what must Y be?
    (a) Y must be true.
    (b) Y must be false.
    (c) Y could be true or false.

8. If "X ∨ Y" is false, then can one of the disjuncts be true?
    (a) Yes
    (b) No

★ 9. If "X ∨ Y" is true, then can one of the disjuncts be false?
    (a) Yes
    (b) No

10. If "X · Y" is false, then can both conjuncts be false?
    (a) Yes
    (b) No

11. If "X ⊃ Y" is true, then which of the following is correct?
    (a) X must be true.
    (b) X must be false.
    (c) X could be true or false.

12. If "X ⊃ Y" is false, then which of the following is correct?
    (a) X must be true.
    (b) X must be false.
    (c) X could be true or false.

★ 13. If "X ⊃ Y" is true, then which of the following is correct?
    (a) Y must be true.
    (b) Y must be false.
    (c) Y could be true or false.

14. If "X ⊃ Y" is false, then which of the following is correct?
    (a) Y must be true.
    (b) Y must be false.
    (c) Y could be true or false.

15. If "X ⊃ Y" is false, then can X be false?
    (a) Yes
    (b) No

16. If "X ⊃ Y" is true, then can Y be false?
    (a) Yes
    (b) No

★ 17. If "X ≡ Y" is true, then which of the following is correct?
    (a) Y must be true.
    (b) Y must be false.
    (c) Y could be true or false.

18. If "X ≡ Y" is true, then which of the following is correct?
    (a) X must be true.
    (b) X must be false.
    (c) X could be true or false.

19. If "X ≡ Y" is false, then must X be false?
    (a) Yes
    (b) No

20. If "X ≡ Y" is false, then must Y be false?
    (a) Yes
    (b) No

Operator Truth Tables and Ordinary Language

We mentioned that the truth table for the wedge establishes an *inclusive disjunction* interpretation of "or." We also pointed out that *exclusive disjunction* uses in ordinary language can be accommodated by spelling them out more fully. Also, the conditional truth table has some less intuitive aspects that we worked through. Throughout the book, we have been balancing the practical needs of logic with its purely abstract nature.

In this sense, logic is similar to mathematics. For example, simple arithmetic has great practical application—everything from simple counting to balancing a checkbook. But we are all aware of the abstract nature of many branches of mathematics. Over many centuries, mathematicians have developed highly sophisticated areas, many of which took decades to find a useful application. In fact, some still have no practical application. However, mathematical excursions into new realms can be stimulating, just like a visit to a new country.

An introduction to logic touches on basic ideas, much like the principles of arithmetic. This is why we are often able to connect logic to ordinary language. Basic logic cannot capture *all* the nuances of ordinary language. But we would not be able to calculate the subtle changes in velocity of a moving object knowing just basic arithmetic. To do that, we would need some calculus. In the same way, while the truth tables for the five logical operators do capture much of ordinary language, we can expect some exceptions.

Start with conjunction. In many cases, the order of the conjuncts is irrelevant to its meaning. Here are two examples:

> Steve is an accountant and he lives in Omaha. $A \cdot O$
> Steve lives in Omaha and he is an accountant. $O \cdot A$

Constructing truth tables for these two statements will reveal an important point:

A	O	$A \cdot O$		O	A	$O \cdot A$
T	T	T		T	T	T
T	F	F		T	F	F
F	T	F		F	T	F
F	F	F		F	F	F

The column of truth values under the dot for "$A \cdot O$" is identical to the column of truth values for "$O \cdot A$." This means that the two statements are *logically equivalent*. (We will have more to say about *logical equivalence* later in this chapter.) Therefore, we can use either of the conjunctions to capture the meaning of both the ordinary language statements.

Now look at two more examples:

> Shirley got her IRS refund this week and bought a new TV. $I \cdot T$
> Shirley bought a new TV and got her IRS refund this week. $T \cdot I$

This time, the implied meanings in ordinary language are different. The first statement can be interpreted as implying that Shirley got her IRS refund and *then* used it to buy a new TV. The second statement can be interpreted as implying that the TV purchase and the IRS refund were unconnected events. A truth-functional interpretation, however, obscures that important difference. From the previous example, we now know that "$I \cdot T$" and "$T \cdot I$" are *logically equivalent*. As these examples illustrate, we should not try to force every ordinary language statement into a truth-functional interpretation.

We can now return to the conditional and connect it to more examples from ordinary language. The truth table for the horseshoe operator defines the truth-functional conditional. (It is also referred to as the *material conditional*.) As we have seen, its truth value depends on only the truth and falsity of the antecedent and consequent. In ordinary language, however, the truth of a conditional statement may depend on an *inferential connection* between the antecedent and consequent. Such a statement should not be translated using the horseshoe operator. Take this example:

> If Boston is in Alaska, then Boston is near the Mexican border.

Most people would rightly consider this statement to be false. After all, Alaska is not near the Mexican border. In fact, Boston is in Massachusetts, and it is not near the Mexican border either. However, if we interpret it truth-functionally by using the horseshoe operator, then the statement is true because the antecedent is false.

Here is another example:

> If Alaska is north of Mexico, then Alaska is a U.S. state.

In this example, both the antecedent and the consequent are true. However, most people would judge the statement to be false based on an error in the inferential connection. In other words, the fact that Alaska is north of Mexico does not automatically make it a U.S. state. After all, Canada is north of Mexico, too. However, if we interpret it truth-functionally by using the horseshoe operator, then the statement is true because both the antecedent and the consequent are true. Once again, we should not try to force every ordinary language statement into a truth-functional interpretation.

Another kind of conditional statement that is common in ordinary language is called a *counterfactual* conditional. Here are some examples:

- If Lady Gaga were married to Barack Obama, then she would be First Lady.
- If the United States had not entered Vietnam in the 1960s and 1970s, then 50,000 of our soldiers would not have died in combat there.
- If Bill Gates has only $100, then he is a millionaire.
- If my house were made entirely of paper, then it could not burn.

The examples are called *counterfactuals* because their antecedents are contrary to the facts. In order to determine their truth value, we need to investigate the inferential nature of the claims through ordinary language. In the first example, we know that the person married to the current president of the United States is traditionally referred to as the First Lady; therefore this counterfactual is true. In the second example, we accept the inference that had the United States not sent any soldiers into Vietnam in the 1960s and 1970s, then no U.S. soldiers would have died in combat there. Therefore, this counterfactual is also true.

However, the third counterfactual example is false because anyone who has only $100 is not a millionaire. The fourth example is also false because a house made of paper certainly could burn. In sum, the first two examples are true but the third and fourth are false.

As these examples illustrate, the truth value of counterfactual conditionals is not related to the truth value of the antecedent and the consequent. However, if we interpret them truth-functionally by using the horseshoe operator, then all four are true because all four antecedents are false. Therefore, counterfactuals should not be translated truth-functionally by using the horseshoe operator.

Much of what we have discussed about conditionals can be applied to biconditionals. (Just as the horseshoe is sometimes called a *material conditional*, the triple bar is sometimes referred to as *material equivalence*.) Again, many statements in ordinary language do not fall under a truth-functional interpretation. Here are a few examples:

- The Mississippi River is in Brazil if and only if it is the longest river in the world.
- Al Gore won the Nobel Prize for physics if and only if he discovered a new subatomic particle.

These two examples are false in an ordinary language interpretation. In the first example, the Mississippi River is not in Brazil, and it is not the longest river in the world. In the second example, Al Gore did not win the Nobel Prize for physics (he won the Nobel Peace Prize), and he did not discover a new subatomic particle. However, if the two examples are interpreted truth functionally using the triple bar operator, then they both are true, because in each case both components have the same truth value.

We do not want to force every ordinary language statement into a truth-functional interpretation. Nevertheless, when we are confident that such an interpretation is called for, then truth-functional propositions are a powerful tool for understanding many of the statements and arguments we encounter every day.

D. TRUTH TABLES FOR PROPOSITIONS

Truth tables for compound statements and for arguments must have a uniform method for displaying work and results. We can start by discussing a compound proposition that has two variables:

$$\sim (P \cdot Q) \lor Q$$

Here there are two different simple propositions (P and Q), each of which can be either true or false (two truth values). As we saw earlier, then, the truth table will have to display four lines ($2 \times 2 = 4$). We first have to fill in those lines for each simple proposition. To complete the truth table, we then need to identify the main operator and a step-by-step method. As we see in this section, that means identifying what we call the *order of operations*.

Arranging the Truth Values

In fact, there is a simple formula to follow to calculate the number of lines for any given proposition: $L = 2^n$. In the formula, L stands for the number of lines in a truth table, and n stands for the number of different simple propositions in the statement. Therefore, a proposition with three different simple propositions would be $L = 2^3$. Written out, this would be $2 \times 2 \times 2 = 8$ lines. A proposition with four different simple propositions would be $L = 2^4$ or $2 \times 2 \times 2 \times 2 = 16$ lines.

We also discussed how to ensure that you have all the correct arrangements of truth values. You begin with the leftmost column and divide the number of lines in half. Since we have a truth table with four lines, the first two lines under the P will contain T and the last two lines will contain F. The next column, Q, will then alternate one T and one F. More generally, the leftmost column has the first half of the lines designated as T and the second half as F. The next column to the right then cuts this in half, again alternating T's and F's. This continues until the final column before the vertical bar has one T and one F alternating with each other:

P	Q	$\sim (P \cdot Q) \vee Q$
T	T	
T	F	
F	T	
F	F	

The Order of Operations

At this point, we need to know the **order of operations**—the order of handling the logical operators within the proposition. The order of operations is a step-by-step method of generating a complete truth table. *Since the main logical operator controls the final determination of the proposition's truth value, it will be the last step.* The main operator in this example is the wedge. Also, we must determine the truth value of whatever is contained within the parentheses before we can deal with the tilde. Therefore, the correct *order of operations* for this example is the following: *dot, tilde, wedge.* Let's work through the order of operations in practice.

First, we determine the truth values for each line under the dot:

P	Q	$\sim (P \cdot Q) \vee Q$
T	T	T
T	F	F
F	T	F
F	F	F

The completed column displays the truth values of the compound proposition "$P \cdot Q$." The next step is the tilde:

Order of operations
The order of handling the logical operators within a proposition; it is a step-by-step method of generating a complete truth table.

P	Q	~ (P · Q) ∨ Q
T	T	F T
T	F	T F
F	T	T F
F	F	T F

The final step is the wedge:

Main operator
↓

P	Q	~(P · Q) ∨ Q	
T	T	F T	T
T	F	T F	T
F	T	T F	T
F	F	T F	T

The box indicates that the main operator represents the entire compound proposition. If this proposition were part of an argument (either a premise or a conclusion), then the results of this truth table would help us decide the argument's validity.

Let's work through a longer truth table. The compound proposition "$R ⊃ (S ∨ \sim P)$" has three different simple propositions. Therefore, we calculate that our truth table

Early Programmers

The first electronic digital computer, ENIAC (Electronic Numerical Integrator and Computer), was developed during World War II in order to compute "firing tables" for calculating the speed and trajectory of field artillery. Six women were hired to do the programming: Frances Bilas, Betty Jean Jennings, Ruth Lictermann, Kathleen McNulty, Elizabeth Snyder, and Marlyn Wescoff. Their task was to get the computer to model all possible trajectories, which required solving complex equations (called *differential equations*). The team had to create their own programming manuals because none existed.

It soon became apparent that they had to alter the huge computer itself in order to match the program with the machine.

Using today's language, they had to create software and hardware at the same time. They had to arrange the computer's complex wires, circuits, cable connections, and vacuum tubes to coordinate the physical steps in the solution with the sequence of equations. Programming ENIAC required understanding both the physical state of the computer *and* logical thinking. As Betty Jennings remarked, it was "a physicalization of *if-then* statements."

Mathematicians, physicists, and other scientists quickly sought out the ENIAC programmers to help with long-standing problems. Computers have handled problems that it would take many lifetimes to solve without them ever since.

will have $L = 2^3$ or 8 lines. We must also make sure that the leftmost column has the first half of the lines designated as T and the second half as F. In this example, the first four lines are T and the next four are F. The next column to the right then cuts this in half, again alternating T's and F's, and the third column will then have one T and one F alternating with each other:

R	S	P	$R \supset (S \vee \sim P)$
T	T	T	
T	T	F	
T	F	T	
T	F	F	
F	T	T	
F	T	F	
F	F	T	
F	F	F	

The next step is to identify the main operator and determine the order of operations. The main operator in this example is the horseshoe, and the order of operations for this example is the following: *tilde, wedge, horseshoe.*

First, we determine the truth values for each line under the tilde:

R	S	P	$R \supset (S \vee \sim P)$
T	T	T	F
T	T	F	T
T	F	T	F
T	F	F	T
F	T	T	F
F	T	F	T
F	F	T	F
F	F	F	T

The next step is the wedge:

R	S	P	$R \supset (S \vee$	$\sim P)$
T	T	T	T	F
T	T	F	T	T
T	F	T	F	F
T	F	F	T	T
F	T	T	T	F
F	T	F	T	T
F	F	T	F	F
F	F	F	T	T

The final step is the horseshoe:

R	S	P	R ⊃ (S v ~ P)
T	T	T	**T** T F
T	T	F	**T** T T
T	F	T	**F** F F
T	F	F	**T** T T
F	T	T	**T** T F
F	T	F	**T** T T
F	F	T	**T** F F
F	F	F	**T** T T

Constructing truth tables for compound propositions requires a step-by-step approach. It is best to be methodical and not try to do more than one thing at a time. First, calculate the number of lines needed. Second, place the T's and F's under the columns for all the simple propositions in the guide. Third, identify the main operator and the order of operations. Fourth, apply your knowledge of the five operators to fill in the truth values according to the order of operations. In the final step, fill in the truth values for the main operator.

CHECK YOUR UNDERSTANDING 7D.1

Create truth tables for the following compound propositions.

    1. $P \cdot \sim Q$

Answer:

P	Q	P · ~ Q
T	T	**F** F
T	F	**T** T
F	T	**F** F
F	F	**F** T

    2. $\sim R \cdot \sim S$

    3. $P \supset Q$

    4. $S \supset \sim Q$

★ 5. $(R \cdot S) \lor Q$

    6. $\sim P \lor (\sim S \lor \sim R)$

    7. $(R \equiv \sim S) \supset P$

    8. $(Q \supset R) \cdot S$

★ 9. $\sim (Q \cdot R) \supset P$

10. $P \vee (S \supset R)$

11. $S \cdot (\sim Q \supset R)$

12. $(Q \supset R) \cdot R$

⭐ 13. $P \equiv (\sim S \vee \sim R)$

14. $\sim P \cdot (S \vee R)$

15. $\sim [(Q \cdot R) \cdot \sim (S \vee R)]$

16. $(R \cdot \sim S) \cdot P$

⭐ 17. $\sim [P \supset (Q \vee R)]$

18. $(Q \cdot R) \equiv (Q \vee \sim S)$

19. $[P \vee (Q \cdot R)] \supset S$

20. $\sim [P \vee (Q \vee R)] \vee \sim (S \vee P)$

Propositions with Assigned Truth Values

A shorter truth table is sometimes possible, provided the simple propositions are assigned specific truth values. For example, suppose the compound proposition "$P \vee \sim S$" has the following truth values assigned: Let P be true and S be false. If the truth values were not assigned, then we would have to create a truth table with four lines. However, with the assigned truth values we need only use one line:

P	S	$P \vee \sim S$
T	F	⊡ T

A good grasp of the truth tables for the five logical operators makes the determination of the truth value for this proposition quite easy.

Let's try another example. Suppose the compound proposition "$R \supset (S \cdot P)$" has the following truth values assigned to the simple propositions: Let R be true, S be false, and P be true. Since there are three simple propositions, a full truth table would require eight lines. But given the assigned truth values we need only to consider one line:

R	S	P	$R \supset (S \cdot P)$
T	F	T	⊡ F

These examples illustrate the importance of having a good understanding of the truth tables for the five logical operators.

Now let's see what happens when truth values are *not* assigned to every simple proposition. For example, suppose the compound proposition "$P \cdot Q$" has P assigned as false, but the truth value for Q is unassigned (meaning it could be true or false). Here is the resulting truth table:

P	Q	P · Q
F	?	F

We are able to determine that the proposition is false because one of the conjuncts is false. Therefore, in this example the truth value of Q does not matter. Of course, this will not always be the case. For example, what if P were true but the truth value for Q remained unassigned? Here is what we would get:

P	Q	P · Q
T	?	?

One of the conjuncts is true, but the other could be true or false. If Q were true, then the proposition is true. On the other hand, if Q were false, then the proposition is false. Therefore, the truth value of the proposition cannot be determined in this case. The reasoning behind this procedure also underlies the indirect truth table technique, which we introduce at the end of the chapter.

CHECK YOUR UNDERSTANDING 7D.2

I. For the following, let P be true, Q be false, R be true, and S be false. Determine the truth value of the compound propositions.

1. $P \cdot \sim Q$

Answer:

P	Q	P · ~ Q
T	F	T T

2. $Q \cdot \sim S$
3. $S \vee \sim Q$
4. $(Q \vee R) \cdot S$
⭐ 5. $P \vee (S \vee R)$
6. $\sim P \vee (\sim S \vee \sim R)$
7. $\sim (Q \cdot R) \cdot \sim (S \cdot P)$
8. $(R \cdot \sim S) \cdot P$
⭐ 9. $[P \vee (Q \cdot R)] \vee \sim S$
10. $\sim [P \vee (Q \vee R)] \vee \sim (S \vee P)$

II. For the following, let P be true, Q be true, R be false, and S is unassigned. Determine the truth value of the compound propositions. If the truth value cannot be determined, then explain why.

1. $P \supset \sim Q$

Answer:

P	Q	P ⊃ ~ Q
T	T	$\boxed{F}$ F

2. $(R \cdot \sim S) \supset Q$

3. $S \vee (\sim Q \supset R)$

4. $(Q \supset R) \cdot S$

⭐ 5. $[P \vee (S \vee R)] \supset \sim Q$

6. $\sim P \supset (\sim S \vee \sim R)$

7. $\sim (Q \cdot R) \supset \sim (S \cdot P)$

8. $(R \cdot \sim S) \supset P$

⭐ 9. $[P \vee (Q \cdot R)] \supset \sim S$

10. $\sim [P \vee (Q \vee R)] \supset \sim (S \vee P)$

E. CONTINGENT AND NONCONTINGENT STATEMENTS

Most of the examples of compound statements that we looked at so far are **contingent statements**: statements that are neither necessarily true nor necessarily false. A truth table for a contingent statement has both true and false results in the main operator column. A simple example is the proposition "*P* ∨ *Q*":

P	Q	P ∨ Q
T	T	T
T	F	T
F	T	T
F	F	F

Contingent statements Statements that are neither necessarily true nor necessarily false (they are sometimes true, sometimes false).

The truth value for this proposition is *contingent* on (it depends on) the truth values of the component parts. The truth table for any contingent proposition contains both true and false results in the main operator column. However, there are some propositions that are *noncontingent*. In **noncontingent statements**, the truth values in the main operator column *do not* depend on the truth values of the component parts. We will look at two kinds of noncontingent statements: *tautologies* and *self-contradictions*.

Noncontingent statements Statements such that the truth values in the main operator column do not depend on the truth values of the component parts.

Tautology

Consider the following statement: "Horses are carnivorous or horses are not carnivorous." Since this is a disjunction, we know that if one of the disjuncts is true, then the entire statement is true. Therefore, if the first disjunct is true, the second disjunct must be false because it is the negation of the first part. The disjunction is then true. The only other possibility is that the first disjunct is false. But this makes the second disjunct true because it is the negation of the first disjunct. Therefore, once again the disjunction is true. Since there are no other possibilities, we have shown that the proposition is necessarily true.

This result follows from the logical form of the proposition. If we let p = *horses are carnivorous*, and $\sim p$ = *horses are not carnivorous*, then the logical form is "$p \lor \sim p$." Here is the truth table:

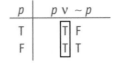

Tautology A statement that is necessarily true.

The truth table shows that the main operator is true whether p is true or false. This type of statement is called a **tautology**—a statement that is necessarily true. Although tautologies are logically true, they are not very useful for conveying information in everyday life. For example, suppose you ask your friend whether she will meet you for dinner tonight and she responds, "Either I will be there or I will not." Her answer is indeed true; in fact, it is necessarily true. However, has she given you any information? Did you learn anything from her response that you did not already know? Tautologies, although necessarily true, are sometimes referred to as "empty truths."

This is one reason why scientific hypotheses should not be tautologies: they would offer no real information about the world, and they would teach us nothing. A scientific hypothesis that turned out to be a tautology would be obviously true, but trivial. Scientific hypotheses should be statements that could turn out to be either true or false, because only then will we learn something about world.

Self-Contradiction

Self-contradiction A statement that is necessarily false.

Another type of noncontingent statement can be illustrated by the following example: "The number 2 is an even number and the number 2 is not an even number." This statement, which is necessarily false, is a **self-contradiction**. We can see this by applying what we have learned about conjunction. If the first conjunct, "The number 2 is an even number" is true, then its negation, the second conjunct is false. Therefore, the conjunction is false. The only other possibility is that the first conjunct is false. In this case, the second conjunct is true. However, once again the conjunction is false.

This result follows from the logical form of the proposition. If we let p = *the number 2 is an even number*, and $\sim p$ = *the number 2 it is not an even number*, then the logical form is "$p \cdot \sim p$." Here is the truth table:

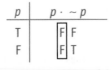

The truth table shows that the main operator is false whether p is true or false. This result illustrates the importance of avoiding self-contradictions when we speak or write. If we contradict ourselves, we are saying something that is necessarily false.

CHECK YOUR UNDERSTANDING 7E

Create truth tables to determine whether each of the following is contingent, a tautology, or a self-contradiction.

   1. $P \vee (Q \cdot \sim Q)$

Answer: Contingent. The truth table reveals that the main operator has both true and false results.

P	Q	$P \vee (Q \cdot \sim Q)$		
T	T	T	F	F
T	F	T	F	T
F	T	F	F	F
F	F	F	F	T

   2. $P \cdot (Q \vee \sim Q)$

   3. $P \vee P$

   4. $P \cdot P$

⭐ 5. $(P \vee \sim P) \vee Q$

   6. $(P \vee \sim P) \cdot Q$

   7. $(R \cdot \sim R) \vee S$

   8. $(R \cdot \sim R) \cdot S$

⭐ 9. $\sim (R \cdot \sim R) \vee \sim (S \vee \sim S)$

  10. $\sim (R \vee \sim R) \cdot \sim (S \cdot \sim S)$

  11. $P \supset (Q \cdot \sim Q)$

  12. $P \cdot (Q \supset \sim Q)$

⭐ 13. $P \supset P$

  14. $\sim P \supset \sim P$

  15. $(P \vee \sim P) \supset P$

  16. $(P \cdot \sim P) \supset P$

⭐ 17. $(R \cdot \sim R) \supset (S \vee \sim S)$

  18. $(R \vee \sim R) \supset (S \vee \sim S)$

  19. $\sim (R \cdot \sim R) \supset \sim (S \cdot \sim S)$

  20. $\sim (R \vee \sim R) \supset \sim (S \vee \sim S)$

F. LOGICAL EQUIVALENCE

Two truth-functional statements may appear different but have identical truth tables. When this occurs, they are called **logically equivalent** statements. In order to compare two statements, identical truth values must be plugged in on each line of the respective truth tables. This is done by placing the two statements next to each other so they can share the same guide for the simple statements. Once this is completed, we compare the truth tables by looking at the truth values under the main operators. Let's compare the following: (1) $P \supset Q$; (2) $P \vee Q$.

P	Q	$P \supset Q$	$P \vee Q$
T	T	T	T
T	F	F	T
F	T	T	T
F	F	T	F

Comparing the final results for the main operators reveals that the second and fourth lines are different. Therefore, these are not logically equivalent statements.

Now let's compare two other statements: (1) $\sim (S \cdot H)$; (2) $\sim S \vee \sim H$.

S	H	$\sim (S \cdot H)$		$\sim S \vee \sim H$		
T	T	F	T	F	F	F
T	F	T	F	F	T	T
F	T	T	F	T	T	F
F	F	T	F	T	T	T

The final result for the main operators shows that they are identical; therefore, these are logically equivalent statements.

You might recall the discussion at the end of Section 7B regarding how best to translate the statement, "Not both Suzuki and Honda are Japanese-owned companies." The statement was translated as "$\sim (S \cdot H)$" because the word "not" was used to deny the conjunction. The results of the foregoing two truth tables show that "$\sim (S \cdot H)$" and "$\sim S \vee \sim H$" are logically equivalent.

We also looked at the English sentence "Neither Ford nor Chevrolet is a Japanese-owned company" at the end of Section 7B. We saw that the statement can be translated as "$\sim (F \vee C)$." A disjunction is false only when both disjuncts are false. Therefore, a denial of a disjunction is the same as when both disjuncts are denied at the same time. This means that "$\sim (F \vee C)$" and "$\sim F \cdot \sim C$" should be logically equivalent.

We can verify this by creating the appropriate truth tables:

F	C	$\sim (F \vee C)$		$\sim F \cdot \sim C$		
T	T	F	T	F	F	F
T	F	F	T	F	F	T
F	T	F	T	T	F	F
F	F	T	F	T	T	T

Comparing the results for the two main operators shows that they are identical, and therefore, the statements are logically equivalent.

CHECK YOUR UNDERSTANDING 7F

Use truth tables to determine whether any of the pairs of statements are logically equivalent.

1. $\sim (P \cdot Q) \mid \sim P \vee \sim Q$

Answer: Logically equivalent. The truth tables have identical results for the main operators.

P	Q		$\sim (P \cdot Q)$		$\sim P$	$\vee$	$\sim Q$
T	T	F	T		F	F	F
T	F	T	F		F	T	T
F	T	T	F		T	T	F
F	F	T	F		T	T	T

2. $\sim (P \vee Q) \mid \sim P \cdot \sim Q$

3. $P \vee Q \mid Q \vee P$

4. $P \cdot Q \mid Q \cdot P$

⭐ 5. $P \vee (Q \vee R) \mid (P \vee Q) \vee R$

6. $P \cdot (Q \cdot R) \mid (P \cdot Q) \cdot R$

7. $P \cdot (Q \vee R) \mid (P \cdot Q) \vee (P \cdot R)$

8. $P \vee (Q \cdot R) \mid (P \vee Q) \cdot (P \vee R)$

⭐ 9. $P \mid \sim \sim P$

10. $P \supset Q \mid \sim Q \supset \sim P$

11. $P \supset Q \mid \sim P \vee Q$

12. $P \equiv Q \mid (P \supset Q) \cdot (Q \supset P)$

⭐ 13. $P \equiv Q \mid (P \cdot Q) \vee (\sim P \cdot \sim Q)$

14. $(P \cdot Q) \supset R \mid P \supset (Q \supset R)$

15. $P \mid P \vee P$

16. $P \mid P \cdot P$

⭐ 17. $\sim (P \cdot Q) \mid \sim P \cdot \sim Q$

18. $\sim (P \vee Q) \mid \sim P \vee \sim Q$

19. $(P \cdot Q) \supset R \mid P \vee (Q \supset R)$

20. $(P \cdot Q) \supset R \mid P \supset (Q \cdot R)$

⭐ 21. $P \equiv Q \,|\, (P \supset Q) \vee (Q \supset P)$

22. $P \equiv Q \,|\, (P \cdot Q) \cdot (\sim P \cdot \sim Q)$

23. $P \supset Q \,|\, \sim P \cdot Q$

24. $P \supset Q \,|\, Q \supset P$

⭐ 25. $P \supset Q \,|\, \sim Q \vee P$

G. CONTRADICTORY, CONSISTENT, AND INCONSISTENT STATEMENTS

Contradictory statements Two statements that have opposite truth values on every line of their respective truth tables.

Logically equivalent statements have identical truth tables. In contrast, two statements that have opposite truth values on every line of their respective truth tables are **contradictory statements**. Consider this pair of statements: (1) "Lincoln was the sixteenth president," and (2) "Lincoln was not the sixteenth president." Translating this pair of statements we get: (1) "L," and (2) "$\sim L$." Let's compare the truth tables:

L	L	$\sim L$
T	T	F
F	F	T

The results reveal that the two statements have opposite truth values on every line of their respective truth tables; therefore, they are contradictory statements.

"Today is not Friday or tomorrow is Saturday," and "Today is Friday and tomorrow is not Saturday." Are these two compound statements contradictory? To answer this question, the compound statements can be translated. The first is "$\sim F \vee S$," and the second is "$F \cdot \sim S$." We can now complete the truth tables:

F	S	$\sim F \vee S$		$F \cdot \sim S$	
T	T	F	T	F	F
T	F	F	F	T	T
F	T	T	T	F	F
F	F	T	T	F	T

The results reveal that the two compound statements have opposite truth values on every line of their respective truth tables; therefore, they are indeed contradictory statements.

Consistent statements Two (or more) statements that have at least one line on their respective truth tables where the main operators are true.

Consistent statements have at least one line on their respective truth tables where the main operators are true. For example, suppose that someone claims that "Robert is over 30 years of age," while another person claims that "Robert is over 40 years of age." According to the definition for consistent statements, are these two statements consistent? Can both statements be true at the same time? If Robert is 42 years old, then both statements are true; therefore, they are consistent.

Here is another pair for analysis: (1) $R \lor B$; (2) $R \lor \sim B$. Truth tables reveal the following:

R	B	$R \lor B$	$R \lor \sim B$
T	T	T	T F
T	F	T	T T
F	T	T	F F
F	F	F	T T

The truth table comparison shows that the main operators are both *true* for line 1 and line 2. Statements are consistent if there is at least one line on their respective truth tables where both the main operators are true; therefore, these two statements are consistent.

Finally, **inconsistent statements** do not have even one line on their respective truth tables where the main operators are true. (However, inconsistent statements can be false at the same time.) In other words, for two statements to be inconsistent, both statements cannot be true at the same time (but they can both be false). For example, suppose that someone claims that "Frances is over 30 years of age," while another person claims that "Frances is under 20 years of age." Are these two statements inconsistent? If Frances is 42 years old, then the first statement is true and the second is false. On the other hand, if Frances is 19 years old, then the second statement is true and the first is false.

It might seem that the two statements are contradictory, but that is not the case. To show this, all we need to do is imagine that Frances is 25 years old. In that case, both statements are false; therefore, they cannot be contradictory. The analysis shows that they are inconsistent.

Here is another pair of statements for comparison: (1) "My car ran out of gas and I do not have money," and (2) "My car ran out of gas if and only if I have money." Translating them, we get: (1) $C \cdot \sim M$, and (2) $C \equiv M$. Here are the truth tables:

C	M	$C \cdot \sim M$	$C \equiv M$
T	T	F F	T
T	F	T T	F
F	T	F F	F
F	F	F T	T

This is a set of inconsistent statements because there is no line where the main operators are both true. (Since both statements are false on line 3, they are not contradictory statements.)

Inconsistent statements
Two (or more) statements that do not have even one line on their respective truth tables where the main operators are true (but they can be false) at the same time.

CHECK YOUR UNDERSTANDING 7G

Use truth tables to determine whether the following pairs are contradictory, consistent, or inconsistent.

1. $A \lor B \mid \sim A \lor B$

Answer: Consistent

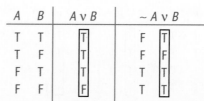

A	B	A ∨ B	~A ∨ B
T	T	T	F T
T	F	T	F F
F	T	T	T T
F	F	F	T T

The truth table comparison reveals that in line 1 and line 3 the main operators are both true. Statements are consistent if there is at least one line on their respective truth tables where the main operators are both true; therefore, the two statements are consistent.

2. $\sim A \cdot B \mid \sim B \lor A$

3. $M \cdot \sim M \mid M$

4. $P \supset Q \mid P \cdot \sim Q$

⭐ 5. $T \equiv U \mid T \cdot U$

6. $P \lor Q \mid \sim (P \lor Q)$

7. $(Q \supset \sim R) \cdot S \mid S \equiv (Q \cdot R)$

8. $Q \lor P \mid \sim Q \supset \sim P$

⭐ 9. $C \cdot D \mid \sim C \lor \sim D$

10. $Q \supset P \mid Q \cdot P$

11. $A \lor B \mid \sim A \lor \sim B$

12. $\sim A \cdot B \mid \sim B \cdot A$

⭐ 13. $M \lor \sim M \mid M$

14. $P \supset Q \mid Q \supset P$

15. $T \equiv U \mid T \lor U$

16. $P \lor Q \mid \sim (P \cdot Q)$

⭐ 17. $(Q \supset \sim R) \supset S \mid S \equiv (Q \cdot R)$

18. $Q \lor P \mid \sim Q \cdot \sim P$

19. $C \cdot D \mid \sim C \supset \sim D$

20. $Q \supset P \mid Q \lor P$

H. TRUTH TABLES FOR ARGUMENTS

We are ready to apply our knowledge of truth tables to the analysis of arguments. We will start using the symbol "/" (called *slash, forward slash,* or *forward stroke*) for "therefore." (The slash symbol will also be used in Chapters 8 and 9.) Here is an example:

$$\sim (P \cdot Q)$$
$$P \qquad / Q$$

The argument has two premises: "$\sim (P \cdot Q)$," and "P." The conclusion is "Q." If it helps, you can imagine that the slash is the line we have used to separate the premises from the conclusion, but angled to the right. In that sense, it still serves to set off the conclusion from the premises.

Validity

The first step is to display the argument so we can apply the truth tables for the operators. Here is the basic structure:

P	Q	$\sim (P \cdot Q)$	P	/ Q
T	T			
T	F			
F	T			
F	F			

The information is displayed to allow a uniform, methodical application of the truth tables for the operators. The truth table is divided into sections. The first two sections are the premises, and the third is the conclusion (indicated by the slash). We complete the truth table by following the same *order of operations* and the *main logical operator* procedures as before. Here is the finished truth table:

P	Q	$\sim (P \cdot Q)$	P	/ Q	
T	T	F T	T	T	
T	F	T F	T	F	√
F	T	T F	F	T	
F	F	T F	F	F	

The final truth value of each statement is either directly under a simple statement or under the main operator of a compound statement. The question of validity hinges on whether any line has true premises and a false conclusion. Since the truth table has revealed all possible cases, we are perfectly situated to decide the question. The second line has true premises and a false conclusion; therefore, the argument is invalid. This result is indicated by the checkmark.

Let's do another one:

$$P \cdot \sim Q$$
$$P \supset \sim S \quad / \sim S$$

This argument contains three simple statements (P, Q, and S); therefore, the truth table will have eight lines. The truth table is completed by following the order of operations and the main logical operator procedures:

P	Q	S	P · ~Q		P ⊃ ~S		/ ~S
T	T	T	F	F	F	F	F
T	T	F	F	F	T	T	T
T	F	T	T	T	F	F	F
T	F	F	T	T	T	T	T
F	T	T	F	F	T	F	F
F	T	F	F	F	T	T	T
F	F	T	F	T	T	F	F
F	F	F	F	T	T	T	T

We inspect the truth table to see whether any line has true premises and a false conclusion. Line 4 has both premises true, but the conclusion is true, too. Lines 1, 3, 5, and 7 have false conclusions, but none of those lines has both premises true. No line has both premises true and the conclusion false; therefore, the argument is valid.

A quick method to inspect a completed truth table is to go down the column that displays the final truth values for the conclusion. You need only inspect those lines where the conclusion is false. In those instances, you then need to see if all the premises are true. The truth table method provides a straightforward, mechanical way to show whether an argument using truth-functional operators is valid or invalid.

Technical Validity

If the conclusion of an argument is a *tautology*, then the conclusion is logically true. As such, the argument is valid because no line of the truth table will have all true premises and a false conclusion. This is an example of a *technically valid argument*. Although valid, this kind of argument comes at a high cost. In that case, the conclusion is trivial—an empty truth that conveys no real information about the world and illuminates nothing.

An argument is also technically valid when at least one of the premises is a *self-contradiction*. No line of the truth table will have all true premises and a false conclusion because the premise with the self-contradiction is logically false. Although the argument is valid, it, too, comes at a high price: the argument is not *sound* (a *sound* argument is one that is *valid* and *has all true premises*).

In a third type of technically valid argument, two premises are *contradictory*. In that case, no line of the truth table will have all true premises and a false conclusion because one of the contradictory premises will be false on every line. However, if we contradict ourselves in the premises, then the argument is not *sound*.

CHECK YOUR UNDERSTANDING 7H

I. Create truth tables to determine whether the following arguments are valid or invalid.

1. *R* v *S*   / *R*

Answer: Invalid

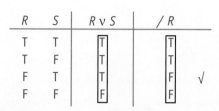

R	*S*	*R* v *S*	/ *R*
T	T	T	T
T	F	T	T
F	T	T	F √
F	F	F	F

The argument is invalid; line 3 has the premise true and the conclusion false. This is indicated by the check mark.

2. *R* · *S*   / *R*

3. ~*P* v ~*S*
   P   / *S*

4. *R* v ~*S*   / *S*

★ 5. ~*R* v ~*S*   / ~*R*

6. ~*R* · ~*S*   / ~*S*

7. ~(~*R* v ~*S*)
   S   / *R*

8. ~(~*R* · ~*S*)
   ~*S*   / ~*R*

★ 9. ~(*R* v *S*)
   ~*R*   / ~*S*

10. ~(*R* · *S*)
    ~*R*   / ~*S*

11. *P* v (*Q* v *S*)   / *P*

12. (*P* · *Q*) v *R*
    ~*Q*   / *R*

★ 13. *S* v (*Q* v *R*)
    ~*Q*
    ~*R*   / *S*

14. (*S* v *Q*) v *R*
    Q
    R   / ~*S*

15. $\sim(\sim S \vee Q) \cdot (P \vee R)$
    $\sim Q$
    $\sim P$
    $\sim R$ $/ \sim S$

II. Create truth tables to determine whether the following arguments are valid or invalid.

1. $P \supset Q$
   P $/ Q$

Answer: Valid

P	Q	$P \supset Q$	P	$/ Q$
T	T	T	T	T
T	F	F	T	F
F	T	T	F	T
F	F	T	F	F

2. $P \supset Q$
   $\sim Q$ $/ \sim P$

3. $P \supset Q$
   $Q \supset R$ $/ P \supset R$

4. $P \vee Q$
   $\sim P$ $/ Q$

⭐ 5. $(P \supset Q) \cdot (R \supset S)$
      $P \vee R$ $/ Q \vee S$

6. $P \cdot Q$ $/ P$

7. P
   Q $/ P \cdot Q$

8. P $/ P \vee Q$

⭐ 9. $R \equiv S$ $/ R$

10. $(R \cdot S) \supset S$ $/ S$

11. $P \equiv (\sim P \vee \sim S)$
    $\sim P$ $/ \sim S$

12. $\sim(R \supset S)$
    $\sim R$ $/ \sim S$

⭐ 13. $\sim(R \cdot S)$
       $\sim R \supset P$ $/ \sim S$

14. $(P \vee Q) \supset S$ $/ P$

15. $(P \cdot Q) \vee (R \supset P)$
    $\sim Q \vee \sim R$ / R

16. $[S \vee (Q \vee R)] \supset Q$
    $\sim Q$
    $\sim R$ / S

★ 17. $[(S \cdot Q) \cdot R] \supset Q$
    Q
    R / $\sim S$

18. $\sim(\sim S \vee Q) \supset (P \vee R)$
    $\sim Q$
    $\sim P$
    $\sim R$ / $\sim S$

19. $P \supset Q$
    $Q \supset P$ / $P \vee Q$

20. $(P \cdot Q) \vee R$
    $\sim Q$ / R

★ 21. $P \supset (Q \vee \sim R)$
    $Q \supset \sim R$ / $P \supset \sim R$

22. $(P \cdot Q) \equiv (R \supset P)$
    $\sim Q \vee \sim R$ / R

23. $P \supset (\sim P \vee \sim S)$
    $\sim P$ / $\sim S$

24. $R \supset S$
    $\sim S$ / R

★ 25. $(P \vee Q) \equiv S$ / P

III. First, translate the following arguments using the logical operators. Second, create truth tables to determine whether the arguments are valid or invalid.

1. Either January or February was the coldest month this year. January was clearly not the coldest month. Therefore, February was the coldest month this year.

Answer: Let *J = January was the coldest month this year,* and *B = February was the coldest month this year.*

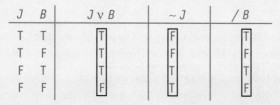

J	B	$J \vee B$	$\sim J$	/ B
T	T	T	F	T
T	F	T	F	F
F	T	T	T	T
F	F	F	T	F

The argument is valid; there is no line where the premises are true and the conclusion is false.

2. Either June or July was the hottest month this year. July was the hottest, so it cannot be June.

3. Either Eddie or Walter is the tallest member of the family. Walter is the tallest, so Eddie is not the tallest.

4. It is not the case that June and September have 31 days. June does not have 31 days; therefore, September does not have 31 days.

★ 5. Unless we stop interfering in other countries' internal affairs we will find ourselves with more enemies than we can handle. We will stop interfering in other countries' internal affairs. So it is safe to conclude that we will not find ourselves with more enemies than we can handle.

6. It is not the case that both Jim and Mary Lynn are hog farmers. Mary Lynn is not a hog farmer, so Jim cannot be one.

7. It is not the case that either Lee Ann or Johnny is old enough to collect Social Security benefits. Since Lee Ann does not collect Social Security benefits, we can conclude that Johnny does not.

8. If the prosecuting attorney's claims are correct, then the defendant is guilty. The defendant is guilty. Therefore, the prosecuting attorney's claims are correct.

★ 9. If the prosecuting attorney's claims are correct, then the defendant is guilty. The defendant is not guilty. Therefore, the prosecuting attorney's claims are correct.

10. If the prosecuting attorney's claims are correct, then the defendant is guilty. The defendant is not guilty. Therefore, the prosecuting attorney's claims are not correct.

11. If the prosecuting attorney's claims are correct, then the defendant is guilty. The defendant is guilty. Therefore, the prosecuting attorney's claims are not correct.

12. If UFOs exist, then there is life on other planets. UFOs do not exist. Thus, it is not the case that there is life on other planets.

★ 13. If UFOs exist, then there is life on other planets. UFOs do not exist. Thus, there is life on other planets.

14. If I am the president of the United States, then I live in the White House. I am not the president of the United States. Therefore, I do not live in the White House.

15. If I live in the White House, then I am the president of the United States. I am not the president of the United States. Therefore, I do not live in the White House.

16. If you take 1000 mg of Vitamin C every day, then you will not get a cold. You get a cold. Thus, you did not take 1000 mg of Vitamin C every day.

★ 17. If you take 1000 mg of Vitamin C every day, then you will not get a cold. You did not get a cold. Thus, you did take 1000 mg of Vitamin C every day.

18. If Robert drove south on I-15 from Las Vegas, then Robert got to Los Angeles. Robert did not go south on I-15 from Las Vegas. Therefore, Robert did not get to Los Angeles.

19. If you did not finish the job by Friday, then you did not get the bonus. You finished the job by Friday. Thus, you did get the bonus.

20. If you finished the job by Friday, then you got the bonus. You did not finish the job by Friday. Thus, you did not get the bonus.

I. INDIRECT TRUTH TABLES

A good understanding of the logical operators gives us the ability to analyze truth-functional statements and arguments more quickly—without having to create full-fledged truth tables. Section 7D introduced some of the principles behind the indirect truth table method. When specific truth values are assigned to simple statements, then a short truth table can be constructed.

Thinking Through an Argument

To get started, we can try thinking our way through an argument. This requires a solid grasp of the truth tables for the five logical operators. Let's start with the following argument:

Stocks will go up in value or we will have a recession.
We will not have a recession.
Stocks will go up in value.

If we let S = *stocks will go up in value*, and R = *we will have a recession*, then the translation is this:

$$S \lor R$$
$$\sim R \qquad / S$$

One way to begin is by figuring out which truth values for the simple statements are needed to make both premises true at the same time. For example, if the first premise $(S \lor R)$ is true, then what can we say about S and R separately? Since this is a disjunction, *at least one* of the disjuncts must be true. We can start by assuming that both S and R are true.

Now if the second premise $(\sim R)$ is true, then the simple statement R must be false; there is no other choice. Once we have determined the specific value for R, we must designate the same value for all instances of R throughout the argument. This means that the R in the first premise is false. Recall that under the assumption that the first premise (a disjunction) was true, at least one of the simple statements (S, R) was true.

But now we have determined that the only way for the second premise to be true is for R to be false.

When we initially assumed the first premise was true, we did not know whether S was true or R was true or both were true. But with the analysis of the second premise, we can determine that, in order for the both premises to be true, S must be true. Finally, if S is true, then the conclusion, S, is true. This means that the argument is valid.

We get the same result by starting with the conclusion and temporarily ignoring the premises. However, if you start with the conclusion, then you must determine which truth value will make it false. Once this is determined, the strategy is then to try to get all the premises true. If it can be done, then the argument is invalid.

Now since the conclusion is the simple statement S, we must assign it the truth value *false*. Therefore, every occurrence of S in the argument is false. Given this, the only way the first premise can be true is if R is true. The second premise is ~ R. Since R has been assigned the truth value *true*, ~ R is false. We have shown that if the conclusion is false, then all the premises cannot be true at the same time. The argument is valid.

A Shorter Truth Table

Now that we have thought our way through an argument using logical operators, we are in position to develop a shortcut method of showing validity or invalidity. An *indirect truth table* assigns truth values to the simple statements of an argument in order to determine if an argument is valid or invalid. Here is an example:

$$\sim(P \cdot Q)$$
$$P \qquad \quad / Q$$

We start by displaying the argument as if we were doing a normal truth table:

P Q	~ (P · Q)	P	/ Q

*The indirect method requires us to look for **any** possibility of true premises and false conclusion.* Since an indirect truth table looks for the shortest way to decide the possibility of true premises and false conclusion, it makes sense to assign truth values to any simple statements that allow us to "lock in" one truth value. In this example, since the conclusion is the simple statement Q, we can start by assigning Q the truth value *false*. The assigned value is placed in the guide on the left side of the truth table:

P Q	~ (P · Q)	P	/ Q
F			F

Notice that the Q in the conclusion has "F" written under it, but not the Q in the first premise. Since the conclusion does not contain any logical operators, we put the truth value directly under the simple statement. However, the Q in the first premise is part of a compound statement. Therefore, we will place truth values only under the operators. To do this, we will rely on the guide to assist us.

The next step is to try to get all the premises true at the same time. Since the second premise is the simple statement *P*, we assign *P* the truth value *true*. This is added to the information in the truth table:

P	Q	~ (P · Q)	P	/ Q
T	F		T̲	F̲

Once again, notice that we placed the truth value for *P* in the guide and under the *P* in the second premise. Since the second premise does not contain any logical operators, we put the truth value directly under the simple statement. All the truth values for the simple statements have been assigned; therefore, the truth table can be completed:

P	Q	~ (P · Q)	P	/ Q
T	F	T̲ F	T̲	F̲ √

The short truth table reveals the possibility of true premises and a false conclusion. Therefore, the argument is invalid. In this example, since the second premise was the simple statement *P*, we could have started by assigning *P* the truth value *true*. The next step would have been to assign the simple statement *Q* in the conclusion the truth value *false*. The resulting truth table would be the same as the earlier one, and it would show that the argument is invalid.

This process has revealed a good strategy for constructing indirect truth tables. Start by assigning truth values to the simple statements, ones that contain no logical operators. But what happens if we get to a point in the assignment of truth values where we have a choice to make? Analysis of the next argument explains the procedure:

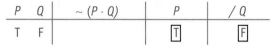

$$\sim P \cdot R$$
$$P \vee \sim Q \quad / Q$$

P	Q	R	~ P · R	P v ~ Q	/ Q
	F			T̲ T	F̲

The indirect truth table starts by assigning the truth value *false* to the simple statement *Q* (the conclusion). The negation sign in the second premise is now determined because the guide informs us that *Q* is false. This information is important. Since the second premise already has a true disjunct, it turns out that no matter what truth value is assigned to *P*, the second premise is true. This allows us to place a box around the "T" under the wedge in the second premise.

However, there are several possibilities to consider for the first premise. Let's take them one at a time. If *P* is true, then first premise is false because the conjunct ~ *P* is false. Let's see what the truth table would look like for this assignment of truth values:

P	Q	R	~ P · R	P v ~ Q	/ Q
T	F		F F̲	T̲ T	F̲

At this point it would be a mistake to say that we have shown that the argument is valid. Recall that the indirect method requires us to look for *any* possibility of true premises and false conclusion. We must consider the possibility that *P* is false before we can make a final determination. Assigning the truth value *false* to *P* does not affect the truth value of the second premise, but it does make one of the conjuncts in the first premise true. We can add this possibility to create a second line in the indirect truth table:

P	Q	R	~P · R	P ∨ ~Q	/ Q
T	F		F F	T T	F
F	F		T	T T	F

The truth value of *R* is now crucial for our analysis. It is possible to make the first premise true by assigning *R* the truth value *true*:

P	Q	R	~P · R	P ∨ ~Q	/ Q	
T	F		F F	T T	F	
F	F	T	T T	T T	F	√

The completed truth table reveals the possibility of true premises and a false conclusion. Therefore, we have shown the argument is invalid. This has been indicated by the check mark to the right of the second line.

Now you can see why this technique is called *indirect truth table*. We purposely assign truth values to the simple statements in order to reveal the possibility of true premises and a false conclusion. A full truth table has every arrangement of truth values. The trade-off is important to recognize. It is less likely that you will get a wrong determination using a full truth table. After all, an indirect truth table considers only a few truth value assignments. Therefore, it is possible to overlook a crucial truth value assignment. *That is why we need to look for any possibility of true premises and a false conclusion.* The indirect truth table method also requires a firm grip on the truth tables for the five logical operators and the flexibility of thinking through possibilities. The full truth table method is more mechanical in nature and proceeds step by step.

Let's look at another example:

$$\sim P \vee Q$$
$$R \supset Q \quad / P \cdot R$$

Since there are no stand-alone simple statements in either the premises or the conclusion, we cannot quickly assign any truth values. The next strategy is to determine which of the compound statements has the least number of ways it can be true (the premises) or false (the conclusion). The idea is to start with whichever compound statement has the fewest number of ways.

The first premise is a disjunction; therefore, there are three ways it can be true. The second premise is a conditional; it has three ways to be true. Next, we turn to the conclusion to determine the number of ways it can be false. Since the conclusion is a conjunction, there are three ways for it to be false. Since all the compound statements have the same number of ways, we can choose any of them to start. Let's try the conclusion:

P	Q	R	~ P v Q	R ⊃ Q	/ P · R
T		F	F	[T]	[F]
F		T	T [T]		[F]
F		F	T [T]	[T]	[F]

The guide on the left lists the three ways that the conclusion can be false. The F's under the dot in the conclusion are put in a box, because they are the result for the main operator in all three lines. The assigned truth values for *P* enable the placement of truth values under the tilde in the first premise. Given this, we can determine the truth value for the main operator in two of the three lines. In other words, since the first premise has at least one disjunct true (the second and third lines), the disjunction is true for those cases. We note this by placing the final truth values in boxes under the wedge. At this point, the first line under the wedge cannot be determined because it might be true or false (depending on the truth value of *Q*).

The assigned truth values for *R* determine truth values for the horseshoe in two of the three lines. In other words, because the antecedent is false on the first and third lines, the compound statement is true. We note this by placing the final truth values in boxes under the horseshoe. At this point, the second line under the horseshoe cannot be determined, because it might be true or false (depending on the truth value of *Q*).

Line 3 is enough to show the argument is invalid; but what if you miss that fact? No problem. When you first start applying the procedure you can easily miss items. The important thing is to continue on with determining the values for *Q*. If we finish the first line and cannot get both premises true, then we are not allowed to make any final decision. We must proceed to the next line. If we cannot get both premises true in that line, then again we cannot make any final decision. If none of the three lines have both premises true and the conclusion false, then the argument is valid.

However, if we get to a line with both premises true and the conclusion false, we can stop—the argument is invalid. Let's look at the first line. The disjunction in the first premise is true if *Q* is true. Let's go ahead and plug in this information:

P	Q	R	~ P v Q	R ⊃ Q	/ P · R	
T	T	F	F [T]	[T]	[F]	√
F		T	T [T]	[F]	[F]	
F		F	T [T]	[T]	[F]	√

Line 1 is complete. As the boxes indicate, both premises are true and the conclusion is false. Therefore, the indirect truth table shows that the argument is invalid. A check mark is placed to the right of the line to indicate this result. (A check mark has been added to indicate that line 3 would have shown the same thing.)

Always remember two points when you construct an indirect truth table for an argument. (1) You have *not* shown that an argument is valid until you have correctly shown that *none* of the available lines contains all true premises and a false conclusion. (2) You have shown that an argument is invalid as soon as you have correctly shown that a line contains *all* true premises and a false conclusion.

CHECK YOUR UNDERSTANDING 7I.1

Use the indirect truth table method to determine whether the following arguments are valid or invalid.

1. $(R \cdot Q) \vee S$
    R
    $\sim Q$ /$\sim S$

2. $(R \vee Q) \cdot S$
    Q
    $\sim R$ /S

Answer for Exercise 1:

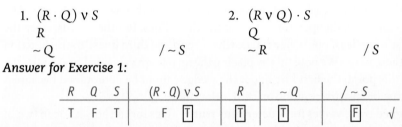

R	Q	S	$(R \cdot Q) \vee S$	R	$\sim Q$	/$\sim S$
T	F	T	F T	T	T	F √

The completed indirect truth table reveals the possibility of true premises and a false conclusion; thus we have shown that the argument is invalid.

3. $(R \cdot Q) \vee S$
    R
    $\sim Q$ /$S \cdot R$

4. $(P \cdot Q) \vee (R \cdot S)$
    Q
    S
    R /P

★ 5. $[P \vee (Q \vee S)] \supset R$
    $\sim P$
    $\sim Q$
    $\sim S$ /$\sim R$

6. $(P \vee Q) \cdot (\sim S \cdot Q)$
    $\sim S$
    $\sim Q$ /$\sim P$

7. $(\sim S \vee \sim Q) \supset \sim R$
    S
    Q /R

8. $R \supset (Q \cdot \sim S)$
    S
    $\sim Q$ /$\sim R$

★ 9. $\sim (P \vee Q) \vee \sim (R \cdot S)$
    $P \cdot Q$
    R /$\sim S$

10. $(P \cdot Q) \vee \sim R$
    $\sim P$
    $\sim Q$ /R

11. $(R \vee S) \supset (P \cdot Q)$
    $\sim S$
    $\sim Q$ /$\sim R$

12. $(R \cdot Q) \vee S$
    R
    Q /$S \cdot R$

★ 13. $(R \vee Q) \supset \sim S$
    $Q \vee S$ /R

14. $(R \vee S) \supset (P \cdot Q)$
    $\sim S \vee \sim Q$ /$\sim R$

15. $\sim (R \vee S) \supset (P \vee Q)$
    $\sim S \vee Q$
    $\sim Q \equiv R$ /$\sim R$

16. $(R \cdot Q) \vee \sim S$
    $R \vee \sim Q$
    $\sim Q \vee \sim S$ /$\sim S \cdot R$

★ 17. $\sim(\sim R \vee \sim Q) \supset \sim S$ 18. $(R \vee \sim S) \supset \sim (P \cdot Q)$
$Q \supset S$ $/\sim R \supset S$ $\sim S \vee \sim Q$ $/\sim R \cdot P$

19. $\sim[\,P \vee (Q \vee S)\,] \supset \sim R$ 20. $(Q \vee S) \supset (\sim R \cdot P)$
$\sim Q \equiv \sim S$ $/\sim R \supset P$ $\sim Q \vee S$ $/\sim Q \supset (S \vee P)$

Necessary and Sufficient Conditions

We can apply the indirect truth table method to illustrate necessary and sufficient conditions. Chapter 3 illustrated that necessary and sufficient conditions can be written as straightforward conditional statements. We saw that a sufficient condition can be understood by using the phrase "is enough for" or "it guarantees." On the other hand, a necessary condition means *essential* or *required*.

Parents often use conditional statements. For example, a parent might say, "If you eat your spinach, then you will get ice cream." Now, suppose the child does not eat the spinach. The parent will probably feel justified in denying the child the ice cream. Here is the parent's argument:

> If you eat your spinach, then you get ice cream.
> <u>You did not eat your spinach.</u>
> You do not get ice cream.

Most parents think that this is a good argument. But let's see. We can have $S = you$ *eat your spinach*, and $I = you$ *get ice cream*.

$$S \supset I$$
$$\sim S \qquad /\sim I$$

We can construct a complete truth table:

S	I	$S \supset I$	$\sim S$	$/\sim I$	
T	T	T	F	F	
T	F	F	F	T	
F	T	T	T	F	√
F	F	T	T	T	

The results show that it is possible for the premises to be true and the conclusion to be false. Therefore, this is an invalid argument.

We can also construct an indirect truth table:

S	I	$S \supset I$	$\sim S$	$/\sim I$	
F	T	T	T	F	√

Once again, the results show that it is possible for the premises to be true and the conclusion to be false. Therefore, this is an invalid argument.

Logically speaking, the children can get the ice cream even if they do not eat the spinach. The reason for this interesting result is that a *sufficient condition* has been given for getting the ice cream: eating the spinach. The first premise sets the sufficient condition. However, since it is an invalid argument, the conclusion could be false even though both premises are true. In other words, it is *not necessary* to eat the spinach to get the ice cream.

Seeing this result might cause smart parents to adjust their argument, since they probably intended to make it necessary to eat the spinach to get the ice cream. This can be accomplished by the parent saying, "If you do not eat your spinach, then you do not get ice cream." Another way of saying the same thing is this: "You will get the ice cream only if you eat your spinach." Now suppose the child does not eat the spinach. The parent will probably feel justified in denying the child the ice cream. This is illustrated in the next argument:

> If you do not eat your spinach, then you do not get ice cream.
> <u>You did not eat your spinach.</u>
> You do not get ice cream.

Here is the translation:

$$\sim S \supset \sim I$$
$$\sim S \qquad / \sim I$$

As before, we can construct a complete truth table:

S	I	~S ⊃ ~I	~S	/ ~I
T	T	F [T] F	[F]	[F]
T	F	F [T] T	[F]	[T]
F	T	T [F] F	[T]	[F]
F	F	T [T] T	[T]	[T]

Since it is not possible for both premises to be true and the conclusion to be false, the argument is valid. Parents will be relieved.

We can also construct an indirect truth table:

S	I	~S ⊃ ~I	~S	/ ~I
F	T	T [F] F	[T]	[F]

There is only one way to get the conclusion false, so that locks in the truth value for *I*. In addition, there is only one way for the second premise to be true: when *S* is false. This means that we do not need to add any more lines. The indirect truth table is complete. Since it is not possible for both premises to be true and the conclusion to be false, the argument is valid.

Since a necessary condition has been established, the children cannot get to the ice cream unless they go through the spinach. However, a new problem has occurred. Imagine that the child actually eats the spinach. In that case the parent would, logically speaking, be justified in *not* giving the ice cream. By setting up a *necessary condition*, the parent is stating that eating the spinach is required in order to get the ice cream. However, even if the spinach is eaten, this does not logically guarantee that the ice cream will be received. This follows because a *sufficient condition* has *not* been established. Therefore, to ensure that parents and children are protected both sufficient and necessary conditions must be set together. For example, the parent might say, "You will get ice cream if and only if you eat your spinach." The biconditional can be translated as "$I \equiv S$."

Now suppose the child eats the spinach. An argument can be created to capture this possibility:

$$I \equiv S$$
$$S \qquad / I$$

As before, we can construct a complete truth table:

S	I	$I \equiv S$	S	/ I
T	T	T	T	T
T	F	F	T	F
F	T	F	F	T
F	F	T	F	F

The truth table shows that the argument is valid. That takes care of the child's expectations.

We can also construct an indirect truth table to show that the argument is valid:

I	S	$I \equiv S$	S	/ I
F	T	F	T	F

There is only one way to get the conclusion false, so that locks in the truth value for *I*. In addition, there is only one way for the second premise to be true: when *S* is true. This means that we do not need to add any more lines. We simply need to determine the truth value of the first premise. Recall that a biconditional is false when the components have different truth values. Therefore, the first premise is false. The indirect truth table is complete. Since it is not possible for both premises to be true and the conclusion to be false, the argument is valid.

Now suppose the child does not eat the spinach. An argument can be created to capture this possibility:

$$I \equiv S$$
$${\sim}S \qquad / {\sim}I$$

We can construct a complete truth table:

S	I	$I \equiv S$	$\sim S$	$/ \sim I$
T	T	T	F	F
T	F	F	F	T
F	T	F	T	F
F	F	T	T	T

The truth table shows that the argument is valid. That takes care of the parent's side of the bargain.

We can also construct an indirect truth table to show that the argument is valid:

I	S	$I \equiv S$	$\sim S$	$/ \sim I$
T	F	F	T	F

Once again, there is only one way to get the conclusion false, so that locks in the truth value for *I*. In addition, there is only one way for the second premise to be true: when *S* is false. This means that we do not need to add any more lines. We simply need to determine the truth value of the first premise. Since the components of the biconditional have different truth values, the biconditional is false. Therefore, the first premise is false. The indirect truth table is complete. Since it is not possible for both premises to be true and the conclusion to be false, the argument is valid.

Argument Form

Earlier in the chapter, we defined a *statement form* as a pattern of statement variables and logical operators such that any uniform substitution of statements for the variables results in a statement. An **argument form** is an arrangement of logical operators and statement variables in which a consistent replacement of the statement variables by statements results in an argument. The result is also called a *substitution instance* of the argument form. In addition, a deductive argument is *formally valid* by nature of its logical form.

Let's look at an example:

> If you give up cigarettes, then you care about your health. You did give up cigarettes. Therefore, you do care about your health.

Let *G = you give up cigarettes*, and *C = you care about your health*.

$$G \supset C$$
$$G \qquad / C$$

We can construct a complete truth table:

G	C	$G \supset C$	G	$/ C$
T	T	T	T	T
T	F	F	T	F
F	T	T	F	T
F	F	T	F	F

Since there is no way to get the conclusion false and both premises true at the same time, the argument is valid. In fact, this argument is a substitution instance of the following valid argument form:

$$p \supset q$$
$$\underline{p}$$
$$q$$

Argument form An arrangement of logical operators and statement variables in which a consistent replacement of the statement variables by statements results in an argument.

This argument form is called ***modus ponens***. Since *modus* means "method" and *po-nens* means "affirming," this valid argument form is also referred to as *affirming the antecedent*. Therefore, any argument whose form is identical to *modus ponens* is valid.

Modus ponens A valid argument form (also referred to as *affirming the antecedent*).

We can also construct an indirect truth table to show the same result:

G	C	G ⊃ C	G	/ C
T	F	F	T	F

Now let's look at a different argument:

> If you give up cigarettes, then you care about your health. You do care about your health. Therefore, you did give up cigarettes.

Once again, let G = *you give up cigarettes*, and C = *you care about your health*.

$$G \supset C$$
$$C \qquad / G$$

We can construct a complete truth table:

G	C	G ⊃ C	C	/ G	
T	T	T	T	T	
T	F	F	F	T	
F	T	T	T	F	√
F	F	T	F	F	

The truth table shows that it is possible to get the conclusion false and both premises true at the same time; therefore, the argument is invalid (as indicated by the check mark). This argument is a substitution instance of the following argument form:

$$p \supset q$$
$$\underline{q \qquad\qquad}$$
$$p$$

This argument form is referred to as the **fallacy of affirming the consequent**, and it is a formal fallacy. This was illustrated by the truth table analysis of the substitution instance.

Fallacy of affirming the consequent An invalid argument form; it is a formal fallacy.

We can also construct an indirect truth table to show the same result:

G	C	G ⊃ C	C	/ G	
F	T	T	T	F	√

Now let's look at another argument:

> If you give up cigarettes, then you care about your health. You do not care about your health. Therefore, you did not give up cigarettes.

Once again, let G = *you give up cigarettes*, and C = *you care about your health*.

$$G \supset C$$
$$\sim C \qquad / \sim G$$

We can construct a complete truth table:

G	C	G ⊃ C	C	/ ~ G
T	T	T	F	F
T	F	F	T	F
F	T	T	F	T
F	F	T	T	T

Since there is no way to get the conclusion false and both premises true at the same time, the argument is valid. In fact, this argument is a substitution instance of the following valid argument form:

$$p \supset q$$
$$\underline{\sim q}$$
$$\sim p$$

Modus tollens A valid argument form (also referred to as *denying the consequent*).

This argument form is called **modus tollens**. Since *modus* means "method" and *tollens* means "denying," this valid argument form is also referred to as *denying the consequent*. Therefore, any argument whose form is identical to *modus tollens* is valid.

We can also construct an indirect truth table to show the same result:

G	C	G ⊃ C	~ C	/ ~ G
F	T	F	T	F

Let's look at one final argument:

> If you give up cigarettes, then you care about your health. You did not give up cigarettes. Therefore, you do not care about your health.

Once again, let G = *you give up cigarettes*, and C = *you care about your health*.

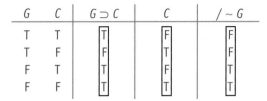

$$G \supset C$$
$$\sim G \qquad / \sim C$$

We can construct a complete truth table:

G	C	G ⊃ C	~ G	/ ~ C	
T	T	T	F	F	
T	F	F	F	T	
F	T	T	T	F	√
F	F	T	T	T	

The truth table shows that it is possible to get the conclusion false and both premises true at the same time; therefore, the argument is invalid (as indicated by the check mark). The argument is a substitution instance of the following argument form:

$$p \supset q$$
$$\underline{\sim p}$$
$$\sim q$$

This argument form is referred to as the **fallacy of denying the antecedent**, and it is a formal fallacy. This was illustrated by the truth table analysis of the substitution instance.

Fallacy of denying the antecedent An invalid argument form; it is a formal fallacy.

We can also construct an indirect truth table to show the same result:

G	C	G ⊃ C	~ G	/ ~ C
F	T	$\boxed{T}$	$\boxed{T}$	$\boxed{F}$ √

The two valid argument forms—*modus ponens* and *modus tollens*—and the two invalid argument forms—the *fallacy of affirming the consequent* and the *fallacy of denying the antecedent*—are developed further in the next chapter.

CHECK YOUR UNDERSTANDING 71.2

First, translate the arguments from English using logical operators. Next, use indirect truth tables to determine whether the arguments are valid or invalid.

1. If either Barbara or Johnny goes to the party, then Lee Ann will not have to pick up Mary Lynn. Barbara is not going to the party. Lee Ann has to pick up Mary Lynn. Therefore, Johnny is not going to the party.

Answer: Let B = *Barbara goes to the party*, J = *Johnny goes to the party*, and L = *Lee Ann has to pick up Mary Lynn*:

$$(B \lor J) \supset \sim L$$
$$\sim B$$
$$L \qquad / \sim J$$

B	J	L	(B ∨ J) ⊃ ~ L)	~ B	L	/ ~ J
F	T	T	T $\boxed{F}$ F	$\boxed{T}$	$\boxed{T}$	$\boxed{F}$

The only way for the conclusion to be false is for *J* to be true. The only way for the third premise to be true is for *L* to be true. The only way for the second premise to be true is for *B* to be false. At this point, all the simple statement truth values have been assigned to the guide on the left. Based on the guide, the first premise is false. Since it is impossible to get all the premises true and the conclusion false at the same time, the argument is valid.

2. Either you take a Breathalyzer test or you get arrested for DUI. You did not take the Breathalyzer test. Therefore, you get arrested for DUI.

3. If animals feel pain or learn from experience, then animals are conscious. Animals do not feel pain. Animals do not learn from experience. Thus, animals are not conscious.

4. If animals feel pain or learn from experience, then animals are conscious. Animals do not feel pain. Animals do not learn from experience. Therefore, animals are conscious.

⭐ 5. If animals are not conscious or do not feel pain, then they do not have any rights. Animals do not have any rights. Animals do not feel pain. Thus, animals are not conscious.

6. If animals are not conscious or do not feel pain, then they do not have any rights. Animals are conscious. Animals do feel pain. Therefore, animals have rights.

7. Either you are right or you are wrong. You are not right. Therefore, you are wrong.

8. If either Bill or Gus or Kate committed the crime, then Mike did not do it and Tina did not do it. Bill did not commit the crime. Gus did not commit the crime. Kate did not commit the crime. Thus, Mike did it.

⭐ 9. If either Elvis or the Beatles sold the most records of all time, then I did not win the contest. The Beatles did not sell the most records of all time. Therefore, I won the contest.

10. If I save $1 a day, then I will not be rich in 10 years. If I save $2 a day, then I will not be rich in 10 years. If I save $3 a day, then I will not be rich in 10 years. I will not save $1 a day. I will not save $2 a day. I will not save $3 a day. Therefore, I will not be rich in 10 years.

11. If X is an even number, then X is divisible by 2. But X is not divisible by 2. Thus, X is not an even number.

12. If X is not an even number, then X is not divisible by 2. But X is divisible by 2. Therefore, X is an even number.

⭐ 13. If Joyce went south on I-15 from Las Vegas, then Joyce got to Los Angeles. Joyce did not go south on I-15 from Las Vegas. Thus, Joyce did not get to Los Angeles.

14. If you did not finish the job by Friday, then you did not get the bonus. You did finish the job by Friday. Therefore, you did get the bonus.

15. If you did finish the job by Friday, then you did get the bonus. You did not finish the job by Friday. Thus, you did not get the bonus.

16. Eddie can vote if, and only if, he is registered. Eddie is registered. Therefore, Eddie can vote.

⭐ 17. Eddie can vote if, and only if, he is registered. Eddie can vote. Thus, Eddie is registered.

18. Eddie can vote if, and only if, he is registered. But Eddie is not registered. Therefore, Eddie cannot vote.

19. Eddie can vote if, and only if, he is registered. Eddie cannot vote. Thus, Eddie is not registered.

20. Linda can think if, and only if, she is conscious. Linda is conscious. Therefore, Linda can think.

Examining Statements for Consistency

Indirect truth tables can be used to determine whether two or more statements are consistent. The procedure draws on the basic strategies behind indirect truth tables but adds one more requirement. If you recall, statements are *consistent* if there is at least one line on their respective truth tables where the statements are true. This is where the strategy diverges from determining the validity of an argument. In other words, the strategy for analyzing arguments is to look for the possibility of true premises and a false conclusion. However, since examining a set of statements for consistency is not dealing with an argument, there are no premises and a conclusion. Let's work through a simple example:

$$P \lor \sim Q$$
$$\sim P \cdot \sim Q$$

The indirect truth table is constructed as before, except that no slash sign indicating a conclusion is used.

P Q	P ∨ ~ Q	~ P · ~ Q

The first step is to determine which of the compound statements has the least number of ways it can be true. The first statement is a disjunction; therefore, there are three ways it can be true. The second statement is a conjunction; there is only one way for it to be true. This narrows the analysis considerably. We lock in the truth values that are needed to get the second statement true:

P Q	P ∨ ~ Q	~ P · ~ Q
F F		T [T] T

We can now go ahead and complete the truth table:

P Q	P ∨ ~ Q	~ P · ~ Q
F F	[T] T	T [T] T

The truth table shows that both statements can be true at the same time; therefore, the statements are consistent.

Let's work through a longer problem this time. Are the following four statements consistent?

$$P \supset \sim Q$$
$$R \lor Q$$
$$\sim R$$
$$Q \supset (P \lor R)$$

The indirect truth table is constructed as before, but this time there are four statements side by side:

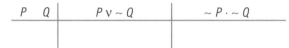

P Q R	P ⊃ ~ Q	R ∨ Q	~ R	Q ⊃ (P ∨ R)

The first step is to determine which of the statements has the least number of ways it can be true. The first is a conditional; therefore, there are three ways it can be true. The second is a disjunction; there are three ways it can be true. The third is the negation of a simple statement; there is only one way for it to be true. This is where we will start. We lock in the truth value that is needed to get the third statement true:

P	Q	R	P ⊃ ~ Q	R ∨ Q	~ R	Q ⊃ (P ∨ R)
		F			T	

The locked-in truth value for R is used to decide the next step. An R appears in the second and fourth statements, so we can look at them. In the fourth statement, the R is part of a disjunction, but the disjunction happens to be the consequent of a conditional. At this point, there are too many possibilities for the fourth statement to be true for us to make any specific determinations. However, the second statement is a disjunction with one of the disjuncts (R) false. Therefore, the only way to get the second statement true is for Q to be true. This information is added to the truth table:

P	Q	R	P ⊃ ~ Q	R ∨ Q	~ R	Q ⊃ (P ∨ R)
	T	F	F	T	T	

This information helps decide what we need to do in the first statement. Since Q is true, the consequent of the conditional is false. Therefore, the only way for the first statement to be true is for P to be false. This information is added to the truth table:

P	Q	R	P ⊃ ~ Q	R ∨ Q	~ R	Q ⊃ (P ∨ R)
F	T	F	T F	T	T	

The guide is complete. Now all we have to do is use the information in the guide to determine the truth value of the fourth statement. If the fourth statement is true, then the set of statements is consistent. On the other hand, if the fourth statement is false, then the set is inconsistent. Once we make that determination, we are finished because we have narrowed down our search by locking in the truth values for all the simple statements. Here is the final result:

P	Q	R	P ⊃ ~ Q	R ∨ Q	~ R	Q ⊃ (P ∨ R)
F	T	F	T F	T	T	F F

The indirect truth table shows that the four statements cannot all be true at the same time. Therefore, the set of statements is inconsistent.

While the process of using indirect truth tables may seem complex at first, it is an efficient way to determine whether an argument is valid or invalid. It is also an efficient way to determine whether sets of statements are consistent or inconsistent. Of course, the technique requires a firm grasp of the truth tables for the five operators. As with most skills, you will become more confident with practice, and applying the technique will go more quickly.

CHECK YOUR UNDERSTANDING 7I.3

Use indirect truth tables to determine whether the following sets of statements are consistent or inconsistent.

1. $A \lor B \mid \sim A \supset B$

Answer: Consistent.

There are three ways to get both statements true, so we can start with either one. Let's try making both A and B true:

A B	$A \lor B$	$\sim A \supset B$
T T	T̄	F T̄

We do not have to try the other two possibilities because the truth table shows that both statements can be true at the same time.

2. $M \cdot \sim N \mid M \mid N \lor P$

3. $R \equiv U \mid \sim R \cdot U \mid R \lor P$

4. $\sim (Q \supset \sim R) \cdot S \mid S \supset \sim (Q \cdot R)$

★ 5. $R \lor (\sim P \cdot S) \mid Q \lor \sim P \mid Q \supset \sim P$

6. $\sim R \supset (Q \supset P) \mid \sim Q \cdot P \mid R \lor \sim Q \mid P \supset R$

7. $\sim A \supset \sim B \mid \sim A \lor B \mid A \cdot \sim B$

8. $(A \cdot B) \lor C \mid \sim B \cdot A \mid \sim C$

★ 9. $\sim M \lor \sim P \mid \sim M \lor Q \mid P \lor R$

10. $P \supset \sim Q \mid Q \supset \sim P \mid Q \lor \sim S$

11. $R \lor (S \equiv U) \mid S \lor R$

12. $P \cdot Q \mid \sim P \supset Q$

★ 13. $\sim (Q \supset R) \supset S \mid S \lor (Q \cdot R)$

14. $Q \lor P \mid Q \cdot R \mid \sim P \supset R$

15. $\sim P \cdot Q \mid \sim P \supset \sim R \mid \sim P \lor (Q \cdot \sim R)$

Summary

- Logical operators: Special symbols that are used to translate ordinary language statements.
- The basic components in propositional logic are statements.
- Simple statement: One that does not have any other statement as a component.
- Compound statement: One that has at least one simple statement as a component.
- The five logical operator symbols: *tilde, dot, wedge, horseshoe,* and *triple bar.*

- The word "not" and the phrase "it is not the case that" are used to deny the statement that follows them (we refer to their use as "negation").
- Conjunction: A compound statement that has two distinct statements (called "conjuncts") connected by the dot symbol.
- Disjunction: A compound statement that has two distinct statements (called "disjuncts") connected by the wedge symbol.
- In ordinary language, the word "if" typically precedes the antecedent of a conditional: "only if" typically precedes the consequent of a conditional. The horseshoe symbol is used to translate a conditional statement.
- Biconditional: A compound statement made up of two conditionals: one indicated by the word "if" and the other indicated by the phrase "only if."
- Well-formed formulas: Compound statement forms that are grammatically correct.
- Main operator: The logical operator that has in its range the largest component or components in a compound statement.
- The truth value of a truth-functional compound proposition is determined by the truth values of its components and the definitions of the logical operators involved. Any truth-functional compound proposition that can be determined in this manner is called a "truth function."
- A statement variable can stand for any statement, simple or complex.
- Statement form: A pattern of statement variables and logical operators.
- Truth table: An arrangement of truth values for a truth-functional compound proposition that displays for every possible case how the truth value of the proposition is determined by the truth values of its simple components.
- Inclusive disjunction: Where both disjuncts can be true at the same time.
- Exclusive disjunction: Where both disjuncts cannot be true at the same time.
- Order of operations: The order of handling the logical operators within a truth-functional proposition; it is a step-by-step method of generating a complete truth table.
- Contingent statements: Statements that are neither necessarily true nor necessarily false (they are sometimes true, sometimes false).
- Noncontingent statements: Statements such that the truth values in the main operator column do not depend on the truth values of the component parts.
- Tautology: A statement that is necessarily true.
- Self-contradiction: A statement that is necessarily false.
- Logically equivalent: When two truth-functional statements appear different but have identical truth tables.
- Contradictory statements: Two statements that have opposite truth values on every line of their respective truth tables.
- Consistent statements: Two (or more) statements that have at least one line on their respective truth tables where the main operators are true.
- Inconsistent statements: Two (or more) statements that do not have even one line on their respective truth tables where the main operators are true.

- Argument form: An arrangement of logical operators and statement variables in which a consistent replacement of the statements variables by statements results in an argument.
- *Modus ponens*: A valid argument form (also referred to as *affirming the antecedent*).
- Fallacy of affirming the consequent: An invalid argument form; it is a formal fallacy.
- *Modus tollens*: A valid argument form (also referred to as *denying the consequent*).
- Fallacy of denying the antecedent: An invalid argument form; it is a formal fallacy.

KEY TERMS

logical operators   289
propositional logic   289
simple statement   289
compound statement   289
negation   291
conjunction   291
disjunction   292
conditional   292
biconditional   293
well-formed formulas   296
main operator   298
truth function   304

statement variable   305
statement form   305
truth table   305
inclusive disjunction   307
exclusive disjunction   307
order of operations   315
contingent statements   321
noncontingent
   statements   321
tautology   322
self-contradiction   322
logically equivalent   324

contradictory
   statements   326
consistent statements   326
inconsistent
   statements   327
argument form   344
modus ponens   345
fallacy of affirming the
   consequent   345
modus tollens   346
fallacy of denying the
   antecedent   347

LOGIC CHALLENGE: A CARD PROBLEM

You have not seen a large number of cards. You are told (and we stipulate that this is true) that each card has a number on one of its sides and a letter on the other side. No card has numbers on both sides, and no card has letters on both sides. You are not told how many cards there are, but you are told that the same number might occur on many different cards. The same letter might also occur on many different cards.

Someone else has been allowed to inspect the cards and makes a claim. "I have looked at all the cards and I have discovered a pattern: *If there is a vowel on one side of the card, then there is an even number on the other side.*" The italicized statement could be true or false.

You will be shown four cards. You will only see one side of each card. If you see a letter, then you know there must be a number on the other side. If you see a number, then you know there must be a letter on the other side. Your task is to turn over *only* the cards that have the *possibility* to make the person's italicized statement *false*. The four cards are displayed as follows:

Which cards (if any) should you turn over?

Chapter 8

Natural Deduction

You and your friends are going to catch a movie at a new mall. You approach a place that seems to be still under construction. Someone remarks casually, "If this is not the new mall, then we are in the wrong place." You stop someone and ask for help. It turns out that you are not at the new mall, so the obvious conclusion is that you are in the wrong place. Let's look at the reasoning:

> If this is not the new mall, then we are in the wrong place.
> <u>This is not the new mall.</u>
> We are in the wrong place.

Seeing the argument displayed this way might help you recognize from Chapter 7 that it is an instance of *modus ponens*. But most people would not stop to identify the form because they would recognize immediately that the conclusion follows from the information at hand.

In fact, in many everyday situations, we recognize when reasoning is correct or incorrect, even when we are not sure whether the information is true or false. We may need help to know whether this is the new mall, but we know why it matters. This type of reasoning is *natural*, in the sense that the practical demands of life require that we have some basic forms of reasoning on which we can all rely. We are subject to the practical demands of reasoning on a daily basis. Everyday situations supply us with information that we quickly analyze. But what if the reasoning and the sheer amount of information become more complicated?

We often use basic forms of reasoning without even being aware of them, but even basic reasoning can throw us a curve if we are not careful. Here is an illustration:

> "Would you tell me, please, which way I ought to go from here?" asked Alice.
> "That depends a good deal on where you want to get to," said the Cheshire Cat.

"I don't much care where—" said Alice.

"Then it doesn't matter which way you go," said the Cat.

"—so long as I get *somewhere*," Alice added as an explanation.

"Oh, you're sure to do that," said the Cat, "if you only walk long enough."

Lewis Carroll, *Alice in Wonderland*

As here, everyday reasoning involves a step-by-step procedure, and it can take care and practice to follow the steps. For example, after adding up the checks you wrote this week, you conclude that you don't have enough money in your checking account to cover everything. You deduce that, unless you want to bounce a check, you had better put some money in the account. In this kind of reasoning, each step follows directly from previous steps. When we get to the final step, we accept that what we have derived is correct, as long as our starting assumptions are correct.

We normally handle everyday arguments without putting them into symbols; in this sense, the reasoning is natural. We can even work our way quite naturally through arguments that involve many steps; but sometimes that gets hard, and we can go astray. In this chapter, we develop a method of proof much like these forms of everyday reasoning; in fact, it is called *natural deduction*. Natural deduction is capable of handling complex arguments that go far beyond simple forms of everyday reasoning. This chapter builds on the natural aspect of our reasoning, so that we can recognize and apply the steps.

A. NATURAL DEDUCTION

Natural deduction is a proof procedure by which the conclusion of an argument is validly derived from the premises through the use of rules of inference. The function of **rules of inference** is to *justify* the steps of a proof. A **proof** (also called a *deduction* or a *derivation*) is a sequence of steps in which each step is either a premise or follows from earlier steps in the sequence according to the rules of inference. A justification of a step includes a rule of inference and the prior steps that were used to derive it. This procedure guarantees that each step follows validly from prior steps. A proof ends when the conclusion of the argument has been correctly derived.

There are two types of rules of inference: *implication rules* and *replacement rules*.

> **Implication rules** are *valid argument forms*. When the premises of a valid argument form occur during a proof, then we can validly derive the conclusion of the argument form as a justified step in the proof. (*Modus ponens* and *modus tollens* are two examples of valid argument forms.)

> **Replacement rules** are *pairs of logically equivalent statement forms*. Whenever one pair member of a replacement rule occurs in a proof step, then we can validly derive the other pair member as a justified step in the proof. For example, the statement form, $\sim (p \cdot q)$ is logically equivalent to $(\sim p \vee \sim q)$.

Both types of rules of inference have the same function—*to ensure the validity of the steps they are used to justify.* A natural deduction proof can begin with any number of

Natural deduction
A proof procedure by which the conclusion of an argument is validly derived from the premises through the use of rules of inference.

Rules of inference
The function of rules of inference is to justify the steps of a proof.

Proof A sequence of steps (also called a deduction or a derivation) in which each step is either a premise or follows from earlier steps in the sequence according to the rules of inference.

Implication rules Valid argument forms that are validly applied only to an entire line.

Replacement rules Pairs of logically equivalent statement forms.

premises. Every step of a proof, except the premises, requires justification. Therefore, a proof is valid if each step is either a premise or is validly derived using the rules of inference.

We saw in Chapter 7 how truth tables and the indirect truth table method allow us to determine whether an argument is valid or invalid. However, one drawback with truth tables is that, as the number of simple statements increases, the number of lines needed to complete the truth table can become overwhelming. Of course, the indirect method can reduce the number of lines. However, the flexibility of the indirect method has the effect that we might overlook an important possibility—and therefore make a wrong determination of an argument.

Natural deduction offers a proof procedure that uses valid argument forms and logically equivalent statement forms. As such, it is a powerful and effective method for proving validity. Of course, the method comes with its own challenges. Mastering the rules of inference takes time, patience, determination, and practice. However, advancing your ability to use natural deduction is no different from learning other skills. For example, learning to talk is a natural part of growing up for most people. But the ability to speak eloquently or in front of a large audience does not come easily, and it usually requires hard work. Likewise, running is something that most children learn naturally. But the ability to run fast enough to win an Olympic gold medal takes immense training and dedication. Similarly, the ability to reason is a natural process in most humans. However, just as learning to run fast or to talk eloquently takes time, there are levels of abstract reasoning that require dedication and training.

B. IMPLICATION RULES I

Chapter 7 showed that every substitution instance of a valid argument form is valid. Since the implication rules are valid argument forms, they preserve truth. In other words, given true premises, the implication rules yield true conclusions. Although you proved the eight implication rules valid in Chapter 7 (*Check Your Understanding 7H.1, II*, exercises 1–8), it will be helpful to discuss their validity in an informal manner. They are referred to as *implication rules* because the premises of the valid argument forms imply their respective conclusions. We will think through the validity of the arguments. This process will add to your understanding of how the implication rules can be used to validly derive steps in a proof.

Modus Ponens (MP)

Chapter 7 introduced *modus ponens* as part of the discussion of argument form. A conditional statement is false when the antecedent is true and the consequent is false. Given this, whenever a conditional statement is true, and the antecedent of that conditional is also true, then we can conclude that the consequent is true. For example, if it is true that "If it rained today, then the street is wet," and if it is also true that "It rained today," we can logically conclude that "the street is wet."

If it rained today, then the street is wet.
It rained today.
The street is wet.

If the first premise is true, then we can rule out the possibility that the antecedent is true and the consequent is false. Now, if the second premise is true, then the antecedent of the first premise is true, too. Given this result, the consequent of the first premise is true. If we let $p =$ *It rained today*, and $q =$ *the street is wet*, we can reveal that the logical form of the argument is *modus ponens*:

Modus Ponens (MP)

$$p \supset q$$
$$\underline{p}$$
$$q$$

The valid argument form **modus ponens** ensures that any uniform substitution in-stance using simple or compound statements results in a valid argument. Here are some examples:

Modus ponens A rule of inference (implication rule).

Valid Applications of *Modus Ponens* (MP)

1. $R \supset (M \vee N)$	1. $(P \cdot Q) \supset (G \cdot \sim D)$	1. $(K \cdot D) \vee F$
2. R	2. $P \cdot Q$	2. $[(K \cdot D) \vee F] \supset (M \vee C)$
3. $M \vee N$	3. $G \cdot \sim D$	3. $M \vee C$

The third example illustrates an important point regarding all eight implication rules: *The order of the required lines is not important.* However, in order for *modus ponens* to be applied validly, it is necessary that both the conditional statement and the antecedent both appear as *complete separate lines.* If we look once again at the third example we see that it has this form:

$$p$$
$$\underline{p \supset q}$$
$$q$$

Since both the conditional statement and its antecedent appear on separate lines, the necessary requirements for *modus ponens* have been met.

When the implication rule of *modus ponens* is used correctly, the result is a valid argu-ment. However, you must be careful to avoid mistaken applications of *modus ponens*. Here are two examples of *invalid* applications:

Invalid Applications of *Modus Ponens* (MP)

1. $(L \supset Q) \vee (R \vee S)$	1. $(L \supset Q) \vee (R \vee S)$
2. L	2. L
3. Q ⊘	3. $R \vee S$ ⊘

A comparison of the three valid applications of *modus ponens* with the two invalid applications pinpoints the problem. In all three valid applications of *modus ponens*, the horseshoe was the main operator of one of the two required lines. However, in both of the invalid applications of *modus ponens* the main operator in line 1 is the wedge. This illustrates an important point: **Implication rules are validly applied only to an entire line**. This point will be emphasized in the discussion of each of the eight implication rules. Failure to adhere to this point is the number one cause of mistakes when first learning to use the implication rules.

Learning to use the rules of inference correctly is similar to learning the rules of any game. Some games have rigid rules, and other games have loose rules. It is quite common for beginners to make mistakes by misapplying the rules. Part of the learning curve of any game is experiencing various situations in which the rules come to play. The examples of invalid applications of the rules of inference are not meant to exhaust all the possible mistakes that might be made. However, they will highlight some common errors and you should use them to help understand how each rule should be used correctly. The rules of inference are precise and the examples will show you how to use them properly. The precision is crucial because the function of all the rules of inference is to ensure that each step in a proof is validly derived.

One final note: You may recall from Chapter 7 that the fallacy of affirming the consequent resembles *modus ponens*. Since it is easy to confuse the two forms, you must be careful not to make this mistake when applying *modus ponens*:

The Fallacy of Affirming the Consequent

$$p \supset q$$
$$\underline{q} \quad \oslash$$
$$p$$

Modus Tollens (MT)

Modus tollens A rule of inference (implication rule).

Chapter 7 also introduced **modus tollens**. Here is its logical form:

Modus Tollens (MT)

$$p \supset q$$
$$\underline{\sim q}$$
$$\sim p$$

Let's substitute the following statement for the first premise: "If it rained today, then the street is wet." We let $p =$ *It rained today*, and $q =$ *the street is wet*. If the first premise is true, then we can rule out the possibility that the antecedent is true and the consequent is false. Now if the second premise, $\sim q$, is true, then q is false. This means that the consequent, q, in the first premise is false. Therefore, p must be false in order for the first premise to remain true. Given these results, the conclusion, $\sim p$, is true.

The form of the argument shows that given a conditional statement and the negation of its consequent we can logically derive the negation of the antecedent as a conclusion. Here are some examples of valid applications:

Valid Applications of *Modus Tollens* (MT)

1. $H \supset (T \lor N)$	1. $(G \cdot D) \supset C$	1. $\sim (F \lor D)$
2. $\underline{\sim (T \lor N)}$	2. $\underline{\sim C}$	2. $\underline{[(T \lor F) \cdot \sim D] \supset (F \lor D)}$
3. $\sim H$	3. $\sim (G \cdot D)$	3. $\sim [(T \lor F) \cdot \sim D]$

As with all the implication rules, you must be careful to avoid mistaken applications of *modus tollens*. Here is an example of an invalid application:

Invalid Application of *Modus Tollens* (MT)

1. $(L \supset Q) \lor (R \lor S)$
2. $\sim Q$ ⊘
3. $\sim L$

In the three examples of valid applications of *modus tollens*, the main operator in one of the required lines is a horseshoe. However, in the example of the invalid application of *modus tollens*, the main operator in line 1 is the wedge. Once again, implication rules are validly applied only to an entire line.

A final note before leaving *modus tollens*: You may recall from Chapter 7 that the fallacy of denying the antecedent resembles *modus tollens*. Since it is easy to confuse the two forms, you must be careful not to make this mistake in applying *modus tollens*:

The Fallacy of Denying the Antecedent

$p \supset q$

$\sim p$

$\sim q$ ⊘

Hypothetical Syllogism (HS)

The implication rule **hypothetical syllogism** relies on conditional statements. Hypothetical syllogism has the following logical form:

Hypothetical syllogism
A rule of inference (implication rule).

Hypothetical Syllogism (HS)

$p \supset q$

$q \supset r$

$p \supset r$

Let's substitute the following for the first premise: "If I live in Atlanta, then I live in Georgia." Let $p = I$ *live in Atlanta*, and $q = I$ *live in Georgia*. Now if $r = I$ *live in the United States*, then the second premise is, "If I live in Georgia, then I live in the United States." If the first premise is true, then the antecedent cannot be true and the consequent false. The same condition holds for the second premise. The only way for the conclusion to be false is for p to be true and r to be false. However, if r is false, then the q in the second premise must be false as well (because that is the only way to keep the second premise true). But that means that the first premise is false because the antecedent is true and the consequent false. This result is in direct conflict with our assumption that the first premise is true. Therefore, if both premises are true, the conclusion is necessarily true.

The following are examples of valid applications of hypothetical syllogism:

Valid Applications of Hypothetical Syllogism (HS)

1. $H \supset (S \lor N)$	1. $[(G \cdot C) \lor P] \supset \sim S$	1. $(M \lor N) \supset (S \lor Q)$
2. $(S \lor N) \supset \sim R$	2. $\sim S \supset M$	2. $(P \lor R) \supset (M \lor N)$
3. $H \supset \sim R$	3. $[(G \cdot C) \lor P] \supset M$	3. $(P \lor R) \supset (S \lor Q)$

Here are two examples of invalid applications:

Invalid Applications of Hypothetical Syllogism (HS)

1. $K \supset (L \lor \sim R)$	1. $(B \lor C) \supset (D \lor E)$
2. $(L \cdot \sim R) \supset M$ ⊘	2. $D \supset (F \lor G)$ ⊘
3. $K \supset M$	3. $(B \lor C) \supset (F \lor G)$

In the first example, the consequent of the first premise, $L \lor \sim R$, is *not identical* to the antecedent of the second premise, $L \cdot \sim R$. Therefore, the application of hypothetical syllogism is used invalidly. In the second example, only part of the consequent of the first premise, D, occurs as the antecedent of the second premise. Therefore, this is also an invalid application of hypothetical syllogism.

Disjunctive Syllogism (DS)

Disjunctive syllogism
A rule of inference
(implication rule).

The implication rule **disjunctive syllogism** has the following logical form:

Disjunctive Syllogism (DS)

$$p \lor q$$
$$\sim p$$
$$q$$

Let's substitute the following for the first premise: "Either CDs are superior to records or DVDs are superior to film." We let $p = CDs$ *are superior to records*, and $q = DVDs$ *are superior to film*. Since the first premise is a disjunction, we know that if it is true, then at least one of the disjuncts is true. Since the second premise is the negation of p ("CDs are *not* superior to records"), p must be false in order for the second premise to be true. This means that in the first premise, q must be true to ensure that the disjunction is true. Thus, the conclusion, q, is true.

The following are examples of legitimate applications of disjunctive syllogism:

Valid Applications of Disjunctive Syllogism (DS)

1. $(R \supset P) \lor S$	1. $G \lor [(H \cdot R) \supset S]$	1. $[\sim S \lor (R \supset B)] \lor (P \cdot Q)$
2. $\sim (R \supset P)$	2. $\sim G$	2. $\sim [\sim S \lor (R \supset B)]$
3. S	3. $(H \cdot R) \supset S$	3. $P \cdot Q$

Here is an example of an invalid application:

Invalid Application of Disjunctive Syllogism (DS)

1. $(F \lor G) \lor H$
2. $\sim F$ ⊘
3. H

Disjunctive syllogism is validly applied when there is a negation of the *entire first disjunct*, not just a part of it. Therefore, the mistake in the example occurs because the negation in the second premise, $\sim F$, is only part of the first disjunct in the first premise, $(F \lor G)$.

Justification: Applying the Rules of Inference

We create proofs using natural deduction by taking the given premises of an argument and deducing whatever is necessary in a step-by-step procedure to prove the conclusion. A complete proof using natural deduction requires a *justification* for each step of the deduction. **Justification** refers to the rule of inference that is applied to every validly derived step in a proof. Here is a simple example:

Justification Refers to the rule of inference that is applied to every validly derived step in a proof.

1. $S \supset P$
2. S 　　　　/ P
3. P 　　　　1, 2, MP

The display of the argument follows the pattern introduced in Chapter 7. The conclusion, indicated by the slash mark, is for reference. The proof is complete when a justified step in the proof displays the conclusion. In this example, the justification for line 3, *the deduced step*, is set off to the right of the line and spells out its derivation; in this case it was derived from lines 1 and 2 using *modus ponens*. The proof is complete.

The next example illustrates the use of multiple rules of inference:

1. $\sim R$
2. $P \supset S$
3. $R \vee \sim S$
4. $\sim P \supset Q$ 　　　/ Q
5. $\sim S$ 　　　　　　1, 3, DS
6. $\sim P$ 　　　　　　2, 5, MT
7. Q 　　　　　　　4, 6, MP

In this example, line 5 is derived from lines 1 and 3 (both of which are premises) by disjunctive syllogism. Line 6 is derived from line 2 (a premise) and line 5 (a derived line) by *modus tollens*. Finally, line 7 is derived from line 4 (a premise) and line 6 (a derived line) by *modus ponens*. The process of justifying each line ensures that a rule of inference is validly applied. It also provides a means for checking the proof. Therefore, the correct application of the rules of inference guarantees that lines 5, 6, and 7 have each been validly deduced.

THE FIRST FOUR IMPLICATION RULES	
Modus Ponens (MP)	**Modus Tollens (MT)**
$p \supset q$ $\underline{p \quad}$ q	$p \supset q$ $\underline{\sim q}$ $\sim p$
Disjunctive Syllogism (DS)	**Hypothetical Syllogism (HS)**
$p \vee q$ $\underline{\sim p \quad}$ q	$p \supset q$ $\underline{q \supset r}$ $p \supset r$

CHECK YOUR UNDERSTANDING 8B

I. The following are examples of what you may encounter in proofs. The last step of each example gives the line numbers needed for its derivation. You are to provide the implication rule that justifies the step.

[1] 1. $P \supset Q$
  2. P /Q
  3. Q 1, 2, _____
Answer: 3. Q 1, 2, MP

[2] 1. $P \supset Q$
  2. $Q \supset R$ /$P \supset R$
  3. $P \supset R$ 1, 2, _____

[3] 1. $R \supset S$
  2. $\sim S$ /$\sim R$
  3. $\sim R$ 1, 2, _____

[4] 1. $(P \cdot Q) \vee (R \supset S)$
  2. $\sim (P \cdot Q)$ /$R \supset S$
  3. $R \supset S$ 1, 2, _____

⭐ [5] 1. $Q \supset (R \vee S)$
  2. $\sim (R \vee S)$ /$\sim Q$
  3. $\sim Q$ 1, 2, _____

[6] 1. $\sim (R \vee S) \supset (P \supset Q)$
  2. $\sim (R \vee S)$ /$P \supset Q$
  3. $P \supset Q$ 1, 2, _____

[7] 1. $(P \cdot Q) \supset R$
  2. $R \supset \sim P$ /$(P \cdot Q) \supset \sim P$
  3. $(P \cdot Q) \supset \sim P$ 1, 2, _____

[8] 1. $(P \supset Q) \supset (R \supset S)$
  2. $\sim (R \supset S)$ /$\sim (P \supset Q)$
  3. $\sim (P \supset Q)$ 1, 2, _____

⭐ [9] 1. $(R \supset S) \vee (P \supset Q)$
  2. $\sim (R \supset S)$ /$P \supset Q$
  3. $P \supset Q$ 1, 2, _____

[10] 1. $\sim P \supset Q$
  2. $\sim Q$ /$\sim \sim P$
  3. $\sim \sim P$ 1, 2, _____

[11] 1. $\sim P \supset \sim Q$
  2. $\sim Q \supset \sim R$ /$\sim P \supset \sim R$
  3. $\sim P \supset \sim R$ 1, 2, _____

[12] 1. $(P \cdot R) \supset \sim S$
    2. $(P \cdot R)$ $/ \sim S$
    3. $\sim S$ 1, 2, _____

⭐ [13] 1. $R \supset (S \vee R)$
     2. $(S \vee R) \supset P$ $/ R \supset P$
     3. $R \supset P$ 1, 2, _____

[14] 1. $R \supset (S \vee R)$
    2. $\sim (S \vee R)$ $/ \sim R$
    3. $\sim R$ 1, 2, _____

[15] 1. $S \vee (P \supset Q)$
    2. $\sim S$ $/ P \supset Q$
    3. $P \supset Q$ 1, 2, _____

II. The following are more examples of what you may encounter in proofs. In these examples the justification (the implication rule) is provided for the last step. However, the step itself is missing. Use the given information to derive the last step of each example.

[1] 1. $(Q \supset S) \vee P$
    2. $\sim (Q \supset S)$
    3.   1, 2, DS

Answer: 3. P 1, 2, DS

[2] 1. $P \supset (Q \vee S)$
    2. P
    3.   1, 2, MP

[3] 1. $(K \vee L) \supset (K \vee N)$
    2. $(K \vee N) \supset (K \vee S)$
    3.   1, 2, HS

[4] 1. $(T \vee R) \supset (Q \vee S)$
    2. $\sim (Q \vee S)$
    3.   1, 2, MT

⭐ [5] 1. $P \vee (Q \cdot S)$
    2. $\sim P$
    3.   1, 2, DS

[6] 1. $(R \vee S) \supset T$
    2. $\sim T$
    3.   1, 2, MT

[7] 1. $(R \vee \sim T) \supset S$
    2. $R \vee \sim T$
    3.   1, 2, MP

[8] 1. $P \supset (Q \vee \sim R)$
    2. $(Q \vee \sim R) \supset \sim S$
    3.   1, 2, HS

★ [9] 1. $(T \supset R) \supset (Q \supset S)$
    2. $\sim (Q \supset S)$
    3   1, 2, MT

[10] 1. $S \supset \sim (\sim R \vee \sim T)$
    2. S
    3.   1, 2, MP

[11] 1. $S \supset \sim (\sim R \vee \sim T)$
    2. $\sim \sim (\sim R \vee \sim T)$
    3.   1, 2, MT

[12] 1. $[P \vee (Q \cdot S)] \vee (\sim Q \cdot \sim P)$
    2. $\sim [P \vee (Q \cdot S)]$
    3.   1, 2, DS

★ [13] 1. $(P \cdot \sim R) \supset Q$
    2. $\sim Q$
    3.   1, 2, MT

[14] 1. $(P \vee Q) \supset \sim R$
    2. $P \vee Q$
    3.   1, 2, MP

[15] 1. $(Q \cdot S) \vee (\sim Q \vee \sim P)$
    2. $\sim (Q \cdot S)$
    3.   1, 2, DS

III. The following examples contain more than one step for which you are to provide the line numbers needed for the derivation and the implication rule as justification.

[1] 1. $P \supset \sim Q$
    2. $R \supset Q$
    3. P / $\sim R$
    4. $\sim Q$
    5. $\sim R$

Answer:
    4. $\sim Q$ 1, 3, MP
    5. $\sim R$ 2, 4, MT

[2] 1. $\sim S$
    2. $Q \supset (S \vee R)$
    3. Q / R
    4. $S \vee R$
    5. R

[3] 1. $(S \cdot M) \supset Q$
    2. $(Q \lor R) \supset (S \cdot M)$
    3. $P \supset (Q \lor R)$ $/ P \supset Q$
    4. $P \supset (S \cdot M)$
    5. $P \supset Q$

[4] 1. $\sim P$
    2. $Q \lor (P \lor R)$
    3. $P \lor \sim Q$ $/ R$
    4. $\sim Q$
    5. $P \lor R$
    6. R

⭐ [5] 1. $R \supset S$
    2. P
    3. $S \supset Q$
    4. $P \supset R$ $/ Q$
    5. $P \supset S$
    6. $P \supset Q$
    7. Q

[6] 1. $S \supset Q$
    2. $\sim R$
    3. S
    4. $Q \supset (R \lor P)$ $/ P$
    5. $S \supset (R \lor P)$
    6. $R \lor P$
    7. P

[7] 1. $\sim Q$
    2. $P \supset Q$
    3. $P \lor (\sim Q \supset R)$ $/ R$
    4. $\sim P$
    5. $\sim Q \supset R$
    6. R

[8] 1. $M \supset \sim Q$
    2. $(P \supset \sim Q) \supset (R \supset \sim L)$
    3. $\sim L \supset S$
    4. $P \supset M$ $/ R \supset S$
    5. $P \supset \sim Q$
    6. $R \supset \sim L$
    7. $R \supset S$

⭐ [9] 1. $R \lor \sim S$
    2. $(P \supset Q) \supset \sim R$
    3. $P \supset L$

      4. $L \supset Q$ / ~ S

      5. $P \supset Q$

      6.   ~ R

      7.   ~ S

[10] 1. $L \lor {\sim} S$

      2. $(P \cdot {\sim} Q) \lor {\sim} R$

      3.   ~ L

      4. $(P \cdot {\sim} Q) \supset S$ / ~ R

      5.   ~ S

      6. $\sim (P \cdot {\sim} Q)$

      7.   ~ R

IV. The following examples contain more than one step for which you are to provide the missing derivation. In each case the implication rule and the lines used for the derivation are provided.

[1] 1. $Q \supset R$

    2. $P \supset Q$

    3. ~ R   / ~ P

    4.   1, 2, HS

    5.   3, 4, MT

Answer:

    4. $P \supset R$ 1, 2, HS

    5. ~ P   3, 4, MT

[2] 1. $Q \supset R$

    2. $P \supset Q$

    3. ~ R   / ~ P

    4.   1, 3, MT

    5.   2, 4, MT

[3] 1. S

    2. $(P \lor Q) \supset R$

    3. $S \supset {\sim} R$ / ~ (P ∨ Q)

    4.   1, 3, MP

    5.   2, 4, MT

[4] 1. $Q \supset R$

    2. ~ P

    3. $P \lor Q$ / R

    4.   2, 3, DS

    5.   1, 4, MP

★ [5] 1. $P \lor {\sim} S$

     2. ${\sim} S \supset (P \supset Q)$

     3. ~ P

     4. $(P \supset Q) \supset R$ / R

    5.   1, 3, DS
    6.   2, 5, MP
    7.   4, 6, MP

[6] 1. $P \supset \sim R$
      2. $R \lor S$
      3. $Q \lor P$
      4. $\sim Q$ / S
      5.   3, 4, DS
      6.   1, 5, MP
      7.   2, 6, DS

[7] 1. $(R \supset S) \lor (L \cdot \sim Q)$
      2. $(P \supset Q) \lor \sim M$
      3. $\sim M \supset \sim (R \supset S)$
      4. $\sim (P \supset Q)$ / $L \cdot \sim Q$
      5.   2, 4, DS
      6.   3, 5, MP
      7.   1, 6, DS

[8] 1. $L \lor R$
      2. $(P \lor Q) \supset S$
      3. $\sim L$
      4. $R \supset (\sim L \supset \sim S)$ / $\sim (P \lor Q)$
      5.   1, 3, DS
      6.   4, 5, MP
      7.   3, 6, MP
      8.   2, 7, MT

★ [9] 1. $S \lor (P \lor Q)$
      2. $\sim (Q \supset R)$
      3. $P \supset (Q \supset R)$
      4. $S \supset P$ / Q
      5.   2, 3, MT
      6.   4, 5, MT
      7.   1, 6, DS
      8.   5, 7, DS

[10] 1. $S \lor \sim R$
      2. $\sim L$
      3. $P \supset (Q \supset R)$
      4. $\sim S$
      5. $\sim L \supset P$ / $\sim Q$
      6.   3, 5, HS
      7.   2, 6, MP
      8.   1, 4, DS
      9.   7, 8, MT

C. TACTICS AND STRATEGY

Now that you have seen how each line of a proof is justified by using the first four implication rules, you are ready to use your knowledge to create your own proofs. However, before you plunge in and thrash about you need to have a few guidelines. Efficient construction of proofs requires that you have an overall goal to keep you focused. You should say, "I need to get here," instead of "I don't much care where," which got Alice off on the wrong foot.

Tactics The use of small-scale maneuvers or devices.

Strategy Referring to a greater, overall goal.

Tactics is the use of small-scale maneuvers or devices, whereas **strategy** is typically understood as referring to a greater, overall goal. For example, in working through a proof, your strategy might be to isolate as many simple statements as possible, or it might be to reduce, to simplify complex statements. These goals can often be accomplished by employing a variety of tactical moves, such as using *modus ponens* to isolate a statement. The same strategic goal might be accomplished by using *modus tollens* or disjunctive syllogism as a tactical move, enabling you to isolate part of a complex statement.

It is extremely helpful to have a strategic sense when employing natural deduction. However, it must be understood that even the best strategies cannot guarantee success. Nevertheless, a well-thought-out strategy, coupled with a firm grasp of the available tactical moves within a proof, will maximize your prospects for successfully completing a proof.

At first, it is often best to simply plug away at tactical moves until you begin to recognize patterns or begin to see more than one move ahead. In this sense, it is like

PROFILES IN LOGIC

Gerhard Gentzen

Although he lived only 36 years, Gerhard Gentzen did remarkable work in logic and the foundations of mathematics. Gentzen (1909–46) was interested in the use of *forms of argument*. He understood that logic and mathematics rely on new forms of argument to help prove new theorems. The need for new forms became that much clearer around the turn of the 20th century, when some of the old forms led to some startling paradoxes and contradictions. The entire foundations of logic and mathematics were threatened. After all, if certainty did not exist in mathematical proofs, then perhaps it might not exist at all.

Gentzen developed the system of *natural deduction* to help secure the consistency of a critical branch of mathematics, number theory. Gentzen's system was also adapted for work in logical analysis. Genzten wanted the term "natural" in logic to mean the same as it does when mathematicians refer to the "natural way of reasoning": We generate rules of argument to derive more theorems. Gentzen's tools allow us to prove the validity of both mathematical and logical arguments. In formal logic proofs, they show how to introduce or eliminate logical operators.

learning to play checkers or chess. The novice player first learns the moves that are permitted. The initial games are usually devoid of any real strategy. Beginners typically move pieces hoping for some tactical advantage in small areas of the checkerboard or chessboard. Real strategy comes only after you have played enough games to begin to understand long-term goals. It takes time and patience to master offensive and defensive skills, the deployment of deception, the ability to think multiple moves ahead, to recognize traps, and to coordinate numerous tactical maneuvers at the same time—in other words, to have a global strategy.

The following guide is offered to help you develop overall strategies, and to apply relevant tactical moves within proofs using the first four implication rules:

STRATEGIES AND TACTICS

Strategy 1: Simplify and isolate
    Tactical Moves—Try using any of the following:
      A. *Modus ponens* (MP)
      B. *Modus tollens* (MT)
      C. Disjunctive syllogism (DS)

Strategy 2: Look for negation
    Tactical Moves—Try using any of the following:
      A. *Modus tollens* (MT)
      B. Disjunctive syllogism (DS)

Strategy 3: Look for conditionals
    Tactical Moves—Try using any of the following:
      A. *Modus ponens* (MP)
      B. *Modus tollens* (MT)
      C. Hypothetical syllogism (HS)

Strategy 4: Look at the conclusion
    Tactical Moves—Try anticipating what you need.
      Try working backward from the conclusion by imagining what the next to last line of the proof might be. Use this to help determine a short-term strategy to derive that line.

Working Through a Proof

The following is an example of a simple completed proof:

$$
\begin{array}{lll}
1. & R \vee (P \supset Q) & \\
2. & P & \\
3. & \sim R & \quad / \, Q \\
4. & P \supset Q & \quad 1, 3, \text{DS} \\
5. & Q & \quad 2, 4, \text{MP}
\end{array}
$$

The proof employs two strategies and two tactics: First, strategy 1 (simplify and isolate) is used to validly derive line 4. This is accomplished by tactically applying disjunctive syllogism to line 1 and line 3. Second, strategy 3 (look for conditionals) is then implemented by the tactical move of *modus ponens* to validly derive line 5. The proof procedure shows that the conclusion follows validly from the premises.

The following is an example of a completed proof with one set of strategies displayed:

1. $R \supset (P \supset Q)$

2. $\sim R \supset \sim L$

3. $(P \supset Q) \supset S$

4. $\sim S$

5. $L \vee (M \supset N)$ / $M \supset N$

6. $R \supset S$ 1, 3, HS   [Strategy 3: Look for conditionals]

7. $\sim R$ 4, 6, MT   [Strategy 2: Look for negation]

8. $\sim L$ 2, 7, MP   [Strategy 1: Simplify and isolate]

9. $M \supset N$ 5, 8, DS   [Strategy 2: Look for negation]

It is quite possible that someone else might use a different set of strategies and tactics to derive the conclusion. In fact, there are often several different proofs that can be constructed, each of which validly derives the conclusion. The main thing to remember is that a proof must use the rules of inference correctly.

CHECK YOUR UNDERSTANDING 8C

I. Use the first four implication rules to complete the proofs. Provide the justification for each step that you derive.

[1] 1. $\sim (P \cdot Q)$
  2. $\sim (R \cdot S) \supset (L \cdot \sim Q)$
  3. $(R \cdot S) \supset (P \cdot Q)$ / $L \cdot \sim Q$

Answer:
  4. $\sim (R \cdot S)$ 1, 3, MT
  5. $L \cdot \sim Q$ 2, 4, MP

[2] 1. $P \supset Q$
  2. $R \supset P$
  3. $\sim Q$ / $\sim R$

[3] 1. P
  2. $R \supset Q$
  3. $P \supset \sim Q$ / $\sim R$

[4] 1. $S \supset (P \cdot Q)$
  2. $(P \cdot Q) \supset R$
  3. $\sim R$ / $\sim S$

★ [5] 1. $\sim P \supset (Q \vee R)$

    2. $(\sim P \supset \sim S) \supset \sim L$
    3. $(Q \vee R) \supset \sim S$ $/ \sim L$

[6] 1. Q
    2. $L \supset (S \supset P)$
    3. $Q \supset (R \supset S)$
    4. L $/ R \supset P$

[7] 1. $P \supset Q$
    2. $(P \supset R) \supset \sim S$
    3. $Q \supset R$
    4. $(\sim Q \supset \sim P) \supset S$ $/ \sim (\sim Q \supset \sim P)$

[8] 1. $S \supset \sim Q$
    2. $P \supset Q$
    3. $R \supset S$
    4. R $/ \sim P$

⭐ [9] 1. $R \vee S$
    2. $\sim (P \vee Q)$
    3. $R \supset (P \vee Q)$
    4. $S \supset (Q \vee R)$ $/ Q \vee R$

[10] 1. $P \vee Q$
     2. $Q \supset \sim R$
     3. $\sim P$
     4. $\sim R \supset \sim S$ $/ \sim S$

[11] 1. $P \supset R$
     2. $\sim S$
     3. $P \vee Q$
     4. $R \supset S$ $/ Q$

[12] 1. $\sim (P \cdot S)$
     2. $\sim R$
     3. $\sim P \supset [P \vee (Q \supset R)]$
     4. $P \supset (P \cdot S)$ $/ \sim Q$

⭐ [13] 1. $P \vee (S \supset Q)$
     2. $\sim Q$
     3. $P \supset Q$
     4. $\sim S \supset R$ $/ R$

[14] 1. $\sim R \vee (P \supset Q)$
     2. $(P \supset Q) \supset (Q \supset \sim R)$
     3. $\sim \sim R$ $/ \sim P$

[15] 1. P
     2. $(Q \supset R) \supset (P \supset Q)$
     3. $P \supset (Q \supset R)$ $/ R$

[16] 1. $L \vee P$
    2. $\sim S$
    3. $P \supset (Q \cdot R)$
    4. $S \vee (L \supset S)$ $/ Q \cdot R$

⭐ [17] 1. $Q \supset P$
    2. S
    3. $(Q \vee \sim R) \supset \sim P$
    4. $S \supset (Q \vee \sim R)$ $/ \sim R$

[18] 1. $(Q \vee R) \supset \sim P$
    2. $\sim P \supset [\, P \vee (Q \supset P)\,]$
    3. $Q \vee R$ $/ R$

[19] 1. $R \supset S$
    2. $(Q \supset S) \supset \sim P$
    3. $\sim P \supset [\, (Q \supset R) \supset (L \vee \sim S)\,]$
    4. $Q \supset R$
    5. $\sim L$ $/ \sim R$

[20] 1. $(P \supset S) \supset \sim Q$
    2. $P \supset R$
    3. $(P \supset R) \supset (R \supset Q)$
    4. $(P \supset Q) \supset (R \supset S)$ $/ \sim P$

II. First, translate the following arguments into symbolic form. Second, use the four implication rules to derive the conclusion of each. Letters for the simple statements are provided in parentheses and can be used in the order they are given.

1. Shane is going to the party, or either Rachel or Max is going. Either Rachel is going to the party or Shane is not going to the party. But Rachel is not going to the party. Therefore, Max is going. (S, R, M)

Answer:

    1. $S \vee (R \vee M)$
    2. $R \vee \sim S$
    3. $\sim R$ $/ M$
    4. $\sim S$ 2, 3, DS
    5. $R \vee M$ 1, 4, DS
    6. M 3, 5, DS

2. If I bet red on roulette, then I will win my bet. If I win my bet, then I will stop betting. If I'm feeling lucky, then I bet red on roulette. I'm feeling lucky. It follows that I will stop betting. (R, W, S, L)

3. If Melinda is a comedian, then she is shy. Either Melinda is a comedian, or if she is not shy, then she is famous. Moreover, Melinda is not shy. Consequently, she is famous. (C, S, F)

4. If we continue to fight, then our supply of troops grows thinner. If our supply of troops grows thinner, then either enlistment slows down or more casualties will occur. But we do continue to fight. Also, enlistment does not slow down. This proves that more casualties will occur. (*F, S, E, C*)

⭐ 5. If my son drinks three sodas, then if he eats some chocolate, then he gets hyper. If he is excited, then my son drinks three sodas. Furthermore, my son is excited, or he either drinks three sodas or he eats some chocolate. But it is not the case that if he eats some chocolate, then he gets hyper. We can conclude that he eats some chocolate. (*S, C, H, E*)

6. If amino acids were found on Mars, then there is life on Mars, then there is life in the universe outside Earth. Either amino acids were found on Mars or we did not look in the best places. If we did not look in the best places, then if amino acids were found on Mars, then there is life on Mars. But it is not the case that amino acids were found on Mars. Thus, there is life in the universe outside Earth. (*A, L, U, P*)

7. Either I am going to the movie or I am studying for the exam. If I study for the exam, then I will not fail the course. But I either fail the course or I will graduate on time. I am not going to the movie. Hence, I will graduate on time. (*M, S, F, G*)

8. If there is a recession and the housing sector does not recover, then the national debt will continue growing. Also, the government invests in public projects or the national debt will not continue growing. Either there is a recession and the housing sector does not recover, or the unemployment rate will not go down. But the government is not investing in public projects. This implies that the unemployment rate will not go down. (*R, H, D, P, U*)

⭐ 9. If Suzy buys a new car or a new motorcycle, then she has to take a loan. If Suzy saves half her weekly salary for a year, then if she doesn't go on an expensive vacation, then she will not have to take a loan. Either she goes on an expensive vacation or she saves half her weekly salary for a year. But Suzy does not go on an expensive vacation. Therefore, it is not the case that either Suzy buys a new car or a new motorcycle. (*C, M, L, S, E*)

10. If your aunt is not a lawyer, then she is an accountant. In addition, if your aunt is an accountant, then if she is tired of her job, then she can teach at our college. Your aunt is either looking for new employment or she cannot teach at our college. But your aunt is not a lawyer. Also, she is not looking for new employment. Therefore, she is not tired of her job. (*L, P, J, C, E*)

D. IMPLICATION RULES II

There are four more implication rules to introduce. As with the first four rules, correct application ensures that valid arguments are derived throughout the proofs. Although these were already proven valid by the truth table method, we will discuss their validity in an informal manner.

Constructive Dilemma (CD)

Constructive dilemma
A rule of inference
(implication rule).

The implication rule **constructive dilemma** is complex because it combines three different logical operators: the horseshoe, the dot, and the wedge. Although the rule can be difficult to grasp at first, working through an example should help you to better understand the logic behind it. First, let's look at the logical form:

Constructive Dilemma (CD)

$$(p \supset q) \cdot (r \supset s)$$
$$\underline{p \lor r}$$
$$q \lor s$$

Let's substitute the following for the first premise:

> If I live in Atlantic City, then I live in New Jersey, *and* if I am a slot machine technician, then I work in a casino.

Let *p = I live in Atlantic City, q = I live in New Jersey, r = I am a slot machine technician,* and *s = I work in a casino.* Substituting for the letters in the argument form for constructive dilemma, the second premise is "I live in Atlantic City or I am a slot machine technician." The conclusion is "I live in New Jersey or I work in a casino." The main operator of the first premise is the dot. Therefore, if the first premise is true, then both conjuncts are true. Since both conjuncts are conditional statements, the antecedents cannot be true and consequents false.

Now, if the second premise is true, then *at least one* of the disjuncts, *p* or *r*, is true. This means that *at least one* of the following must be true: "I live in Atlantic City," or "I am a slot machine technician." Given this, *at least one* of the antecedents in the first premise is true (*p* or *r*). Since we previously eliminated the possibility of true antecedent and false consequent in both conditionals of the first premise, we now know that *at least one* of *q* or *s* must be true. In other words, *at least one* of the following must be true: "I live in New Jersey," or "I work in a casino." This analysis shows that if the premises are true, then the conclusion is true, because it is a disjunction with *at least one* true disjunct (*q* or *s*).

The following are examples of valid applications of constructive dilemma:

Valid Applications of Constructive Dilemma (CD)

1. $(S \supset Q) \cdot (M \supset N)$	1. $[\sim G \supset (P \cdot R)] \cdot [\sim D \supset (H \cdot F)]$
2. $\underline{S \lor M}$	2. $\underline{\sim G \lor \sim D}$
3. $Q \lor N$	3. $(P \cdot R) \lor (H \cdot F)$

Here are two examples of invalid applications:

Invalid Applications of Constructive Dilemma (CD)

1. $(S \supset \sim P) \lor (Q \supset \sim R)$	1. $(S \supset M) \cdot [(F \cdot G) \supset H]$
2. $\underline{S \lor Q}$ ⊘	2. $\underline{S \lor F}$ ⊘
3. $\sim P \lor \sim R$	3. $M \lor H$

In the first example of an invalid application, the main operator in premise 1 is the wedge. However, for constructive dilemma to work correctly the main operator must be a dot. In the second example, the statement, $F \cdot G$, is an antecedent, but premise 2 only has F as the second disjunct. But in order for constructive dilemma to be used correctly, the second disjunct in premise 2 has to be the entire antecedent, $F \cdot G$. Since this is not the case, this is an invalid application of constructive dilemma.

Simplification (Simp)

The implication rule **simplification** has the dot as the main operator. The logical form of this rule is the following:

Simplification A rule of inference (implication rule).

Simplification (Simp)

$$\frac{p \cdot q}{p}$$

Let's substitute the following for the premise: "Oak trees are deciduous, and pine trees are conifers." Let $p = Oak\ trees\ are\ deciduous$, and $q = pine\ trees\ are\ conifers$. If the premise is true, then *both* conjuncts are true. Since the conclusion is merely one of the conjuncts, it is true. The following are examples of valid applications of the rule of simplification:

Valid Applications of Simplification (Simp)

1. $(H \vee D) \cdot (F \vee G)$	1. $\sim (B \supset D) \cdot Q$	1. $M \cdot [\,S \vee (G \supset C)\,]$
2. $H \vee D$	2. $\sim (B \supset D)$	2. M

Here is an example of an invalid application:

Invalid Application of Simplification (Simp)

1. $(P \cdot Q) \vee (R \supset S)$
2. P ⊘

Since the main operator in line 1 is a wedge, the logical form is $p \vee q$. However, simplification cannot be used validly with a disjunction.

Conjunction (Conj)

The implication rule **conjunction** can be stated quite simply: Any two true statements can be joined conjunctively with the result being a true statement. Recall that a conjunction is true only when both conjuncts are true. For example, if the statement "June has 30 days" and the statement "Apples are fruit" are both true statements, then it follows that "June has 30 days and apples are fruit." If we let $p = June\ has\ 30\ days$, and $q = apples\ are\ fruit$, then the argument is revealed as an instance of the implication rule conjunction:

Conjunction A rule of inference (implication rule).

Conjunction (Conj)

$$\frac{\begin{array}{c} p \\ q \end{array}}{p \cdot q}$$

If both premises are true, then p and q are true. Therefore, the conjunction of p and q is true. A correct application of the implication rule results in a valid argument. Here are some examples:

Valid Applications of Conjunction (Conj)

1. G	1. $B \supset J$	1. $S \lor D$
2. $H \lor K$	2. $L \supset \sim F$	2. M
3. $G \cdot (H \lor K)$	3. $(B \supset J) \cdot (L \supset \sim F)$	3. $(P \cdot Q) \supset R$
		4. $(S \lor D) \cdot M$
		5. $(S \lor D) \cdot [(P \cdot Q) \supset R]$
		6. $M \cdot [(P \cdot Q) \supset R]$
		7. $[(S \lor D) \cdot M] \cdot [(P \cdot Q) \supset R]$

The third example offers an illustration of the various ways that conjunction can be used. For example, lines 4, 5, and 6 were derived by using two premises. However, line 7 was derived from line 4, a derived line, and line 3, a premise.

Here is an example of a invalid application of conjunction:

Invalid Application of Conjunction (Conj)

1. S
2. $P \supset R$
3. $S \cdot P$ ⦸

The mistake here is in thinking that conjunction allows you to conjoin part of a line. Like all the implication rules, conjunction has to be applied to an entire line. The rule permits you to conjoin any two complete lines, either premises or derived lines.

Addition (Add)

Addition A rule of inference (implication rule).

The implication rule **addition** can be stated this way: Any true statement, either a premise or a derived line, can be joined *disjunctively* with any other statement. The reasoning behind this is that a disjunction is true if at least one of the disjuncts is true. For example, if it is true that "Mt. Everest is the tallest mountain on Earth," then it is also true that "Mt. Everest is the tallest mountain on Earth or butterflies are carnivorous." If we let p = *Mt. Everest is the tallest mountain on Earth*, and q = *butterflies are carnivorous*, we reveal the logical form:

Addition (Add)

$$\frac{p}{p \lor q}$$

If the premise is true, then p is true. Since a disjunction is true if at least one of its disjuncts is true, we can validly deduce $p \lor q$. This means that even if we add (disjunctively) a false statement, such as the one in the example (q = *butterflies are carnivorous*), the resulting derivation $p \lor q$ is true because at least one of the disjuncts is true.

It is important to remember that the *rule of addition can only be used with a disjunction as the main operator* for an entire line. Here are some examples of valid applications:

Valid Applications of Addition (Add)

1. S
2. $S \vee (Q \cdot R)$

1. R
2. $R \vee (Q \supset T)$

1. $M \supset N$
2. $(M \supset N) \vee (Q \cdot \sim P)$

1. $\sim D \cdot T$
2. $(\sim D \cdot T) \vee [\,(P \supset R) \cdot S\,]$

In all four examples the entire first line was used for the application of addition. If only part of a line is used, then the result is an invalid application. Here is an example:

Invalid Application of Addition (Add)

1. $(P \cdot Q) \supset (R \cdot S)$
2. $(P \cdot Q) \vee T$ ⊘

The mistake occurs because only part of line 1 was used (the antecedent). For this example, the only way to correctly apply the rule of addition to line 1 is to derive a *disjunction* with $(P \cdot Q) \supset (R \cdot S)$ as the first disjunct. For example, we could validly derive the following using addition: $[\,(P \cdot Q) \supset (R \cdot S)\,] \vee \sim D$.

Here is another example of a mistake in applying the rule:

Invalid Application of Addition (Add)

1. $P \supset (\sim Q \vee S)$
2. $R \vee D$ ⊘

The rule of addition *does not* allow you to just add anything you wish from nothing. It allows you to create a disjunction *only with an already established line.*

THE EIGHT IMPLICATION RULES	
Modus Ponens (MP)	**Modus Tollens (MT)**
$p \supset q$ p q	$p \supset q$ $\sim q$ $\sim p$
Hypothetical Syllogism (HS)	**Disjunctive Syllogism (DS)**
$p \supset q$ $q \supset r$ $p \supset r$	$p \vee q$ $\sim p$ q
Constructive Dilemma (CD)	**Simplification (Simp)**
$(p \supset q) \cdot (r \supset s)$ $p \vee r$ $q \vee s$	$p \cdot q$ p
Conjunction (Conj)	**Addition (Add)**
p q $p \cdot q$	p $p \vee q$

Since we added four more implication rules to the original set, we need to update our strategies and tactics guide:

Strategy 1: Simplify and isolate
    Tactical Moves—Try using any of the following:
      A. *Modus ponens* (MP)
      B. *Modus tollens* (MT)
      C. Disjunctive syllogism (DS)
      D. Simplification (Simp)

Strategy 2: Look for negation
    Tactical Moves—Try using any of the following:
      A. *Modus tollens* (MT)
      B. Disjunctive syllogism (DS)

Strategy 3: Look for conditionals
    Tactical Moves—Try using any of the following:
      A. *Modus ponens* (MP)
      B. *Modus tollens* (MT)
      C. Hypothetical syllogism (HS)
      D. Constructive dilemma (CD)

Strategy 4: Look at the conclusion
    Tactical Moves—Try anticipating what you need.
    Try working backward from the conclusion by imagining what the next to last line of the proof might be. Use this to help determine a short-term strategy to derive that line.

Strategy 5: Add whatever you need
    Tactical Moves—Try using addition (Add).

Strategy 6: Combine lines
    Tactical Moves—Try using conjunction (Conj).

CHECK YOUR UNDERSTANDING 8D

    I. The following are more examples of what you may encounter in proofs. The last step of each example gives the line numbers needed for its derivation. You are to provide the implication rule that justifies the step. This will give you practice using the second set of four implication rules.

[1] 1. $(P \supset Q) \cdot (R \supset S)$
     2. $P \lor R$ / $Q \lor S$
     3. $Q \lor S$ 1, 2, _____
Answer: 1, 2, CD

[2] 1. $(P \supset R) \cdot (Q \supset R)$ / $P \supset R$
     2. $P \supset R$ 1, _____

[3] 1. $T \lor U$
     2. $\sim P$ / $(T \lor U) \cdot \sim P$
     3. $(T \lor U) \cdot \sim P$ 1, 2, _____

[4] 1. R $/ R \lor (P \cdot \sim Q)$
    2. $R \lor (P \cdot \sim Q)$ 1, _____

★ [5] 1. $\sim P$
    2. $T \supset U$ $/ \sim P \cdot (T \supset U)$
    3. $\sim P \cdot (T \supset U)$ 1, 2, _____

[6] 1. $\sim (P \lor Q) \cdot R$ $/ \sim (P \lor Q)$
    2. $\sim (P \lor Q)$ 1, _____

[7] 1. $(\sim P \supset Q) \cdot (\sim R \supset S)$
    2. $\sim P \lor \sim R$ $/ Q \lor S$
    3. $Q \lor S$ 1, 2, _____

[8] 1. P $/ P \lor \sim Q$
    2. $P \lor \sim Q$ 1, _____

★ [9] 1. P
    2. Q $/ P \cdot Q$
    3. $P \cdot Q$ 1, 2, _____

[10] 1. $(S \lor P) \cdot M$ $/ S \lor P$
    2. $S \lor P$ 1, _____

[11] 1. $[(P \cdot R) \supset \sim S] \cdot [(P \lor R) \supset \sim T]$
    2. $(P \cdot R) \lor (P \lor R)$ $/ \sim S \lor \sim T$
    3. $\sim S \lor \sim T$ 1, 2, _____

[12] 1. $P \supset Q$ $/ (P \supset Q) \lor \sim (R \lor S)$
    2. $(P \supset Q) \lor \sim (R \lor S)$ 1, _____

★ [13] 1. P
    2. $(R \supset S) \lor Q$ $/ P \cdot [(R \supset S) \lor Q]$
    3. $P \cdot [(R \supset S) \lor Q]$ 1, 2, _____

[14] 1. $(\sim P \supset Q) \cdot (\sim R \supset S)$ $/ \sim P \supset Q$
    2. $\sim P \supset Q$ 1, _____

[15] 1. $(S \supset P) \cdot [R \supset (\sim Q \cdot L)]$
    2. $S \lor R$ $/ P \lor (\sim Q \cdot L)$
    3. $P \lor (\sim Q \cdot L)$ 1, 2, _____

II. The following are more examples of what you may encounter in proofs. In these examples the justification (the implication rule) is provided for the last step. However, the step itself is missing. Use the given information to derive the last step of each example. This will give you practice using the second set of four implication rules.

[1] 1. $(S \supset T) \cdot (P \supset Q)$
    2. $S \lor P$
    3.   1, 2, CD

Answer: 3. $T \vee Q$ 1, 2, CD

[2] 1. $(M \supset P) \cdot K$
     2.   1, Simp

[3] 1. $P \vee Q$
     2. $S \vee T$
     3.   1, 2, Conj

[4] 1. $\sim (S \vee T)$
     2.   1, Add

★ [5] 1. $P \cdot (Q \supset R)$
     2.   1, Simp

[6] 1. $(R \vee S) \cdot (P \supset Q)$
     2. $S \vee Q$
     3.   1, 2, Conj

[7] 1. $[P \supset (R \vee L)] \cdot [S \supset (Q \vee M)]$
     2. $P \vee S$
     3.   1, 2, CD

[8] 1. $\sim S$
     2.   1, Add

★ [9] 1. $P \supset Q$
     2. $R \vee S$
     3.   1, 2, Conj

[10] 1. $[P \vee (\sim R \vee \sim S)] \cdot (Q \supset R)$
      2.   1, Simp

[11] 1. $(\sim R \supset \sim S) \cdot (\sim P \supset \sim Q)$
      2. $\sim R \vee \sim P$
      3.   1, 2, CD

[12] 1. $(S \supset \sim Q)$
      2. $\sim (\sim P \cdot \sim Q)$
      3.   1, 2, Conj

★ [13] 1. $(\sim P \vee \sim S) \cdot (\sim L \supset \sim R)$
      2.   1, Simp

[14] 1. $P \supset \sim (\sim S \vee \sim L)$
      2.   1, Add

[15] 1. $[\sim L \supset (\sim Q \vee \sim R)] \supset \sim S$
      2. $P \supset \sim Q$
      3.   1, 2, Conj

III. Use the eight implication rules to complete the proofs. Provide the justification for each step that you derive.

[1] 1. $Q \supset (P \lor R)$
     2. $Q \cdot S$ $/ P \lor R$

Answer: 1. $Q \supset (P \lor R)$

     2. $Q \cdot S$ $/ P \lor R$
     3. Q 2, Simp
     4. $P \lor R$ 1, 3, MP

[2] 1. $R \supset (P \lor Q)$
     2. $S \lor \sim (P \lor Q)$
     3. $\sim S$ $/ \sim R$

[3] 1. $(M \supset P) \cdot (S \lor Q)$
     2. $R \supset M$ $/ R \supset P$

[4] 1. $[(M \cdot R) \lor S] \supset (P \lor Q)$
     2. M
     3. R $/ P \lor Q$

★ [5] 1. P
     2. $(P \lor Q) \supset R$
     3. $R \supset S$ $/ S$

[6] 1. $P \lor (M \lor R)$
     2. $M \supset S$
     3. $R \supset Q$
     4. $\sim P$ $/ S \lor Q$

[7] 1. $(M \lor \sim P) \supset (Q \lor \sim S)$
     2. $M \cdot \sim R$ $/ Q \lor \sim S$

[8] 1. $P \cdot R$
     2. $(P \supset Q) \cdot (R \supset S)$ $/ Q \lor S$

★ [9] 1. $P \cdot (S \lor Q)$
     2. $(P \lor R) \supset M$ $/ M$

[10] 1. $\sim (Q \cdot R)$
      2. $P \lor S$
      3. $[P \supset (Q \cdot R)] \cdot (S \supset L)$
      4. S $/ L$

[11] 1. $(M \lor Q) \supset \sim P$
      2. M
      3. $P \lor S$ $/ S \cdot (M \lor Q)$

[12] 1. $\sim P \cdot D$
     2. $P \lor (Q \cdot R)$
     3. $P \lor (S \cdot L)$ / $Q \cdot S$

★ [13] 1. $(P \supset Q) \cdot (R \supset S)$
     2. $P \lor L$
     3. $(L \supset M) \cdot (N \supset K)$ / $Q \lor M$

[14] 1. $(P \lor R) \supset S$
     2. $P \cdot Q$ / $P \cdot S$

[15] 1. $R \lor (P \lor S)$
     2. $\sim R$
     3. $P \supset Q$
     4. $\sim R \supset (S \supset L)$ / $Q \lor L$

[16] 1. $Q \supset S$
     2. $\sim R \cdot P$
     3. $P \supset Q$
     4. P / $S \cdot \sim R$

★ [17] 1. $S \lor P$
     2. $(R \lor S) \supset L$
     3. $(P \lor Q) \supset R$
     4. $\sim S$ / L

[18] 1. $(P \cdot Q) \supset R$
     2. $Q \cdot \sim S$
     3. $Q \supset (P \cdot S)$ / R

[19] 1. $(R \lor S) \lor (\sim L \cdot M)$
     2. $(P \cdot Q) \supset \sim (R \lor S)$
     3. $\sim L$
     4. $(\sim L \lor M) \supset (P \cdot Q)$ / $(\sim L \cdot M) \cdot \sim L$

[20] 1. $N \supset \sim L$
     2. $\sim P \cdot K$
     3. $(\sim P \lor Q) \supset (\sim R \supset S)$
     4. $\sim L \supset M$
     5. $N \lor \sim R$ / $\sim R \supset S$

★ [21] 1. $R \supset P$
     2. $(Q \cdot \sim R) \supset (S \cdot \sim R)$
     3. $\sim P$
     4. $P \lor Q$ / S

[22] 1. $R \supset S$
     2. $P \supset \sim Q$
     3. $\sim Q \supset R$
     4. $P \cdot Q$ / $R \cdot S$

[23] 1. $(R \lor Q) \supset [P \supset (S \equiv L)]$
    2. $(P \lor Q) \supset R$
    3. $P \cdot S$ $/ S \equiv L$

[24] 1. $P \lor (Q \supset R)$
    2. $(S \lor L) \supset (Q \cdot M)$
    3. $Q \supset \sim P$
    4. $S \cdot N$ $/ R$

★ [25] 1. $(M \lor N) \supset (P \cdot K)$
     2. $(P \lor \sim Q) \supset [(R \supset L) \cdot S]$
     3. M $/ P \cdot (R \supset L)$

[26] 1. $R \supset \sim S$
    2. $(\sim Q \cdot \sim S) \supset L$
    3. P
    4. $P \supset \sim Q$
    5. $(R \cdot L) \supset M$
    6. R $/ M$

[27] 1. $\sim P \cdot (N \supset L)$
    2. $\sim Q \cdot (\sim K \equiv J)$
    3. $(\sim P \cdot \sim Q) \supset [(\sim P \lor R) \supset (S \cdot M)]$ $/ S \cdot \sim Q$

[28] 1. $(Q \cdot R) \lor \sim P$
    2. $R \supset S$
    3. $[\sim P \cdot \sim (Q \cdot R)] \supset (L \supset \sim Q)$
    4. $\sim (Q \cdot R) \supset (\sim Q \supset R)$
    5. $\sim (Q \cdot R) \cdot \sim M$ $/ L \supset S$

★ [29] 1. $P \cdot \sim Q$
     2. $(P \lor \sim R) \supset (\sim S \cdot M)$
     3. $(\sim S \cdot P) \supset (P \supset N)$ $/ N$

[30] 1. $\sim P \supset Q$
    2. $R \cdot (S \supset L)$
    3. $(Q \cdot \sim M) \supset (R \supset \sim L)$
    4. $\sim P \cdot \sim K$
    5. $\sim P \supset \sim M$ $/ \sim L$

IV. First, translate the following arguments into symbolic form. Second, use the eight implication rules to derive the conclusion of each. Letters for the simple statements are provided in parentheses and can be used in the order given.

   1. If Samantha got a transfer, then if her company has a branch in Colorado, then Samantha lives in Denver. Either Samantha lives in Denver or she got a transfer. But Samantha does not live in Denver. It follows that her company does not have a branch in Colorado. (S, C, D)

Answer:

[1] 1. $S \supset (C \supset D)$
    2. $D \vee S$
    3. $\sim D$ $/ \sim C$
    4. S 2, 3, DS
    5. $C \supset D$ 1, 4, MP
    6. $\sim C$ 3, 5, MT

2. Credit card fees continue to go up. If credit card fees continue to go up, then if customers stop making payments on their cards, then either credit card companies lose customers or the companies lower the fees. However, it is not the case that either credit card companies lose customers or the companies lower the fees. Therefore, either customers do not stop making payments on their cards or the companies lower the fees. (*F, S, L, W*)

3. If 3D movies are making large profits, then movie companies are producing what people want to see and the movie companies are creating jobs. Either movie ticket sales are going up or it is not the case that movie companies are producing what people want to see and the movie companies are creating jobs. But movie ticket sales are not going up. If 3D movies are not making large profits and movie ticket sales are not going up, then Hollywood will start making different kinds of movies and movie companies will start being more creative. Thus, Hollywood will start making different kinds of movies. (*P, M, J, S, H, C*)

4. Paris has many art museums, and they are not expensive to visit. However, if Paris has many art museums, then either they are expensive to visit or they get large crowds. Furthermore, if they are expensive to visit or they get large crowds, then they are not worth seeing. Therefore, either they are not worth seeing or they are not expensive to visit. (*A, E, L, W*)

★ 5. Baseball is not the most popular sport or hockey is not the most popular sport. If advertisers continue to pay high costs for television commercial time, then the advertisers expect to see an increase in sales. If baseball is not the most popular sport, then the number of baseball fans is small, and if hockey is not the most popular sport, then hockey is not appealing to advertisers. If the number of baseball fans is small or hockey is not appealing to advertisers, then the advertisers cannot expect to see an increase in sales. Therefore, advertisers will not continue to pay high costs for television commercial time. (*B, H, P, S, F, A*)

6. Cell phones are expensive, but they do not break down quickly. If cell phones are made cheaply, then they break down quickly. If cell phones are worth the added cost, then they have a high resale value. If cell phones are expensive, then either they are made cheaply or they are worth the added cost. It follows that either cell phones break down quickly or they have a high resale value. (*E, B, C, A, H*)

7. If exercise is important for health, then you should have a regular exercise routine. Staying healthy saves you money. If staying healthy saves you money, then

you can afford good exercise equipment. If you can afford good exercise equipment, then you will use the equipment. So either you will use the equipment or you should have a regular exercise routine. (*E, R, H, A, U*)

8. If natural disasters will continue to increase, then the country's infrastructure will deteriorate and costs for repairing the damage will slow the economy. If global warming is affecting the world's weather, then natural disasters will continue to increase. If the country's infrastructure will deteriorate and costs for repairing the damage will slow the economy, then we must find alternative sources of energy. Thus, if global warming is affecting the world's weather, then we must find alternative sources of energy. (*N, I, R, G, A*)

⭐ 9. If social networking is a global phenomenon, then it is able to connect people with diverse backgrounds. If people can better understand different cultures, then the social networking folks will not stereotype different cultures. Social networking is a global phenomenon. If social networking is able to connect people with diverse backgrounds, then people can better understand different cultures. Therefore, the social networking folks will not stereotype different cultures. (*G, C, U, S*)

10. If both government corruption and corporate corruption can be eliminated, then the economy will not stagnate. If dishonest people are elected, then the economy will stagnate. Furthermore, both government corruption and corporate corruption can be eliminated. Thus, government corruption can be eliminated and dishonest people are not elected. (*G, C, E, D*)

E. REPLACEMENT RULES I

The implication rules are valid argument forms, but the replacement rules are pairs of logically equivalent statement forms (they have identical truth tables). According to the **principle of replacement**, logically equivalent expressions may replace each other within the context of a proof. The ten replacement rules were proven to be logically equivalent statement forms by you in *Check Your Understanding 7F* (exercises 1–16). Unlike the eight implication rules that are restricted to entire lines of a proof, replacement rules have no such restriction. They can be used either for an entire line or a part of a line.

> **Principle of replacement** Logically equivalent expressions may replace each other within the context of a proof.

De Morgan (DM)

Two sets of logically equivalent statement forms are named after the logician Augustus De Morgan:

De Morgan (DM)

$$\sim (p \cdot q) :: (\sim p \vee \sim q)$$
$$\sim (p \vee q) :: (\sim p \cdot \sim q)$$

De Morgan A rule of inference (replacement rule).

The new symbol "::" is used in all the replacement rules; it means "logically equivalent." *De Morgan replacement rules can be used validly only with conjunction or disjunction.* Let's examine the first pair. We can use the statement "It is not the case that both Judy likes riding roller coasters and Eddie likes riding roller coasters" as a substitution for the left side of the first pair: $\sim (p \cdot q)$. The original statement is logically equivalent to this statement: "Either Judy does not like riding roller coasters or Eddie does not like riding roller coasters." The original statement and the second statement express the same proposition: that *at least one* of the two people mentioned does not like to ride roller coasters.

The second pair of De Morgan can be understood in a similar manner. For example, the statement "It is not the case that either Judy or Eddie likes riding roller coasters" is logically equivalent to "Judy and Eddie do not like riding roller coasters." These two statements express the same proposition: that both of the people mentioned do not like to ride roller coasters.

The replacement rules offer some flexibility. For example, the pairs of statement forms that make up the replacement rules can be used in either direction. In other words, if a left member of a pair occurs in a proof, then it can be replaced by the right member. Likewise, if a right member of a pair occurs in a proof, then it can be replaced by the left member.

Here is an example of a valid application of the rule:

Valid Application of De Morgan (DM)

1. $\sim (A \cdot B) \supset C$
2. $\sim A \cdot M$ $/ C$
3. $\sim A$ 2, Simp
4. $\sim A \vee \sim B$ 3, Add
5. $\sim (A \cdot B)$ 4, DM
6. C 1, 5, MP

The strategy used for the proof was to try to derive the antecedent of line 1 in order to be able to use *modus ponens* to derive the conclusion. The first step was to isolate $\sim A$. Next, the rule of addition was used. The application of De Morgan allowed the valid derivation of the antecedent of the first premise.

The next two examples show invalid applications:

Invalid Applications of De Morgan (DM)

1. $\sim (A \cdot B)$ 1. $\sim C \vee \sim D$
2. $\sim A \cdot \sim B$ 🚫   2. $\sim (C \vee D)$ 🚫

The two invalid applications *do not result in logically equivalent statements.* This point is crucial, because the invalid applications *do not yield valid inferences.* The proof procedure of natural deduction requires that every step of a proof is a valid derivation. But in both invalid examples, line 2 *does not validly follow* from line 1. (You might want to try constructing truth tables to verify that the derivations in each example are not logically equivalent to the original statements.)

Commutation (Com)

The principle behind **commutation** can be easily illustrated. For example, it should be clear that the following two disjunctive statements are logically equivalent:

Commutation A rule of inference (replacement rule).

1. Either digital music is better than analog music or plasma TVs are expensive items.
2. Either plasma TVs are expensive items or digital music is better than analog music.

The same can be said for the following two conjunctive statements:

3. Digital music is better than analog music, and plasma TVs are expensive items.
4. Plasma TVs are expensive items, and digital music is better than analog music.

It should be obvious that the order of the disjuncts in the first set does not affect the truth value of the compound statements. Also, the order of the conjuncts in the second set does not affect the truth value of those compound statements. Once again, truth tables can verify these claims. The examples illustrate the form of the rule:

Commutation (Com)

$$(p \lor q) :: (q \lor p)$$
$$(p \cdot q) :: (q \cdot p)$$

The two pairs of logically equivalent statement forms illustrates that commutation can be used only with disjunction or conjunction. Here is an example of a valid application:

Valid Application of Commutation (Com)

1. $M \supset (P \lor Q)$
2. $S \cdot M$ / $P \lor Q$
3. $M \cdot S$ 2, Com
4. M 3, Simp
5. $P \lor Q$ 1, 4, MP

The strategy was to recognize that the M in line 2 could eventually be used to get the antecedent of the first premise. The first tactical move used commutation (Com) on line 2. The statement in line 3 is inferred from that in line 2. The inference is valid because the two sentences are logically equivalent. The second tactical move used the rule of simplification on line 3 to isolate the M.

The next example shows an invalid application:

Invalid Application of Commutation (Com)

1. $M \supset (P \lor Q)$
2. $(P \lor Q) \supset M$ ⊘

This example attempted to apply commutation to a conditional. However, commutation can be used validly only with disjunction or conjunction. Therefore, the derivation is invalid. (You might want to try constructing a truth table to verify that the derivation in line 2 of the invalid example is not logically equivalent to the statement in line 1.)

The two replacement rules under commutation can help by expanding the use of disjunctive syllogism and simplification. For example, disjunctive syllogism justifies deriving only one of the disjuncts:

> 1. $p \vee q$
> 2. $\sim p$ $/ \; q$
> 3. q 1, 2, DS

In other words, if $p \vee q$ is on one line and $\sim q$ is on another line, then disjunctive syllogism does not permit the derivation of p. However, when commutation is used correctly this can be accommodated. Here is how the two rules of inference can work together:

> 1. $p \vee q$
> 2. $\sim q$ $/ \; p$
> 3. $q \vee p$ 1, Com
> 4. p 2, 3, DS

Similarly, the implication rule simplification justifies deriving only one of the conjuncts:

> 1. $p \cdot q$ $/ \; p$
> 2. p 1, Simp

In other words, if $p \cdot q$ is on one line, then simplification does not permit the derivation of q. However, when commutation is used correctly this can be accommodated. Here is how the two rules of inference can work together:

> 1. $p \cdot q$ $/ \; q$
> 2. $q \cdot p$ 1, Com
> 3. q 2, Simp

Association (Assoc)

Association A rule of inference (replacement rule).

Association allows the use of parentheses to group the component parts of certain complex truth-functional statements in different ways without affecting the truth value. The following two pairs of logically equivalent statement forms show the logical form of the rule:

Association (Assoc)

$$[\, p \vee (q \vee r) \,] :: [\, (p \vee q) \vee r \,]$$
$$[\, p \cdot (q \cdot r) \,] :: [\, (p \cdot q) \cdot r \,]$$

As an example, suppose we let $p = $ *Walter will vote in the next election*, $q = $ *Sandy will vote in the next election*, and $r = $ *Judy will vote in the next election*. If we join these three statements and create disjunctions, we get the following:

Either Walter will vote in the next election or Sandy will vote in the next election or Judy will vote in the next election.

When parentheses are used to group the first two simple statements together, then the second occurrence of the wedge becomes the main operator: $(p \lor q) \lor r$. On the other hand, if we use parentheses to group the second and third simple statements together, then the first occurrence of the wedge becomes the main operator: $p \lor (q \lor r)$. These different groupings have no effect on the truth value of the complex statement. As with all the replacement rules, you can consult the truth tables for these logically equivalent statement forms from Chapter 7.

Here are two examples of valid applications:

Valid Applications of Association (Assoc)

1. $(P \lor Q) \supset S$		1. $(M \cdot \sim Q) \supset \sim S$	
2. $\sim M$		2. $M \cdot (\sim Q \cdot R)$	$/ \sim S$
3. $(M \lor P) \lor Q$	$/ S$	3. $(M \cdot \sim Q) \cdot R$	2, Assoc
4. $M \lor (P \lor Q)$	3, Assoc	4. $M \cdot \sim Q$	3, Simp
5. $P \lor Q$	2, 4, DS	5. $\sim S$	1, 4, MP
6. S	1, 5, MP		

In the first example, line 4 is validly derived from line 3. This step is justified because it uses association correctly. The overall strategy of the proof involved separating the M from the P. In turn, the $\sim M$ in line 2 was used in the application of disjunctive syllogism.

In the second example, the strategy was to try to derive the antecedent of line 1. This required two tactical moves. First, association validly replaced the grouping in line 2. Second, simplification validly isolated $M \cdot \sim Q$ (the antecedent of the first premise).

A word of caution: Association yields a valid derivation only when the affected logical operators in the two statements are either both disjunctions or else both conjunctions. The next two examples show invalid applications:

Invalid Applications of Association (Assoc)

1. $(P \cdot \sim Q) \lor R$	1. $P \cdot (\sim Q \lor R)$
2. $P \cdot (\sim Q \lor R)$ ⊘	2. $(P \cdot \sim Q) \lor R$ ⊘

These two examples did not heed the caution. A mixture of conjunction and disjunction was used, resulting in invalid derivations. The two invalid applications do not result in logically equivalent statements. This point is crucial because the invalid applications do not yield valid inferences. (You might want to try constructing truth tables to verify that in both examples the derivations are not logically equivalent to the original statements.)

Distribution (Dist)

The replacement rule **distribution** can be illustrated by the following statement:

Motorcycles are loud, and either trucks or buses get poor gas mileage.

Distribution A rule of inference (replacement rule).

If we let p = *Motorcycles are loud*, q = *trucks get poor gas mileage*, and r = *buses get poor gas mileage*, we get $p \cdot (q \lor r)$. Since the main operator is a conjunction, if the compound statement is true, then both conjuncts are true. This means that p is true, and *at least one* of the disjuncts, q or r, is true. Given this, the following disjunction is true:

> Motorcycles are loud and trucks get poor gas mileage, or motorcycles are loud and buses get poor gas mileage.

The logical form of this complex statement is $(p \cdot q) \vee (p \cdot r)$. Therefore, if $p \cdot (q \vee r)$ is true, then $(p \cdot q) \vee (p \cdot r)$ is true. This result is the first pair of the following logically equivalent statement forms:

Distribution (Dist)

$$[\,p \cdot (q \vee r)\,] :: [\,(p \cdot q) \vee (p \cdot r)\,]$$
$$[\,p \vee (q \cdot r)\,] :: [\,(p \vee q) \cdot (p \vee r)\,]$$

The second pair of statement forms can be understood in a similar manner. Consider the complex statement, "Motorcycles are loud or both trucks and buses get poor gas mileage." If we let $p = $ *Motorcycles are loud*, $q = $ *trucks get poor gas mileage*, and $r = $ *buses get poor gas mileage*, we get $p \vee (q \cdot r)$. Since the main operator is the wedge, the compound statement is true if at least one of the disjuncts is true. Therefore, if the first disjunct, p, is true, then $(p \vee q)$ is true and $(p \vee r)$ is true. On the other hand, if the second disjunct is true, then both q and r are true. Therefore, once again, $(p \vee q)$ is true and $(p \vee r)$ is true.

Here are two examples of valid applications:

Valid Applications of Distribution (Dist)

1. ~ $(M \cdot N)$			1. ~ C	
2. $M \cdot (N \vee P)$	/ $M \cdot P$		2. $A \vee (C \cdot D)$	/ A
3. $(M \cdot N) \vee (M \cdot P)$	2, Dist		3. $(A \vee C) \cdot (A \vee D)$	2, Dist
4. $M \cdot P$	1, 3, DS		4. $A \vee C$	3, Simp
			5. $C \vee A$	4, Com
			6. A	1, 5, DS

In the first example, the strategy was to try to get the M and N of the second premise together. Distribution justified the derivation in line 3. This produced a disjunction to which disjunctive syllogism was applied. In the second example, the strategy was to isolate A. A tactical move placed the A and C together in such a way that the ~ C in the first line was used. Therefore, distribution was a key tactical move in completing the proof.

Again a caution: Distribution can be used *only with conjunction and disjunction*. The next two examples illustrate invalid applications:

Invalid Applications of Distribution (Dist)

1. $B \vee (C \cdot D)$	1. $(M \cdot N) \vee (M \cdot P)$
2. $(B \vee C) \vee (B \vee D)$ ⊘	2. $M \cdot (N \cdot P)$ ⊘

In the first example, the main operator in line 1 is a wedge. An attempt was made to use distribution on line 1. However, the mistake occurred because the main operator in line 2 (the derived line) is a wedge. But in order to use distribution correctly on line

1, the result would have to be a dot as the main operator: $(B \lor C) \cdot (B \lor D)$. Therefore, the mistake resulted in an invalid application.

In the second example, a correct application of distribution would have given this result for line 2: $M \cdot (N \lor P)$. However, the mistake occurred because the derived line used a dot in the second conjunct: $(N \cdot P)$. This was a misapplication of distribution. (You might want to try constructing truth tables to verify that the derivations in both examples are not logically equivalent to the original statements.)

Double Negation (DN)

The replacement rule **double negation** justifies the introduction or elimination of pairs of negation signs, because the replacements result in valid derivations. This line of reasoning is revealed in the following form:

Double negation A rule of inference (replacement rule).

Double Negation (DN)

$$p :: {\sim}{\sim}p$$

For example, the contradiction of the statement "Golf is a sport" is the statement "It is not the case that golf is a sport." Following the same procedure, the contradiction of "It is not the case that golf is a sport" can be written as "It is not the case that it is not the case that golf is a sport." This means that the statement "Golf is a sport" is logically equivalent to the statement "It is not the case that it is not the case that golf is a sport."

Here are two examples of valid applications:

Valid Applications of Double Negation (DN)

1. $(Q \lor R) \supset {\sim}P$			1. $P \supset Q$	
2. P	/ ${\sim}(Q \lor R)$		2. R	
3. ${\sim}{\sim}P$	2, DN		3. ${\sim}P \supset {\sim}R$	/ Q
4. ${\sim}(Q \lor R)$	1, 3, MT		4. ${\sim}{\sim}R$	2, DN
			5. ${\sim}{\sim}P$	3, 4, MT
			6. P	5, DN
			7. Q	1, 6, MP

In the first example, the tactical move was to apply double negation to P in order to derive the negation of the consequent of the first premise. In turn, this allowed *modus tollens* to be used to derive the conclusion.

In the second example, a similar strategy was employed. Since line 2 is the negation of the consequent in line 3, double negation was used to derive ${\sim}{\sim}R$ from its logically equivalent pair member R. Double negation was then used a second time in line 6 to derive P from its logically equivalent pair member ${\sim}{\sim}P$. This example clearly illustrates what was stated earlier: replacement rules can be applied *left-to-right* or *right-to-left*.

The next example illustrates an invalid application:

Invalid Application of Double Negation (DN)

$$\frac{1.\ (Q \lor R)}{2.\ {\sim}({\sim}Q \lor {\sim}R)} \ \oslash$$

Line 2 is a misapplication of double negation. You might want to try constructing a truth table to verify that "~ (~ Q ∨ ~ R)" is *not* logically equivalent to "(Q ∨ R)." In this example, a correct application of double negation would give this result for line 2: ~ ~ (Q ∨ R).

THE FIRST FIVE REPLACEMENT RULES	
De Morgan (DM)	**Commutation (Com)**
~ ($p \cdot q$) :: (~ p ∨ ~ q) ~ (p ∨ q) :: (~ $p \cdot$ ~ q)	(p ∨ q) :: (q ∨ p) ($p \cdot q$) :: ($q \cdot p$)
Association (Assoc)	**Distribution (Dist)**
p ∨ (q ∨ r) :: (p ∨ q) ∨ r $p \cdot$ ($q \cdot r$) :: ($p \cdot q$) $\cdot r$	$p \cdot$ (q ∨ r) :: ($p \cdot q$) ∨ ($p \cdot r$) p ∨ ($q \cdot r$) :: (p ∨ q) $\cdot$ (p ∨ r)
Double Negation (DN)	
p :: ~ ~ p	

The strategy and tactics guide is updated to reflect the addition of first five replacement rules:

STRATEGIES AND TACTICS

Strategy 1: Simplify and isolate
    Tactical Moves—Try using any of the following:
    A. Simplification (Simp)
    B. *Modus ponens* (MP)
    C. *Modus tollens* (MT)
    D. Disjunctive syllogism (DS)
Strategy 2: Look for negation
    Tactical Moves—Try using any of the following:
    A. *Modus tollens* (MT)
    B. Disjunctive syllogism (DS)
    C. De Morgan (DM)
    D. Double negation (DN)
Strategy 3: Look for conditionals
    Tactical Moves—Try using any of the following:
    A. *Modus ponens* (MP)
    B. *Modus tollens* (MT)
    C. Hypothetical syllogism (HS)
    D. Constructive dilemma (CD)
Strategy 4: Add whatever you need
    Tactical Moves—Try using addition (Add)
Strategy 5: Combine lines
    Tactical Moves—Try using conjunction (Conj)
Strategy 6: Regroup
    Tactical Moves—Try using any of the following:
    A. Commutation (Com)
    B. Association (Assoc)
    C. Distribution (Dist)

CHECK YOUR UNDERSTANDING 8E

I. The following are examples of what you might encounter in proofs. The last step of each example gives the number of the step needed for its derivation. You are to provide the justification (the replacement rule) in the space provided. This will give you practice using the first five replacement rules.

[1] 1. $\sim (S \cdot R)$
    2. $\sim S \vee \sim R$ 1, _____

Answer: 2. $\sim S \vee \sim R$ 1, DM

[2] 1. $S \vee P$
    2. $P \vee S$ 1, _____

[3] 1. $R \vee (S \vee P)$
    2. $(R \vee S) \vee P$ 1, _____

[4] 1. $P \cdot (S \vee Q)$
    2. $(P \cdot S) \vee (P \cdot Q)$ 1, _____

★ [5] 1. S
    2. $\sim \sim S$ 1, _____

[6] 1. $\sim P \vee \sim Q$
    2. $\sim (P \cdot Q)$ 1, _____

[7] 1. $P \vee (Q \cdot R)$
    2. $(Q \cdot R) \vee P$ 1, _____

[8] 1. $(P \vee Q) \vee R$
    2. $P \vee (Q \vee R)$ 1, _____

★ [9] 1. $(P \cdot Q) \vee (P \cdot R)$
    2. $P \cdot (Q \vee R)$ 1, _____

[10] 1. $\sim \sim Q$
    2. Q 1, _____

[11] 1. $\sim (\sim Q \vee R)$
    2. $\sim \sim Q \cdot \sim R$ 1, _____

[12] 1. $(P \vee Q) \cdot (P \vee R)$
    2. $P \vee (Q \cdot R)$ 1, _____

★ [13] 1. $(S \cdot Q) \cdot R$
    2. $S \cdot (Q \cdot R)$ 1, _____

[14] 1. $\sim [(P \cdot Q) \vee (R \cdot S)]$
    2. $\sim (P \cdot Q) \cdot \sim (R \cdot S)$ 1, _____

[15] 1. $[(P \cdot Q) \vee (R \cdot S)] \cdot [(L \cdot M) \vee (N \cdot K)]$
    2. $[(L \cdot M) \vee (N \cdot K)] \cdot [(P \cdot Q) \vee (R \cdot S)]$ 1, _____

II. The following are more examples of what you might encounter in proofs. In these examples the justification (the replacement rule) is provided for the last line; however, the line itself is missing. Use the given information to derive the last line of each example. This will give you more practice using the first five replacement rules.

[1] 1. $S \cdot R$

    2.   1, Com

Answer: 2. $R \cdot S$ 1, Com

[2] 1. $(S \lor P) \cdot (S \lor Q)$

    2.   1, Dist

[3] 1. $\sim\sim Q$

    2.   1, DN

[4] 1. $(R \cdot S) \cdot P$

    2.   1, Assoc

★ [5] 1. $\sim P \cdot \sim Q$

    2.   1, DM

[6] 1. $\sim\sim(P \cdot R)$

    2.   1, DN

[7] 1. $P \cdot Q$

    2.   1, Com

[8] 1. $P \lor (Q \cdot R)$

    2.   1, Dist

★ [9] 1. $(R \lor S) \lor (P \supset Q)$

    2.   1, Assoc

[10] 1. $\sim(\sim P \lor \sim Q)$

    2.   1, DM

[11] 1. $P \cdot [\,(S \supset R) \lor (Q \supset L)\,]$

    2.   1, Dist

[12] 1. $\sim[\,(\sim P \cdot \sim Q) \lor (\sim R \cdot \sim S)\,]$

    2.   1, DM

★ [13] 1. $[\,R \supset (P \cdot Q)\,] \lor (L \lor M)$

    2.   1, Assoc

[14] 1. $[\,(S \lor R) \supset Q\,] \lor \sim[\,(\sim P \lor L) \supset K\,]$

    2.   1, Com

[15] 1. $S \lor [\,P \cdot (Q \supset M)\,]$

    2.   1, DN

III. Use the eight implication rules and the five replacement rules to complete the proofs. Provide the justification for each step that you derive.

[1] 1. $\sim (S \cdot L)$
    2. $(Q \cdot R) \supset (M \equiv N)$
    3. $P \supset (Q \cdot R)$
    4. $(M \equiv N) \supset (S \cdot L)$ $/ \sim P$
Answer: 5. $\sim (M \equiv N)$ 1, 4, MT
    6. $\sim (Q \cdot R)$ 2, 5, MT
    7. $\sim P$ 3, 6, MT

[2] 1. $\sim S$
    2. $R \supset (S \lor Q)$
    3. $R \cdot L$ $/ Q$

[3] 1. $\sim (\sim P \lor \sim Q)$
    2. $(P \cdot Q) \supset (R \lor S)$ $/ R \lor S$

[4] 1. $S \supset (L \lor M)$
    2. $(P \cdot Q) \supset \sim R$
    3. $(S \lor P) \cdot (S \lor Q)$ $/ (L \lor M) \lor \sim R$

⭐ [5] 1. $P \supset (Q \cdot R)$
     2. $\sim Q \cdot S$ $/ \sim P$

[6] 1. $(P \lor Q) \supset \sim (R \equiv S)$
    2. $R \equiv S$ $/ \sim P$

[7] 1. $[S \supset (L \cdot M)] \cdot [P \supset (M \cdot Q)]$
    2. $S \lor P$ $/ M$

[8] 1. $P \supset (Q \cdot R)$
    2. $P \cdot (S \lor R)$
    3. $L \supset (M \equiv P)$ $/ (Q \cdot R) \lor (M \equiv P)$

⭐ [9] 1. $\sim (P \cdot Q)$
     2. $(\sim P \lor \sim Q) \supset (R \cdot S)$
     3. $(R \lor \sim Q) \supset \sim T$ $/ \sim T$

[10] 1. $P \cdot Q$
     2. $(P \lor R) \supset (S \cdot L)$
     3. $(S \cdot L) \supset (R \lor S)$ $/ R \lor S$

[11] 1. $(P \lor Q) \lor \sim R$
     2. $[(P \lor Q) \supset Q] \cdot (\sim R \supset S)$
     3. $\sim P$ $/ Q \lor (S \cdot \sim R)$

[12] 1. $P \cdot \sim Q$
     2. $R \supset Q$ $/ \sim R \cdot P$

⭐ [13] 1. $\sim P$
     2. $Q \vee (R \cdot P)$ / Q

[14] 1. $S \supset (Q \cdot M)$
     2. $S \vee (P \cdot L)$
     3. $P \supset (Q \cdot R)$ / $Q \cdot (M \vee R)$

[15] 1. P
     2. $(R \vee Q) \cdot S$
     3. $P \supset (L \equiv M)$
     4. $(L \equiv M) \supset \sim (S \cdot R)$ / $S \cdot Q$

[16] 1. $P \supset \sim Q$
     2. $(P \cdot R) \vee (P \cdot S)$
     3. $L \vee Q$ / L

⭐ [17] 1. $P \vee Q$
     2. $(R \cdot S) \cdot L$ / $[(L \cdot R) \cdot P] \vee [(L \cdot R) \cdot Q]$

[18] 1. $(P \vee Q) \supset \sim R$
     2. $S \cdot R$ / $\sim P$

[19] 1. P
     2. $Q \vee (R \vee S)$
     3. $R \supset \sim P$ / $Q \vee S$

[20] 1. $\sim R$
     2. $(Q \supset R) \cdot (S \supset L)$
     3. Q / $\sim M \vee L$

⭐ [21] 1. $P \supset \sim \sim R$
     2. $P \cdot \sim (S \cdot R)$ / $\sim S$

[22] 1. $\sim P \cdot Q$
     2. $\sim (\sim P \cdot \sim R)$
     3. $(R \vee S) \supset \sim (L \vee M)$ / $\sim (M \vee L)$

[23] 1. $\sim P$
     2. $(Q \vee \sim R) \supset (P \cdot S)$ / R

[24] 1. $\sim P$
     2. $(P \cdot Q) \vee (R \cdot S)$ / $\sim (P \vee \sim R)$

⭐ [25] 1. $\sim (P \cdot Q)$
     2. R
     3. $[S \supset (P \cdot Q)] \cdot (R \supset L)$
     4. $S \vee R$ / $\sim P \supset (\sim Q \cdot L)$

[26] 1. $P \vee (Q \supset R)$
     2. $P \supset R$
     3. $\sim Q \supset S$
     4. $\sim R$ / $S \vee K$

[27] 1. $(P \vee Q) \supset R$
    2. $\sim R$
    3. $\sim S \supset (Q \vee R)$ / S

[28] 1. $P \supset Q$
    2. $R \vee P$
    3. $S \supset (L \vee \sim R)$
    4. $S \cdot \sim L$ / Q \vee M

★ [29] 1. $P \supset \sim Q$
    2. $P \cdot (R \vee Q)$
    3. $R \supset S$ / S

[30] 1. $P \supset Q$
    2. $\sim (L \vee \sim P)$
    3. $L \vee S$ / Q \cdot S

[31] 1. $(Q \vee S) \supset \sim P$
    2. $Q \vee (R \cdot S)$
    3. $(Q \vee R) \supset \sim L$
    4. $K \supset (L \vee P)$ / \sim K

[32] 1. $(P \vee Q) \supset \sim R$
    2. $P \cdot (S \vee R)$
    3. $(N \cdot M) \cdot L$ / N \cdot S

★ [33] 1. $\sim (J \equiv Q) \cdot R$
    2. $[S \supset (L \cdot M)] \vee (N \cdot J)$
    3. $[S \supset (L \cdot Q)] \supset (J \equiv M)$ / $(J \vee K) \cdot (R \vee \sim H)$

[34] 1. $\sim [(\sim P \vee \sim Q) \vee (R \vee \sim S)]$
    2. $P \supset (R \vee L)$ / L

[35] 1. $(R \cdot M) \supset L$
    2. $(\sim M \vee Q) \supset \sim (R \cdot S)$
    3. $R \cdot \sim L$ / $\sim (L \vee S)$

IV. First, translate the following arguments into symbolic form. Second, use the eight implication rules to derive the conclusion of each. Letters for the simple statements are provided in parentheses and can be used in the order given.

  1. Maggie is single. Since it is not the case that Maggie is divorced and she is single, we can conclude that Maggie is not divorced. (*S, D*)

Answer:

[1] 1. S
    2. $\sim (D \cdot S)$ / $\sim D$
    3. $\sim D \vee \sim S$ 2, DM
    4. $\sim S \vee \sim D$ 3, Com
    5. $\sim \sim S$ 1, DN
    6. $\sim D$ 4, 5, DS

2. If you do not change the oil in your car regularly, then if take your car in for required maintenance, then any car repairs will be covered by the warranty, and it is not the case that if you did take your car in for required maintenance, then any car repairs are covered by the warranty. Therefore, you did change the oil in your car regularly. (O, M, W)

3. Humans are not by nature competitive but they are cooperative. If humans are cooperative, then either they can work together peacefully or they are by nature competitive. We can infer that humans can work together peacefully. (C, O, P)

4. If you have a good retirement plan, then you do not need to worry about inflation. You either have a good retirement plan or you make wise investments or else you plan to work for a long time. If you either make wise investments or you plan to work for a long time, then you do not need to borrow money later in life. Therefore, it is not the case that you need to worry about inflation and you need to borrow money later in life. (R, I, W, L, B)

★ 5. Accidents are not avoidable and long-term health care is often required, or else accidents are not avoidable and first aid is sometimes available. But first aid is sometimes not available. Therefore, long-term health care is often required. (A, L, F)

6. If it did not snow last night, then we can go hiking. If we get visitors, then we cannot paint the spare bedroom this weekend. It is not the case that we do not get visitors, and it snowed last night. Therefore, either we can go hiking or we cannot paint the spare bedroom this weekend. (S, H, V, P)

7. If either scandals are rampant in politics or incompetence is rewarded at election time, then the government is not effective. Either the government is effective but scandals are rampant in politics, or else government is effective and there are barely enough competent people to run things. We can conclude that there are barely enough competent people to run things. (S, I, E, C)

8. If the results of your experiment are not replicable, then the results are not accepted by scientists. If it is not the case that both the results are accepted by scientists and there is any evidence of experimental error, then the results are accepted by scientists. But there is not any evidence of experimental error. Therefore, the results of your experiment are replicable. (R, A, E)

★ 9. If your novel is well written, then your book will get good reviews and it might be made into a movie. Your novel is well written and it is pulp fiction, or else your novel is well written and it is soon forgotten by the reading public. We can conclude that your novel is well written and it might be made into a movie. (N, R, M, P, F)

10. If it is not the case that she is either a citizen or a permanent resident, then she still has certain basic rights. If she is currently applying for asylum and she has not overstayed her visa, then she is not a permanent resident and she is not a citizen. Moreover, she is currently applying for asylum and she has not overstayed her visa. Therefore, she still has certain basic rights. (C, P, R, A, V)

F. REPLACEMENT RULES II

There are five additional replacement rules for us to consider. As with the first five sets, a correct application ensures that derivations will be valid arguments.

Transposition (Trans)

One way to see how **transposition** functions is to recall the discussion of necessary and sufficient conditions. For example, the statement "If you get at least a 90 on the exam, then you get an A" is logically equivalent to the statement "If you did not get an A, then you did not get at least a 90 on the exam." The logical form of this set of statements is captured by the replacement rule:

Transposition A rule of inference (replacement rule).

Transposition (Trans)

$$(p \supset q) :: (\sim q \supset \sim p)$$

Here are two examples of valid applications of the rule:

Valid Applications of Transposition (Trans)

1. $S \supset \sim Q$		1. $S \cdot \sim M$	
2. $P \supset Q$	$/ S \supset \sim P$	2. $(P \lor R) \supset M$	$/ \sim P \cdot \sim R$
3. $\sim Q \supset \sim P$	2, Trans	3. $\sim M \supset \sim (P \lor R)$	2, Trans
4. $S \supset \sim P$	1, 3, HS	4. $\sim M \cdot S$	1, Com
		5. $\sim M$	4, Simp
		6. $\sim (P \lor R)$	3, 5, MP
		7. $\sim P \cdot \sim R$	6, DM

In the first example, transposition was used tactically on line 2 to derive $\sim Q$ as an antecedent of a conditional statement. This created the opportunity to apply hypothetical syllogism to validly derive the conclusion.

In the second example, the strategy was to recognize that $\sim M$ could be derived on a separate line. Given this, the tactical move of transposition on line 2 set up $\sim M$ as the antecedent of a conditional. Once that was achieved the final result was within reach.

The next example shows an invalid application:

Invalid Application of Transposition (Trans)

1. $\sim P \supset \sim Q$	
2. $P \supset Q$	🚫

The mistake occurs because the negation signs were eliminated without transposing the antecedent and consequent. (You might want to try constructing a truth table to verify that the derivation in line 2 is not logically equivalent to the statement in line 1.)

Material Implication (Impl)

Material implication can be illustrated by the following two statements:

Material implication A rule of inference (replacement rule).

1. If you get fewer than 60 points, then you fail the exam.
2. Either you do not get fewer than 60 points or you fail the exam.

Truth tables can verify that these are logically equivalent statements. They have the following forms:

Material Implication (Impl)

$$(p \supset q) :: (\sim p \vee q)$$

Here are two examples of valid applications of the rule:

Valid Applications of Material Implication (Impl)

1. $\sim R$	/ $(R \supset S) \vee P$	1. B	
2. $\sim R \vee S$	1, Add	2. $(B \supset C) \vee D$	/ $C \vee D$
3. $R \supset S$	2, Impl	3. $(\sim B \vee C) \vee D$	2, Impl
4. $(R \supset S) \vee P$	3, Add	4. $\sim B \vee (C \vee D)$	3, Assoc
		5. $\sim \sim B$	1, DN
		6. $C \vee D$	4, 5, DS

In the first example, material implication allowed the derivation of a conditional statement in line 3. This change was needed in order to get the statement into the same form as appears in the conclusion.

In the second example, the overall strategy was to ensure that C could be joined with D in a disjunction, as indicated by the conclusion. Since material implication allows the derivation of a disjunction from a conditional statement, the tactical move in line 3 helped to eventually derive the conclusion.

The next two examples are invalid applications:

Invalid Applications of Material Implication (Impl)

1. $S \supset R$	1. $\sim D \vee G$
2. $\sim S \cdot R$ ⊘	2. $\sim (D \supset G)$ ⊘

In the first example, the mistake occurs from using a dot instead of a wedge. In the second example, the mistake occurs from the incorrect placement of the tilde. (You might want to try constructing truth tables to verify that the derivations in both examples are not logically equivalent to the original statements.)

Material Equivalence (Equiv)

Material equivalence
A rule of inference
(replacement rule).

In Chapter 7, the truth table for **material equivalence** revealed that $p \equiv q$ is true when p and q are both true and when p and q are both false. With this in mind, let's look at the two forms for the replacement rule:

Material Equivalence (Equiv)

$$(p \equiv q) :: (p \supset q) \cdot (q \supset p)$$
$$(p \equiv q) :: (p \cdot q) \vee (\sim p \cdot \sim q)$$

For the first pair, if p and q are both true, then $(p \supset q)$ and $(q \supset p)$ are true, because in both instances the antecedent and consequent are true. Likewise, if p and q are both false, then $(p \supset q)$ and $(q \supset p)$ are once again true, because in both instances the antecedent and the consequent are false. Also, if p is true and q is false, then $(p \supset q)$

is false. In that case, the conjunction is false. Likewise, if p is false and q is true, then $(q \supset p)$ is false. In that case, too, the conjunction is false. Therefore, $(p \equiv q)$ is logically equivalent to $(p \supset q) \cdot (q \supset p)$.

For the second pair, if p and q are both true, then $(p \cdot q)$ is true; therefore, the disjunction $(p \cdot q) \lor (\sim p \cdot \sim q)$ is true. If p and q are both false, then $(\sim p \cdot \sim q)$ is true; therefore, the disjunction $(p \cdot q) \lor (\sim p \cdot \sim q)$ is again true. Now, if p is true and q is false, then $(p \cdot q)$ and $(\sim p \cdot \sim q)$ are both false. In that case, the disjunction is false. Likewise, if p is false and q is true, then $(p \cdot q)$ and $(\sim p \cdot \sim q)$ are both false. In that case, too, the disjunction is false. Therefore, $(p \equiv q)$ is logically equivalent to $(p \cdot q) \lor (\sim p \cdot \sim q)$.

Here are two examples of valid applications:

Valid Applications of Material Equivalence (Equiv)

1. $\sim S$		1. $C \equiv D$	
2. $(\sim Q \lor \sim R) \supset S$	/ $Q \equiv R$	2. $(C \cdot D) \supset \sim P$	
3. $\sim(\sim Q \lor \sim R)$	1, 2, MT	3. P	/ $\sim C$
4. $\sim\sim Q \cdot \sim\sim R$	3, DM	4. $(C \cdot D) \lor (\sim C \cdot \sim D)$	1, Equiv
5. $Q \cdot R$	4, DN (twice)	5. $\sim\sim P \supset \sim (C \cdot D)$	2, Trans
6. $(Q \cdot R) \lor (\sim Q \cdot \sim R)$	5, Add	6. $P \supset \sim (C \cdot D)$	5, DN
7. $Q \equiv R$	6, Equiv	7. $\sim (C \cdot D)$	3, 6, MP
		8. $\sim C \cdot \sim D$	4, 7, DS
		9. $\sim C$	8, Simp

In the first example, since the conclusion is $Q \equiv R$, the overall strategy was to derive one of the two logically equivalent pairs. That meant that if $Q \cdot R$ is isolated, then addition can be used to derive the necessary part. Therefore, rather than use material equivalence as a tactical move within the body of the proof, it was used to derive the final step.

The next two examples are invalid applications:

Invalid Applications of Material Equivalence (Equiv)

1. $G \equiv H$		1. $(M \supset Q) \lor (Q \supset M)$	
2. $(G \cdot H) \cdot (\sim G \cdot \sim H)$ ⊘		2. $M \equiv Q$ ⊘

In the first example, the mistake in line 2 was making the main operator a dot instead of a wedge. In the second example, line 1 has a wedge as the main operator. But in order for the rule to be applied correctly, there had to be a dot as the main operator. (You might want to try constructing truth tables to verify that the derivations in both examples are not logically equivalent to the original statements.)

Exportation (Exp)

Consider the following statement: "If it snows this afternoon and we buy a sled, then we can go sledding." This is logically equivalent to the statement "If it snows this afternoon, then if we buy a sled, then we can go sledding." Here are the forms of these two statements:

Exportation A rule of inference (replacement rule).

Exportation (Exp)

$$(p \cdot q) \supset r :: p \supset (q \supset r)$$

Here are two examples of valid applications:

Valid Applications of Exportation (Exp)

1. Q		1. G	
2. $(Q \cdot R) \supset S$	/ $\sim R \lor S$	2. $H \supset (K \supset \sim G)$	/ $\sim H \lor \sim K$
3. $Q \supset (R \supset S)$	2, Exp	3. $(H \cdot K) \supset \sim G$	2, Exp
4. $R \supset S$	1, 3, MP	4. $\sim \sim G$	1, DN
5. $\sim R \lor S$	4, Impl	5. $\sim (H \cdot K)$	3, 4, MT
		6. $\sim H \lor \sim K$	5, DM

In the first example, exportation was used tactically to derive a conditional statement with Q as the antecedent. This led to the eventual derivation of the conclusion. In the second example, exportation was used tactically to derive a conditional statement with $\sim G$ as the consequent. Once again, this led to the eventual derivation of the conclusion.

The next two examples are invalid applications:

Invalid Applications of Exportation (Exp)

1. $Q \supset (R \supset S)$		1. $(D \cdot G) \supset H$
2. $Q \supset (R \cdot S)$	🚫	2. $(D \supset G) \supset H$	🚫

PROFILES IN LOGIC

Augustus De Morgan

When asked how old he was, Augustus De Morgan (1806–71), ever the mathematician, once remarked, "I was x years old in the year x-squared." (De Morgan was 43 years old in the year 1849.) One of De Morgan's main interests was in the problem of transforming thoughts into symbols. Although trained as a mathematician, De Morgan read widely in many other fields. From years of intense studies, De Morgan realized that all scientific and mathematical fields advanced only when they had a robust system of symbols.

De Morgan is also credited with establishing a mathematical basis for understanding Aristotelian categorical syllogisms. For example, from the premises "Some D are J" and "Some D are N," we cannot validly conclude that "Some J are N." However, De Morgan showed, from the premises "Most D are J" and "Most D are N," we can validly conclude that "Some J are N." In fact, De Morgan provides a mathematical formula for this problem. Let the number of D's $= x$, the number of D's that are J's $= y$, and the number of D's that are N's $= z$. From this we can conclude that *at least* $(y + z) - x$ J's are N's.

De Morgan recognized what had hindered the development of logic from Aristotle's time—the lack of a system of logical symbols. De Morgan argued that logic and mathematics should be studied together so that the disciplines can learn from each other. When he taught mathematics, he always included logical training as part of the curriculum.

There are two mistakes in the first example. They can be illustrated by comparing line 2 with a *correct* application: $(Q \cdot R) \supset S$. In other words, one mistake placed the dot between the R and S, and the second was the misplacement of the horseshoe. (You might want to try constructing truth tables to verify that the derivations in both examples are not logically equivalent to the original statements.)

Tautology (Taut)

A tautology is a statement that is necessarily true. The principle behind the replacement rule **tautology** can be illustrated by considering the following statement: "August has 31 days." If this statement is true, then the *disjunction* "August has 31 days or August has 31 days" is true. The truth tables for these statements are identical, so they are logically equivalent statements.

Tautology A rule of inference (replacement rule).

Similarly, if the statement "August has 31 days" is true, then the *conjunction* "August has 31 days and August has 31 days" is true. Once again, the truth tables for these statements are identical, so they are logically equivalent statements.

Here are the forms for the rule:

Tautology (Taut)

$$p :: (p \lor p)$$
$$p :: (p \cdot p)$$

Here are two examples of valid applications:

Valid Applications of Tautology (Taut)

1. $(Q \supset S) \cdot (R \supset S)$		1. $P \supset R$	
2. $Q \lor R$	/ S	2. $P \lor (Q \cdot P)$	/ R
3. $S \lor S$	1, 2, CD	3. $(P \lor Q) \cdot (P \lor P)$	2, Dist
4. S	3, Taut	4. $(P \lor P) \cdot (P \lor Q)$	3, Com
		5. $P \lor P$	4, Simp
		6. P	5, Taut
		7. R	1, 6, MP

In the first example, tautology was used to derive the final step of the proof. In the second example, tautology was used as a tactical move to isolate P in order for *modus ponens* to be applied to derive the conclusion.

The next example is an invalid application:

Invalid Application of Tautology (Taut)

1. $S \supset (Q \lor S)$
2. $S \supset Q$ ⊘

The mistake occurs because the two instances of S are not directly connected with each other with either a disjunction or a conjunction as the main operator. (You might want to try constructing a truth table to verify that the derivation in line 2 is not logically equivalent to the statement in line 1.)

THE TEN REPLACEMENT RULES	
De Morgan (DM)	**Commutation (Com)**
$\sim (p \cdot q) :: (\sim p \vee \sim q)$ $\sim (p \vee q) :: (\sim p \cdot \sim q)$	$(p \vee q) :: (q \vee p)$ $(p \cdot q) :: (q \cdot p)$
Association (Assoc)	**Distribution (Dist)**
$p \vee (q \vee r) :: (p \vee q) \vee r$ $p \cdot (q \cdot r) :: (p \cdot q) \cdot r$	$p \cdot (q \vee r) :: (p \cdot q) \vee (p \cdot r)$ $p \vee (q \cdot r) :: (p \vee q) \cdot (p \vee r)$
Double negation (DN)	**Transposition (Trans)**
$p :: \sim \sim p$	$(p \supset q) :: (\sim q \supset \sim p)$
Material implication (Impl)	**Material equivalence (Equiv)**
$(p \supset q) :: (\sim p \vee q)$	$(p \equiv q) :: (p \supset q) \cdot (q \supset p)$ $(p \equiv q) :: (p \cdot q) \vee (\sim p \cdot \sim q)$
Exportation (Exp)	**Tautology (Taut)**
$(p \cdot q) \supset r :: p \supset (q \supset r)$	$p :: (p \vee p)$ $p :: (p \cdot p)$

The strategy and tactics guide is updated to reflect all the rules of inference:

STRATEGIES AND TACTICS USING THE RULES OF INFERENCE
Strategy 1: Simplify and isolate
Tactical Moves—Try using any of the following:
A. Simplification (Simp)
B. *Modus ponens* (MP)
C. *Modus tollens* (MT)
D. Disjunctive syllogism (DS)
Strategy 2: Look for negation
Tactical Moves—Try using any of the following:
A. *Modus tollens* (MT)
B. Disjunctive syllogism (DS)
C. De Morgan (DM)
D. Double negation (DN)
E. Transposition (Trans)
F. Material implication (Impl)
Strategy 3: Look for conditionals
Tactical Moves—Try using any of the following:
A. *Modus ponens* (MP)
B. *Modus tollens* (MT)
C. Hypothetical syllogism (HS)
D. Constructive dilemma (CD)
E. Material implication (Impl)
F. Material equivalence (Equiv)
G. Exportation (Exp)
Strategy 4: Add whatever you need
Tactical Moves—Try using addition (Add)

STRATEGIES AND TACTICS USING THE RULES OF INFERENCE (continued)

Strategy 5: Combine lines
    Tactical Moves—Try using conjunction (Conj)
Strategy 6: Regroup
    Tactical Moves—Try using any of the following:
      A. Commutation (Com)
      B. Association (Assoc)
      C. Distribution (Dist)
      D. Tautology (Taut)

CHECK YOUR UNDERSTANDING 8F

I. The following are examples of what you may encounter in proofs. The last step of each example gives the line number needed for its derivation. You are to provide the replacement rule that justifies the step. This will give you practice using the second group of replacement rules.

[1] 1. $R \supset S$
    2. $\sim S \supset \sim R$ 1, _____

Answer: 2. $\sim S \supset \sim R$ 1, Trans

[2] 1. $(S \cdot R) \supset Q$
    2. $S \supset (R \supset Q)$ 1, _____

[3] 1. $P \supset Q$
    2. $\sim P \vee Q$ 1, _____

[4] 1. R
    2. $R \vee R$ 1, _____

⭐ [5] 1. $R \equiv S$
    2. $(R \supset S) \cdot (S \supset R)$ 1, _____

[6] 1. $\sim P \supset \sim Q$
    2. $Q \supset P$ 1, _____

[7] 1. $(P \cdot Q) \vee (\sim P \cdot \sim Q)$
    2. $P \equiv Q$ 1, _____

[8] 1. $P \supset (Q \supset R)$
    2. $(P \cdot Q) \supset R$ 1, _____

⭐ [9] 1. $\sim P \vee Q$
    2. $P \supset Q$ 1, _____

[10] 1. $P \cdot P$
    2. P 1, _____

[11] 1. $[(P \lor Q) \cdot R] \supset (S \lor L)$
     2. $(P \lor Q) \supset [R \supset (S \lor L)]$ 1, _____

[12] 1. $(P \cdot Q) \supset R$
     2. $\sim R \supset \sim (P \cdot Q)$ 1, _____

⭐ [13] 1. $(S \lor L) \equiv (Q \lor K)$
      2. $[(S \lor L) \cdot (Q \lor K)] \lor [\sim (S \lor L) \cdot \sim (Q \lor K)]$ 1, _____

[14] 1. $(M \cdot \sim P) \lor (M \cdot \sim P)$
     2. $M \cdot \sim P$ 1, _____

[15] 1. $\sim [P \lor (Q \cdot R)] \lor (S \cdot L)$
     2. $[P \lor (Q \cdot R)] \supset (S \cdot L)$ 1, _____

II. The following are more examples of what you may encounter in proofs. In these examples the justification (the replacement rule) is provided for the last step. However, the step itself is missing. Use the given information to derive the last step of each example. This will give you more practice using the second group of replacement rules.

[1] 1. $\sim S \supset \sim R$
    2.   1, Trans
Answer: 2. $R \supset S$ 1, Trans

[2] 1. $(R \cdot S) \lor (\sim R \cdot \sim S)$
    2.   1, Equiv

[3] 1. $Q \cdot Q$
    2.   1, Taut

[4] 1. $R \supset (S \supset P)$
    2.   1, Exp

⭐ [5] 1. $\sim S \lor P$
     2.   1, Impl

[6] 1. $[(P \lor Q) \supset (S \lor R)] \cdot [(S \lor R) \supset (P \lor Q)]$
    2.   1, Equiv

[7] 1. $(S \lor S) \cdot (S \lor S)$
    2.   1, Taut

[8] 1. $\sim [(Q \lor L) \cdot \sim K] \lor (M \supset P)$
    2.   1, Impl

⭐ [9] 1. $(R \lor K) \equiv (Q \lor S)$
     2.   1, Equiv

[10] 1. $\sim (P \cdot Q) \supset \sim (S \lor Q)$
     2.   1, Trans

III. Complete the following proofs. Provide the justification for each step that you derive. Note: Each proof will require you to use *one implication rule* and *one replacement rule* to complete the proof.

[1] 1. $(\sim T \vee \sim R) \supset S$
    2. $\sim (T \cdot R)$ / S

Answer:
    3. $\sim T \vee \sim R$ 2, DM
    4. S 1, 3, MP

[2] 1. $S \supset P$
    2. $\sim P \vee (R \cdot Q)$ / $S \supset (R \cdot Q)$

[3] 1. $T \vee S$
    2. $\sim \sim R$ / $(T \vee S) \cdot R$

[4] 1. $(\sim T \supset S) \cdot (R \supset P)$
    2. $T \supset R$ / $S \vee P$

★ [5] 1. $S \supset (P \supset Q)$
    2. $\sim Q$ / $\sim (S \cdot P)$

[6] 1. $(T \vee Q) \vee S$
    2. $\sim T$ / $Q \vee S$

[7] 1. $S \vee (T \cdot R)$ / $S \vee T$

[8] 1. $S \vee S$ / $S \vee T$

★ [9] 1. $P \equiv S$ / $P \supset S$

[10] 1. $\sim T \supset \sim P$
    2. $T \supset S$ / $P \supset S$

[11] 1. $\sim (T \vee S) \supset (P \vee Q)$
    2. $\sim T \cdot \sim S$ / $P \vee Q$

[12] 1. $P \vee S$
    2. $\sim S$ / P

★ [13] 1. $(S \cdot T) \cdot R$ / S

[14] 1. $T \cdot (S \vee R)$
    2. $\sim (T \cdot S)$ / $T \cdot R$

[15] 1. $(R \cdot P) \vee (\sim R \cdot \sim P)$
    2. $(R \equiv P) \supset T$ / T

IV. Use all the rules of inference (eight implication rules and ten replacement rules) to complete the proofs. Provide the justification for each step that you derive.

[1] 1. $(S \vee \sim P) \vee R$
    2. $\sim S$ / $P \supset R$

Answer:
    3. $S \vee (\sim P \vee R)$ 1, Assoc
    4. $\sim P \vee R$ 2, 3, DS
    5. $P \supset R$ 4, Impl

[2] 1. $\sim P$
    2. $(Q \vee P) \vee R$ / $Q \vee R$

[3] 1. $\sim (P \cdot P)$ / $P \supset Q$

[4] 1. $Q \vee R$
    2. $[Q \supset (S \cdot P)] \cdot [R \supset (P \cdot L)]$ / P

⭐ [5] 1. $\sim Q \supset \sim P$
    2. $(P \cdot R) \supset S$
    3. P / $Q \vee S$

[6] 1. $P \supset Q$
    2. $(R \cdot S) \supset P$
    3. R / $S \supset Q$

[7] 1. $P \vee (T \cdot R)$
    2. $S \supset \sim (P \vee T)$ / $\sim S$

[8] 1. $\sim (S \vee Q)$ / $\sim P \supset \sim S$

⭐ [9] 1. $\sim P \cdot Q$
    2. $Q \supset (R \supset P)$ / $\sim R$

[10] 1. $\sim P$
     2. $\sim Q \supset P$
     3. $\sim Q \vee (\sim P \supset R)$ / $R \vee S$

[11] 1. $P \vee Q$
     2. $(Q \supset R) \cdot (T \supset A)$
     3. $(P \supset B) \cdot (C \supset D)$ / $B \vee R$

[12] 1. $P \supset (\sim Q \cdot \sim R)$
     2. $R \supset Q$ / $\sim P$

⭐ [13] 1. $[P \supset (Q \cdot R)] \cdot [S \supset (L \cdot Q)]$
     2. $P \cdot R$ / $Q \cdot (R \vee L)$

[14] 1. $\sim P \supset (Q \vee R)$ / $(\sim P \cdot \sim Q) \supset R$

[15] 1. $P \supset (Q \cdot R)$
     2. $Q \supset \sim R$ / $P \supset S$

[16] 1. $T \supset (R \cdot S)$
     2. $R \supset (S \supset P)$ / $(P \vee \sim T) \vee Q$

⭐ [17] 1. $\sim (P \cdot Q) \supset (R \vee S)$
     2. $\sim P \vee \sim Q$
     3. T / $(T \cdot R) \vee (T \cdot S)$

[18] 1. $\sim (P \cdot Q)$
     2. $(P \cdot Q) \vee (R \cdot S)$ / $Q \vee S$

[19] 1. $P \supset (Q \vee R)$
     2. $S \supset \sim (Q \vee R)$ / $\sim (P \cdot S)$

[20] 1. $T \vee S$
    2. $\sim T$
    3. $(S \vee S) \supset (\sim P \vee R)$ $/ \sim R \supset \sim P$

⭐ [21] 1. $(P \vee Q) \vee \sim R$
    2. $[(P \vee Q) \supset Q] \cdot (\sim R \supset S)$
    3. $\sim P$ $/ Q \vee (S \cdot \sim R)$

[22] 1. $(\sim P \vee Q) \supset R$
    2. $(S \vee R) \supset P$
    3. $P \supset Q$ $/ Q$

[23] 1. $P \supset Q$
    2. $R \supset (S \supset P)$
    3. $Q \supset \sim P$ $/ \sim R \vee \sim S$

[24] 1. $\sim Q$
    2. $R \supset Q$
    3. $\sim S \supset M$
    4. $R \vee (S \supset Q)$ $/ M \vee K$

⭐ [25] 1. $\sim P \supset Q$
    2. $\sim R \supset \sim (\sim S \vee P)$
    3. $Q \supset \sim S$ $/ R$

[26] 1. $\sim P$
    2. $(Q \supset P) \cdot (S \supset L)$
    3. Q $/ M \supset L$

[27] 1. $T \equiv R$
    2. $(\sim R \supset \sim T) \supset (P \cdot \sim S)$ $/ \sim S \vee T$

[28] 1. $P \supset (Q \vee R)$
    2. $(S \vee T) \supset R$
    3. $\sim Q \cdot \sim R$ $/ \sim P \cdot \sim (S \vee T)$

⭐ [29] 1. $\sim R \vee \sim S$
    2. $P \vee [Q \vee (R \cdot S)]$
    3. $L \supset \sim P$ $/ L \supset Q$

[30] 1. $(P \cdot Q) \supset R$
    2. P
    3. $\sim Q \vee S$ $/ \sim Q \cdot (R \vee S)$

[31] 1. $(P \vee Q) \supset S$
    2. $R \vee (P \vee Q)$
    3. $\sim R$
    4. $\sim T \supset R$ $/ S \equiv T$

[32] 1. $\sim P \supset (Q \vee R)$
    2. $(S \vee Q) \supset R$
    3. $\sim R$ / P

⭐ [33] 1. $S \supset Q$
    2. $R \cdot S$
    3. $Q \supset (L \vee \sim R)$ / L

[34] 1. $C \supset F$
    2. $A \supset B$
    3. $\sim F \cdot A$
    4. $\sim C \supset (B \supset D)$ / $B \cdot D$

[35] 1. $\sim P \vee Q$
    2. $R \cdot (S \vee P)$
    3. $\sim S$ / Q

[36] 1. $P \vee Q$
    2. $[P \supset (R \cdot S)] \cdot (Q \supset L)$
    3. $\sim (R \cdot S)$
    4. Q / $\sim R \vee (\sim S \cdot L)$

⭐ [37] 1. $Q \vee (P \supset S)$
    2. $S \equiv (R \cdot T)$
    3. $P \cdot \sim Q$ / $P \cdot R$

[38] 1. $P \supset (R \vee S)$
    2. $\sim [(\sim P \vee \sim Q) \vee (R \vee \sim L)]$ / S

[39] 1. $(Q \vee S) \supset \sim P$
    2. $Q \vee (R \cdot S)$
    3. $(Q \vee R) \supset \sim L$
    4. $K \supset (L \vee P)$ / $\sim K$

[40] 1. R
    2. $\sim (P \cdot \sim Q)$
    3. $P \vee S$
    4. $\sim (R \cdot S)$ / Q

⭐ [41] 1. $P \vee R$
    2. $\sim P \vee (Q \cdot R)$
    3. $R \supset (Q \cdot S)$ / $Q \cdot S$

[42] 1. $\sim S$
    2. $\sim P \supset \sim Q$
    3. $Q \cdot (R \vee S)$ / $P \cdot R$

[43] 1. $Q \cdot S$
    2. $(Q \cdot \sim P) \supset \sim R$
    3. $Q \supset \sim P$
    4. $(S \cdot T) \supset (P \vee R)$ / $\sim T$

[44] 1. $\sim P \vee Q$
   2. $(P \vee R) \cdot S$
   3. $\sim (R \vee L)$ / Q

⭐ [45] 1. $P \supset Q$
    2. $Q \supset \sim (R \vee P)$
    3. $\sim S \supset Q$
    4. $S \supset (M \supset L)$
    5. R
    6. $M \vee P$ / L

[46] 1. $\sim S \supset (N \supset T)$
   2. $\sim S \cdot (R \supset S)$
   3. $(\sim M \cdot \sim N) \supset (\sim O \vee \sim P)$
   4. $(Q \vee \sim R) \supset \sim M$
   5. $(\sim R \cdot \sim S) \supset (\sim \sim O \cdot \sim T)$ / $\sim P$

[47] 1. $\sim A \cdot \sim B$
   2. $\sim D \supset A$
   3. $M \supset [(N \vee O) \supset P]$
   4. $Q \supset (S \vee T)$
   5. $(\sim Q \vee \sim R) \supset (M \cdot N)$
   6. $\sim D \vee \sim (S \vee T)$ / $P \cdot \sim B$

[48] 1. $(\sim Q \vee \sim S) \supset T$
   2. $(M \vee N) \supset [(O \vee P) \supset (\sim Q \cdot R)]$ / $M \supset (O \supset T)$

⭐ [49] 1. $\sim (S \supset Q)$
    2. $(M \cdot N) \supset (O \vee P)$
    3. $\sim [O \vee (N \cdot P)]$
    4. $N \equiv \sim (Q \cdot R)$ / $\sim (M \vee Q)$

[50] 1. $\sim (R \vee S)$
   2. $\sim (M \cdot N) \vee \sim (O \cdot P)$
   3. $\sim (O \cdot M) \supset S$
   4. $(Q \cdot R) \equiv \sim P$ / $\sim (N \cdot T)$

V. First, translate the following arguments into symbolic form. Second, use the implication rules and the replacement rules to derive the conclusion of each. Letters for the simple statements are provided in parentheses and can be used in the order given.

  1. Science will eventually come to an end. If science comes to an end and metaphysical speculation runs rampant, then intellectual progress will end. However, it is not the case that either intellectual progress will end or we stop seeking epistemological answers. Therefore, metaphysical speculation will not run rampant. (S, M, I, E)

Answer:
    1. S
    2. $(S \cdot M) \supset I$
    3. $\sim (I \vee E)$ / $\sim M$

4.	$\sim I \cdot \sim E$	3, DM
5.	$\sim I$	4, Simp
6.	$\sim (S \cdot M)$	2, 5, MT
7.	$\sim S \vee \sim M$	6, DM
8.	$\sim \sim S$	1, DN
9.	$\sim M$	7, 8, DS

2. Either dolphins or chimpanzees are sentient beings. If chimpanzees can solve complex problems, then chimpanzees are sentient beings. If dolphins can learn a language, then dolphins are sentient beings. Chimpanzees can solve complex problems, and dolphins can learn a language. So, we must conclude that both chimpanzees and dolphins are sentient beings. (D, C, S, L)

3. If sports continue to dominate our culture, then it is not the case that either we will mature as a society or we will lose touch with reality. We will mature as a society, or we will both decline as a world power and we will we lose touch with reality. Therefore, sports will not continue to dominate our culture. (S, M, L, D)

4. If people know how to read and they are interested in the history of ideas, then they will discover new truths. If people do not know how to read, then they cannot access the wisdom of thousands of years. But people can access the wisdom of thousands of years. Thus, if they are interested in the history of ideas, then they will discover new truths. (R, H, D, W)

⭐ 5. That movie will not win the Academy Award for best picture. Therefore, if the governor of our state is not impeached, then that movie will not win the Academy Award for best picture. (M, G)

6. If the world's population continues to grow, then if birth control measures are made available in every country, then the world's population will not continue to grow. Hence, if the world's population continues to grow, then birth control measures are not made available in every country. (P, B)

7. Either my roommate did not pay his phone bill or he did not pay this month's rent, or else he got a part-time job. If it is not the case that my roommate pays his phone bill and he pays this month's rent, then he moves out. But he did not move out. It follows that he got a part-time job. (P, R, J, M)

8. Either it is not the case that if the thief entered through the basement door, then she picked the lock, or else the door was not locked. If the thief entered through the basement door, then she picked the lock, if and only if the door was locked. This suggests that it is not the case that if the thief entered through the basement door, then she picked the lock. (B, P, L)

⭐ 9. If there is a raging fire in the attic, then there is a constant supply of oxygen to the room. If there is a raging fire in the attic, then a window must have been left open. If there is a raging fire in the attic, then a window must have been left open and there is a constant supply of oxygen to the room. (F, O, W)

10. Either we do not get a new furnace or else we repair the roof or we spend the money to overhaul the car's engine. If we sell the house, then it is not the case that if we do get a new furnace, then we repair the roof. However, we did not spend the money to overhaul the car's engine. Therefore, we did not sell the house. (*F, R, C, S*)

11. If all languages have a common origin, then there are grammatical similarities among languages and common root words among all languages. If there are grammatical similarities among languages, then if there are some distinct dialects, then there are not common root words among all languages. This implies that if all languages have a common origin, then there are not some distinct dialects. (*O, G, R, D*)

12. Either the administration does not cut the budget for social services or the administration reduces the defense budget. If the administration does cut the budget for social services, then it lowers the tax rate. Thus, if the administration does cut the budget for social services, then it lowers the tax rate and it reduces the defense budget. (*S, D, T*)

★ 13. It is not the case that either humans are always healthy or humans stay young forever. If humans are immortal, then it is not the case that either humans do not stay young forever or humans are always healthy. We can conclude that humans are not immortal. (*H, Y, I*)

14. If you get malaria, then you can get very sick and you can die. Therefore, if you get malaria, then you can die. (*M, S, D*)

15. It is not the case that either witchcraft is real or astrology is considered a science. If the majority of people are not superstitious or they believe things without evidence, then astrology is considered a science. It follows that people are superstitious. (*W, A, S, E*)

G. CONDITIONAL PROOF

The proof procedure we have been using is capable of handling most valid arguments. However, some arguments have conclusions that can be derived only by a *conditional proof*. **Conditional proof** is a strategic method that starts by assuming the antecedent of a conditional statement on a separate line and then proceeds to derive the consequent on a separate line.

This method is used in conjunction with the rules of inference. Consider this example:

> 1. Q
> 2. $P \supset (Q \supset R)$ $\quad$ / $P \supset R$

Notice that the conclusion is a conditional statement. The conditional proof procedure is displayed in a special way to distinguish its role in a natural deduction proof. The first step is to assume the antecedent of the conclusion:

Conditional proof A method that starts by assuming the antecedent of a conditional statement on a separate line and then proceeds to validly derive the consequent on a separate line.

1. Q
2. $P \supset (Q \supset R)$ / $P \supset R$
     3. P *Assumption (CP)*

Note that line 3 is indented. It is shown this way because it was *not* derived from any other line—it was *not validly deduced*. On the contrary, we are *assuming* the truth of line 3. This is also why this line is justified as *Assumption (CP)*. All of our proofs to this point have contained lines that were either given premises or statements derived from previous lines, which, in turn, were justified by the implication rules or replacement rules. This procedure and requirement ensured that each line in a derived proof is a valid argument. However, in the foregoing example, line 3 has not been proven. It is therefore an *assumption* on our part, and is justified as such.

We now have the opportunity to explore the consequences of our assumption. We can ask, "If *P*, then what follows?" At this point, we are free to use the implication rules and the replacement rules, as long as we acknowledge that any derivations that rely on line 3 are the result of the assumption. Therefore, we will have to keep indenting any lines that rely on line 3. The next steps in the proof are as follows:

1. Q
2. $P \supset (Q \supset R)$ / $P \supset R$
     3. P *Assumption (CP)*
     4. $Q \supset R$ 2, 3, MP
     5. R 1, 4, MP

At this point, we have all the necessary ingredients to complete our proof. We started out by assuming *P* (the antecedent of the conclusion) and from this we derived *R* (the consequent of the conclusion). The next line in the proof combines these results.

1. Q
2. $P \supset (Q \supset R)$ / $P \supset R$
     3. P *Assumption (CP)*
     4. $Q \supset R$ 2, 3, MP
     5. R 1, 4, MP
6. $P \supset R$ 3–5, CP

Our proof is now complete. Line 6 is a *conditional statement* and it has been derived by a sequence of steps from line 3 through line 5. Note the difference in notation for the lines of the proof. Whereas line 4 uses a *comma*, line 6 uses a *dash*. The dash indicates that the *entire CP sequence* was used to derive the step.

Line 6 ends the conditional proof sequence, and the result is *discharged*, meaning that it no longer needs to be indented. The conditional proof sequence starts with an assumption, and the final result of the *CP* sequence is a conditional statement. This is why line 6 must be justified by listing the entire sequence. What the proof shows is that the conclusion can be validly derived from the original premises.

Conditional proof can be used in a variety of ways. For example, it is possible to have a conditional proof *within* another conditional proof. The following example illustrates this point.

1. $\sim P \supset Q$
2. $\sim R \vee [\sim P \supset (\sim Q \vee \sim U)]$ $/ R \supset (U \supset P)$

The antecedent of the main operator in the conclusion is R. We can start a *CP* by assuming R. In fact, the second premise is a disjunction that has $\sim R$ as the first disjunct. However, if we use material implication (Impl) on the second premise, then we can derive another conditional with R as the antecedent.

Now, if we start the *CP*, and somewhere within the indented lines we use material implication on premise 2, we cannot use that result outside the *CP*. *Since every line in a CP sequence is based on an assumption, it is not valid outside that assumption.* Therefore, as a general strategy when using *CP*, look to see if you need to use the implication rules and the replacement rules on the given premises before you start the *CP* sequence. This strategy is illustrated by line 3 in the following display. Line 4 starts the *CP* sequence:

1. $\sim P \supset Q$
2. $\sim R \vee [\sim P \supset (\sim Q \vee \sim U)]$ $/ R \supset (U \supset P)$
3. $R \supset [\sim P \supset (\sim Q \vee \sim U)]$ 2, Impl
    4. R Assumption (CP)
    5. $\sim P \supset (\sim Q \vee \sim U)$ 3, 4, MP

At this point, we need to survey what we have and where we are going. The conclusion is a conditional statement. The antecedent is R, but the consequent happens to be a conditional statement as well. Line 4 provides the antecedent of the conclusion. Several options are available. We can try a second use of *CP*. This gives us two further choices: We can start by assuming either U or $\sim P$. Let's think ahead a few steps. If we start with U, then we will probably have to add Q somewhere along the line in order to isolate P. However, if we start with $\sim P$, then we can immediately get $\sim Q \vee \sim U$ from line 5. Perhaps transposition (Trans) can then come into play. Let's try $\sim P$ and see how far we can get:

1. $\sim P \supset Q$
2. $\sim R \vee [\sim P \supset (\sim Q \vee \sim U)]$ $/ R \supset (U \supset P)$
3. $R \supset [\sim P \supset (\sim Q \vee \sim U)]$ 2, Impl
    4. R Assumption (CP)
    5. $\sim P \supset (\sim Q \vee \sim U)$ 3, 4, MP
        6. $\sim P$ Assumption (CP)
        7. $\sim Q \vee \sim U$ 5, 6, MP
        8. Q 1, 6, MP
        9. $\sim \sim Q$ 8, DN
        10. $\sim U$ 7, 9, DS

We are getting close to the consequent of the conclusion, so we can now discharge the second assumption:

1. $\sim P \supset Q$
2. $\sim R \vee [\sim P \supset (\sim Q \vee \sim U)]$ / $R \supset (U \supset P)$
3. $R \supset [\sim P \supset (\sim Q \vee \sim U)]$ 2, Impl
   > 4. R *Assumption (CP)*
   > 5. $\sim P \supset (\sim Q \vee \sim U)$ 3, 4, MP
   >> 6. $\sim P$ *Assumption (CP)*
   >> 7. $\sim Q \vee \sim U$ 5, 6, MP
   >> 8. Q 1, 6, MP
   >> 9. $\sim \sim Q$ 8, DN
   >> 10. $\sim U$ 7, 9, DS
   > 11. $\sim P \supset \sim U$ 6–10, CP

Using transposition (Trans) on line 11 gives the desired consequent and makes it possible to complete the proof.

1. $\sim P \supset Q$
2. $\sim R \vee [\sim P \supset (\sim Q \vee \sim U)]$ / $R \supset (U \supset P)$
3. $R \supset [\sim P \supset (\sim Q \vee \sim U)]$ 2, Impl
   > 4. R *Assumption (CP)*
   > 5. $\sim P \supset (\sim Q \vee \sim U)$ 3, 4, MP
   >> 6. $\sim P$ *Assumption (CP)*
   >> 7. $\sim Q \vee \sim U$ 5, 6, MP
   >> 8. Q 1, 6, MP
   >> 9. $\sim \sim Q$ 8, DN
   >> 10. $\sim U$ 7, 9, DS
   > 11. $\sim P \supset \sim U$ 6–10, CP
   > 12. $U \supset P$ 11, Trans
13. $R \supset (U \supset P)$ 4–12, CP

Line 4 started one conditional proof sequence. But before it was completed, another conditional proof sequence began with line 6. Note that *both* lines have been justified: *Assumption (CP)*.

In addition to showing an assumption, the use of indentation with conditional proofs lets us know that no line within the *CP* sequence can be used outside the sequence. This means that you cannot use any line within the sequence 6–10 after line 11. Also, if the proof were longer, you could not use any line within the sequence 4–12 after line 13. This requirement should make sense, if we think about what *CP* does. Since every line in a *CP* sequence is based on an assumption, the lines are not valid outside that assumption. This is why every *CP* sequence must end with a conditional statement. Once the *CP* is completed, we can use the discharged conditional statement, because its validity is based on a series of steps that have been carefully contained within the rules of the natural deduction proof procedure. (Of course, you can discharge more than one line from a *CP* sequence. For example, line 11, $\sim P \supset \sim U$, was discharged and justified as 6–10, CP. If needed in a proof, we could have also discharged a new line; for example, $\sim P \supset Q$ would be justified as 6-8, CP.)

Another way to use conditional proof is to have more than one *CP* sequence within a proof, but with each sequence separate, as in the following example:

1. $(\sim R \lor \sim Q) \cdot (R \lor P)$
2. $P \supset \sim S$
3. $Q \lor S$ $/ P \equiv Q$

If we apply material equivalence, then we can see that the conclusion is logically equivalent to $(P \supset Q) \cdot (Q \supset P)$. Since the conclusion is the *conjunction* of two *conditionals*, we might try assuming the antecedent of each one to see what we can derive. Of course, before we start *CP*, we should consider whether the given premises could offer us any interesting results.

We can start the proof as follows:

1. $(\sim R \lor \sim Q) \cdot (R \lor P)$
2. $P \supset \sim S$
3. $Q \lor S$ $/ P \equiv Q$
4. $\sim R \lor \sim Q$ 1, Simp
5. $(R \lor P) \cdot (\sim R \lor \sim Q)$ 1, Com
6. $R \lor P$ 5, Simp
7. P Assumption (CP)
8. $\sim S$ 2, 7, MP
9. $S \lor Q$ 3, Com
10. Q 8, 9, DS
11. $P \supset Q$ 7–10, CP

At this point in our proof we have deduced the first part of the conjunction: $(P \supset Q) \cdot (Q \supset P)$. We now need to derive the second part.

1. $(\sim R \lor \sim Q) \cdot (R \lor P)$
2. $P \supset \sim S$
3. $Q \lor S$ $/ P \equiv Q$
4. $\sim R \lor \sim Q$ 1, Simp
5. $(R \lor P) \cdot (\sim R \lor \sim Q)$ 1, Com
6. $R \lor P$ 5, Simp
7. P Assumption (CP)
8. $\sim S$ 2, 7, MP
9. $S \lor Q$ 3, Com
10. Q 8, 9, DS
11. $P \supset Q$ 7–10, CP
12. Q Assumption (CP)
13. $\sim \sim Q$ 12, DN
14. $\sim Q \lor \sim R$ 4, Com
15. $\sim R$ 13, 14 DS
16. P 6, 15 DS
17. $Q \supset P$ 12–16, CP
18. $(P \supset Q) \cdot (Q \supset P)$ 11, 17, Conj
19. $P \equiv Q$ 18, Equiv

As before, we must ensure that any individual line within the two *CP* sequences (7–10, and 12–16) are not used anywhere outside of the *CP* sequences. In addition, each discharged step (line 11 and line 17) is correctly formulated to be the result of a CP sequence, namely, a conditional statement.

CHECK YOUR UNDERSTANDING 8G

I. Apply conditional proof (CP) to the following arguments. Use the implication rules and the replacement rules.

[1] 1. $P \supset Q$ $/ P \supset (S \supset Q)$

Answer:

    1. $P \supset Q$ $/ P \supset (S \supset Q)$
      2. P Assumption (CP)
      3. Q 1, 2, MP
      4. $Q \vee \sim S$ 3, Add
      5. $\sim S \vee Q$ 4, Com
      6. $S \supset Q$ 5, Impl
    7. $P \supset (S \supset Q)$ 2–6, CP

[2] 1. $U \supset \sim Q$ $/ (P \cdot R) \supset \sim (U \cdot Q)$

[3] 1. $P \vee Q$
    2. $R \supset \sim Q$ $/ R \supset P$

[4] 1. $R \supset \sim S$
    2. $(\sim S \vee P) \supset \sim Q$ $/ R \supset \sim Q$

⭐ [5] 1. $(P \cdot Q) \supset S$
    2. $P \supset Q$ $/ P \supset S$

[6] 1. $P \supset (\sim Q \cdot \sim R)$ $/ \sim P \vee \sim R$

[7] 1. $P \supset Q$
    2. $P \supset R$ $/ P \supset [(Q \cdot R) \vee \sim S]$

[8] 1. $\sim P$
    2. $(Q \vee R) \supset S$
    3. $L \supset (\sim P \supset \sim S)$ $/ L \supset \sim (Q \vee R)$

⭐ [9] 1. $P \supset (Q \cdot R)$
    2. $S \supset (Q \cdot T)$ $/ (S \vee P) \supset Q$

[10] 1. Q
    2. $P \supset [\sim Q \vee (R \supset S)]$ $/ (P \cdot R) \supset S$

[11] 1. $\sim P$
    2. $Q \supset R$
    3. $R \supset S$ $/ Q \supset (S \cdot \sim P)$

[12] 1. $(P \lor Q) \supset S$ $/ \sim S \supset [(R \lor \sim P) \cdot (R \lor \sim Q)]$

★ [13] 1. $[(P \lor Q) \lor R] \supset (S \lor L)$
     2. $(S \lor L) \supset (M \lor K)$ $/ Q \supset (M \lor K)$

[14] 1. $P \supset (Q \cdot R)$ $/ (S \supset P) \supset (S \supset R)$

[15] 1. $(P \lor Q) \supset R$
     2. $L \supset (S \cdot P)$ $/ L \supset R$

[16] 1. $(P \cdot Q) \lor (R \cdot S)$
     2. $R \supset L$ $/ \sim P \supset L$

★ [17] 1. $Q \supset \sim P$
     2. $\sim P \lor (Q \lor R)$ $/ P \supset (R \lor \sim S)$

[18] 1. P
     2. $(P \lor P) \supset [Q \supset \sim (R \lor S)]$ $/ Q \supset \sim S$

[19] 1. $(P \lor \sim Q) \lor R$
     2. $\sim Q \supset \sim S$ $/ \sim R \supset (S \supset P)$

[20] 1. $\sim P$
     2. $Q \supset (R \supset P)$
     3. $\sim R \supset (S \lor P)$ $/ Q \supset S$

★ [21] 1. $[(A \cdot B) \cdot C] \supset D$ $/ A \supset [B \supset (C \supset D)]$

[22] 1. $(P \lor Q) \supset R$
     2. $S \supset (P \cdot K)$ $/ \sim R \supset \sim S$

[23] 1. $P \supset (Q \lor R)$
     2. $\sim Q \supset (R \supset \sim P)$ $/ P \supset (P \supset Q)$

[24] 1. $P \supset Q$ $/ \sim (Q \lor S) \supset \sim P$

★ [25] 1. $(P \lor Q) \supset (R \cdot S)$
     2. $(R \lor \sim L) \supset [M \cdot (K \lor N)]$ $/ P \supset [R \cdot (K \lor N)]$

[26] 1. $\sim (P \cdot \sim Q)$
     2. $\sim P \supset \sim R$
     3. $(R \cdot Q) \supset S$ $/ R \supset S$

[27] 1. P
     2. $Q \cdot R$
     3. $S \supset [\sim R \lor (P \supset \sim L)]$ $/ S \supset \sim L$

[28] 1. $P \supset (Q \cdot R)$
     2. $S \supset (\sim Q \cdot R)$ $/ P \supset \sim S$

★ [29] 1. $R \supset \sim U$
     2. $P \supset (Q \lor R)$
     3. $(Q \supset S) \cdot (S \supset T)$ $/ P \supset (\sim U \lor T)$

[30] 1. $\sim P \supset Q$
2. $\sim (Q \cdot \sim S)$
3. $R \supset (P \supset S)$ $/ R \supset S$

[31] 1. $\sim P \vee (Q \supset R)$
2. P
3. $\sim Q \supset S$ $/ \sim S \supset R$

[32] 1. $D \supset E$
2. $E \supset F$
3. $A \supset [C \vee (D \cdot \sim B)]$ $/ A \supset (C \vee F)$

[33] 1. $P \supset Q$
2. $(P \cdot Q) \equiv S$ $/ P \equiv S$

[34] 1. $P \cdot Q$
2. $P \supset \sim (R \cdot S)$
3. $Q \supset (R \vee S)$ $/ R \equiv \sim S$

[35] 1. $\sim P \supset (R \supset \sim T)$
2. $U \supset (\sim Q \supset \sim R)$
3. $\sim Q \cdot T$ $/ \sim R \vee (\sim U \cdot P)$

II. First, translate the following arguments into symbolic form. Second, use the implication rules, the replacement rules, and conditional proof to derive the conclusion of each. Letters for the simple statements are provided in parentheses and can be used in the order given.

1. If you travel to other countries, then you can learn another language. In addition, if you travel to other countries, then you can test your ability to adapt. So if you travel to other countries, then you can test your ability to adapt and you can learn another language. (C, L, A)

Answer:

[1] 1. $C \supset L$
2. $C \supset A$ $/ C \supset (A \cdot L)$
> 3. C Assumption (CP)
> 4. A 2, 3, MP
> 5. L 1, 3, MP
> 6. $A \cdot L$ 4, 5, Conj
7. $C \supset (A \cdot L)$ 3–6, CP

2. If animals are conscious, then they are self-aware and they can feel pain. If animals can feel pain and they are conscious, then they have certain rights. It follows that if animals are conscious, then they have certain rights. (C, S, P, R)

3. If call center representatives are rude, then they are not trained correctly. If call center representatives are rude, then if they are not trained correctly, then customers have a right to complain. So, if call center representatives are rude, then customers have a right to complain. (R, T, C)

4. If either your credit card information is stolen or your e-mail is hacked, then identity theft can occur. If either legal issues arise or monetary loses occur, then you are a victim of fraud and your credit card information is stolen. If legal issues arise, then identity theft can occur. (*C, E, I, L, M, F*)

★ 5. If a movie has a low budget, then it can still win the Academy Award for best picture. If a movie stars an unknown actor, then if the producer is just starting out in show business, then a movie has a low budget. Therefore, if a movie stars an unknown actor, then if the producer is just starting out in show business, then it can still win the Academy Award for best picture. (*L, A, U, P*)

H. INDIRECT PROOF

Indirect proof can be used to derive either the conclusion of an argument or an intermediate line in a proof sequence. The technique starts by assuming the *negation* of the statement to be derived, and then deriving a contradiction on a subsequent line. The indirect proof sequence is then discharged by negating the *assumed* statement. The reasoning behind the procedure is straightforward: If in the context of a proof the negation of a statement leads to an absurdity—a *contradiction*—then we have *indirectly* established the truth of the original statement. (That is why the procedure is sometimes called *reductio ad absurdum*, which means reduction to the absurd.)

This procedure also needs to be displayed in a special way to distinguish its role in a natural deduction proof. The display is similar to that of conditional proof, in that the indirect proof sequence starts with an assumption. The following illustrates this method of indirect proof:

> **Indirect proof** A method that starts by assuming the negation of the required statement and then validly deriving a contradiction on a subsequent line.

```
1. ~ M ⊃ ~ N
2. (~ L · ~ M) ⊃ N          / L ∨ M
    3. ~ (L ∨ M)            Assumption (IP)
    4. ~ L · ~ M            3, DM
    5. N                    2, 4, MP
    6. ~ M · ~ L            4, Com
    7. ~ M                  6, Simp
    8. ~ N                  1, 7, MP
    9. N · ~ N              5, 8, Conj
10. ~ ~ (L ∨ M)            3–9, IP
11. L ∨ M                  10, DN
```

Line 3 begins the sequence; it is indented and justified as *Assumption (IP)*. Line 9 displays the goal of all *IP* sequences, which is to *derive a contradiction*. Line 10 discharges the *IP* sequence by negating the assumption that started the sequence: line 3. The final result is the statement that we wished to prove. As with *CP*, we cannot use any line within an *IP* sequence outside that sequence as part of our overall proof.

Here is another example of how indirect proof can be used:

```
 1. D ⊃ C
 2. A v (B · C)
 3. A ⊃ D                          / C
        4. ~ C                     Assumption (IP)
        5. ~ D                     1, 4, MT
        6. ~ A                     3, 5, MT
        7. B · C                   2, 6, DS
        8. C · B                   7, Com
        9. C                       8, Simp
       10. ~ C · C                 4, 9, Conj
11. ~ ~ C                          4–10, IP
12. C                              11, DN
```

Line 4 begins the indirect proof sequence; it is indented and justified as *Assumption (IP)*. Line 10 is the contradiction derived in the *IP* sequence. Line 11 discharges the *IP* sequence by negating the assumption that started the sequence: line 4.

The methods of indirect proof and conditional proof can *both* be used in a proof. Here is an example:

```
 1. ~ (P · ~ Q) v (P ⊃ R)          / P ⊃ (Q v R)
     2. P                          Assumption (CP)
          3. ~ (Q v R)             Assumption (IP)
          4. ~ Q · ~ R             3, DM
          5. ~ Q                   4, Simp
          6. P · ~ Q               2, 5, Conj
          7. ~ ~ (P · ~ Q)         6, DN
          8. P ⊃ R                 1, 7, DS
          9. R                     2, 8, MP
         10. ~ R · ~ Q             4, Com
         11. ~ R                   10, Simp
         12. R · ~ R               9, 11, Conj
     13. ~ ~ (Q v R)               3–12, IP
     14. (Q v R)                   13, DN
15. P ⊃ (Q v R)                    2–14, CP
```

Line 2 started a *CP* sequence by assuming the antecedent of the conclusion. This meant that if we were able to derive the consequent of conditional in the conclusion, then we could discharge the *CP*. At that point in the proof, an indirect proof sequence was started by negating the consequent in the conclusion. The overall strategy was to try to derive a contradiction; this would establish the truth of the original statement. Once this was accomplished, the *IP* sequence was discharged. The final step of the proof discharged the *CP* sequence. As the proof illustrates, each sequence of *IP* and *CP* has been correctly discharged, and no line within either sequence has been used outside that sequence. The proof shows that the conclusion follows from the premises.

CHECK YOUR UNDERSTANDING 8H

I. Apply indirect proof to the following arguments. Use the implication rules and the replacement rules. You can also use conditional proof, if needed.

[1] 1. $P \supset \sim (P \vee Q)$ / $\sim P$

Answer:

    1. $P \supset \sim (P \vee Q)$ / $\sim P$
      2. P *Assumption (IP)*
      3. $\sim (P \vee Q)$ 1, 2, MP
      4. $\sim P \cdot \sim Q$ 3, DM
      5. $\sim P$ 4, Simp
      6. $P \cdot \sim P$ 2, 5, Conj
    7. $\sim P$ 2–6, IP

[2] P / $Q \vee \sim Q$

[3] 1. $P \supset (Q \cdot S)$
    2. $\sim S$ / $\sim P$

[4] 1. $P \supset Q$
    2. $R \supset P$
    3. $\sim Q$ / $\sim R$

⭐ [5] 1. $\sim Q \vee P$
    2. $\sim (P \vee S)$ / $\sim Q$

[6] 1. $(Q \supset Q) \supset S$ / S

[7] 1. $P \vee (\sim P \supset Q)$
    2. $\sim Q$ / P

[8] 1. $P \supset Q$
    2. $P \vee (Q \cdot S)$ / Q

⭐ [9] 1. $[P \supset (Q \cdot R)] \cdot (S \supset L)$
    2. S / L

[10] 1. $(P \vee \sim P) \supset \sim Q$
    2. $R \supset Q$ / $\sim R$

[11] 1. $(R \vee S) \supset (\sim P \cdot \sim Q)$
    2. P / $\sim R$

[12] 1. $R \vee S$
    2. $Q \supset \sim R$
    3. $P \supset Q$
    4. $\sim S$ / $\sim P$

⭐ [13] 1. $\sim P \supset \sim (Q \vee \sim P)$ / P

[14] 1. $P \vee (Q \cdot P)$
    2. $P \supset R$ / R

[15] 1. $S \supset \sim (\sim Q \lor P)$
      2. $Q \equiv P$ $/ \sim S$

[16] 1. $P \lor Q$
      2. $(S \lor Q) \supset P$ $/ P$

⭐ [17] 1. $\sim P \cdot \sim T$
        2. $\sim (P \cdot \sim Q) \supset R$ $/ R \lor T$

[18] 1. $P \lor \sim (Q \cdot S)$ $/ Q \supset (S \supset P)$

[19] 1. $Q \supset \sim R$
      2. $P \lor Q$
      3. $\sim P \supset (Q \supset R)$ $/ P$

[20] 1. $(\sim Q \supset \sim S) \cdot (\sim S \supset S)$ $/ Q$

⭐ [21] 1. $P \supset (\sim P \equiv \sim Q)$
        2. $\sim P \lor \sim Q$ $/ \sim P$

[22] 1. $A \supset B$
      2. $A \supset C$
      3. $\sim B \lor \sim C$ $/ \sim A$

[23] 1. $(P \lor Q) \supset (L \cdot \sim M)$
      2. $\sim L \lor M$ $/ \sim (P \cdot K)$

[24] 1. $\sim P \supset Q$
      2. $\sim R \supset (\sim P \cdot \sim S)$
      3. $\sim S \supset \sim Q$ $/ R$

⭐ [25] 1. $P \supset Q$
        2. $(R \cdot S) \lor L$
        3. $L \supset \sim Q$ $/ (\sim S \lor \sim R) \supset \sim P$

[26] 1. $(P \lor Q) \supset R$
      2. $\sim S \supset (Q \lor R)$
      3. $\sim R$ $/ S$

[27] 1. $(\sim D \lor E) \supset (A \cdot C)$
      2. $(A \lor B) \supset (C \supset D)$ $/ D$

[28] 1. $(P \equiv \sim Q) \equiv R$
      2. $(P \lor S) \supset (R \cdot \sim Q)$
      3. $P \equiv \sim S$
      4. $R \supset \sim P$ $/ \sim P$

⭐ [29] 1. $P \supset Q$
        2. $\sim R \supset (P \cdot S)$
        3. $S \supset \sim Q$ $/ R$

[30] 1. $(P \cdot Q) \lor (R \cdot S)$ $/ Q \lor S$

[31] 1. $\sim P \supset \sim (Q \supset P)$
  2. $\sim R \supset (\sim P \supset \sim Q)$ $/ R \vee P$

[32] 1. $P \supset Q$ $/ Q \supset [P \supset (P \cdot Q)]$

★ [33] 1. $(P \supset Q) \supset \sim (S \supset R)$
   2. $\sim (P \vee T)$ $/ S$

[34] 1. $P \supset (Q \cdot S)$
  2. $Q \supset (R \vee \sim S)$
  3. $P \vee (Q \supset R)$ $/ Q \supset R$

[35] 1. $G \supset (E \cdot F)$
  2. $A \supset B$
  3. $A \vee G$
  4. $(B \vee C) \supset D$ $/ D \vee E$

II. First, translate the following arguments into symbolic form. Second, use the implication rules, the replacement rules, and indirect proof to derive the conclusion of each. Letters for the simple statements are provided in parentheses and can be used in the order given.

1. My car is not fuel-efficient and it is not reliable. Consequently, my car is fuel-efficient if and only if it is reliable. (*F, R*)

Answer:

[1] 1. $\sim F \cdot \sim R$ $/ F \equiv R$
  2. $\sim (F \equiv R)$ Assumption (IP)
  3. $\sim [(F \cdot R) \vee (\sim F \cdot \sim R)]$ 2, Equiv
  4. $\sim (F \cdot R) \cdot \sim (\sim F \cdot \sim R)$ 3, DM
  5. $\sim (\sim F \cdot \sim R) \cdot \sim (F \cdot R)$ 4, Com
  6. $\sim (\sim F \cdot \sim R)$ 5, Simp
  7. $(\sim F \cdot \sim R) \cdot \sim (\sim F \cdot \sim R)$ 1, 6, Conj
  8. $\sim \sim (F \equiv R)$ 2–7, IP
  9. $F \equiv R$ 8, DN

2. If she finished her term paper on time, then she does not have to work on it over spring break. Either she does have to work on it over spring break or she did not finish her term paper on time and she gets a lower grade. Therefore, she did not finish her term paper on time. (*F, S, L*)

3. If the murder happened in the hotel room, then there are bloodstains somewhere in the room. It follows that it is not the case that the murder happened in the hotel room and there are not bloodstains somewhere in the room. (*M, B*)

4. If criminals are not put on trial, then they are likely to commit worse crimes. If criminals are put on trial and they are acquitted, then they are likely to commit worse crimes. Since criminals are acquitted, we can conclude that criminals are likely to commit worse crimes. (*T, W, A*)

★ 5. It is not the case that Sam did not get the job offer and he is still working at the factory. If Sam did not get the job offer, then he is still working at the factory. We can infer that Sam did get the job offer. (*J, F*)

Summary

- Natural deduction: A proof procedure by which the conclusion of an argument is validly derived from the premises through the use of rules of inference.
- There are two types of rules of inference: implication rules and replacement rules. The function of rules of inference is to justify the steps of a proof.
- Proof: A sequence of steps in which each step is either a premise or follows from earlier steps in the sequence according to the rules of inference.
- Implication rules are valid argument forms. They are validly applied only to an entire line.
- Tactics: The use of small-scale maneuvers or devices.
- Strategy: Typically understood as referring to a greater, overall goal.
- Principle of replacement: Logically equivalent expressions may replace each other within the context of a proof.
- Replacement rules: Pairs of logically equivalent statement forms.
- Conditional proof (CP): A method that starts by assuming the antecedent of a conditional statement on a separate line and then proceeds to validly derive the consequent on a separate line.
- When the result of a conditional proof sequence is discharged it no longer needs to be indented.
- Indirect proof (IP): A method that starts by assuming the negation of the required statement and then validly deriving a contradiction on a subsequent line.

KEY TERMS

natural deduction 355	justification 361	commutation 387
rules of inference 355	tactics 368	association 388
proof 355	strategy 368	distribution 389
implication rules 355	constructive	double negation 391
replacement rules 355	dilemma 374	transposition 399
modus ponens 357	simplification 375	material implication 399
modus tollens 357	conjunction 375	material equivalence 400
hypothetical	addition 376	exportation 401
syllogism 359	principle of	tautology 402
disjunctive	replacement 385	conditional proof 413
syllogism 360	De Morgan 386	indirect proof 421

LOGIC CHALLENGE: THE TRUTH

Three of your friends, Wayne, Eric, and Will, want to know what you have learned in your logic class, so you think of a demonstration. You will leave the room and they are to choose among themselves whether to be a *truth-teller* or a *liar*. Every statement a truth-teller makes is *true*, and every statement a liar makes is *false*. You leave the room and then after a short while return. You then ask Wayne this question: "Are you a truth-teller or a liar?" Before he answers, you tell him that he is to whisper the answer to Eric. After hearing the answer, Eric announces this: "Wayne said that he is a truth-teller. He is indeed a truth-teller, and so am I." Upon hearing this, Will says the following: "Don't believe Eric, he is a liar. I am a truth-teller."

Use your reasoning abilities to determine who is a truth-teller and who is a liar.

Chapter 9
Predicate Logic

In the course of a semester like this one, you encounter a dizzying number of new faces and things to learn. You are still probably trying to sort them out. To help, it is only natural to ask what the members of a group share. What are their common characteristics—or do the members of a group instead display significant differences? The results can be humorous:

> Dogs come when they're called. Cats take a message and get back to you.
>
> Mary Bly, quoted in *Boundaries—Where You End and I Begin* by Anne Katherine

Or our statement can be serious indeed:

> Great minds discuss ideas; average minds discuss events; small minds discuss people.

When statements like these are strung together, they sometimes form an argument. This chapter introduces a new tool for analyzing complex arguments, the symbolic system called *predicate logic.*

We have examined many types of statements and arguments. For example, categorical logic analyzes arguments using Venn diagrams and rules. The basic components of categorical syllogisms are *terms*, and validity is determined by arrangement of the terms within an argument. For example:

> All computers are inorganic objects. Some computers are conscious beings. Therefore, some inorganic objects are conscious beings.

On the other hand, propositional logic analyzes arguments using truth tables and natural deduction. The basic components are *statements*, and validity is determined by arrangement of the statements within an argument. Here is an example:

> If toxic waste is not properly secured, then it poses a health hazard. Nuclear power plants and petroleum refineries produce toxic waste. Nuclear power

plants and petroleum refineries do not always properly secure their toxic waste. Therefore, nuclear power plants and petroleum refineries pose health hazards.

In this chapter, we take one more step. Many arguments combine the distinctive features of both categorical *and* propositional logic. For example:

A person can be elected to the U.S. Senate if and only if that person is at least 30 years of age and is a U.S. citizen. Barbara Boxer is a U.S. senator from California. Therefore, Barbara Boxer is at least 30 years of age and is a U.S. citizen.

The validity of these arguments cannot easily be determined by the individual methods of categorical or propositional logic. A new method of proof is needed. As we saw earlier, George Boole began connecting some features of categorical logic with features of propositional logic. A key idea is the modern interpretation of universal categorical statements as conditional statements. For example, "All cheetahs are mammals" can be interpreted as follows: *For any object, if that object is a cheetah, then it is a mammal.* This kind of interpretation accomplishes two things. First, it eliminates existential import, because a conditional statement makes no existence claim. Second, it places validity nearer to the modern idea of logical form.

Gottlob Frege took the decisive step in connecting categorical logic with propositional logic in the late nineteenth century. Frege demonstrated clearly how the special features of the two logics could be combined, using quantifiers, as **predicate logic**.

Predicate logic is flexible. It enables us to analyze arguments about individuals (for example, *Socrates*), properties of individuals (*Socrates was a Greek philosopher*), and relations between individuals (*Socrates was the teacher of Plato*). Predicate logic is also capable of expressing complex and precise language in a formal manner. In fact, some of the basic principles of predicate logic are used in computer programming and mathematics. The principles have even been adapted to artificial intelligence programs. Predicate logic has advanced through rigorous analysis of symbol arrangement and through the development of special rules. Of course, the main concern is still the same as the other areas of logic—the validity of arguments.

Predicate logic
Integrates many of the features of categorical and propositional logic. It combines the symbols associated with propositional logic with special symbols that are used to translate predicates.

A. TRANSLATING ORDINARY LANGUAGE

Our study of predicate logic begins by establishing a foundation for correct translations of ordinary language statements. We start by introducing techniques for translating *singular statements*, *universal statements*, and *particular statements*. We give special attention to the meaning of ordinary language statements.

Singular Statements

You may recall that a singular statement is about a specific person, place, time, or object. We distinguish individuals from the characteristics that are asserted of them. Since *predicates* are the fundamental unit in predicate logic, uppercase letters (*A, B, C, . . . ,*

X, Y, Z), called **predicate symbols** are used. For example, in the statement "Abraham Lincoln was a lawyer," the subject is "Abraham Lincoln" and the predicate is "... was a lawyer." Here are some more examples of ordinary language predicates:

> . . . is an athlete
> . . . is a bachelor
> . . . is a Congressperson
> . . . is a state

The *subject* of a singular statement is translated using lowercase letters (*a, b, c, ..., u, v, w*). These lowercase letters, called **individual constants**, act as names of individuals. (Notice that the lowercase letters for individual constants stop at the letter *w*. That's because the lowercase letters, *x, y,* and *z* play a special role in predicate logic. That role will be explained soon.)

The system used for translating singular statements puts the capital letter first (the symbol designating the characteristic predicated), followed by a lowercase letter (the symbol denoting the individual). For example, "Abraham Lincoln was a lawyer" can be translated as *La*.

Here are some more translations:

Statement in English	Symbolic Translation
Arnold Schwarzenegger was a governor.	*Ga*
Maria Sharapova is an athlete.	*Am*
The Arctic Circle is not warm.	*~Wa*
Nevada is a desert.	*Dn*

Predicate logic offers a powerful way of capturing more ordinary language into precise statement and argument analysis. For example, the singular statement "Joe Biden is vice president of the United States" asserts that one individual person has a specific characteristic. In this statement, the subject "Joe Biden," denotes a particular individual. The predicate "... vice president of the United States," designates a specific characteristic. It is possible for the same subject and predicate to occur in a variety of singular statements. Some of these assertions will be true, and some will be false. For example, "Joe Biden is a Republican" is a false statement. The statement contains the same subject as the earlier statement, but it contains a different predicate. The statement "Tom Cruise is vice president of the United States" is false. The statement contains the same predicate as the earlier example, but it contains a different subject.

More complex statements can be translated by using the basic apparatus of propositional logic. Here are some examples:

Statement in English	Symbolic Translation
Carly is either a fashion designer or a dancer.	*Fc* v *Dc*
If Shane is an honor student, then he is bright.	*Hs* ⊃ *Bs*
Bill can get the job if and only if he is honest and loyal.	*Jb* ≡ (*Hb* · *Lb*)
John will win the contest only if he does not panic.	*Cj* ⊃ *~Pj*

Universal Statements

Universal statements either affirm or deny that every member of a subject class is a member of a predicate class. This is accomplished by translating the universal statements in the following way:

Universal Statement Form	Boolean Interpretation
All S are P.	*If anything is an S, then it is a P.*
No S are P.	*If anything is an S, then it is not a P.*

The interpretations can be translated using the horseshoe. However, we need a new symbol to capture the idea that universal statements assert something about *every member of the subject class*. That symbol is called the **universal quantifier**. This is where the three lowercase letters (*x*, *y*, and *z*) previously set aside come into play. When one of the letters is placed within parentheses—for example, (*x*)— it gets translated as "for any *x*." The three designated lowercase letters are called **individual variables**.

We can now complete the translation of the two universal statement forms:

Statement Form	Symbolic Translation	Verbal Meaning
All S are P.	$(x)(Sx \supset Px)$	*For any x, if x is an S, then x is a P.*
No S are P.	$(x)(Sx \supset \sim Px)$	*For any x, if x is an S, then x is not a P.*

Using this information, let's do a simple translation:

All humans are moral agents. $(x)(Hx \supset Mx)$

In the symbolic translation $(x)(Sx \supset Px)$, both S and P are predicates. This is illustrated by the verbal meaning. When we say, "For any *x*, if *x* is an S, then *x* is a P," the capital letters in both the antecedent and the consequent are both predicates. Here are some additional examples:

Statement in English	Symbolic Translation
No humans are moral agents.	$(x)(Hx \supset \sim Mx)$
All alcoholic drinks are depressants.	$(x)(Ax \supset Dx)$
No French fries are healthy foods.	$(x)(Fx \supset \sim Hx)$
All magazines are glossy publications.	$(x)(Mx \supset Gx)$
No millionaires are tax evaders.	$(x)(Mx \supset \sim Tx)$

Let's look at one of the examples: $(x)(Hx \supset \sim Mx)$. The variables in this statement are **bound variables**, meaning that they are governed by a quantifier. But what happens when we remove the quantifier? The result is this: $Hx \supset \sim Mx$. This is an example of a **statement function**, an expression that does not make any universal or particular assertion about anything; therefore, it has no truth value. Statement functions are simply patterns for a statement. The variables in statement functions are **free variables**, meaning that they are not governed by any quantifier.

Universal quantifier The symbol used to capture the idea that universal statements assert something about every member of the subject class.

Individual variables The three lowercase letters, *x*, *y*, and *z*.

Bound variables Variables governed by a quantifier.

Statement function An expression that does not make any universal or particular assertion about anything; therefore, it has no truth value. Statement functions are simply patterns for a statement.

Free variables Variables that are not governed by any quantifier.

The placement of a quantifier in front of an expression is important. For example, consider these two expressions:

$(x)(Rx \supset Fx)$
$(x)Rx \supset Fx$

In the first example, the quantifier governs everything in parentheses. Therefore, both variables are bound. However, in the second example, the quantifier governs only Rx, so it is a bound variable. Therefore, Fx is a free variable. There is a simple rule to follow: A quantifier governs only the expression immediately following it.

Particular Statements

Particular statements either affirm or deny that at least one member of a subject class is a member of a predicate class. If you recall from categorical logic in Chapters 5 and 6, particular statements involve existential import. Boolean translations are accomplished in the following way:

Universal Statement Form	Boolean Interpretation
Some S are P.	*At least one thing is an S and it is also a P.*
Some S are not P.	*At least one thing is an S and it is not a P.*

Notice that while the translations for universal statements are conditional statements, the translations for particular statements are conjunctions. Therefore, the symbolic translations use the dot. However, we need another new symbol to capture the idea of existence. The **existential quantifier** is formed by putting a backward E in front of a variable, and then placing them in parentheses: $(\exists x)$. This gets translated as "there exists an x such that." We combine the existential quantifier with the dot symbol to translate particular statements.

Existential quantifier
Formed by putting a backward E in front of a variable, and then placing them both in parentheses.

Statement Form	Translation	Verbal Meaning
Some S are P.	$(\exists x)(Sx \cdot Px)$	*There exists an x such that x is an S and x is a P.*
Some S are not P.	$(\exists x)(Sx \cdot \sim Px)$	*There exists an x such that x is an S and x is not a P.*

Using this information, let's do a simple translation:

Some battleships are monstrosities. $(\exists x)(Bx \cdot Mx)$

The translation can be read in the following way: Something exists that is both a battleship and a monstrosity. Here are some additional examples:

Statement in English	Symbolic Translation
Some birds are not flyers.	$(\exists x)(Bx \cdot \sim Fx)$
Some hermits are introverts.	$(\exists x)(Hx \cdot Ix)$
Some sweeteners are addictive products.	$(\exists x)(Sx \cdot Ax)$
Some divers are not fearless people.	$(\exists x)(Dx \cdot \sim Fx)$

SUMMARY OF PREDICATE LOGIC SYMBOLS	
A–Z	predicate symbols
a–w	individual constants
x, y, and z	individual variables
(x), (y), (z)	universal quantifiers
$(\exists x)$, $(\exists y)$, $(\exists z)$	existential quantifiers

Paying Attention to Meaning

Some statements in ordinary language are more complex than the statements we have been examining. For example, consider this statement:

> All thoroughbreds are either brown or gray.

The statement contains both categorical and propositional elements. To symbolize this statement requires a close examination of the statement's meaning. We can interpret the statement as expressing the following: *If anything is a thoroughbred, then either it is brown or it is gray.* If we let $T = thoroughbred$, $B = brown$, and $G = gray$, then we get this translation:

> All thoroughbreds are either brown or gray. $(x)[Tx \supset (Bx \vee Gx)]$

Here is another statement that requires careful consideration:

> Thoroughbreds and mules are quadrupeds.

Even though the word "and" appears in the statement, the statement is *not* asserting that anything is *both* a thoroughbred and a mule. Instead, the meaning of the statement is this: *If anything is either a thoroughbred or a mule, then that individual is a quadruped.* Therefore, if we let $T = thoroughbreds$, $M = mules$, $Q = quadrupeds$, we get this translation:

> Thoroughbreds and mules are quadrupeds. $(x)[(Tx \vee Mx) \supset Qx]$

Here are some more examples of translations:

1. There are plastic bags. $(\exists x)(Bx \cdot Px)$
2. There are cloth bags. $(\exists x)(Bx \cdot Cx)$
3. UFOs exist. $(\exists x)Ux$

Notice that the statement in example 3 merely asserts that a class of objects exists. Therefore, it can be translated by using one predicate and an existential quantifier.

In predicate logic, the **domain of discourse** is the set of individuals over which a quantifier ranges. A domain (or *universe*) of discourse can be *restricted* (specified) or *unrestricted*. For example, if we restrict the domain of discourse to humans, we get this translation:

Domain of discourse
The set of individuals over which a quantifier ranges.

4. Everyone is good. $(x)(Gx)$

However, if the domain of discourse is unrestricted, then the translation of the statement is different:

5. Everyone is good. $(x)(Hx \supset Gx)$

The domain of discourse is specified within the translation itself. The translation can be read as follows: For any x, if x is a human, then x is good. Here are some more examples of translations using unrestricted domains:

6.	Termites are insects.	$(x)(Tx \supset Ix)$
7.	Termites are eating your house.	$(\exists x)(Tx \cdot Ex)$
8.	Children are not judgmental.	$(x)(Cx \supset \sim Jx)$
9.	Some children are starving.	$(\exists x)(Cx \cdot Sx)$

The statement in example 6 asserts something of the entire class of termites. Therefore, it is translated by using a universal quantifier. In contrast, the statement in example 7 asserts something only about some termites. Therefore, it is translated by using an existential quantifier. Here are two more examples:

10.	Only guests are welcome.	$(x)(Wx \supset Gx)$
11.	None but the brave are lonely.	$(x)(Lx \supset Bx)$

The statement in example 10 uses the word "only." You might recognize this as an *exclusive* proposition. When this kind of statement gets translated as a conditional statement the class term after the word "only" becomes the consequent. In other words, persons are welcome only if they are guests.

The statement in example 11 uses the words "none but." This, too, is an *exclusive* proposition. When it gets translated as a conditional statement the class term after the words "none but" becomes the consequent. In other words, persons are lonely only if they are brave.

Here are two other examples:

12.	Not one student failed the midterm exam.	$\sim (\exists x)(Sx \cdot Fx)$ or $(x)(Sx \supset \sim Fx)$
13.	It is not the case that every student graduates	$\sim (x)(Sx \supset Gx)$ or $(\exists x)(Sx \cdot \sim Gx)$

The statements in examples 12 and 13 can be translated by using either a universal or existential quantifier. This illustrates an important point: A universal statement is equivalent to a negated existential statement, and an existential statement is equivalent to a negated universal statement. In other words, the universal translation of example 12 can be read this way: *No students failed the midterm exam.* This is equivalent to the original statement: *Not one student failed the midterm exam.*

Here are a few examples to illustrate how the logical operators of propositional logic can be combined to form compound arrangements of universal and particular statements:

14.	If some Academy Award movies are films not worth watching, then all movies are films capable of disappointing audiences.	$(\exists x)(Ax \cdot \sim Wx) \supset (x)(Mx \supset Dx)$
15.	If all science fiction writers are philosophers, then some philosophers are famous.	$(x)(Sx \supset Px) \supset (\exists x)(Px \cdot Fx)$

CHECK YOUR UNDERSTANDING 9A

Translate the following statements into symbolic form. You can use the predicate letters that are provided.

1. Ginger is a spice. (*G*, *S*)

Answer: $(x) (Gx \supset Sx)$

2. Curry chicken is pungent. (*C*, *P*)

3. Rabbits are sexually active. (*R*, *S*)

4. Sir Lancelot was a member of the Round Table. (*R*)

★ 5. Steve McQueen was not an Academy Award winner. (*A*)

6. Only if Joe runs the mile under 4 minutes will he qualify. (*M*, *Q*)

7. The Taj Mahal is one of the Seven Wonders of the Modern World. (*S*)

8. Diamonds are the hardest substance on Earth. (*D*, *H*)

★ 9. Used cars are good if and only if they were well maintained and have low mileage. (*U*, *G*, *M*, *L*)

10. Broiled salmon tastes good. (*S*, *G*)

11. Textbooks are my friends. (*T*, *F*)

12. Pittsburgh is cold only if it has a bad winter. (*C*, *W*)

★ 13. Cell phones are not universally admired products. (*C*, *U*)

14. Susan will pass the exam only if she is well prepared. (*E*, *W*)

15. Only if Fidelix gets here by 8:00 PM will he be admitted. (*G*, *A*)

16. All deciduous trees are colorful trees during autumn. (*D*, *C*)

★ 17. No coconuts are pink fruit. (*C*, *P*)

18. Some short stories are not about people. (*S*, *P*)

19. If anything is alive, then it is aware of its environment. (*A*, *E*)

20. Every volcano is a dangerous thing. (*V*, *D*)

★ 21. Labyrinths are amazing structures. (*L*, *A*)

22. Not even one student showed up for the pep rally. (*S*, *P*)

23. Only registered voters are allowed to vote. (*R*, *V*)

24. Every DUI citation is a serious offense. (*D*, *S*)

★ 25. Basketball players are not comfortable in bunk beds. (*B*, *C*)

26. No MP3 players are good birthday gifts. (*M*, *B*)

27. All knitted underwear is warm and comfortable. (*K*, *W*, *C*)

28. No knitted underwear is a bikini substitute. (*K*, *B*)

★ 29. Some SUVs are not environmentally friendly vehicles. (*S*, *E*)

30. Some buses are not comfortable transportation. (*B*, *C*)

31. Whales are a protected species. (*W*, *P*)

32. No movie ratings are accurate pieces of information. (*M*, *A*)

★ 33. Fanatics never compromise. (*F*, *C*)

34. Only graduates can participate in the commencement. (*G*, *P*)

35. A person is medically dead if and only if there is not detectable brain stem activity. (*P*, *D*, *B*)

36. Not one representative returned my call. (*R*, *C*)

★ 37. All whole numbers are either even or odd. (*W*, *E*, *O*)

38. Anything that is either sweet or crunchy is tasty. (*S*, *C*, *T*)

39. None but qualified staff members are permitted to enter the work area. (*Q*, *P*)

40. Some hurricanes are violent. (*H*, *V*)

★ 41. If some TV shows are worth watching, then every TV show is informative. (*T*, *W*, *I*)

42. No pessimists are happy. (*P*, *H*)

43. Tom is sleeping if and only if Jerry is awake. (*S*, *A*)

44. Nothing bad lasts forever. (*B*, *L*)

★ 45. Everything that is alive is mortal. (*A*, *M*)

46. Only pleasant people are happy people. (*P*, *H*)

47. Both Plato and Socrates were philosophers. (*P*)

48. If Sam is not late for class, then he will not miss the exam. (*C*, *E*)

★ 49. Whenever both Tim and Sarah are at the meetings, then neither Frank nor Rachel is at the meetings. (*M*, *S*)

50. Isaac Newton was either a scientist or a mathematician, or else he was both. (*S*, *M*)

51. None but cats are predators. (*C*, *P*)

52. Whenever Joe smokes he coughs. (*S*, *C*)

★ 53. If Paul is not a poker player, then he is not a gambler. (*P*, *G*)

54. Neither motorcycles nor mopeds are stable vehicles. (*M*, *P*, *S*)

55. Whenever Jake is late for supper, then he cries. (*S*, *C*)

56. If Chris goes to the party, then he will have fun. (*P*, *F*)

⭐ 57. Both Shane and Agatha are dancers, but neither one is a professional. (D, P)

58. Everything is expensive. (E)

59. All animals can think. (A, T)

60. It is not the case that birds are either mammals or crustaceans. (B, M, C)

B. FOUR NEW RULES OF INFERENCE

The translations from ordinary language provide experience with the symbols of predicate logic. In addition, we have been able to use the logical operators of propositional logic. However, in order to construct proofs in predicate logic, a few additional rules are needed.

Two of these new rules remove quantifiers, and two introduce quantifiers. One of the rules that remove quantifiers is for universal quantifiers, and the other is for existential quantifiers. These are generally used at the beginning of a sequence of steps. On the other hand, one of the rules that introduce quantifiers is for universal quantifiers, and the other is for existential quantifiers. These are generally used at the end of a sequence of steps.

Universal Instantiation

Some arguments in ordinary language are obviously valid, but they cannot be proven with just the rules of inference that were introduced in Chapter 8. Here is an example:

> Steven Hawking is a physicist. All physicists are logical thinkers. Therefore, Steven Hawking is a logical thinker.

Symbolizing the argument reveals why we don't yet have the means to prove its validity:

1. Ps
2. $(x)(Px \supset Lx)$ $/ Ls$

The rules of inference that we have so far cannot be applied to derive the conclusion. For example, we cannot apply *modus ponens* to lines 1 and 2, because the rule requires a conditional statement. However, line 2 is *not* a conditional; it is a *universally quantified statement*. What we need is something that allows us to remove the universal quantifier, and derive $Ps \supset Ls$. If we can derive this step, then *modus ponens* can be applied (with premise 1). The sequence will end with a valid derivation of the conclusion.

In order to understand the process involved, we need to look at a few simple examples. Let's use the quantified statement in the foregoing argument:

$$(x)(Px \supset Lx)$$

If we remove the universal quantifier, then we get a statement function with two free occurrences of the x-variable:

$$Px \supset Lx$$

If we replace the *x*-variable with the constant *s*, then we get an *instance* of the original quantified statement:

$$Ps \supset Ls$$

The process is called **instantiation**, and the *s* that is introduced is called the **instantial letter**. When instantiation is applied to a quantified statement, the quantifier is removed, and *every variable that was bound by the quantifier* is replaced by the same instantial letter. We can now say that a substitution instance of a statement function can be validly deduced from the universally quantified statement by the rule of **universal instantiation** (UI).

We can now complete the proof of the argument:

1. *Ps*
2. (*x*)(*Px* ⊃ *Lx*)   / *Ls*
3. *Ps* ⊃ *Ls*   2, UI
4. *Ls*   1, 3, MP

As always, we have to be careful not to misapply the process of instantiation. Here are some examples:

Misapplications of Instantiation
Original quantified statement: (*x*)(*Px* ⊃ *Lx*)

Invalid Derivations:
A. (*x*)(*Ps* ⊃ *Ls*)
B. *Ps* ⊃ *Lr*   ⊘
C. *Ps* ⊃ *Lx*

The mistake in A is the result of not removing the universal quantifier. The mistake in B is the result of not replacing every variable that was bound by the quantifier by the same instantial constant. The mistake in C is the result of not replacing the second bound *x*-variable by the instantial letter.

Universal Generalization

We saw how a rule provided for the removal of a quantifier. Now we can look at a rule that provides the introduction of a quantifier. Consider this argument:

All private universities are self-funded institutions. All self-funded institutions are taxed. Therefore, all private universities are taxed.

The argument can be translated and symbolized as follows:

1. (*x*)(*Px* ⊃ *Sx*)
2. (*x*)(*Sx* ⊃ *Tx*)   / (*x*)(*Px* ⊃ *Tx*)

Both the premises and the conclusion are universally quantified statements. We might anticipate an application of hypothetical syllogism during the proof sequence. However, we must first remove the universal quantifier from both premises—and that requires a new strategy.

Let's start with the first premise. Since it is a universally quantified statement, we could begin by listing applications of UI. For example:

$$Pa \supset Sa$$
$$Pb \supset Sb$$
$$Pc \supset Sc$$
. . . and so on.

In other words, *any* arbitrarily selected individual can be substituted uniformly in the statement function that results from removing the universal quantifier. We can therefore substitute a *variable* instead of a constant. The same reasoning applies to the second premise as well.

Based on this reasoning, we can now introduce a new rule. **Universal generalization** (UG) holds that you can validly deduce the universal quantification of a statement function from a substitution instance only when the instantial letter is a variable. Here is the completed proof that incorporates the new rule:

1. $(x)(Px \supset Sx)$
2. $(x)(Sx \supset Tx)$ / $(x)(Px \supset Tx)$
3. $Py \supset Sy$ 1, UI
4. $Sy \supset Ty$ 2, UI
5. $Py \supset Ty$ 3, 4, HS
6. $(x)(Px \supset Tx)$ 5, UG

> **Universal generalization** A rule by which you can validly deduce the universal quantification of a statement function from a substitution instance with respect to the name of any arbitrarily selected individual (subject to restrictions).

As always, we have to be careful not to misapply the rule. Here are some examples:

Misapplications of UG

A. 1. $My \supset Ry$
    2. $(x)(Mx \supset Ry)$ ⊘

B. 1. $Md \supset Rd$
    2. $(x)(Mx \supset Rx)$ ⊘

The mistake in A is the result of not replacing every instance of *y* with *x*. The mistake in B is the result of the instantial letter in line 1 being a constant (*d*) instead of a variable.

Existential Generalization

We saw how UG provided for the introduction of a universal quantifier. Now we can look at a rule that provides the introduction of an existential quantifier. Consider this argument:

All carbon-based organisms are mortal creatures. Will Smith is a carbon-based organism. Therefore, there is at least one mortal creature.

The argument can be translated and symbolized as follows:

1. $(x)(Cx \supset Mx)$
2. Cw / $(\exists x)Mx$

This looks like a perfect setup for *modus ponens*. If we apply UI to line 1, then we can easily derive the conclusion:

1. $(x)(Cx \supset Mx)$
2. Cw / $(\exists x)Mx$

3. $Cw \supset Mw$ 1, UI
4. Mw 2, 3, MP
5. $(\exists x)Mx$ 4, EG

The deduction of Mw on line 4 reveals an instance of at least one mortal creature (in this instance, Will Smith). This result provides the rationale for deriving the conclusion, which just states that there is at least one mortal creature.

Existential generalization (EG) is a rule that permits us to existentially generalize an instance of a quantified formula, and it proceeds just that way. It can also be applied to a variable as well as a constant. Here is an example:

Existential generalization A rule that permits the valid introduction of an existential quantifier from either a constant or a variable.

1. $(x)(Cx \supset Mx)$
2. $(x)Cx$ / $(\exists x)Mx$
3. $Cy \supset My$ 1, UI
4. Cy 2, UI
5. My 3, 4, MP
6. $(\exists x)Mx$ 5, EG

According to line 5, any arbitrary individual is an M; therefore, we can validly deduce that at least one thing is an M. Of course, we presuppose a basic, but reasonable, assumption of predicate logic: *At least one thing exists in the universe.* Without this assumption, even the instantiation in line 4 would be impossible.

As always, we have to be careful not to misapply the rule. Here are some examples:

Misapplications of EG

A. 1. $Mx \cdot Rx$ B. 1. $Md \cdot Rd$
   2. $(\exists y)(My \cdot Rx)$ ⊘   2. $(\exists y)My \cdot Ry$ ⊘

The mistake in A is the result of not replacing every instance of x with y. The mistake in B is the result of the existential quantifier not being applied to the entire line.

We have seen two kinds of generalization: universal and existential. Universal generalization requires that every occurrence of the instantial letter must be replaced with the quantifier variable. On the other hand, existential generalization requires only that at least one of the instantial letters must be replaced with the quantifier variable.

Existential Instantiation

We saw how UI provided for the removal of a universal quantifier. Now we can look at a rule that provides the removal of an existential quantifier. Consider this argument:

> All breakfast cereals are rich in fiber. Some breakfast cereals are kid's foods. Therefore, some kid's foods are rich in fiber.

The argument can be translated as follows:

1. $(x)(Bx \supset Rx)$
2. $(\exists x)(Bx \cdot Kx)$ / $(\exists x)(Kx \cdot Rx)$

The beginning strategy is to remove the quantifiers in both premises. You already know that UI can be applied to line 1. We can interpret line 2 as stating that there exists something that is both a *B* and a *K*. **Existential instantiation** (EI) is a rule that permits giving a *name* to the thing that exists. The name can then be represented by a constant. For example, we can replace the *x*-variable in line 2 with the instantial letter *c*. This creates the next step in the proof:

Existential instantiation A rule that permits giving a name to a thing that exists. The name can then be represented by a constant.

1. $(x)(Bx \supset Rx)$
2. $(\exists x)(Bx \cdot Kx)$ $/ (\exists x)(Kx \cdot Rx)$
3. $Bc \cdot Kc$ 2, EI

At this point we can apply UI to line 1:

1. $(x)(Bx \supset Rx)$
2. $(\exists x)(Bx \cdot Kx)$ $/ (\exists x)(Kx \cdot Rx)$
3. $Bc \cdot Kc$ 2, EI
4. $Bc \supset Rc$ 1, UI

We applied EI to line 2 before we applied UI to line 1, because there are certain restrictions to EI. The restrictions ensure that we do not create an invalid step in the proof. For example, if we use UI before EI, then we derive $Bc \supset Rc$. If we do this, then we cannot use the same constant *c*, for EI. Here is the reason: If UI establishes the constant *c* before EI, then we are *not* justified in assuming the thing that is a *B* and a *K* (from the existential quantifier) has the same name as the thing instantiated by UI. We have to assign the EI instantiation a different name. However, by applying EI first and establishing a name, we are justified in giving the UI instantiation the same name, because the universal quantifier can be instantiated to *any* arbitrary individual, including the one named by the EI. (In addition, the existential name cannot occur in the line that indicates the conclusion to be derived.) Having established this restriction on EI, we can complete the proof:

1. $(x)(Bx \supset Rx)$
2. $(\exists x)(Bx \cdot Kx)$ $/ (\exists x)(Kx \cdot Rx)$
3. $Bc \cdot Kc$ 2, EI
4. $Bc \supset Rc$ 1, UI
5. Bc 3, Simp
6. Rc 4, 5, MP
7. $Kc \cdot Bc$ 3, Com
8. Kc 7, Simp
9. $Kc \cdot Rc$ 6, 8, Conj
10. $(\exists x)(Kx \cdot Rx)$ 9, EG

As always, we have to be careful not to misapply the rule. Here are some examples:

Misapplications of EI

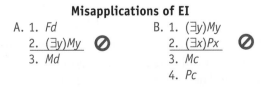

A. 1. Fd
    2. $(\exists y)My$
    3. Md

B. 1. $(\exists y)My$
    2. $(\exists x)Px$
    3. Mc
    4. Pc

The mistake in A is the result of using the instantial letter *d* that appeared earlier in the proof sequence in line 1. A similar mistake occurs in B. The instantial letter *c* is validly derived on line 3. However, its use on line 4 violates the restriction that prohibits using an instantial letter that appeared earlier in the proof sequence.

Summary of the Four Rules

We can now summarize the four new rules of inference. This will require the introduction of a few new symbols: $\mathcal{S}x$, $\mathcal{S}y$, and $\mathcal{S}a$. The first two symbols are used to represent *any statement function* (any symbolic arrangement containing individual *variables*). The third symbol is used to represent *any statement* (any symbolic arrangement containing individual *constants*). Here are the four predicate logic rules:

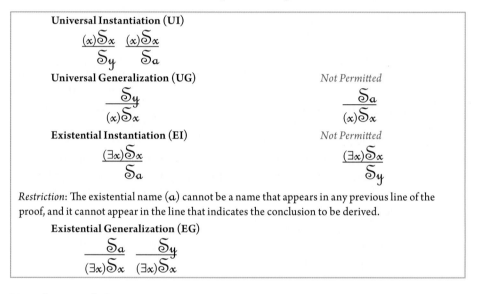

Universal Instantiation (UI)

$$\frac{(x)\mathcal{S}x}{\mathcal{S}y} \quad \frac{(x)\mathcal{S}x}{\mathcal{S}a}$$

Universal Generalization (UG)   *Not Permitted*

$$\frac{\mathcal{S}y}{(x)\mathcal{S}x} \qquad\qquad \frac{\mathcal{S}a}{(x)\mathcal{S}x}$$

Existential Instantiation (EI)   *Not Permitted*

$$\frac{(\exists x)\mathcal{S}x}{\mathcal{S}a} \qquad\qquad \frac{(\exists x)\mathcal{S}x}{\mathcal{S}y}$$

Restriction: The existential name (a) cannot be a name that appears in any previous line of the proof, and it cannot appear in the line that indicates the conclusion to be derived.

Existential Generalization (EG)

$$\frac{\mathcal{S}a}{(\exists x)\mathcal{S}x} \quad \frac{\mathcal{S}y}{(\exists x)\mathcal{S}x}$$

Tactics and Strategy

The most important thing to remember when doing proofs in predicate logic is not to misapply the rules. The four new rules of inference mesh smoothly with the previous rules of inference in Chapter 8. Therefore, your familiarity with the previous rules should help you create proofs in predicate logic.

One more basic principle needs to be reinforced. The four new rules are similar to the eight implication rules in an important way: *They can be applied only to an entire line of a proof (either a premise or a derived line).* Let's look at how this affects strategy in a proof. Consider this argument:

1. $Pg \cdot Rg$
2. $(\exists x)Px \supset (x)(Rx \supset Sx)$ / Sg

One strategic goal is to instantiate the information in line 2. However, line 2 is a conditional statement. In other words, the entire line is governed neither by the existential quantifier nor the universal quantifier. In fact, the existential quantifier governs only the antecedent, while the universal quantifier governs only the consequent. Therefore, we cannot apply either EI or UI to line 2.

Line 1 provides the means to solve our problem. The first step is to derive *Pg* on a separate line by simplification. Next, we can apply EG to derive the consequent of line 2. From there, the proof will proceed smoothly.

1. $Pg \cdot Rg$
2. $(\exists x)Px \supset (x)(Rx \supset Sx)$ / Sg
3. Pg 1, Simp
4. $(\exists x)Px$ 3, EG
5. $(x)(Rx \supset Sx)$ 2, 4, MP
6. $Rg \supset Sg$ 5, UI
7. $Rg \cdot Pg$ 1, Com
8. Rg 7, Simp
9. Sg 6, 8, MP

The following strategy and tactics guide can be used with the four new rules of inference for predicate logic:

STRATEGIES AND TACTICS

Strategy 1: Look at the conclusion
    Tactical moves—
        A. If you need to perform universal generalization (UG) on the last line of the proof, try using universal instantiation (UI) on the premises to instantiate a variable. (UG can be used only on a variable, not on a constant.)
        B. If you need to perform existential generalization (EG) on the last line of the proof, try using both UI and EI on the premises. (Be sure to use EI first.)

Strategy 3: Look at the premises
    Tactical moves—
        A. If the premises have universal quantifiers, then try using universal instantiation (UI). Determine whether you need to instantiate a variable or a constant. (You may instantiate the same variable for more than one premise.)
        B. If the premises have more than one existential quantifier, try using existential instantiation (EI). (Make sure not to instantiate a letter that occurs earlier in the proof.)

Strategy 3: Remember that the four predicate logic rules can be applied only to an entire line in a proof (either a premise or a derived line).
    Tactical Moves—
        A. Try using simplification to separate two conjuncts. You can then use either EI or UI to instantiate whatever you need.
        B. Try deriving the antecedent of a conditional on a separate line, and then derive the consequent by *modus ponens*. You can then use either EI or UI to instantiate whatever you need.

CHECK YOUR UNDERSTANDING 9B

I. The proofs for the following arguments have been given. Choose the correct rule for the missing justifications.

[1] 1. $(y)(Py \supset Sy)$
     2. $(\exists y)(Py \cdot Ty)$ / $(\exists y)(Ty \cdot Sy)$

3.	$Pa \cdot Ta$	2,
4.	Pa	3, Simp
5.	$Pa \supset Sa$	1,
6.	Sa	4, 5, MP
7.	$Ta \cdot Pa$	3, Com
8.	Ta	7, Simp
9.	$Ta \cdot Sa$	6, 8, Conj
10.	$(\exists y)(Ty \cdot Sy)$	9,

Answer:

The justification for line 3: **EI**
The justification for line 5: **UI**
The justification for line 10: **EG**

[2]

1.	$(x)(Nx \supset Mx)$	
2.	$(x)(Mx \supset Ox)$	
3.	Na	/ Oa
4.	$Na \supset Ma$	1,
5.	$Ma \supset Oa$	2,
6.	$Na \supset Oa$	4, 5, HS
7.	Oa	3, 6, MP

[3]

1.	$(\exists x)(Px \cdot Qx)$	
2.	$(x)(Px \supset Rx)$	/ $(\exists x)(Qx \cdot Rx)$
3.	$Pa \cdot Qa$	1,
4.	$Pa \supset Ra$	2,
5.	Pa	3, Simp
6.	Ra	4, 5, MP
7.	$Qa \cdot Pa$	3, Com
8.	Qa	7, Simp
9.	$Qa \cdot Ra$	6, 8, Conj
10.	$(\exists x)(Qx \cdot Rx)$	9,

II. In the following proofs the correct justification has been given for the rule. You are to supply the missing information in the line.

[1]

1.	$(x)(Kx \supset \sim Sx)$	
2.	$(\exists x)(Sx \cdot Wx)$	/ $(\exists x)(Wx \cdot \sim Kx)$
3.		2, **EI**
4.		1, **UI**
5.	Sa	3, Simp
6.	$\sim \sim Sa$	5, DN
7.	$\sim Ka$	4, 6, MT
8.	$Wa \cdot Sa$	3, Com
9.	Wa	8, Simp
10.	$Wa \cdot \sim Ka$	7, 9, Conj
11.		10, **EG**

Answer:

> The information in line 3: *Sa · Wa*
> The information in line 4: *Ka ⊃ ~ Sa*
> The information in line 11: (∃x)(Wx · ~ Kx)

[2] 1. (∃x)(Px · Qx)
    2. (∃x) (Rx · Sx)
    3. [(∃x) Px · (∃x) Rx] ⊃ Ta   / Ta
    4.   1, EI
    5.   2, EI
    6. *Pa*   4, Simp
    7. *Rb*   5, Simp
    8.   6, EG
    9.   7, EG
    10. (∃x) Px · (∃x) Rx   8, 9, Conj
    11. `Ta`   3, 10, MP

III. Use the rules of inference to derive the conclusion of each argument.

[1] 1. (x)(Sx ⊃ Tx)
    2. (x)(Tx ⊃ ~ Ux)   / (x)(Sx ⊃ ~ Ux)

Answer:

    3. Sx ⊃ Tx   1, UI
    4. Tx ⊃ ~ Ux   2, UI
    5. Sx ⊃ ~ Ux   3, 4, HS
    6. (x) (Sx ⊃ ~ Ux)   5, UG

[2] 1. (∃x) Gx ⊃ (x) Hx
    2. *Ga*   / *Ha*

[3] 1. *Ta*
    2. (x) (Sx ⊃ ~ Tx)   / ~ *Sa*

[4] 1. (x) (Px ⊃ ~ Qx)
    2. *Qa*   / ~ *Pa*

★ [5] 1. (∃x) Hx
    2. (x)(Hx ⊃ Px)   / (∃x)(Hx · Px)

[6] 1. *Fa · ~ Ga*
    2. (x) [Fx ⊃ (Gx ∨ Hx)]   / *Ha*

[7] 1. (x) (Sx ⊃ Tx)
    2. (x) (Tx ⊃ Px)
    3. *Sa*   / (∃x) Px

[8] 1. (x)[(Fx ∨ Gx) ⊃ Hx]
    2. ~ *Ha*   / (∃x) ~ Gx

★ [9] 1. (x)(Ux ⊃ Sx)
    2. (∃x)(Ux · Tx)   / (∃x)(Tx · Sx)

[10] 1. $(\exists x)(Fx \cdot \sim Gx)$
      2. $(x)(Hx \supset Gx)$ $/ (\exists x)(Ax \cdot \sim Hx)$

[11] 1. $Ha \lor Hb$
      2. $(x)(\sim Cx \supset \sim Hx)$ $/ Ca \lor Cb$

[12] 1. $(x)[(Fx \lor Gx) \supset Hx]$
      2. $(\exists x)\, Fx$
      3. $(x)\, Lx \supset \sim (\exists x)\, Hx$ $/ \sim (x)\, Lx$

⭐ [13] 1. $(\exists x)(Px \cdot Qx)$
      2. $(x)(Px \supset Rx)$ $/ (\exists x)(Qx \cdot Rx)$

[14] 1. $(x)[(Fx \cdot Gx) \supset Hx]$
      2. $(\exists x)\, Fx$
      3. $(x)\, Gx$ $/ (\exists x)\, Hx$

[15] 1. $(\exists x)(Tx \cdot \sim Mx)$
      2. $(x)[Tx \supset (Rx \lor Mx)]$ $/ (\exists x)\, Rx$

[16] 1. $(\exists x)(Sx \cdot Tx)$
      2. $(x)(Px \supset \sim Sx)$ $/ (\exists x)(Tx \cdot \sim Px)$

⭐ [17] 1. $(x)[\sim (Fx \lor Gx) \supset Hx]$
      2. $(x)(Hx \supset Lx)$
      3. $(x) \sim Fx$ $/ (x)(Gx \lor Lx)$

[18] 1. $(\exists x)\, Px \supset (\exists x)\, Kx$
      2. $(\exists x)\, Mx \supset (x)\, Nx$
      3. $Mc \cdot Pc$ $/ (\exists x)(Nx \cdot Kx)$

[19] 1. $(x)(Lx \supset Fx)$
      2. $(\exists x)(Lx \cdot \sim Hx)$
      3. $(x)[(Fx \cdot \sim Gx) \supset Hx]$ $/ (\exists x)\, Gx$

[20] 1. $Ha \cdot \sim Hb$
      2. $Fa \cdot Fb$
      3. $(x)[Fx \supset (Gx \equiv Hx)]$ $/ Ga \cdot \sim Gb$

IV. First, translate the following arguments. Second, use the rules of inference to derive the conclusion of each argument.

1. If something is heavy, then it is not glass. If something is fragile, then it is glass. Therefore, if something is heavy, then it is not fragile. (H, G, F)

    1. $(x)(Hx \supset \sim Gx)$
        $(x)(Fx \supset Gx)$ $/ (x)(Hx \supset \sim Fx)$

Answer:

    1. $(x)(Hx \supset \sim Gx)$
    2. $(x)(Fx \supset Gx)$ $/ (x)(Hx \supset \sim Fx)$

3. $Hy \supset\, \sim Gy$ 1, UI
4. $Fy \supset Gy$ 2, UI
5. $\sim Gy \supset\, \sim Fy$ 4, Trans
6. $Hy \supset\, \sim Fy$ 3, 5, HS
7. $(x)(Hx \supset\, \sim Fx)$ 6, UG

2. Either Anna is a graduate or Ben is a graduate. Those who are not finished are not graduates. Thus, either Anna is finished or Ben is finished. (G, F)

3. Some boxers are dancers. All boxers are courageous. Consequently, some dancers are courageous. (B, D, C)

4. Something is fearless. Everything that is fearless is both strong and disciplined. It follows that something is both strong and disciplined. (F, S, D)

★ 5. Nothing is rare. Everything is either beautiful or expensive if and only if it is rare. Therefore, everything is expensive if and only if it is beautiful. (R, B, E)

C. CHANGE OF QUANTIFIER

The four new rules of inference allow us to prove the validity of many different types of arguments. However, there are still some arguments that require us to generate an additional rule of inference. Here is an example:

> Either some hallucinations are illusions, or else some visions are ghosts. However, it is not the case that there are any ghosts. Therefore, there are some illusions.

Translating the argument reveals the difficulty:

1. $(\exists x)(Hx \cdot Ix) \lor (\exists x)(Vx \cdot Gx)$
2. $\sim (\exists x) Gx$ / $(\exists x) Ix$

The second premise has a tilde in front of the existential quantifier. However, we cannot instantiate the statement until the tilde is removed. Once the tilde is removed, we can then use instantiation to help derive the conclusion. A new rule, called **change of quantifier**, allows the removal or introduction of negation signs. The rule is a set of four logical equivalences, and their function is similar to replacement rules. In other words, they can be applied to part of a line or to an entire line. We can use a symbol introduced earlier, $\mathcal{S}x$, to help generalize the logical equivalences.

Change of quantifier
The rule allows the removal or introduction of negation signs. (The rule is a set of four logical equivalences).

CHANGE OF QUANTIFIER (CQ)
$(x)\, \mathcal{S}x\, ::\, \sim (\exists x)\, \sim\!\mathcal{S}x$
$\sim (x)\, \mathcal{S}x\, ::\, (\exists x)\, \sim\!\mathcal{S}x$
$(\exists x)\, \mathcal{S}x\, ::\, \sim (x)\, \sim\!\mathcal{S}x$
$\sim (\exists x)\, \mathcal{S}x\, ::\, (x)\, \sim\!\mathcal{S}x$

Armed with this new rule, we can now complete the proof:

1. (∃x) (Hx · Ix) ∨ (∃x) (Vx · Gx)
2. ~ (∃x) Gx   / (∃x) Ix
3. (x) ~ Gx   2, CQ
4. ~ Gx   3, UI
5. ~ Gx ∨ ~ Vx   4, Add
6. ~ Vx ∨ ~ Gx   5, Com
7. ~ (Vx · Gx)   6, DM
8. (x) ~ (Vx · Gx)   7, UG
9. ~ (∃x) (Vx · Gx)   8, CQ
10. (∃x) (Vx · Gx) ∨ (∃x) (Hx · Ix)   1, Com
11. (∃x) (Hx · Ix)   9, 10, DS
12. Ha · Ia   11, EI
13. Ia · Ha   12, Com
14. Ia   13, Simp
15. (∃x) Ix   14, EG

As indicated by proof, we needed to apply the rule at two separate steps in the sequence. The first application occurred on line 3, and it used the fourth pair of logical equivalences. The second application occurred in line 9, and it also used the fourth pair of logical equivalences.

A few more examples will illustrate further applications of the rule:

1. ~ Ca
2. (∃x) (Ax ∨ Bx) ⊃ (x) Cx   / (x) ~ (Ax ∨ Bx)
3. (∃x) ~ Cx   1, EG
4. ~ (x) Cx   3, CQ
5. ~ (∃x) (Ax ∨ Bx)   2, 4, MT
6. (x) ~ (Ax ∨ Bx)   5, CQ

The change of quantifier rule was applied twice in the proof sequence. The first application occurred on line 4, and it used the second pair of logical equivalences. The second application occurred in line 6, and it used the fourth pair of logical equivalences. Here is another example:

1. (x) ~ Bx ⊃ (x) ~ Cx
2. (∃x) (Ax · Dx) ⊃ ~ (∃x) Bx   / (∃x) (Ax · Dx) ⊃ ~ (∃x) Cx
3. (∃x) (Ax · Dx) ⊃ (x) ~ Bx   2, CQ
4. (∃x) (Ax · Dx) ⊃ (x) ~ Cx   1, 3, HS
5. (∃x) (Ax · Dx) ⊃ ~ (∃x) Cx   4, CQ

The change of quantifier rule was applied twice in the proof sequence. The first application occurred on line 3, and it used the fourth pair of logical equivalences. However, notice that the rule was applied only to the consequent of line 3. This illustrates that the rule can be applied to part of a line. The second application occurred in line 5, and it also used the fourth pair of logical equivalences. Once again, the rule was applied only to the consequent of line 4.

CHECK YOUR UNDERSTANDING 9C

I. For each of the following, use the change of quantifier rule. This will give you practice using the pairs of logical equivalences.

1. ~ (∃x) (Tx · Rx)

Answer: (x) ~ (Tx · Rx)

2. ~ (x) (Px ⊃ ~ Sx)

3. ~ (∃x) ~ (Jx · ~ Kx)

4. ~ (x) ~ (Dx ⊃ Gx)

⭐ 5. (x) ~ (Px ⊃ Qx)

6. (∃x) ~ (Px · Qx)

7. ~ (x) (Px ⊃ ~ Qx)

8. (∃x) (Px · Qx)

⭐ 9. (x) ~ (Px ⊃ Qx)

10. ~ (∃x) ~ (Jx · ~ Kx)

II. Use the change of quantifier rule and the other rules of inference to construct proofs for the following arguments.

[1] 1. ~ (x) Fx
    2. (x) Gx ⊃ (x) Fx   / (∃x) ~ Gx

Answer:

1. ~ (x) Fx
2. (x) Gx ⊃ (x) Fx   / (∃x) ~ Gx
3. ~ (x) Gx   1, 2, MT
4. (∃x) ~ Gx   3, CQ

[2] ~ (∃x) Dx   / Da ⊃ Ga

[3] 1. (x) ~ Gx
    2. (x) Fx ⊃ (∃x) Gx   / (∃x) ~ Fx

[4] 1. (∃x) Gx ⊃ (x) Fx
    2. Ga ∨ (x) ~ Hx
    3. ~ (x) Fx ∨ (∃x) ~ Fx   / ~ Hb

⭐ [5] 1. ~ (∃x) Gx
    2. (∃x) Fx ∨ (∃x) (Gx · Hx)   / (∃x) Fx

[6] 1. (y) [(~ By ∨ Cy) ⊃ Dy]
    2. ~ (x) (Ax ∨ Bx)   / (∃z) Dz

[7] 1. ~ (x) Fx
    2. Ga ≡ Hb
    3. (∃x) ~ Fx ⊃ ~ (∃x) Gx   / ~ Hb

[8] 1. $(\exists y)\,(\sim By \lor \sim Ay)$
    2. $(x)\,[(Ax \lor Bx) \supset Cx]$
    3. $(\exists z) \sim (Dz \lor \sim Bz)$ / $(\exists w)\,Cw$

★ [9] 1. $\sim (x)\,Gx$
    2. $(x)\,(Fx \supset Gx)$
    3. $\sim (x)\,Hx \lor (x)\,Fx$ / $(\exists x) \sim Hx$

[10] 1. $(\exists x)\,(Cx \cdot \sim Bx)$
    2. $(x)\,(\sim Dx \lor Ax)$
    3. $(x)\,(Ax \supset Bx)$ / $(\exists x)\,(Cx \cdot \sim Dx)$

[11] 1. $(x)\,[(Hx \lor Lx) \supset Mx]$
    2. $(x)\,[Fx \supset (Gx \lor Hx)]$ / $(x)\,[(Fx \cdot \sim Gx) \supset Mx]$

[12] 1. $\sim (\exists x)\,(Fx \cdot \sim Gx)$
    2. $\sim (\exists x)\,(Gx \cdot \sim Hx)$ / $(x)\,(Fx \supset Hx)$

★ [13] 1. $\sim (\exists x)\,Lx$
    2. $(\exists y)\,My$
    3. $(x)\,[(Kx \supset \sim Mx) \lor La]$ / $\sim (y)\,Ky$

[14] 1. $\sim (\exists x)\,Dx$
    2. $(\exists x)\,(Bx \cdot Cx) \lor (\exists x)\,(Fx \cdot Dx)$ / $(\exists x)\,Cx$

[15] 1. $(\exists x) \sim Hx \supset (\exists x)\,Gx$
    2. $(x)\,Fx \supset (\exists x)\,Gx$
    3. $(x)\,[(Fx \cdot Hx) \supset La]$ / La

III. First, translate the following arguments. Second, use the change of quantifier rules and the other rules of inference to derive the conclusion of each argument.

1. It is not true that something is sweet. Therefore, if something is sweet, then it is artificial. (S, A)

Answer:

[1] 1. $\sim (\exists x)\,Sx$ / $(x)\,(Sx \supset Ax)$
    2. $(x) \sim Sx$ 1, CQ
    3. $\sim Sx$ 2, UI
    4. $\sim Sx \lor Ax$ 3, Add
    5   $Sx \supset Ax$ 4, Impl
    6. $(x)\,(Sx \supset Ax)$ 5, UG

2. If something is either concrete or steel, then everything is heavy. But something is not heavy. We can conclude that it is false that something is concrete. (C, S, H)

3. Not everything is either not a tragedy, or it is a joke. It is not true that some stories are jokes. Thus, something is not a story. (T, J, S)

4. Not all clowns are funny. It is false that some mimes are not clowns. Therefore, something is not a mime. (C, F, M)

★ 5. It is false that something is either an herb or a garnish. If anything is both a fragrance and not a garnish, then something is an herb. Therefore, everything is a fragrance. (H, G, F)

D. CONDITIONAL AND INDIRECT PROOF

We saw in Chapter 8 that some arguments in propositional logic can be proven valid by conditional proof or indirect proof. The two methods can also be used with arguments containing quantifiers.

Conditional Proof

A conditional proof sequence in predicate logic uses the same indenting technique as in propositional logic. Also, the process of discharging a CP sequence remains the same. However, some special features can arise within both a predicate logic conditional proof and a predicate logic indirect proof. We can get started by looking at a valid argument that uses quantifiers:

1. $(x) (Ax \supset Bx)$ / $(\exists x) (Ax \cdot Cx) \supset (\exists x) Bx$

Since the conclusion is a conditional statement, we can assume the antecedent in the first line of a conditional sequence. Once this is done, we can use any of the instantiation or generalization rules within the indented sequence. When the desired line is derived, it is discharged as a conditional statement in which the first line of the CP sequence is the antecedent, and the last line of the CP sequence is the consequent. Here is the completed proof:

1. $(x) (Ax \supset Bx)$ / $(\exists x) (Ax \cdot Cx) \supset (\exists x) Bx$
2. $(\exists x) (Ax \cdot Cx)$ Assumption CP
3. $Ag \cdot Cg$ 2, EI
4. Ag 3, Simp
5. $Ag \supset Bg$ 1, UI
6. Bg 4, 5, MP
7. $(\exists x) Bx$ 6, EG
8. $(\exists x) (Ax \cdot Cx) \supset (\exists x) Bx$ 2–7, CP

Our proof is done, but sometimes a new restriction to universal generalization (UG) is needed if we are to avoid invalid deductions.

Universal Generalization (UG)

$$\frac{Sy}{(x)Sx}$$

Restriction: *Universal generalization cannot be used within an indented proof sequence, if the instantial variable is free in the first line of that sequence.*

Let's look at a proof that obeys the restriction:

```
1. (x) (Cx ⊃ Dx)                  / (x) Cx ⊃ (x) Dx
   ┌ 2. (x) Cx                     Assumption CP
   │ 3. Cx                         2, UI
   │ 4. Cx ⊃ Dx                    1, UI
   │ 5. Dx                         3, 4, MP
   └ 6. (x) Dx                     5, UG
7. (x) Cx ⊃ (x) Dx                 2–6, CP
```

In the proof, the variable *x* is bound by a universal quantifier in line 2 (the first line of the indented sequence). Therefore, when UI is applied to line 2, we validly derive an *arbitrarily selected individual* in line 3. When *Dx* is subsequently derived in line 5, the result is based on the arbitrarily selected individuals in both lines 3 and 4. Therefore, UG is applied correctly.

But what happens if we start a CP assumption with a free variable? In that case, the free variable *does not name an arbitrary individual*, because a free variable *names an individual that is assumed to have a particular property*. Therefore, we cannot bind that variable using universal generalization. Let's look at an example that fails to obey the restriction:

```
1. (x) Cx ⊃ (x) Dx                / (x) (Cx ⊃ Dx)
   ┌ 2. Cx                         Assumption CP
   │ 3. (x) Cx                     2, UG (Invalid: x is free in line 2) ⊘
```

In the first line of the CP sequence (line 2), the variable *x* is free. Since it was not derived by UI, it is not an arbitrarily selected individual. Therefore, line 3 is invalidly derived because it fails to conform to the restriction on UG.

Indirect Proof

An indirect proof (IP) sequence in predicate logic uses the same indenting technique that was established in propositional logic. Also, the process of discharging an IP sequence remains the same. However, the restriction for using universal generalization (UG) regarding free variables applies equally to an indirect proof sequence.

We can get started by looking at an argument that uses quantifiers:

```
 1. (∃x) Fx
 2. (x) (Fx ⊃ Gx)                 / (∃x) Gx
    ┌ 3. ~ (∃x) Gx                 Assumption IP
    │ 4. (x) ~ Gx                  3, CQ
    │ 5. Fa                        1, EI
    │ 6. Fa ⊃ Ga                   2, UI
    │ 7. Ga                        5, 6, MP
    │ 8. ~ Ga                      4, UI
    └ 9. Ga · ~ Ga                 7, 8, Conj
10. ~ ~ (∃x) Gx                    3–9, IP
11. (∃x) Gx                        10, DN
```

The indirect proof sequence begins on line 3 by negating the conclusion. We can apply the same strategy for all indirect proofs: try to derive a contradiction, and then discharge the IP sequence by negating the assumption. Line 3 has a negation in front of the existential quantifier. Therefore, we have to apply the change of quantifier rule to line 3 before we can begin an instantiation. Once the basic groundwork is in place, the proof can be completed.

The two techniques of CP and IP can be combined in one proof in predicate logic, as long as we use the rules of inference properly. Here is an example:

1. $(x) [Gx \supset (Fx \cdot Hx)]$ / $(\exists x) (Fx \lor Gx) \supset (\exists x) Fx$
2. $(\exists x) (Fx \lor Gx)$ Assumption CP
3. $\sim (\exists x) Fx$ Assumption IP
4. $(x) \sim Fx$ 3, CQ
5. $Fa \lor Ga$ 2, EI
6. $\sim Fa$ 4, UI
7. Ga 5, 6, DS
8. $Ga \supset (Fa \cdot Ha)$ 1, UI
9. $Fa \cdot Ha$ 7, 8, MP
10. Fa 9, Simp
11. $Fa \cdot \sim Fa$ 6, 10, Conj
12. $\sim \sim (\exists x) Fx$ 3–11, IP
13. $(\exists x) Fx$ 12, DN
14. $(\exists x) (Fx \lor Gx) \supset (\exists x) Fx$ 2–13, CP

The overall strategy is to start with a CP sequence by assuming the antecedent of the conditional statement that we want to derive. The goal of this strategy is to validly

Gottlob Frege

Gottlob Frege (1848–1925) was one of the most original and influential modern thinkers. For Frege, "every mathematician must be a philosopher, and every philosopher must be a mathematician," and his monumental attempt to reduce mathematics to logic connected the two fields forever. Frege believed in the *a priori* nature of mathematics and logic, which meant that both fields could be developed by reason alone. Ironically, his work led to the discovery of logical and mathematical paradoxes that revolutionized the foundations of mathematics.

Frege developed the logic of quantifiers, the distinction between constants and variables, and the first modern clarification of sense and reference. For example, the term "dog" refers to all sorts of four-legged friends, but its sense, or meaning, is not the same as any of them—or even all of them taken together. Just look it up! And those are just a few of his original insights. In fact, the important and influential field of mathematical logic can be traced to Frege's pioneering work.

derive the consequent of the conditional, and then discharge the CP sequence. In order to derive the consequent, we use an IP sequence as a tactic to derive a contradiction within the IP sequence. This provides the means to derive the consequent within the CP sequence.

CHECK YOUR UNDERSTANDING 9D

I. Use either *conditional proof* or *indirect proof* to derive the conclusions of the following arguments.

1. $(\exists x)\ (Sx \lor Px\ ) \supset (x)\ Tx$
   $(\exists x)\ Qx \supset (\exists x)\ (Rx \cdot Sx)$ $/ (x)(Qx \supset Tx)$

Answer:

1.	$(\exists x)\ (Sx \lor Px\ ) \supset (x)\ Tx$	
2.	$(\exists x)\ Qx \supset (\exists x)\ (Rx \cdot Sx)$	$/ (x)(Qx \supset Tx)$
3.	Qx	Assumption (CP)
4.	$(\exists x)\ Qx$	3, EG
5.	$(\exists x)\ (Rx \cdot Sx)$	2, 4, MP
6.	$Rb \cdot Sb$	5, EI
7.	$Sb \cdot Rb$	6, Com
8.	Sb	7, Simp
9.	$Sb \lor Pb$	8, Add
10.	$(\exists x)\ (Sx \lor Px)$	9, EG
11.	$(x)\ Tx$	1, 10, MP
12.	Tx	11, UI
13.	$Qx \supset Tx$	3–12, CP
14.	$(x)(Qx \supset Tx)$	13, UG

[2] 1. $(x)\ (Fx \supset Gx)$ $/ (x)\ Fx \supset (x)\ Gx$

[3] 1. $(x)\ (Bx \supset Cx)$ $/ \sim (x)\ Cx \supset \sim (x)\ Bx$

[4] 1. $(x) \sim Dx$
    2. $\sim (\exists x)\ Bx \supset (\exists x)\ (Cx \cdot Dx)$ $/ (\exists x)\ Bx$

⭐ [5] 1. $(x)\ (Fx \supset Hx)$
    2. $(x)\ (Fx \supset Gx)$ $/ (x)\ [Fx \supset (Gx \cdot Hx)]$

[6] 1. $(x)\ Hx \lor (x)\ Kx$ $/ (x)\ (\sim Hx \supset Kx)$

[7] 1. $(x)\ (Bx \supset Dx)$
    2. $(x)\ (Bx \supset Cx)$ $/ (x)\ [Bx \supset (Cx \cdot Dx)]$

[8] 1. $(\exists x)\ Fx$
    2. $(x)\ (Fx \supset Gx)$ $/ (\exists x)\ Gx$

⭐ [9] 1. $\sim (\exists y)\ Ky \supset \sim (\exists z)\ Mz$
    2. $(\exists x)\ [Hx \supset (y) \sim Ky]$ $/ (x)\ Hx \supset (z) \sim Mz$

[10] 1. $(x) [Sx \vee (Bx \cdot \sim Fx)]$
      2. $(x) Fx$ $/ (x)(Cx \supset Sx)$

[11] 1. $(x) [(Hx \vee Lx) \supset Mx]$
      2. $(x) [(Fx \vee Gx) \supset Hx]$ $/ (x) (Fx \supset Mx)$

[12] 1. $(y) Ly$
      2. $(x) (Lx \supset \sim Mx)$ $/ (z) \sim Mz$

⭐ [13] 1. $(x) [Gx \supset (Hx \cdot Lx)]$ $/ (x) (Fx \supset Gx) \supset (x) (Fx \supset Lx)$

[14] 1. $\sim (\exists x) Lx \supset (\exists x) Mx$
      2. $(x) (Lx \supset Mx)$ $/ \sim (x) \sim Mx$

[15] 1. $(\exists x) Hx \supset (\exists x) (Gx \cdot Lx)$
      2. $(x)(Fx \supset Hx)$ $/ (\exists x) Fx \supset (\exists x) Gx$

[16] 1. $(\exists x) Dx \supset (x) Fx$
      2. $(\exists x) Bx \supset (\exists x) (Cx \cdot Dx)$ $/ (x) (Bx \supset Fx)$

⭐ [17] 1. $(\exists x) (Dx \vee Mx) \supset (x) Fx$
      2. $(\exists x) Bx \supset (\exists x) (Cx \cdot Dx)$ $/ (x) (Bx \supset Fx)$

[18] 1. $La \vee Lb$
      2. $(x) (Lx \supset Mx)$ $/ (\exists x) Mx$

[19] 1. $(x) [(Hx \vee Lx) \supset Mx]$
      2. $(x) [Fx \supset (Gx \vee Hx)]$ $/ (x) [(Fx \cdot \sim Gx) \supset Mx]$

[20] 1. $(x) [Bx \equiv (y) Cy]$ $/ (x) Bx \vee (x) \sim Bx$

II. First, translate the following arguments. Second, use either *conditional proof* or *indirect proof* to derive the conclusions of each argument.

  1. Either Anabelle is a cat or Bob is a cat. All cats are mammals. Therefore, there is a mammal. (C, M)

Answer:

    1. $Ca \vee Cb$
    2. $(x) (Cx \supset Mx)$ $/ (\exists x) Mx$

3. $\sim (\exists x) Mx$		*Assumption IP*
4. $(x) \sim Mx$		3, CQ
5. $Ca \supset Ma$		2, UI
6. $Cb \supset Mb$		2, UI
7. $(Ca \supset Ma) \cdot (Cb \supset Mb)$		5, 6, Conj
8. $Ma \vee Mb$		1, 7, CD
9. $\sim Ma$		4, UI
10. Mb		8, 9, DS
11. $\sim Mb$		4, UI
12. $Mb \cdot \sim Mb$		10, 11, Conj

  13. $\sim \sim (\exists x) Mx$ 3–12, IP
  14. $(\exists x) Mx$ 13, DN

2. All beagles are canines. Also, all puppies are animals. It follows that all beagle puppies are canines and animals. (*B, C, P, A*)

3. Everything is fragile. Everything is either sweet, or else bitter and not fragile. Therefore, something is either not cold or sweet. (*F, S, B, C*)

4. There is something that is either not tired or hungry only if everything is jolly. Everything is tired or grouchy only if miserable. Therefore, everything is miserable or everything is jolly. (*T, H, J, G, M*)

★ 5. All UFOs are spaceships. There is a spaceship only if there is an alien. We can conclude that there is a UFO only if there is an alien. (*U, S, A*)

E. DEMONSTRATING INVALIDITY

There are two methods for demonstrating invalidity in predicate logic. However, neither of the methods is mechanical in the way that a complete truth table or a Venn diagram can be used to determine the invalidity of an argument. One of the methods we can use draws on the ability to create *counterexamples*. You already have some experience with this method from Chapter 1. The second method is called the *finite universe method*. It consists in creating models using increasing numbers of individuals in order to show an argument is invalid.

Counterexample Method

A counterexample to an argument is a substitution instance of an argument form that has actually true premises and a false conclusion. (The counterexample method was introduced in Chapter 1.) A good way to create a counterexample is to use objects that are known by just about everyone; the idea is to create statements whose truth value is readily acceptable. Thinking of counterexamples challenges our creativity, but it is rewarding when you finally think of a good example. Sometimes it takes a while to think of just the right thing to solve a problem. But as with most skills, practice makes it easier because the training strengthens our ability to think through a problem. Here is an example using quantifiers:

1. $(x) (Fx \supset Gx)$
2. $(\exists x) (Hx \cdot \sim Gx)$ $/ (\exists x) (Fx \cdot \sim Hx)$

One way to begin thinking about the argument is to notice that the argument refers to three different groups of objects. Next, we can translate the statements into English to get a feel for them. For example, the first premise can be translated as "Every *F* is a *G*." In other words, if the first premise is true, then the *F* group is included in the *G* group (or else we can say that *F* is a subset of *G*). The second premise can be translated as "There is at least one *H* that is not a *G*." In other words, if the second premise is true, then at least one member of the *H* group is not included in the *G* group. Finally, the conclusion can be translated as "There is at least one *F* that is not an *H*." Now, at this point we have to change our thinking process a bit. Our goal is to try to get the conclusion false and the premises true. In other words, if the conclusion is false, then it *is not the case that* at least one member of the *F* group is *not included* in the *H* group. In other words, if the conclusion is false, then *all* the members of *F are* members of *H*.

Now that we have the pieces drawn out, we can begin putting them together to create a counterexample. Since we want to get the conclusion to be a false statement, we need to have *every member of F be a member of H*. Here is one possibility: If we let *F = children*, and *H = humans*, then we get "Some children are not humans." This is obviously false, because every child is a human. In addition, we now need only to think of something to fit the *G* group. Let's see what we have so far:

All children are _____.
Some humans are not _____.
Therefore, some children are not humans.

We need something that will make both premises true. There are several things that can fit. Here, we offer just one solution: let *G = persons under 21 years of age*.

All children are persons under 21 years of age.
Some humans are not persons under 21 years of age.
Therefore, some children are not humans.

The premises are true, and the conclusion is false. Therefore, the counterexample to the original argument shows that it is invalid.

Let's try another example that may seem plausible, but is it? To find out, we again look for a counterexample:

1. $(x) (Dx \supset Kx)$
2. $\sim Da$ $/ \sim Ka$

This example has a singular statement in the second premise and in the conclusion. When this occurs we should think of an individual who is well known. In this way, the truth value of the statements we create will be obvious. For example, the first premise can be translated as "Every *D* is a *K*." In other words, if the first premise is true, then the *D* group is included in the *K* group. The second premise can be translated as "*a* is not a *D*." In other words, if the second premise is true, then the individual *a* is not a member of *D*. Finally, the conclusion can be translated as "*a* is not a *K*." Recall that our goal is to try to get the conclusion false and the premises true. In other words, if the conclusion is false, then the individual *a* is a member of the *K* group. Here is one substitution instance:

All United States senators are humans.
Jon Stewart is not a United States senator.
Therefore, Jon Stewart is not a human.

The premises are true, and the conclusion is false. Therefore, the counterexample to the original argument shows that it is invalid.

The counterexample method works well with simple invalid predicate logic arguments. However, as arguments get more complex, the method can become quite challenging. The next method for showing invalidity can handle the complex cases.

Finite Universe Method

A valid argument that uses quantifiers is valid for any number of individuals, with just one stipulation: there is at least one individual in the universe. In order to show that an argument that uses quantifiers is invalid, a model containing at least one individual needs to reveal the possibility of true premises and a false conclusion. If an argument using quantifiers is invalid, it is always possible to create such a model. This is referred to as the **finite universe method**, or *possible universe method*, of showing invalidity.

Finite universe method The method of demonstrating invalidity that assumes a universe, containing at least one individual, to show the possibility of true premises and a false conclusion.

We first establish a set of individuals that are said to exist in the possible universe of the given model. We then use the indirect truth table method to determine invalidity. However, before we get to arguments, we need to develop a few basic building blocks.

Let's imagine a universe that contains only one individual. Imagine further that this individual is bald. If we assign the letter *a* to this individual, then we get *Ba*. An interesting

PROFILES IN LOGIC

Bertrand Russell

It is hard to imagine a philosopher with as long and interesting a life as Bertrand Russell (1872–1970). His influence stretched from logic and philosophy to literature and social issues.

Russell collaborated with Alfred Whitehead in the monumental *Principia Mathematica*, in which they tried to reduce mathematics to formal logic. They thought that all *mathematical truths* could be translated into *logical truths*, and all *mathematical proofs* could be translated as *logical proofs*. Russell was also instrumental in clarifying the basics of predicate logic. He firmly believed that by using logic philosophers could reveal the *logical form* of ordinary language statements. This would go a long way in resolving many problems caused by the ambiguity and vagueness of ordinary language.

However, Russell's writing was not limited to technical aspects of logic and philosophy. He wrote many successful books that popularized philosophical thinking, with a gift for explaining difficult subjects in clear language. He was awarded the Nobel Prize for Literature in 1950, "in recognition of his varied and significant writings in which he champions humanitarian ideals and freedom of thought."

Russell was not one to hide away in academia. He fought passionately for many social causes throughout his life and was imprisoned for 5 months in 1918 as a result of antiwar protests. Forty-three years later, in 1961, he was again imprisoned for participating in antinuclear protests.

Russell believed that education was essential for social progress: "Education is the key to the new world." We need to understand nature and each other. He was highly critical of superstitious beliefs of any kind. If we rely on evidence instead of superstitions, then we can make social progress: "It is undesirable to believe a proposition when there is no ground whatever for supposing it true."

Russell summed up his life in this statement: "Three passions, simple but overwhelmingly strong, have governed my life: the longing for love, the search for knowledge, and unbearable pity for the suffering of mankind."

thing occurs: The existential statement "Something is bald" and the universal statement "Everything is bald" are equivalent. In other words, in this universe containing one individual, $(\exists x)\,Bx$ is equivalent to $(x)\,Bx$. We can formalize the results as follows:

(x) Bx is *conditionally equivalent* to Ba
(∃x) Bx is *conditionally equivalent* to Ba

We use the expression "conditionally equivalent" because the equivalence is in *this* possible universe. In other words, it is not unconditionally equivalent. We will assign the symbol "-CE-" to the expression "conditionally equivalent."

Now what happens in a universe containing two individuals? Let's assign the letter *a* to one individual, and the letter *b* to the other individual. In this universe, the universal statement "Everything is bald" can be symbolized as follows:

(x) Bx -CE- Ba · Bb

In a universe containing two individuals, if *everything is bald*, then both individuals are bald. This result is symbolized by using a *conjunction*. However, in the universe containing two individuals, the existential statement "Something is bald" gets symbolized differently:

(∃x) Bx -CE- Ba ∨ Bb

In the universe containing two individuals, if *something is bald*, then *at least one* individual is bald. This result is symbolized by a *disjunction*. The general thrust of the procedure should now be clear: As the number of individuals in the possible universe increases, they are joined by a *conjunction* for a universal statement. However, they are joined by a *disjunction* for an existential statement.

Let's extend this idea even further. Suppose we have a universe containing three individuals, and we have the statement $(x)(Fx \supset Gx)$. These are the results:

(x)(Fx ⊃ Gx) -CE- [(Fa ⊃ Ga) · (Fb ⊃ Gb) · (Fc ⊃ Gc)]

In this universe, the statement $(\exists x)\,(Fx \cdot Gx)$ has this result:

(∃x) (Fx · Gx) -CE- [(Fa · Ga) ∨ (Fb · Gb) ∨ (Fc · Gc)]

Indirect Truth Tables

We are now in position to show the invalidity of an argument. The following example will illustrate the procedure:

(x) (Hx ⊃ Mx)
(x) (Rx ⊃ Mx)   / (x) (Rx ⊃ Hx)

We can try a universe containing one individual, represented by the letter *a*:

Ha ⊃ Ma
Ra ⊃ Ma   / Ra ⊃ Ha

The first step is to determine whether to start with a premise or with the conclusion. Recall that the most efficient way to proceed is to start with whatever has the least number of possible cases. For this example, since the conclusion is a conditional statement, there is only one way for the conclusion to be false—when the antecedent is true and the consequent false. We assign the appropriate truth values to the guide on the left:

Ha	Ma	Ra	Ha ⊃ Ma	Ra ⊃ Ma	/ Ra ⊃ Ha
F		T	[T]		[F]

The assignment of truth values makes the first premise true because the antecedent is false. Now if *Ma* is true, then the second premise is true. We add this information to complete the truth table:

Ha	Ma	Ra	Ha ⊃ Ma	Ra ⊃ Ma	/ Ra ⊃ Ha	
F	T	T	[T]	[T]	[F]	√

The assignment of truth values in a universe containing one individual reveals the possibility of true premises and false conclusion. Therefore, the argument is invalid. This result has been indicated by the check mark to the right of the line.

Let's try an argument with a universal statement in the premise and an existential statement in the conclusion:

$$(x) \ (Cx \supset Dx) \qquad\qquad / \ (\exists x) \ (Cx \cdot Dx)$$

We can try a universe containing one individual:

Ca	Da	Ca ⊃ Da	/ Ca · Da	
F	T	[T]	[F]	√

The assignment of truth values shows that the argument is invalid. But what if a universe containing one individual does not show that an argument is invalid? In that case, we must try a universe containing two individuals. Here is an example:

All fanatics are dangerous people. There is at least one fanatic. Therefore, everything is dangerous.

We can translate it and get the following:

$$(x) \ (Fx \supset Dx)$$
$$(\exists x) \ Fx \qquad\qquad\qquad / \ (x) \ Dx$$

We first try a universe containing one individual:

Fa	Da	Fa ⊃ Da	Fa	/ Da
T	F	[F]	[T]	[F]

The conclusion is false when *Da* is false. The second premise is true when *Fa* is true. However, these assignments make the first premise false. Therefore, this universe is not sufficient to show the argument is invalid. Therefore, we next try a universe containing two individuals:

Fa	Da	Fb	Db	(Fa ⊃ Da) · (Fb ⊃ Db)	Fa ∨ Fb	/ Da · Db	
T	T	F	F	T [T] T	[T]	[F]	√

The truth table shows the possibility of true premises and a false conclusion. Therefore, the argument is invalid. The finite universe method can be summed up in three steps:

1. Try a universe containing one individual. If the argument is shown to be invalid, you are finished. Otherwise, go to step 2.
2. Try a universe containing two individuals. If the argument is shown to be invalid, you are finished. Otherwise, go to step 3.
3. Try a universe containing three individuals. If the argument is still not shown to be invalid, then go back and check your work for any simple mistakes. Going beyond a universe containing three individuals can make the indirect truth tables difficult to manage. Therefore, if you suspect that the argument is valid, then try proving its validity using the rules of inference.

CHECK YOUR UNDERSTANDING 9E

I. Use the *counterexample* method to show the invalidity of the following arguments.

[1] 1. $(x)(Cx \supset Dx)$
    2. $(\exists x) Cx$ / $(x) Dx$

Answer:

Every puppy is a dog.
There is a puppy.
Therefore, everything is a dog.

[2] 1. $(x)(Dx \supset Fx)$ / $(\exists x) Dx \supset (x) Fx$

[3] 1. $(x)(Fx \supset {\sim}Hx)$
    2. $(\exists x) Gx$
    3. $(\exists x) Fx$ / $(\exists x)(Gx \cdot {\sim}Hx)$

[4] 1. $(\exists x) Lx$ / $(x) Lx$

⭐ [5] 1. $(\exists x)(Gx \cdot Hx)$ / $(x)(Gx \supset Hx)$

[6] 1. $(x)(Dx \supset {\sim}Lx)$
    2. $(x)(Dx \supset Gx)$ / $(x)(Lx \supset {\sim}Gx)$

[7] 1. $(x)(Bx \supset Cx)$
    2. $(x)(Bx \supset Dx)$ / $(x)(Cx \supset Dx)$

[8] 1. $(\exists x)(Fx \cdot Gx)$
    3. $(\exists x)(Hx \cdot {\sim}Gx)$ / $(\exists x)(Fx \cdot {\sim}Hx)$

⭐ [9] 1. $(x)(Fx \supset Gx)$ / $(x) Fx \lor (x) Gx$

[10] 1. $(\exists x) Lx$
     2. $(\exists x) Dx$ / $(\exists x)(Lx \cdot Dx)$

II. Use the *finite universe method* to show the invalidity of the following arguments.

[1] 1. $(x) (Px \supset \sim Qx)$
    2. $(x) (Qx \supset \sim Rx)$ $/ (x) (Px \supset \sim Rx)$

Answer:

A universe containing one individual:

$Pa \supset \sim Qa$
$Qa \supset \sim Ra$ $/ Pa \supset \sim Ra$

The following truth value assignments show the argument is invalid:

Pa	Qa	Ra	$Pa \supset \sim Qa$	$Qa \supset \sim Ra$	$/ Pa \supset \sim Ra$	
T	F	T	T T	T F	F F	√

[2] 1. $(x) (Dx \lor Fx)$
    2. $(x) Dx$ $/ (x) \sim Fx$

[3] 1. $(\exists x) (Px \cdot \sim Qx)$
    2. $(x) (Rx \supset \sim Qx)$ $/ (x) (Rx \supset Px)$

[4] 1. $(x) (Fx \supset Hx)$
    2. $(x) \sim Fx$ $/ (x) \sim Hx$

★ [5] 1. $(x) (Lx \supset Mx)$
      2. $(x) Mx$ $/ (x) Lx$

[6] 1. $(x) (Gx \lor Hx)$ $/ (x) Gx$

[7] 1. $(x) (Dx \supset Gx)$
    2. $(\exists x) Gx$ $/ (x) Dx$

[8] 1. $(x) (Cx \supset \sim Dx)$ $/ (x) (Dx \supset Cx)$

★ [9] 1. $(x) (Hx \supset Fx)$
      2. $(x) (Fx \supset Gx)$ $/ (x) (Gx \supset Hx)$

[10] 1. $\sim (x) Fx \supset (\exists y) Gy$ $/ (x) Fx \supset (\exists y) Gy$

[11] 1. $(\exists x) (Fx \cdot \sim Dx)$
     2. $(\exists x) (Cx \cdot Dx)$ $/ (x) (Fx \supset \sim Cx)$

[12] 1. $\sim (x) (Mx \supset Kx)$ $/ (x) Mx \supset (x) Kx$

★ [13] 1. $(\exists x) (Gx \cdot Lx)$
       2. $(\exists x) (Gx \cdot Hx)$ $/ (x) (Lx \supset Hx)$

[14] 1. Ga
     2. $(x) (Lx \supset Gx)$ $/ La$

[15] 1. $(\exists x) (Gx \cdot \sim Dx)$
     2. $(\exists x) (Hx \cdot \sim Fx)$
     3. $(\exists x) (Dx \cdot Hx)$ $/ (\exists x) (Gx \cdot Hx)$

III. First, translate the following arguments. Second, use the *finite universe method* to show they are invalid.

1. All diamonds are carbon. Graphite is carbon. Thus, diamonds are graphite. (D, C, G)

Translation: 1. $(x) (Dx \supset Cx)$

    2. $(x) (Gx \supset Cx)$ $/ (x) (Dx \supset Gx)$

A universe containing one individual:

        1. $Da \supset Ca$

        2. $Ga \supset Ca$ $/ Da \supset Ga$

Da	Ca	Ga	$Da \supset Ca$	$Ga \supset Ca$	$Da \supset Ga$
T	T	F	$\boxed{T}$	$\boxed{T}$	$\boxed{F}$

2. All horses are mammals. Some horses are pets. Therefore, all pets are mammals. (H, M, P)

3. All problem-solvers and all thinkers have minds. Computers are problem-solvers. Thus, computers are thinkers. (P, T, M, C)

4. Every dancer and every singer is right-brained. There is at least one singer. Thus, everyone is right-brained. (D, S, R)

★ 5. Some CEOs are not people blindly devoted to profits. Some women are CEOs. Therefore, some people blindly devoted to profits are not women. (C, B, W)

F. RELATIONAL PREDICATES

The system of predicate logic developed thus far is capable of handling many kinds of statements and arguments. So far, however, we have been using **monadic predicates**, such as Fx, Gy, and Hz. These are one-place predicates that assign a characteristic to an individual. But we know that ordinary language is extremely complex. For example, consider this argument:

> Saul is older than Pablo. In addition, Pablo is older than Chang. Of course, it is true of anything that if one thing is older than a second thing, and the second thing is older than a third thing, then the first thing is older than the third thing. It follows that Saul is older than Chang.

An essential part of the argument is the phrase "is older than." A translation of this phrase requires a **relational predicate**, which establishes a connection between individuals. For example, a binary relation connects two individuals, such as the phrase "is older than." As you can imagine, relations can exist between three or more individuals. However, we will concentrate on binary relations.

A translation of an ordinary language statement that uses relational predicates often provides a guide to the symbols. These guides are written in a special way, and they are

Monadic predicate A one-place predicate that assigns a characteristic to an individual thing.

Relational predicate Establishes a connection between individuals.

used to help understand the translation. For example, the phrase "is older than" can be translated as *Oxy*. This is read as "*x* is older than *y*." A complete guide to the translation of the earlier argument is written in this style:

> *Oxy*: *x* is older than *y*; *s*: Saul; *p*: Pablo; *c*: Chang

We can now translate the argument:

> *Osp*
> *Opc*
> (*x*) (*y*) (*z*) [(*Oxy* · *Oyz*) ⊃ *Oxz*]   / *Osc*

We will defer the proof of the argument until the next section. For now, we will concentrate on translating ordinary language using relational predicates.

Translations

Translating ordinary language using relational predicates requires paying close attention to the placement of the logical symbols. Here are some examples that involve relations among specifically named individuals:

> 1. Kelly is married to Rick.   *Mkr*
> 2. Peter is the father of Helen.   *Fph*
> 3. Kris loves Morgan.   *Lkm*

These three examples illustrate some general features of relations. The first is an example of a **symmetrical** relationship. In other words, if Kelly is married to Rick, then Rick is married to Kelly. If we let *Mxy*: *x* is married to *y*, then the form of the symmetrical relationship is as follows:

$$(x)\ (y)\ (Mxy \supset Myx)$$

Symmetrical Illustrated by the following: If A is married to B, then B is married to A.

The second example illustrates an **asymmetrical** relationship. In other words, if Peter is the father of Helen, then Helen is *not* the father of Peter. If we let *Fxy*: *x* is the father of *y*, then the form of the asymmetrical relationship is as follows:

$$(x)\ (y)\ (Fxy \supset \sim Fyx)$$

Asymmetrical Illustrated by the following: If A is the father of B, then B is not the father of A.

When a relationship is neither symmetrical nor asymmetrical, then it is **nonsymmetrical**. The third example is an illustration of a nonsymmetrical relationship. In other words, if Kris loves Morgan, then Morgan may or may not love Kris. (Given this, we do not create a form of the nonsymmetrical relationship.)

Nonsymmetrical When a relationship is neither symmetrical nor asymmetrical, then it is nonsymmetrical. Illustrated by the following: If Kris loves Morgan, then Morgan may or may not love Kris.

Here is another example of an ordinary language statement that uses specifically named individuals:

> If the Eiffel Tower is taller than the Washington Monument, and the Washington Monument is taller than the Lincoln Memorial, then the Eiffel Tower is taller than the Lincoln Memorial.

This example is an illustration of a **transitive** relationship. In general terms, if A is taller than B, and B is taller than C, then A is taller than C. If we let *Txy*: *x* is taller than *y*, then the form of the transitive relationship is as follows:

Transitive Illustrated by the following: If A is taller than B, and B is taller than C, then A is taller than C.

$$(x)\ (y)\ (z)\ [(Txy \cdot Tyz) \supset Txz]$$

Of course, not all relations are transitive. For example, "the mother of" is an **intransitive** relationship. In general terms, if A is the mother of B, and B is the mother of C, then A is *not* the mother of C. If we let Mxy: x is the mother of y, then the form of the intransitive relationship is as follows:

$$(x)\ (y)\ (z)\ [(Mxy \cdot Myz) \supset\ \sim Mxz]$$

When a relationship is neither transitive nor intransitive, then it is **nontransitive**. Here is an example:

Kris loves Morgan and Morgan loves Terry.

This illustrates a nontransitive relationship. In other words, if Kris loves Morgan and Morgan loves Terry, then Kris may or may not love Terry. (Given this, we do not create a form of the nontransitive relationship.)

We can now examine some translations of ordinary language statements that do not use specifically named individuals. Here is an example:

Someone helps everyone.

Although it is a short sentence, there is a lot of logical information that has to be unpacked. The translation will include an existential quantifier (for "someone") and a universal quantifier (for "everyone"). Let's begin the translation by rephrasing the statement using some symbols:

There is an x such that x is a person, and for every y, if y is a person, then x helps y.

The rephrased statement is a blueprint for the construction of the final translation:

$$(\exists x)\ [Px \cdot (y)\ (Py \supset Hxy)]$$

The translation keeps all the logical symbols in order and captures the relations in the English sentence. Here is another example:

Everyone flatters someone.

You probably already realized that the translation will include a universal quantifier (for "everyone") and an existential quantifier (for "someone"). Once again, it helps to begin the translation by rephrasing the statement:

For any x, if x is a person, then there is a y such that y is a person and x flatters y.

The rephrased statement is the basis for the final translation:

$$(x)\ [Px \supset (\exists y)(Py \cdot Fxy)]$$

Let's look at another example:

No one cheats everyone.

The translation will have two universal quantifiers (one for "no one" and one for "everyone"). We can begin the translation by rephrasing the statement:

Intransitive Illustrated by the following: If A is the mother of B, and B is the mother of C, then A is not the mother of C.

Nontransitive Illustrated by the following: If Kris loves Morgan and Morgan loves Terry, then Kris may or may not love Terry.

For every x, if x is a person, then it is not true that for every y, if y is a person, x cheats y.

The rephrased statement is the basis for the translation:

$$(x) [Px \supset \sim (y)(Py \supset Cxy)]$$

There is an alternate translation that is logically equivalent to the one above. In order to construct the alternative translation, the original statement needs to be rephrased in a different way:

It is not the case that there is an x such that x is a person, and for every y, if y is a person, then x cheats y.

The rephrased statement is the basis for the following translation:

$$\sim (\exists x) [Px \cdot (y) (Py \supset Cxy)]$$

One more example will illustrate another kind of translation that is possible using relational predicates:

No one influences anyone.

Once again, we begin the translation by rephrasing the statement:

For any x, if x is a person, then for any y, if y is a person, x does not influence y.

The translation has two universal quantifiers:

$$(x) [Px \supset (y)(Py \supset \sim Ixy)]$$

There is an alternate translation that is logically equivalent to the one above. Once again, in order to construct the alternative translation, the original statement needs to be rephrased in a different way:

It is not the case that there is an x such that x is a person, and there is a y such that y is a person, and x influences y.

The translation has two existential quantifiers:

$$\sim (\exists x) [Px \cdot (\exists y) (Py \cdot Ixy)]$$

The following is a summary of some of the examples presented. You can use it as a guide to help with translations.

English Statement	Translation
Kelly is married to Rick.	Mkr
Peter is the father of Helen.	Fph
Kris loves Morgan.	Lkm
Someone helps everyone.	$(\exists x) [Px \cdot (y) (Py \supset Hxy)]$
Everyone flatters someone.	$(x) [Px \supset (\exists y)(Py \cdot Fxy)]$
No one cheats everyone.	$(x) [Px \supset \sim (y)(Py \supset Cxy)]$
	or
	$\sim (\exists x) [Px \cdot (y) (Py \supset Cxy)]$
No one influences anyone.	$(x) [Px \supset (y)(Py \supset \sim Ixy)]$
	or
	$\sim (\exists x) [Px \cdot (\exists y) (Py \cdot Ixy)]$

CHECK YOUR UNDERSTANDING 9F.1

Translate the following statements into symbolic form.

1. Every play by William Shakespeare is either a tragedy or a history.
   (*Pxy*: *x* is a play by *y*; *Tx*: *x* is a tragedy; *Hx*: *x* is a history; *s*: William Shakespeare)

Answer: $(x) [Pxs \supset (Tx \lor Hx)]$

2. No one in this city is a relative of George Washington.
   (*Cx*: *x* is in this city; *Rxy*: *x* is a relative of *y*; *w*: George Washington)

3. Sam cannot jump higher than everyone on the team.
   (*Fxy*: *x* can jump higher than *y*; *Tx*: *x* is on the team; *s*: Sam)

4. Some strange disease killed Leo.
   (*Kxy*: *x* killed *y*; *Sx*: *x* is strange; *Dx*: *x* is a disease; *l*: Leo)

★ 5. Something destroyed everything.
   (*Dxy*: *x* destroyed *y*)

6. There is a barber who shaves all those barbers who do not shave themselves.
   (*Bx*: *x* is a barber; *Sxy*: *x* shaves *y*)

7. Anyone older than Florence is older than Ralph.
   (*Oxy*: *x* is older than *y*; *f*: Florence; *r*: Ralph)

8. If anyone fails the exam, then everyone will blame someone.
   (*Fx*: *x* fails the exam; *Bxy*: *x* will blame *y*)

★ 9. Anyone who reads Tolstoy reads Dostoevsky.
   (*Rxy*: *x* reads *y*; *t*: Tolstoy; *d*: Dostoevsky)

10. No one is smarter than Isaac.
    (*Sxy*: *x* is smarter than *y*; *i*: Isaac)

11. Jane is taller than Lester.
    (*Txy*: *x* is taller than *y*; *j*: Jane; *l*: Lester)

12. No one is a sister of everyone.
    (*Sxy*: *x* is a sister of *y*)

★13. Everyone is a child of someone.
    (*Cxy*: *x* is a child of *y*)

14. Sharon has at least one brother.
    (*Bxy*: *x* is a brother of *y*; *s*: Sharon)

15. Steve has no living relatives.
    (*Lx*: *x* is living; *Rxy*: *x* is a relative of *y*; *s*: Steve)

16. Someone is the uncle of every United States senator.
    (*Sx*: *x* is a United States senator; *Uxy*: *x* is the uncle of *y*)

★ 17. Every grandparent is the parent of a parent of someone.
     (*Gx*: *x* is a grandparent; *Pxy*: *x* is a parent of *y*)

18. No one ate anything.
    (*Axy*: *x* ate *y*)

19. Anyone who is not faster than Mabel is not faster than Sophie.
    (*Wxy*: *x* is faster than *y*; *m*: Mabel; *s*: Sophie)

20. Every retired steelworker lives on some fixed income.
    (*Rx*: *x* is retired; *Sx*: *x* is a steelworker; *Lxy*: *x* lives on *y*; *Fy*: *y* is a fixed income)

Proofs

The inference rules that have been introduced can be used with relational predicates. However, in a few special situations, the relational predicates and overlapping quantifiers place restrictions on some of the rules. But before we get to the restrictions, let's take a look at a proof that is straightforward. The example is the argument that was introduced earlier, only now applied to relational predicates. Here is the argument:

> Saul is older than Pablo. In addition, Pablo is older than Chang. Of course, it is true of anything that if one thing is older than a second thing, and the second thing is older than a third thing, then the first thing is older than the third thing. It follows that Saul is older than Chang.

1. *Osp*
2. *Opc*
3. *(x) (y) (z) [(Oxy · Oyz) ⊃ Oxz]*   / *Osc*
4. *(y) (z) [(Osy · Oyz) ⊃ Osz]*   3, UI
5. *(z) [(Osp · Opz) ⊃ Osz]*   4, UI
6. *(Osp · Opc) ⊃ Osc*   5, UI
7. *Osp · Opc*   1, 2, Conj
8. *Osc*   6, 7, MP

Notice that in lines 4, 5, and 6, each time UI was applied, the leftmost quantifier was eliminated: line 4 eliminated (*x*); line 5 eliminated (*y*); finally, line 6 eliminated (*z*). The proof sequence applied the rules of inference to premises with relational predicates and overlapping quantifiers. No restrictions were placed on the rules in the proof.

A New Restriction

The next example shows how instantiation and generalization can proceed with overlapping quantifiers.

1. *(∃x) (y) (Axy ⊃ Bxy)*
2. *(x) (y) Axy*   / *(∃x) (y) Bxy*
3. *(y) (Acy ⊃ Bcy)*   1, EI
4. *(y) Acy*   2, UI

5. $Acy \supset Bcy$ 3, UI
6. Acy 4, UI
7. Bcy 5, 6, MP
8. $(y) Bcy$ 7, UG
9. $(\exists x)(y) Bxy$ 8, EG

The proof followed the normal way of using instantiation by applying EI to line 1 before applying UI. The important step for us to examine occurs in line 8. The instantial variable y in line 8 was derived from line 3. The crucial aspect of line 3 is that the instantial variable y *is not free* in line 3. We can formalize this discussion as an additional restriction placed on UG:

Universal Generalization (UG)

$$\frac{\mathcal{S}y}{(x)\mathcal{S}x}$$

Restriction 1: *Universal generalization cannot be used within an indented proof sequence, if the instantial variable is free in the first line of the sequence.*

Restriction 2: *Universal generalization cannot be used if the instantial variable y is free in any line that was obtained by existential instantiation (EI).*

Universal instantiation (UI) gets applied in the same manner as before. However, you must be careful not to violate the basic technique when applying it to certain relations. For example, here is how UI works without any relations involved:

1. $(x)(Fx \supset Hx)$
2. $Fy \supset Hy$ 1, UI

The important thing to notice is that the instantial variable y is free in line 2. The same kind of result needs to follow when you apply UI to a relation. Here is an example of a correct application of UI:

1. $(x)(\exists y) Gxy$
2. $(\exists y) Gxy$ 1, UI Valid: The instantial variable x is free in line 2.

Here is an example of an *incorrect* application of UI:

1. $(x)(\exists y) Gxy$
2. $(\exists y) Gyy$ 1, UI **Invalid:** The instantial variable y is not free in line 2; it is bound by the existential quantifier.

Change of Quantifier

We apply the change of quantifier rule to overlapping quantifiers step by step. The following example illustrates the correct technique:

1. $\sim (\exists x)(y) Gxy$
2. $(x) \sim (y) Gxy$ 1, CQ
3. $(x)(\exists y) \sim Gxy$ 2, CQ

The first application of the rule moved the tilde and switched the existential quantifier to a universal quantifier. The second application moved the tilde and switched the universal quantifier to an existential quantifier.

Conditional Proof and Indirect Proof

The next example illustrates how the conditional proof method can be applied in essentially the same manner as before. The addition of relational predicates and overlapping quantifiers do not affect the method, as long as the rules of inference and restrictions are followed.

1.	(x) [(y) Fxy ⊃ Ga]	/ (x) (y) Fxy ⊃ Ga
2.	(x) (y) Fxy	Assumption CP
3.	(y) Fby ⊃ Ga	1, UI
4.	(y) Fby	2, UI
5.	Ga	3, 4, MP
6.	(x) (y) Fxy ⊃ Ga	2–5, CP

The next example illustrates how the indirect proof method can be applied. Once again, the addition of relational predicates and overlapping quantifiers do not affect the method, as long as the rules of inference and restrictions are followed.

1.	(x) [(Fx · Gx) ⊃ Hax]	
2.	(x) (Fx ⊃ ~ Hxx)	
3.	Fa	/ ~ Ga
4.	Ga	Assumption IP
5.	(Fa · Ga) ⊃ Haa	1, UI
6.	Fa · Ga	3, 4, Conj
7.	Haa	5, 6, MP
8.	Fa ⊃ ~ Haa	2, UI
9.	~ Haa	3, 8, MP
10.	Haa · ~ Haa	7, 9, Conj
11.	~ Ga	4–10, IP

CHECK YOUR UNDERSTANDING 9F.2

Use the rules of inference to derive the conclusions of the following arguments. You can use conditional proof or indirect proof.

[1] 1. (∃x) [Lx · (y) (My ⊃ Pxy)]   / (∃x) [Lx · (Mb ⊃ Pxb)]

Answer:

1.	(∃x) [Lx · (y) (My ⊃ Pxy)]	/ (∃x) [Lx · (Mb ⊃ Pxb)]
2.	La · (y) (My ⊃ Pay)	1, EI
3.	La	2, Simp
4.	(y) (My ⊃ Pay) · La	2, Com
5.	(y) (My ⊃ Pay)	4, Simp
6.	Mb ⊃ Pab	5, UI
7.	La · (Mb ⊃ Pab)	3, 6, Conj
8.	(∃x) [Lx · (Mb ⊃ Pxb)]	7, EG

[2] 1. (x) $(Fax \lor Fxa)$ / Faa

[3] 1. (x) $[Fx \supset (y)$ $Hxy]$
     2. Fa / (y) Hay

[4] 1. (x) (y) $(Fxy \supset Fyx)$
     2. Fab / Fba

⭐ [5] 1. (x) (y) $(Fxy \supset \sim Fyx)$
       2. Fba / $\sim Fab$

[6] 1. $(\exists x)$ (y) $\sim Gxy$
     2. (x) $(\exists y)$ $Fxy \supset (x)$ $(\exists y)$ Gxy / $(\exists x)$ (y) $\sim Fxy$

[7] 1. (x) $(\exists y)$ $\sim Mxy$
     2. (x) (y) $(Lx \supset Mxy)$ / $(\exists x)$ $\sim Lx$

[8] 1. $(\exists x)$ $[Fx \cdot (y)$ $(Fy \supset Gyx)]$ / $(\exists x)$ $(Fx \cdot Gxx)$

⭐ [9] 1. $\sim (\exists x)$ $[Fx \cdot (\exists y)$ $(Fy \cdot Bxy)]$ / (x) $[Fx \supset (y)$ $(Fy \supset \sim Bxy)]$

[10] 1. $(\exists x)$ $[Mx \cdot (y)$ $(My \supset Pxy)]$ / $(\exists x)$ Pxx

[11] 1. $(\exists x)$ (y) Cxy
      2. (x) $(\exists y)$ $(Cxy \supset Dxy)$ / $(\exists x)$ $(\exists y)$ Dxy

[12] 1. (x) $[Fx \supset (y)$ $(Gy \supset Hxy)]$
      2. $Fa \cdot \sim Hab$ / $\sim Gb$

⭐ [13] 1. (x) $(\exists y)$ $(Mx \cdot Py)$ / (x) Mx

[14] 1. $(\exists x)$ $Lx \supset \sim (\exists y)$ Py
      2. (x) $(Lx \supset Mx)$ / (x) $[(\exists y)$ $Ly \supset \sim Px]$

[15] 1. $(La \cdot Ma) \cdot \sim Pab$
      2. (x) $\{(Lx \cdot Mx) \supset (y)$ $[(\sim Ly \cdot My) \supset Pxy]\}$ / $Mb \supset Lb$

[16] 1. $(\exists x)$ (y) $\sim Mxy$
      2. (x) $(\exists y)$ $Lxy \supset (x)$ $(\exists y)$ Mxy / $(\exists x)$ (y) $\sim Lxy$

⭐ [17] 1. Fa / (x) $[(Gx \cdot Hxa) \supset (\exists y)$ $(Fy \cdot Hxy)]$

[18] 1. $(\exists x)$ $Fx \supset (\exists y)$ Gy
      2. $(\exists x)$ $\{Fx \cdot (y)$ $[(Gy \lor Hy) \supset Lxy]\}$ / $(\exists x)$ $(\exists y)$ Lxy

[19] 1. $(\exists x)$ $\{Fx \cdot (y)$ $[(Fy \cdot Dxy) \supset Hxy]\}$
      2. (x) $[Fx \supset (\exists y)$ $(Fy \cdot Dxy)]$ / $(\exists x)$ $(\exists y)$ $[(Fx \cdot Fy) \supset Hxy]$

[20] 1. $(\exists x)$ Fx / $\sim (\exists x)$ $\{Fx \cdot (y)$ $[Fy \supset (Hxy \equiv \sim Hyy)]\}$

G. IDENTITY

There is a special kind of relation that occurs in ordinary language that can be illustrated by the following argument:

> Lewis Carroll wrote *Alice in Wonderland*. But Lewis Carroll is Charles Lutwidge Dodgson. Therefore, Charles Lutwidge Dodgson wrote *Alice in Wonderland*.

Identity A binary relation that holds between a thing and itself.

The argument involves *identity*. The **identity** relation is sometimes defined as a binary relation that holds between a thing and itself. In this example, the conclusion indicates an identity between the person who is Lewis Carroll and the person who is Charles Lutwidge Dodgson. We will use the identity symbol "$=$" to translate statements involving the identity relation. For example:

> Lewis Carroll is Charles Lutwidge Dodgson. $l = c$

The translation is quite short compared to the statement in English. However, this will not always be the case. Many ordinary language statements that use identity relations require long arrangements of symbols. This is necessary in order to spell out the details. Several kinds of identity relations need to be explored, so let's get started.

Simple Identity Statements

An assertion that one named individual is identical to another named individual is common in ordinary language. The Lewis Carroll-Charles Lutwidge Dodgson identity relation is one example. In this case, the assertion is that the name "Lewis Carroll" and the name "Charles Lutwidge Dodgson" *designate the same person*. Here are some more examples:

> Michelle Obama is Michelle LaVaughn Robinson. $m = r$
> Bono is Paul Hewson. $b = p$
> The Mississippi River is Old Man River. $m = o$
> Mount Everest is Sagarmatha. $e = s$

We can modify the identity symbol to translate a negated identity statement. Here is the technique:

> Brad Pitt is not Jennifer Aniston. $b \neq j$
> Mount Everest is not K2. $e \neq k$
> Muhammad Ali is not Will Smith. $m \neq w$

The symbol "$\neq$" is a shorthand way of writing the negation of an identity. For example, instead of writing $\sim (a = b)$, we can simply write $a \neq b$. There are many kinds of ordinary language statements that require more elaborate arrangements. We will examine some of the most common types.

"Only"

Recall that statements with the word "only" can be rewritten as straightforward categorical statements. Here is an example:

Original: Only government-issued IDs are valid documents.
Rewritten: All valid documents are government-issued IDs.

In the example, the term that follows "only" is a plural noun ("government-issued IDs"). However, there are many examples in ordinary language where the word or words following "only" designate an individual. These kinds of statements require a more complex translation. Here is an example:

Only John F. Kennedy was a Catholic U.S. president

If we unpack the statement's meaning, two things are clear: first, that John F. Kennedy was a Catholic U.S. president; and second, that *if anyone* was a Catholic U.S. president, then that person is John F. Kennedy. The translation needs to capture these two points. If we let Cx: x was a Catholic, Ux: x was a U.S. president, and j: John F. Kennedy, then the translation is the following:

Only John F. Kennedy was a Catholic U.S. president. $Cj \cdot Uj \cdot (x) [(Cx \cdot Ux) \supset x = j]$

The translation can be read this way: John F. Kennedy was a Catholic U.S. president, and if anyone was a Catholic U.S. president, then that person is identical to John F. Kennedy. The translation uses the dot, the horseshoe, the identity sign, and a universal quantifier.

As illustrated in the translation, parentheses are used a bit differently when translating identity relations. For example, there are some cases where we will be able to write the following: $Fs \cdot Hs \cdot Fr \cdot Hr$. Normally, we must separate the three dots by using parentheses. The same modification to the use of parentheses holds for a string of disjunctions. In addition, instead of writing $(x = j) \cdot (f = h) \cdot (x = y)$, we can simplify it to $x = j \cdot f = h \cdot x = y$. Finally, instead of $Gx \supset (x = j)$, we can write $Gx \supset x = j$.

"The Only"

Statements with the phrase "the only" can be rewritten as categorical statements. Here is an example:

Original: The only students in the course are seniors.
Rewritten: All students in the course are seniors.

In the example, the term that follows "the only" is a plural noun ("students"). However, if the ordinary language statement designates an individual, then the translation is more complex. Here is an example that requires careful analysis before attempting a translation:

The only student who passed the driver's exam is Mary.

The translation has to capture the following two points: Mary did not fail the driver's exam; all the other students did fail. If we let Sx: x is a student, Px: x passed the driver's exam, and m: Mary, then the translation is the following:

$$Sm \cdot Pm \cdot (x) [(Sx \cdot Px) \supset x = m]$$

The translation can be read this way: Mary is a student and Mary passed the driver's exam, and if any student passed the driver's exam, then that student is Mary. This has the same meaning as the original statement.

"No . . . Except"

Some statements that use the phrase "No . . . except" are similar to those that use "the only." Here is an example:

> No employee except George is late for work.

The translation has to capture the following points: George is late for work; no other employee is late for work. If we let Ex: x is an employee, Lx: x is late for work, and g: George, then the translation is the following:

$$Eg \cdot Lg \cdot (x) \, [(Ex \cdot Lx) \supset x = g]$$

The translation can be read this way: George is an employee and George is late for work, and if any employee is late for work, then that employee is George. This has the same meaning as the original statement.

"All Except"

Statements that use the phrase "All except" are similar to ones that use "No. . . except" and "the only," but there is a slight difference. Here is an example:

> All the states except Hawaii are located in North America.

The translation has to capture the following points: Hawaii is not located in North America; all the other states are located in North America. If we let Sx: x is a state, Lx: x is located in North America, and h: Hawaii, then the translation is the following:

$$Sh \cdot {\sim} Lh \cdot (x) \, [(Sx \cdot x \neq h) \supset Lx \,]$$

The translation can be read this way: Hawaii is a state and Hawaii is not located in North America, and if any state is not identical to Hawaii, then that state is located in North America. This has the same meaning as the original statement.

Here is another example:

> All the reindeers except Rudolph are allowed to join in reindeer games.

If we let Rx: x is a reindeer, Ax: x is allowed to join in reindeer games, and r: Rudolph, then the translation is the following:

$$Rr \cdot {\sim} Ar \cdot (x) \, [(Rx \cdot x \neq r) \supset Ax]$$

The translation can be read this way: Rudolph is a reindeer and Rudolph is not allowed to join in reindeer games, and if any reindeer is not identical to Rudolph, then that reindeer is allowed to join in reindeer games. This has the same unfortunate meaning as the original statement.

Superlatives

There are some statements that contain *superlatives* (a form of an adjective used to indicate the greatest degree of the quality described by the adjective). Here are some common examples of superlatives: *fastest, tallest, oldest, lightest,* and *warmest.* If you say "Death Valley is the hottest place on Earth," then you are claiming that no other place on Earth is hotter than Death Valley. If we let Px: x is a place on Earth, Hxy: x is hotter than y, and d: Death Valley, then the translation is the following:

$$Pd \cdot (x) \ [(Px \cdot x \neq d) \supset Hdx]$$

The translation can be read this way: Death Valley is a place on Earth, and if anything is a place on Earth and not identical to Death Valley, then Death Valley is hotter than it.

Here is another example:

Burj Khalifa is the tallest structure in the world.

If we let Sx: x is a structure in the world, Txy: x is taller than y, and b: Burj Khalifa, then the translation is the following:

$$Sb \cdot (x) \ [(Sx \cdot x \neq b) \supset Tbx]$$

The translation can be read this way: Burj Khalifa is a structure in the world, and if anything is a structure in the world and not identical to Burj Khalifa, then Burj Khalifa is taller than it.

"At Most"

Some ordinary language statements that use the phrase "at most" can be translated without using numerals. Here is an example:

There is at most one president.

Notice that the statement does not assert that there really are any objects that have the property of being a president. The statement asserts only that *if* any objects have that property, then the maximum number of objects is one. The translation will thus include universal quantifiers and the horseshoe. If we let Px: x is a president, then the translation is the following:

$$(x) \ (y) \ [(Px \cdot Py) \supset x = y]$$

It may seem odd that the translation uses two universal quantifiers to translate the phrase "at most one." The idea behind the translation is that if there are two items, then they are identical. The translation can be read this way: For any x and any y, if x is a president, and y is a president, then x is identical to y.

Following this principle, the phrase "at most two" would get translated by using three universal quantifiers. Here is an example:

There are at most two unicorns.

If we let Ux: x is a unicorn, then the translation is the following:

$$(x)\ (y)\ (z)\ [(Ux \cdot Uy \cdot Uz) \supset (x = y \lor x = z \lor y = z)]$$

The translation can be read this way: For any x, any y, and any z, if x is a unicorn, and y is a unicorn, and z is a unicorn, then either x is identical to y, or x is identical to z, or y is identical to z.

"At Least"

Ordinary language statements that use the phrase "at least" can also be translated without using numerals. Here is an example:

There is at least one honest politician.

Statements that use the phrase "at least" assert that the objects having the property in question actually exist. Their translation will include existential quantifiers. However, the translations will use a number of quantifiers equal to the number of objects mentioned in the original statement. Therefore, if we let Hx: x is honest, and Px: x is a politician, then the translation is the following:

$$(\exists x)\ (Hx \cdot Px)$$

We can now translate the statement "There are at least two honest politicians." As before, let Hx: x is honest, and Px: x is a politician:

There are at least two honest politicians.
$$(\exists x)\ (\exists y)\ (Hx \cdot Px \cdot Hy \cdot Py \cdot x \neq y)$$

The translation has to ensure that the two objects are distinct. Therefore, the equal sign with a slash through it is used to indicate that x and y are not identical. The translation can be read this way: There exists an x and there exists a y such that x is an honest politician and y is an honest politician, and x is not identical to y. This has the same meaning as the original statement.

"Exactly"

Ordinary language statements that use the word "exactly" can often be translated as a combination of "at least" and "at most." Here is an example:

There is exactly one pizza in the oven.

The statement is actually asserting two things: There is *at least* one pizza in the oven, and there is *at most* one pizza in the oven. The translation will therefore include both an existential quantifier and a universal quantifier. If we let Px: x is a pizza, and Ox: x is in the oven, then the translation is the following:

$$(\exists x)\ \{Px \cdot Ox \cdot (y)\ [(Py \cdot Oy) \supset x = y]\}$$

We can now translate the statement "There are exactly two pizzas in the oven." As before, let Px: x is a pizza, and Ox: x is in the oven:

$$(\exists x)\ (\exists y)\ \{Px \cdot Ox \cdot Py \cdot Oy \cdot x \neq y \cdot (z)\ [(Pz \cdot Oz) \supset (z = x \lor z = y)]\}$$

The translation has to ensure that the two objects are distinct. In other words, there are *at least* two pizzas. Therefore, the equal sign with a slash through it is used to indicate that *x* and *y* are not identical. In addition, the translation has to ensure that there are *at most* two pizzas. The universal quantifier was used for this purpose. The translation can be read this way: There exists an *x* and there exists a *y* such that *x* is a pizza in the oven and *y* is a pizza in the oven, and *x* is not identical to *y*, and for any *z*, if *z* is a pizza in the oven, then either *z* is identical to *x* or *z* is identical to *y*. This has the same meaning as the original statement.

Definite Descriptions

Sometimes we refer to a person by *name* (for example, "Matt Groening") and sometimes we refer to the same person by a *description* (for example, "the creator of *The Simpsons*"). This type of description is called a **definite description** because it describes an individual person, place, or thing. Definite descriptions are found in ordinary language. For example, "Matt Groening is the creator of *The Simpsons*." In this example, the statement asserts that one, and only one, person is the creator of *The Simpsons*.

A translation of a statement with a definite description needs to accomplish several tasks. Let's examine these tasks by way of the example:

Matt Groening is the creator of *The Simpsons*.

The translation has to show that *exactly one* person created *The Simpsons*. In order to do this, the translation must show two things: *At least one* person created *The Simpsons*, and *at most one* person created *The Simpsons*. If we let *Cxs*: *x* created *The Simpsons*, and *m*: Matt Groening, then the translation is the following:

$$(\exists x)\ [Cxs \cdot (y)\ (Cys \supset y = x) \cdot x = m\ ]$$

The translation can be read this way: There exists an *x* such that *x* is the creator of *The Simpsons*, and for any *y*, if *y* is the creator of *The Simpsons*, then *y* is identical to *x*, and *x* is identical to *m*. This has the same meaning as the original statement.

Here is another example:

Shane's mother adores him.

Of course, the sentence does not bother to mention that *exactly one* person is Shane's mother, but the translation has to show just that. In other words, *at least one* person is Shane's mother, and *at most one* person is Shane's mother. If we let *Mxs*: *x* is the mother of Shane, and *Axs*: *x* adores Shane, then the translation is the following:

$$(\exists x)\ [Mxs \cdot (y)\ (Mys \supset y = x) \cdot Axs]$$

The translation can be read this way: There exists an *x* such that *x* is the mother of Shane, and for any *y*, if *y* is the mother of Shane, then *y* is identical to *x*, and *x* adores Shane. This has the same meaning as the original statement.

Here is another example:

The present king of the United States is tall.

Definite description
Describes an individual person, place, or thing.

The sentence can be interpreted to mean that there is one and only one present king of the United States and he is tall. Let's diagram this interpretation: let *Pxu*: *x* is the present king of the United States, *Tx*: *x* is tall.

$$(\exists x) \ [Pxu \cdot (y) \ (Pyu \supset y = x) \cdot Tx]$$

This type of statement has important historical significance. The interest for logicians has focused on the truth value of such statements. The philosopher Bertrand Russell proposed one solution: A statement containing a definite description asserts that a specific object exists, and there is only one such object, and the object has the particular characteristic. Under Russell's solution, the foregoing statement is false.

Summary of Identity Translations

Simple Identity Statement

Michelle Obama is Michelle LaVaughn Robinson.

$m = r$

Only

Only John F. Kennedy was a Catholic U.S. president.

$Cj \cdot Uj \cdot (x) \ (Cx \cdot Ux \supset x = j)$

The Only

The only student who passed the driver's exam is Mary.

$Sm \cdot Pm \cdot (x) \ [(Sx \cdot Px) \supset x = m]$

No . . . Except

No employee except George is late for work.

$Eg \cdot Lg \cdot (x) \ [(Ex \cdot Lx) \supset x = g]$

All Except

All the states except Hawaii are located in North America.

$Sh \cdot {\sim} Lh \cdot (x) \ [(Sx \cdot x \neq h) \supset Lx]$

Superlatives

Death Valley is the hottest place on Earth. $Pd \cdot (x) \ [(Px \cdot x \neq d) \supset Hdx]$

At Most

There is at most two unicorns. $(x) \ (y) \ (z) \ [(Ux \cdot Uy \cdot Uz) \supset (x = y \lor x = z \lor y = z)]$

At Least

There are at least two honest politicians. $(\exists x) \ (\exists y) \ (Hx \cdot Px \cdot Hy \cdot Py \cdot x \neq y)$

Exactly

There are exactly two pizzas in the oven. $(\exists x) \ (\exists y) \ \{Px \cdot Ox \cdot Py \cdot Oy \cdot x \neq y \cdot (z) \ [(Pz \cdot Oz) \supset (z = x \lor z = y)]\}$

Definite Descriptions

Shane's mother adores him. $(\exists x) \ [Mxs \cdot (y) \ (Mys \supset y = x) \cdot Axs \ ]$

CHECK YOUR UNDERSTANDING 9G.1

Translate the following statements into symbolic form.

1. Stephanie Kwolek invented Kevlar.
   (*Ixk*: *x* invented Kevlar; *s*: Stephanie Kwolek)

Answer: $(\exists x)\,[Ixk \cdot (y)\,(Iyk \supset y = x) \cdot x = s]$

2. There is at most one moon orbiting around Earth.
   (*Mx*: *x* is a moon; *Ox*: *x* is orbiting around Earth)

3. There is exactly one happy professor.
   (*Hx*: *x* is happy; *Px*: *x* is a professor)

4. Only Tammy is the editor of the *Daily Scoop*.
   (*Ex*: *x* is the editor of the *Daily Scoop*; *t*: Tammy)

⭐ 5. Joseph Conrad is Jozef Teodor Konrad Korzeniowski.
   (c, k)

6. The only child in the playground is Stella.
   (*Cx*: *x* is a child; *Px*: *x* is in the playground; *s*: Stella)

7. All patients except Lou hate medicine.
   (*Px*: *x* is a patient; *Hx*: *x* hates medicine; *l*: Lou)

8. Antarctica is the coldest continent on Earth.
   (*Px*: *x* is a place on Earth; *Cxy*: *x* is colder than *y*; *a*: Antarctica)

⭐ 9. There is at least one famous scientist.
   (*Fx*: *x* is famous; *Sx*: *x* is a scientist)

10. No president except James Buchanan was a bachelor.
    (*Px*: *x* is a president; *Bx*: *x* is a bachelor; *j*: James Buchanan)

11. George Eliot is Mary Ann Evans.
    (g, m)

12. All states except Hawaii get snow.
    (*Sx*: *x* is a state; *Wx*: *x* gets snow; *h*: Hawaii)

⭐ 13. There are at least two pirates.
    (*Px*: *x* is a pirate)

14. The youngest Nobel Laureate is Lawrence Bragg.
    (*Nx*: *x* is a Nobel Laureate; *Yxz*: *x* is younger than *z*; *b*: Lawrence Bragg)

15. Only Egypt has the Sphinx.
    (*Sx*: *x* has the Sphnix; *e*: Egypt)

16. Alexander Fleming discovered penicillin.
    (*Cxp*: *x* discovered penicillin; *f*: Alexander Fleming)

⭐ 17. The only villain in the movie was Krutox.
    (*Vx*: *x* is a villain; *Mx*: *x* is in the movie; *k*: Krutox)

18. No planet in our solar system except Earth is habitable.
    (*Px*: *x* is a planet; *Sx*: *x* is in our solar system; *Hx*: *x* is habitable; *e*: Earth)

19. There are exactly two senators from California.
    (*Sx*: *x* is a senator; *Cx*: *x* is from California)

20. There are at most two senators from New York.
    (*Sx*: *x* is a senator; *Nx*: *x* is from New York)

Proofs

We know how to translate identity statements. However, a special kind of identity relation needs to be developed in order to construct some proofs. The idea that *anything is identical to itself* is expressed by the **reflexive** property. This idea can be symbolized as follows:

$$(x)\ Ixx$$

The statement can be read as "For any *x*, *x* is identical to itself." Not all relations are reflexive. For example, *nothing can be taller than itself*. This is an example of an **irreflexive** relationship; it can be symbolized as follows:

$$(x) \sim Txx$$

The statement can be read as "For any *x*, *x* is not taller than itself." When a relationship is neither reflexive nor irreflexive, then it is **nonreflexive**. For example, if a person loves someone else, but does not love himself, then the relation is not reflexive. On the other hand, if a person loves someone else, and loves herself, then the relation is not irreflexive.

We can now generate three special rules for proofs using the identity relation (Id).

1. <u>Premise</u>   2. $a = b :: b = a$ 3. Sa
   $a = a$ $\underline{a = b}$
                                                                 Sb

a, b are any individual constants

Rule 1 expresses the *reflexive* property (*anything is identical to itself*). This rule permits the insertion of a self-identity on any line of a proof after a premise.

Rule 2 is a replacement rule. It is a special case of a *symmetrical* relationship used for the identity relation. Rule 2 permits the replacement of $a = b$ with $b = a$, or $a \neq b$ with $b \neq a$.

Finally, Rule 3 is a special case of the *transitive* property. Rule 3 allows us to infer from $a = b$, and $b = c$, that $a = c$.

An important part of the identity relation rules is captured in "*a, b* are any individual constants." This means that the three rules *cannot* be applied to variables (*x, y, z*). Let's look at a simple argument:

> Anything that is identical to Moby Dick is a whale. It follows that Moby Dick is a whale.

Reflexive The idea that *anything is identical to itself* is expressed by the reflexive property.

Irreflexive An example of an irreflexive relationship is expressed by the statement "Nothing can be taller than itself."

Nonreflexive When a relationship is neither reflexive nor irreflexive.

If we let *Wx*: *x* is a whale, and *m*: Moby Dick, then we can translate the argument:

$(x) (x = m \supset Wx)$ / *Wm*

Here is the completed proof:

1. $(x) (x = m \supset Wx)$ / *Wm*
2. $m = m \supset Wm$ 1, UI
3. $m = m$ Id
4. *Wm*   2, 3, MP

Identity Rule 1 permits the insertion of a self-identity on any line of a proof after a premise. Since the rule is applied directly into the proof, no other line number is needed. However, the other two identity rules require reference to a line or lines.

We can use the identity rule in a conditional proof or an indirect proof. Here is an example:

1. $\sim (Cb \supset Db)$
2. $Ca \supset Da$ / $\sim (a = b)$
    3. $a = b$ Assumption IP
    4. $Cb \supset Db$ 2, 3, Id
    5. $\sim (Cb \supset Db) \cdot (Cb \supset Db)$ 1, 4, Conj
6. $\sim (a = b)$ 3–5, IP

The justification for line 4 includes a reference to both line 2 and line 3 because it applied the third identity rule. The basic techniques of indirect proof are the same for proofs using the identity rules. Therefore, the IP sequence is discharged in the usual way.

CHECK YOUR UNDERSTANDING 9G.2

Use the rules of inference to derive the conclusions of the following arguments. You can use conditional proof or indirect proof.

[1] 1. *Fa*
   2. $(y) (Fy \supset Gy)$
   3. $a = b$ / *Gb*

Answer:
1. *Fa*
2. $(y) (Fy \supset Gy)$
3. $a = b$ / *Gb*
4. $Fa \supset Ga$ 2, UI
5. *Ga*   1, 4, MP
6. *Gb*   3, 5, Id

[2] 1. *Ha*
   2. $\sim Hb$ / $\sim (a = b)$

[3] 1. Hc
    2. $a = b \supset c = d$
    3. $b = a$ / Hd

[4] 1. $(x)\,(x = a)$
    2. $(\exists x)\,(x = b)$ / $b = a$

⭐ [5] 1. Fb
    2. $(x)\,(Fa \supset x \neq a)$ / $a \neq b$

[6] 1. $(x)\,(x = a)$
    2. Da / $Db \cdot Dc$

[7] 1. $Ha \cdot Hb$
    2. $(x)\,(Hx \supset {\sim} Lxx)$
    3. Lab / ${\sim}(a = b)$

[8] 1. $Fc \cdot Gca$
    2. $(\exists x)\,\{(Fx \cdot Gxa) \cdot (y)\,[(Fy \cdot Gya) \supset y = x] \cdot Hxb\}$ / Hcb

⭐ [9] 1. ${\sim} Lb$
    2. $(x)\,[Hx \supset (Lx \cdot x = b)]$ / ${\sim} Ha$

[10] 1. Ca
    2. $(x)\,(Cx \supset (\exists y)\,Dyx)$
    3. $(y)\,{\sim} Dyb$ / ${\sim}(a = b)$

[11] 1. $(x)\,(x = b \supset Gx)$
    2. $(x)\,(Fx \supset x = a)$
    3. $a = b$ / $(x)\,(Fx \supset Gx)$

[12] 1. $(\exists x)\,(Cx \cdot Dx)$
    2. $(x)\,(Cx \supset x = a)$
    3. $(x)\,(Dx \supset x = b)$ / $a = b$

⭐ [13] 1. $(Fb \cdot Gab) \cdot (x)\,[(Fx \cdot Gax) \supset x = b]$
    2. $(\exists x)\,[(Fx \cdot Gax) \cdot Hx]$ / Hb

[14] 1. $Ca \cdot Fb$
    2. $(x)\,(Cx \supset Dx)$
    3. $(x)\,(Fx \supset Gx)$
    4. $b = a$ / $Db \cdot Ga$

[15] 1. $(\exists x)\,(y)\,(Hxy \cdot x = a)$
    2. $(x)\,(\exists y)\,(Hxy \supset x = y)$ / Haa

[16] 1. $(x)\,(Gx \supset Hx)$
    2. $Fa \cdot {\sim} Hb$
    3. $(x)\,(Fx \supset Gx)$ / ${\sim}(a = b)$

⭐ [17] 1. $(Fb \cdot Hab) \cdot (x)\,[(Fx \cdot Hax) \supset x = b]$
    2. $(\exists x)\,\{(Fx \cdot Gx) \cdot (y)\,[(Fy \cdot Gy) \supset y = x] \cdot Hax\}$
                  / $(\exists x)\,\{(Fx \cdot Gx) \cdot (y)\,[(Fy \cdot Gy) \supset y = x] \cdot x = b\}$

[18] 1. $\sim (x) \sim (Hx \cdot Lx)$
　　　2. $(y) [\sim (y = a) \supset \sim Hy]$
　　　3. $(z) [\sim (z = b) \supset \sim Lz]$　　　　　　　$/ a = b$

[19] 1. $(Da \cdot \sim Ha) \cdot (x) [(Dx \cdot x \neq a) \supset Hx]$
　　　2. $(Db \cdot \sim Lb) \cdot (x) [(Dx \cdot x \neq b) \supset Lx]$
　　　3. $a \neq b$　　　　　　　　　　　　　　$/ La \cdot Hb$

[20] 1. $(\exists x) (y) [(\sim Hxy \supset x = y) \cdot Lx]$　　$/ (x) \{\sim Lx \supset (\exists y) [\sim (y = x) \cdot Hyx]\}$

Summary

- Predicate logic: Integrates many of the features of categorical and propositional logic. It combines the symbols associated with propositional logic with special symbols that are used to translate predicates.
- Predicates: The fundamental units in predicate logic. Uppercase letters, called "predicate symbols," are used to symbolize the units.
- The subject of a singular statement is translated using lowercase letters. The lowercase letters, called "individual constants," act as names of individuals.
- Universal quantifier: The symbol that is used to capture the idea that universal statements assert something about every member of the subject class.
- The three lowercase letters, x, y, and z, are individual variables.
- Bound variables: Variables governed by a quantifier.
- Statement function: An expression that does not make any universal or particular assertion about anything; therefore, it has no truth value. Statement functions are simply patterns for a statement.
- Free variables: The variables in statement functions; they are not governed by any quantifier.
- Existential quantifier: Formed by putting a backward E in front of a variable, and then placing them both in parentheses.
- Domain of discourse: The set of individuals over which a quantifier ranges.
- When instantiation is applied to a quantified statement, the quantifier is removed, and every variable that was bound by the quantifier is replaced by the same instantial letter.
- A substitution instance of a statement function can be validly deduced from the universally quantified statement by the rule of universal instantiation (UI).
- Universal generalization (UG): The rule by which we can validly deduce the universal quantification of a statement function from a substitution instance with respect to the name of any arbitrarily selected individual (subject to restrictions).
- Existential generalization (EG): The rule that permits the valid introduction of an existential quantifier from either a constant or a variable.
- Existential instantiation (EI): The rule that permits giving a name to a thing that exists. The name can then be represented by a constant.

- The four new rules of predicate logic are similar to the eight implication rules, in that they can be applied only to an entire line of a proof (either a premise or a derived line).
- Change of quantifier rule: Allows the removal or introduction of negation signs. The rule is a set of four logical equivalences.
- Universal generalization cannot be used within an indented proof sequence, if the instantial variable is free in the first line of the sequence.
- A counterexample to an argument is a substitution instance of an argument form that has actually true premises and a false conclusion.
- The finite universe method of demonstrating invalidity assumes a universe, containing at least one individual, to show the possibility of true premises and a false conclusion.
- Monadic predicate: A one-place predicate that assigns a characteristic to an individual thing.
- Relational predicate: Establishes a connection between individuals.
- Symmetrical relationship: Can be illustrated by the following: If A is married to B, then B is married to A.
- Asymmetrical relationship: Can be illustrated by the following. If A is the father of B, then B is *not* the father of A.
- Nonsymmetrical: When a relationship is neither symmetrical nor asymmetrical. For example: If Kris loves Morgan, then Morgan may or may not love Kris.
- Transitive relationship: Can be illustrated by the following: If A is taller than B, and B is taller than C, then A is taller than C.
- Intransitive relationship: Can be illustrated by the following: If A is the mother of B, and B is the mother of C, then A is *not* the mother of C.
- Nontransitive relationship: Can be illustrated by the following: If Kris loves Morgan and Morgan loves Terry, then Kris may or may not love Terry.
- Identity relation: A binary relation that holds between a thing and itself.
- Definite description: Describes an individual person, place, or thing.
- Reflexive property: The idea that *anything is identical to itself.*
- Irreflexive relationship: Can be illustrated by the following expression: "Nothing can be taller than itself."
- Nonreflexive: When a relationship is neither reflexive nor irreflexive.

KEY TERMS

LOGIC CHALLENGE: YOUR NAME AND AGE, PLEASE

Three friends are riding home on a bus when they notice someone they haven't seen for many years. Raul says, "Look, there's *Mary*. She is our age, 26." Renee responds, "Actually, her name is *Marcie*. She is 2 years younger than us." Rachel laughs and says, "Her name is *not Mary*. She is 2 years older than us."

It turns out that Raul, Renee, and Rachel have each made *one true* and *one false* statement regarding the person in question. If so, determine the correct name and age of the person referred to by the three friends.

Part IV

INDUCTIVE LOGIC

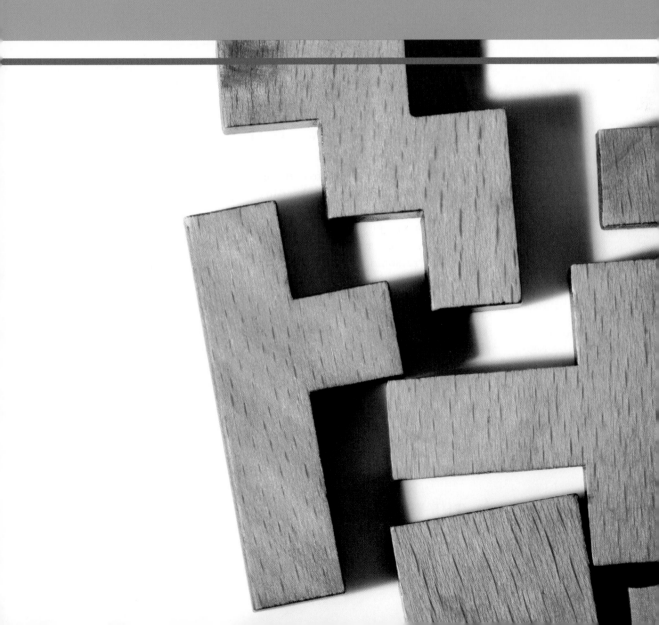

Chapter 10

Analogical Arguments

A. *The Framework of Analogical Arguments*
B. *Analyzing Analogical Arguments*
C. *Strategies of Evaluation*

A good analogy opens up new ways of thinking. For Thomas Paine, whose writings spurred on the American Revolution, an analogy could open one's mind to reason itself:

> To argue with a man who has renounced the use and authority of reason, and whose philosophy consists in holding humanity in contempt, is like administering medicine to the dead, or endeavoring to convert an atheist by scripture.
>
> Thomas Paine, *Common Sense*

Analogy To draw an analogy is simply to indicate that there are similarities between two or more things.

To draw an **analogy** is simply to indicate that there are similarities between two or more things. You might be more inclined to buy a particular car if you had good experience with a similar model. On the other hand, you might decide *not* to buy that model because of the poor performance of the last car you owned. In each case, we reason that, because two cars share some relevant characteristics, they might also share others.

Analogical reasoning One of the most fundamental tools used in creating an argument. It can be analyzed as a type of inductive argument—it is a matter of probability, based on experience, and it can be quite persuasive.

Analogical reasoning is one of the most fundamental tools used in creating an argument, and it can be quite persuasive. It can be analyzed as a type of inductive argument: it is a matter of *probability*, based on experience. For example, another car of the same model may not perform the same as yours. However, if an analogical argument is strong, then the probability that the conclusion is true is high.

Analogical reasoning plays a major part in legal decisions. Suppose a court has ruled that college students may not be restrained from speaking out about cuts in scholarships. A different court may conclude, by analogical reasoning, that the same group cannot be stopped from holding a peaceful rally because a rally is similar to speaking. An argument from an older legal decision, like this one, is said to appeal to *precedent*. When spelled out in detail, the analogy will identify those respects in which the older decision and the current one are alike. (We will return to legal arguments in the next chapter.) This chapter explores how analogical arguments work and how they can be evaluated.

A. THE FRAMEWORK OF ANALOGICAL ARGUMENTS

We know that ordinary language arguments often require rewriting, and that in turn requires a close reading to determine the premises and conclusion. We will construct a general framework that can guide our analysis and evaluation of analogical reasoning.

Every analogical argument has three defining features. First, it must refer to characteristics that two (or more) things have in common. Second, it must identify a new characteristic in one of the things being compared. Finally, it concludes that the other thing in the comparison probably has the new characteristic as well. The framework for an **analogical argument** translates these features into premises and a conclusion:

ANALOGICAL ARGUMENTS: A FRAMEWORK
Premise 1: X and Y have characteristics *a, b, c*...in common.
Premise 2: X has characteristic *k*.
Therefore, *probably* Y has characteristic *k*.

Analogical argument
The argument lists the characteristics that two (or more) things have in common and concludes that the things being compared probably have some other characteristic in common.

Example 1

A father buys his son, Mike, a shirt that (naturally) the son does not like. The father justifies his decision:

> I bought the shirt for you because your friend Steve has one like it, and you guys wear your hair the same, wear the same kind of pants and shoes, and like the same music and television programs. Since Steve must like his shirt, I thought that you would like the shirt, too.

If we let S = *Steve*, M = *Mike*, *a* = *you guys wear your hair the same*, *b* = *wear the same kind of pants*, *c* = *shoes*, *d* = *the same music*, *e* = *television programs*, and *f* = *the shirt*, then the father's analogical reasoning can be displayed.

> Premise 1: S and M have *a, b, c, d,* and *e* in common.
> Premise 2: S likes *f*.
> Therefore, *probably* M will like *f*.

The force of an analogical argument works through the two premises, and each plays a specific role. Premise 1 takes two different objects (in this case, people) and shows how they are similar by listing certain characteristics that the two objects have in common. If premise 1 does its job effectively, then we should begin to see the two objects as overlapping:

Premise 1

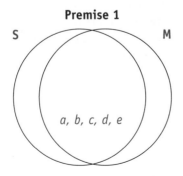

The circles represent the two people referred to in the argument (Steve and Mike). The lowercase letters stand for the five characteristics that they have in common, and these are placed in the area where the two circles overlap.

At this point premise 2 is introduced to make a claim regarding one of the two objects: S has a new characteristic that was not listed in premise 1. In other words, the two premises work together. Premise 1 shows that S and M have several characteristics in common (*a, b, c, d,* and *e*). Premise 2 points out that S has an additional characteristic, namely *f*, which is somewhere in the S circle. The conclusion is that M very probably has characteristic *f*, too.

Premise 1, if effective, persuades us that S and M overlap. Premise 2 places the *f* inside S, as a matter of historical fact. The conclusion asserts that *f* should be applied to M as well. The goal is for us to accept this picture:

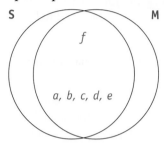

However, our conclusion could still be false, because *f* could actually be placed in at least two different locations:

What Premise 2 Really Says

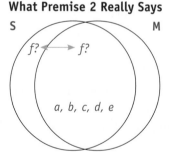

Always remember that the analogical argument does not claim that S and M are identical, but only that they are similar. Premise 2 merely states that *f* is in S, but it is possible that characteristic *f* is not in M. Given this, the conclusion might be false, even if the premises are assumed to be true:

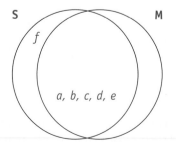

In sum, an analogical argument can only claim, at best, that it is *probable* that *f* is in M, and this probability rests heavily on the first premise and its relevance to the conclusion. The way to assess the strength of the analogical argument is to determine the degree of support that the first premise provides for the conclusion, as we will see in the rest of this chapter. For now, though, we will continue applying the general framework to reveal the reasoning behind analogical arguments.

Example 2

Analogical arguments can be about people, places, times, and animate or inanimate objects. Let's look at an example involving defective tires.

> *Premise 1*: The steel-belted tires that have been involved in blowouts (T) and the steel-belted tires on your automobile (Y) have the following attributes in common: *a*, same size; *b*, same tread design; *c*, same manufacturer; *d*, same place of manufacture; *e*, on same type of vehicle; and *f*, same recommended tire pressure.
>
> *Premise 2*: The steel-belted tires involved in blowouts (T) have been determined to be *g*, defective.
>
> *Conclusion*: Therefore, *probably* the steel-belted tires on your automobile (Y) are *g*, defective.

First, we use the framework for analogical arguments to extract the relevant information:

> Premise 1: T and Y have *a, b, c, d, e,* and *f,* in common.
> <u>Premise 2: T has *g.*</u>
> Therefore, *probably* Y has g.

The force of the analogical argument works through the two premises. The idea is to get us to agree that the two things being compared share several characteristics. The first premise can be depicted as follows:

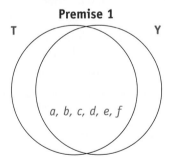

Premise 2 introduces a new characteristic attached to T. As in our earlier example, we can actually draw two different pictures of the argument:

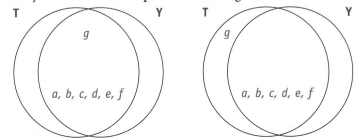

Premise 1, if effective, persuades us that T and Y overlap. Premise 2 places the *g* inside T (historical fact). However, it is possible for the conclusion to be false, even if the premises are assumed to be true. Since premise 2 merely states that *g* is in T, it could turn out that *g* is not in Y. How likely is it that *g* is in Y? In other words, how strong is the analogical argument? The rest of this chapter will concentrate on specific techniques for determining the strength of analogical arguments.

CHECK YOUR UNDERSTANDING 10A

I. Reveal the framework of the analogical argument in each example by determining what would go in the premises and the conclusion.

1. We know that humans are capable of highly abstract thinking by their ability to understand and use complex concepts. Recent research on dolphins has revealed that dolphins have brains almost identical in size to humans. Dolphins have a body size nearly identical to humans. Experiments have shown that dolphins can understand verbal commands and sign language instructions, which humans can do quite easily. Like humans, dolphins have a strong sense of self-identity, because it has been shown that dolphins can recognize themselves in mirrors and when shown their image on a TV screen. Therefore, it is highly probable that dolphins are capable of highly abstract thinking.

Answer:

Premise 1: X, humans, and Y, dolphins, have the following attributes in common: *a*, dolphins have brains almost identical in size to humans; *b*, dolphins have a body size nearly identical to humans; *c*, dolphins can understand verbal commands and sign language instructions, which humans can do quite easily; *d*, like humans, dolphins have a strong sense of self-identity, because it has been shown that dolphins can recognize themselves in mirrors and when shown their image on a TV screen.

Premise 2: We know that X, humans, are *e*, capable of highly abstract thinking by their ability to understand and use complex concepts.

Conclusion: Therefore, it is highly probable that Y, dolphins, are *e*, capable of highly abstract thinking.

The structure of the argument can now be displayed

> X and Y have *a, b, c, d*, in common.
> X has *e*.
> Therefore, *probably* Y has *e*.

2. Chimpanzees are certainly capable of feeling pain. They will avoid negative feedback (electrical shocks) in a laboratory setting when given the opportunity to do so. When one chimpanzee is injured, others will recognize the pain behavior

and try to comfort and help the injured member of the group. Chimpanzees that have been given pain-relief medicine soon after an injury connect the medicine to the relief from pain, because when injured again they will give the sign for the medicine. Humans display all of these behaviors as well. There are legal and ethical constraints that protect humans from experimentation without their consent. Therefore, chimpanzees should be afforded the same protections.

3. When a dog has killed or severely injured a human for no apparent reason, we feel justified in killing the dog in order to stop it from doing more damage. We don't try to figure out the psychological reasons for its violent behavior, whether it hates its mother or father. We just figure it is part of its genetic makeup and it cannot be changed. We don't lock the dog up for 5 years to life with the possibility of parole. Humans who kill or injure other humans for no apparent reason are like those dogs. We should feel justified in killing them in order to stop them from doing more damage.

4. England and Japan have much lower overall crime rates than the United States. The United States has 20 times more homicides than England and 30 times more than Japan. All three countries have large populations, are highly industrialized, and are in the top five in economic strength among the world's countries. In addition, all three countries are democracies, have separate branches of government, and a large prison system. But England and Japan have strict gun control legislation. If the United States wants to lower its homicide rate, then it has to pass strict gun control legislation.

★ 5. I am a junior at Lincoln Heights High School. My parents make me do all the housework, like taking out the trash (every night), laundry (every Monday), dishes, vacuuming, washing the car, and cleaning up the rooms. My kid brother, who is in fifth grade, doesn't have to do anything. But he eats the same food as me, has his own bedroom like me, and gets the same amount of allowance as me. If I have to do so much work, then he should, too.

6. The recent unearthing of some bones in central China has been the source of much controversy. Some experts are claiming that it is the oldest evidence of a human ever discovered, because it predates the next earliest fossil by 20,000 years. The experts claim that the cranial area is the same as the earliest agreed upon fossil of a human. The jawbone matches human fossils of a later date. Crude tools were found near the bones. The teeth match the later human fossils. If the oldest recognized bones have been declared to be human, then these must be human as well.

7. The government gives billions to big farming companies to *not* grow crops, in order to keep prices stable. Thus consumers are protected—at least so say the farmers. I run a business. I have a small area where I raise worms. Like the big businesses, I too have expenses. I pay for help, buy equipment, purchase supplies, suffer losses, pay taxes, pay utilities, and am subject to the laws of supply and

demand. If they can get money for not growing crops, then I would be more than willing to get money from the government, so I can stop growing those slimy worms!

8. A computer program developed by some Pittsburgh professors at Carnegie-Mellon University has beaten the world chess champion Garry Kasparov. Computer programs are used to help diagnose diseases and predict economic trends and the winners in horse races and other sports. They can calculate and analyze, in a few seconds, problems that no human could do in a lifetime. Advanced computer programs have been shown the ability to learn from experience and adapt to new situations. They can understand language and communicate concepts and ideas. Any human who can do these things is considered to possess consciousness. Some computer programs should be given the same designation.

★ 9. Fruit has many attributes that are good for your health. Fruit provides energy, roughage, sugars, citric acid, vitamins, and minerals. The new candy bar Chocolate Peanut Gooies provides energy, roughage, sugar, citric acid, vitamins, and minerals. How can it not be good for your health too?

10. *Planet X24: Our Last Hope*, the new movie by director Billy Kuberg, has just been released. It's his fourth sci-fi film. His other three had newcomers in the starring roles, were based on novels by Joel Francis Hitchmann, opened in summer, and had huge marketing tie-ins. This new movie has an unknown in the lead role, is based on a novel by Joel Francis Hitchmann, is opening in the summer, and has huge marketing tie-ins. Each of Kuberg's first three sci-fi films grossed over $550 million. I predict this new film will do about the same amount of business.

11. I already ate apples, oranges, peaches, and cherries from her fruit stand, and I enjoyed all of them. I am going to try her pears. I am sure I will enjoy them.

12. I took Philosophy 101, 102, 103, and 104 and got an A in each course. I am going to take Philosophy 105, so I expect to get an A in that course as well.

★ 13. Evidence indicates that adding fertilizer helps fruit trees and vegetable plants to grow better. Seaweed is a plant. Therefore, adding fertilizer should help seaweed grow better.

II. Reveal the framework of the analogical argument in each example by determining what would go in the premises and the conclusion.

1. A study by U.S. and Korean researchers including Harvard Business School's Jordan Siegel found that if you operate in a sexist country full of educated, talented women, it makes good business sense to tap them for management roles. . . . It's depressing how governments don't realize that failing to harness half of populations holds back growth. Planes that need two engines to fly don't take off when one isn't working, so why do nations think they can thrive in our madly competitive world with one engine?

William Pesek, "Sexism That Irks Goldman Is Boon for Savvy CEOs"

Answer:

1. *Premise 1:* X, planes with two engines, and Y, nations, have the following attributes in common: *a*, they both have two crucial components.

Premise 2: We know that X, planes with two engines, *e*, do not take off when one engine isn't working.

Conclusion: Therefore, probably Y, nations, are *e*, not capable of taking off economically in a competitive world without utilizing the talent of women.

The structure of the argument:

> X and Y have *a* in common.
> <u>X has *e*.</u>
> Therefore, probably Y has *e*.

2. You expect far too much of a first sentence. Think of it as analogous to a good country breakfast: what we want is something simple, but nourishing to the imagination. Hold the philosophy; hold the adjectives; just give us a plain subject and verb and perhaps a wholesome, nonfattening adverb or two.

    Larry McMurtry, Some Can Whistle

3. Students should be allowed to look at their textbooks during examinations. After all, surgeons have X-rays to guide them during an operation, lawyers have briefs to guide them during a trial, carpenters have blueprints to guide them when they are building a house. Why, then, shouldn't students be allowed to look at their textbooks during an examination? Max Shulman, "Love Is a Fallacy"

4. Like other colonial peoples, adolescents are economically dependent on the dominant society, and appear in its accounts as the beneficiaries of its philanthropy. Like them also, adolescents are partly dependent because of their immature stage of development, but even more because of restrictions placed upon them by the dominant society.... Nevertheless, "teen-agers" do have money.... They scrounge it from home or earn it at odd times, and this, too, contributes to their colonial status. The "teen-age" market is big business. We all share an economic interest in the dependency of the "teen-ager." The school is interested in keeping him off the streets and in custody. Labor is interested in keeping him off the labor market. Business and industry are interested in seeing that his tastes become fads and in selling him specialized junk that a more mature taste would reject. Like a dependent native, the "teen-ager" is encouraged to be economically irresponsible because his sources of income are undependable and do not derive from his personal qualities. Edgar F. Friedenberg, Coming of Age in America

★ 5. Many orthodox people speak as though it were the business of sceptics to disprove received dogmas rather than of dogmatists to prove them. This is, of course, a mistake. If I were to suggest that between the Earth and Mars there is a china teapot revolving about the sun in an elliptical orbit, nobody would be able to disprove my assertion provided I were careful to add that the teapot is too small to be revealed even by our most powerful telescopes. But if I were to go on to say that, since my assertion cannot be disproved, it is intolerable presumption on the part of human reason to doubt it, I should rightly be thought to be talking nonsense. If, however, the existence of such a teapot were affirmed in ancient books, taught as the sacred truth every Sunday, and instilled into the minds of children at school, hesitation to believe in its existence would become a mark of eccentricity and entitle the doubter to the attentions of the psychiatrist in an enlightened age or of the Inquisitor in an earlier time. It is customary to suppose that, if a belief is widespread, there must be something reasonable about it. I do not think this view can be held by anyone who has studied history.

Bertrand Russell, "Is There a God?"

B. ANALYZING ANALOGICAL ARGUMENTS

Four criteria can be used to analyze the strength of an analogical argument. Each involves looking specifically at the first premise. We look at the *number of things* referred to in the premise, the *variety* of those things, the *number of characteristics* claimed to be similar, and the *relevance* of those characteristics.

First, the strength of an analogical argument is related to the *number of things* referred to in the first premise. A large number of examples of the same kind, with the same item, will serve to establish the conclusion with a much higher degree of probability than if the conclusion were based on one instance alone. In example 1 before, if the father had compared his son to a number of friends rather than just to Steve, and if all the friends had worn the same shirt, then this would increase the probability that the conclusion is true. In example 2 before, presumably an adequate number of instances of defective tires have been examined to make the conclusion probably true.

There is rarely a simple numerical ratio between the number of instances and the probability of the conclusion. Say, if one analogical argument refers to two instances, and a second refers to ten instances, we cannot claim that the conclusion in the second is exactly five times as probable as the first.

Second, the strength of an analogical argument is related to *variety of things* referred to in the first premise. In example 1, if the father could show that a lot of people of different ages seem to be wearing the shirt in question, then this would seem to make the shirt desirable to more people, and it might raise the probability that Mike would like the shirt. In example 2, if it can be shown that defective tires were made in many locations and at different times, then this variety in the place and time of manufacture would increase the likelihood that defective tires are on your automobile. This additional evidence would increase the probability that the conclusion is true.

Third, the strength of an analogical argument is related to the *number of characteristics* that are claimed to be similar between the things being compared. All things being equal, the greater the number of characteristics listed in the first premise the more probable the conclusion will be. In example 1, premise 1 lists five characteristics.

Example 2 lists six characteristics in its first premise. This does not mean that the conclusion of the second argument is 20% more likely to be true. There is no simple mathematical formula for judging the probability of the conclusion based on the number of characteristics in the first premise.

Fourth and last, the strength of an analogical argument is related to the *relevance of the characteristics* referred to in the first premise. Some characteristics may have no real bearing on the analogy, and the weight of each characteristic has to be determined on its own merits. In fact, relevance is the single most important criterion on which to judge the strength of an analogical argument. An argument based on a single *relevant* characteristic between two things will be far more convincing than an argument based on ten *irrelevant* characteristics between ten things. However, determining relevance is not always easy. This is why it is important to make arguments by analogy strong enough to withstand scrutiny.

The relevance of any particular characteristic in the premises depends on how it is related to the conclusion of an argument. Take, for example, the color of a car:

A. My Ford Fusion Hybrid and your Hummer are the same color. My vehicle averages 40 miles per gallon of gasoline. Therefore, your vehicle will probably average 40 miles per gallon of gasoline.

B. My Toyota Camry and your Nissan Sonata are the same color. My daughter likes the color of my car. Therefore, my daughter will probably like the color of your car, too.

In A, the characteristic that the two vehicles have in common (the color) is not relevant to gas mileage, so it does not offer support for the conclusion. However, in B, the characteristic that the two cars have in common (the color) *is* relevant to whether the daughter will like the color, so it does offer support to the conclusion.

Relevance is often the most crucial factor, even when the things being compared have several things in common. Here are two more examples:

C. My sister's Chevrolet Volt Hybrid and her boyfriend's Dodge Ram pickup truck are the same color, they were both bought on the same day, and they have the same kind of financing deal. My sister's car averages 50 miles per gallon of gasoline. Therefore, her boyfriend's truck will probably average 50 miles per gallon of gasoline.

D. My father's Toyota Prius and my mother's Honda Civic Hybrid have the same engine size. My father's car averages 48 miles per gallon of gasoline. Therefore, my mother's car will probably average 48 miles per gallon of gasoline.

In C, three characteristics are listed in the first premise, while only one characteristic is referred to in the first premise of D. But since none of the three characteristics in C are relevant to gas mileage, together they offer no support for the conclusion. However, in D, the single characteristic referred to in the first premise is relevant to gas mileage, so by itself it offers some support for the conclusion.

Of course, in another argument engine size may not be relevant. This is why we must be careful to assess each characteristic in its relationship to a particular argument.

Note, too, that some characteristics might be relevant and others might not. Again, each characteristic has to be evaluated in relation to the argument in which it appears.

Criteria for Analyzing Analogical Arguments

1. The strength of an analogical argument is related to the *number of things* referred to in the first premise. A large number of examples of the same kind, with the same item, establish the conclusion with a much higher degree of probability than would be the case if the conclusion were based on one instance alone.
2. The strength of an analogical argument is related to the *variety of things* referred to in the first premise. If the first premise shows some variety among the things being compared, then it might make the conclusion more likely.
3. The strength of an analogical argument is related to the *number of characteristics* that are claimed to be similar between the things being compared. All things being equal, the greater the number of characteristics listed in the first premise, the more probable the conclusion.
4. The strength of an analogical argument is related to the *relevance of the characteristics* referred to in the first premise. These characteristics must carry weight when it comes to deciding the probability of the conclusion.

CHECK YOUR UNDERSTANDING 10B

I. You have already revealed the framework of the analogical arguments in *Check Your Understanding 10A*. Now analyze those same arguments by applying the four criteria for the strength of the argument: (1) Determine the number of things referred to in the first premise; (2) assess the variety of things referred to in the first premise; (3) list the number of characteristics that are claimed to be similar between the things being compared; (4) determine the relevance of the characteristics.

Refer back to *Check Your Understanding 10A, I*, for the exercises. The first exercise and a solution is provided here:

1. We know that humans are capable of highly abstract thinking by their ability to understand and use complex concepts. Recent research on dolphins has revealed that dolphins have brains almost identical in size to humans. Dolphins have a body size nearly identical to humans. Experiments have shown that dolphins can understand verbal commands and sign language instructions, which humans can do quite easily. Like humans, dolphins have a strong sense of self-identity, because it has been shown that dolphins can recognize themselves in mirrors and when shown their image on a TV screen. Therefore, it is highly probable that dolphins are capable of highly abstract thinking.

Answer:

(1) Dolphins and humans (we are not told how many dolphins were studied).
(2) We are not given specific information on the age, sex, or species of the dolphins studied.

(3) Brain size; body size; ability to understand verbal commands; ability to understand sign language; strong sense of self-identity.

(4) Of all the characteristics referred to, *body size* seems the least relevant to the question of highly abstract thinking.

II. Analyze the arguments from Part II of *Check Your Understanding 10A* by applying the four criteria introduced in this section: (1) Determine the number of things referred to in the first premise; (2) assess the variety of things referred to in the first premise; (3) list the number of characteristics that are claimed to be similar between the things being compared; (4) determine the relevance of the characteristics.

Refer back to *Check Your Understanding 10A, II*, for the exercises. The first exercise and a solution is provided here:

1. A study by U.S. and Korean researchers including Harvard Business School's Jordan Siegel found that if you operate in a sexist country full of educated, talented women, it makes good business sense to tap them for management roles. . . . It's depressing how governments don't realize that failing to harness half of populations holds back growth. Planes that need two engines to fly don't take off when one isn't working, so why do nations think they can thrive in our madly competitive world with one engine?

William Pesek, "Sexism That Irks Goldman Is Boon for Savvy CEOs"

Answer:

1. (a) *Number of entities*: Planes with two engines; nations.
   (b) *Variety of instances:* Planes differ in size, structure and use; nations differ in size, economies, cultures, and languages.
   (c) *Number of characteristics*: Planes operating with one engine; countries that do not employ educated, talented women.
   (d) *Relevancy*: The characteristic of a plane needing two engines to operate effectively, and a nation needing to use all its qualified workers to compete in the world's marketplace is probably related to both instances.

III. For the following argument by analogy, consider alternative scenarios. For each of these, decide whether it *strengthens*, *weakens*, or is *irrelevant* to the original argument. Do each one independently of the others.

Imagine that an auto mechanic says the following:

You car has ABS brakes manufactured by Skidmore Brake Company. Unfortunately, that company is no longer in business. Research has shown that the brakes made by that company failed to work in at least 1000 cases. The brakes failed in cars, trucks, and SUVs. Therefore, I recommend that you replace your ABS brake system.

1. What if there had been only 10 recorded cases of brake failure with those particular brakes?

Answer: Weakens the argument. The number of entities in the premises is now decreased substantially.

2. What if the recorded cases of failure had all been in cars and you have a truck?

3. What if the majority of the recorded cases of brake failure involved red cars, but your car is blue?

4. What if none of the recorded cases of failure involved SUVs, and you have an SUV?

5. What if the brakes in your car are only 1 month old?

C. STRATEGIES OF EVALUATION

Three strategies can further help determine the strength of analogical arguments. We look in turn at *disanalogies*, *counteranalogies*, and the *unintended consequences* of analogies.

Disanalogies

The first strategy involves the obvious fact that any two distinct things have differences between them. These differences can be exploited and, if significant, can severely

PROFILES IN LOGIC

David Hume

The ideas of David Hume (1711–76) echo throughout modern philosophy, but one of his most memorable contributions to logic concerns reasoning by analogy. In his *Dialogues Concerning Natural Religion*, Hume dissects a famous analogical argument. The *design argument*—which many people still use today—starts with the idea that objects like watches could not have randomly assembled themselves. Anything so orderly and intricate had to be designed and built for a specific purpose by an intelligent creature. In the same way, observation of the universe reveals an orderly design and purpose. It follows by analogy that it was designed and built for a specific purpose by an intelligent creature, namely God.

Hume provides several criticisms of the design argument. First, he points out, watches and other man-made objects are very different from much of the universe, which in fact exhibits great disorder and randomness. These flaws in the analogy (relevant disanalogies) weaken the analogical argument.

Second, Hume offered a counteranalogy. He points out that some forms of animal life and vegetation do reveal order, but they are still the result of natural processes without any intentional intelligent design or purpose.

Third, Hume notes, the argument by design has unintended consequences. Since we human designers of watches are finite creatures, then probably God is finite; since we are imperfect, then perhaps God is imperfect; since groups of designers and builders create watches, then many gods were needed to create our universe. Since humans can create imperfect products, perhaps our universe "is a botched creation of an inferior deity who afterwards abandoned it, ashamed of the poor quality of the product."

weaken any analogical argument. To point out differences between two things is to reveal **disanalogies**.

Disanalogies To point out differences between two things.

As we saw earlier, the function of premise 1 of an analogical argument is to point out similarities between the two things. Disanalogies can affect the degree of overlap between the two things in question by acknowledging significant and relevant differences between them. If effective, this strategy lowers the probability that the characteristic attached to the thing referred to in premise 2 is also attached to the thing referred to in the conclusion. In example 1, the son Mike could point out differences between himself and Steve. These differences might include the following: *p*, the color of shirts they wear; *q*, the logos (or lack of logos) on the shirts they typically wear; *r*, the food they like; and *v*, the movies they like. Pointing out the disanalogies (differences) de-emphasizes the overlap between the two, as illustrated here:

Disanalogies and Overlap

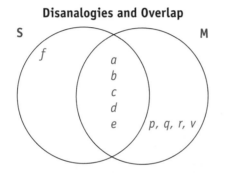

Notice that the strategy of pointing out disanalogies does not directly affect the original characteristics (*a* through *e*) listed in premise 1. Those characteristics remain in the area where S and M overlap. Rather, the new picture reveals that, *if* we can effectively point out relevant differences between S and M, then even if Steve likes his shirt (*f*), the probability, according to our new picture, is that *f* is *not* in M (Mike does not like the shirt). If we look back at the overlap *without* disanalogies, we can see how disanalogies can reduce the likelihood that the conclusion is true.

Overlap Without Disanalogies

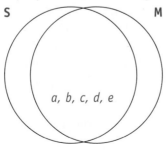

Counteranalogy

A second type of evaluation relies on a **counteranalogy**—a new, competing argument—one that compares the thing in question to *something else*. This new argument

Counteranalogy A new, competing argument—one that compares the thing in question to something else.

may lead to a conclusion that contradicts the conclusion of the original argument. In example 1, for instance, suppose that Mike's mother insists she predicted all along that Mike would *not* like the shirt his father bought. Her reasoning might run like this:

> Mike (M) is more like Nick (N) because they both wear the same kind of pants (*a*); like the same music (*b*); like the same television programs (*c*); like the same colors (*d*); wear the same kinds of logos (*e*); like the same kinds of food (*f*); and like the same movies (*g*). Nick does *not* like that kind of shirt (*h*); therefore, probably Mike will not like it.

This completely new, competing analogical argument is pictured here:

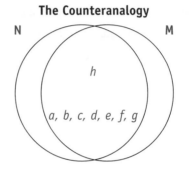

A counteranalogy, appropriately enough, *counters* the original analogical argument. In fact, there is no limit to the number of counteranalogies we can create from a given analogy. Of course, we are still faced with the prospect of weighing, judging, and evaluating the competing strengths of two analogies. And all the counteranalogies, as well as the original analogy, are subject to disanalogies as well.

Unintended Consequences

Unintended consequences
Something that is a direct result of an analogy, but that is unacceptable to the person presenting the analogy.

The third strategy of evaluating an analogy is the discovery of **unintended consequences**. If you can point to something that is a direct result of an analogy, but that is unacceptable to the person presenting the analogy, then you can put that person in a difficult position. They have "painted themselves into a corner." The discovery forces the person either to accept the unintended consequence or to weaken the original analogy. For example, suppose Mike says the following:

> O.K., Dad, you are correct, Steve and I are very much alike. But since Steve likes smoking cigarettes, you won't mind if I start smoking, too, right?

The father might respond by saying the following:

> Steve's parents don't seem to care what he does, but I care what you do. Besides, Steve's parents are rich and can give him more spending money than we can give you. Also, Steve doesn't seem too interested in personal grooming and the odor associated with smoking cigarettes, but you are very particular about the scent you give off. Therefore, I do mind if you smoke.

Mike's father sounds reasonable, but he is really pointing out disanalogies. He is thus effectively weakening his own original analogical argument by admitting there are relevant differences between Steve and Mike.

Combining Strategies

Let's see how disanalogies, counteranalogies, and unintended consequences can affect our analysis of a more extended analogical argument—the kind that played out in the media in 2011 after turmoil in North Africa. Suppose a TV political commentator demands that the United States take military action:

> The United States should go into Libya and topple the Qaddafi regime. If your own neighbors threatened your property, stockpiled dangerous weapons, disparaged our form of government and our social customs, and threatened our very way of life, then you would feel justified in going into their house and stopping them—by force, if necessary. Libya has threatened us as well as its neighboring countries, it has stockpiled dangerous weapons, it has disparaged our form of government and our social customs, and it has threatened our very way of life. If there is no way to solve the problem diplomatically, then we are justified in going there to stop them, by force, if necessary.

Let X = *a family living in the United States*, L = *the foreign country in question*, *a* = *threatened their neighbor's property*, *b* = *stockpiled dangerous weapons*, *c* = *disparaged our form of government*, *d* = *disparaged our social customs*, *e* = *threatened our very way of life*, and *f* = *we would feel justified in going in and stopping them—by force, if necessary*. We can then reconstruct the argument:

> X and L have *a, b, c, d,* and *e* in common.
> <u>In the case of X, *f.*</u>
> Therefore, in the case of L, *probably f.*

We can now draw the analogical argument:

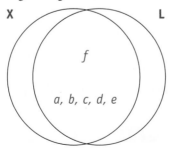

On the same TV program, another talking head might respond by saying this:

> You are comparing apples to oranges. A family living in the United States is subject to the laws of this country; this is not the case with foreign countries. We cannot impose, nor can we enforce, our laws on another country. If your neighbor threatens your property, you are afforded the protection of our government. A threat by one U.S. citizen on another, if taken seriously,

is grounds for immediate action by our government. Although a threat by a recognized sovereign nation should cause us to be ready for any eventuality, it does not give us the right to go in with force.

This commentator is pointing out differences and is using disanalogies to weaken the original analogy. Of course, we should pay close attention to the relevance of the characteristics in both the original analogy and the disanalogy to see how much weight we should give to each. We can then determine for ourselves the strength of the original analogy.

A different commentator might respond like this:

Libya is more like Vietnam when we first got involved. Vietnam was a divided country, at war with itself, with one side asking for our help and the other side telling us to keep out. North Vietnam received military and financial assistance from the Soviet Union, while Russia has stood against invading Libya today. We suffered too many deaths and wounded in Vietnam. We are told that a protracted war with Libya will result in many deaths and wounded as well. In Vietnam, we stayed too long, and in the end, the results were not what we had hoped for. This will happen again if we go into Libya. Many people feel that we should not have gone into Vietnam in the first place. Therefore, we should not go into Libya.

This commentator is using a counteranalogy to show that a completely different conclusion can be reached. As we have seen, a counteranalogy is subject to the three strategies of evaluation: (1) its strength can be questioned by pointing out disanalogies between Vietnam and Libya; (2) unintended consequences of the analogy might be discovered; and (3) a new counteranalogy could also be constructed.

One final commentator might have her say:

I agree that we should go into Libya and topple the regime by force. Of course, this will mean that some other countries, like Russia or China, will not join in. Some countries may even sever economic and diplomatic ties with us, as they have forcefully repeated. In turn, this will make our economy suffer. But that's the price we have to be willing to pay for protecting ourselves by force.

This illustrates the strategy of pointing out some unintended consequences of the analogy. Of course the original talking head might find these results acceptable; but if the last commentator is wise enough, and knows the opponent well, then she is sure to think of consequences that she knows her opponent will find unacceptable.

STRATEGIES FOR EVALUATING ANALOGICAL ARGUMENTS
Disanalogy: To point out the *differences* between the two (or more) things referred to in the first premise of an analogical argument.
Counteranalogy: To create a completely new, competing, analogical argument.
Unintended consequences of an analogy: To point to something that is a direct result of the original analogy, but that is unacceptable to the person presenting that analogy.

CHECK YOUR UNDERSTANDING 10C

I. You revealed the framework of the analogical arguments in *Check Your Understanding 10A*. Next, you analyzed those arguments in *Check Your Understanding 10B*. Now, you are in position to conclude your evaluation of those arguments by using the three strategies illustrated in this section: (a) point out any relevant disanalogies between the things being compared; (b) construct a counteranalogy; (c) determine any unintended consequences of the analogy.

Refer back to *Check Your Understanding 10A, I*, for the exercises. The first exercise and a solution is provided here:

1. We know that humans are capable of highly abstract thinking by their ability to understand and use complex concepts. Recent research on dolphins has revealed that dolphins have brains almost identical in size to humans. Dolphins have a body size nearly identical to humans. Experiments have shown that dolphins can understand verbal commands and sign language instructions, which humans can do quite easily. Like humans, dolphins have a strong sense of self-identity, because it has been shown that dolphins can recognize themselves in mirrors and when shown their image on a TV screen. Therefore, it is highly probable that dolphins are capable of highly abstract thinking.

Answer:

    (a) Disanalogies: Humans display complex speech patterns and can create completely new forms. Mathematical skills, which are taken as a hallmark of abstract thinking, are not mentioned as one of the dolphins' abilities; poetry, art, music and other aesthetic abilities have not been shown to exist in dolphins.

    (b) Counteranalogy: Dolphins are more like dogs. They both have highly sensitive senses of smell; they both have extraordinary sensitivity to sounds that humans cannot detect; they both can learn to react correctly to certain signs or verbal commands; they both seem to bond well with humans; they both are able to learn tricks of performance. Since there is no evidence that dogs are capable of highly abstract thinking, dolphins probably do not have that ability either.

    (c) Unintended consequences: If dolphins are capable of highly abstract thinking, then perhaps they should be afforded rights similar to humans. They should not be kept and raised in captivity and be subject to experiments like those mentioned in the article. The researchers should get informed consent agreements with the dolphins before embarking on any further experiments.

II. Analyze the arguments from Part II of *Check Your Understanding 10A* by applying the criteria introduced in this section. For each of the following arguments, (a) point out any relevant disanalogies between the things being compared; (b) construct a counteranalogy; and (c) determine any unintended consequences of the analogy.

Refer back to *Check Your Understanding 10A, II*, for the exercises. The first exercise and a solution is provided here:

1. A study by U.S. and Korean researchers including Harvard Business School's Jordan Siegel found that if you operate in a sexist country full of educated,

talented women, it makes good business sense to tap them for management roles. . . . It's depressing how governments don't realize that failing to harness half of populations holds back growth. Planes that need two engines to fly don't take off when one isn't working, so why do nations think they can thrive in our madly competitive world with one engine?

William Pesek, "Sexism That Irks Goldman Is Boon for Savvy CEOs"

Answer:

1. *(a) Disanalogies*: Airplane engines and humans are quite different—in size, function, structure, and motivation in the case of humans. Airplane engines are mechanical; humans are organic.
   (b) Counteranalogy: Nations are like genes. The dominant gene wins out and the recessive gene is not used. So, only one aspect of a nation is needed to compete.
   (c) Unintended consequences: When engines fail they are discarded or put on the scrap heap. So, if humans fail, do we discard them?

Summary

- To draw an analogy is simply to indicate that there are similarities between two or more things.
- Analogical reasoning is one of the most fundamental tools used in creating an argument. It can be analyzed as a type of inductive argument—it is a matter of probability, based on experience, and it can be quite persuasive.
- An analogical argument is analyzed by revealing the general framework of the argument. The argument lists the characteristics that two (or more) things have in common and concludes that the things being compared probably have some other characteristic in common.
- If an analogical argument is strong, then it raises the probability that the conclusion is true.
- Four criteria are used to analyze the first premise of an analogical argument: (1) The strength of an analogical argument is related to the number of things referred to in the first premise. (2) The strength of an analogical argument is related to the variety of things referred to in the first premise. (3) The strength of an analogical argument is related to the number of characteristics that are claimed to be similar between the things being compared. (4) The strength of an analogical argument is related to the relevance of the characteristics referred to in the first premise.
- Disanalogies: To point out differences between two or more things.
- Counteranalogy: A new, competing argument—one that compares the thing in question to something else.
- If you can point to something that is a direct result of an analogy, but that is unacceptable to the person presenting the analogy, then you can put that person

in a difficult position. An unintended consequence of an analogy is something that is a direct result of an analogy, but that is unacceptable to the person presenting the analogy.

LOGIC CHALLENGE: BEAT THE CHEAT

While walking downtown, you come across a very excited group of people. They have gathered around a loud man who is challenging them to a bet. You watch as the man holds up two cards; one is blank, and the other has an X written on it. He then quickly places them face down on a small table and shuffles their positions many times. He is willing to bet $10 that no one can locate the card with the X. Another man steps forward and puts $10 down on the table and chooses one of the cards. He turns it over, reveals that it is blank, and promptly loses $10. Three other people try and they each fail, too.

By now you are convinced that the game is a scam. The man is obviously palming or hiding the card with the X and putting two blank cards down on the table. Suddenly, you realize that you can beat the cheat. You ask the crowd how many people lost $10, and then you challenge the cheat to bet that amount for one game.

You win the bet and return everyone's lost $10. How did you do it?

Chapter 11

Legal Arguments

You have probably seen the old image of *Justice* wearing a blindfold and holding a balance. The image is meant to evoke an ideal. Justice, it says, has nothing to do with stereotypes or emotional appeals. The law should be blind to any sort of prejudice. Yet legal debates often involve politically and emotionally charged issues, such as gay marriage, crime, or abortion. When civil rights protesters were met with violence, the courts were called to decide legal arguments. When fears of terrorism led to imprisonment without trial and, some say, even torture, the courts again had to decide what must be done. And when citizens then protest court decisions, they are exercising a right protected by law.

In fact, disputes like these help explain the ideal of blind justice. The process of making legal decisions has evolved to emphasize rationality and impartiality, because we depend on it for our everyday safety, security, and well-being. Although legal debates often involve emotional issues, legal discourse has evolved patterns and conventions that we can recognize. Legal arguments can be understood once you are able to grasp the underlying logic, and our reasoning skills can complement our understanding of the practical demands of the law.

This chapter looks at the logical foundation of legal arguments. We will explore the use of *conditional statements, necessary and sufficient conditions, disjunction, conjunction,* and the role of *analogies*. We will see how inductive analysis helps explains legal reasoning.

A. DEDUCTIVE AND INDUCTIVE REASONING

The logical basis of legal arguments has a long history. According to Aristotle, writing in the 4th century BC, "The law is reason free from passion." The defining documents of the United States clearly describe the rights of citizens, and the duties and responsibilities of government. The Constitution spells out in detail guidelines for many legal issues and their remedies in Amendment 5:

> No person shall be held to answer for a capital, or otherwise infamous crime, unless on a presentment or indictment of a Grand Jury, except in cases arising in the land or naval forces, or in the Militia, when in actual service in time of War or public danger; nor shall any person be subject for the same offense to be twice put in jeopardy of life or limb; nor shall be compelled in any criminal case to be a witness against himself, nor be deprived of life, liberty, or property, without due process of law; nor shall private property be taken for public use, without just compensation.

Legislative bodies usually enact laws, which then get expressed in formal documents. Federal laws are also referred to as *statutes*. In charging individuals with crimes, for example, federal prosecutors must make a judgment that a statute is applicable to the case at hand. An average reader may not find that judgment so easy. Take this example:

> **Crimes and Criminal Procedure**
> **US Code—Section 111: Assaulting, resisting, or impeding certain officers or employees.**
> **(a) In General —Whoever**
>   (1) forcibly assaults, resists, opposes, impedes, intimidates, or interferes with any person designated in section 1114 of this title while engaged in or on account of the performance of official duties; or . . .

And that's just the first clause. Fortunately, the ability to recognize a few basics will let you engage in reasoned debates about the meaning and intent of laws like these. **Appellate courts** are courts of appeal that review the decisions of lower courts. Legal briefs to these courts may also look complicated, but they, too, rely on the same kind of reasoning.

Appellate courts Courts of appeal that review the decisions of lower courts.

In law, deductive reasoning generally means going from the *general* to the *specific*—that is, from the statement of a *rule* to its application to a particular legal case. Although this definition is too narrow to capture all the varieties of deductive reasoning in logic, for legal purposes it serves the intended goal. On the other hand, many law textbooks refer to inductive reasoning as the process of going from the *specific* to the *general*. It comes into play whenever we move from a *specific case* or legal opinion to a *general rule*. Again, although this legal use, too, is narrow, it is a legitimate part of the larger class of inductive reasoning in logic.

B. CONDITIONAL STATEMENTS

Conditional statements play a major role in *legal reasoning*, which is also referred to as **rule-based reasoning**. Once you recognize a conditional statement, you have a powerful tool for assessing the strengths or weaknesses of the legal argument quickly and precisely. (Conditional statements were introduced in Chapter 3 and further developed in Chapter 7.)

Rule-based reasoning Legal reasoning is also referred to as "rule-based reasoning."

When legal terminology contains the words "if" or "only if," then the application of necessary and sufficient conditions can often assist in unraveling the legal issues. Let's work through some examples to sharpen our skills. Think of them as exercises, much like sit-ups. The point is *not* to have done them; rather it is to help you get into overall good condition. Here is an example:

> A judge may admit evidence of a prior conviction, if it falls within either of two categories.

Although we do not yet know the "two categories" mentioned in the statement, the key word is "if"; it alerts us that we are dealing with a conditional statement. Since the "if" always precedes the antecedent, it must be placed first when we reconstruct the given sentence. In our example, we could rewrite the sentence as follows:

> If evidence of a prior conviction falls within either of two categories, then it may be admitted.

Here is another example:

> If the judge has refused to admit into evidence a piece of evidence, that information cannot be considered when deciding a case.

Although the word "then" is absent, you should recognize that this is a conditional statement. We can easily reconstruct the sentence by placing the word "then" in the appropriate place.

In examples of rule-based legal reasoning, you should pay attention to the possibility of the existence of conditional statements. We already know that the word "if" is a good indicator. We also know that certain statements in ordinary language can be translated into a conditional statement using the word "if." The phrases *every time, whenever, all cases where, given that,* and *in the event of* all indicate a conditional statement. If we encounter, say, the statement, "*Whenever* the judge has refused to admit into evidence a piece of evidence, that information cannot be considered when deciding a case," we can recognize this as an instance of a conditional statement.

C. NECESSARY AND SUFFICIENT CONDITIONS

Before we see how conditional statements relate to legal concerns, we need to review both kinds of conditions. As we saw in Chapter 3, a sufficient condition is one such that, *if* the antecedent is true, then the consequent will be true as well. Now suppose that the state law in which you are driving states that anyone caught driving with a blood alcohol level above 0.08% will be subject to a citation for *driving while intoxicated* (DWI) or, in some states, *driving under the influence* (DUI). If you are stopped by the police and agree to take a breath-analyzer test, then the following indicates a sufficient condition.

> If your blood alcohol level exceeds 0.08%, then you are cited for DWI.

In other words, anyone caught driving with a blood alcohol level above 0.08% has met a *sufficient condition* for being issued a citation for DWI. Compare these results with a new case:

> If you are cited for DWI, then your blood alcohol level exceeds 0.08%.

Even though it might be true that you were cited for a DWI, this is *not sufficient* information to determine that your blood alcohol level exceeds 0.08%. You might have refused to take a breath-analyzer test, so your blood alcohol level was not determined. Or you might have been given a variety of field sobriety tests, such as walking a straight line and turning, standing on one foot, or closing your eyes and touching the tip of your nose. If in the officer's opinion you failed the field sobriety test, then you may have been cited for DWI.

A necessary condition is essential, mandatory, or required for another thing to be realized. Here is a simple example of a necessary condition:

> If you are allowed to vote in the presidential election, then you are at least 18 years old.

According to the law, you must be at least 18 years of age in order to be able to vote in a presidential election. Therefore, being at least 18 years of age is a *necessary condition*

PROFILES IN LOGIC

Cesare Beccaria

Cesare Beccaria (1738–94), wrote a short but influential book, *On Crimes and Punishments*, to provide a clear foundation for the criminal justice system. Theoretical justifications for the punishment of criminals have a long history: *retribution* (revenge, or "an eye for an eye"); *rehabilitation* (reforming the offender into a productive member of society); *incapacitation* (simply removing the offender from society); and *deterrence* (discouraging others from committing crimes). Since Beccaria thought that the only justification for punishment was to create a better society, he advocated deterrence as the fundamental justification for punishment.

For Beccaria, two basic principles must be rigorously followed for deterrence to work effectively—*certainty* and *celerity*. "Certainty" means that everyone in the society must see that laws will be strictly enforced and that punishment will be consistent. In other words, identical punishments must follow identical crimes. For that reason,

Beccaria argued, judges should not have the power to alter any punishment. "Celerity" means that punishment should occur swiftly. People need to connect a specific punishment to a specific crime (*certainty*)—and to connect it immediately (*celerity*). "A punishment may not be an act of violence, of one, or of many, against a private member of society; it should be public, immediate, and necessary, the least possible in the case given, proportioned to the crime, and determined by the laws."

Beccaria argued that the most damaging crimes are committed by those who have gained the greatest benefits from society. In today's terms, this means that white-collar crimes are the most damaging. In support of this idea, Beccaria argued that most people are not likely to imitate violent crimes. However, seeing wealthy criminals abusing their positions in society for personal gain, and often getting light punishment for it, tears the fabric of society.

to vote. In other words, if you are not at least 18 years of age, then you are not allowed to vote in the presidential election. Compare the above results with a new example:

> If you are not allowed to vote in the presidential election, then you are not at least 18 years old.

Even if you are *not* allowed to vote in the presidential election, we *cannot* say for sure that you are *not* at least 18 years old. There are many other reasons why you might not be allowed to vote as well. Perhaps you missed the deadline for registering, or you were convicted of a certain felony.

D. DISJUNCTION AND CONJUNCTION

The legal use of *disjunction* is illustrated by an "either/or" test, in which at least one component be satisfied. Here is one possible example:

> A lawyer is not permitted to get a contingent fee in child custody cases or divorce cases.

If we let C = *child custody cases*, and D = *divorce cases*, then we can write:

> A lawyer is *not* permitted to get a contingent fee for C *or* D.

C or D is a *sufficient* condition for the lawyer *not* to be allowed to get a contingent fee. Thus, the rule sets the condition that a particular result will occur *if* a case falls within one of two possibilities. The word "if" is essential here. It alerts us that we are dealing with sufficient conditions and a conditional statement. If we let "L" stand for the phrase "A lawyer is *not* permitted to get a contingent fee," we then reconstruct the logical form:

> If (C or D), then L.

This is a compound statement and it contains three simple statements (represented by the letters "C," "D," and "L"). We can now picture the rule:

This picture can also be interpreted as indicating that we have an *exclusive* disjunction, because C and D do not overlap. This means that C and D cannot both occur at the same time. (As an exercise in legal thinking, do you think that this is correct when it comes to our hypothetical lawyer? Does the rule clearly indicate that we are dealing with exclusive disjunction? Why or why not?)

A *rule* containing a conjunction specifies a test, with *necessary conditions* that must be met for the rule to apply. Suppose a rule defines "burglary" as having five components, *all of which must be met* for a case to fall under the definition. If even one of the five parts is not met, then the burglary rule should not be applied. Necessary conditions and conjunctions specify logical, and in this case legal, commitments that are specific and comprehensive.

E. ANALYZING A COMPLEX RULE

We now have the logical tools to analyze a complex legal rule. For example, Rule 609(a) of the Federal Rules of Evidence deals with questioning the character of a witness for truthfulness. We will paraphrase the rule to highlight the grounds for the possible impeachment of a witness by evidence of a conviction of a crime:

> Evidence that a witness has been convicted of a crime shall be admitted if either (1) the crime was punishable by death or imprisonment in excess of one year under the law under which he/she was convicted, and its **probative value** of admitting this evidence outweighs its **prejudicial effect** to the accused, or (2) that establishing the elements of the crime required proof or admission of an act of dishonesty or false statement by the witness, regardless of punishment.

Probative value
Evidence that can be used during a trial to advance the facts of the case.

Prejudicial effect
Evidence that might cause some jurors to be negatively biased toward a defendant.

The term "probative value" refers to evidence that can be used during a trial to advance the facts of the case. The term "prejudicial effect" describes evidence that might cause some jurors to be negatively biased toward a defendant. For example, the defendant might belong to a religious group that is not popular.

A complete analysis will of necessity take many steps. However, at the end we will have revealed the logic behind this complex rule. We start by highlighting in italics all the logical operators at work:

> Evidence that a witness has been convicted of a crime shall be admitted *if* either (1) the crime was punishable by death *or* imprisonment in excess of one year under the law under which he/she was convicted, *and* its probative value of admitting this evidence outweighs its prejudicial effect to the accused, *or* (2) that establishing the elements of the crime required proof *or* admission of an act of dishonesty *or* false statement by the witness, regardless of punishment.

We can use the logical operators to outline the rule:

Evidence that a witness has been convicted of a crime shall be admitted (E) *if* it meets *either* criterion A *or* B:

Criterion A: The evidence shall be admitted *if* both A1 *and* A2 are true:
    A1. The prior conviction was punishable by either a or b:
        a. Death
        b. Imprisonment in excess of one year
    A2. Its probative value outweighs its prejudicial effect.
Criterion B: The evidence shall be admitted *if* it involved either of the following:
    B1. Establishing the elements of the crime required *proof* of either a or b, as follows:
        a. An act of dishonesty by the witness
        b. A false statement by the witness

B2. Establishing the elements of the crime required an *admission* of either
a or b:
a. An act of dishonesty by the witness
b. A false statement by the witness

Given this, the overall logical structure of this rule is simple: If either A or B, then E. (In symbolic notation: $(A \vee B) \supset E$). From this basic structure we can recognize that this rule designates both A and B as *sufficient conditions* for E. This means that the antecedent of the conditional statement will be satisfied if either A or B is found to be true.

Our next step is to analyze both A and B into their components. Criterion A is very complex, but we can see that three logical operators are involved (*if; and; or*). We are told that A is realized whenever two further conditions are true at the same time: A1 and A2. Thus, *if* both A1 *and* A2 are true, then A will be true (we already know that if A is true then E will be true).

On closer inspection, we see that A1 is itself complex: it contains "or." This tells us that A1 can be realized in either of two ways—when either A1a is true or A1b is true. A2 is a bit more complicated, because it asks us to gauge the relative value of two things. We are told that the court must be able to determine that A2a, the probative value, outweighs A2b, the prejudicial effect. Of course, we would need to know the facts of the case before we could determine the actual value of each component; a judge would have to decide. However, we can still understand the logic behind this requirement. In order for A2 to hold, A2a must be greater than A2b.

We can now combine our analysis into one result for criterion A:

If [(A1a, the prior conviction was punishable by death, *or* A1b, by imprisonment in excess of one year), *and* (A2a, its probative value outweighs A2b, its prejudicial effect)], *then* E, evidence of a prior conviction shall be admitted.

As we have outlined, we must acknowledge that E can be realized even if A does not occur, because the rule asserts that B is sufficient to bring about E. As before, let E = *evidence of a prior conviction may be admitted*. We notice that B can be realized if either B1 or B2 is the case. So either B1 or B2 is sufficient for B to occur. However, for a complete analysis we need to explore B1 and B2. It turns out that B1 can occur if either B1a is the case (*proof* of an act of dishonesty by the witness), *or* B1b is the case (*proof* of a false statement by the witness). Similarly, B2 can occur if either B2a is the case (*admission* of an act of dishonesty by the witness), *or* B2b is the case (*admission* of a false statement by the witness). This analysis results in the following conditional statement:

If [(B1a, *proof* of an act of dishonesty by the witness, *or* B1b, *proof* of a false statement by the witness), *or* (B2a, *admission* of an act of dishonesty by the witness, *or* B2b, *admission* of a false statement by the witness)], *then* E, evidence of a prior conviction shall be admitted.

Our analysis of a complex rule is complete. It has revealed the existence of sufficient and necessary conditions, the use of conjunction, disjunction, and conditional statements. It has shown what must occur in order for the rule to be applied. Taking apart legal rules this way allows us to see how the rules work by showing the logical foundation of the legal reasoning. We can then see both the strengths and weaknesses of a legal position by asking whether the facts at hand fit the rule. As we move back and forth between the statements and the logical operators, we become more sensitive to the subtleties of legal language and its logical structure.

CHECK YOUR UNDERSTANDING 11E

For each exercise you are to explain the logical apparatus used in a particular rule of evidence. Follow the method of analysis that we did for Rule 609(a) of the Federal Rules of Evidence. Highlight any logical operators when available. Rewrite and reconstruct the statements whenever necessary in order to reveal the logic of the rule. (All the exercises are adapted from the Federal Rules of Evidence.)

1. RULE 603. OATH OR AFFIRMATION
Before testifying, every witness shall be required to declare that the witness will testify truthfully, by oath or affirmation administered in a form calculated to awaken the witness' conscience and impress the witness' mind with the duty to do so.

Answer:

Highlight logical operators:

Before testifying, every witness shall be required to declare that the witness will testify truthfully, by oath **or** affirmation administered in a form calculated to awaken the witness' conscience **and** impress the witness' mind with the duty to do so.

Reconstruct the statements in order to reveal the logic of the rule:

If (T) testifying, then either (O) a witness shall be required to declare that the witness will testify truthfully by oath or (A) a witness shall be required to declare that the witness will testify truthfully by affirmation, and (C) administered in a form calculated to awaken the witness' conscience and (D) administered in a form calculated to impress the witness' mind with the duty to do so.

If T, then (O or A) and (C and D)

2. RULE 605. COMPETENCY OF JUDGE AS WITNESS
The judge presiding at the trial may not testify in that trial as a witness.

3. RULE 606(A). COMPETENCY OF JUROR AS WITNESS—AT THE TRIAL.
A member of the jury may not testify as a witness before that jury in the trial of the case in which the juror is sitting. If the juror is called so to testify, the opposing party shall be afforded an opportunity to object out of the presence of the jury.

4. RULE 606(B). COMPETENCY OF JUROR AS WITNESS—INQUIRY INTO VALIDITY OF VERDICT OR INDICTMENT.
Upon an inquiry into the validity of a verdict or **indictment** (a formal accusation presented by a grand jury), a juror may not testify as to any matter or statement occurring during the course of the jury's deliberations or to the effect of anything upon that or any other juror's mind or emotions as influencing the juror to assent to or dissent from the verdict or indictment or concerning the juror's mental processes in connection

Indictment A formal accusation presented by a grand jury.

therewith. But a juror may testify about (1) whether extraneous prejudicial information was improperly brought to the jury's attention, (2) whether any outside influence was improperly brought to bear upon any juror, or (3) whether there was a mistake in entering the verdict onto the verdict form. A juror's **affidavit** (a written statement signed before an authorized official), or evidence of any statement by the juror may not be received on a matter about which the juror would be precluded from testifying.

⭐ 5. RULE 608(A). EVIDENCE OF CHARACTER AND CONDUCT OF WITNESS—OPINION AND REPUTATION EVIDENCE OF CHARACTER.

The credibility of a witness may be attacked or supported by evidence in the form of opinion or reputation, but subject to these limitations: (1) the evidence may refer only to character for truthfulness or untruthfulness, and (2) evidence of truthful character is admissible only after the character of the witness for truthfulness has been attacked by opinion or reputation evidence or otherwise.

6. RULE 608(B). EVIDENCE OF CHARACTER AND CONDUCT OF WITNESS—SPECIFIC INSTANCES OF CONDUCT.

Specific instances of the conduct of a witness, for the purpose of attacking or supporting the witness' character for truthfulness, other than conviction of crime as provided in Rule 609, may not be proved by extrinsic evidence. They may, however, in the discretion of the court, if probative of truthfulness or untruthfulness, be inquired into on cross-examination of the witness (1) concerning the witness' character for truthfulness or untruthfulness, or (2) concerning the character for truthfulness or untruthfulness of another witness as to which character the witness being cross-examined has testified. The giving of testimony, whether by an accused or by any other witness, does not operate as a waiver of the accused's or the witness' privilege against self-incrimination when examined with respect to matters that relate only to character for truthfulness.

7. RULE 609(B) IMPEACHMENT BY EVIDENCE OF CONVICTION OF CRIME—TIME LIMIT.

Evidence of a conviction under this rule is not admissible if a period of more than ten years has elapsed since the date of the conviction or of the release of the witness from the confinement imposed for that conviction, whichever is the later date, unless the court determines, in the interests of justice, that the probative value of the conviction supported by specific facts and circumstances substantially outweighs its prejudicial effect. However, evidence of a conviction more than 10 years old as calculated herein, is not admissible unless the proponent gives to the adverse party sufficient advance written notice of intent to use such evidence to provide the adverse party with a fair opportunity to contest the use of such evidence.

8. RULE 609(C) IMPEACHMENT BY EVIDENCE OF CONVICTION OF CRIME—EFFECT OF PARDON, ANNULMENT, OR CERTIFICATE OF REHABILITATION.

Evidence of a conviction is not admissible under this rule if (1) the conviction has been the subject of a pardon, annulment, certificate of rehabilitation, or other equivalent procedure based on a finding of the rehabilitation of the person convicted, and that person has not been convicted of a subsequent crime which was punishable by death or imprisonment in excess of one year, or (2) the conviction has been the subject of a pardon, annulment, or other equivalent procedure based on a finding of innocence.

⭐ **9. RULE 609(D) IMPEACHMENT BY EVIDENCE OF CONVICTION OF CRIME— JUVENILE ADJUDICATIONS.**

Evidence of juvenile adjudications is generally not admissible under this rule. The court may, however, in a criminal case allow evidence of a juvenile adjudication of a witness other than the accused if conviction of the offense would be admissible to attack the credibility of an adult and the court is satisfied that admission in evidence is necessary for a fair determination of the issue of guilt or innocence.

10. RULE 609(E) IMPEACHMENT BY EVIDENCE OF CONVICTION OF CRIME— PENDENCY OF APPEAL.

The pendency of an appeal therefrom does not render evidence of a conviction inadmissible. Evidence of the pendency of an appeal is admissible.

11. RULE 610. RELIGIOUS BELIEFS OR OPINIONS

Evidence of the beliefs or opinions of a witness on matters of religion is not admissible for the purpose of showing that by reason of their nature the witness' credibility is impaired or enhanced.

12. RULE 611(A). MODE AND ORDER OF INTERROGATION AND PRESENTATION—CONTROL BY COURT.

The court shall exercise reasonable control over the mode and order of interrogating witnesses and presenting evidence so as to (1) make the interrogation and presentation effective for the ascertainment of the truth, (2) avoid needless consumption of time, and (3) protect witnesses from harassment or undue embarrassment.

⭐ **13. RULE 611(B). MODE AND ORDER OF INTERROGATION AND PRESENTATION—SCOPE OF CROSS-EXAMINATION.**

Cross-examination should be limited to the subject matter of the direct examination and matters affecting the credibility of the witness. The court may, in the exercise of discretion, permit inquiry into additional matters as if on direct examination.

14. RULE 611(C). MODE AND ORDER OF INTERROGATION AND PRESENTATION—LEADING QUESTIONS.

Leading questions should not be used on the direct examination of a witness except as may be necessary to develop the witness' testimony. Ordinarily leading questions should be permitted on cross-examination. When a party calls a hostile witness, an adverse party, or a witness identified with an adverse party, interrogation may be by leading questions.

15. RULE 612. WRITING USED TO REFRESH MEMORY

Except as otherwise provided in criminal proceedings by section 3500 of title 18, United States Code, if a witness uses a writing to refresh memory for the purpose of testifying, either (1) while testifying, or (2) before testifying, if the court in its discretion determines it is necessary in the interests of justice, an adverse party is entitled to have the writing produced at the hearing, to inspect it, to cross-examine the witness thereon, and to introduce in evidence those portions which relate to the testimony of the witness.

16. RULE 613(A). PRIOR STATEMENTS OF WITNESSES—EXAMINING WITNESS CONCERNING PRIOR STATEMENT.

In examining a witness concerning a prior statement made by the witness, whether written or not, the statement need not be shown nor its contents disclosed to the witness at that time, but on request the same shall be shown or disclosed to opposing counsel.

⭐ 17. RULE 613(B). PRIOR STATEMENTS OF WITNESSES—EXTRINSIC EVIDENCE OF PRIOR INCONSISTENT STATEMENT OF WITNESS.

Extrinsic evidence of a prior inconsistent statement by a witness is not admissible unless the witness is afforded an opportunity to explain or deny the same and the opposite party is afforded an opportunity to interrogate the witness thereon, or the interests of justice otherwise require. This provision does not apply to admissions of a party-opponent as defined in rule 801(d)(2).

18. RULE 614(A). CALLING AND INTERROGATION OF WITNESSES BY COURT—CALLING BY COURT.

The court may, on its own motion or at the suggestion of a party, call witnesses, and all parties are entitled to cross-examine witnesses thus called.

19. RULE 614(B). CALLING AND INTERROGATION OF WITNESSES BY COURT—INTERROGATION BY COURT.

The court may interrogate witnesses, whether called by itself or by a party.

20. RULE 614(C). CALLING AND INTERROGATION OF WITNESSES BY COURT—OBJECTIONS.

Objections to the calling of witnesses by the court or to interrogation by it may be made at the time or at the next available opportunity when the jury is not present.

⭐ 21. RULE 615. EXCLUSION OF WITNESSES

At the request of a party the court shall order witnesses excluded so that they cannot hear the testimony of other witnesses, and it may make the order of its own motion. This rule does not authorize exclusion of (1) a party who is a natural person, or (2) an officer or employee of a party which is not a natural person designated as its representative by its attorney, or (3) a person whose presence is shown by a party to be essential to the presentation of the party's cause, or (4) a person authorized by statute to be present.

F. ANALOGIES

Legal reasoning probably could not work without using analogies. It relies on **precedent** (a judicial decision that can be applied to later cases), and the use of similar cases. Lawyers' arguments and judges' written opinions usually contain reasoning by analogy as an essential component. (Chapter 10 introduced analogical reasoning.)

Once you know where and how a legal argument uses analogies, you gain a foothold to start your analysis of the case at hand. You should always look for the logical components involved in legal reasoning, because the more you begin to see them, the more quickly you can apply them. With a little practice, you will find that they become comfortable and reliable.

Analogical reasoning is one of the most fundamental tools used in the legal profession. Lawyers try to find **rules of law**, or legal principles that have been applied to historical cases. Along with this, the lawyers must show that the facts of the current case are sufficiently similar to the precedent. Because they share relevant characteristics, they should share the same legal outcome. Therefore, the lawyers argue, the judge should make the same decision as laid down in the precedent.

A rational decision will choose a course of action that has the highest probability of being correct. If an analogical argument is strong, then it raises the probability that the conclusion is true. For example, once a court has decided that members of a group may not be restrained from *speaking*, another court is likely to conclude, by analogical reasoning, that the same group cannot be stopped from *parading*. In other words, the court holds that parading and speaking share relevant characteristics. Arguments like this, from precedent, will identify those respects in which the older cases and the current case are closely alike.

Knowing how to reconstruct the analogy's structure allows you to uncover the mechanisms at work in legal reasoning. Let's imagine that lawyers are arguing a case about that parade, which we will designate as case A. One of the lawyers might argue that case B, a case previously decided by the courts about free speech, and case A, the present case, have many points in common. She would have to illustrate clearly the common points to the court by referring to the facts in A and B. She then shows that case B has already been decided by having rule Z applied to it. She then concludes that rule Z should be applied to the present case A. Therefore, she has argued by analogy that case B should be used as a precedent in deciding case A.

However, the argument is strong only if cases A and B are judged to be similar enough for the rule to apply. Of course, an opposing lawyer will try to show that cases A and B contain substantial differences. He will argue that rule Z *should not* be applied to the present case, because the two cases are *not* similar enough for the rule to be applied. He must point out relevant differences (disanalogies) between case authority (the prior case) and the case being currently adjudicated in order to justify a different result.

Of course, it is not always easy to identify the *relevant* characteristics in a particular legal case. Ultimately, a judge (or an appeals court) will have to decide what kinds of similarities and differences are legally significant. A lawyer argues that significant relevant *similarities* exist, and the opposing lawyer argues that significant relevant *differences* exist. Even then, however, there still remain the *logical* issues regarding the uses of analogies. We can engage in a logical assessment of the legal analogies and offer a reasonable, informed opinion.

Precedent A judicial decision that can be applied to later cases.

Rules of law The legal principles that have been applied to historical cases.

Let's examine a fictional case, *Judy B. v. Quickoilz*:

> Judy B. had the oil changed in her car at a company called Quickoilz. While driving home, the oil light came on and the engine temperature gauge began to rapidly rise. She quickly stopped the car, looked underneath, and saw that the screw in the oil pan was missing. All the oil had been lost and the car was overheating. She lived in a rural area outside Las Vegas, and it was 117 degrees outside. She had a baby on board, and instead of trying to walk the five miles to her home, with no water, she decided to keep driving the car. She managed to get the car to within 100 yards of her house before the engine seized up. The engine was ruined, so she sued Quickoilz.

Plaintiff The person who initiates a lawsuit.

Judy B. is the **plaintiff**, or person initiating the lawsuit, and Quickoilz is the defendant in the case. During the hearing, Judy's lawyer argues that Quickoilz is fully responsible for the damage to the engine, since they must have improperly replaced the oil pan screw. Therefore, Quickoilz should be required to pay the entire bill for a new engine replacement.

Quickoilz's lawyer argues that Judy B. is ultimately responsible for the engine failure. He claims that if she had turned off the car as soon as the oil light came on and the temperature gauge began rising, then the engine would not have been damaged. Since she willingly and knowingly kept driving, she assumed responsibility for the consequences. Quickoilz's lawyer then cites a rule of law, which we shall call "AR-1: Assumption of Risk":

> A plaintiff has voluntarily accepted or exposed him or herself to a risk of damage, injury, or loss, whenever he or she understands that the condition or situation is clearly dangerous, but nevertheless makes the decision to act. In all such cases, the defendant in the case may raise the issue of the plaintiff's knowledge and appreciation of the danger as an affirmative defense. If successful, the application of the assumption of risk as an affirmative defense shall result in either a reduction or complete elimination of the damages assessed against the defendant.

Quickoilz lawyer then refers the court to a past case, *The Spyder v. Kaufman Brothers*:

> A man calling himself *The Spyder* attempted to climb to the top of a fifty-story office building owned by the Kaufman brothers. The plaintiff did this without the permission of the owners of the building. He managed to get thirty feet off the ground when he stepped on a ledge that collapsed under him. He fell to the ground and broke his pelvis. He sued the building's owners for damages, and argued that they were responsible for letting a defective ledge go unrepaired.

> The defendant's lawyer argued that Rule AR-1 should be applied, because the man had voluntarily accepted and exposed himself to a risk of injury; he clearly understood that the situation was dangerous, but nevertheless he made the decision to climb the building. The court agreed with the defendant's argument that Rule AR-1 was applicable to this case and found in favor of the defendant.

Quickoilz's lawyer then argues that *The Spyder v. Kaufman Brothers* case should be applied to the present case. Applying the language of Rule AR-1, "Judy B. voluntarily accepted and exposed herself to damage or loss; she clearly understood that the situation was dangerous, but nevertheless she made the decision to drive the car." Therefore, since she voluntarily assumed the risk, she bears responsibility for the engine damage. Thus, Rule AR-1 is applicable, and the court should decide in favor of the defendant.

In response, the plaintiff's lawyer argues that Judy B. was caught in a dilemma—a decision that had to be made between two choices, either of which would lead to an unwanted result. (For more details on dilemmas, see Chapter 3.)

> *The Spyder v. Kaufman Brothers* does *not* apply to the present case, because the facts of the two cases are substantially different. In *The Spyder v. Kaufman Brothers* the plaintiff voluntarily placed himself in the dangerous situation. But Judy B.'s decision was not made voluntarily. It was the defendant's negligence that put her between a rock and a hard place. She could either keep driving the car and expose the engine to damage, or start walking in 117 degrees heat with no water and expose herself and her baby to serious physical harm. Her decision was *not* voluntary, because she was caught in a dilemma not of her own making. The two choices were forced on her by Quickoilz's negligence; they were not initiated by Judy B.

The plaintiff's lawyer then refers the court to another past case, which we will call *Eddie W. v. Ian R.*:

> Eddie W. jumped in front of a swerving car in order to get his child out of harm's way. The parent was injured and sued the driver to recover medical bills. The defendant in the case, Ian R., invoked AR-1 (the assumption of risk rule as described above), claiming that the parent voluntarily chose the action that led to the injury. The court rejected the defendant's argument that the parent had voluntarily assumed the risk, and held instead that the action of the driver forced the parent to save the child, as any parent would naturally do; therefore, the parent's actions were not voluntary.

Judy B.'s lawyer argues that the court's decision in *Eddie W. v. Ian R.* should be used in the present case. Rule AR-1 is not applicable to this case, he says, and therefore the court should decide in favor of the plaintiff.

Both the defendant and the plaintiff use analogical reasoning. Both sides refer to a rule of law, and both sides cite cases that could be used as precedent. Let's diagram the arguments:

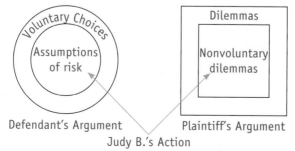

The defendant's argument is illustrated by the large circle representing the class of human actions called "voluntary choices" and the smaller circle representing the class of human actions called "assumptions of risk." We can see that every instance of an assumption of risk falls within the larger class of voluntary choices. This follows because many everyday voluntary choices assume *no* risk—such as which book to read or what to have for dinner. So, although every assumption of risk is also a voluntary choice, not every voluntary choice is an assumption of risk. The defendant concludes that Judy B.'s action should be placed inside the class of "assumptions of risk."

Judy B.'s lawyer has argued that her decision was not voluntary. This is seen in the right side of the diagram, which illustrates the difference between *assumption of risk* (which requires a *voluntary choice*), and a *dilemma* forced upon the plaintiff (which absolves her of voluntary choice).

The plaintiff's argument is illustrated by the large rectangle representing the class of situations called "dilemmas" and the smaller rectangle representing the class of situations called "nonvoluntary dilemmas." We can see that every instance of a non-voluntary dilemma falls within the larger class of dilemmas. Many dilemmas are self-imposed—for example, asking two people out on a date at the same time. Whoever you choose, someone will be hurt by your action. So, although every nonvoluntary dilemma is a dilemma, not every dilemma is a nonvoluntary dilemma. The plaintiff concludes that Judy B.'s action should be placed inside the class of "nonvoluntary dilemmas."

G. THE ROLE OF PRECEDENT

State and federal appeals courts, state supreme courts, and the Supreme Court of the United States all render decisions and opinions that we can analyze with our logical tools. We look for instances of analogical reasoning, sufficient and necessary conditions, and logical operators such as conjunction, disjunction, negation, and conditional statements.

The use of a prior court decision as a precedent can be understood as a species of analogical reasoning. Arguing that a prior case should be applied to a present case requires pointing out the relevant similarities of the two cases. The legal use of analogical reasoning is subject to all the same constraints as in everyday use. It can be analyzed and evaluated for its strengths and weaknesses using the criteria for judging analogical arguments.

We will look at an actual U.S. Supreme Court decision. The case involved an Oregon jury that determined that Honda had to pay $5 million to plaintiffs who had suffered injuries while driving an ATV. That sounds like a lot of money, but there were horrible injuries. Are "punitive damages" in the millions crucial to protecting consumers? Is there such a thing as "excessive damages"? It was up to the Supreme Court to decide. First, we provide a summary of the case. This is not an official part of either the actual court opinion or the dissenting opinion. It is the abstract, or *syllabus*, offered by the court's Reporter of Decisions. It names the justice who wrote the opinion of court, as well as those who joined the opinion. It also mentions who wrote the dissenting opinion and who joined in the dissent.

Second, we give the opening sections of the Opinion of the Court. This introduces the court's reasoning, along with important legal and historical background.

Third, we leave an edited version of the remainder of the Opinion of the Court to the exercises, so that you can practice applying what you know. Each exercise contains only part of a complex court opinion. However, when you are finished, you will have analyzed the entire decision.

Fourth, the dissenting opinion provides the material for another set of exercises. You will see the entire legal procedure as it unfolds. Since the dissenting opinion offers criticism of the opinion, you will see how courts wrestle with difficult decisions. Go to it!

SUPREME COURT OF THE UNITED STATES

HONDA MOTOR CO. v. OBERG

Argued April 20, 1994 — Decided June 24, 1994
Syllabus

After finding petitioner Honda Motor Co., liable for injuries that respondent Oberg received while driving a three-wheeled all-terrain-vehicle manufactured and sold by Honda, an Oregon jury awarded Oberg $5 million in punitive damages, over five times the amount of his compensatory damages award. In affirming, both the Oregon State Court of Appeals and the Oregon State Supreme Court rejected Honda's argument that the punitive damages award violated due process because it was excessive and because Oregon courts have no power to correct excessive verdicts under a 1910 Amendment to the State Constitution, which prohibits judicial review of the amount of punitive damages awarded by a jury "unless the court can affirmatively say there is no evidence to support the verdict."

The decision of Supreme Court of the United States: "The judgment is reversed, and the case is remanded to the Oregon Supreme Court for further proceedings not inconsistent with this opinion. *It is so ordered*."

Justice *Stevens, J.*, delivered the opinion of the Court, in which *Blackmun, O'Connor, Scalia, Kennedy, Souter*, and *Thomas, J.J.*, joined. *Scalia, J.*, filed a concurring opinion. Justice *Ginsburg, J.*, filed a dissenting opinion, in which *Rehnquist, C. J.*, joined.

OPINION OF THE COURT

An amendment to the Oregon Constitution prohibits judicial review of the amount of punitive damages awarded by a jury, "unless the court can affirmatively say there is no evidence to support the verdict." The question presented is whether that prohibition is consistent with the Due Process Clause of the Fourteenth Amendment. We hold that it is not.

Petitioner Honda Motor Co. manufactured and sold the three-wheeled all-terrain vehicle that overturned while respondent was driving it, causing him severe and permanent injuries. Respondent brought suit alleging that petitioner knew or should have known that the vehicle had an inherently and unreasonably dangerous design. The jury found petitioner liable and awarded respondent $919,390.39 in compensatory damages and punitive damages of $5 million. The compensatory damages, however, were reduced by 20% to $735,512.31, because respondent's own negligence contributed to the accident. On appeal, relying on our then recent decision in *Pacific Mut. Life Ins. Co. v. Haslip*, 499 U. S. 1 (1991), petitioner argued that the award of punitive damages violated the Due Process Clause of the Fourteenth Amendment, because the punitive damages were excessive and because Oregon courts lacked the power to correct excessive verdicts.

The Oregon Court of Appeals affirmed, as did the Oregon Supreme Court. The latter court relied heavily on the fact that the Oregon statute governing the award of punitive damages in product liability actions and the jury instructions in this case contain substantive criteria that provide at least as much guidance to the factfinders as the Alabama statute and jury instructions that we upheld in *Haslip*. The Oregon Supreme Court also noted that Oregon law provides an additional protection by requiring the plaintiff to prove entitlement to punitive damages by clear and convincing evidence rather than a mere preponderance. Recognizing that other state courts had interpreted *Haslip* as including a "clear constitutional mandate for meaningful judicial scrutiny of punitive damage awards," the Court nevertheless declined to "interpret *Haslip* to hold that an award of punitive damages, to comport with the requirements of the Due Process Clause, always must be subject to a form of postverdict or appellate review that includes the possibility of remittitur." It also noted that trial and appellate courts were "not entirely powerless" because a judgment may be vacated if "there is no evidence to support the jury's decision," and because "appellate review is available to test the sufficiency of the jury instructions."

We granted *certiorari*, to consider whether Oregon's limited judicial review of the size of punitive damage awards is consistent with our decision in *Haslip*. Our recent cases have recognized that the Constitution imposes a substantive limit on the size of punitive damage awards. *Pacific Mut. Life Ins. Co. v. Haslip; TXO Production Corp. v. Alliance Resources, Corp.* Although they fail to "draw a mathematical bright line between the constitutionally acceptable and the constitutionally unacceptable," a majority of the Justices agreed that the Due Process Clause imposes a limit on punitive damage awards. A plurality assented to the proposition that "grossly excessive" punitive damages would violate due process, while Justice O'Connor, who dissented because she favored more rigorous standards, noted that "it is thus common ground that an award may be so excessive as to violate due process." In the case before us today we are not directly concerned with the character of the standard that will identify unconstitutionally excessive awards; rather we are confronted with the question of what procedures are necessary to ensure that punitive damages are not imposed in an arbitrary manner. More specifically, the question is whether the Due Process Clause requires judicial review of the amount of punitive damage awards.

The opinions in both *Haslip* and *TXO* strongly emphasized the importance of the procedural component of the Due Process Clause. In *Haslip*, the Court held that the common law method of assessing punitive damages did not violate procedural due process. In so holding, the Court stressed the availability of both "meaningful and adequate review by the trial court" and subsequent appellate review. Similarly, in *TXO*, the plurality opinion found that the fact that the "award was reviewed and upheld by the trial judge" and unanimously affirmed on appeal gave rise "to a strong presumption of validity." Concurring in the judgment, Justice Scalia (joined by Justice Thomas) considered it sufficient that traditional common law procedures were followed. In particular, he noted that 'procedural due process' requires judicial review of punitive damages awards for reasonableness. . . ."

All of those opinions suggest that our analysis in this case should focus on Oregon's departure from traditional procedures. We therefore first contrast the relevant common law practice with Oregon's procedure, which that State's Supreme Court once described as "a system of trial by jury in which the judge is reduced to the status of a mere monitor." We then examine the constitutional implications of Oregon's deviation from established common law procedures.

Judicial review of the size of punitive damage awards has been a safeguard against excessive verdicts for as long as punitive damages have been awarded. One of the earliest reported cases involving exemplary damages, *Huckle v. Money*, (1763), arose out of King George III's attempt to punish the publishers of the allegedly seditious *North Briton,* No. 45. The King's agents arrested the plaintiff, a journeyman printer, in his home and detained him for six hours. Although the defendants treated the plaintiff rather well, feeding him "beef steaks and beer, so that he suffered very little or no damages," the jury awarded him £300, an enormous sum almost three hundred times the plaintiff's weekly wage. The defendant's lawyer requested a new trial, arguing that the jury's award was excessive. Plaintiff's counsel, on the other hand, argued that "in cases of tort . . . the Court will never interpose in setting aside verdicts for excessive damages." While the court denied the motion for new trial, the Chief Justice explicitly rejected plaintiff's absolute rule against review of damages amounts. Instead, he noted that when the damages are "outrageous" and "all mankind at first blush must think so," a court may grant a new trial "for excessive damages." In accord with his view that the amount of an award was relevant to the motion for a new trial, the Chief Justice noted that "[u]pon the whole, I am of opinion the damages are not excessive."

Subsequent English cases, while generally deferring to the jury's determination of damages, steadfastly upheld the court's power to order new trials solely on the basis that the damages were too high. *Fabrigas v. Mostyn*, (1773), Damages "may be so monstrous and excessive, as to be in themselves an evidence of passion or partiality in the jury"); *Sharpe v. Brice*, (1774), "It has never been laid down, that the Court will not grant a new trial for excessive damages in any cases of tort"; *Leith v. Pope*, (1779), "[I]n cases of tort the Court will not interpose on account of the largeness of damages, unless they are so flagrantly excessive as to afford an internal evidence of the prejudice and partiality of the jury"); *Hewlett v. Cruchley*, (1813), "[I]t is now well acknowledged in all the Courts of *Westminster-hall,* that whether in actions for criminal conversation, malicious prosecutions, words, or any other matter, if the damages are clearly too large, the Courts will send the inquiry to another jury."

CHECK YOUR UNDERSTANDING 11G

I. The following passages are from the *Opinion of the Court.* They continue the Court's opinion and lay out the reasons for the majority decision. Some of the passages have been edited to simplify the task at hand. In many instances we have omitted reference to case numbers (e.g., *Hurtado v. California*, 110 U.S. 516, 538 is reduced to *Hurtado v. California*). On the one hand, we have tried to keep as much of the legal arguments and apparatus intact; on the other hand, we tried to emphasize the logic at play.

Your job is to describe the reasoning involved in each passage. You can do this by illustrating the logic involved. You should look for uses of logical operators such as conjunction, disjunction, negation, and conditional statements; sufficient and necessary conditions; and the analogical reasoning involved in the Court's arguments.

1. Respondent calls to our attention the case of *Beardmore v. Carrington*, in which the court asserted that "there is not one single case, (that is law), in all the books to be found, where the Court has granted a new trial for excessive damages in actions for torts." Respondent would infer from that statement that 18th century common law did not provide for judicial review of damages. Respondent's argument overlooks several crucial facts. First, the *Beardmore* case antedates all but one of the cases cited in the previous paragraph. Even if respondent's interpretation of the case were correct, it would be an interpretation the English courts rejected soon thereafter.

Answer:

Three items can be used to get started: first, the passage uses analogical reasoning (*Beardmore v. Carrington*); second, it uses the logical operators "not" and "if"; third, it contains the word "infer."

The respondent argued that the case of *Beardmore v. Carrington* offers a precedent for the court not to grant a new trial. The court in *Beardmore* asserted that "there is **not** one single case, (that is law), in all the books to be found, where the Court has granted *a new trial* for excessive damages in actions for torts." However, in its opinion the U.S. Supreme Court argued that the respondent's inference "that 18th century common law did **not** provide for *judicial review of damages*" was faulty. The opinion pointed out that the "respondent's *argument overlooks several crucial facts*": First, *Beardmore* came before (antedates) *all but one of the cases* cited. Second, "even **if** respondent's interpretation of the case were correct, [then] it would be an interpretation the English courts rejected soon thereafter." In other words, although the respondent's interpretation of the court's assertion in *Beardmore* might be correct, the assertion was rejected by later courts.

2. Second, *Beardmore* itself cites at least one case which it concedes granted a new trial for excessive damages, *Chambers v. Robinson*, although it characterizes the case as wrongly decided.

3. Third, to say that "there is not one single case . . . in all the books" is to say very little, because then, much more so than now, only a small proportion of decided cases was reported. For example, the year *Beardmore* was decided only 16 Common Pleas cases are recorded in the standard reporter.

4. Finally, the argument respondent would draw, that 18th century English common law did not permit a judge to order new trials for excessive damages, is explicitly rejected by *Beardmore* itself, which cautioned against that very argument: "We desire to be understood that this Court does not say, or lay down any rule that there never can happen a case of such excessive damages in tort where the Court may not grant a new trial."

5. Common law courts in the United States followed their English predecessors in providing judicial review of the size of damage awards. They too emphasized the deference ordinarily afforded jury verdicts, but they recognized that juries sometimes awarded damages so high as to require correction. In 1822, Justice Story ordered a new trial unless the plaintiff agreed to a reduction in his damages. In explaining his ruling, he noted: "As to the question of excessive damages, I agree, that the court may grant a new trial for excessive damages. . . . It is indeed an exercise of discretion full of delicacy and difficulty. But if it should clearly appear that the jury have committed a gross error, or have acted from improper motives, or have given damages excessive in relation to the person or the injury, it is as much the duty of the court to interfere, to prevent the wrong, as in any other case." *Blunt v. Little*.

6. In the 19th century, both before and after the ratification of the Fourteenth Amendment, many American courts reviewed damages for "partiality" or "passion and prejudice." Nevertheless, because of the difficulty of probing juror reasoning, passion and prejudice review was, in fact, review of the amount of awards. Judges would infer passion, prejudice, or partiality from the size of the award. *Taylor v. Giger*: "In actions of tort . . . a new trial ought not to be granted for excessiveness of damages, unless the damages found are so enormous as to shew that the jury were under some improper influence, or were led astray by the violence of prejudice or passion."

7. Nineteenth century treatises similarly recognized judges' authority to award new trials on the basis of the size of damage awards. "[E]ven in personal torts, where the jury find *outrageous damages*, clearly evincing partiality, prejudice and passion, the court will interfere for the relief of the defendant, and order a new trial"); "The court again holds itself at liberty to set aside verdicts and grant new trials . . . whenever the damages are so excessive as to create the belief that the jury have been misled either by passion, prejudice, or ignorance"); When punitive damages are submitted to the jury, "the amount which they may think proper to allow will be accepted by the court, unless so exorbitant as to indicate that they have been influenced by passion, prejudice or a perverted judgment."

8. Modern practice is consistent with these earlier authorities. In the federal courts and in every State, except Oregon, judges review the size of damage awards. See *Dagnello v. Long Island R. Co.*, citing cases from all 50 States except Alaska, Maryland, and Oregon.

9. There is a dramatic difference between the judicial review of punitive damages awards under the common law and the scope of review available in Oregon. An Oregon trial judge, or an Oregon Appellate Court, may order a new trial if the jury was not properly instructed, if error occurred during the trial, or if there is no evidence to support any punitive damages at all. But if the defendant's only basis for relief is the *amount* of punitive damages the jury awarded, Oregon

provides no procedure for reducing or setting aside that award. This has been the law in Oregon at least since 1949 when the State Supreme Court announced its opinion in *Van Lom v. Schneiderman*, definitively construing the 1910 amendment to the Oregon Constitution. In that case the court held that it had no power to reduce or set aside an award of both compensatory and punitive damages that was admittedly excessive.

10. Respondent argues that Oregon's procedures do not deviate from common law practice, because Oregon judges have the power to examine the size of the award to determine whether the jury was influenced by passion and prejudice. This is simply incorrect. The earliest Oregon cases interpreting the 1910 amendment squarely held that Oregon courts lack precisely that power. No Oregon court for more than half a century has inferred passion and prejudice from the size of a damages award, and no court in more than a decade has even hinted that courts might possess the power to do so.

11. Finally, if Oregon courts could evaluate the excessiveness of punitive damage awards through passion and prejudice review, the Oregon Supreme Court would have mentioned that power in this very case. Petitioner argued that Oregon procedures were unconstitutional precisely because they failed to provide judicial review of the size of punitive damage awards.

12. Respondent also argues that Oregon provides adequate review, because the trial judge can overturn a punitive damage award if there is no substantial evidence to support an award of punitive damages. This argument is unconvincing, because the review provided by Oregon courts ensures only that there is evidence to support *some* punitive damages, not that there is evidence to support the amount actually awarded. While Oregon's judicial review ensures that punitive damages are not awarded against defendants entirely innocent of conduct warranting exemplary damages, Oregon, unlike the common law, provides no assurance that those whose conduct is sanctionable by punitive damages are not subjected to punitive damages of arbitrary amounts. What we are concerned with is the possibility that a guilty defendant may be unjustly punished; evidence of guilt warranting some punishment is not a substitute for evidence providing at least a rational basis for the particular deprivation of property imposed by the State to deter future wrongdoing.

13. Oregon's abrogation of a well-established common law protection against arbitrary deprivations of property raises a presumption that its procedures violate the Due Process Clause. As this Court has stated from its first Due Process cases, traditional practice provides a touchstone for constitutional analysis. Because the basic procedural protections of the common law have been regarded as so fundamental, very few cases have arisen in which a party has complained of their denial. In fact, most of our Due Process decisions involve arguments that traditional procedures provide too little protection and that additional

safeguards are necessary to ensure compliance with the Constitution. Nevertheless, there are a handful of cases in which a party has been deprived of liberty or property without the safeguards of common law procedure. When the absent procedures would have provided protection against arbitrary and inaccurate adjudication, this Court has not hesitated to find the proceedings violative of Due Process.

14. Of course, not all deviations from established procedures result in constitutional infirmity. As the Court noted in *Hurtado*, to hold all procedural change unconstitutional "would be to deny every quality of the law but its age, and to render it incapable of progress or improvement." A review of the cases, however, suggests that the case before us is unlike those in which abrogations of common law procedures have been upheld.

    In *Hurtado*, for example, examination by a neutral magistrate provided criminal defendants with nearly the same protection as the abrogated common law grand jury procedure. Oregon, by contrast, has provided no similar substitute for the protection provided by judicial review of the amount awarded by the jury in punitive damages. . . . If anything, the rise of large, interstate and multinational corporations has aggravated the problem of arbitrary awards and potentially biased juries.

15. Punitive damages pose an acute danger of arbitrary deprivation of property. Jury instructions typically leave the jury with wide discretion in choosing amounts, and the presentation of evidence of a defendant's net worth creates the potential that juries will use their verdicts to express biases against big businesses, particularly those without strong local presences. Judicial review of the amount awarded was one of the few procedural safeguards which the common law provided against that danger. Oregon has removed that safeguard without providing any substitute procedure and without any indication that the danger of arbitrary awards has in any way subsided over time. For these reasons, we hold that Oregon's denial of judicial review of the size of punitive damage awards violates the Due Process Clause of the Fourteenth Amendment.

16. Respondent argues that Oregon has provided other safeguards against arbitrary awards and that, in any event, the exercise of this unreviewable power by the jury is consistent with the jury's historic role in our judicial system.

    Respondent points to four safeguards provided in the Oregon courts: the limitation of punitive damages to the amount specified in the complaint, the clear and convincing standard of proof, pre-verdict determination of maximum allowable punitive damages, and detailed jury instructions.

17. The first, limitation of punitive damages to the amount specified, is hardly a constraint at all, because there is no limit to the amount the plaintiff can request, and it is unclear whether an award exceeding the amount requested could be set aside. See *Tenold v. Weyerhaeuser Co:* Oregon Constitution bars court from

examining jury award to ensure compliance with $500,000 statutory limit on noneconomic damages.

18. The second safeguard, the clear and convincing standard of proof, is an important check against unwarranted imposition of punitive damages, but, like the "no substantial evidence" review discussed above, it provides no assurance that those whose conduct is sanctionable by punitive damages are not subjected to punitive damages of arbitrary amounts.

19. Regarding the third purported constraint, respondent cites no cases to support the idea that Oregon courts do or can set maximum punitive damage awards in advance of the verdict. Nor are we aware of any court which implements that procedure.

20. Respondent's final safeguard, proper jury instruction, is a well established and, of course, important check against excessive awards. The problem that concerns us, however, is the possibility that a jury will not follow those instructions and may return a lawless, biased, or arbitrary verdict.

In support of his argument that there is a historic basis for making the jury the final arbiter of the amount of punitive damages, respondent calls our attention to early civil and criminal cases in which the jury was allowed to judge the law as well as the facts. As we have already explained, in civil cases, the jury's discretion to determine the amount of damages was constrained by judicial review. The criminal cases do establish—as does our practice today—that a jury's arbitrary decision to acquit a defendant charged with a crime is completely unreviewable. There is, however, a vast difference between arbitrary grants of freedom and arbitrary deprivations of liberty or property. The Due Process Clause has nothing to say about the former, but its whole purpose is to prevent the latter. A decision to punish a tortfeasor by means of an exaction of exemplary damages is an exercise of state power that must comply with the Due Process Clause of the Fourteenth Amendment. The common law practice, the procedures applied by every other State, the strong presumption favoring judicial review that we have applied in other areas of the law, and elementary considerations of justice, all support the conclusion that such a decision should not be committed to the unreviewable discretion of a jury.

II. The next set of passages is from the *footnotes* to the *Opinion of the Court*. They offer additional examples of the majority's decision-making process. Once again, you are to describe the reasoning involved in each passage. Illustrate the logical apparatus involved (the uses of logical operators), and the analogical reasoning that constitutes the Supreme Court's arguments.

1. The jury instructions in the original Oregon trial, in relevant part, read: "Punitive damages may be awarded to the plaintiff in addition to general damages to punish wrongdoers and to discourage wanton misconduct. In order for plaintiff to recover punitive damages against the defendant[s], the plaintiff

must prove by clear and convincing evidence that defendant[s have] shown wanton disregard for the health, safety, and welfare of others. . . . If you decide this issue against the defendant[s], you may award punitive damages, although you are not required to do so, because punitive damages are discretionary. In the exercise of that discretion, you shall consider evidence, if any, of the following: First, the likelihood at the time of the sale [of the three-wheeled vehicle] that serious harm would arise from defendants' misconduct. Second, the degree of the defendants' awareness of that likelihood. Third, the duration of the misconduct. Fourth, the attitude and conduct of the defendant[s] upon notice of the alleged condition of the vehicle. Fifth, the financial condition of the defendant[s]. And the amount of punitive damages may not exceed the sum of $5 million."

Answer:

The passage presents a series of rules that must be followed for two issues: (1) "In order for plaintiff to recover punitive damages against the defendant," and (2) the jury's exercise of discretion if they decide against the defendant.

(A) In order for plaintiff to recover punitive damages against the defendant[s], (B) the plaintiff must prove by clear and convincing evidence that defendant[s have]shown wanton disregard for the health, safety, and welfare of others. . . . **If** (C) you decide this issue against the defendant[s], [**then**] (D) you may award punitive damages, although you are **not** required to do so, **because** punitive damages are discretionary. In the exercise of that discretion, you shall consider evidence, **if** any, of the following: (E) First, the likelihood at the time of the sale [of the three-wheeled vehicle] that serious harm would arise from defendants' misconduct. (F) Second, the degree of the defendants' awareness of that likelihood. (G) Third, the duration of the misconduct. (H) Fourth, the attitude and conduct of the defendant[s] upon notice of the alleged condition of the vehicle. (I) Fifth, the financial condition of the defendant[s]. **And** (J) the amount of punitive damages may not exceed the sum of $5 million.

> A only if B.
> If C, then (D or not D).
> If C, then [(E or F or G or H or I) and J].

2. As in many early cases, it is unclear whether this case (*Fabrigas v. Mostyn*) specifically concerns punitive damages or merely ordinary compensatory damages. Since there is no suggestion that different standards of judicial review were applied for punitive and compensatory damages before the twentieth century, no effort has been made to separate out the two classes of case.

3. The amended Article VII, §3, of the Oregon Constitution provides: "In actions at law, where the value in controversy shall exceed twenty dollars, the right of trial by jury shall be preserved, and no fact tried by a jury shall be otherwise reexamined in any court of this State, unless the court can affirmatively say there is no evidence to support the verdict."

4. The Oregon Supreme Court in *Van Lom v. Schneiderman* stated the following: "The court is of the opinion that the verdict of $10,000.00 is excessive. Some members of the court think that only the award of punitive damages is excessive; others that both the awards of compensatory and punitive damages are excessive. Since a majority are of the opinion that this court has no power to disturb the verdict, it is not deemed necessary to discuss the grounds for these divergent views."

5. The Oregon Supreme Court in *Van Lom v. Schneiderman* stated the following: "The guaranty of the right to jury trial in suits at common law, incorporated in the Bill of Rights as one of the first ten amendments of the Constitution of the United States, was interpreted by the Supreme Court of the United States to refer to jury trial as it had been theretofore known in England; and so it is that the federal judges, like the English judges, have always exercised the prerogative of granting a new trial when the verdict was clearly against the weight of the evidence, whether it be because excessive damages were awarded or for any other reason.

6. Respondent cites as support for its argument *Chicago, R. I. & P. R. Co. v. Cole*. In that case, the Court upheld a provision of the Oklahoma Constitution providing that "the defense of contributory negligence . . . shall . . . be left to the jury." *Chicago, R. I.* provides little support for respondent's case. Justice Holmes' reasoning relied on the fact that a State could completely abolish the defense of contributory negligence. This case, however, is different, because the *TXO* and *Haslip* opinions establish that States cannot abolish limits on the award of punitive damages.

7. Respondent also argues that empirical evidence supports the effectiveness of these safeguards. It points to the analysis of an *amicus* showing that the average punitive damage award in a products liability case in Oregon is less than the national average. While we welcome respondent's introduction of empirical evidence on the effectiveness of Oregon's legal rules, its statistics are undermined by the fact that the Oregon average is computed from only two punitive damage awards. It is well known that one cannot draw valid statistical arguments from such a small number of observations.

   Empirical evidence, in fact, supports the importance of judicial review of the size of punitive damage awards. The most exhaustive study of punitive damages establishes that over half of punitive damage awards were appealed, and that more than half of those appealed resulted in reductions or reversals of the punitive damages. In over 10 percent of the cases appealed, the judge found the damages to be excessive.

8. Judicial deference to jury verdicts may have been stronger in 18th century America than in England, and judges' power to order new trials for excessive damages more contested. Nevertheless, because this case concerns the Due

Process Clause of the Fourteenth Amendment, 19th century American practice is the "crucial time for present purposes." As demonstrated above, by the time the Fourteenth Amendment was ratified in 1868, the power of judges to order new trials for excessive damages was well established in American courts. In addition, the idea that jurors can find law as well as fact is not inconsistent with judicial review for excessive damages.

III. The next set of passages is from the *dissenting opinion* by Justice Ginsberg. They offer examples of the reasons for dissenting from the majority opinion. Once again, some of the passages have been edited to simplify the task at hand. As before, you are to describe the reasoning involved in each passage. Illustrate the logical apparatus involved (the uses of logical operators) and the analogical reasoning that constitutes the dissenting opinion.

1. Where the factfinder is a jury, its decision is subject to judicial review to this extent: The trial court, or an appellate court, may nullify the verdict if reversible error occurred during the trial, if the jury was improperly or inadequately instructed, or if there is no evidence to support the verdict. Absent trial error, and if there is evidence to support the award of punitive damages, however, Oregon's Constitution, Article VII, §3, provides that a properly instructed jury's verdict shall not be reexamined. Oregon's procedures, I conclude, are adequate to pass the Constitution's due process threshold. I therefore dissent from the Court's judgment upsetting Oregon's disposition in this case.

Answer:

(A) Where the factfinder is a jury, its decision is subject to judicial review to this extent: (B) The trial court, **or** an appellate court, may nullify the verdict **if** (C) reversible error occurred during the trial, **if** (D) the jury was improperly **or** inadequately instructed, **or if** (E) there is no evidence to support the verdict. (F) Absent trial error, **and if** (G) there is evidence to support the award of punitive damages, however, [**then**] (H) Oregon's Constitution, Article VII, §3, provides that a properly instructed jury's verdict shall **not** be reexamined. (I) Oregon's procedures, I **conclude**, are adequate to pass the Constitution's due process threshold. (J) I **therefore** dissent from the Court's judgment upsetting Oregon's disposition in this case.

> If A, then [if (C or D or E), then B].
> If (F and G), then H.
> Therefore I.
> Therefore J.

2. To assess the constitutionality of Oregon's scheme, I turn first to this Court's recent opinions in *Haslip*, and *TXO*. The Court upheld punitive damage awards in both cases, but indicated that due process imposes an outer limit on remedies of this type. Significantly, neither decision declared any specific procedures or substantive criteria essential to satisfy due process. In *Haslip*, the Court expressed concerns about "unlimited jury discretion, or unlimited judicial discretion for

that matter, in the fixing of punitive damages," but refused to "draw a mathematical bright line between the constitutionally acceptable and the constitutionally unacceptable. . . ." And in *TXO*, a majority agreed that a punitive damage award may be so grossly excessive as to violate the Due Process Clause. In the plurality's view, however, "a judgment that is a product" of "fair procedures . . . is entitled to a strong presumption of validity."

3. The procedures Oregon's courts followed in this case satisfy the due process limits indicated in *Haslip* and *TXO*; the jurors were adequately guided by the trial court's instructions, and Honda has not maintained, in its full presentation to this Court, that the award in question was "so 'grossly excessive' as to violate the Federal Constitution."

4. Several preverdict mechanisms channeled the jury's discretion more tightly in this case than in either *Haslip* or *TXO*. First, providing at least some protection against unguided, utterly arbitrary jury awards, respondent Oberg was permitted to recover no more than the amounts specified in the complaint, $919,390.39 in compensatory damages and $5 million in punitive damages. The trial court properly instructed the jury on this damage cap. No provision of Oregon law appears to preclude the defendant from seeking an instruction setting a lower cap, if the evidence at trial cannot support an award in the amount demanded. Additionally, if the trial judge relates the incorrect maximum amount, a defendant who timely objects may gain modification or nullification of the verdict.

5. Second, Oberg was not allowed to introduce evidence regarding Honda's wealth until he "presented evidence sufficient to justify to the court a prima facie claim of punitive damages. During the course of trial, evidence of the defendant's ability to pay shall not be admitted unless and until the party entitled to recover establishes a prima facie right to recover [punitive damages]." This evidentiary rule is designed to lessen the risk "that juries will use their verdicts to express biases against big businesses," to take into account "[t]he total deterrent effect of other punishment imposed upon the defendant as a result of the misconduct."

6. Third, and more significant, as the trial court instructed the jury, Honda could not be found liable for punitive damages unless Oberg established by "clear and convincing evidence" that Honda "show[ed] wanton disregard for the health, safety and welfare of others." [Governing product liability actions, see §41.315(1): "Except as otherwise specifically provided by law, a claim for punitive damages shall be established by clear and convincing evidence."] "[T]he clear and convincing evidence requirement," which is considerably more rigorous than the standards applied by Alabama in *Haslip* and West Virginia in *TXO*, "constrain[s] the jury's discretion, limiting punitive damages to the more egregious cases." Nothing in Oregon law appears to preclude a new trial order if the trial judge, informed by the jury's verdict, determines that his charge did not adequately explain what the "clear and convincing" standard means.

7. Fourth, and perhaps most important, in product liability cases, Oregon requires that punitive damages, if any, be awarded based on seven substantive criteria: "(a) The likelihood at the time that serious harm would arise from the defendant's misconduct; (b) [t]he degree of the defendant's awareness of that likelihood; (c) [t]he profitability of the defendant's misconduct; (d) [t]he duration of the misconduct and any concealment of it; (e) [t]he attitude and conduct of the defendant upon discovery of the misconduct; (f) [t]he financial condition of the defendant; and (g) [t]he total deterrent effect of other punishment imposed upon the defendant as a result of the misconduct, including, but not limited to, punitive damage awards to persons in situations similar to the claimant's and the severity of criminal penalties to which the defendant has been or may be subjected."

8. These substantive criteria (*a* through *g* in question 7), and the precise instructions detailing them, gave the jurors "adequate guidance" in making their award far more guidance than their counterparts in *Haslip* and *TXO* received. In *Haslip*, for example, the jury was told only the purpose of punitive damages (punishment and deterrence) and that an award was discretionary, not compulsory. We deemed those instructions, notable for their generality, constitutionally sufficient.

⭐ 9. The Court's opinion in *Haslip* went on to describe the checks Alabama places on the jury's discretion *postverdict*—through excessiveness review by the trial court, and appellate review, which tests the award against specific substantive criteria. While postverdict review of that character is not available in Oregon, the seven factors against which Alabama's Supreme Court tests punitive awards strongly resemble the statutory criteria Oregon's juries are instructed to apply. And this Court has often acknowledged, and generally respected, the presumption that juries follow the instructions they are given. As the Supreme Court of Oregon observed, *Haslip* "determined only that the Alabama procedure, as a whole and in its net effect, did not violate the Due Process Clause."

10. The Oregon court also observed, correctly, that the Due Process Clause does not require States to subject punitive damage awards to a form of postverdict review "that includes the possibility of remittitur." Because Oregon requires the factfinder to apply objective criteria, moreover, its procedures are perhaps more likely to prompt rational and fair punitive damage decisions than are the *post hoc* checks employed in jurisdictions following Alabama's pattern.

11. The Supreme Court of Oregon's conclusions are buttressed by the availability of at least some postverdict judicial review of punitive damage awards. Oregon's courts ensure that there is evidence to support the verdict: "If there is no evidence to support the jury's decision—in this context, no evidence that the statutory prerequisites for the award of punitive damages were met—then the trial court or the appellate courts can intervene to vacate the award."

12. The State's courts have shown no reluctance to strike punitive damage awards in cases where punitive liability is not established, so that defendant qualifies for judgment on that issue as a matter of law. In addition, punitive damage awards may be set aside because of flaws in jury instructions. See *Honeywell v. Sterling Furniture Co*: setting aside punitive damage award because it was prejudicial error to instruct jury that a portion of any award would be used to pay plaintiff's attorney fees and that another portion would go to State's common injury fund. As the Court acknowledges, "proper jury instructio[n] is a well established and, of course, important check against excessive awards."

13. In short, Oregon has enacted legal standards confining punitive damage awards in product liability cases. These state standards are judicially enforced by means of comparatively comprehensive preverdict procedures but markedly limited postverdict review, for Oregon has elected to make fact-finding, once supporting evidence is produced, the province of the jury. . . . The Court today invalidates this choice, largely because it concludes that English and early American courts generally provided judicial review of the size of punitive damage awards. The Court's account of the relevant history is not compelling.

14. I am not as confident as the Court about either the clarity of early American common law, or its import. Tellingly, the Court barely acknowledges the large authority exercised by American juries in the 18th and 19th centuries. In the early years of our Nation, juries "usually possessed the power to determine both law and fact." *Georgia v. Brailsford*: Chief Justice John Jay, trying a case in which State was party, instructed jury it had authority "to determine the law as well as the fact in controversy." And at the time trial by jury was recognized as the constitutional right of parties "[i]n [s]uits at common law," U.S. Constitution, Amendment 7, the assessment of "uncertain damages" was regarded, generally, as exclusively a jury function.

15. More revealing, the Court notably contracts the scope of its inquiry. It asks: Did common law judges claim the power to overturn jury verdicts they viewed as excessive? But full and fair historical inquiry ought to be wider. The Court should inspect, comprehensively and comparatively, the procedures employed—at trial *and* on appeal—to fix the amount of punitive damages. Evaluated in this manner, Oregon's scheme affords defendants like Honda *more* procedural safeguards than 19th century law provided.

16. Oregon instructs juries to decide punitive damage issues based on seven substantive factors and a clear and convincing evidence standard. When the Fourteenth Amendment was adopted in 1868, in contrast (see *Haslip*), "no particular procedures were deemed necessary to circumscribe a jury's discretion regarding the award of [punitive] damages, or their amount." The responsibility entrusted to the jury surely was not guided by instructions of the kind Oregon has enacted.

17. Furthermore, common law courts reviewed punitive damage verdicts extremely deferentially, if at all. See *Day v. Woodworth*: assessment of "exemplary, punitive, or vindictive damages . . . has been always left to the discretion of the jury, as the degree of punishment to be thus inflicted must depend on the peculiar circumstances of each case"; *Missouri Pacific R. Co. v. Humes*: "[t]he discretion of the jury in such cases is not controlled by any very definite rules"; *Barry v. Edmunds*: in "actions for torts where no precise rule of law fixes the recoverable damages, it is the peculiar function of the jury to determine the amount by their verdict." True, 19th century judges occasionally asserted that they had authority to overturn damage awards upon concluding, from the size of an award, that the jury's decision must have been based on "partiality" or "passion and prejudice." But courts rarely *exercised* this authority.

18. Because Oregon's procedures assure "adequate guidance from the court when the case is tried to a jury," (*Haslip*), this Court has no cause to disturb the judgment in this instance, for Honda presses here only a *procedural* due process claim. True, in a footnote to its petition for *certiorari*, not repeated in its briefs, Honda attributed to this Court an "assumption that procedural due process requires [judicial] review of *both* federal substantive due process and state law excessiveness challenges to the size of an award." But the assertion regarding "state law excessiveness challenges" is extraordinary, for this Court has never held that the Due Process Clause requires a State's courts to police jury fact-findings to ensure their conformity with state law. And, as earlier observed, the plurality opinion in *TXO* disavowed the suggestion that a defendant has a federal due process right to a correct determination under state law of the "reasonableness" of a punitive damages award.

19. Honda further asserted in its *certiorari* petition footnote: "Surely . . . due process (not to mention Supremacy Clause principles) requires, at a minimum, that state courts entertain and pass on the federal law contention that a particular punitive verdict is so grossly excessive as to violate substantive due process. Oregon's refusal to provide even that limited form of review is particularly indefensible." But Honda points to no definitive Oregon pronouncement postdating this Court's precedent setting decisions in *Haslip* and *TXO* demonstrating the hypothesized refusal to pass on a federal law contention.

20. It may be that Oregon's procedures guide juries so well that the "grossly excessive" verdict Honda projects in its *certiorari* petition footnote never materializes. [Between 1965 and the present, awards of punitive damages in Oregon have been reported in only two products liability cases, including this one.] If, however, in some future case, a plea is plausibly made that a particular punitive damage award is not merely excessive, but "so 'grossly excessive' as to violate the Federal Constitution," *TXO*, and Oregon's judiciary nevertheless insists that it is powerless to consider the plea, this Court might have cause to grant review. No such

case is before us today, nor does Honda, in this Court, maintain otherwise (size of award against Honda does not appear to be out of line with awards upheld in *Haslip* and *TXO*).

⭐ 21. To summarize: Oregon's procedures adequately guide the jury charged with the responsibility to determine a plaintiff's qualification for, and the amount of, punitive damages, and on that account do not deny defendants procedural due process; Oregon's Supreme Court correctly refused to rule that "an award of punitive damages, to comport with the requirements of the Due Process Clause, *always* must be subject to a form of postverdict or appellate review" for excessiveness; the verdict in this particular case, considered in light of this Court's decisions in *Haslip* and *TXO*, hardly appears "so 'grossly excessive' as to violate the substantive component of the Due Process Clause," *TXO*. Accordingly, the Court's procedural directive to the state court is neither necessary nor proper. The Supreme Court of Oregon has not refused to enforce federal law, and I would affirm its judgment.

IV. The next set of passages is from the *footnotes* to the *dissenting opinion*. They offer additional examples of the dissenting opinion's decision-making process. Once again, you are to describe the reasoning involved in each passage. Illustrate the logical apparatus involved (the uses of logical operators) and the analogical reasoning that constitutes the Supreme Court's arguments.

1. The *Haslip* jury was told that it could award punitive damages if "reasonably satisfied from the evidence" that the defendant committed fraud.

Answer:

(A) The *Haslip* jury was told that it could award punitive damages **if** (B) "reasonably satisfied from the evidence" that the defendant committed fraud.

If B, then A.

No argument is put forward in this passage. The statement is meant to help clarify the facts of the case.

2. The trial court in the Oregon case instructed the jury as follows: "Punitive damages: If you have found that plaintiff is entitled to general damages, you must then consider whether to award punitive damages. Punitive damages may be awarded to the plaintiff in addition to general damages to punish wrongdoers and to discourage wanton misconduct.

3. The trial judge did not instruct the jury on the following factors: (1) The "profitability of [Honda's] misconduct," or (2) the "total deterrent effect of other punishment" to which Honda was subject. Honda objected to an instruction on factor (1), which it argued was phrased "to assume the existence of misconduct," and expressly waived an instruction on factor (2), on the ground that it had not previously been subject to punitive damages. In its argument before the Supreme Court of Oregon, Honda did not contend that the trial court failed to instruct the jury concerning the criteria, or "that the jury did not properly apply those criteria."

4. The trial judge in *Haslip* instructed the jury as follows:

"Now, if you find that fraud was perpetrated then in addition to compensatory damages you may in your discretion, when I use the word discretion, I say you don't have to even find fraud, you wouldn't have to, but you may, the law says you may award an amount of money known as punitive damages.

"This amount of money is awarded to the plaintiff but it is not to compensate the plaintiff for any injury. It is to punish the defendant. Punitive means to punish or it is also called exemplary damages, which means to make an example. So, if you feel or not feel, but if you are reasonably satisfied from the evidence that the plaintiff[s] . . . ha[ve] had a fraud perpetrated upon them and as a direct result they were injured [then] in addition to compensatory damages you may in your discretion award punitive damages. . . .

"Should you award punitive damages, in fixing the amount, you must take into consideration the character and the degree of the wrong as shown by the evidence and necessity of preventing similar wrong."

Summary

- Legal arguments can be appreciated and understood when you are able to grasp the underlying logic. Legal discourse has evolved patterns and conventions that we can recognize and apply to specific legal cases.
- Appellate courts: Courts of appeal which review the decisions of lower courts.
- A rule that specifies a test with mandatory elements lists all the necessary conditions that must be met in order for the rule to be applicable.
- In law, deductive reasoning generally means as going from the *general* to the *specific*—that is, from the statement of a *rule* to its application to a particular legal case.
- Many law textbooks refer to inductive reasoning as the process of going from the *specific* to the *general*. It comes into play whenever we move from a specific case or legal opinion to a general rule.
- Legal reasoning is also called "rule-based reasoning."
- Probative value: Evidence that can be used during a trial to advance the facts of the case.
- Prejudicial effect: Evidence that might cause some jurors to be negatively biased toward a defendant.
- Indictment: A formal accusation presented by a grand jury.
- Affidavit: A written statement signed before an authorized official.
- Legal reasoning, relying as it does on precedent (a judicial decision that can be applied to later cases) and similar cases, often relies on analogies.
- Rules of law: The legal principles that have been applied to historical cases.
- Plaintiff: The person who initiates a lawsuit.

KEY TERMS

appellate courts 509	**prejudicial effect** 513	**precedent** 518
rule-based reasoning 509	**indictment** 515	**rules of law** 519
probative value 513	**affidavit** 516	**plaintiff** 520

LOGIC CHALLENGE: A GUILTY PROBLEM

Imagine that you are a private investigator specializing in determining the truth value of suspects' statements to the police. You are shown a videotape of four suspects accused of robbing a quick-loan store. The four suspects happen to know each other. When you view the videotape, you are allowed to hear each suspect make only one statement.

> *Alice*: Benny did it.
> *Benny*: David did it.
> *Connie*: I did not do it.
> *David*: What Benny said about me is false.

Assume that only one person did it and only one of the four statements is true. If so, determine the following two things:

1. Who committed the crime?
2. Which one of the statements is true?

Chapter 12

Moral Arguments

On a gut level, moral arguments are about right and wrong, and they can quickly become demanding, commanding, and heated. "Thou shalt not kill." "Abortion is wrong." "Leave your sister alone." However, value judgments enter a lot that we do and say—and so does the word "should." "You should remember to wash your hands before eating." "I should really be studying for that test tomorrow." "I should never have bought that stupid car."

To make things more complicated, some arguments rely solely on *factual claims* for support, some arguments rely solely on *value judgments* for support, and some arguments rely on a mixture of the two. "You take one more step, and you're in deep trouble." "You should stop lying, because you will quickly lose your credibility." "Without affordable health care, thousands of Americans will die." Where exactly do the factual claims end and the value judgments begin?

As usual, the first step in analyzing an argument is clarifying the premises and conclusion. Imagine that you want to take a vacation to Los Angeles from your home in New York. You discuss it with two friends, who offer their advice. One friend mentions the fact that you can fly from the East Coast of the United States to the West Coast nonstop in about 6 hours. He then adds another piece of information by citing the fact that it would take about 4 days to drive the same distance across the United States (factoring in time needed to eat and sleep). From this, he concludes that you *should* fly rather than drive to Los Angeles. Here is the argument:

> You can fly from New York to Los Angeles in about 6 hours. It takes about 4 days to drive the same distance. You *should* fly rather than drive.

However, the second friend might agree with the two premises just described, but she comes to the opposite conclusion—that you *should* drive instead of fly.

> You can fly from New York to Los Angeles in about 6 hours. It takes about 4 days to drive the same distance. You *should* drive rather than fly.

Can these differences be explained by just the facts involved? Obviously, both arguments use the same factual claims in the premises. However, the word "should" appears in both conclusions, but it is found nowhere in the premises. What is the justification for its introduction? The exploration of the difference between facts and values, as well as words such as "should" and "ought," starts our discussion of moral arguments. Let's begin.

A. VALUE JUDGMENTS

Value judgment A claim that a particular human action or object has some degree of importance, worth, or desirability.

A **value judgment** is a claim that a particular human action or object has some degree of importance, worth, or desirability. Let's see how value judgments enter into our discussion of your travel plans.

Justifying "Should"

Justifying the use of the word "should" in the conclusion of both arguments requires an introduction of new information in the premises. Since both arguments are missing this important ingredient, we can treat them as enthymemes (Chapter 3 introduced enthymemes and missing information). For the first argument, a possible implied premise is that *you probably want to make the trip as quickly as possible*. Adding this as a new premise would make the first argument strong. On the other hand, for the second argument, a possible implied premise is that *you probably want to see as much of the country as possible*. Adding this new information would make the second argument strong.

Both argument reconstructions deliberately supplied a premise designed to make each argument strong. When you have the time to reflect more thoroughly about the available options, then you might decide that you do want to see as much of the country as possible. In that case, the added premise in the first argument would be false, so the argument would not be cogent. However, the added premise in the second argument would be true, so that would yield a cogent argument.

In these two examples, the word "should" in the conclusion was justified as following from a *desired goal*. The intent of each argument was to offer good reasons why you should choose one method of transportation over another. The evaluation of the arguments hinged on how well the arguments match the intended goal. Notice that *if* you had decided that you wanted to make the trip as quickly as possible, then the added premise in the first argument would be true and the argument would be cogent. It would also follow that the added premise in the second argument would be false and the argument would not be cogent.

But what happens if we eliminate the intended goal of the trip? What if, instead, you and your friends were just talking about travel in general? Now suppose that one of your friends remarked that he hated driving long distances, while another friend remarked that she loved taking long road trips. These would be instances of value judgments.

Types of Value Judgments

There are many types of value judgments. For example, moral value judgments place emphasis on human actions or behaviors by asserting that they are *good, bad, right*, or *wrong*. Here are some examples of moral claims:

1. Murder is wrong.
2. You should always tell the truth.
3. Torturing prisoners is an immoral act.
4. Extracting information by torture in order to save lives is the morally right thing to do.

A second type of value judgment concerns matters of personal taste or value. For example, one person might say "Anchovies taste great" while another might say "Anchovies taste terrible." *Neither of these two statements asserts any facts about anchovies.* At best, they are an assertion of a person's feelings about the taste of anchovies. Examine the following three sentences:

5. Anchovies taste great.
6. Anchovies taste terrible.
7. Anchovies are small fish belonging to the herring family.

Sentence 7 is the only one of the three that *asserts something factual* about anchovies. If they are members of the herring family, then the statement is true, otherwise the statement is false. The first two sentences may appear to assert something about anchovies, but they do not. If you hate the taste of anchovies you might imagine that everyone else does too, and are amazed that anyone would find the taste desirable. On the other hand, if you love the taste of a certain kind of ice cream you might be surprised that other people do not share your personal value judgment. We would like our personal value judgments to be *universally shared* and are often surprised when they are not. So, for example, when you introduce your favorite ice cream to a friend and she says that "it is just OK," you might ask her to take another bite, hoping that she will change her mind and agree with your value judgment.

Another way of describing the set of three sentences regarding anchovies is to label the first two *subjective* and the third *objective*. In other words, the first two sentences *refer to the person* making the claim about anchovies and are, therefore, *subjective* claims. As such, these claims can be rewritten to bring out this point:

8. Anchovies taste great *to me*.
9. Anchovies taste terrible *to me*.

Now, these two statements can be considered either true or false, but their truth value cannot be determined by an examination of the facts concerning anchovies. These *subjective* statements are true if the persons uttering the statements are accurately describing how anchovies taste *to them*, otherwise they are false. Contrast those two statements with the third statement whose *objective* truth value can be determined by the facts concerning anchovies.

Now look closely at the next statement:

Killing another human being is always wrong.

It is fair to say that when most people make this claim they intend it to be an objective assertion. It is not likely that they would think that it was anything like the assertions regarding the taste of anchovies. Nevertheless, it is obviously a value judgment; more specifically, a *moral value judgment*. It is used typically in the following way:

You *should not* kill a human being.

Here we have another instance of the word "should." It is being used as a directive for how you *ought to* act toward other humans. When the words *should* and *ought* are used in a moral setting, the resulting statements are also referred to as *prescriptive* or *normative*. **Prescriptive** means "to offer advice." In a medical setting, a physician may prescribe medicine or a course of treatment. In a moral setting, advice may be offered either by specifying a particular action that ought to be performed, or by providing general moral rules, principles, or guidelines that should be followed.

Normative means establishing standards for correct moral behavior; determining norms or rules of conduct. Given this, we can see that the statement "You *should not* kill a human being" has a different function than the earlier example "You *should* drive across the United States." There, the emphasis was surely not in any way connected to a moral decision. Therefore, different types of value judgments have decidedly different roles to play in the construction and analysis of arguments. Since we are interested in moral reasoning we need to explore how moral value judgments function in the construction, analysis, and evaluation of moral arguments.

> **Prescriptive** The term means "to offer advice."

> **Normative** Establishing standards for correct moral behavior; determining norms or rules of conduct.

Taste and Value

To get started, let's imagine that someone is trying to persuade you that incest is morally wrong. He might resort to empirical research that indicates nearly all cultures view incest as morally wrong. This evidence is then used to conclude that "You should not commit incest." Now compare this result with the following scenario. Let's imagine that someone is trying to persuade you that anchovies taste terrible. She might resort to surveys that show that most people do not like the taste of anchovies. This evidence is then used to conclude that "You should not like anchovies."

Most people agree that there is a substantial difference between the *incest* and *anchovies* examples, because they believe there is a fundamental difference between a moral value judgment and one involving personal taste. Of course, both arguments are classified as value judgments, and both arguments have the word "should" in the conclusion. But suppose a close friend claims that the two cases are *not* fundamentally different; in other words, he thinks that *all value judgments are the same*. In fact, he believes that since empirical evidence is irrelevant in the anchovy argument, then it is also irrelevant in the incest argument. Therefore, we need to think seriously about two questions:

A. Are the two uses of "should" really that different?

B. If so, in what fundamental ways are they different?

We can start out by assessing the use of the empirical data. For the anchovy example, no matter if you were the only person on earth who liked the taste of anchovies, we would think it foolish for anyone to claim that *you should not like them*. Since personal taste of foods is subjective, any supposed "objective" evidence regarding other humans is actually just a tally of their personal tastes. On the other hand, the empirical data regarding cultural attitudes toward incest seems to be appealing to an objective fact and not just a tally of personal feelings. Nevertheless, we still need to determine the supposed "objective" nature of a moral judgment. In other words, if it is objective, then how do we come to that decision? To help us gain insight into the nature and complexity of moral claims, we need to look next at some moral theories, the subject of the next section.

CHECK YOUR UNDERSTANDING 12A

Determine whether the following statements are factual claims or value claims. If a statement makes a value claim, then determine if it is a moral value claim or a personal value claim.

1. Capital punishment is wrong.

Answer: Moral value claim

2. Your answer to the homework problem is wrong.

3. Pizza is the most delicious kind of food on the planet.

4. Euthanasia is an acceptable act.

★ 5. The movie *Inception* won four Academy Awards.

6. The movie *Inception* was confusing and difficult to follow.

7. Venison is deer meat.

8. Eating meat is wrong.

★ 9. Air travel is boring.

10. Air travel is the safest way to travel.

11. Anyone afraid of flying is irrational.

12. Tax evasion is a criminal offense.

★ 13. Not paying taxes is a justified form of protest.

14. Giving big corporations tax breaks is welfare for the millionaires.

15. Microsoft employs the most workers of any software company in the United States.

B. MORAL THEORIES

There are many different kinds of moral theories. Some theories offer ways of determining whether a human action is morally right or wrong by placing emphasis on the outcome of the action. These theories look to the ultimate consequences of our actions as the focal point for moral deliberations. On the other hand, some theories reject any consideration of the outcome of an action and instead hold that moral acts are right or wrong in themselves. In addition, some moral theories try to combine these two types of approaches. There are even theories that hold that *all* moral judgments are relative to individuals, cultures, and societies. In this section, we will look at six moral theories: *emotivism, egoism, utilitarianism, deontology, situation ethics,* and *relativism.*

Emotivism

Consider the following claims:

- Murder is morally wrong.
- You ought always to tell the truth.
- You ought not to steal.

To most people these seem like perfectly understandable and meaningful *moral statements.* It would be easy to take a survey and get people's responses to each statement. But it is unlikely that you will find many people who say that they do not understand the statements at all. Now compare the three foregoing claims with three different statements:

- Harrisburg is the capital of Pennsylvania.
- The Eiffel Tower is in Paris, France.
- Mount Everest is the fourth tallest mountain in the world.

Once again, most people would think these to be perfectly understandable and meaningful *factual statements.* Also, it would be easy to take a survey and get people's responses to each of these statements. And again, it is unlikely that you will find many people who say that they do not understand the statements at all. Now suppose we ask people how they would *verify* the truth or falsity of the *factual* statements. It should be an easy task for most people, because each of the statements refers to objective facts of the world. Therefore, appropriate and uncontroversial empirical support would be readily available.

But now suppose we ask people how they would *verify* the truth or falsity of the *moral* statements. This would not be as easy, because it is not obvious that each of the moral statements refers to any kind of objective facts of the world. Therefore, appropriate and uncontroversial empirical support would not be readily available.

Emotivism A theory that asserts that moral value judgments are merely expressions of our attitudes or emotions.

Difficulties such as these are addressed by **emotivism**, a theory that asserts that moral value judgments are merely expressions of our attitudes or emotions. Emotivism thus bypasses the problem of objectively verifying the truth or falsity of moral value judgments. If a moral judgment is an expression of one's personal emotions, then it is not an assertion of a fact in the objective sense, but rather a description of your emotional state. Supporters of emotivism often point out that we currently have no reliable means of verifying the accuracy of anyone's subjective statements. The important thing to remember is that emotivism rejects any notion that moral value judgments are in any way descriptions of objective moral facts. Therefore, moral value judgments are no different from other personal value judgments, for example, expressions of taste, such as the utterance "Apples taste delicious (*to me*)."

Thus, for emotivism, moral statements are nothing but expressions of what we personally like and dislike, or of what we approve and disapprove. As such, they can be used to persuade others to have the same moral feelings that we have; this is similar to hoping that others will like the same ice cream that we do. So, according to emotivism, when you say, "Murder is wrong," you are not referring to anything objective; this and all other moral value judgments assert nothing factual about the world.

However, emotivism raises some important practical considerations. How do we talk about related moral and legal issues, such as blame, responsibility, and praise? How do we decide when there is a legitimate moral dispute? Since emotivism holds that moral judgments are merely pronouncements of personal taste, then any dispute about a case of child negligence, for example, would be reduced to assertions about each individual's personal feelings. If emotivism is correct, there would be no objective moral aspect to consider in the case.

Consequentialism

Consequentialism refers to a *class* of moral theories in which the moral value of any human action or behavior is determined exclusively by its outcomes. In other words, consequentialist theories hold that a human action is judged morally right or wrong, good or bad, solely on the end result of the action. Similarly, people are judged to be morally good or bad strictly by the consequences of their actions.

Consequentialist theories are based on **teleology**, the philosophical belief that the value of an action or object can be determined by looking at the purpose or the end of the action or object. (The term "teleology" comes from *telos*, meaning *end*, so it is the study of the end, purpose, or design of an object or human action.) We will look at two consequentialist theories: *egoism* and *utilitarianism*.

Egoism

As the name indicates, **egoism** is the basic principle that everyone should act in order to maximize his or her own individual pleasure or happiness. Egoism reduces the moral value of an act to the outcome of its consequences to one person, the acting agent. (Since "ego" means *the self* the moral theory is really just *self-ism*.) Egoism's moral directive is quite simple: *All humans ought to pursue their own personal pleasure.*

It is interesting to consider whether an unintended, but potentially positive consequence of egoism is possible. If everyone consistently followed the directive of egoism, could this increase the overall happiness of the society as a whole? Some argue that since we cannot know with certainty how our actions will affect other people, we

Consequentialism A class of moral theories in which the moral value of any human action or behavior is determined exclusively by its outcomes.

Teleology The philosophical belief that the value of an action or object can be determined by looking at the purpose or the end of the action or object.

Egoism The basic principle that everyone should act in order to maximize his or her own individual pleasure or happiness.

should not even attempt to consider them. By consistently pursuing our own pleasure or happiness, we are doing our best to maximize the overall happiness of society. As evidence for this position, quite often the best intentions go in vain. As a consequence, if we give up the chance to pursue our own pleasure, then we risk the possibility that no happiness will be achieved. How often has it happened that a seemingly good deed has failed to achieve its goal? (There is a popular paraphrase of a line in Robert Burns's poem, "To a Mouse": "The best laid plans of mice and men often go astray.") Therefore, we *ought* always to pursue our own happiness.

Of course, since we cannot know precisely all the future consequences of our actions, we cannot be certain that our own pursuit of pleasure or happiness will end with a good result. An action may result in a short-term pleasure, but if repeated often enough, it might lead to long-term unhappiness and pain. Think of alcohol and drug addiction.

These considerations point to two major problems with consequentialist theories. First, how do we *define* what would be *happiness* or *pleasure* for everyone (or for egoism, my own happiness or pleasure)? And second, how do we *measure* or quantify amounts or degrees of *happiness* or *pleasure*? For example, is the happiness or the pleasure of a child comparable to that of an adult? What measuring device, scale, or chart can we consult to determine the levels, degree, or extent of happiness or pleasure in an individual (for egoism), or for society as a whole, or even between cultures?

Utilitarianism

Another specific and important example of a consequentialist moral theory (and therefore, teleological) is *utilitarianism*. Although there are many varieties of utilitarianism, they all agree on a few fundamental principles. The most important principle for **utilitarianism** can be summed up in the famous dictum "the greatest good for the greatest number." Any action or human behavior is to be judged by its outcomes—specifically, whether it brought about the greatest good to the greatest number of people. (The name *utilitarianism* is derived from the term "utility," which means *usefulness*.) Since utilitarianism is a moral theory, it concentrates on the usefulness of human actions and behaviors. It asks how they affect the overall good or happiness in a society. (Compare this with the term "public utilities," which typically refers to organizations that supply water or electricity, which are useful and beneficial to society.)

> **Utilitarianism** It can be summed up in the famous dictum "the greatest good for the greatest number."

Utilitarianism (like egoism, for that matter) is grounded on the psychological assumption that the great driving force of human behavior is the *avoidance of pain* and the *seeking of pleasure*. So, from the psychological evidence supporting this view of human nature, utilitarianism derives its moral directive: *All humans ought to act in order to maximize the greatest pleasure or happiness for the greatest number of people.*

> **Universalizable** When the same principles hold for all people at all times.

According to utilitarianism, every human action is **universalizable**, meaning that the same principles hold for all people at all times. More simply, "What if everyone did that?" The underlying sentiment is utilitarian because it appeals to the outcome of our actions. Generally speaking, the question is mostly used in a rhetorical way, in that it appeals to the possible *negative* effects of certain actions. For example, you throw a piece of litter on the ground and are asked, "What would happen if everyone littered?" Since the end result of everyone performing that action would be an unwanted situation, we are then instructed not to litter.

Jeremy Bentham, one of the foremost defenders of utilitarianism, thought that we could measure or quantify the results of our actions. Bentham counseled us to do the following:

1. Determine the possible actions available to you in any given situation.
2. List all the people your action will affect. (Be sure to include yourself in the list.)
3. Calculate the total amount of pleasure derived as the outcome of each possible action.
4. Calculate the total amount of pain derived as the outcome of each possible action.
5. Subtract the amount of pain from the amount of pleasure derived as the outcome of each possible action.
6. You ought to choose the action whose outcome results in the greatest amount of pleasure.

However, the same problems associated with consequentialist theories are relevant for Bentham's six-step procedure. First, we need clear definitions of "happiness" and "pleasure," definitions that cut across individuals, cultures, and societies. Second, it is one thing for Bentham to say that we should *measure* or *quantify* the amount of pleasure and pain as a result of our possible actions, but it is quite another thing to tell us how we are to do this. Bentham fails to provide the tools necessary for such an undertaking. He instead provides loose guidelines, such as the *intensity* and *duration* of the pleasure or pain. But this just moves the question back one step. Bentham does not provide a clear method for measuring or quantifying the *intensity* or *duration* of our own levels or amounts of pain and pleasure, let alone for all the other people our actions will affect. Is it even possible, in principle, to quantify the *intensity* and *duration* of a child's pain or pleasure, and then be able to compare it to that of an adult?

Nevertheless, many people do try to apply Bentham's ideas, even if they are not familiar with the specifics of his theory. People often attempt to weigh the pros and cons of their actions. We sometimes try to gauge the extent of the pain and pleasure that will result, even though we do not have a clear-cut system of quantifying them. We often use our decidedly nonquantitative "calculations" to justify our actions, and we do often try to maximize the greatest happiness for the greatest number.

Deontology

A deontological moral theory is radically different from a consequentialist theory. We know that consequentialist theories emphasize the results of our actions. A deontological theory rejects any emphasis on the results or outcomes of an action, and instead recognizes the *role of duty*. **Deontology** holds that duty to others is the first and foremost moral consideration, and it lays the groundwork for discovering those duties. (The root word "deon" means *duty* or *obligation*, so *deontology* is the study of duties.)

Deontology The theory that duty to others is the first and foremost moral consideration.

An important distinction for deontology is that performing a particular duty does not have to have any immediate positive consequence. In this sense, a recognized duty (for example, telling the truth) is an instance of what Immanuel Kant called a **categorical imperative**. The basic idea is that your actions or behavior toward others should always be such that *you would want everyone to act in the same manner.* In this context, "categorical" means *absolute* and *unconditional*, and "imperative" means *command* or *obligation*. In other words, a categorical imperative is an absolute and universal moral law. For example, telling the truth would be a categorical imperative, because it is something that each individual would want everyone to do. However, even if it is a universal moral law to always tell the truth, we cannot expect that good consequences will result every time we apply the moral law. This can be seen in the saying that "the truth often hurts." Therefore, a deontological theory is quite different from a consequentialist moral theory that is based on the outcomes of our actions.

Deontology and consequentialism can also be distinguished by exploring two moral uses of the word "ought." Consequentialist theories rely on a *conditional ought.* For example, the statement "You ought to tell the truth" would be correct only if this would result in the best possible outcome in a given situation. Therefore, consequentialist theories place *conditions* on the use of *ought.* On the other hand, deontological theories rely on an *unconditional ought.* For example, the statement "You ought to tell the truth" would *always* be applicable, *with no exceptions no matter what the outcome.* For deontology, all moral rules are universal, they have no exceptions, and they are absolutely binding to all people. In other words, it is your unconditional duty to always tell the truth.

Situation Ethics

Situation ethics agrees that there can be general, even objective, moral rules; however, it holds that we should not rigidly apply those rules to every possible situation. This is similar to the legal principle that reminds us to distinguish the letter of the law from the spirit of the law. Although laws are designed to help prevent unwanted behavior, it is also true that most laws have exceptions. For example, suppose someone is rushing to the hospital with an injured relative. The driver might slow down at a red light (just enough to make sure there is no oncoming traffic) and then proceed through the intersection without having come to a full stop. The letter of the law has been broken, but the spirit of the law has not. The law is meant to deter flagrant violations of running through red lights, and as such is meant to make driving safe for all concerned. But the violation in question was clearly not flagrant; in fact, the driver made sure no one was coming before continuing on.

Situation ethics asks us to acknowledge that each situation has some unique characteristics. Because of this obvious fact, we must learn to balance the letter and the spirit of any moral rule that might be applicable to present situation. Therefore, situation ethics calls for flexibility when making our moral decisions.

Categorical imperative
The basic idea is that your actions or behavior toward others should always be such that you would want everyone to act in the same manner.

Situation ethics
Although there can be general, even objective, moral rules, we should not rigidly apply those rules to every possible situation.

Relativism

Relativism makes two claims:

1. All moral value judgments are determined by an individual's personal beliefs or by a society's beliefs toward actions or behavior.
2. There are no objective or universal moral value judgments.

This means that all moral judgments are either *subjective* (when applied to an individual) or *intersubjective* (when applied to a society or societies). In neither case is the moral judgment objective. For example, the statement "Stealing is wrong" means that the individual who utters the statement disapproves of stealing, or the community in general disapproves of stealing, or both. Moral judgments are therefore reduced to subjective determinations of an individual's or a society's attitudes toward a particular behavior.

Adherents of relativism point to profound cultural and ethical differences among societies. For example, some cultures developed in the difficult terrain of the arctic. Those people survived the yearlong harsh conditions and became meat eaters, simply because there was no vegetation. By the relativist light, it would be absurd to expect them to be vegetarians and to hold that they are somehow morally deficient. Similarly, some nomadic cultures found it impossible to raise too many children at the same time, or to raise children who would not be able to quickly survive on their own. Consequently, infanticide was a regularly practiced way of life. Again, the relativist concludes that we cannot judge their actions and behaviors by our ethical standards that were developed over centuries in far different environments and under completely different circumstances.

Relativists also point out that most people's moral beliefs were conditioned by some combination of their immediate family and the society in which they were raised. Therefore, your individual moral beliefs are determined for the most part by where and when you were raised, just like the language you learned. In addition, relativists emphasize the difficult (and they think impossible) problem of judging between two competing moral systems. Relativists point out that every set of moral beliefs is judged by its adherents to be superior to all other sets of moral beliefs. Thus, relativists stress the point that there are no objective criteria that we could apply to decide which moral system is "correct."

Contrasting Moral Theories

The many different moral theories can be illustrated by analyzing a hypothetical situation. A large cruise ship sinks and twenty people manage to make it to a small lifeboat. However, there are only enough provisions to keep ten people alive for at most a few days. Also, the lifeboat will capsize if all twenty people are allowed to enter it. The officer in charge decides that ten adult males will have to swim away from the lifeboat in order to give the remaining ten people a chance to survive.

Relativism First, all moral value judgments are determined by an individual's personal beliefs or by a society's beliefs toward actions or behavior. Second, there are no objective or universal moral value judgments.

A consequentialist might agree that the decision was morally justified based on a calculation of the best possible outcome for the most people. On the other hand, a deontologist might disagree with the decision. The deontologist could invoke the categorical imperative that our actions or decisions should never purposely or consciously harm innocent people. Finally, a relativist would argue that there is no one right answer.

CHECK YOUR UNDERSTANDING 12B

Answer "true" or "false" to the following statements.

1. A utilitarian argument for capital punishment might be that it benefits society by eliminating dangerous individuals.

Answer: True

2. Every moral theory is based on the determination of how a person's act either produces pleasure or avoids pain.

3. An ethical theory is teleological if it relies on duties and responsibilities to others.

4. The fact that pleasure, pain, and happiness are different for each person is a problem for deontological theories.

⭐ 5. Consequentialist moral theories are based on our duties to others.

6. Deontological theories hold that one should always act so as to produce the greatest happiness for the greatest number of people.

7. Utilitarianism holds that since moral values are relative to individuals and cultures, therefore, there can be no universal moral principles.

8. Emotivism holds that moral judgments must be based on the consequences of our acts.

⭐ 9. A categorical imperative is a rule relative to a particular culture or religion.

10. Egoism holds that every rule should be obeyed without exception and without regard for any possible negative consequences of the act.

11. Situation ethics holds that all value judgments are merely expressions of our feelings about certain human behaviors.

12. Relativism holds that universal ethical principles do not exist.

⭐ 13. A criticism of utilitarianism is that we can never know all the consequences of our actions.

14. A criticism of deontology is that we do not have a way to measure pleasure and pain.

15. An important factor for teleological moral theories is the motive behind a particular act or behavior.

C. THE NATURALISTIC FALLACY

As we saw earlier, some moral theories use facts about human nature as the basis for moral value judgments. They rely on psychological and biological evidence to argue that human behavior can be reduced to two forces: the desire for pleasure (or happiness) and the avoidance of pain. The basic principle for all *naturalistic* moral theories, such as egoism and utilitarianism, is captured by the **naturalistic moral principle**:

> Since it is *natural* for humans to desire pleasure (or happiness) and to avoid pain, we can conclude that human behavior *ought* to be directed to these two ends.

The argument has been criticized for falling prey to the **naturalistic fallacy**: *value judgments cannot be logically derived from statements of fact.* This line of criticism (also known as the "is-ought" distinction) was originally presented by David Hume, but the name *naturalistic fallacy* was coined by G. E. Moore. The criticism begins by drawing a line between factual statements and value judgments. On one side of the line are the factual statements, and on the other side of the line are value judgments. In other words, an ethical pronouncement that you *ought to do* something *cannot* be logically deduced from statements that assert only *what is the case.*

The fallacious use of the naturalistic moral principle can be illustrated by a few examples. We know that *factual statements* assert that something is or is not the case, and they are decided by empirical investigations. For example, we could gather data about human eating habits and determine the following fact: Most humans get pleasure from eating ice cream. Since we have discovered a fact about humans, we can apply the naturalistic moral principle to create this argument:

> It *is* true that most humans get pleasure from eating ice cream. Therefore, humans *ought* to eat ice cream.

Our data gathering about human eating habits might also reveal this fact: Most humans do not like the taste of anchovies. Once again, if we have discovered a fact about humans, then we can apply the naturalistic moral principle:

> It *is* the case that most humans do not like the taste of anchovies. Therefore, humans *ought not* to eat anchovies.

Once we recognize that these are two instances of the *naturalistic fallacy,* then we can assert that the "ought" in the two conclusions does not follow logically from the "is" in the premises. In addition, the truth value of the premises does not help the arguments. We know that humans often do things that are damaging to their bodies; for example, there are numerous negative addictions. However, many of the addictions give intense pleasure that can last for a long time. According to egoism, the addict's actions are morally acceptable (at least in the short term). In addition, since Bentham's *intensity* and *duration* criteria have been met, then, according to utilitarianism, this provides the justification for claiming that the addict "ought" to perform the act.

Of course, a more complete analysis of the addict's situation would have to include the pain and suffering of any close relatives that are affected by the addict's behavior.

Naturalistic moral principle Since it is natural for humans to desire pleasure (or happiness), and to avoid pain, human behavior ought to be directed to these two ends.

Naturalistic fallacy Value judgments cannot be logically derived from statements of fact.

Nevertheless, how do we quantify the intensity and duration of the pleasure for the addict, and then subtract the quantity of pain and suffering of the relatives? Also, what if the addict has no close relatives to consider? Finally, what can we conclude about so-called "victimless crimes"? For example, since *it is a fact* that many people like to gamble, can we then conclude that *they ought to gamble*?

D. THE STRUCTURE OF MORAL ARGUMENTS

Moral arguments generally have conclusions that assert some moral position or action, such as "You ought to do X," or "It is wrong to do Y." In its simplest form, these are the requirements for a moral argument:

1. There is at least one premise describing a particular situation where a decision to act will be made by someone (this is a nonmoral statement).
2. There is at least one premise that supplies a moral rule, principle, or command.
3. The conclusion asserts that a specific action should be performed.

Of course, not all moral arguments come in complete packages. Some have missing premises or conclusions, but these are generally easily filled in by those familiar with the context in which the moral argument occurs. The moral premise is necessary for two reasons:

1. It fills in the gap described by the "is-ought" problem.

Jeremy Bentham

Happiness, for Jeremy Bentham (1748–1832), is achieved by maximizing pleasure and minimizing pain. Bentham was influenced by the social upheavals of the Industrial Revolution. Although qualified to practice law, he chose not to; instead, he tried to influence society by his writings. His *Introduction to the Principles of Morals and Legislation* contains the details of "the greatest happiness principle."

Bentham's thinking combined the clarification of concepts with rigorous deductive argument. He chose reason over tradition, and rationality over authority. He also championed a scientific description of human nature. His emphasis on "pleasure and pain" as the prime motivations for human

behavior anticipated the modern approach to modifying that behavior, though *positive* and *negative feedback*—in other words, rewards and punishment. "Nature has placed mankind under the governance of two sovereign masters, *pain* and *pleasure*. It is for them alone to point out what we ought to do, as well as to determine what we shall do."

Upon his death, Bentham had tens of thousands of unpublished pages of material that he hoped would eventually be published. He left the bulk of his considerable fortune to help support the University College, London. According to his instructions, his body was to be preserved and displayed sitting in a chair. In fact, you can visit Bentham at the university today.

2. It supplies the general moral rule or principle needed to derive a specific moral action or behavior. In other words, it provides the moral grounds for *why you ought to do X.*

In order to see how the moral and nonmoral premises work, consider these four arguments:

A. Some prisoners of war have been tortured while in U.S. custody. Therefore, the United States should stop torturing prisoners of war.

B. Some prisoners of war have been tortured while in U.S. custody. Therefore, the United States should not stop torturing prisoners of war.

C. Some prisoners of war have been tortured while in U.S. custody. The United States has signed an agreement to abide by the Geneva Convention. The United States is violating the Geneva Convention, which prohibits the torture of prisoners of war. Therefore, the United States should stop torturing prisoners of war.

D. Some prisoners of war have been tortured while in U.S. custody. The United States is gaining valuable information from the torture of prisoners of war. Anything the United States can do to fight the war on terror should be permitted. Therefore, the United States should not stop torturing prisoners of war.

In arguments A and B the single nonmoral premise describes a reported fact about U.S. treatment of prisoners of war. It is easily seen that neither the conclusion in argument A, nor the conclusion in B, follows from the single premise. However, arguments C and D have premises that attempt to provide the necessary moral justification for their respective conclusions. As with most moral arguments, the moral premises are generally the point of departure for further argumentation and analysis. Nevertheless, many times the nonmoral issues drive the force of analysis. For example:

> Our mother has been in a coma for several months and is being kept alive by life-sustaining equipment. The attending physician's opinion is that the coma is irreversible. There appears to be little or no brain activity in our mother. Therefore, we should ask the physician to take our mother off the life-sustaining equipment.

It is possible that other relatives might disagree with the conclusion for a variety of moral and nonmoral reasons. For example, they might point out that the physician cannot be certain that the patient will never come out of the coma. They might argue that little or no brain activity is a measure of what is occurring in the patient's brain, but not in her mind. Also, the equipment to measure brain activity is only our best guide today as to what is happening in a person's brain. They might point out that surely more powerful equipment will be developed in future that will give us a better picture of what is occurring in the brain. In other words, the argument against taking the patient off the life-sustaining equipment may be over the factual or empirical nature of the status of the coma, and not a moral debate over "pulling the plug." In fact, it is possible that all the relatives will agree to the decision to let the mother die if they can agree on the nature and extent of the coma.

When starting to analyze moral arguments it often helps to see them as deductive. This simplifies the logical analysis into *valid, invalid, sound,* and *unsound.* For example, many moral arguments have this structure:

> X is Y.
> Anything Y is morally wrong.
> X is morally wrong.

For example, let X = *killing an innocent human,* and Y = *murder*:

> Killing an innocent human is murder.
> Murder is morally wrong.
> Killing an innocent human is morally wrong.

To see another example, this time let X = *stealing,* and Y = *taking other people's property without their consent*:

> Stealing is taking other people's property without their consent.
> Taking other people's property without their consent is morally wrong.
> Stealing is morally wrong.

Since both examples result in valid arguments, the remaining question is one of soundness. The first premise in both arguments is considered by most people to be merely definitional. One premise defines "killing," and the other defines "stealing." As such, their truth value would probably not be much debated. But in order to determine soundness, we must be able to decide the truth value of the second premise of each argument. Here is where we run into problems. The second premise of each of the two arguments is a moral value judgment. We already discussed the problems with determining the truth value of this kind of statement. The statement is not merely definitional; nor does it seem to assert a fact of the world. Therefore, the soundness issue will usually be a difficult hurdle to overcome.

So, should we treat some moral arguments as deductive? One reason to do this is that many people feel strongly that moral rules or principles are universal. Hence, the logical intent of an argument using a general moral rule as a premise must be to have the moral action prescribed in the conclusion to follow with necessity. And this indeed is how many people perceive or intend their moral arguments to be interpreted.

Of course, we can also classify some moral arguments as inductive, instead of deductive. Let's see how the logical analysis and evaluation would proceed. For example, suppose you come across a research survey that asked a large number of Christians, chosen at random, to state their beliefs concerning several social issues. You might read the following statistic: "Ninety percent of Christians believe that stem cell research is morally wrong." Now, perhaps you know someone who is a Christian; if so, you might create this argument:

> **E.** Ninety percent of Christians believe that stem cell research is morally wrong. Gerry is a Christian. Therefore, Gerry *probably* believes that stem cell research is wrong.

This is a straightforward inductive argument. If the premises are assumed to be true, then we can classify it as a strong argument. In addition, if the research was well conducted and we have reason to believe that the evidence in the first premise is factually true, then we can also classify the argument as cogent. But now look at the next argument:

> **F.** Ninety percent of Christians believe that stem cell research is morally wrong. Gerry is a Christian. Therefore, Gerry *ought* to believe that stem cell research is wrong.

This is a not a straightforward inductive argument. The "ought" in the conclusion of argument F is quite different from the word "probably" in the conclusion of argument E. The conclusion of E merely asserts that a high statistical probability can be attached to the claim that "Gerry believes that stem cell research is wrong." Of course, the conclusion is not necessarily true, but that is not a requirement of a strong inductive argument. The premises in argument E, if true, do provide strong statistical evidence for the conclusion.

On the other hand, the conclusion of F does not assert anything about a statistical probability that can be attached to the claim that "Gerry believes that stem cell research is wrong." Instead, the conclusion of F offers a moral prescription of what Gerry *ought* to do. Here again we see an *ought statement* derived from an *is statement*. But perhaps the argument is missing some key information, and we can provide the missing moral link:

> **G.** Ninety percent of Christians believe that stem cell research is morally wrong. Gerry is a Christian. Every Christian ought to believe what the vast majority Christians believe. Therefore, Gerry *ought* to believe that stem cell research is wrong.

The added premise seems to fill in the missing gap between the "is" in the premises and the "ought" in the conclusion. However, now the argument is no longer inductive, it is deductive. Thus, we are back to determining its validity and soundness.

Let's add one more twist to the argument. Suppose we change the conclusion:

> **H.** Ninety percent of Christians believe that stem cell research is morally wrong. Gerry is a Christian. Every Christian ought to believe what the vast majority of Christians believe. Therefore, Gerry *probably ought* to believe that stem cell research is wrong.

This would have the appearance of making the argument inductive once again. Nevertheless, there is something extremely odd about the phrase "probably ought." Moral prescriptions about what we ought to do are not generally couched in terms of what we *probably ought to do*, but rather of what we *ought to do*, with no added qualifications.

You can apply the discussion thus far to two last examples, to deepen your understanding:

> **I.** Seventy-five percent of Americans believe that abortions are sometimes morally justified. Maxine is an American. Therefore, Maxine *probably* believes that abortions are sometimes morally justified.
>
> **J.** Seventy-five percent of Americans believe that abortions are sometimes morally justified. Maxine is an American. Therefore, Maxine *ought* to believe that abortions are sometimes morally justified.

E. ANALOGIES AND MORAL ARGUMENTS

Analogies are often used in moral arguments as a way to support a moral prescription in the conclusion. Like all analogical reasoning, the premises of an analogical moral argument try to link two or more situations that call for a moral decision or determination to be made. The idea is to persuade others that they should (or should not) perform a certain action (or hold a certain belief), because the present case is similar to a previously determined moral situation. Thus, analogical moral arguments are attempts to point out that our moral actions (or beliefs) should be consistent. The following is an analogical moral argument:

> You believe that every human embryo or fetus is a human being. You believe that abortion is wrong, because it is the murder of an innocent human being. Yet you also believe that abortion is morally permissible in cases of rape and incest. But a human embryo or fetus conceived by an act of rape or incest is no less an innocent human being than one conceived by an act of consensual sex. Therefore, you *ought* to believe that abortion is *not* morally permissible in cases of rape and incest.

The point of the premises is to force someone into recognizing the inconsistency of holding (1) that *every* human embryo or fetus is a human being and (2) that an embryo or fetus conceived by incest or rape is *not* an innocent human being. In other words, people who hold (1) and (2) would need to explain why and how a fetus conceived by rape or incest is different from a fetus that was conceived through consensual sex. They would have to explain how the act of conception in the case of rape or incest causes the resulting fetus to be excluded from the class of innocent human beings.

Let's look at another example of an analogical moral argument:

> You told me that you think that using marijuana is morally wrong, not because it is illegal, but because it is addictive and physically harmful after long-term use. But you regularly drink alcohol, even though you are aware of studies that show that it is addictive and physically harmful after long-term use. Therefore, you *ought* not to drink alcohol, because it is morally wrong.

As in the previous example, the intent of the premises is to force others into recognizing that they hold inconsistent positions. (1) They believe that using marijuana is morally wrong, because it is addictive and physically harmful after long-term use. (2) They regularly drink alcohol, even though they are aware of studies that show that it is addictive and physically harmful after long-term use. Hence, they would have to explain how regularly drinking alcohol is different from using marijuana in order to justify its continued use on moral grounds. Furthermore, the first premise precludes them from replying that the illegality of marijuana is the relevant moral difference. (You might compare this analogical moral argument with the *tu quoque* fallacy discussed in Chapter 4.)

In sum, we can reconstruct, analyze, and evaluate analogical moral arguments by using the same techniques as for nonmoral analogical arguments. We can evaluate the strengths and weaknesses of analogical moral arguments by assessing the relevant instances in the premises. We can also apply the familiar techniques of looking for disanalogies, counteranalogies, and any unintended consequences of the analogy. These logical analysis techniques allow us to understand how analogical moral arguments function—and how they can be evaluated for degrees of strength.

CHECK YOUR UNDERSTANDING 12E

Discuss the following moral issues in light of the ideas put forward in this chapter. Use the moral theories described in this chapter to construct arguments regarding the following issues. Choose a moral theory and construct an argument by applying it to an issue. Then take a different moral theory and apply it to a different issue. Discuss the strength of the arguments you construct in light of the discussions regarding each particular theory you use. Try to use each moral theory at least twice.

1. downloading music illegally	7. welfare	⭐ 13. freedom of speech
2. gambling	8. giving to charities	14. smoker's rights
3. state-run lotteries	⭐ 9. animal rights	15. prostitution
4. rehabilitation of criminals	10. abortion	16. cheating on exams
⭐ 5. stealing	11. capital punishment	⭐ 17. birth control
6. murder	12. affirmative action	18. telemarketing

Answer to #1: downloading music illegally
Your answers will depend on the particular moral theory you choose for each issue. Here is an example that applies *Utilitarianism*:

Argument: *Downloading music illegally* denies artists (music composers, lyricists, and musicians) a fair share of any royalties for their original work. It also reduces the income of the companies that produced and marketed the music. Without royalties artists lose incentive to create new music, and without sales music companies cannot afford to produce new music. The immediate pleasure derived from those listening to illegally downloaded music does not outweigh the pain of the artists and company employees who will not be able to survive a continued economic loss. The long-term effect is that artists and music companies will no longer produce new music.

Discussion of the argument: Not everyone downloads music illegally. Enough people are willing to buy music to ensure that artists get some royalties and to keep music companies in business. Also, with the explosion of the Internet, some artists now self-publish their work or even offer it for free. The idea is to gain a following of loyal fans willing to pay a small fee directly to the artist, instead of buying music from a company at a higher cost. In some cases this income will match the artist's royalty derived from a contract in which the music company keeps the lion's share of the profits.

F. JUSTIFYING MORAL PREMISES

We could ask that a moral premise itself be justified. Let's explore two ways of doing this. First, it has often been held that moral rules are "self-evident." A classic example is in the second paragraph of the Declaration of Independence:

> We hold these truths to be self-evident, that all men are created equal, that they are endowed by their Creator with certain unalienable rights; that among these are life, liberty, and the pursuit of happiness.

Self-evident truths are often defined as statements to which any *rational* person would give assent. The clearest examples are found in mathematics, and especially in the axioms of geometry. René Descartes, the inventor of analytic geometry, referred to self-evident truths as "clear and distinct ideas." But the axioms of geometry are *not* value judgments—they do not assert what we ought to do.

In fact, rational humans can disagree with parts of the Declaration of Independence. For example, an atheist might agree that we have the unalienable rights of "life, liberty, and the pursuit of happiness," but disagree strongly that these rights have been endowed in humans "by their Creator." Others will say that the term "unalienable rights" is too strong and obviously false. "Unalienable" means something that cannot be either taken away or given away. But in the United States, some states *take away the life* of citizens by the act of execution. Also, convicted felons often have their *liberty* and *pursuit of happiness* taken away by incarceration. It has also been observed that the self-evident truths in the declaration referred only to white, property-owning males. Why did the self-evident truths and unalienable rights endowed by the Creator not apply to all humans—including women, nonwhites, and non-property owners? In fact, questions of just this type were the basis for amendments to the U.S. Constitution.

It is also true that perfectly rational people can, and often do, disagree on *moral actions*. For example, rational disagreement occurred during the deliberations in the Truman administration on whether to drop the atomic bomb on Hiroshima and Nagasaki in 1945. Arguments on both sides of the debate appealed to the facts regarding the state of the ongoing war in the Pacific (the nonmoral premises), but also to moral principles. One side argued that the devastating effects of the atomic bomb would cause Japan to surrender quickly. This would bring an immediate end to the war, saving millions of lives. The other side argued that killing hundreds of thousands of noncombatants in the two cities was inherently immoral and an act of terror, and thus dropping the bomb could not be justified by the outcome.

Another method of supplying reasons or backing for a moral principle is to look for empirical evidence. With a suitable definition of "murder," we might find that it is universally agreed that murder is wrong. However, any appeal to the facts regarding human moral belief suffers from two problems. First, science itself provides evidence that humans evolved through a complex series of "accidents," including random genetic mutations and chance environmental changes. If this is so, then moral value judgments arose through accidents and are contingent on these facts. Second, any empirical backing to the moral premise immediately falls prey to the naturalistic fallacy (the *is-ought* problem).

CHECK YOUR UNDERSTANDING 12F

The following passages are taken from various sources. Identify the moral arguments in each passage, and use any of the theories discussed in this chapter in your analysis of the arguments.

1. But across action sports, where individuality is prized, many are uncomfortable with rules or restrictions. "I respect that everyone should wear a helmet, like I wear a helmet," professional snowboarder Keir Dillon says. "But I don't think it should be mandated. For me, I always get worried about mandating or having governing bodies over our sport."

   Matt Higgins, "Head Games"

Answer:

Argument: Everyone should wear a helmet, [just as] I wear a helmet. [However,] I always get worried about mandating or having governing bodies over our sport. [Therefore,] I don't think it [wearing a helmet] should be mandated.

Discussion: *Situation ethics* holds that we should not rigidly apply rules to every possible situation. Although wearing a helmet reduces the likelihood of injuries, we should allow individual riders the freedom to choose for themselves. The governing bodies of the sport can strongly suggest that riders use helmets, but should not mandate their use; we should allow for exceptions.

2. With over 1 billion people, China should have a greater voice on the issue of world peace. Norway is only a small country, but it must be in the minority concerning the conception of freedom and democracy. Hence, the selection of the "Nobel Peace Prize" should be open to the people in the world.

   Ed Flanagan, "Big PR Goof? China's Confusing Confucius Prize," *NBC News*

3. "Never did get you for stealing that money?"
   "I didn't consider it stealing."
   "It didn't belong to you."
   "I needed a road stake. Like that bank in New Mexico. I needed a road stake, and there it was. I never robbed no citizen or took a man's watch!"
   "It's all stealing."

   From the screenplay of the 1969 movie *True Grit*

4. While most people took Internet access for granted as a constant, the suddenness of Egypt's Internet shutdown raises the question: Is access to the Internet a human right? "There are certain technological advances that are such leaps forward in human evolution that they do, in fact, become human rights. Vaccines, for example. Potable water. I believe the Internet has become one as well," said John Addis.

   Wilson Rothman, "Is Internet Access a Human Right?" *Technolog*

⭐ 5. After more than three years of pressure from shareholders, religious groups and blacks, the Colgate-Palmolive Company announced yesterday that it would rename Darkie, a popular toothpaste that it sells in Asia, and redesign its logotype, a minstrel in blackface. "It's just plain wrong," Reuben Mark, chairman and chief executive of Colgate-Palmolive, said about the toothpaste's name and logotype. "It's just offensive. The morally right thing dictated that we must change."

Douglas C. McGill, "Colgate to Rename a Toothpaste," New York Times

6. It is frequently stated that illicit drugs are "bad, dangerous, destructive," or "addictive," and that society has an obligation to keep them from the public. But nowhere can be found reliable, objective scientific evidence that they are any more harmful than other substances and activities that are legal. In view of the enormous expense, the carnage and the obvious futility of the "drug war," resulting in massive criminalization of society, it is high time to examine the supposed justification for keeping certain substances illegal.

Benson B. Roe, MD, "Why We Should Legalize Drugs"

7. The violent behavior caused by drugs won't magically stop because the drugs are legal. Legal PCP isn't going to make a person less violent than illegally purchased PCP. So, crimes committed because of drugs will increase as the number of drug users will increase with the legalization of drugs. The psychopathic behavior that drugs cause will not somehow magically stop because drugs are legal.

Carolyn C. Gargaro, "Drugs"

8. And yet, while young men's failures in life are not penalizing them in the bedroom, their sexual success may, ironically, be hindering their drive to achieve in life. Don't forget your Freud: Civilization is built on blocked, redirected, and channeled sexual impulse, because men will work for sex. Today's young men, however, seldom have to. As the authors of last year's book *Sex at Dawn: The Prehistoric Origins of Modern Sexuality* put it, "Societies in which women have lots of autonomy and authority tend to be decidedly male-friendly, relaxed, tolerant, and plenty sexy." They're right. But then try getting men to do anything.

Mark Regnerus, "Sex Is Cheap," Slate

9. "It's interesting because different cultures have different views on concussions and different views on identifying concussions, or even what the symptoms are that may suggest concussion," Dr. Ruben Echemendia recently told reporters. "So we know from our research, for example, that the reporting of symptoms varies by language of origin." Echemendia's group has determined that players from different nationalities and cultural backgrounds report concussions in different manners. Different cultures also put more or less importance around different symptoms, Echemendia explained. One culture may not consider a headache to be important and won't report it, but they will report dizziness. Meanwhile, headaches can be one of the indicators for post-concussion syndrome.

Pierre LeBrun, "National Hockey League Has Unique Off-Ice Concussion Foe"

10. The list of growing jobs is heavy on nurturing professions, in which women, ironically, seem to benefit from old stereotypes and habits. Theoretically, there is no reason men should not be qualified. But they have proved remarkably unable to adapt. Over the course of the past century, feminism has pushed women

to do things once considered against their nature— first enter the workforce as singles, then continue to work while married, then work even with small children at home. Many professions that started out as the province of men are now filled mostly with women—secretary and teacher come to mind. Yet I'm not aware of any that have gone the opposite way. Nursing schools have tried hard to recruit men in the past few years, with minimal success. Teaching schools, eager to recruit male role models, are having a similarly hard time. The range of acceptable masculine roles has changed comparatively little, and has perhaps even narrowed as men have shied away from some careers women have entered. And with each passing day, they lag further behind.

Hanna Rosin, "The End of Men," Atlantic

11. Let me make my somewhat seditious proposal explicit: We should not call ourselves "atheists." We should not call ourselves "secularists." We should not call ourselves "humanists," or "secular humanists," or "naturalists," or "skeptics," or "anti-theists," or "rationalists," or "freethinkers," or "brights." We should not call ourselves anything. We should go under the radar—for the rest of our lives. And while there, we should be decent, responsible people who destroy bad ideas wherever we find them. Now, it just so happens that religion has more than its fair share of bad ideas. And it remains the only system of thought, where the process of maintaining bad ideas in perpetual immunity from criticism is considered a sacred act. This is the act of faith. And I remain convinced that religious faith is one of the most perverse misuses of intelligence we have ever devised. So we will, inevitably, continue to criticize religious thinking. But we should not define ourselves and name ourselves in opposition to such thinking. So what does this all mean in practical terms? Well, rather than declare ourselves "atheists" in opposition to all religion, I think we should do nothing more than advocate reason and intellectual honesty—and where this advocacy causes us to collide with religion, as it inevitably will, we should observe that the points of impact are always with specific religious beliefs—not with religion in general. There is no religion in general. Sam Harris, "The Problem with Atheism," Washington Post

12. *Lotteries Bilk the Poor*: Last week, the Mega Millions lotto paid what was described in media reports as a "$380 million" jackpot. Actually the number reflects an annuity that pays $380 million over 26 years. The present value of the annuity, the only figure that matters, is $240 million—heady enough. Any money sum can be made to appear to roughly twice as great by expressing the number as a long-term annuity. If your employer offered you $50,000 this year, or $80,000 conveyed as one payment of $3,000 annually for each of the next 26 years—the same proportion as the Mega Millions markup—which would you choose? The media should not sensationalize lottery numbers by using the phony figures the lotto companies promote. But that's the least of the problems with lotteries, whose financial structure—spectacularly low chances of winning for players, combined with riches for those administering the lottos—make

them, as a wag once said, "a tax on the stupid." As TMQ wrote two years ago of state-sponsored lotteries, "There is almost no chance you will win, while total assurance you will lose the average of $190 annually that Americans throw away on government-run roulette. Worse, public lotteries, with their glitzy false promises of instant wealth, are a tax on poverty—as David Brooks of *The New York Times* has noted, households with an income of less than $13,000 spend an average of $645 annually on scratch-off tickets, meaning the poor are the main group throwing away cash at government lotto sites." Government, which ought to aid the poor, instead cynically markets lottos to the poor—with false promises of instant wealth, plus a high concentration of lotto sales outlets in low-income neighborhoods. The goal of this cynicism? Wealth for lotto companies and kickbacks—excuse me, consulting fees—for the politicians and government bureaucrats involved.

Gregg Easterbrook, "The Next Step"

Summary

- Some arguments rely solely on factual claims for support, some arguments rely solely on value judgments for support, and some arguments rely on a mixture of the two.
- Value judgment: A claim that a particular human action or object has some degree of importance, worth, or desirability.
- Prescriptive: In a moral setting, advice may be offered either by specifying a particular action that ought to be performed, or by providing general moral rules, principles, or guidelines that should be followed.
- Normative: Establishing standards for correct moral behavior; determining norms or rules of conduct.
- Emotivism: Holds that moral value judgments are merely expressions of our attitudes or emotions.
- Consequentialism: A class of moral theories in which the moral value of any human action or behavior is determined exclusively by its outcomes.
- Teleology: The philosophical belief that the value of an action or object can be determined by looking at the purpose or the end of the action or object.
- Egoism: The basic principle that everyone should act in order to maximize his or her own individual pleasure or happiness.
- The most important principle for utilitarianism can be summed up in the famous dictum "the greatest good for the greatest number."
- According to utilitarianism, every human action is "universalizable," meaning that the same principles hold for all people at all times.
- Deontology: Holds that duty to others is the first and foremost moral consideration, and it lays the groundwork for discovering those duties.

- The basic idea of a categorical imperative is that your actions or behavior toward others should always be such that you would want everyone to act in the same manner.
- Situation ethics agrees that there can be general, even objective, moral rules. However, it holds that we should not rigidly apply those rules to every possible situation.
- Relativism makes two claims: First, all moral value judgments are determined by an individual's personal beliefs or by a society's beliefs toward actions or behavior. Second, there are no objective or universal moral value judgments.
- Naturalistic moral principle: Since it is natural for humans to desire pleasure (or happiness), and to avoid pain, human behavior ought to be directed to these two ends.
- Naturalistic fallacy: Value judgments cannot be logically derived from statements of fact.

KEY TERMS

value judgment   542
prescriptive   544
normative   544
emotivism   546
consequentialism   547
teleology   547

egoism   547
utilitarianism   548
universalizable   548
deontology   549
categorical
   imperative   550

situation ethics   550
relativism   551
naturalistic moral
   principle   553
naturalistic fallacy   553

LOGIC CHALLENGE: DANGEROUS CARGO

You own a small resort on a tropical island where the only way on and off is by boat. Three of your guests, Leo, Aries, and Aquarius, had a bad weekend and they are standing by the boat dock with their luggage demanding to get off the island as quickly as possible. Leo, Aries, and Aquarius are all relatives who came together in one car, which is parked on the mainland. Over the last few days, old childhood squabbles surfaced, which threaten to escalate into violence.

To make things worse, a further difficulty arises. Your large boat is broken, and the small boat can hold only you and one passenger. As soon as the three guests hear this, they make more demands. Leo says, "Don't leave me alone either here or at the car with Aries." Upon hearing this, Aquarius says, "Well, you'd better not leave me alone either here or at the car with Leo." How can you get the three relatives to their car while meeting their demands?

Chapter 13

Statistical Arguments and Probability

Television commercials are fond of claims like this:

- Four out of five dentists recommend the ingredient found in our toothpaste.
- Our diet cola has 30% fewer calories.
- Get up to 70% off our previously low prices on selected items.
- American children watch an average of 5 hours of television a day. That means that they have watched an average of 5000 hours of television before entering first grade. Our *Early Reading Program* DVDs are fun and educational at the same time. So why not let your child's television viewing help prepare them for their first days in school. Don't let your children fall behind. Give them the right head start.

After the commercials end, a short news update might announce this: "A recent survey reveals that the incumbent mayor, who is running for reelection and who is being investigated for alleged ties to a securities fraud scandal, trails his opponent: 34% of those surveyed said they will vote for the mayor; 62% said they will vote for his opponent; and 4% said that they haven't made up their minds."

Evaluating arguments that rely on statistical evidence requires that we can correctly interpret the statistical evidence as it is presented. However, in many everyday arguments the words "average" and "percentage" are ambiguous because we are not told how the average or percentage was derived. (Chapter 4 already discussed the *fallacy of misleading precision*.) Information as to how statistical figures are computed is just as crucial for evaluating many statistical arguments. This chapter supplies the tools we need to make those evaluations. We then introduce probability.

A. SAMPLES AND POPULATIONS

Suppose a criminal justice researcher wants to know the conviction rate in felony cases in the state where she teaches. She compiles this statistic: 70% of a sample of defendants in criminal cases were found guilty. Let's look at how this statistic might be used in an argument:

> Seventy percent of a *sample* of defendants in criminal cases were found guilty. Therefore, probably 70% of *all* defendants in criminal cases are found guilty.

But how was the sample gathered? How large was the sample? Was it a random sample? Is there any evidence that the sample is not representative of the population of all defendants? Our answers to these questions will help determine the strength of the argument. Therefore, we need to know as much as we can about the research that was conducted.

Population refers to any group of objects, not just a human population. A **sample** is a subset, or part, of a population. If the population in question is the student body of a large urban university (say, 10,000 students), then a sample would be any portion of that population. A **representative sample** accurately reflects the characteristics of the population as a whole. Let's see what that takes.

Imagine that a senior class in sociology is told to determine the student population's opinion on a proposed tuition increase. Two members of this class decide to work together. They each interview two students in the remaining three classes that day, for a total of 12 students. They discover that 10 students are opposed to the tuition increase. Armed with this data they make a bold generalization:

> Eighty-three percent of a *sample* of students is opposed to a tuition increase. Therefore, probably 83% of the student *population* is opposed to a tuition increase.

The teacher points out that they have based their generalization on a small sample. A sample size of 12, relative to a student body of 10,000, is small and extremely unlikely to be representative of the population. This is an example of the *fallacy of hasty generalization* (see Chapter 4).

There is no simple formula for calculating the ratio of sample size to population to ensure a representative sample. However, when a sample size is small relative to the size of the population, other factors (which we will soon discuss) can help ensure that a representative sample has been achieved. Without the necessary equipment to strengthen it, however, a small sample weakens the argument.

Our intrepid students go back to work to gather more data. This time they make sure they gather a large sample. They begin polling more students in their classes, and they poll students from their dormitory. Their sample size swells to over 300 students. Analyzing the data prompts them to make a new argument:

> Seventy-six percent of a *sample* of 300 students is opposed to a tuition increase. Therefore, probably 76% of the student *population* is opposed to a tuition increase.

Population Any group of objects, not just human populations.

Sample A subset of a population.

Representative sample A sample that accurately reflects the characteristics of the population as a whole.

Their teacher does not question the sample size, but does inquire into which students were polled. The researchers admit that the vast majority of those polled in their upper-level classes are probably either juniors or seniors. Also, they live in a dorm reserved for juniors, seniors, and graduate students. These admissions weaken the argument, because the sample is not representative of all students: It is *biased* toward upperclassmen. This is an example of the *fallacy of biased sample* (see Chapter 4). It means that both freshmen and sophomores are underrepresented in the sample. If the researchers had restricted their conclusion to upperclassmen, then their argument would be stronger. Since the researchers wanted to generalize to the entire student population, their sample was biased, because it excluded certain subsets of that population.

The researchers go back to work and supplement their data by polling an appropriate number of freshmen and sophomores. Their new data yields a new argument:

> Seventy-two percent of a *sample* of 500 students is opposed to a tuition increase. Therefore, probably 72% of the student *population* is opposed to a tuition increase.

The teacher remarks that both the sample size and the distribution of students' year in school strengthen the argument. However, one more problem is uncovered. This is not a *random sample*. The researchers polled only students to whom they had easy access. To get a **random sample**, you must ensure that *every member of the population has an equal chance of getting in*. A random sample strengthens the likelihood that the sample represents the population.

Random sample Where every member of the population has an equal chance of getting into the sample.

CHECK YOUR UNDERSTANDING 13A

For the following passages, first identify the *sample* and *population* in the passages. Next, discuss whether the sample is representative of the population referred to in the conclusion. Analyze for sample size, potential bias, and randomness. Determine how your answers to these questions affect the strength of the arguments.

1. I am never going to buy another Hinckley car again. I had one and so did my sister. Both our cars were constantly in the shop. They had electrical and carburetor problems that caused them to stall all the time with no warning. Then we would have to get them towed, because they wouldn't start again. I am sure that all Hinckley cars have the same kinds of problems; that's why I won't buy one no matter what the price.

Answer:

Sample: Two Hinckley cars.
Population: All Hinckley cars.
Sample size: Two cars are a very small sample when we are discussing potentially millions of cars. This reduces the likelihood that the sample is representative of the population.

Potential bias: The sample excludes any cars that other owners might praise. It doesn't allow for the possibility of evidence that would go against its claims. This reduces the likelihood that the sample is representative of the population.

Randomness: This is not a random sample, because not every Hinckley car had an equal chance of getting into the sample. This reduces the likelihood that the sample is representative of the population.

2. A veterinarian kept track, for 1 year, of all the dogs brought in for testing after they had bitten someone. Out of 132 dogs brought in, pit bulls accounted for 67% of all attacks resulting in bite wounds to people. The veterinarian concluded that pit bulls are twice as likely to bite someone as all other dog breeds combined.

3. A study of psychiatric outpatients at a major hospital in Chicago showed that patients given counseling, plus some form of drug therapy, stayed in the program only one-third as long as those given just counseling. For three years the researchers followed 1600 patients; half were given only counseling and the other half were given counseling and drug treatment. The group given counseling and drugs felt confident that they could now cope with their problems and left the program, while the group given just counseling stayed in the program three times longer.

4. There have been over 4000 UFO sightings around the world in the past 5 years alone. Our analysis of these cases shows that 78% of the sightings have never been adequately explained by any government agency in any country where the sightings occurred. The number of sightings that appear to be hoaxes, or where the credibility of the eyewitnesses is under question, is insignificant. Given this information, we can confidently say that UFOs are real and the sightings are unequivocally of extraterrestrial spaceships manned by organisms far more advanced than earthlings.

5. A random study of 6000 urban public high school seniors throughout the United States has confirmed what many have long suspected. The students were given the same verbal, mathematical, perceptual, and manual dexterity test that was given 20 years ago to high school seniors. The Bincaid-Forbush test had not been used for over 15 years, so the researchers thought that it could be a good way of comparing the results of the preceding generation (many of whom are probably the parents of today's seniors) with the current crop of students. As expected, verbal and math scores have declined by 20% in today's students.

   Surprisingly, the perceptual and manual dexterity scores of today's students are 34% higher than their parents' generation. The researchers speculate that the rise of computers and arcade video games can explain both results. They hypothesize that verbal and math skills have deteriorated because video games require very little reading or calculating. However, these games require superior perceptual and manual dexterity skills, and thus give today's students much more exposure to this kind of skill development.

6. I have closely examined ninety-three wars that took place within the last 200 years. I use the word "war" to include both external conflicts (between two or more countries) and internal or civil wars. In 84% of those cases the wars were precipitated by a recent change in the government. Specifically, those 84% occurred soon after a conservative leader of that country took over from someone who was more liberal. The terms "conservative" and "liberal" are applied after examining and rating the leader on a scale from 1 to 10 for variables related to economic beliefs, religious pronouncements, social welfare programs, military buildup, judicial appointments, immigration laws, and the treatment of criminals. From these results, we can safely conclude that approximately four out of every five future wars around the world will occur after a conservative leader replaces a liberal leader.

7. Eight out ten people surveyed chose Slacker Soda over the next four most popular brands of soft drink. It is clear that America has spoken. Eighty percent of all Americans can't be wrong. Don't you think that you should start drinking Slacker Soda?

8. Research on people's dreams shows that they are not visions of the future. A group of psychologists monitored thirty volunteers for one year. The volunteers were told to keep a daily log only of the dreams they could clearly recall. They were also told to record anything that happened within a few days of the dream that they felt corresponded to the dream (to determine if they thought the dream was a premonition). On average, the volunteers recorded three dreams a night. In 1 year the researchers had over 25,000 dreams to analyze. They found that less than 1% of the dreams could be accurately correlated with a subsequent event in the dreamer's life (and these were usually trivial events). They concluded that humans' dreams do not come from the future, they do not offer a glimpse of some inevitable occurrence, nor do they act as a warning so we can avoid unpleasant events.

9. From 1903 to 2008, whenever the American League won the World Series, cigarette sales rose 20% over the previous year. But when the National League won the World Series, liquor sales rose 25% for the next year. Stock buyers pay heed! Watch who wins the World Series, and then buy or sell accordingly.

10. A study of college majors has revealed some interesting results. The study looked at more than 20,000 students who were accepted to U.S. law schools and medical schools for the past 20 years. The highest *percentage* of any major to be accepted to both law and medical schools was philosophy majors. The researchers speculate that this can be partially explained by the fact that philosophy majors have to take numerous logic courses and to write critical papers using logical reasoning. Since both the LSAT and MCAT (the law school and medical school standardized tests required of all applicants) have a *logical reasoning* section, philosophy majors are better prepared and tend to score higher on that section. The researchers encourage those planning to apply to law or medical school to take as many philosophy courses that they can.

B. STATISTICAL AVERAGES

Imagine that, in class one day, your instructor tells you that a slide will appear on screen, showing a room with people whose average age is 45. Now, if you are around 20 years of age, you might anticipate that the people on the slide will look somewhat like your parents. To your surprise, you see five very young children and six people who look to be your grandparents' age. To you, none of the people appear even close to 45 years of age; everyone is either much too young or much too old. One of your classmates is equally puzzled and complains to the teacher: The class was misled. You were told that the average age in the slide would be 45, so it should depict a middle-aged person, right? Yet not even one person looks middle-aged.

In fact, the average age given was correct. Your teacher lists the ages of the people in the picture:

The Ages of the Five Younger People	The Ages of the Six Older People
5	76
5	77
4	78
3	79
2	80
	86

If we add the ages in the first column, we get 19. The second column adds up to 476. Together they add up to 495, which is the total age of the eleven people. We now divide the *total age* by the *number of people* to get the *average age*; this gives us $495 \div 11 = 45$. The average age of the eleven people in the slide is indeed 45.

This type of statistical average, called the *mean*, is one way to describe a set of data. The **mean** is determined by adding the numerical values in the data for the objects examined, then dividing by the number of objects. In our example, the mean, or average age, was determined by adding the people's ages (to get 495) and then dividing by the number of people (in this case, 11). When newspapers, magazines, and other nontechnical sources refer to the "average" of a set of numerical data, they usually intend the mean. You have probably run into claims like these (whether or not they are true):

- The average yearly salary of a National Basketball Association (NBA) player is $5 million.
- The top ten movie stars average $20 million per movie.
- High school teachers in the United States average $30,000 a year.
- The top fifteen corporation CEOs in the United States averaged $50 million in stock compensation last year.
- The average yearly income for U.S. teenagers is $2000.

Since calculating the mean uses simple arithmetic techniques (adding and dividing), it is normally the first kind of average that we are taught in school. (In fact, it is also referred to as the *arithmetical mean*.) As we saw in the slide example, the *mean* can be psychologically misleading, even when it is perfectly accurate. If you, too, felt misled, you can appreciate how easily statistics can be used to manipulate our ideas. For most people, "average" easily calls up an image rather than data. And the image that you have

Mean A statistical average that is determined by adding the numerical values in the data concerning the examined objects, then dividing by the number of objects that were measured.

of a 45-year-old depends partly on your own age. A teenager's conception of someone who is 45 will surely differ from the perspective of a person who really is 45. People around 85 years of age will probably envision someone who is 45 as quite young. Very young children may not have a clear picture of a 45-year-old at all.

To see this more fully, imagine that your teacher promises another slide, and it, too, will have eleven people whose average age is 45. At this point, you might try to avoid picturing in your mind what the people will look like, since your first guess was way off the mark. As soon as the slide appears, however, you see that all of the people look around the same age and not unlike your parents. Your teacher lists the ages of the people in the new picture:

The Ages of the Eleven People in the Second Slide

41	46
42	47
43	47
43	47
44	47
	48

To calculate the mean of this second set of values, we once again add all eleven ages, and once again the result is 495. We now divide 495 by the total number of people to get $495 \div 11 = 45$. Sure enough, the mean age of the eleven people in the second slide is 45. As far as this one "average" is concerned, there is no difference between the two sets of people on the two slides. Of course, there is still a great gap between the ages of the younger and older people in the first slide, while the people in the second slide differ very little in their ages. That is why knowing the *mean* can tell us only so much.

Fortunately, additional kinds of *average* can add to our understanding of the data. The **median**, for one, is determined by locating the value that breaks the entire set of data in half. In other words, 50% of the data is above the median, and 50% is below it. For the people in the first slide, the *median* age is 76. Exactly five values are smaller than 76 (5, 5, 4, 3, 2), and exactly five values are greater than 76 (77, 78, 79, 80, 86). In contrast, for the people in the second slide, the *median* age is 46. You can easily check for yourself that half the values are smaller than 46 (41, 42, 43, 43, 44), and half are larger (47, 47, 47, 47, 48).

Let's put what we know about the ages of the two sets of people together:

Slide 1: Mean = 45; Median = 76
Slide 2: Mean = 45; Median = 46

Having information about the median age often greatly expands our understanding. To see why, suppose you discuss what happened in class with your roommates later that night. If you give them only the *mean* age (45), then they would have no way to differentiate between the two groups of people. However, let's see what happens when you provide them with the *median* age of the groups. Since the median age is 76 for the people on slide 1, half are older than 76 and half younger than 76. Thus, the younger

Median A statistical average that is determined by locating the value that separates the entire set of data in half.

people must be very young in order for the mean age to be 45. Although your room-mates would not know the exact ages of the eleven people involved, they can correctly infer that the slide includes children.

However, the results for slide 2 are not as informative. If you tell your roommates that the mean is 45 and the median is 46, then what can they conclude? Remember, they did not see the slides, and you did not tell them what you saw. Can they conclude that all the people are in their 40s? No, they could not do this. The ages might be clustered in the 40s, or they might instead be more like the ages in the first slide—sharply divided between older people and children. Take the following set of numbers:

  1, 2, 3, 4, 5, 46, 84, 86, 87, 88, 89

Here, the numbers again total 495, and the *mean* is again 495 ÷ 11 = 45. But what about the median age? Well, since there are exactly five values smaller than 46 (1, 2, 3, 4, 5) and exactly five values larger than 46 (84, 86, 87, 88, 89), the median is exactly the same as for slide 2.

Blaise Pascal

Blaise Pascal (1623–62) achieved much in a short life. In science, he became convinced that a vacuum exists, an idea not generally accepted at the time. In mathematics, Pascal did crucial work on many topics, including conic sections (such as circles and ellipses, the orbit of the planets). Have you ever seen a triangle like this one,

```
            1
          1   1
        1   2   1
      1   3   3   1
    1   4   6   4   1
  1   5  10  10   5   1
```

where we obtain a number in each new row by adding the pairs of numbers above it? This arithmetical triangle simplifies a remarkable range of calculations, from algebra to statistics, and today it is called *Pascal's triangle*. In probability, he laid the very foundations, in letters to and from Pierre Fermat, of *a priori* probability. The foundation of probability is built on the solutions to two related questions: (1) How often can we expect two sixes to appear when we throw a pair of dice? (2) What odds should someone give that will ensure a minimum profit in dice games?

Pascal's most famous work, however, is in philosophy, and it is also his most personal. His *Pensées* recounts his thoughts on human suffering—but here, too, he tries to ground all-too-human questions in mathematics and logic. In this book, Pascal manages to use his insights into probability theory as a basis for religious belief. He derived a betting proposition that has come to be known as *Pascal's wager*: If God exists and you believe, he argued, then you win everything. If God exists and you don't believe, then you lose everything. Pascal concludes that part of the human predicament is that we are *compelled to gamble.*

For an odd number of items like these, it is easy to find the median; you simply find the number in the middle of the set. However, an even number of items requires two more quick steps. Suppose a data set consists of these six numbers:

8, 11, 17, 33, 36, 40

The first step is to locate the *two values* that together make up the middle of the set. Here 17 and 33 make up the middle, because there are two values to the left of them (8, 11) and two to the right (36, 40). The second step is to *add* the two middle values; in this case we get $17 + 33 = 50$. The final step is to *divide* this number by two (the number of items we added together). The result is $50 \div 2 = 25$. Hence the median for these six numbers is 25. (For practice, how does the median compare to the mean for those six numbers?)

There is one more type of average that you should know. The **mode** is the value that occurs most. For example, for slide 1 the mode is 5, because that value occurs twice and no other value occurs more than once. For slide 2 above the mode is 47, because it occurs four times (43 occurs twice, but this time it is not the mode).

Mode A statistical average that is determined by locating the value that occurs most.

If two values have the same number of instances, then we call the data *bimodal*, like this set:

4, 6, 10, 10, 22, 35, 35, 56

The numbers 10 and 35 each occur twice, and all the other values occur only once. In much the same way, if three different values occur the most, the set is *trimodal*. Let's look at all three measures of average age for the two slides:

Slide 1: Mean = 45; Median = 76; Mode = 5
Slide 2: Mean = 45; Median = 46; Mode = 47

Once again, let's see how the new information regarding the *mode* affects your roommates' understanding. (Remember: They do not have access to the slides or to the actual ages for each group.) Your roommates were able to infer from the mean and median, that group 1 had five very young children; in fact, from the mode, they can infer that *at least two* are 5 years old. However, your roommates could not infer very much before about group 2. Now, thanks to the mode, they know that *at least two* are 47 years old. They can begin to suspect that the ages are somewhat close together.

Unfortunately, they cannot know just *how* close. Knowing the mean, median, and mode still often gives a limited picture. To understand the *amount of diversity* within a group, we need a more powerful statistical tool, as we see in the next section.

CHECK YOUR UNDERSTANDING 13B

I. Determine the *mean, median,* and *mode* for the following sets of values:

1. [2, 3, 4, 4, 8, 10]
Answer: Mean: 5.17; Median: 4; Mode: 4

2. [3, 5, 7, 9, 11, 11, 11]

3. [1, 2, 3, 3, 5, 7, 11, 13, 13]

4. [10, 20, 30, 40]

⭐ 5. [100, 110, 200, 200, 210, 300]

II. Determine the *mean, median,* and *mode* for the following sets of incomes:

1. [$6,000, $42,000, $42,000, $120,000]

Answer: Mean: $52,500; Median: $42,000; Mode: $42,000

2. [$100,000, $100,000, $100,000, $3 million, $5 million]

3. [$10, $10, $10, $10]

4. [$7, $77, $777, $7777]

⭐ 5. [50 cents, $1, $1,000, $1,000, $4,000]

III. Determine the *mean, median,* and *mode* for the following sets of grade point averages (GPAs):

1. [2.14, 2.49, 3.26, 3.26, 3.78, 3.99]

Answer: Mean: 3.15; Median: 3.26; Mode: 3.26

2. [1.88, 2.03, 2.56, 2.89, 3.64, 3.89]

3. [3.25, 3.25, 3.25, 3.75, 3.75]

4. [1.00, 2.00, 3.00, 4.00]

⭐ 5. [2.86, 2.96, 3.16, 3.16, 3.26, 3.36]

IV. Determine the *mean, median,* and *mode* for the following sets of heights (in inches):

1. [37″, 45″, 48″, 67″, 67″, 78″, 86″]

Answer: Mean: 61.14″; Median: 67″; Mode: 67″

2. [38″, 40″, 44″, 45″, 49″, 52″]

3. [23″, 27″, 27″, 27″, 29″, 29″]

4. [30″, 31″, 32″, 33″, 34″, 35″, 36″]

⭐ 5. [24″, 27″, 28″, 74″, 74″, 80″, 80″]

C. STANDARD DEVIATION

The **standard deviation** is a measure of the *amount of diversity* in a set of numerical values. Consider a bell-shaped, or *normal,* curve. Although the numerical values are spread throughout the curve, the majority of the values are clustered around the *mean*:

Standard deviation A measure of the amount of diversity in a set of numerical values.

A Bell Curve

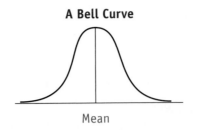

Mean

We call that spread or clustering the *distribution*. Let's see how to interpret the standard deviation to understand that distribution for a normal curve.

Dividing the Curve

As you can see, an equal number of values are found on both sides of the mean; this gives the curve its bell shape. Statisticians have developed a way of dividing the area under the curve into equal parts:

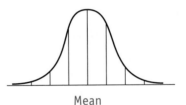

Mean

The areas to the *right* of the mean represent values that are *larger* than the mean, and the areas to the *left* represent values that are *smaller* than the mean. Each of the areas constitutes one standard deviation from the mean. Thus, the area directly to the right of the mean is designated as +1 SD (standard deviation), the next area to the right is +2 SD, and the third area is +3 SD. Similarly, the area directly to the left of the mean is designated as −1 SD, the next area to the left is −2 SD, and the third area is −3 SD:

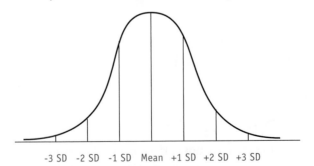

-3 SD   -2 SD   -1 SD   Mean   +1 SD   +2 SD   +3 SD

If you look closely, you can observe that area from +1 SD to −1 SD makes up the largest portion of the bell curve. In fact, this area contains approximately 68% of all the data. This means that approximately 34% of the data is in the +1 SD area, and approximately 34% is in the −1 SD area. The next two areas, +2 SD and −2 SD, each contain approximately 13.5% of the data, for a total of 27%. Therefore, the four areas from +2 SD to −2 SD contain approximately 95% of all the data. The +3 SD and the −3 SD areas each contain approximately 2.3% of the data, for a total of 4.6%. The grand total of all six areas is approximately 99.5%. The remaining 0.4% lie at the extreme ends:

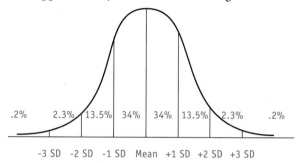

Apparently, a bell curve has few values indeed at the extremes. We can see this easily by adding color, to illustrate the total area captured by each SD:

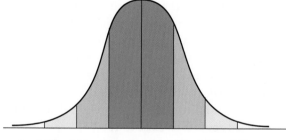

The two dark blue areas contain the data for +1 SD and −1 SD; the next two areas contain the data for +2 SD and −2 SD; the next two areas contain the data for +3 SD and −3 SD; and the two small areas at each end of the curve contain the fewest members—the extreme limits.

The Size of the Standard Deviation

Another way to look at the diversity is to ask how far from the mean we need to go to get a given percentage of the values. For example, you take a test for which the possible scores range anywhere from 0 to 100 (in whole numbers). You learn later that a graph of the scores takes the form of a normal curve, so the scores are spread equally on both sides of the mean. Let's imagine that the mean score was 50. You would then know that approximately 34% of the scores were within +1 SD from the mean, and approximately 34% of the scores were within −1 SD from the mean. Therefore, approximately 68% of all the scores fell with these two areas. *But how far from the mean do we have to go to get that 68%?*

The answer lies in the *size* of the standard deviation—in our picture, the width of each vertical slice in the bell curve. Suppose you are now told that the standard deviation was 15 points. This tells us how far we have to go from the mean to get each area of the curve. *The larger the size of the standard deviation, the larger the diversity; the smaller the size of the standard deviation, the smaller the diversity.*

In our example, the mean was 50, and to get the value for +1 SD, you simply *add* 15 to the mean: $50 + 15 = 65$. To get the value for −1 SD you must *subtract* 15 points from the mean, because this area contains numbers that are smaller than the mean: $50 − 15 = 35$. Therefore, approximately 68% of the scores fell within the range of 35–65.

The range of scores in the next two areas is calculated in much the same way. Since the standard deviation is 15, to get +2 SD means that we have to go $15 × 2 = 30$ points away from the mean. This time, you thus *add* 30 to the mean: $50 + 30 = 80$. To get the value for −2 SD you must *subtract* 30 points from the mean: $50 − 30 = 20$. Therefore, approximately 95% of the scores fell within the range of 20–80.

What about the range of scores in the 3 SD range? To get +3 SD, we have to go 15 $× 3 = 45$ points away from the mean: $50 + 45 = 95$. To get −3 SD, we have to subtract 45 points from the mean: $50 − 45 = 5$. We now know that approximately 99.5% of the scores fell within the range of 5–95. If you scored 100, you were very special.

Let's compare these results with another example. Suppose the same test is given to another class. A graph of the scores once again takes the form of a normal curve, with a mean of 50. We might think that this group scored much the same as yours. But now suppose that the standard deviation for the second group was 3. Since *the smaller the size of the standard deviation, the smaller the diversity*, you can immediately infer that the second class has very little difference in its scores. In that group, you would have been very special if you had come even close to 100.

We can calculate the SD ranges to verify our inference. To get the value for +1 SD, you *add* 3 to the mean: $50 + 3 = 53$. To get the value for −1 SD, you *subtract* 3 points from the mean: $50 − 3 = 47$. Therefore, approximately 68% of the scores fell within the range of 47–53. This means that 68% of the scores were separated by only 6 points (47–53). Compare this to your own class, in which 68% of the scores were separated by 30 points (35–65).

The range of scores in the next two areas is easily calculated. To get the value for +2 SD, you *add* 6 to the mean: $50 + 6 = 56$. To get the value for −2 SD, you *subtract* 6 points from the mean: $50 − 6 = 44$. Therefore, approximately 95% of the scores fell within the range of 44–56. This means that 95% of the scores were separated by only 12 points (44–56). In contrast, in your class, 95% of the scores were separated by 60 points (20–80).

Finally, let's determine the range of scores in the 3 SD area. To get the value for +3 SD, you *add* 9 to the mean: $50 + 9 = 59$. To get the value for −3, SD you *subtract* 9 points from the mean: $50 − 9 = 41$. Therefore, approximately 99.5% of the scores fell within the range of 41–59. This means that 99.5% of the scores were separated by only 18 points (41–59). Again, compare this to your class, in which 99.5% of the scores were separated by 90 points (5–95).

The graph of the second group is a normal curve, but its shape has to reflect its lack of diversity. It must show that scores are relatively close to the mean. In practice, that means that the curve is very narrow, *because the size of the deviation is small:*

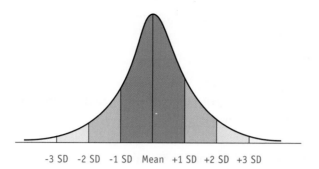

-3 SD   -2 SD   -1 SD   Mean   +1 SD   +2 SD   +3 SD

Since the range of scores for each SD was quite small, the sides of the curve slope down very sharply from the top—once again indicating the small diversity in the group.

How to Calculate the Standard Deviation

In real-life research, the amount of data can be enormous, but computers can do the calculations quickly, efficiently, and with little chance of error. (Handheld calculators programmed to do statistical calculations can handle smaller data sets.) Still, finding the standard deviation has just six steps. Let's do a simple calculation ourselves to see how it works. We will use the following small set of values as our reference.

[1, 3, 8, 17, 22, 33, 42]

STEP 1: Calculate the mean value. The sum of the seven numbers in our set is 126. We divide this by the number of items in the set to get the mean: $126 \div 7 = 18$.

STEP 2: Calculate the difference between each value in the set and the mean value. A value that is smaller than the mean will result in a negative difference; a value greater than the mean will result in a positive difference; a value that is identical to the mean will result in a 0. Here are the results for our set (the boldface numbers are the values in our data set):

1 − 18 = −17	**17** − 18 = −1	**42** − 18 = 24
3 − 18 = −15	**22** − 18 = 4	
8 − 18 = −10	**33** − 18 = 15	

STEP 3: Multiply each difference by itself. This means that we are *squaring the differences.*

Why is squaring necessary to get the amount of variation? Why not just add the differences? To see why, take a worst-case scenario. Suppose that there were only four values in a set of data, and the mean was 20. If the values of the four members of the set were 18, 19, 21, and 22, then the differences would be −2, −1, 1, and 2. Adding these four numbers gives us a result of 0—but there is some small variation nonetheless. To get a meaningful result, we must change a negative value into a positive value by squaring, so all the results will be positive numbers.

In our problem, squaring the differences $(-17, -15, -10, -1, 4, 15, 24)$ gives 289, 225, 100, 1, 16, 225, and 576.

STEP 4: Add the results of the squaring process in step 3. The sum of the seven numbers (289, 225, 100, 1, 16, 225, 576) is 1432.

STEP 5: Divide the result of step 4 by *one fewer* than the number of members in the set. This gives us the following result: $1432 \div 6 = 238.7$. This result is called the *total variance*.

STEP 6: The square root of the total variance is the standard deviation. The square root of 238.7 is 15.4. Therefore, the set of values $[1, 3, 8, 17, 22, 33, 42]$ has a standard deviation of 15.4.

THE SIX STEPS TO THE STANDARD DEVIATION

Step 1: Calculate the mean value.
Step 2: Calculate the difference between each value in the set and the mean value.
Step 3: Multiply each difference by itself (square each difference).
Step 4: Add the results of the squaring process in step 3.
Step 5: Divide the result of step 4 by one fewer than the number of members in the set.
Step 6: The square root of the total variance is the standard deviation.

CHECK YOUR UNDERSTANDING 13C

Since you have already calculated the mean value of each set of data in *Check Your Understanding 13B*, you have already finished step 1 of calculating the standard deviation. Now perform steps 2–6 and complete the determination of the standard deviation for each set of data. Refer back to *Check Your Understanding 13B* for the exercises. The first exercise and a solution are provided here:

  I. 1. $[2, 3, 4, 4, 8, 10]$
Answer: The standard deviation is 3.13.

    Step 1: 5.17
    Step 2: $2 - 5.17 = -3.17$ $4 - 5.17 = -1.17$
              $3 - 5.17 = -2.17$ $8 - 5.17 = 2.83$
              $4 - 5.17 = -1.17$ $10 - 5.17 = 4.83$
    Step 3: 10.05, 4.71, 1.37, 1.37, 8.01, 23.33
    Step 4: 48.84
    Step 5: 9.77
    Step 6: 3.13

D. WHAT IF THE RESULTS ARE SKEWED?

So far we have looked at normal curves. While real-life data do not always fit perfectly bell-shaped curves, the same basic principles apply in calculating the standard deviation. The problem lies in interpreting and applying the unexpected results.

Many measurements involve "objective" criteria for some "naturally occurring" phenomenon. For example, you can measure the height of every student in class and determine the mean, median, mode, and standard deviation. A ruler or tape measure is equally objective, whether it is in inches or centimeters. But not all measuring devices are objective—especially when it comes to human capabilities. For example, many people have challenged whether I.Q. exams truly measure intelligence. Perhaps intelligence is not even quantifiable or not just one simple thing. For many children, the results of some verbal and mathematical I.Q. exams give substantially different results from tests that do not rely on the same verbal skills.

At least some physical skills lend themselves to objective measurement. For example, we can measure the amount of time for each class member to run 100 yards, to swim 50 meters, or to throw a baseball. We can measure how much weight each student can lift, or even many types of hand and finger dexterity. We can then determine the amount of variation.

However, when it comes to nonphysical skills, things can get more difficult. Teachers try very hard to create tests that will accurately determine the level of understanding. But we all know from experience that something can go very wrong. For example, suppose a teacher decides on the following scale for determining grades on an upcoming exam:

A 90–100
B 80–89
C 70–79
D 60–69
F 0–59

After the exam, the teacher then calculates the mean and the standard deviation. Here is one possible distribution of grades:

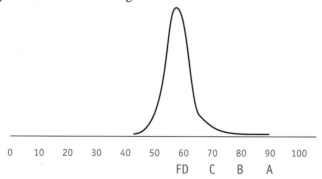

The mean appears to be around 54, and we can see that most of the class got an F. Only a very small percentage of the class received an A, B, or C grade. (F and D are right next to each other at the bottom of the graph, because 59 starts the F range and 60 is the lowest possible score for a D.)

If the class results reflected a normal curve, the mean would instead be somewhere over the C range. There would then be a smaller number of D and B grades, followed by an even smaller number of F and A grades. The actual results lean far to the left of what we had anticipated, and they are said to be *skewed*. How should we understand the outcome? Students might interpret the graph to mean that the exam was *too hard*. On the other hand, the teacher might conclude that the class had not prepared adequately for the exam. Either way, the teacher might decide to *curve* the results of the exam, by simply sliding the existing curve to the right:

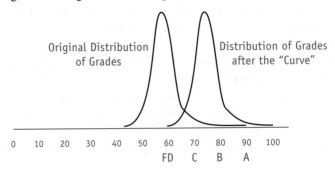

This places the mean over the C range. The teacher can then adjust the original grading scale to get an appropriate number of A, B, D, and F grades.

What, however, if the results of the exam had produced this graph?

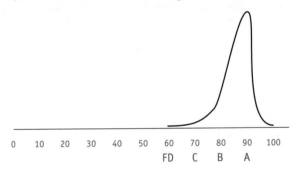

Here the mean appears to be around 91, and we can see that most of the class got an A. Only a very small percentage received an F, D, or C. If we expected a normal curve, we instead find a curve that is *skewed* far to the right. The students might explain the results as the outcome of their having studied diligently for the exam. On the other hand, the teacher might conclude that the test that was *too easy*. This time, the teacher might decide to curve the results by sliding the existing curve to the left:

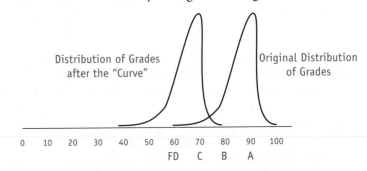

This movement of the curve places the mean over the C range. The teacher can then easily adjust the original grading scale to get an appropriate number of A, B, D, and F grades.

As you can see, data analysis often leads to new questions—and disagreement about the answers. In our two examples, did the original results accurately measure what the class knew? Have the new curves produced more accurate pictures? How can we best decide?

These kinds of questions need to be asked and debated whenever we have to interpret complex statistical data. Social policy, such as federal funding for early childhood training, often depends on the results of statistical studies. For some administrations, statistical data justified an increase in the amount of money for preschools. Other administrations have used statistical data to justify a decrease in the amount of money available. They relied on different data, but also on different interpretations.

E. THE MISUSE OF STATISTICS

Statistics can mislead us either intentionally or unintentionally. Statements containing quantitative terms are often interpreted differently than those containing qualitative terms. For example:

1. The latest album by the Green Biscuits is number one in sales this year.
2. The latest album by the Green Biscuits is the best album this year.

Most people would accept statement 1 at face value because they assume that the statistics were compiled objectively and accurately. However, the word "best" in statement 2 is vague. Even when an album wins awards people often argue about the subjective nature of the voting process.

We saw in Chapter 4 that the fallacy of misleading precision occurs when a claim appears to be statistically significant but is not. Statistics can be accurate, but they can also be easily misinterpreted. For example, suppose you read the following:

> Since we began advertising on the Internet, sales of our Premium Widgets have increased 400% over the first quarter. Stock options will be offered only for a limited time, so this might be your best chance to invest in our growing company.

Put your checkbook away. More information is needed to evaluate the claim. For example, suppose we find that the company sold a total of two Premium Widgets during the first quarter (at $10 each), and the company lost a million dollars. A 400% increase in sales means that they sold eight Premium Widgets during the second quarter (for a whopping $80 in sales), and they still lost a lot of money. The statistics are accurate, but if you misinterpret the information, then you might make a bad investment.

Statistics can mislead in other ways as well. A recent article on the *Psychology Today* website stirred up so much controversy that it was taken off in a matter of days. "Why Are Black Women Less Physically Attractive than Other Women?" reported on a study that measured the "physical attractiveness of its respondents both objectively and subjectively." According to Satoshi Kanazawa, an evolutionary psychologist at the London School of Economics, the respondents were asked to rate themselves on a four-point scale: "1 = not at all, 2 = slightly, 3 = moderately, 4 = very." Although each respondent used the same four-point scale, Kanazawa correctly labeled the rating *subjective* because the respondents applied their own standards of attractiveness when rating themselves.

The same respondents were then interviewed. Kanazawa tells us that each interviewer rated the physical attractiveness of each respondent *objectively* on a five-point scale: "1 = very unattractive, 2 = unattractive, 3 = about average, 4 = attractive, 5 = very attractive." We are told that each respondent was "measured three times by three different interviewers over seven years." According to Kanazawa, the results show that black women are "far less attractive than white, Asian, and Native American women."

Kanazawa also offered an "explanation" for the results: Black women have a higher level of testosterone than other races. Since women with high levels of testosterone have more masculine features, they are "therefore less physically attractive."

Why did the article stir so much controversy? In fact, the study itself relies on faulty reasoning in more ways than one. First, Kanazawa incorrectly labels the rating done by the interviewers "objective." The scale used by the interviewers is not objective in the sense that using inches or centimeters to measure height, for example, is objective. Instead, the so-called objective scale (1–5 rating of physical attractiveness) was applied based on the *subjective* opinion of the interviewers. The interviewers did not "measure" the physical attractiveness of the women in the same way they might have measured the women's height using a yardstick that would ensure that all the interviewers got the same result.

Second, we are told that only three interviewers did the rating. In addition to this being an extremely small number of interviewers used to gather data, we are not told the race of the interviewers. Without this information, the potential for biased results exists, especially since the rating system used by the interviewers was inherently subjective.

Third, Kanazawa offered an "explanation" for something that had not even been shown to be true. The title of his article reflects his *unjustified conclusion* that a fact has been revealed that needs explaining.

CHECK YOUR UNDERSTANDING 13E

Analyze the statistical reasoning in each passage.

1. In general, however, the financial odds still greatly favor a person with a college degree. The Bureau of Labor Statistics estimates that median weekly earnings for a person with a bachelor's degree was $1,025 in 2009, compared with just $626 for those with only a high school diploma.

   Allison Linn, "Is It Worth It to Go to College?"

Answer:

Since the Bureau of Labor Statistics has access to large amounts of data, we can assume that the size of the data set is adequate. The *median* weekly income for persons with a bachelor's degree was $1,025 (in 2009); therefore we know that 50% of that data set made more than that amount and 50% made less. For those with only a high school diploma, 50% of that data set made more than $626 a week and 50% made less.

On the surface, the difference between $1,025 and $626 is substantial. However, we are not told either the *mean* or the *standard deviation* in the two sets of data. Without that information, we cannot determine the amount of diversity in the sets. In addition, people with bachelor's degrees in engineering and computer science average three to four times the yearly salary of many social science majors. The article does not distinguish between majors. It therefore may misleadingly suggest that any kind of bachelor's degree puts you in a position to make substantially more than a person with only a high school diploma.

2. A study finds that Best Actress Oscar winners have a 63% chance of their marriages ending sooner than nonwinners. The median marriage duration was 4.30 years; 9.51 for nonwinners.   Ken McGuffin, "The Oscar Curse?"

3. Reuters Legal compiled a tally of reported decisions in which judges granted a new trial, denied a request for a new trial, or overturned a verdict, in whole or in part, because of juror actions related to the Internet. The data show that since 1999 at least 90 verdicts have been the subject of challenges, because of alleged Internet-related juror misconduct. More than half of the cases occurred in the last two years. Judges granted new trials or overturned verdicts in 28 criminal and civil cases—21 since January 2009. In three-quarters of the cases in which judges declined to declare mistrials, they nevertheless found Internet-related misconduct on the part of jurors. These figures do not include the many incidents that escape judicial notice.   "As Jurors Go Online, U.S. Trials Go Off Track," Reuters

4. Alberto Contador might face a one-year doping suspension and be stripped of his 2010 Tour de France title. . . . . Contador, whose sample contained 50 picograms (trillionths of a gram) of a banned substance, is being diagnosed as a little bit pregnant in a context where there shouldn't be any ambiguity. When Contador offered the explanation that he had consumed tainted beef purchased in Spain, . . . statistics about Clenbuterol contamination in the food and water supply were debated. One authority didn't swallow the steak story. Christiane Ayotte, longtime director of the WADA-accredited lab in Montreal, was blunt with reporters in an informal media briefing in mid-October. "You'll never find a ton of [Clenbuterol] because the doses are really small," Ayotte said then, calling the beef excuse implausible. "Most of the samples are below 1 nanogram—a billionth of a gram."   Bonnie D. Ford, "Why Contador Case Sets Bad Precedent"

5. It's possible to see procrastination as the quintessential modern problem. It's also a surprisingly costly one. Each year, Americans waste hundreds of millions of dollars because they don't file their taxes on time. The Harvard economist David Laibson has shown that American workers have forgone huge amounts of money in matching 401(k) contributions because they never got around to signing up

for a retirement plan. Seventy percent of patients suffering from glaucoma risk blindness because they don't use their eyedrops regularly. Procrastination also inflicts major costs on businesses and governments. The recent crisis of the euro was exacerbated by the German government's dithering, and the decline of the American auto industry, exemplified by the bankruptcy of General Motors was due in part to executives' penchant for delaying tough decisions.

James Surowiecki, "Later: What Does Procrastination Tell Us About Ourselves?"

6. Another argument for Zenyatta is that she brought more mainstream coverage to the Sport.... The numbers simply do not support that. In 2004, Smarty Jones was attempting to join Seattle Slew as the only undefeated Triple Crown winners in history; a record crowd of 120,139 showed up to see his Belmont. Compare that to the 72,739 who came to Churchill Downs on Nov. 6 to see if Zenyatta would retire undefeated.... A search of news archives shows far more was written about Smarty Jones throughout the course of 2004 than Zenyatta in 2010: 7,350 articles for Smarty Jones; 2,260 articles for Zenyatta.

Amanda Duckworth, "Facts vs. Feelings"

7. There's been a lot of misinformation thrown around during Michigan's rather hastily arranged price tag debate. The governor cited research offered up by a group called the Coalition for Retail Pricing Modernization saying price tag application cost Michigan stores $2.2 billion annually. The governor cited the cost as a cause of Michigan's downtrodden economy. The questionable research extrapolates from a 2007 economics paper, which found that prices in an area of New York that then required price tags were about 10 percent higher than stores in nearby New Jersey, which didn't. It ignored other factors which make New York stores pricier. Then, the group calculated 10 percent of Michigan store sales to arrive at the $2.2 billion. The back-of-the-envelope calculation was cited by the governor in his arguments, but derided by consumer advocates. "The true cost of placing price stickers on Michigan groceries is a small fraction of $2 billion," said Edgar Dworsky.
Bob Sullivan, "Another Nail in the Coffin of Price Tags"

F. PROBABILITY THEORIES

Statements and arguments that include the word "probability" also play a large part in conversations, material, and other media. On any given day you might read these items:

- The probability of winning the Grand Prize in the Powerball Lottery is 1 in 195,249,054. (www.powerball.com)
- Drawing on new data and new methodologies, the Working Group on California Earthquake Probabilities (WG02) has concluded that there is a 0.62 probability (i.e., a 62% probability) of a strong earthquake striking the greater San Francisco Bay Region (SFBR) over the next 30 years (2003–2032). (U.S. Geological Survey)

- Strictly speaking, the probability of doomsday isn't any higher than it is on any normal Wednesday, but there's been a fair bit of kerfuffle and hullabaloo over the CERN Large Hadron Collider (LHC) and whether it will create a black hole that will destroy the entire planet. (Matt Blum, "The Large Hadron Collider Will Not Destroy the World Tomorrow, or Ever")

Evaluating statements and arguments that rely on probabilities requires that we accurately interpret the information. However, like "average," the word "probability" is ambiguous, and we need to know exactly how the word is being used. Three theories can help provide some clarity.

A Priori Theory

Sometimes we can determine whether something is true or false without having any experience of the things involved. Our knowledge is then said to be *a priori*. For example, the statement "All bachelors are unmarried males" is true by definition, even if we have never actually seen a bachelor. Similarly, we know *a priori* that "all unicorns have one horn."

The *a priori* **theory of probability** ascribes to a simple event a fraction between 0 and 1; the denominator of this fraction is the number of equally possible, or **equiprobable,** outcomes, and the numerator is the number of outcomes in which the event in question occurs. Probability calculations using the *a priori*, or classical, theory rely on two major assumptions:

> **A priori theory of probability** Ascribes to a simple event a fraction between 0 and 1.

> **Equiprobable** When each of the possible outcomes has an equal probability of occurring.

1. All possible outcomes of a given situation can be determined.
2. Each possible outcome has an equal probability of occurring.

Consider a coin toss. We can quickly calculate the probability of the coin coming up heads (or tails) because we assume two things: There are just two possible outcomes, heads or tails; and each of these two possible outcomes has an equal probability of occurring. We can state that probability as a fraction by making the number of desired, or *positive*, outcomes the numerator and the number of *all* possible outcomes the denominator. Thus, the probability of heads is 1/2 (or 50%, or 0.5, or 50-50), because there is just one positive outcome (heads) and just two possible outcomes (heads and tails).

It is not surprising that the *a priori* theory originated with games of chance. Coin tosses, dice, and lotteries are all subject to *a priori* calculations. The assumption of equiprobable outcomes is really the assumption of randomness. This does not mean that any actual coin, dice, or lottery is perfectly random. Rather, our calculations are based on *a priori* assumptions, even before actual experiments prove them right or wrong.

Take a single event, like a single toss. (We return to combinations of events, or *compound* events, later in the chapter.) Dice usually come in pairs (one of a pair of dice is called a *die*), and we can ask, "What is the probability of a die coming up 4 on the next (or any) toss?" Assuming that all outcomes are equiprobable ensures that it is a fair game, governed by randomness. We also assume that the die has six sides, that only one of the numerals (1, 2, 3, 4, 5, or 6) occurs on each of the six faces, and that landing on an edge will not count as a legitimate outcome. With those assumptions, the one positive outcome (4) becomes the numerator, and all the possible outcomes become the denominator, giving us the fraction 1/6. What is the probability that an even number will come up on any toss of the die? Now there are three positive outcomes (2, 4, and 6), and so the probability of an even number coming up is 3/6, or 1/2.

Relative Frequency Theory

Relative frequency theory of probability
The theory that some probabilities can be computed by dividing the number of favorable cases by the total number of observed cases.

The **relative frequency theory of probability** relies on direct observation of events. According to this theory, probabilities can be computed by dividing the number of favorable cases by the total number of observed cases.

Actuarial tables rely on relative frequency theory. Although insurance schemes go back at least 2000 years, the probability methods needed were developed only after the year 1650. Companies that offered insurance for ships bringing goods to a country needed to know how many ships successfully returned to port. Accurate empirical research was necessary to determine the number of ships leaving port, the number of ships arriving safely back, as well as the amount of goods successfully imported. Over time, adequate information enabled insurers to charge just enough for insurance to make it affordable to shipping companies, as well as guaranteeing a profit to the insurance company. Charging too much for insurance would scare away potential customers, while charging too little would mean that the insurance company would not have enough money to pay off claims.

Direct observation is especially important when we cannot know *a priori* all the possible positive and negative outcomes. For example, to know the probability that a 20-year-old female will live to age 65 requires thousands of observations of 20-year-old females to see how many actually live to age 65. Researchers might track 10,000 20-year-old females for the next 45 years to see how many were still alive. On the other hand, the researchers might go back 45 years and get a list of 10,000 females who were 20 years old at that time. They then would need to find out how many of those 10,000 females were still alive today.

The total number of observed cases (10,000) becomes the denominator of a fraction, while the positive outcomes (those actually living to age 65) becomes the numerator. Therefore, if 9200 females were still alive at age 65, the fraction would be 9200/10,000. This can be reduced to 92/100, which means that there is a 92% chance that a 20-year-old female will live to age 65, according to the historical data. The frequency of a 20-year-old female living to age 65 is *relative* to the set of observed cases, which explains the name *relative frequency theory*. Here is the formula for this method:

$$Pr\ (A) = p/tn$$

The formula tells us that the probability of an event, *Pr (A)*, is equal to the number of positive outcomes, *p*, divided by the total number of observed cases, *tn*.

It is important not to misapply probability calculations. An insurance company that issues a policy to a 20-year-old female is not predicting that this particular individual has a 92% chance of living to age 65. This individual is considered a member of the class of 20-year-old females, so her probability of living to age 65 is relative to the probability regarding the entire class, which in this case is 92%. The insurance company is not only insuring this one particular 20-year-old female, they hope to insure thousands. The monthly premium the insurance company charges each female is calculated to guarantee the company will have enough to pay off the 8% of the females who will die before age 65, plus ensure the company a profit.

Subjectivist Theory

Sometimes neither *a priori* nor relative frequency methods work. In a race with ten horses, *a priori* calculations would tell us that the favorite should win only 10% of the time. (The favorite is the horse that has the most money bet on it.) Clearly this is not the case, since favorites in horse races win approximately 1/3 of the time. Professional sports gamblers also cannot rely so simply on statistical, historical data. A team's win-loss record is certainly relevant to predicting how the team will do in the future. However, the number of variables affecting the outcome of a sporting event is immense. The team playing this year is not identical to last year's team. Players come and go, get older, and get injured. The horses in the Kentucky Derby probably have never all raced together before—and never in the Kentucky Derby. (Horses get only one chance to run in the Kentucky Derby—when they are 3 years old.) To calculate the odds, we must interpret the historical data subjectively.

The **subjectivist theory of probability** is based on a lack of total knowledge regarding an event. This does not mean that the probability calculations are mere guesses. They often rely on relative frequency data. Professional gamblers and professional stock market investors rely on years of experience to sift and weigh the pertinent information. They need that experience to cope with not only the mounds of data, but also with their partial ignorance.

Suppose the favorite wins approximately 1/3 of the time (33%) in horse races. Is it therefore wise to bet the favorite in every race? Wouldn't you be assured of picking the winner 33% of the time? The answer to the second question is "yes," but the answer to the first question is "no." Although this system will ensure that you will have a winning ticket 1/3 of the time, you also have a losing ticket 2/3 of the time. In addition, the favorite has the most money bet on it, so the payoff is the smallest of all the potential payoffs. You would need to get 2:1 odds *just to break even*, but favorites pay far less than that, on average. For example, suppose you make a $2 bet on the favorite in nine races. You will have invested a total of $18. Since favorites pay approximately $4 to win, and since you will win only 1/3 of the time (or three races), you will get back around $12. Therefore, you will lose approximately $6 for each $18 invested.

Sometimes we use probability calculations to refer to events, but they can be used to refer to our statements as well. In a sense, two different situations are occurring at the same time. For example, suppose I draw a marble at random from a jar containing five red, five black, and five green marbles, and I ask you to guess the color. Let's imagine that the marble has already been picked and I can see that it is red, but you cannot see it. From my perspective, the probability of its being red is 1, because I have

Subjectivist theory of probability The theory that some probability determinations are based on the lack of total knowledge regarding an event.

total knowledge of the outcome. From your perspective, all three colors have equal probability (1/3), because you lack certain information. If you say "The marble is red," then your *statement* has a 1/3 chance of being true, from your perspective. From my perspective, your statement *is* true. Therefore, probability is intimately connected to the availability of relevant information regarding an event.

G. PROBABILITY CALCULUS

Probability calculus The branch of mathematics that can be used to compute the probabilities of complex events from the probabilities of their component events.

Probability calculus refers to the rules for calculating the probability of compound events from the probability of simple events. The results can be displayed as fractions, percentages, ratios, or a number between 0 and 1.

For example, what is the probability that the next toss of a coin will come up either heads or tails? (We already stipulated that landing on edge will not count as a legitimate outcome.) Since there are two positive outcomes (heads or tails), and two possible outcomes (heads or tails), the fraction is 1/1 or just 1. This corresponds to our notion of a *tautology*, a noncontingent statement. (Recall from Chapter 7 that a contingent statement is neither necessarily true nor necessarily false.) At the opposite end of the probability spectrum is the probability that the coin will come up *both* heads and tails at the same time. Since the positive outcomes are 0, the fraction is 0/2, or just 0. This corresponds to our notion of a *self-contradiction*, another kind of noncontingent statement. However, most of our examples will be about contingent events.

Conjunction Methods

When we need to calculate the probability of two or more events occurring together (*A and B*), we rely on one of two conjunction methods: the *restricted* or the *general*. Each conjunction method provides a formula for a simple calculation of joint occurrences.

Restricted conjunction method The method that is used in situations dealing with two or more independent events, where the occurrence of one event has no bearing whatsoever on the occurrence or nonoccurrence of the other event.

The **restricted conjunction method** is used when two or more events are *independent of each other*: The occurrence of one event has no bearing whatsoever on the occurrence or nonoccurrence of the other event. For example, tails on one toss of the coin has no effect on the probability of tails (or heads, for that matter) occurring on the next toss; these are independent events. Here is the formula for the probability of occurrence of two independent events:

$$Pr\ (A\ and\ B) = Pr\ (A) \times Pr\ (B)$$

Why must we multiply the probability of the first occurrence (*A*) times the probability of the second occurrence (*B*)? The coin toss example provides the justification. Suppose a coin is tossed two times. *A priori* assumptions allow us to list all the possible outcomes:

Toss 1	**Toss 2**
Heads	Heads
Tails	Tails
Heads	Tails
Tails	Heads

Of course, these four possible combinations can go in any order. According to the list, the conjunction *tails and tails* occurs once. Since there are four possible outcomes, the probability is 1/4 for the occurrence of *tails and tails*. The formula should give the identical results. The formula shows that the probability of *tails and tails*, *Pr (A and B)*, is equal to the probability of tails (toss 1) *times* the probability of tails (toss 2). Since the probability of the positive outcome tails is 1/2 for each independent event, we multiply $1/2 \times 1/2$ to get the *Pr (A and B)* = 1/4, which is identical to the result in the list of possible outcomes.

What is the probability that 4 will come up in two successive throws of a die? The restricted conjunction formula gives this result:

$$Pr\ (A\ and\ B) = 1/6 \times 1/6$$

Under the *a priori* assumption of equiprobable outcomes, the probability of each independent occurrence of 4 is calculated as 1/6. Therefore, the final determination that 4 will come up in any two successive throws of the die is $1/6 \times 1/6 = 1/36$. This can be verified by listing all the possible outcomes. The list might start with the possibility that the first toss will be 1. Six possibilities are conjoined with this result (since any of the six numbers could come up in the second toss). Since the same number of possibilities can be conjoined with any of the six numbers occurring on the first toss, there would be thirty-six total possible outcomes, of which only one would correspond to the joint occurrence of *4 and 4*. This result, 1/36, matches the result from our formula. Although both methods are reliable, the formula is obviously more efficient and convenient than generating lists of possibilities.

The **general conjunction method** facilitates the calculation of the probability of two (or more) events occurring together, regardless of whether the events are independent. Two (or more) events are *not* independent when the occurrence of one event affects the probability of the other event. In these cases, the probability of subsequent events is dependent on prior events. For example, if a jar contains ten marbles, five red and five black, then what is the probability of picking two red ones in succession *if we do not put the first marble back into the jar*? Since we are reducing the number of marbles from ten to nine, the probability of picking a second red marble becomes dependent on our first pick.

Given the jar of marbles, the probability that the first marble picked will be red is 5/10, or 1/2. However, if the first marble is red and is not put back into the jar, then there will be only nine marbles left, four of which will be red. So, now, the probability that the second marble picked will be red changes to 4/9. Here is the formula for the general conjunction method:

$$Pr\ (A\ and\ B) = Pr\ (A) \times Pr\ (B,\ if\ A)$$

With this formula, it is easy to compute the probability that two red marbles will be picked in succession. The probability that the first marble picked will be red, *Pr (A)*, is 1/2. The probability that the second marble picked will be red, *Pr (B, if A)*, is 4/9. Therefore, the probability that two red marbles will be picked in succession, under these conditions, is $1/2 \times 4/9 = 4/18$, or 2/9:

$$Pr\ (A\ and\ B) = 1/2 \times 4/9$$

General conjunction method The method that is used for calculating the probability of two or more events occurring together, regardless of whether the events are independent or not independent.

What is the probability that the first three marbles picked from our jar will all be red? If the first two marbles are red, then there eight marbles are left in the jar, of which three are red. The formula gives these results:

$$Pr\ (A\ and\ B\ and\ C) = 1/2 \times 4/9 \times 3/8$$

Therefore, the probability that three red marbles will be picked in succession, under these conditions, is $1/2 \times 4/9 \times 3/8 = 12/144$, or $1/12$.

Disjunction Methods

When we need to calculate the probability that either one of two or more events will occur ($A\ or\ B$), we rely on one of two disjunction methods: the *restricted* or the *general*. Each disjunction method provides a formula for easy calculation of either one of two independent events.

Restricted disjunction method The method that is used when two (or more) events are independent of each other, and the events are mutually exclusive.

There are two requirements for using the **restricted disjunction method**: (1) the situation must involve two or more events that are independent of each other, and (2) the events must be **mutually exclusive** (if one event occurs then the other cannot). Here is the formula:

$$Pr\ (A\ or\ B) = Pr\ (A) + Pr\ (B)$$

Mutually exclusive Two events, such that if one event occurs, then the other cannot.

Suppose five green marbles are added to the jar already containing five red and five black marbles. The formula can be used to compute the probability of picking *either a red or a black marble*. The probability of picking red, $Pr\ A$, is $5/15$, or $1/3$. The probability of picking black is the same, $5/15$, or $1/3$. Therefore, we get this result:

$$Pr\ (A\ or\ B) = 1/3 + 1/3$$

So the probability of picking *either a red or a black* marble is $1/3 + 1/3 = 2/3$. What is the probability of picking *a red, or black, or green* marble? Since we get $1/3 + 1/3 + 1/3 = 1$, it is a *certainty* that you will pick one of the three colored marbles.

What is the probability that you will throw *either a 4 or an odd number*, if you throw one die? The formula gives this result:

$$Pr\ (A\ or\ B) = 1/6 + 1/2$$

The probability of throwing a 4, $Pr\ (A)$, is $1/6$ for a six-sided die, and the probability of throwing an odd number is $1/2$. Therefore, the probability that you will throw *either a 4 or an odd number* is $1/6 + 1/2 = 1/6 + 3/6 = 4/6$, or $2/3$.

General disjunction method The method that is used for calculating the probability when two or more events are not mutually exclusive.

The **general disjunction method** is used when two or more events are not mutually exclusive. Here is the formula:

$$Pr\ (A\ or\ B) = [Pr\ (A) + Pr\ (B)] - [Pr\ (A) \times Pr\ (B)]$$

The formula is complex, but it works. For example, suppose we wanted to compute the probability that tails will come up in either of the first two tosses of a coin. Since these are independent events, the probability of tails coming up on the first toss, $Pr\ (A)$, is $1/2$; the same probability, $1/2$, exists for the second toss, $Pr\ (B)$. But these are *not* mutually exclusive events. The *restricted disjunction formula* would give this result:

$$Pr\ (A\ or\ B) = 1/2 + 1/2$$

This would mean that the probability of a tails coming up in either of the first two tosses would be $1/2 + 1/2 = 1$. But surely this cannot be correct. Let's look once again at the list of possibilities for tossing a coin two times:

Toss 1	Toss 2
Heads	Heads
Tails	Tails
Heads	Tails
Tails	Heads

The list yields four possibilities, three of which contain at least one tails coming up. This means that the probability of tails coming up in either of the first two tosses is 3/4. The *general disjunction formula* should give the same result:

$$Pr\ (A\ or\ B) = [1/2 + 1/2] - [1/2 \times 1/2]$$

The fractions in the first set of brackets *add up* to 1. The *product* of the fractions in the second set of brackets is 1/4. Therefore, the probability of getting tails in either of two tosses is $1 - 1/4 = 3/4$. The complexity of the general disjunction formula pays off.

Suppose we pick from our jar of five red, five black, and five green marbles. What is the probability of getting a black marble in either of two picks—provided we return the first marble picked back into the jar? The formula gives this result:

$$Pr\ (A\ or\ B) = [1/3 + 1/3] - [1/3 \times 1/3]$$

The first set of brackets gives $1/3 + 1/3 = 2/3$. The second set of brackets gives $1/3 \times 1/3 = 1/9$. We can change 2/3 into 6/9 to allow the subtraction of the second bracket. Our final result is $6/9 - 1/9 = 5/9$. This is the probability of getting a black marble in either of two picks from the jar.

Negation Method

Once we know the probability of the occurrence of an event, we can easily calculate the probability of the event *not* occurring. Here is the **negation method** formula:

$$Pr\ (\sim A) = 1 - Pr\ (A)$$

For example, as we saw earlier with the restricted conjunction method, the probability of getting two tails in successive tosses of a coin is 1/4. Using this information, the negation formula allows us to calculate the probability that two tails in succession will not occur:

$$Pr\ (\sim A) = 1 - 1/4$$

Therefore, the probability that two tails will not occur in succession is $1 - 1/4 = 3/4$.

Negation method The method that is used once the probability of an event occurring is known; it is then easy to calculate the probability of the event not occurring.

The general disjunction method calculations showed that the probability of tails coming up in either of the first two coin tosses is 3/4. Applying this information to the negation formula lets us calculate the probability that tails will *not* come up in either of the first two tosses:

$$Pr\ (\sim\!A) = 1 - 3/4$$

Therefore, the probability that tails will *not* occur in either of the first two tosses is $1 - 3/4 = 1/4$. This agrees with the list of possibilities, because the only way at least one tails will *not* come up in two successive tosses is if two heads come up. The probability of that happening is 1/4.

CHECK YOUR UNDERSTANDING 13G

1. A deck of fifty-two playing cards containing two red queens and two black queens is thoroughly shuffled. Determine the probability of picking one card at random and getting a black queen.

Answer: $2/52 = 1/26$. There are two black queens and fifty-two cards.

2. Determine the probability of picking one card at random and getting any queen.

3. Determine the probability of picking two cards at random (without replacing the first one picked) and getting any two queens.

4. Determine the probability of picking two cards at random (without replacing the first one picked) and getting both black queens.

★ 5. Determine the probability that two people randomly chosen will both be born on the same day of the week.

6. Determine the probability that four people randomly chosen will all be born on the same day of the week.

7. Determine the probability that two people randomly chosen will both be born in the same month of the year.

8. Determine the probability that four people randomly chosen will all be born in the same month of the year.

★ 9. Determine the probability that two people randomly chosen will both have their Social Security numbers end with an odd number.

10. Determine the probability that four people randomly chosen will all have their Social Security numbers end with an odd number.

11. Imagine that there are two identical-looking opaque jars, but one contains a red marble and the other contains a black marble. Suppose you are allowed to pick a marble from any jar you wish. You record the results (red or black marble picked), replace the marble, and have the jars' positions randomly mixed again.

The procedure is repeated until you have picked three times. Determine the probability that you will pick the red marble *at least once.*

12. Imagine a box of fifteen CDs contains these types of music: four jazz CDs, four classical CDs, three rap CDs, three reggae CDs, one disco CD. If two CDs are drawn, but the first CD is *not* put back into the box before the second is picked, determine the probability that both CDs will be jazz.

13. From the information give in #12, if two CDs are drawn, but the first CD *is* put back into the box before the second is picked, determine the probability that both CDs will be jazz.

14. From the information give in #12, if two CDs are drawn, but the first CD is *not* put back into the box before the second is picked, determine the probability that *neither* CD will be jazz.

15. From the information give in #12, if two CDs are drawn, but the first CD *is* put back into the box before the second is picked, determine the probability that *neither* CD will be jazz.

16. If you know only that George Washington was born in February, what is the probability that, if given one guess, you will correctly pick the day of the week he was born? What if he was born in a leap year?

17. In a normal deck of fifty-two playing cards there are four aces: two red and two black. What is the probability that a single card chosen at random will be a red ace? That it will be any ace at all?

18. What is the probability that the ages of two people, chosen at random, will both be even numbers?

19. What is the probability that the ages of five people, chosen at random, will all be even numbers?

20. Without looking up their actual birth dates, calculate the probability that Abraham Lincoln and John Kennedy were both born in leap years.

21. Without looking up their actual birth dates, calculate the probability that Abraham Lincoln, John Kennedy, Ronald Reagan, and George W. Bush were all born in leap years.

22. Imagine that there is an opaque jar that contains two red marbles and three black marbles, and you are going to reach in and pick one of the marbles. Determine the probability that you will pick a red marble in the first try.

23. Imagine that there is an opaque jar that contains two red marbles and three black marbles and you are going to reach in and pick one of the marbles. If you pick a marble, but do not replace it, then determine the probability that you will pick both red marbles in the first two picks.

24. Suppose there are two indistinguishable envelopes, one containing a $1 bill, and the other a $100 bill. You pick one envelope, its contents are revealed to you,

and the money is replaced. You do this again two more times, for a total of three picks. What is the probability that you will pick the envelope with the $100 bill at least once?

★ 25. Suppose you have a drawer of socks in these colors and amounts:

three black socks
four white socks
four brown socks
three orange socks
one red sock

If you draw two socks in succession, without replacing the first before the second draw, then what is the probability that both socks will be brown?

H. TRUE ODDS IN GAMES OF CHANCE

In a "fair" game of chance, the payoff odds of winning guarantee that, in the long run, the gambler will break even. The ability to calculate true odds will allow you to determine whether you are playing a fair game or whether the odds are stacked against you. We know that a coin toss has an equal probability of coming up heads or tails, so each has a probability of 1/2. If you bet $1 on each toss of the coin, you will *win* the same number of times that you will *lose*, in the long run. Since there are one out of two chances of winning, one out of two chances of losing, true odds for this game are one-to-one, written as 1:1. So for every dollar you bet, you will get $1, if you win. If you lose, then your dollar is taken away.

As we calculated earlier, the probability of 4 coming up on one toss of a die is 1/6. Using the negation formula, we determine the probability that 4 will *not* come up as 5/6. Therefore, if you bet that 4 will come up, you must *receive* odds of 5:1 to ensure a fair bet. On the other hand, if you bet that 4 will *not* come up then you must be willing to *give* 5:1 odds.

Most casino games do not provide true odds. This should not be surprising, since the casinos would not survive if there were an equal chance of winning or losing on their games. To ensure a winning margin, casino games offer odds stacked in their favor, odds designed to guarantee that the casino will win, in the long run. For example, the majority of American roulette wheels contain eighteen red numbers and eighteen black numbers, arranged from 1 to 36. In addition, there are two green numbers, 0 and 00. Since there are a total of thirty-eight possible outcomes, the probability of red coming up is 18/38. The probability that red will *not* come up is, therefore, 20/38 (eighteen black numbers plus two green numbers). As we can see, if you bet red, the odds are slightly against your winning. However, the casino will only offer you 1:1 odds for this bet (meaning that you will get a dollar back for each dollar you bet). After thousands of such bets the casino is guaranteed to come out ahead.

If you decide to place your bet on your lucky number, what will happen? The casino is willing to give you 35:1 odds for this bet. But since there are thirty-eight numbers, the odds are once again not true. Odds have to deviate only slightly away from true odds to provide the casino with a winning margin, especially with millions of bets taken annually.

I. BAYESIAN THEORY

A major advance in probability theory and method came when Thomas Bayes was able to unite much of the probability calculus and the relative frequency theory into a method for calculating conditional probability. **Conditional probability** is the calculation of the probability of an event *if* another event has already happened. Bayes's ideas proved so useful that they have been applied to everything from risk assessment and hypothesis testing to the probability of false positives in disease testing. Bayes's theory is also used extensively in judging the predictive ability of exams and other measures. For example, formulas are available to determine whether the SAT is a useful predictor of success in college.

Conditional probability
The calculation of the probability of an event if another event has already happened.

In fact, a single conditional probability formula combines the restricted disjunction method, the general conjunction method, the negation method, and the relative frequency theory. The general conjunction method already introduced the idea of conditional probability. It allowed us to calculate the probability of one event occurring *if another event occurred first*. What Bayes's theory does is to expand this basic conditional to include relative frequency. Here is the formula we will be using:

$$Pr\ (A,\ if\ B) = \frac{Pr\ (B,\ if\ A) \times Pr\ (A)}{Pr\ (B)}$$

This formula allows us to calculate the conditional probability of two mutually exclusive and exhaustive events. As defined earlier, *mutually exclusive* means they both cannot happen at the same time; *exhaustive* means there are no other possibilities. For example, consider this problem:

> A teacher calculates that 80% of the students who passed had perfect attendance. Meanwhile 10% of students who did *not* pass had perfect attendance. Of the total number of students in all her classes, 75% passed the courses. What is the correct interpretation of the data? Is perfect attendance a good predictor of passing the courses?

This problem fulfills the requirements we have set forth. There are two possibilities for each event: (1) passing or not passing, and (2) perfect attendance or not perfect attendance. Together, they form a set of mutually exclusive and exhaustive events (a student cannot both pass and not pass, and a student cannot both have perfect attendance and not have perfect attendance).

If A = *passing the course* and B = *perfect attendance*, we can use the data to fill in the formula. We want to determine the probability of passing, *if perfect attendance is achieved*, which is written *Pr (A, if B)*. Suppose this data is provided:

(1) The probability of perfect attendance, if they passed the course, is 80%, or 0.80, which can be written as *Pr (B, if A) = 0.80*

(2) The probability of perfect attendance, if they did *not* pass the course, is 10%, or 0.10, which can be written as *Pr (B, if ~A) = 0.10*

(3) The probability of passing the course is 75%, or 0.75, which can be written as *Pr (A) = 0.75*

This information can now be applied directly to the general formula:

$$Pr \ (A, \ if \ B) = \frac{(0.80 \times 0.75)}{Pr \ (B)}$$

$$= \frac{0.60}{Pr \ (B)}$$

A new formula is needed to calculate the *Pr (B)*, one that allows us to calculate the *total probability*:

$$Pr \ (B) = [Pr \ (B, \ if \ A) \times Pr \ (A)] + [Pr \ (B, \ if \ {\sim}A) \times Pr \ ({\sim}A)]$$

This formula can be interpreted by using information from the example. The probability of B (*perfect attendance*) is defined through a set of conditional relationships. The left set of brackets relates B to A (*passing*), while the right set of brackets relates B to ~A (*not passing*). Since A and ~A are mutually exclusive, the *total probability* of B (*perfect attendance*) can be calculated by determining the complete relationship with A and ~A. Since *Pr (A) = 0.75*, the negation formula can be used to calculate that *Pr (~A) = 0.25*. Placing this information into the formula gives us *Pr (B)*:

$$Pr \ (B) = (0.80 \times 0.75) + (0.10 \times 0.25)$$
$$Pr \ (B) = 0.60 + 0.025$$
$$Pr \ (B) = 0.625$$

Adding this information to the previous calculations gives this result:

$$Pr \ (A, \ if \ B) = \frac{0.60}{0.625}$$

$$Pr \ (A, \ if \ B) = 0.96$$

Therefore, perfect attendance is a strong measure for predicting who will pass the course.

CHECK YOUR UNDERSTANDING 13I

Use the discussion in this section and apply the Bayes's formula to the following situations.

1. Shane did a survey of his friends. The results showed that 60% own a video game console, and 40% own a laptop computer; but interestingly, none of his friends own both items. He also found out that 20% of the video game console owners have Twitter accounts, but that 70% of the laptop owners have Twitter accounts. Using all the information given, calculate the probability that a friend who has a Twitter account is a laptop owner.

Answer:

Pr = probability; L = laptop; T = Twitter account; V = video game console:

$$Pr\ (L, if\ T) = \frac{Pr\ (L) \times Pr\ (T, if\ L)}{[Pr\ (L) \times Pr\ (T, if\ L)] + [Pr\ (V) \times Pr\ (T, if\ V)]}$$

$$= \frac{0.4 \times 0.7}{(0.4 \times 0.7) + (0.6 \times 0.2)}$$

$$= \frac{0.28}{0.28 + 0.12}$$

$$= \frac{0.28}{0.4}$$

$$= .7$$

2. Frances is supposed to arrive at work by 9:00 AM. She leaves for work at 8:00 AM 40% of the time, but she leaves for work at 8:30 AM 60% of the time. On the days she leaves for work at 8:00 AM, she arrives by 9:00 AM 70% of the time. But for the days she leaves for work at 8:30 AM, she arrives by 9:00 AM 30% of the time. If she arrived at work by 9:00 AM today, then what is the probability that she left for work at 8:00 AM?

3. A student has a number of books that she purchased for her classes: 70% of her books cost under $100, and 30% of her books cost $100 or more. Of the books that cost under $100, 10% are hardbacks and 90% are paperbacks. Of the books that cost $100 or more, 80% are hardbacks and 20% are paperbacks. She recently loaned one of her hardback books to a friend. Using all the information given, calculate the probability that the book she loaned to her friend cost under $100.

4. Carly took her car to a garage for inspection and the mechanic said that her engine needed some major work. Since her car was old, Carly was not sure if she wanted to invest the money in the repairs. The mechanic said that if she did the repairs, then there was a 25% probability that the engine will break down within the next 25,000 miles. But if she did not do the repairs, then there was a 67% probability that the engine will break down within the next 25,000 miles. Suppose that Carly's car engine did break down within the next 25,000 miles. Calculate the probability that she did the repairs.

★ 5. Imagine that a researcher gathers data on a new test for high school seniors, the Multiphasic Aptitude Diagnostic (MAD) test. He wants to determine whether scoring above 1200 on the MAD test is a good predictor of graduating college with a GPA greater than 3.5. He calculates that 70% of the students who graduated with a GPA greater than 3.5 scored above 1200 on the MAD test. The data also indicate that 25% of students who did *not* graduate with a GPA greater than 3.5 scored above 1200 on the MAD test. The percentage of students who graduated with a GPA greater than 3.5 was 10%. What is the correct interpretation of the data? Is scoring above 1200 on the MAD test a good predictor of graduating college with a GPA greater than 3.5?

Summary

- Evaluating arguments that rely on statistical evidence requires that we can correctly interpret the statistical evidence as it is presented.
- Population: Any group of objects, not just human populations.
- Sample: A subset of a population.
- Representative sample: A sample that accurately reflects the characteristics of the population as a whole.
- Random sample: When every member of the population has an equal chance of getting into the sample.
- Mean: The statistical average that is determined by adding the numerical values in the data concerning the examined objects, then dividing by the number of objects that were measured.
- Median: The statistical average that is determined by locating the value that separates the entire set of data in half.
- Mode: The statistical average that is determined by locating the value that occurs most.
- Standard deviation: Describes the amount of diversity in a set of numerical values.
- Probability calculations using the *a priori* theory rely on hypothetical reasoning based on two major assumptions. The first is that all the possible outcomes can be determined, and the second is that each of the possible outcomes has an equal probability of occurring (equiprobable).
- In the relative frequency theory, some probabilities can be computed by dividing the number of favorable cases by the total number of observed cases.
- Reliance on statistical, historical data is not the same as relative frequency applications. Calculations of this kind fall under the subjective theory of probability, where determinations are based on the lack of total knowledge regarding an event.
- Probability calculus: A branch of mathematics that can be used to compute the probabilities of complex events from the probabilities of their component events.
- The restricted conjunction method is used in situations dealing with two or more independent events, where the occurrence of one event has no bearing whatsoever on the occurrence or nonoccurrence of the other event.
- The general conjunction method is used for calculating the probability of two or more events occurring together, regardless of whether the events are independent or not independent.
- The restricted disjunction method is used when two (or more) events are independent of each other, and the events are mutually exclusive (if one event occurs then the other cannot).
- The general disjunction method is used for calculating the probability of occurrence of two or more events that are not mutually exclusive.

- The negation method is used once the probability of an event occurring is known; it is then easy to calculate the probability of the event not occurring.
- Conditional probability: The calculation of the probability of an event if another event has already happened.

KEY TERMS

population   567
sample   567
representative sample   567
random sample   568
mean   571
median   572
mode   574
standard deviation   575
a priori theory   587

equiprobable   587
relative frequency
   theory   588
subjectivist theory   589
probability calculus   590
restricted conjunction
   method   590
general conjunction
   method   591

restricted disjunction
   method   592
mutually exclusive   592
general disjunction
   method   592
negation method   593
conditional
   probability   597

LOGIC CHALLENGE: THE SECOND CHILD

You are at a playground and happen to strike up a conversation with a stranger. You are told that he is there to watch his daughter play basketball. When you ask if he has any other children, he tells you that he has one more child. What is the probability that the second child is a female?

Chapter 14
Causality and Scientific Arguments

Medical research has uncovered the cause of many diseases and how to treat them. In fact, the news and the Internet are filled with the latest discoveries—but not all the claims you meet are unambiguous or true. Here are some items that you might have come across:

> Electronic cigarettes, which are increasingly used worldwide, are said to be unsafe and pose health risks, a new study suggests.
>
> "Electronic Cigarettes Pose Health Risks," Bernama.com

> It might be the potlucks, it might be those long hours sitting in pews, but whatever the cause, a new study presented this week shows a link between religious activity and weight gain.
>
> Diane Mapes, "Praise the Lard? Religion Linked to Obesity in Young Adults," Msnbc.com

> Girls, but not boys, who walk or bike to school instead of getting a ride perform better in tests of verbal and math skills, according to a new study of teens living in Spanish cities. And the longer the commute, the higher the test scores.
>
> "Girls Who Walk, Bike to School Do Better in Tests," Reuters

> A new report from British scientists suggests that long-term, low-dose aspirin use may modestly reduce the risk of dying of certain cancers, though experts warn the study isn't strong enough to recommend healthy people start taking a pill that can cause bleeding and other problems.
>
> "Aspirin May Cut Cancer Deaths, but Caution Urged," Associated Press

The search for causes is a large part of science, medicine, and everyday life as well. Cause-effect relationships are at the heart of physics, chemistry, biology, and many other fields. In everyday life you might look for why your car is stalling in traffic, why your computer suddenly stopped working, or why your stomach is aching. However, the word "cause" has several meanings, and in everyday situations the possibility of ambiguity arises. For example, parents often tell their children that they must take vitamins, because vitamins will help them grow. The claim is not that vitamins alone will cause children to grow; it is that vitamins are a *necessary condition* for children's growth. In another situation a child might complain of a stomachache. The parent could suggest that the child stop drinking so much soda. Of course, the parent could also give the child some medicine to ease the pain. The parent relies on an understanding that several methods of reducing or eliminating the stomachache are possible. In other words, the parent is offering a *sufficient condition* to bring about a desired effect.

Necessary and sufficient conditions may both be present. For example, the ideal gas law holds that as the pressure of a gas rises (or falls), so does its temperature. In other words, the rising (or falling) pressure is both a sufficient and a necessary condition for the rising (or falling) temperature of the gas.

We begin by discussing cause-effect relationships. We see how John Stuart Mill developed basic principles of causality and scientific investigation. The rest of the chapter will focus on scientific theories and hypotheses, how they are tested in experiments, how they differ from superstition—and why they provide the best way to understand the physical world.

A. CAUSALITY

A *cause* is a set of conditions that bring about an effect. For example, imagine that a window in your house breaks. If we saw a rock hit the window, we probably would claim that the rock was *the cause* of the broken window. For practical purposes, for assigning blame perhaps, this is a normal claim to make. However, for a deeper understanding of causality, we need to consider some alternatives.

If we take the same rock and strike a similar window, we would expect to get similar results. That already tells us something about what we expect of a cause-effect relationship: *same cause, same effect*. However, if we throw the rock so that it barely grazes the window, then the window might not break. Alternatively, we could keep the rock the same and the angle at which it strikes the window the same, but change the velocity with which it strikes the window. In other words, we just throw the rock more softly. Again, it might not break the window. The weight of the rock, the "angle of incidence," and the velocity are all parts of the event, and all of them can vary. In a scientific experiment, they are the *variables*.

What we originally called *the cause* has evolved into a **causal network**, a set of conditions that bring about an effect. By changing the parts of the event, the variables, we can achieve different results. For example, by varying the velocity of the rock, or by varying the angle of incidence of the rock, or by using rocks of various densities, we can discover the set of conditions that are involved in cause-effect relationships. This holds for the window itself, which is surely part of the event. By conducting experiments, we can find the necessary range of glass density and strength needed to bring about a desired effect—if it is our house, to keep the window from breaking. However,

Causal network A set of conditions that bring about an effect.

we must be sure to eliminate factors that are *not* necessary for the effect to have happened, such as the time of day, the color of the window frame, or the color of the rock. This is how we establish the set of *necessary and sufficient conditions* that constitute the cause of the event in question.

Normal state The historical information regarding an object.

We single out the rock as the cause because we are able to establish the **normal state** of a system. If the window has been in an unbroken state for some time, then that is its normal state. As soon as it breaks, an **abnormal state** is established. Any change from the normal state requires explanation, typically a causal one. The causes of the change include many factors—the density of the rock, the velocity, the angle of incidence, and so on. Together these establish the causal network.

Abnormal state A drastic change in the normal state regarding an object.

A **precipitating cause** is the object or event directly involved in bringing about an effect. In our example, it would be safe to call the rock the precipitating cause of the broken window. We then add to the precipitating cause the causal network in order to have a complete scientific explanation of the cause-effect relationship.

Precipitating cause The object or event directly involved in bringing about an effect.

On the other hand, a **remote cause** is something that is connected to the precipitating cause by a chain of events. We can trace the chain of events back in time depending on our needs. For example, we might not be interested in determining how the rock came to hit the window if we are scientists or engineers developing stronger windows. However, we may very much want to know the remote cause in order to assign blame and recover the cost of repairs. Now let's imagine that some children had been playing baseball. Without thinking, and for no real reason other than curiosity and a dare from another player, the pitcher picked up a rock and tossed it at the batter. The batter hit the rock, which then hit the window. If we were interested in assigning blame for legal purposes, we could charge the batter, the pitcher, and perhaps the player who instigated the dare.

Remote cause Something that is connected to the precipitating cause by a chain of events.

A legal test to determine the cause of an event is not the same as a scientific one. For scientific purposes, to determine the *physical cause* of the broken window, we need only consider the precipitating cause and the causal network, not the remote causes. Of course, a trial often calls on scientific testimony. However, for legal purposes the remote causes would probably be emphasized—in our example, the chain of events that led to the rock hitting the window. In a trial, too, to prove cause and effect, we would have to show that we suffered harm, like the broken window. On the other hand, a scientific investigation would be interested simply in what happened when the rock hit the window.

These same issues appear in other cases. If someone is found dead under suspicious circumstances, the police will probably have an autopsy performed. The medical expert performing the autopsy seeks the physical cause of death—the precipitating cause and its effects on the body. So far, there need be no moral or legal issues involved. However, if it is determined that death was by poison, then the police will have to investigate if it was self-administered or was left by someone else. They will also ask if the poison was administered accidentally or deliberately. If there is evidence of a crime, then the police and district attorney will look for the remote causes of the death.

B. MILL'S METHODS

Is there a best way to discover causes? And if we found the right method, would it be what we call science? Many scientists and philosophers have suggested what they thought would be the most efficient and reliable way to conduct experiments. John Stuart Mill proposed one influential program in his book *A System of Logic*. Mill presents five methods of experimental inquiry (also called "canons," which means general principles). They are the *method of agreement*, the *method of difference*, the *joint method of agreement and difference*, the *method of residues*, and the *method of concomitant variations*. As you will soon see, his principles are the basis for many of the causal inductive arguments people make in everyday life.

Method of Agreement

The **method of agreement** looks at two or more instances of an event to see what they have in common. For example, if four people eat at a restaurant, but only three get food poisoning, then the method of agreement tells us to investigate what the three instances have in common. We can create a chart to display the data:

Method of agreement
The method that looks at two or more instances of an event to see what they have in common.

Instances of the **Effect**		Fish	Spaghetti	Ham	Bread	Appetizer	Soda	Beer	Wine
					Possible Causes				
John	Food poisoning		√		√	√		√	
Robert	Food poisoning	√				√	√		
Christina	Food poisoning			√	√	√			√

The check marks indicate when a condition has been met. A blank space under an item indicates that a condition has not been met. For example, the chart indicates that John had the spaghetti, bread, appetizer, and beer. We also know from the chart that he did *not* have fish, ham, soda, or wine. We see that all three cases of food poisoning have just one thing in common: the appetizer. Therefore, of the eight conditions under investigation, the appetizer is the probable cause of the food poisoning.

Whenever a series of similar, but unexplained events occur, we are likely to wonder what they have in common. However, the method of agreement does not provide conclusive proof that we have found the cause. It can offer only partial, tentative inductive evidence. For example, the three people who came down with food poisoning might have had other features in common, and we simply overlooked them. All three victims might have had water (tap or bottled), or they might have grabbed a mint at the cash register just before leaving. Maybe the three ate something even before going to the restaurant. Or perhaps their utensils were not washed properly.

The method of agreement may also run into trouble because it depends on how we decide to list things. Consider the possibility that two *different* items on our chart caused the food poisoning. For example, what if both the fish and the bread were contaminated, but not the appetizer? Could this explain why the three got sick? Since Robert ate the fish, this explains one instance. And since John and Christina both ate the bread, this would explain the remaining two instances of food poisoning. This is why experimental data can offer evidence to support a claim that something is a cause, but still leave a measure of uncertainty.

Let's look at another example. Suppose a mechanic has four cars towed to her garage in less than 1 hour, and the car owners all complain that their car just began sputtering and then stalled. Once again, we can draw a chart to see the results:

Instances of the **Effect**	Possible Causes				
	Spark Plugs	Generator	Water in Gasoline	Alternator	Carburetor
Car 1 Stopped running	√		√		
Car 2 Stopped running			√		
Car 3 Stopped running	√		√		
Car 4 Stopped running			√		

We can now interpret the results. In two instances, the spark plugs had to be replaced (car 1 and car 3). There were no instances in which the generator, alternator, or carburetor showed signs of being defective. But in all four cases water was found in the gasoline tank. The mechanic can use this information to do follow-up research. For example, she might find that all four drivers had recently bought gas from the same nearby gas station. She could then refill the tanks with good gas and see the result. The mechanic could also replace the two sets of old spark plugs to see if the cars start. Here the method of agreement adds something to our investigation: It allows the mechanic to follow up on the initial results. It helps narrow the search, once we have the right background information to know which of the hundreds of possible variables are relevant. However, if an event is truly novel, then background knowledge will not be much help.

Method of Difference

Method of difference
The method that looks for what all the instances of an event do not have in common.

The **method of difference** looks instead for what all the instances of an event do *not* have in common. If they have everything in common except one item, then that item is a likely cause.

Let's examine that unfortunate group of diners at a different meal. This time we need to investigate all four people to locate the *difference* between the three who got food poisoning and the one person who did not get it. We are really looking at the *absence* of food poisoning. Once again, we can create a chart to display the data:

Instances of the **Effect**	Possible Causes			
	Hamburger	French Fries	Tea	Pie
John Food poisoning	√	√	√	√
Robert Food poisoning	√	√	√	√
Christina Food poisoning	√	√	√	√
Kristin *No food poisoning*	√		√	√

We look for a single condition that was present when the effect occurred and that was absent when the effect did not occur. We see that there is only one circumstance that differentiates Kristin, who does not have food poisoning, from the three other people—the French fries. We conclude that, of the four circumstances under investigation, the French fries are the probable cause of the food poisoning.

The method identifies a *sufficient condition* as the probable cause. However, it still does not provide conclusive proof. Once again, we might have disregarded or overlooked other variables that differ among the four people. Those other possibilities have still not been ruled out.

Joint Method of Agreement and Difference

The **joint method of agreement and difference** combines our first two approaches. If two or more instances of an event have only one thing in common, while the instances in which it does *not* occur all share the absence of that thing, then the item is a likely cause.

Adding the results of the method of agreement and the method of difference into one analysis strengthens our claim. We can highlight the results in two colors to illustrate how each method is to be applied:

Joint method of agreement and difference If two or more instances of an event have only one thing in common, while the instances in which it does not occur all share the absence of that thing, then the item is a likely cause.

Instances of the **Effect**		Possible Causes							
		Fish	Spaghetti	Ham	Bread	Appetizer	Soda	Beer	Wine
John	Food poisoning		√		√	√		√	
Robert	Food poisoning	√				√	√		
Christina	Food poisoning			√	√	√			√
Kristin	*No food poisoning*	√			√				√

Instances of the **Effect**		Possible Causes							
		Fish	Spaghetti	Ham	Bread	Appetizer	Soda	Beer	Wine
John	Food poisoning		√		√	√		√	
Robert	Food poisoning	√				√	√		
Christina	Food poisoning			√	√	√			√
Kristin	*No food poisoning*	√			√				√

The three light blue boxes show the results of the method of agreement, while the single dark blue box shows the results of the method of difference. First, *the effect must always be present when the cause is present.* In each case in light blue, the cause, the appetizer, is present. This identifies a necessary condition. Second, *the effect must always be absent when the cause is absent.* The dark blue box shows that food poisoning is absent when the cause, the appetizer, is absent. This identifies a sufficient condition.

Our conclusion has a higher probability of being correct than if we had used either of the first two methods alone. The method of agreement by itself could not rule out the possibility that two different items listed on our chart caused the food poisoning.

Perhaps both the fish and the bread were contaminated, but not the appetizer. The joint method eliminates this possibility. In the dark blue box, Kristin ate the fish and the bread and did not get food poisoning. Therefore, neither of those items could be a cause of the illness.

The joint method allows us to assert that the appetizer was a *sufficient condition* for food poisoning. The joint method also allows us to assert that the appetizer was a *necessary condition*.

The same principles apply to our example of stalled cars:

	Possible Causes				
Instances of the **Effect**	Spark Plugs	Generator	Water in Gasoline	Alternator	Carburetor
Car 1 Stopped running	√		√		
Car 2 Stopped running			√		
Car 3 Stopped running	√		√		
Car 4 Stopped running			√		
Car 5 *Did not stop running*					

	Possible Causes				
Instances of the **Effect**	Spark Plugs	Generator	Water in Gasoline	Alternator	Carburetor
Car 1 Stopped running	√		√		
Car 2 Stopped running			√		
Car 3 Stopped running	√		√		
Car 4 Stopped running			√		
Car 5 *Did not stop running*					

Again, the four light blue boxes show the results of the method of agreement, while the dark blue box shows the results of the method of difference. First, *the method of agreement requires that the effect must always be present when the cause is present.* In each case in light blue, the cause, water in the gasoline, is present whenever the car stopped running. Second, *the method of difference requires that the effect must always be absent when the cause is absent.* In the dark blue box, the effect (the car stopping) is absent when the cause, water in the gasoline, is absent.

Again our conclusion has a higher probability than with each of the first two methods considered alone. The joint method allows us to assert that water in the gasoline was probably both a *sufficient condition* and a *necessary condition* for the effect.

Method of Residues

Method of residues The method that subtracts from a complex set of events those parts that already have known causes.

The **method of residues** subtracts from a complex set of events those parts that already have known causes. Whatever remains (the "residue") is a likely cause of the remaining effect.

Suppose your roommate returns from a party with a stomachache, headache, and a rash. You piece together the food and drinks that your roommate consumed and form this list: hot dogs, pizza, chips, pretzels, macadamia nuts, and soda. Soda always gives him a headache, so that explains one symptom. He sometimes gets a stomachache from hot dogs, so that could account for another symptom. He does not remember ever having had a reaction to pizza, chips, or pretzels. That leaves just two things—the nuts and the rash. Sure enough, this was the first time he had eaten macadamia nuts, so the rash probably was caused by an allergic reaction to them. He plans on visiting the campus medical clinic to get tested for allergies to verify his conclusion.

We can again follow the reasoning by drawing a chart:

Possible Causes of the Symptoms						
Symptoms	Hot Dogs	Pizza	Chips	Pretzels	Macadamia Nuts	Soda
Stomachache	√	x	x	x	x	x
Headache	x	x	x	x	x	√
Rash	x	x	x	x	√	x

However, we need to interpret this chart differently from the previous examples. With the method of residues, we are actively drawing on our background knowledge. For example, we concluded from past experience that hot dogs were the probable cause of the stomachache, so we place a check mark in a blue box to indicate that cause-effect relationship. Similarly, the two x's in the hot dogs column indicate that hot dogs had not been connected before to either a headache or rash.

We also concluded from past experience that soda was the probable cause of the headache, so we place a check mark in a blue box to indicate a causal connection. The two x's in the soda column indicate that soda has not been connected previously to either a stomachache or rash. In the columns for pizza, chips, and pretzels we find only x's because they have not been connected before to any of the symptoms.

The method of residues tells us to subtract from a complex set of events those parts that are already understood. We have done just that for the stomachache and headache. We also eliminate items that have no previous connection to any of the symptoms. Whatever remains, we conclude, is the most likely cause of the remaining effect. In this case, the macadamia nuts are the probable cause of the rash. We place the check mark in a red box to indicate that this causal connection is newly discovered.

Method of Concomitant Variations

The **method of concomitant variations** looks for two factors that vary together. If a variation of one part of an event accompanies a variation in another part of the event, then the two parts are probably causally connected. (The word "concomitant" means *accompanying*.)

This method looks for a **correlation**, or correspondence between two sets of objects, events, or sets of data. For example, suppose a car company wants to determine the speed

Method of concomitant variations The method that looks for two factors that vary together.

Correlation A correspondence between two sets of objects, events, or sets of data.

at which a particular car gets the best gas mileage. Many automatic transmissions have three gears that shift up and down, depending on the car's speed and the revolutions per minute (RPM) of the engine. In a simple experiment, a test car is equipped with a special one-gallon gasoline tank. The car will go around a test track and maintain a fixed speed until it uses up that single gallon of gasoline. The number of miles traveled will determine the car's mileage at that speed, in miles per gallon (MPG). The engineers then repeat the test run at different speeds to see which gives the best mileage.

This example involves isolating one variable, *speed*. The engineers thus make sure to keep tire size, tire pressure, the weather, road conditions, and other factors constant throughout the experiment, in order to see how speed affects the gas mileage of this one car model. Of course, many variables affect gas mileage, and the same method could test for those as well. The engineers could increase or decrease the tire size, for example, while keeping other variables constant. Regardless, in each case they are looking for a *correlation*—between a given variable and gas mileage.

Focusing for now on speed and mileage, suppose we make a chart of the results for the company's most popular subcompact car:

	Miles per Hour (MPH)								
	0	10	20	30	40	50	60	70	80
Miles per gallon of gasoline (MPG)	0	12	18	25	35	37	29	25	21

The first column indicates the worst possible driving situation, just sitting with the car idling. When the gallon of gasoline is used up, the car will have traveled exactly 0 miles at 0 MPH, so its MPG will also be 0. You can see that the MPG increases steadily until it reaches its peak at 37 MPG, when the car's speed is 50 MPH. It then decreases steadily for speeds over 50 MPH.

The method of concomitant variations looks for correlations, but the correlation can be either positive or negative. In other words, the two variables must change together, but they may change in the same direction or in opposite directions. In this example, in the range from 0 to 50 MPH we observe a positive correlation between speed and MPG. From 50 to 80 MPH, we see a negative correlation.

Once the method has found a correlation, it can help reveal a cause-effect relationship. Here we observe a complex relationship between speed and gas mileage, but why? Perhaps the explanation lies in the car's three gears. Because the lowest two gears are used to accelerate from a standing position, a lower MPG is found from 10 to 40 MPH. The engine needs the most power to get moving, so it consumes a lot of gasoline. If you ever rode a 10-speed bicycle, you know that when you start out at the lowest gears, you need a lot of energy to turn the pedals. As your speed increases, and you shift through higher gears, the power needed to turn the pedals decreases, and you reach a "sweet spot." Perhaps the same principle holds true for cars, too—and in fact it does. With the results in hand, the engineers can do further tests to confirm that causal relationship.

All cars have a "sweet spot" as well. This is the speed at which the car runs most efficiently, and of course it varies considerably from car to car, especially with engine size and car weight. The sweet spot typically occurs soon after the car shifts into its highest gear. After that, further acceleration will usually cause a decrease in MPG. We can see just that in the chart for the range from 50 to 80 MPH. These results, too, are comparable to what we find for a 10-speed bicycle.

As we can already see, the method of concomitant variations has its limits. It can point to a causal relationship, but that still leaves work to be done to discover why. The results can even be misleading, because neither variable may prove to be the cause of the other. A basic principle of science holds that *every cause-effect relationship is a case of correlation, but not every correlation is a cause-effect relationship*. In other words, causality requires correlation, but correlation does not require causality. For example, there is a high correlation between Sundays and Mondays: One always follows directly after the other. But Sundays do not cause Mondays to occur. There is a high correlation between a person's weight and pants size. But your weight does not cause your pants size to be what it is, nor does your pants size cause you to weigh a certain amount. Of course, the *reason* you buy a certain pants size is your weight. Nevertheless there is no direct cause-effect relationship between your weight and the pants.

CHECK YOUR UNDERSTANDING 14B

I. Identify whether the intended causality in the following statements is a necessary condition, a sufficient condition, or both a necessary and a sufficient condition:

1. Drinking polluted water will cause you to get stomach cramps.
Answer: Sufficient condition

2. Releasing a helium balloon will cause it to rise up to the sky.

3. Slowly dissolving a throat lozenge in your mouth will cause you to stop coughing.

4. Smothering a fire with dirt will cause the fire to go out.

⭐ 5. Hitting a glass window with a baseball will cause the window to break.

6. Turning the key in the ignition will cause a car to start.

7. Throwing a cup onto a concrete pavement will cause the cup to break.

8. Getting bit by a mosquito will cause you to get malaria.

⭐ 9. Jumping into a swimming pool will cause you to get wet.

10. Pulling the plug from the socket will cause a television to stop working.

II. Answer "true" or "false" to the following:

1. A causal network is the degree of probability that we assign to an event occurring.
Answer: False

2. A remote cause is something that is connected to the precipitating cause by a chain of events.

3. A correlation is a sufficient condition for making a causal claim.

4. The method of residues tells us that if two or more instances in which an event occurs have only one thing in common, while the two or more instances in which it does not occur all have the absence of that thing, then the item in which the two sets of instances differ is causally connected to the event.

⭐ 5. The method of agreement tells us that if all the instances in which the event under investigation occurs, and an instance in which it does not occur, have everything in common except one item, then that item is causally connected to the event.

6. The method of difference tells us that if two or more instances of an event under investigation have only one thing in common, then the circumstance in which all the instances agree is causally connected to the given event.

7. The method of concomitant variations tells us that if a variation of one part of an event accompanies a variation in another part of the event, either in direct or inverse proportion, then the two parts are causally connected.

8. The joint method of agreement and difference tells us that if you subtract from any complex set of events those parts that are already understood to be the effects of known causes, then what remains is causally connected to the remaining effect.

⭐ 9. Since the word "cause" has several meanings, when it is used in everyday situations the possibility of ambiguity arises.

10. Mill's methods provide conclusive proof of causality.

III. Determine which of Mill's methods matches the descriptions that follow:

1. If you subtract from any complex set of events those parts that are already understood to be the effects of known causes, then what remains is causally connected to the remaining effect.

Answer: The method of residues

2. If all the instances in which the event under investigation occurs, and an instance in which it does not occur, have everything in common except one item, then that item is causally connected to the event.

3. If a variation of one part of an event accompanies a variation in another part of the event, either in direct or inverse proportion, then the two parts are causally connected.

4. If two or more instances of an event under investigation have only one thing in common, then the circumstance in which all the instances agree is causally connected to the given event.

⭐ 5. If two or more instances in which an event occurs have only one thing in common, while the two or more instances in which it does not occur all have the absence of that thing, then the item in which the two sets of instances differ is causally connected to the event.

IV. For each of the following cases, do three things. First, construct a chart based on the information given for each case. Second, determine which of Mill's methods apply to each case. Third, determine the conclusion that can be derived from the method.

1. Tom and Marsha both bought new cars. They chose the same make and model, with the same size engine and automatic transmission and same tire size. They both buy the gas at the same station and use the same octane gas. Tom drives his car exclusively in the city, while Marsha does mainly highway driving. However, when they compared gas mileage, Marsha's car averages 35 miles per gallon (MPG), but Tom's car averages only 26 MPG.

Answer:

			Possible Causes						
The **Effect**	Make	Model	Engine Size	Automatic Transmission	Tire Size	Gas Station	Gas Octane	City Driving	Highway Driving
Tom 26 MPG	√	√	√	√	√	√	√	√	
Marsha 35 MPG	√	√	√	√	√	√	√		√

The chart displays the *method of difference*. We can conclude that city driving is the probable cause of Tom's car averaging 26 MPG, and highway driving is the probable cause of Marsha's car averaging 35 MPG.

2. A student majoring in physics wanted to see if a relationship exists between height above or below sea level and the boiling point of water. Her experiments result in the following data: At sea level, water boils at approximately 212 degrees F; at 500 feet above sea level, water boils at approximately 211 degrees F; at 1000 feet above sea level, water boils at approximately 210 degrees F; at 500 below sea level, water boils at approximately 213 degrees F; and at 1000 feet below sea level, water boils at approximately 214 degrees F.

3. Louis received at least a score of 90 on all four math exams this semester. He tried to determine why he did so well. He had different meals the night before the exams; he studied a different number of hours; two times he studied with friends and two times he didn't. The only thing that he remembered doing before all four exams was getting at least 8 hours of sleep the night before.

4. Judy's electric bill averaged $200 a month for 3 months. She noticed that she used the air conditioner in the bedroom all night. For the next 2 months she decided to try to sleep without using the air conditioner. The electric bill for those 2 months averaged $75 a month.

★ 5. Sam had $250 in his wallet on Friday afternoon. By Sunday night he had only $10 left. He recalled spending $60 on a dinner and a date Friday night. Then he spent $70 on groceries, $40 on gas for his car, and lent $50 to a friend. He didn't recall spending any more money, so the only thing he could think of was that he must have lost the $20 somewhere.

6. Frank's three dogs suddenly started having fleas. They get baths at different times and he uses different dog shampoos on them since they have very different hair types. They eat different kinds of food and like different doggie snacks. But last week a neighbor's dog got into the back yard and all three dogs played with it. The flea problem occurred soon after.

7. Two students who share the same dorm room received coupons in the mail for a free meal at a restaurant that recently opened near campus. However, the two students across the hall in the same dorm did not get any coupons. All four are juniors, they all have cafeteria passes, and they have lived in the same dorm for two years. The two students who received coupons in the mail remember participating in a survey at the student union the previous month. The other two students did not fill out the survey forms.

8. Jake's house was quite hot in the summer. He tried adding insulation to the attic, and it helped some the next summer. He added sunscreens to the windows, and that helped, too. He planted six large shade trees, and the house was even somewhat cooler. He added aluminum siding to the house, but it didn't get any cooler.

★ 9. Two tomato plants were started from the same batch of seeds. They were all placed in the same kind of soil, given the same watering schedule and same amount of water, and had the same access to sun. Only one of the plants was sprayed with a fertilizer once a week; the other plant never received the fertilizer. The plant that received the fertilizer produced twice as many pounds of tomatoes as the nonfertilized plant.

10. After Luke washes his T-shirts, it takes 25 minutes to dry in a heavy-duty dryer. Whenever he adds his underwear and socks to the T-shirts load, it takes 50 minutes to dry. If he adds his jeans to the underwear, socks, and T-shirts load, it takes an hour and a half to dry.

11. Max heard a buzzing sound that sounded like it came from an electronic source. He switched off the TV, but the sound did not go away. He turned off his computer, but the sound persisted. He switched off the lights in the room, but he still heard the sound. He decided that the sound must be coming from the next-door apartment.

12. Chris noticed that for the entire spring semester she had a backache on Tuesdays and Thursdays, but not on the other three school days. On all 5 days she walked the same route to school and back home, and she spent the same amount of hours on campus. She ate similar meals each day and did similar exercise routines. She got the same amount of sleep each night and slept in the same bed each night. But she did note that on Tuesdays and Thursdays she had to carry four heavy textbooks in her backpack instead of only two small books on the other 3 school days.

⭐ 13. TreShawn boiled an egg for 3 minutes. Opening it, he found that it was quite runny. He tried boiling another egg for 4 minutes; it was a little thicker, but still not what he wanted. He boiled another egg for 5 minutes, and it was exactly what he wanted. He then decided to try to get a hard-boiled egg. After adding an additional minute of boiling to each subsequent egg, he determined that the hard-boiled egg he liked took 10 minutes of boiling.

14. Leslie wanted to try to spend less money, so she gathered information about her spending habits. According to her bank records she averaged ten ATM withdraws amounting to $200 a month. She decided to keep the ATM card at home except for Saturdays. For the next 3 months she averaged four withdraws amounting to $80 a month.

15. Five friends (let's call them *1, 2, 3, 4,* and *5*) each lost approximately six pounds in the last month. Friends *2, 4,* and *5* eat meat; friends *1* and *3* are vegetarians; *1, 3, 4,* and *5* drink coffee regularly; *2* drinks nothing but tea; *2, 3,* and *5* work full time; *1* and *4* work part time; *1, 3, 4,* and *5* take night classes; *2* does not take any classes. They have all been meeting three times a week at a gym where they do intense aerobic routines.

C. LIMITATIONS OF MILL'S METHODS

Mill's basic principles can be adapted to a variety of settings in both science and everyday life. In fact, we shall see how they help understand the process of science. However, the methods all have their limitations, especially if they are applied in a simplistic way. Suppose a person woke up 3 mornings in a row with a terrible hangover. He carefully lists what he had the 3 previous nights: Gin and tonic water, vodka and tonic water, and whisky and tonic water. Applying the method of agreement, he concludes that the tonic water caused the hangovers.

Similar mistakes can be made using the method of difference. For example, suppose someone drove to work each day for a year; but with the price of gas getting so high, she decided to start walking to work to save some money. At the end of the workday the manager announces that, because of the economic downturn, everyone will have to take a 10% pay cut. On the way home she reconstructs the evidence. For 1 year, she drove her car to work, and each day there was no pay cut. She walked to work for 1 day, and her pay was cut 10%. She concludes that walking to work caused the pay cut. (For a related discussion, see the *false cause fallacies* section in Chapter 4.)

Although Mill's methods do not provide conclusive proof of causality, they are helpful in discovering correlations and potential causes. However, they still rely heavily on background knowledge in order to get started. Experimenters must list what they think are *relevant* similarities or differences among sets of objects or events. The methods are thus not very helpful in discovering new cause-effect relationships. After all, if we have never encountered a factor before, or never seen it as a cause, we can easily overlook or reject it. Finally, Mill's methods can show only a correlation, but correlation does not guarantee causation. At best, a correlation reveals a probable case of causality. Mill's methods can help reveal a *necessary* ingredient in causation (a *correlation*), they do not by themselves provide *sufficient* evidence of causation.

The ability to discover causes is a powerful tool. When we know how part of the world works, we can often create things that will benefit us, such as vaccines, antibiotics, and cures for diseases. Discovering the cause of malaria enabled scientists to create drugs to fight the disease. Scientists are trying other new approaches as well:

> Scientists working on malaria have found a way of genetically manipulating large populations of mosquitoes that could dramatically reduce the spread of the deadly disease, . . . making genetic changes to a few mosquitoes and then allowing them to breed; genetic alterations could spread through large mosquito populations in just a few generations.
>
> Kate Kelland, "Scientists Tweak Mosquito Genes to Fight Malaria," Reuters

Knowing that certain types of mosquitoes carry the disease to humans has not yet enabled us to eradicate the disease. A complex, worldwide problem like malaria requires a multipronged solution. However, without knowing the cause, we could not even think of rational ways of combating the disease.

Discovering causes also expands our ability to correctly predict the future. If we know what causes things to break, collapse, or burn, then we can often predict their life span. Although we cannot predict with perfect accuracy when any water heater will break, for example, we can use statistical data on similar models to predict the average life expectancy. This information helps you determine when to purchase a new water heater.

Similarly, physicians can often predict with great accuracy how a disease will run its course. This knowledge allows decisive action by targeting the cause and administering potential remedies. Of course, many phenomena are very complex, and our knowledge of the underlying causes may not yet allow accurate predictions. This is especially true for many social issues, such as poverty, crime, and domestic and international conflicts:

> Predictions usually deal with events—who will win an election, whether or not a country will go to war, the specification of a new invention; they center on decisions. Yet such predictions, while possible, cannot be formalized, i.e., made subject to rules. The prediction of events is inherently difficult. Events are the intersect of social vectors (interests, forces, pressures, and the like). While one can to some extent assess the strength of these vectors individually, one would need a "social physics" to predict the exact crosspoints where decisions and forces combine. . . . Forecasting is possible where there are regularities and recurrences of phenomena (these are rare), of where there are persisting trends whose direction, if not an exact trajectory, can be plotted with statistical time-series or be formulated as historical tendencies. Necessarily, therefore, one deals with probabilities and an array of possible

projections. But the limitations of forecasting are also evident. The further one reaches ahead in time with a set of forecasts, the greater the margin for error, since the fan of the projections widens.

Daniel Bell, *The Coming of the Post-Industrial Society*

As we saw, Mill's methods can only reveal evidence of probable causes; they provide no real explanatory power. Discovering instances of causation is an important step in understanding the world—but it is only part of what we need. We also need to understand *how* and *why* particular instances of causation function as they do. Answers to these questions take us beyond being able to identify cause-effect relationships. We must develop theories and hypotheses—the basis of scientific reasoning.

D. THEORETICAL AND EXPERIMENTAL SCIENCE

We sometimes need an explanation that not only captures certain facts, but also gives us a way of discovering new ones. This is what a good **hypothesis** does. It provides an explanation for known facts and provides a way to test our explanation. In addition, a good hypothesis can foster new technologies, which in turn create new ways of exploring the world. These inventions allow us to make more precise observations and to discover new facts.

> **Hypothesis** Provides an explanation for known facts and a way to test an explanation.

PROFILES IN LOGIC

John Stuart Mill

John Stuart Mill (1806–73) believed that the advance of knowledge went hand in hand with advances in human freedom and equality. For Mill, logic plays a crucial role in that advancement. Deductive logic tells us if our reasoning is correct, and inductive logic is our best guide to discovering new truths. Since our inductive inferences are a combination of our current experiences and our memory, the conclusions do not follow with necessity. Although our inductive reasoning is subject to error, Mill argued that a scientific approach to knowledge, however fallible, is superior to superstitious beliefs that direct observation shows to be false.

Mill argued that our ability to recognize patterns existing in nature is the foundation of our discovering the "laws of nature," which in turn are shown to be accurate through our ability to explain and predict. Science advances by assuming that *causes* exist and that we can discover them.

Mill believed that we will find the best ways to live by carefully observing the way the world is. "Few human creatures would consent to be changed into any other lower animals, for a promise of the fullest allowance of a beast's pleasures; no intelligent human being would consent to be a fool, no instructed person would be an ignoramus, no person of feeling and conscience would be selfish and base, even though they should be persuaded that the fool, the dunce, or the rascal is better satisfied with his lot than they are with theirs."

The interplay of science and technology is a complex process, but it thus follows a repeating pattern:

Facts $\rightarrow$ Hypothesis $\rightarrow$ Technology $\rightarrow$ New hypothesis $\rightarrow$ New facts. . . .

For example, the creation of better and stronger lenses allowed Galileo to see clearly the surface of our moon, and to discover some moons of Jupiter. The new information that Galileo gathered by using the improved telescopes helped refute the then generally accepted view of the universe and Earth's place in it.

There are two aspects of science—*theoretical* and *experimental*—and each has an important role to play in our knowledge of the physical world. **Theoretical science** proposes explanations for observations of natural phenomena, while **experimental science** tests those explanations. Both theoretical science and experimental science are involved in the development of new inventions and technologies that may allow us to gather new data and new facts about the physical world.

Theoretical science
Proposes explanations for natural phenomena.

Experimental science
Tests the explanations proposed by theoretical science.

The impact of experimental science and theoretical science that occurred during Galileo's time can be seen throughout the ensuing centuries. For example, recent advances in technology are forcing us to rethink our theories of mind and consciousness; this is especially true in the role that genetics plays in human behavior. We are achieving greater and greater insight into the physiology and chemistry of the brain thanks to such advancements as magnetic resonance imaging (MRI) and computerized axial tomography (CAT) scans. These reveal structures and processes never before seen, which forces us to create new hypotheses of the mind.

Theoretical science, in turn, can have sweeping consequences as well. The *theoretical* breakthrough regarding the structure of DNA, made by James Watson and Francis Crick, provided *experimental* scientists with clues about where to look, what to look for, and what could be predicted based on consequences of the theoretical work. The early twentieth century saw the rise of Albert Einstein's theories of space-time, as well as quantum theory (the physics of subatomic particles). These theories led to many unexpected and unique predictions about the world. When experimental results verified both Einstein's theories and quantum physics, they opened new horizons for understanding the world and our place in it.

Chapter 2 explained how theoretical definitions assign a meaning to a term and assist in understanding how a term fits into a general theory. For example, Mendel's theory of inheritance contains a set of definitions of key terms, such as "trait," "dominant," and "recessive." A theory is scientific if it generates hypotheses that can be tested. A theory that produces untestable hypotheses is not a scientific theory. A fruitful scientific theory is one that generates multiple *confirmed* hypotheses. In contrast, a theory that repeatedly generates *refuted* hypotheses is not useful. The words "confirmed" and "refuted" are not identical to "true" and "false" when they are used to describe hypotheses. Instead, they mean that we have some evidence that *supports* one hypothesis and *denies* the other hypothesis.

The important factor for any theory is its ability to let the physical world decide. A controlled experiment opens the possibility of letting the physical world answer unambiguously "yes" or "no" to our hypotheses. A successful scientific theory also provides fertile ground for invention and experimentation. For example, recently the most precise measurements of an electron ever made suggest that it's nearly perfectly spherical. The laser experiments conducted by researchers at Imperial College London took 10 years to design and complete. One of the researchers made the point well:

> We're really pleased that we've been able to improve our knowledge of one of the basic building blocks of matter. It's been a very difficult measurement to make, but this knowledge will let us improve our theories of fundamental physics. People are often surprised to hear that our theories of physics aren't "finished," but in truth they get constantly refined and improved by making ever more accurate measurements.   ScienceDaily.com

A scientific theory functions like an abstract tool. Physical tools often come with manuals that tell you how to operate the tool safely and effectively. The manuals speak in general terms to let you know which tasks are appropriate. Physical tools can be useful for some tasks and useless for others. For example, a hammer is good for driving nails into wood, but it's not good for delicate brain surgery. Through trial and error we learn the limits of tools.

Just as we do not expect any physical tool to solve all our problems, we should not expect a scientific theory to answer every possible question. For example, because Mendel's theory of inheritance failed to correctly predict a few outcomes for a small set of inherited traits in humans, it was abandoned. However, several decades later scientists realized that Mendel's theory was indeed useful for explaining and predicting many kinds of inheritance problems, but of course not all. In fact, Mendel's theory offers a simple and accurate explanation for why some diseases reappear after a few generations. In many cases the theory can accurately predict the probability that a child will inherit a disease based on the genetic profile of the parents.

Over time we have learned where Mendel's theory works—and where it doesn't. But we are able to learn something about the world only because the hypotheses it generates are testable. This is why experimentation is so important. Scientific experiments and repeated testing under strict controls provide the best method for determining the success, failure, or limitations of a theory. We learn from success, but also from failure.

E. INFERENCE TO THE BEST EXPLANATION

The logician Charles S. Peirce argued that it is a common human trait to infer explanations for our experience, especially for events with recurring patterns. He called this process **abduction**. But what happens when people infer different explanations for the same facts. How do we decide which explanation is correct? In **inference to the best explanation**, we reason from the premise that a hypothesis would explain certain facts to the conclusion that the hypothesis is the best explanation for those facts. Scientists define "best" as *the most probable explanation*, and to learn what is most probable, they make more observations and conduct experiments. We can see science as an interrelated set of elements, all of which support each other in the quest to understand the physical world. Together, they make up the scientific method.

Abduction The process that occurs when we infer explanations for certain facts.

Inference to the best explanation When we reason from the premise that a hypothesis would explain certain facts to the conclusion that the hypothesis is the best explanation for those facts.

For example, suppose that there was no snow in your yard when you went to sleep, but when you woke up there was snow in the yard. This is a fact, and one explanation is that it snowed last night. A second explanation is that your friends have executed an elaborate prank by placing artificial snow in your yard. How do we decide which explanation is best? We had better gather more evidence.

The idea is to force the explanation to predict something else that we do not know yet. For example, we might look around the neighborhood to see if there is snow anywhere besides your yard. If there is snow everywhere in the neighborhood, then it is unlikely that your friends would have been able to get hold of that much artificial snow. If snow is everywhere in the neighborhood, then we say that the snow hypothesis has been *confirmed* and the prank hypothesis has been *refuted*. Gathering additional evidence is an ongoing process. Only in exceptional cases can a single confirmation or refutation establish a definitive answer. Instead, the accumulation of evidence after repeated experiments points us in the right direction.

To see why we cannot determine the best explanation based solely on what we already know, take the two hypotheses to explain the snow in your yard. The reasoning might go as follows:

- If it snowed last night, then there is snow in your yard. There is snow in your yard. Therefore, it snowed last night.
- If your friends played a prank on you last night, then there is snow in your yard. There is snow in your yard. Therefore, your friends played a prank on you last night.

Both arguments commit the fallacy of affirming the consequent; they are, therefore, both invalid. This is why we need evidence that goes beyond the known facts. We need to think of things that we can do that will allow us to gather new facts, and this additional information will help us decide which explanation is better.

The same process can be seen in a criminal trial. The prosecution needs to gather important and relevant incriminating evidence in order to convince the jury of the guilt of the defendant. But what proves guilt "beyond a reasonable doubt"? It may take several additional pieces of evidence. Of course, the defense will do its best to discredit the prosecution's evidence.

In biology, Charles Darwin's reasoning was partly based on his inference that, although natural selection was not the only explanation for the diversity of species, as far as he could determine, it was the best explanation. In fiction, Sherlock Holmes often made this remark: "Once you eliminate the impossible, whatever remains, no matter how improbable, must be the truth." The private detective started his reasoning process with a set of facts. Next, he devised various hypotheses—his possible suspects. Holmes's subsequent investigations and research led him to a series of new facts that, one by one, allowed him to eliminate hypotheses until one remained—the best explanation. (Holmes referred to his method as "deduction," but he repeatedly used the process of abduction.)

Our hypotheses are only as good as our imagination. We might fail to think of the correct hypothesis. In this sense, abduction has many of the drawbacks that we saw with Mill's methods. Whether we hit on the correct hypothesis often depends on our background knowledge, our wit, and our imagination. This is why breakthroughs in science and other fields often take so long. It sometimes takes several generations for someone to think of the correct hypothesis or to devise a new way of gathering evidence—a novel experiment—that will point us in the right direction.

Peirce's ideas apply to a recent tragedy. Many explanations for the earthquake and the devastating tsunami that struck Japan in 2011 have been proposed. Here are three:

- The disasters are God's way of punishing the Japanese for their attack on Pearl Harbor.
- The Japanese built the nuclear plants too close to the ocean.
- Japan is located on the Pacific "rim of fire," which is one of the world's major geological fault lines. It has a long history of powerful earthquakes and massive tsunamis, and similar disasters have been documented for centuries.

The first hypothesis does nothing to explain the dozens of earthquakes and tsunamis that have occurred in the same places in Japan going back several centuries—long before the attack on Pearl Harbor. The second hypothesis might help explain why the nuclear power plants were damaged by the earthquake and tsunami. They were built too close to the ocean. However, it does nothing to explain the cause of the earthquake and the tsunami. The third hypothesis provides a causal explanation based on historical data, contemporary knowledge of the causes of earthquakes and tsunamis, and their probability.

In cases like this, perhaps we can pay attention to Peirce's advice: "Facts cannot be explained by a hypothesis more extraordinary than these facts themselves; and of various hypotheses the least extraordinary must be adopted" (quoted in *The Play of Musement* by Thomas Sebeok).

F. HYPOTHESIS TESTING, EXPERIMENTS, AND PREDICTIONS

Hypotheses are sometimes easy to propose but difficult to test. Exploring this idea will allow us to see how experiments and predictions help us understand the world. This, in turn, will enable us to analyze scientific reasoning in greater detail.

Controlled Experiments

The best way to test a hypothesis is with a **controlled experiment**—an experiment in which multiple experimental setups differ by only one variable. You might have recognized that the principle behind this kind of research is Mill's method of difference. In fact, many of Mill's methods have been adapted for modern scientific research. This should not be surprising, since we know that the methods are useful for revealing instances of correlation and uncovering potential causes.

In everyday life, many variables affect the outcome of a given situation, often making strong cause-effect claims very difficult. But a laboratory setting can reduce the

Controlled experiment
One in which multiple experimental setups differ by only one variable.

Experimental group
The group that gets the variable being tested.

Control group The group in which the variable being tested is withheld.

number of variables. For example, suppose we want to see the effect of a new fertilizer on plant growth. The idea is to make things as similar as possible—except for one variable. The researchers need to control the plant seeds, growing areas, soil, amount of water, and available sunlight, making sure that these items are as similar as possible for every plant in the experiment. One group of plants, the **experimental group**, is given a precise amount of a fertilizer, which the other group, the **control group**, does not get. At the end of the experiment, the plants in the two groups are compared. Any statistical difference between the groups—for example, size or crop yield—might then be ascribed to the fertilizer. Further tests must then duplicate all the experimental factors. These *repeated trials* are necessary before the effects of the fertilizer, positive or negative, can be accepted as definitive.

Through this painstaking attention to detail and methodical procedure, controlled laboratory experiments help scientists to uncover causal relationships. A scientific theory must stand up to the severest testing we can devise. It must provide coherent and effective explanations. It must provide correct predictions repeatedly, and help us to discover new facts about the world. When opponents of Darwin's theory of evolution by natural selection call it "only a theory," they ignore what a theory means in science. They ignore how much it predicts, the repeated success of its predictions, and the breadth of causal relationships that it has helped biologists to discover.

Determining Causality

Of course, many things can affect the results of an experiment, forcing scientists to go to great lengths to ensure that nothing disrupts the experimental setting. In addition, since a controlled experiment is by definition "artificial," the results may not match real life. For example, quite often laboratory experiments that test new drugs are conducted on animals whose physiology does not match that of humans. Consequently, positive (or negative) results with the laboratory animals may not match what we would find if the drug were given to humans. This is why taking the results of controlled laboratory experiments and proclaiming that similar connections exist in the outside world is so problematic. Most scientists candidly admit that their promising lab results may not fit the world at large. Unfortunately, popularized versions of laboratory results are sometimes disseminated mistakenly to the public. This is why we often see claims that a cure for a disease has been found, or that scientists have isolated the cause of a disease, only to be disappointed later on.

In understanding the complex nature of causality, we can point to five criteria:

CRITERIA FOR DETERMINING CAUSALITY
1.   There should be a *correlation* between the *cause* and the *effect*.
2.   The cause should precede the effect.
3.   The cause should be in the *proximity* of the effect.
4.   A set of *necessary* and *sufficient* conditions should exist.
5.   *Alternative explanations* should be ruled out.

None of the five criteria alone is sufficient to establish a cause-effect relationship. Instead, it is the weight of the answers to all five criteria that together establishes the grounds for a satisfactory cause-effect relationship.

As we saw earlier, a correlation alone cannot establish a causal relationship. For example, there is a strong correlation between a barometer falling and a storm. There is also a strong correlation between people putting on swimsuits and getting wet. In neither case do we have a causal relationship.

The second criterion cautions us to consider the time lag between the cause and the effect. The longer the time between the cause and the effect, the more the situation can be interrupted by other variables that might have brought about the effect. This same note of caution is realized in the third criterion. The greater the spatial distance between the cause and the effect the greater the chance of other variables interfering.

The fourth criterion derives its meaning from the results of our discussion of necessary and sufficient conditions. In other words, the criterion requires that a claim that "X caused Y" must be backed by two things: (1) X was *sufficient* to bring about Y; and (2) X was *necessary* for Y (without X, Y would *not* have occurred).

The fifth criterion, the ability to rule out plausible alternative explanations, is the glue that unifies the set. Any causal claim can be challenged by suggestions of alternative potential causes. (We saw this earlier in the example of the two competing hypotheses for the snow in your yard.) Therefore, a strong causal claim should be backed up by evidence that confirms the hypothesis, and evidence that refutes (or disconfirms) rival, alternative causal claims.

Each of these five criteria has its place in science. They can also help us see how scientific explanations are vastly different from superstitious beliefs.

G. SCIENCE AND SUPERSTITION

Even in science, a causal hypothesis is often extremely difficult to test directly. Although it may say something about the world that is either true or false (for example, "The disease was caused by a parasite"), we cannot simply look at a hypothesis and directly determine its truth or falsity. We must force the hypothesis to do something—to put itself out on a limb, so to speak. This is accomplished by getting the hypothesis to make a *prediction*.

The Need for a Fair Test

A proposed experiment is simply another way of asking the question "What if we do this?" For example, if your car does not start, someone might suggest that you have a dead battery. Although the suggestion (which is a hypothesis or conjecture) is either true or false, we cannot discover the answer by looking at the battery. What we can do is propose a simple experiment: What if we try the headlights? The person who hypothesized that we have a dead battery would be forced to predict that the headlights would not work (in most cars the headlights need power from the battery). If the headlights come on as normal, then the prediction is false, and we would have evidence to refute (disconfirm) the hypothesis. However, if the headlights do not come on as normal, then the prediction is true and we would have evidence to support (confirm) the hypothesis.

We can try different experiments in order to get different predictions. For example, if we disconnect the battery, take it to a garage, and hook it up to a battery tester (the experiment), the dead-battery hypothesis would predict that the battery would have little or no power. Again, this prediction is either true or false, and the results can be used to confirm or disconfirm the hypothesis. Another possible experiment would be to try to start the car using jumper cables that are attached to another car's battery. If the dead-battery hypothesis is correct, the car should then start. The truth or falsity of this prediction will again be the indirect evidence that confirms or refutes the hypothesis.

Predictions are crucial to our understanding of the truth of hypotheses. In fact, even a hypothesis that does not make an explicit causal claim should be tested. Since predictions are generally specific statements that are testable, they provide the means for determining, *indirectly*, the truth or falsity of the hypothesis. After an experiment is completed, we can take the truth value of the prediction and trace it back to its source, the hypothesis. Therefore, the fate of the hypothesis rests on the fate of the prediction.

When considering scientific results, we must make decisions about the relevance of the available evidence. We need to have criteria that will eliminate evidence that is misleading or irrelevant. These criteria must also help us to decide how much weight to give each piece of evidence. This is required if we are to judge accurately the strength of a causal argument. Here are three requirements for acceptable predictions that ensure that a fair test of a causal hypothesis has been conducted:

REQUIREMENTS FOR A FAIR TEST OF A CAUSAL HYPOTHESIS
1. The prediction should be *verifiable*. 2. The prediction should *not* be *trivial*. 3. The prediction should have a *logical connection* to the hypothesis.

Verifiable Predictions

Verifiable prediction
One where the prediction, if it is true, must include an observable event.

A **verifiable prediction** is a prediction that, if it is true, includes an observable event. Suppose there is a house where all the people living there got sick for no apparent reason. Two causal hypotheses are put forward:

Hypothesis 1: A high degree of radioactivity in the house is causing the illness.
Hypothesis 2: A disease-causing ghost is haunting this house.

Many people smile when they encounter hypothesis 2, but not when they read hypothesis 1. The two hypotheses are statements that could be either true or false. Also, neither hypothesis can be tested directly by simply looking around the house, because both of the conjectured entities are things that are invisible to the unaided human eye (radioactivity and ghosts). But are both hypotheses equally testable and verifiable?

An advocate of hypothesis 1 might predict that if we take a Geiger counter and go around the house (the experiment), then we will find a high reading of radioactivity. If the Geiger counter is operating correctly, and we do get a high reading, then we can safely say that the prediction is true; therefore, the hypothesis has some evidence to support, or confirm, it. However, if there is no sign of radioactivity, then the prediction is false, and we would have evidence to disconfirm (or refute) the hypothesis. A verifiable prediction does not have to be true, only verifiable. There must be a method for deciding, clearly and objectively, the truth or falsity of the prediction.

We would accept the evidence for or against hypothesis 1 because Geiger counters are an established source of scientific evidence. Their reliability has been repeatedly confirmed. In fact, they were invented as a way of detecting what is invisible to human eyes. Geiger counters provide one source of empirical evidence in the complex field of subatomic particles and quantum physics. We understand how Geiger counters work, and we trust them to be a good source of objective evidence. There is also a well-established theoretical framework that secures their place in the scientific community.

Let's turn now to hypothesis 2. What would function as a device that is comparable to the Geiger counter? Short of a *Ghostbusters*-type gadget, there seems to be no comparable method of gathering evidence for the ghost hypothesis. A ghost hypothesis defender might say "But of course the ghost is invisible, so it is impossible to detect." Yet exactly the same challenge confronted hypothesis 1, since we cannot see radioactivity either. Nevertheless, we are able to gather indirect physical evidence to decide if the radioactivity is actually there. In addition, although radioactivity is invisible, we know that it is a part of the physical world and is therefore subject to detection.

Our knowledge of the physical reality of radioactivity also allows us to determine how it causes illness. We have learned how radioactivity affects human tissue and alters human cells, often leading to tragic results. The ghost hypothesis provides no comparable understanding. For example, if ghosts are not only invisible, but also immaterial (not part of the physical world), as many ghost hypotheses allege, then it would be extremely difficult to explain how ghosts could physically affect us. Quite often ghost stories are filled with inconsistencies. For example, a movie might depict a ghost walking unimpeded through doors or walls, but in the next instant the ghost is seen climbing stairs. If the ghost is truly immaterial, then it should not be able to interact with any material objects.

We can assert, then, that a prediction does not meet the first requirement whenever there is no acceptable method to check objectively the truth value of the prediction. Therefore, we need not accept as evidence someone's subjective claim that he can see ghosts.

Nontrivial Predictions

The first requirement for a fair test of a causal hypothesis turns on predictions of future observations and future experiments. The second requirement turns on what we already know and wish to explain. A **nontrivial prediction** requires reference to background knowledge, which is everything we know to be true. It includes all facts and hypotheses

Nontrivial prediction
The prediction requires reference to background knowledge, which is everything we know to be true.

that have already been confirmed or disconfirmed. Of course, background knowledge changes over time. Therefore, to decide if a prediction satisfies the second requirement, it is necessary to judge it in the light of what we know at the time it is put forth.

Suppose I claim to have the power to see the future (hypothesis). Of course, my claim is either true or false. Now, having understood and accepted the first requirement for a fair test of a hypothesis, you correctly ask me to provide some evidence. That is easy enough for me to do. If all you want is a prediction that is verifiable, then I predict that tomorrow the sun will come up. If you have only the first requirement to use, then you are forced to accept my prediction as being a fair test of the hypothesis. Therefore, the claim that I have the power to see the future will most probably turn out to be true. However, this should *not* be acceptable. We want to avoid situations such as this; we want to be able to eliminate predictions like this one, ones that are highly likely to be true. This is just what the second requirement effectively does. It provides a way of handling predictions that should not be used as evidence. Without the second requirement, we would be forced to accept almost anything as evidence, as long as it is merely verifiable (as long as it satisfied the first requirement). Although the first requirement is a necessary condition, by itself it is not a sufficient condition to ensure a fair test of a hypothesis.

Let's get back to the hypothesis that I have the power to see the future. The second requirement for predictions allows us to eliminate predictions that we consider trivial, and hence carry no weight. This new requirement forces me to revise my original prediction ("The sun will come up tomorrow") because as it stands, even if it turns out true (which is a near certainty), it will carry no weight in support of my hypothesis.

PROFILES IN LOGIC

Charles S. Peirce

C. S. Peirce (1839–1914) is recognized as the greatest American philosopher-mathematician. He did outstanding work in both logic and mathematics, creating many of the notations used today. According to Peirce, the conclusions of mathematics follow by necessity, but logic is broader still, because it investigates any and all kinds of arguments.

In philosophy he founded *pragmatism*, the application of scientific methods and results to philosophical problems. Peirce coined the term "abduction" to an all-encompassing activity—generating hypotheses in order to explain facts and to deduce predictions. Deduction and induction alone, he believed, are not sufficient to complete logic.

Peirce stressed the use of truth tables as a way to reveal the logic behind truth-functional operators. Although it took the work of others, most notably the philosopher Ludwig Wittgenstein (1889–1951), before truth tables were fully accepted, this system became the perfect tool for something else as well: It helped in creating computers. The system of truth values (true and false) is a foundation of computer languages and hardware applications.

Accepting this criticism now forces me to be more specific. I offer this prediction as evidence of my power to see the future:

> Tomorrow, at exactly 1:35 PM, it will start raining on the steps of the U.S. Capitol building. Then it will stop raining at exactly 1:57 PM. But it will rain only on the steps of the Capitol building; it will not rain anywhere else in Washington, D.C.

Would you accept this as a good test? Is this prediction trivial? What we know about the weather should lead us to say that the prediction, being so specific about something that is as unpredictable as the weather in a specific part of a city, is nontrivial. This is all that the second requirement asks of a prediction. Furthermore, the prediction meets the first requirement, because it is easily verifiable. Therefore, according to the first two requirements, this would be a fair test of the hypothesis. Of course, when my prediction turns out to be false, then you would have good evidence that refutes my hypothesis. Therefore, you should be willing to accept the challenge, because it is almost certain that my prediction will fail.

The history of Halley's Comet illustrates the principles we have been describing. Applying part of Isaac Newton's theories, Edmund Halley hypothesized that comets reappear in regular cycles. In 1705, Halley predicted that a comet would appear in the year 1758 in a precise location of the sky. In order to judge whether his prediction was trivial, we have to consider, not what we know to be true today, but rather what the background knowledge was in 1705. Halley's hypothesis was not yet part of what was known to be true. Therefore, his prediction was considered, at that time, unlikely to be true.

If Halley had predicted that a comet would appear *somewhere* in the sky *sometime* in the 1750s, this would have been a trivial prediction, because many comets had been observed throughout recorded history. The phrase "*somewhere* in the sky," is vague, and the range of dates—"*sometime* in the 1750s"—is too long to offer any precision to the prediction. Therefore, when Halley's specific, and unlikely, prediction did in fact turn out to be true (in the location and time predicted), scientists had good justification for claiming that his hypothesis was also true (based on the confirming evidence).

Halley's hypothesis then became part of the background knowledge, something scientists knew to be true. Therefore, after 1758, if anyone predicted that Halley's Comet would reappear in another 76 years, this would have been considered likely to be true. Therefore, future predictions regarding the return of Halley's Comet do not carry the same weight as the initial one. Each correct prediction confirms the hypothesis to some extent, but the weight diminishes with each subsequent confirmation. When background knowledge changes, then our decisions regarding the second requirement often change as well.

Connecting the Hypothesis and Prediction

The third requirement for an acceptable prediction ensures that there is a connection between the hypothesis and the prediction. This is necessary, because we want to transfer the truth value from the prediction back to the hypothesis. We therefore need a direct link.

To derive a prediction from a hypothesis, we must first develop an experiment that will test the hypothesis. We cannot simply take a hypothesis and deduce a prediction straight away. For example, Halley's hypothesis simply stated that comets are part of Newtonian particle systems. From this claim nothing much can be predicted. However, Halley consulted the information about comets that had been gathered over many centuries. He noticed a pattern: A comet appeared in a specific place in the sky in 1682, 1606, and 1530. Halley conjectured that they were instances of the same comet. In other words, from the available data and his hypothesis that comets return, he was able to calculate the next return of the comet. This process enabled Halley to make a specific prediction. Of course, the prediction could have turned out to be false. However, when the prediction did turn out to be true, then the truth value could be transferred back to the hypothesis as confirmation. (Unfortunately, Halley did not live long enough to see his hypothesis confirmed.)

Science and Superstition

These examples illustrate the vast difference between science and superstition. Our knowledge of the world has allowed us to shed some beliefs that were based on a general lack of understanding of the physical world. For example, although we do not yet know everything about human diseases, we do know enough to say that they are caused by physical processes.

Of course, some individuals refuse to accept medical and scientific advances. These people often stubbornly refuse to allow medical treatment for their children, for example. The result is that sometimes society has to step in and provide the medical assistance that might cure the disease, or at least reduce the symptoms, and needless pain and suffering. Still others refuse to accept evolution or global warming. Their beliefs have practical and political consequences.

Evolutionary theory faces an ongoing battle. Based on the standards that we have been discussing in this chapter, there should be no question that evolutionary theory is scientific. It is highly testable, it has been tested repeatedly, and it has been tremendously successful and fruitful in explaining a large part of the world. Creationism or "intelligent design" cannot make the same claims. It does not generate testable hypotheses and is not fruitful in explaining anything new about the physical world. It does not meet the basic criteria for a scientific theory as set forth in this chapter.

Physical tools and inventions are usually put through rigorous tests in order to learn the conditions under which they are likely to fail. When, how, and why they fail unlocks part of nature's secrets. This knowledge provides the basis for improving our inventions. The same holds for scientific theories. Our scientific knowledge of the world advances by confronting our theories with new problems. If the theory fails, then we can improve it. However, a nonscientific theory insulates itself from failure—it does not help us learn anything new about the world.

Applying the criteria for testing hypotheses can help expose false beliefs. For example, some people have claimed to be able to perform *mental telepathy*, the act of sending and receiving thoughts. A few believers have accepted the challenge of displaying their "powers" in controlled scientific experiments. One simple test is to place two people in separate rooms and show one of them a series of cards. The cards might be pictures of animals, they might have numbers written on them, or they can be ordinary playing cards. If experimental subjects can perform mental telepathy, then they should score higher on their responses than non-telepathists.

Suppose you were told that someone in another room is going to turn over a random series of ten cards. Your job is to guess what is written on each card. You are told that each card has one number written on it. To make it easy, the numbers run from 1 to 10, and no number occurs twice. Using simple probability, we can see that you should guess correctly approximately 10% of the time. Repeated experiments have shown this to be the case.

The self-proclaimed mental telepathists who agreed to be tested under strict experimental conditions scored no higher than other subjects. When confronted with the results, some subjects refused to accept the outcome. They resorted to *ad hoc* rescue of their belief ("*ad hoc*" means "for this specific purpose"); an *ad hoc* rescue is an attempt to save a belief that has been confronted with refuting evidence. For example, subjects might say, skeptics (like the experimenters) give off "negative waves" that interfere with the positive telepathic waves. In other words, subjects may say in defense that there is something about a scientific experiment that causes the failure. And, yes, there is indeed something about a well-controlled scientific experiment: It reveals the truth.

A rational and scientific approach can reveal the utter foolishness of many nonscientific beliefs. For example, based on his cryptic calculations and reading of the Bible, Harold Camping predicted that the "rapture" would occur on May 21, 2011. We were told that all good Christians would ascend to heaven that day, while everyone else would be left behind to suffer until the end of the world. Camping predicted that God would completely destroy the Earth (and presumably the entire universe) after 5 months, on October 21, 2011. If you are reading this after the due date, then Camping was wrong.

Camping has a history of failed predictions about the end of the world. He previously predicted that it would occur on May 21, 1988. When that day came and went he then predicted that it would end on September 7, 1994. After each of his first two failed predictions, Camping resorted to *ad hoc* rescue. He proclaimed that he had miscalculated, but that his basic system was correct. It just needed some fine-tuning. (To be fair, Camping is not the only one to fail miserably in his predictions; failed predictions of the end of the world litter the pages of history.)

Although Camping's system of calculations and predictions based on his interpretations of the Bible are scientifically bankrupt, they are not economic failures. His Family Radio and ministry have generated more than $100 million in donations, some of it from people who sold everything they had because of their fervent belief in Camping's predictions. This is an example where an understanding of sound reasoning and sound claims can have enormous practical consequences.

The Allure of Superstition

The allure of superstitions and their psychological hold on humans are not difficult to understand. Here is one explanation of why superstitions are so easily formed, and why they are so difficult to remove:

> It was in 1947 that a dozen pigeons gave researchers at the University of Indiana what was to prove the most fundamental insight into the roots of superstition and magic—even, many would argue, of religion itself. These birds were put on restricted rations, so that before long their body weight had fallen by 25% and they were permanently hungry. When each bird had, in the words of Professor Burrhus Frederic (B.F.) Skinner, been "brought to a stable state of hunger," it found itself spending several minutes every day in a special cage. At one end of the cage was an automatic food hopper, linked to a timer so that it would swing into place every 15 seconds, and remain in place for five seconds before disappearing.
>
> Crucial to the set-up was the fact that, no matter what the pigeon did, the food came and went at set intervals. For the purpose of the experiment was to observe what affect its comings and goings had on the pigeons. And, sad to say, it made them—and, by extension, us—look somewhat foolish.
>
> Before long, one of the pigeons had begun making strange counterclockwise turns in the intervals between the hopper's arrivals. Others indulged in repetitive head movements, while two birds developed a complicated pendulum motion of the head and body. By the end of the experiment, six of the eight subjects were performing elaborate routines, clearly with the intention of hastening the return of the food. In each case, the routine grew out of some action that the bird had just happened to be performing when the hopper appeared.
>
> Describing what is now regarded as a classic experiment, Skinner was in no doubt as to the mechanism involved: "The bird behaves as if there were a causal relation between its behavior and the presentation of food, although such a relation is lacking." . . . "The experiment," he said, "might be said to demonstrate a sort of superstition."
>
> David Newnham, "Hostages to Fortune," *Guardian*

It is the interplay of hypotheses, data, experiments, and predictions that establishes authentic scientific understanding of the world. We cannot deduce a prediction only from a hypothesis; we cannot make a prediction only from data; and we cannot get a prediction only from an experiment. A scientific prediction is the offspring of hypotheses, data, and experiments; it is a direct logical consequence that may or may not actually fit the real world. If the prediction turns out to be true, then the hypothesis is confirmed (to some degree). If the prediction turns out to be false, then the hypothesis is refuted.

Notice that in this process we transfer the truth value to the hypothesis. (It is said to be *confirmed* or *disconfirmed*.) But what about the experiment's role in the process?

Could something have gone wrong with the experimental setup? These are very important questions. If the prediction is a product of the hypothesis, data, and the experiment, then why is the hypothesis saddled with the results? Part of the answer lies in our ability to check directly the experimental setup and the data. This is another reason why the results of a single experiment are never taken as a final proof. Scientific experiments must be repeated and the results must be replicated. It is the cumulative aspect of scientific research in the light of repeated and rigorous testing over long periods of time and under varying conditions that makes science our best guide to understanding the physical world.

It is important to remember that the application of the scientific method attempts to confirm or refute a hypothesis. As such, this process should always be considered partial and tentative. The weight we give to a confirmation or refutation is never all or nothing. We must accumulate evidence over a long time. If we make mistakes, they will be revealed by the results of repeated experiments.

CHECK YOUR UNDERSTANDING 14G

I. Answer "true" or "false" to the following:

1. Inference to the best explanation produces a valid argument.
Answer: False

2. Experimental science proposes explanations for observations of natural phenomena.

3. The process of abduction occurs when we infer explanations for certain facts.

4. A good hypothesis provides an explanation of facts and gives us a way of discovering new facts.

★ 5. The results of experiments are used to confirm (support) or disconfirm (refute) a hypothesis.

6. A controlled experiment tries to establish a causal link between several variables at once.

7. A prediction must be unlikely to be true based on our background knowledge.

8. The control group is the group that gets the variable being tested.

★ 9. Each of the five criteria for establishing causality is a sufficient condition for supporting a causal claim.

10. A prediction must be something that is verifiable means that it must be true.

II. Create two different hypotheses to explain the circumstances in each of the following situations. For each hypothesis, think of an experiment that would result in additional evidence that could be used to either confirm or refute the hypothesis. (*Note:*

It is often possible to devise a single experiment to test more than one hypothesis at the same time, but it is not required.)

1. You come home to find that the lights in your apartment do not work. You then determine that nothing that requires electricity works in your apartment.

Answer:

Hypothesis 1: The circuit breaker in your fuse box tripped off.
Experiment 1: Check the fuse box settings.
Hypothesis 2: There is no electricity in other apartments on your floor due to a main circuit malfunction.
Experiment 2: Call the building superintendent to see if other apartments are affected.

2. A credit card company calls to tell you that your payment is overdue. However, you know that you sent them a check by mail more than a week ago.

3. You turn the key in the ignition of your car and the car does not start. In fact, there is just a small clicking sound when you turn the key.

4. After washing your clothes at the Laundromat, you place everything in a dryer and put in enough money for one hour of drying time. You return in 1 hour to find that your clothes are still as wet as when you first put them in the dryer.

⭐ 5. You go away for a 2-week vacation and ask your friend to water your houseplants. When you return you see that the plants are dying.

6. You are a salesclerk in a clothing store. A customer comes in and complains that you did not give her the correct change when she purchased a few items less than half an hour ago.

7. You are driving your car when suddenly you notice that the gas gauge is almost at empty. However, you know that you just filled up the gas tank yesterday and you have not driven the car since then.

8. You had a soft-boiled egg and a coffee with milk, but no sugar for breakfast; then you had a cheeseburger and yogurt shake for lunch. On your way home your stomach begins to ache.

⭐ 9. You are using your cell phone to talk to your mother when the connection suddenly ends. You try dialing your mother's number, but you cannot get a dial tone on the phone.

10. Arrangements have been made for you to meet your friend at a certain movie theater. Before leaving your house, you verified the time and place, and your friend said that he was taking a taxi to meet you. The movie is about to start in 5 minutes and your friend has not arrived. Neither one of you has a cell phone.

III. Analyze the following fictional case studies by picking out the hypothesis, experiment, and prediction. Does the evidence offered in the case study confirm or disconfirm the hypothesis? How much weight would you give to the evidence? If a causal claim is being put forward, then analyze the strength of the argument by checking for any reasonable alternative explanations or other possible facts which, if uncovered, would weaken the causal claim.

1. There have been reports from around the world of some extraordinary "operations." It seems that people with cancerous tumors have been "cured" without any incisions made. When captured on film, the "doctor" seems to be pressing on the patient's body where the tumor is located. Suddenly, blood begins to ooze and the tumor appears to be removed. When cleaned, the patient shows no sign of having been cut. Skeptical researchers did some checking. They performed two simple experiments. First, they tested the material supposedly taken from the patient's body. The patients and their "doctors" claimed that they were cancerous tumors. Results of laboratory analysis showed that the material and blood were from a pig. The second experiment was to take the patients back to the clinic or hospital where the tumors were first noticed, and where records and X-rays were available, in order to see if the tumors had been removed. In all cases, the tumors were exactly where they had originally been; none had been removed.

Answer:

Hypothesis: Cancerous tumors can be physically removed by "surgery," but without any incision.

Experiment: There are two experiments. (A) Test the material (supposedly) taken from the patient to determine its composition. (B) Check the patients to see if the tumors had been removed.

Prediction: The "doctors" and the believing patients (those putting forth the hypothesis) should predict the following: (a) the material will be human cancerous tissue; (b) the tumors will no longer be in the patient.

Confirm/Disconfirm: Since both predictions were false, the evidence gathered from the experiments disconfirms the hypothesis. The evidence carries a lot of weight, because the scientific results are objective and can be accepted as a clear refutation of the hypothesis.

Alternative Explanations: A reasonable explanation is that the "doctors" were scam artists or sleight-of-hand tricksters preying on desperate people.

2. Recently, some physiological psychologists have hypothesized that something in the blood of schizophrenics causes their abnormal behavior. In order to test their conjecture they took some blood from a patient who had been receiving treatment for acute schizophrenia. The researchers then took two groups of spiders that regularly spin uniformly geometrical webs. One group of spiders was given a small injection of the blood, while the other group was left untouched. For the next 2 weeks, the spiders given the blood produced bizarre, asymmetrical webs, which one researcher called *surreal*. The other group spun their normal webs. The

researchers are claiming that this supports their contention that there is some, as yet unknown, factor in the schizophrenic's blood that caused the spider's unusual behavior, and is causing the abnormal behavior in the human subject.

3. I decided to revisit the "executive monkey syndrome" hypothesis. Many years ago some researchers stumbled onto what they thought was evidence that the psychological pressure of "command decisions" caused illness. They restrained two monkeys in chairs. One monkey was provided with a button that, if pressed at the right time, would stop an electrical shock given to both monkeys at the same time. This was the "executive monkey." The other monkey had no way to stop the shock. The executive monkey learned quickly that it could stop the shock from occurring, and it seemed preoccupied with timing the button pressing. This went on for some weeks. Once the experiment was completed, autopsies on the two monkeys revealed that the "executive" had stomach ulcers while the other monkey had none. However, subsequent research has failed to duplicate these results.

4. If you bought a condo in the wrong tower, you were unlucky. It has been revealed that tenants living in one of the two *Sublime Inn* towers are suffering from a mysterious disease. It is believed that the disease is linked to a fungus growing in the air-conditioning system of the tower. The towers are both 5 years old and were built by the same contractor, yet there is no sign of the fungus in the other tower. Engineers, medical personnel, and others are looking for any other difference between the two towers, or between the tenants themselves, that could explain what is happening.

★ 5. Joe's car would not start. He wondered why. His friend said the battery was dead. Joe replaced the battery. The car started. The friend said that this proved he was right.

6. Joe's car would not start. He wondered why. His friend said the battery was dead. Joe turned on the car's headlights. They came on with normal intensity. Joe knew that it was not the battery.

7. "The garlic is what does it," says Ralph. He was referring to his dog, Balboa, now 14 years of age. "I started mixing a clove of garlic into his dog food ever since he was a puppy. There were six puppies in the litter when he was born. I've kept track of Balboa's sisters and brothers and all of them died before they were 10 years old. He's the last one left. The garlic's what done it."

8. The study of twins separated at birth confirms that genetics controls your destiny. Researchers tracked down a set of twins, now 25 years old, and checked for similarities. Both males eat the same brand of cereal, smoke the same brand of cigarettes, have each married a nurse, work as auto mechanics, and are registered Democrats, and yet neither twin has ever come in contact with the other. The only possible cause of these remarkable similarities is that they have the identical genetic makeup.

★ 9. For the past 2 weeks, every time Becky's cat, Melanie, sat on her lap, Becky started sneezing uncontrollably. Thinking that she was becoming allergic to her cat, Becky tried an experiment. She gave the cat to her neighbor for a day; during that time, she did not sneeze. As soon as the cat returned and sat on Becky's lap, she began sneezing. Becky started taking some over-the-counter allergy medicine, and the sneezing stopped. What Becky did not know was that the bottle of a new kind of flea powder her husband started using a few weeks earlier had broken, and so he bought the powder they had always used before. Becky continues to take the allergy medicine.

10. Pete was videotaping his sister Nancy while she was walking toward the line of people waiting to go on a roller-coaster ride. Nancy fell hard on the concrete and broke her arm. After getting the arm set and placed in a cast, Pete watched the video to see if he could determine why Nancy fell. Nancy had maintained that someone had pushed her from behind. However, when Pete replayed the video recording of the event, he could not see anyone near her. The next day he decided to go back to the park to see if he could find something that might have made Nancy trip and fall. Using the video as a guide, he located the spot where she fell; however, he could not find a hole in the ground or any uneven surface that might have cause her to fall. Pete concluded that Nancy must have lost her balance as she was walking.

Summary

- The word "cause" has several meanings, and in everyday situations the possibility of ambiguity arises.
- Causal network: A set of conditions that bring about an effect.
- Normal state: The historical information regarding an object.
- Abnormal state: A drastic change in the normal state. Any change from the normal state requires an explanation, typically a causal one.
- Precipitating cause: The object or event directly involved in bringing about an effect.
- Remote cause: Something that is connected to the precipitating cause by a chain of events.
- Method of agreement: The method that looks at two or more instances of an event to see what they have in common.
- Method of difference: The method that looks for what all the instances of an event do not have in common.
- Joint method of agreement and difference: If two or more instances of an event have only one thing in common, while the instances in which it does *not* occur all share the absence of that thing, then the item is a likely cause.
- Method of residues: The method that subtracts from a complex set of events those parts that already have known causes.

- Method of concomitant variations: The method that looks for two factors that vary together.
- Correlation: A correspondence between two sets of objects, events, or sets of data.
- Although Mill's methods do not provide conclusive proof of causality, the five methods are helpful in discovering correlations and potential causes.
- A good hypothesis provides an explanation for known facts and a way to test an explanation.
- Theoretical science proposes explanations for natural phenomena, while experimental science tests those explanations.
- The process of abduction occurs when we infer explanations for certain facts.
- Inference to the best explanation: When we reason from the premise that a hypothesis would explain certain facts to the conclusion that the hypothesis is the best explanation for those facts.
- Controlled experiment: One in which multiple experimental setups differ by only one variable.
- Experimental group: The group that gets the variable being tested.
- Control group: The group in which the variable being tested is withheld.
- Five criteria need to be considered to fully appreciate the complexity of causality: (1) There should be a correlation between the cause and the effect. (2) The cause should precede the effect. (3) The cause should be in the proximity of the effect. (4) A set of necessary and sufficient conditions should exist. (5) Alternative explanations should be ruled out.
- The weight of our answers to all five criteria together establishes the grounds for a satisfactory cause-effect relationship.
- We can test a hypothesis by getting it to make a prediction. Predictions are either true or false; the results are used to confirm (support) or disconfirm (refute) the hypothesis.
- Three requirements ensure a fair test of the causal hypothesis: (1) The prediction should be something that is verifiable. (2) The prediction should be unlikely to be true based on our background knowledge. (3) There should be a connection between the hypothesis and the prediction.
- Verifiable prediction: The prediction, if it is true, must include an observable event.
- Nontrivial prediction: Requires reference to background knowledge, which is everything we know to be true.
- The weight we give to a confirmation or refutation is never all-or-nothing. We need to accumulate evidence over a long time.

KEY TERMS

LOGIC CHALLENGE: THE SCALE AND THE COINS

You are given ten large canvas bags of identical-looking coins. Nine of the bags contain coins that weigh 1 ounce each, and one bag contains coins that weigh 1.1 ounces each. Because of the small difference in weight, you cannot distinguish the 1-ounce coin from the 1.1-ounce coin just by holding them in your hands. And since they look identical in shape and size, they cannot be distinguished that way either.

You are given a scale. You can place on the scale as much or as little of the contents of the bags that you wish, and it will display the total weight placed on it. However, you are permitted to use the scale only once. You will get only one chance to figure out which bag has the 1.1-ounce coins. How would you solve the problem?

Chapter 15

Analyzing a Long Essay

A. *Childbed Fever*
B. *Vienna*
C. *Miasm and Contagion*
D. *Semmelweis's Account of the Discovery*
E. *Initial Questions*
F. *A New Interpretation*

A long essay may draw on many of the strategies that we have examined. It may also fall into more than one failure in logic or more than one informal fallacy. Consider a case study in the history of medicine. It includes analogical, statistical, and causal reasoning. Scientific theories, hypotheses, experiments, and predictions all play a prominent role; so does refuting and confirming evidence. Is the essay convincing? You will decide. As you read, you can apply many of the logical skills that you have learned to identify and reconstruct its arguments. You will be able to analyze governmental reaction and the social policies that were enacted in the face of an ongoing tragedy.

The essay format allows for a comprehensive series of arguments and analyses within the context of a single complex issue. You will face complex arguments in your career, in politics, and in ordinary life almost every day. We hope that you will thoroughly enjoy facing them. We hope, too, that your practice throughout this book makes you a more engaged and effective reader. (*Note*: The paragraphs have been numbered so that you can easily locate specific passages while working on the *Check Your Understanding* exercises.)

A. CHILDBED FEVER

1. The following is a reconstruction of the reasoning, research, and experiments that enabled Ignac Semmelweis to find the cause of childbed fever. Semmelweis claimed that his discovery (that the so-called disease was actually blood poisoning) was a leap of the imagination that came to him after an extensive experimental process whereby he eliminated many false causes. Semmelweis's written account has become the "received view" and is accepted by nearly all writers on the subject. Upon close analysis, however, Semmelweis's written account reveals several important gaps; in addition, it does not mesh with other historical information.

2. This paper will propose two main points: (1) Semmelweis's final discovery came later than even he realized. (2) The discovery was arrived at by circumstances that have been overlooked by the received view. The reconstruction and analysis begins with a brief description of the "lying-in" (maternity) hospital of Vienna, where Semmelweis did his work. Since Semmelweis began working on the problem of childbed fever (also called *puerperal fever*) from the standpoint of the prevailing theories of disease, it will be necessary to sketch a profile of the two major competing theories of the 1840s, *miasm* and *contagion*. Following the background information, a detailed look at Semmelweis's own report of the discovery will be undertaken. Finally, the crucial gaps in the received view will be filled in by an alternative account of the discovery.

B. VIENNA

3. In 1784, Joseph II made a decree setting up the lying-in hospital of Vienna. His mother had been worried about the number of illegitimate births in Vienna, which was almost equal to the number of legitimate births for quite a number of years. Concerned that the young girls and their newborn might not be getting the best care, the decree stated that a secure place of refuge was to be provided for "the many seduced females who are under the compulsion of shame and necessity, and for the preservation of the blameless, unborn offspring which they carry in their wombs, so that they may at least be brought to Holy Baptism" [11, p. 335]. (*Note:* The references in brackets are to the bibliography at the end of this chapter.) It is ironic that this charitable act would eventually lead to the tremendous number of deaths from childbed fever that took the lives of the very women the lying-in hospital was set up to protect in the first place. There were indeed a great number of deaths to mothers, and as the fever did not normally affect the newly born, this left many children without mothers. It would appear from this that there were a great number of children who had to grow up without mothers. "During the period of Semmelweis' service in the first division, and for some 20 years before, for that matter, there was a surfeit of motherless infants, because of the high mortality rate from puerperal fever among the new mothers. This was however nicely canceled by the frightful mortality rate in the foundling hospital" [11, p. 339]. From 1784 to 1838 there were 183,955 infants admitted to the foundling hospital, 146,920 of whom died.

4. In 1840, the Vienna Hospital set up two divisions in the obstetric department. The first clinic was staffed by doctors and medical students doing intern work in obstetrics, while the second employed midwives who had no duties other than assisting in the care of the patients and in deliveries. Admissions to the clinics were as follows: On Tuesday, Thursday, and Saturday patients were admitted to the second clinic; on Sunday, Monday, Wednesday, and Friday patients were admitted to the first clinic. When Semmelweis began his investigation, the rates of death from puerperal fever were approximately 12% monthly for the first clinic, but only 3% for the second clinic. Semmelweis was interested in finding answers to two questions: What was the cause of childbed fever, and why did more deaths occur as a result of childbed fever in the

first clinic than in the second? Many people had proposed answers, but none of the explanations had proven to work. It is against the background of these proposed explanations that Semmelweis began his research.

CHECK YOUR UNDERSTANDING 15B

1. According to the information in paragraph 3, what was the reason for setting up the lying-in hospital of Vienna? Was it successful?

Answer: The mother of Joseph II was worried about the high number of illegitimate births in Vienna. The concern was that young girls and their newborn might not be getting the best care. It was not successful because of the high mortality rate from puerperal fever among the new mothers. In addition, the mortality rate in the foundling hospital was also very high (of the 183,955 infants admitted, 146,920 died).

2. Describe how the two clinics in the lying-in hospital were staffed. (paragraph 4)

3. How were admissions handled in the two clinics? (paragraph 4)

4. At the beginning of Semmelweis's investigation what were the rates of death from puerperal fever for the two clinics? (paragraph 4)

⭐ 5. What were Semmelweis's initial questions? (paragraph 4)

C. MIASM AND CONTAGION

Childbed fever Also called *puerperal fever,* was universally believed to be a disease peculiar to women.

5. Until Semmelweis made his discovery, **childbed fever** (also called *puerperal fever*) was universally believed to be a disease peculiar to women. In order to get the disease, it was thought that two conditions had to be realized. First, the woman had to be pregnant, and second, she had to come in contact with the cause (whatever it was). Both conditions were thought to be necessary; being pregnant was not sufficient, and coming in contact with the cause was not enough either. It was believed that nonpregnant women never got puerperal fever. Thus, the prevalent view was that childbed fever was a *specific disease* that affected only pregnant women.

Miasm theory Postulated that diseases were carried by the air; that certain combinations of the basic elements in the atmosphere were potentially harmful to humans.

6. In the early 1800s, the explanations given for the spread of childbed fever fell mainly under two dominant theories of disease: miasm and contagion. Quite simply, **miasm theory** postulated that diseases were carried by the air; certain combinations of the basic elements in the atmosphere were potentially harmful to humans. This theory sought to explain why diseases, such as plagues, occurred in certain areas and not in others. In other words, "Miasmatic diseases result from the invasion of infectious agents from without, which cannot always be traced either directly or indirectly to some other case of the same disease" [1, p. 59].

Contagion theory Held that a contagious disease is one transmissible from individual to individual by immediate or direct contact.

7. As an alternative, **contagion theory** (at least in the early 1800s) held that "a contagious disease is one transmissible from individual to individual by immediate or direct

contact" [1, p. 59]. It should be kept in mind that **infectious** is understood as being distinct from **contagious**, in that the former is the broader of the two. Whereas *infectious* refers to the *causation* of the disease, *contagious* refers only to the *manner of transmission*.

Infectious Refers to the causation of a disease.

Contagious Refers to the *manner of transmission* of a disease.

8. The debate between these two dominant theories took a definite geographic flavor. The British regarded childbed fever as a *contagion*, and thus their methods of combating it were different from those practiced on "the Continent" (Europe), where *miasm* theory held sway. In England, doctors who came in contact with patients washed their hands in a solution of chlorinated water in order to destroy any contagion that might be around. However, the British considered childbed fever to be a *specific disease* that was contagious. They were under the assumption, similar to that held on the Continent, that childbed fever affected *only* pregnant women. The British belief that childbed fever was a specific contagious disease was erroneous; nevertheless, their method of treatment against childbed fever was successful. What was needed, and what no one had ever done, was to recognize the fever as a *symptom* and not as a disease.

9. Although the majority of doctors in England thought childbed fever to be a contagion, some did side with miasm theory. These physicians took precautions to clean up sewage and foul odors in and around hospitals. They used chlorinated water in various solutions as a disinfectant. They often built their lying-in hospitals away from dumps and other areas where foul odors could be found. The fact that both systems of combating childbed fever had some success further complicated the debate between the two opposing sides.

10. It is difficult to characterize accurately the climate in Vienna regarding the debate between miasm and contagion. Both theories were being revised and both sides were shifting their ground as diverse forms of evidence became more available. An important historical point must also be kept in mind—the extreme difficulty Semmelweis had in getting his discovery accepted in 1847. Semmelweis could not use *germ theory* as support, because Pasteur's experimental results would not be universally accepted for another 16 years. "The concepts of bacteriology—which would have added credibility to Semmelweis's findings—awaited Pasteur's work; and the concepts which reigned instead—miasm, epidemic constitution and telluric influences (contagion)—made acceptance of Semmelweis's (theory) improbable" [7, p. 12].

11. It is against this historical backdrop that we find Semmelweis in the obstetric department of the Vienna Hospital, understandably appalled by the great number of deaths from childbed fever. He set himself the task of finding its cause.

CHECK YOUR UNDERSTANDING 15C

1. What two conditions were thought to be necessary in order for a woman to contract childbed fever? (paragraph 5)

Answer: First, the woman had to be pregnant, and second, she had to come in contact with the cause (whatever it was). Both conditions were thought to be necessary.

2. Was the prevalent view that childbed fever was a specific disease that affected only pregnant women? (paragraph 5)

3. Explain miasm theory. (paragraph 6)

4. Explain contagion theory. (paragraph 7)

★ 5. Describe the distinction between *infectious* and *contagious*. (paragraph 7)

6. How did the British view childbed fever? How did they combat it? How did the British view differ from thinking on the Continent? (paragraphs 8 and 9)

7. Why couldn't Semmelweis use Pasteur's germ theory as support for his ideas? (paragraph 10)

D. SEMMELWEIS'S ACCOUNT OF THE DISCOVERY

12. Since Semmelweis was looking for the *cause* of childbed fever, he began testing some obvious implications of the miasm view to see if it could explain why the rates of death in the two divisions were so radically different. If the fever was caused by something in the atmosphere, as miasm theory suggested, then why did it not strike the second clinic as well? Since the two clinics had a corridor in common, one might reasonably conclude that the atmosphere should be the same in both clinics, and thus the rates of death should be similar as well. Semmelweis also wondered why the fever occurred more in women who were admitted on Sundays, Mondays, Wednesdays, and Fridays (the first clinic). Surely the fever did not happen to enter the atmosphere only on those 4 days.

13. However, perhaps women came in contact with puerperal fever miasms in the atmosphere *outside* the hospital. Semmelweis rejected this similar idea, because it would mean that it was equally likely for all women to get the fever. If the fever was contracted outside the hospital, then the rates in the two clinics should be the same regardless of the day the women were admitted.

14. It was well known that the rate of the fever in the population at large had never reached the high percentage that it had in the hospital. If childbed fever was like cholera—if it was a true epidemic—then why did it not appear like one? It should have been relatively easy to find similar degrees of fever outside the hospital, if the miasm theory of atmospheric epidemics was correct; but the statistics did not bear this out. In addition, epidemics have periodic intermissions. They usually do not continue for long periods of time, and they were thought to be seasonal. But the high rate of fever, at least in the first clinic, had not regressed since the two clinics were set up. Since there was no periodic remission accompanying the changes of the seasons, then puerperal fever did not seem like a true epidemic.

15. Statistics from other hospitals and lying-in clinics revealed yet another curious result. In places where there was no medical teaching, other than midwifery, the rate

of death by puerperal fever was usually (but not always) very low. Even in cities where the rate was high in a hospital where general medicine was practiced and taught, the rate was usually lower where no medical teaching was done. If the epidemic theory was correct, then how could it account for two completely different rates in the same city? Semmelweis's early conclusion to these preliminary studies was that puerperal fever was **endemic**: a disease that was the result of causes *within the hospital* from endemic noxious agents. Semmelweis now faced the task of testing the many conjectures that fell within the group of endemic causes.

Endemic A disease that is confined to a specific place.

16. The first endemic explanation that Semmelweis checked was overcrowding. It turned out that there was no real difference between the two clinics in terms of number of patients per available area. If anything, the second clinic might at times have been more crowded than the first, because women were becoming aware of the great chance of death that accompanied admission to the first clinic. Semmelweis relates that women would fall down on their knees and beg not to be admitted to the first clinic. It was said that women who had not known of the admission procedure, and who were told that they had come on the day that women were being admitted to the dreaded first clinic, actually fainted at the prospect. But Semmelweis argued that the rate had been high long before it had become common knowledge. As a matter of fact, the high rate in the first clinic was clearly documented from the time the two clinics were formed. The first clinic was consistently higher than the second in both the incidence of childbed fever and the number of deaths. Therefore, terror could not account for the high rates in the early years of the clinic.

17. Since Semmelweis did not have his own apartment, he slept in a room that was close to the first clinic. He noticed one night that the priest who had to deliver last rites to a dying patient went through the first clinic. Semmelweis became disturbed when he was aroused from sleep by the ringing of the bell. He felt sorrow at the thought of some patient's imminent death. He wondered if the women lying in the first clinic were as affected by this as he was and, if so, if this might be the cause of the high rate of childbed fever. If he, a healthy person, were sorrowed by the incident, then how much more might a woman who was in a highly emotional and sensitive state be affected? He knew that the priest went only through the first clinic, not the second, on his way to hospital calls. Having spoken to the priest about this and made him aware of the grave peril, Semmelweis was able to convince the priest to go a different way and to stop ringing the bell. However, this experiment did not unearth the true cause.

18. It was suggested to Semmelweis that perhaps the first clinic contained more poor patients. If so, the poverty of the patients might have caused them to be unhealthy before they were admitted. However, Semmelweis could find no facts to support this idea.

19. Another idea was that the first clinic had happened to admit more unmarried young women than the second clinic. Although no explanation was given as to why this

should cause more cases of childbed fever, nevertheless Semmelweis tested it anyway. Once again, Semmelweis could find no substantiation for this claim.

20. Another explanation had been circulating for some time as well. Perhaps the doctors and medical students were "rougher" in handling women than the midwives, who, being women, were more apt to treat the patients in a gentle manner. Semmelweis responded that the fetal body was much rougher on women through delivery than were the male doctors' examinations.

21. A different, but related, idea was that the women were embarrassed by being examined by men, but not by the midwives. Semmelweis rejected this idea, because he could not see why modesty should cause anything like a disease.

22. Semmelweis's investigations showed that patients in both clinics received the same kinds of medical attention and treatment when necessary. For example, the women in the first clinic were required to walk back to their beds 3 hours after delivery. But this policy was followed in the second clinic as well.

23. Could poor ventilation be the cause? Semmelweis determined that the ventilation was the same in both clinics.

24. Could the linen be a factor? Perhaps it was of a different kind or laundered differently. Semmelweis determined that the linen was the same and was laundered at the same place.

25. Could food be the answer? The food for both clinics was prepared in the same place and the diets were the same.

26. If there were an unlimited number of possible explanations of the death rate (and by the look of things, this is what Semmelweis seems to have faced), then he could eliminate as many as he liked without getting any closer to the truth. He doubted that he would ever stumble on the answer. Semmelweis felt that he was grasping at straws.

27. One day a colleague pointed out something that Semmelweis had not noticed. The procedure in the second clinic, but not in the first clinic, was to have women assume a lateral position for delivery. Semmelweis immediately implemented the use of the lateral position in the first clinic. Every delivery was performed this way in the hope that the death rate in the two divisions would be comparable. But this experiment failed to change the death rate in the first clinic. The high rate in the first clinic seemed immune to change, however hard Semmelweis tried to lower it.

28. There seemed to be an unending supply of explanations for Semmelweis to test. One popular belief was that conception itself was to blame for childbed fever. That is, the women in the first clinic had a different experience that brought about their present condition. Semmelweis commented on this idea:

> Recent investigators have indeed accused the *conception itself* as the factor in producing the puerperal processes, in that the effect of the *Spirma Virile* postulates a series of metamorphoses and stimulates many, in part unknown, changes in the blood. I do not consider that I am laboring under any illusion

when I make the assertion that those individuals, who have borne in the second clinic, were preceded by a conception also. [15, p. 380]

29. Semmelweis also considered the birth act itself. Possible causes of childbed fever were protracted labor, death of the fetus, and the wounding of the inner surface of the uterus by the fetus. However, Semmelweis pointed out that all these effects could be seen in both clinics. The outcomes of the birth act had to be similar in both divisions.

30. Additional aspects of childbed fever were puzzling as well. For one, when labor lasted 24 hours or more, puerperal fever almost always occurred, especially in first pregnancies. Semmelweis writes, "I did not know, to be sure, why this happened, but I saw it happen often; the fact was the more inexplicable, because it was not repeated in the second division under similar circumstances" [15, p. 381].

31. With the power of hindsight, let us see what would have happened in the first clinic. If there was a protracted labor, and if it lasted for, let us say, 2 days, what was likely to happen? Since there were two shifts of medical students in the first clinic, there would be four clinic visits in a 2-day period. Each shift had at least five students, plus a physician examining the patient. This would amount to at least twenty-four examinations of the patient. We can easily see why these cases almost always resulted in childbed fever, because the chance of blood poisoning was great. This is especially so since the physicians and students did not take care to disinfect their hands before the examinations were conducted.

32. In addition, in these cases of protracted labor the child, too, was usually affected with childbed fever-like symptoms and died along with its mother. Semmelweis came to believe that the symptoms occurred in both *female* and *male* babies. Semmelweis was the first to notice this: "The anatomical findings in the cadavers of such newborn were identical to the dead bodies of puerperae (the mothers) who succumbed to puerperal fever. To recognize the changes in the bodies of the puerperae, and not to recognize the identical changes in the bodies of the newborn, invalidates the pathological anatomy" [15, p. 381]. Semmelweis tells us that these early clues gave him the first real breakthrough: He stopped thinking of puerperal fever as occurring only in pregnant women.

33. Through painstaking effort and thought, Semmelweis had acquired new facts that strengthened his rejection of the previous conjectures. "The many etiologic factors which have been cited as productive of childbed fever among the mothers are impossible of acceptance with reference to the newborn. The newborn were probably unafraid of the first division, because its evil reputation was unknown to them; and the injured sense of modesty, because they are born in the presence of men, would be less liable to do harm among the newborn" [15, p. 383].

34. Semmelweis thought that he might be finally getting close to the answer. He had conducted numerous experiments to weed out the false conjectures. He had some important new facts, which he could not yet explain; but he was aware that these facts were necessary to finding the true cause of childbed fever.

35. The scandal surrounding the notorious first clinic and its appalling number of deaths had reached its peak, and this poor reputation was a blemish on the otherwise highly acclaimed Vienna Hospital. Something had to be done, and the government did what most governments do in times of crisis: It formed a commission to investigate the situation. The commission, consisting of nonmedical people, went to the head of the clinic for advice. Its conclusion was that the medical students were rougher than the midwives. The commission further stated that the foreign students were roughest of all. What was the remedy? Get rid of the foreign students. As a result, the staff in the first clinic was cut in half, from about forty students down to around twenty. And for the next 4 months the death rate did indeed go down in the first clinic—from an average of 12% to 3%. Given this result, the commission felt justified, and the government was satisfied. (Once again, with hindsight we can understand the sudden drop. Fewer students meant fewer examinations; thus, the chance of infection was reduced.)

36. However, the remaining staff began making up for lack of help, and Semmelweis did more than his share of work. Little by little the death rate rose again. After 5 months it was right back at 12%. What was the commission's reaction to this turn of events? It concluded that childbed fever must be an epidemic. Semmelweis's comment to all this: "Everything was uncertain, everything was inexplicable; only the enormous number of deaths was an indubitable fact" [15, p. 390].

37. Just when it appeared that Semmelweis was beginning to get some interesting information, he was relieved of his position. He had been hired as a substitute in February 1846, a position that lasted until October 1846, when he expected to get his own 2-year assistantship. However, this did not happen, and it meant that he would have to wait 2 more years to get the assistantship back. Without the position he could not try his ideas, because he no longer would have free access to and control over the first clinic. He continued his autopsy work and performed other duties in the hospital where needed, but he longed to return to his search. He gave up hope of continuing on at Vienna, and so he began studying English with the idea of going to Dublin Hospital. However, before he could begin anything new he got back the assistantship. The doctor who had taken his job back got an offer from another hospital. So, after a 5-month delay, Semmelweis was able to resume his study.

38. Naturally he was relieved by this news, and having admitted to being depressed during those 5 months, he was given permission to go on a vacation. He and a few friends went to Venice for 3 weeks. Semmelweis related how this period was calming and he forgot all about the problem awaiting him at the lying-in hospital and, instead, concentrated on the beautiful paintings and fantastic surroundings of Venice.

39. When he reached Vienna he was given some shocking news; his good friend Dr. Kolletschka had died. Kolletschka had been performing a routine autopsy when an assistant accidentally cut Kolletschka's finger, and he died within 2 weeks. Semmelweis studied the autopsy findings in great detail. This is where Semmelweis tells us he made the discovery of the cause of childbed fever:

a. Kolletschka . . . was stuck in the finger by a student, with a knife which was used during the post-mortem. . . . [He] then became ill with lymphangitis and phlebitis in the same upper extremity and died . . . of bilateral pleuritis, pericarditis, peritonitis, and meningitis, and some days before his death a metastasis formed in one eye. . . . [T]here was forced on my mind with irresistible clarity in this excited state the identity of this disease, of which Kolletschka died, with that which I had seen so many hundred puerperae die. The puerperae died likewise of phlebitis, lymphangitis, peritonitis, pleuritis, pericarditis, and meningitis, and metastases were also formed in them.

b. Day and night this picture of Kolletschka's disease pursued me, and with ever increasing determination, I was obliged to acknowledge the identity of the disease, from which Kolletschka died, with that of which I saw so many puerperae die.

c. From the identity of the pathological findings in the cadavers of the newborn with the pathological findings in the women, who died from childbed fever, we had concluded earlier, and we think rightly, that the newborn died also of childbed fever, or in other words, the newborn died of the same disease as did the puerperae. Since we came upon the identical results in the pathological findings of Kolletschka as in the puerperae, then the conclusion that Kolletschka died of the same disease from which I had seen so many hundred puerperae die, likewise was justified. The . . . cause of Kolletschka's illness was known, that is to say, the wound produced by the autopsy knife was contaminated at the same time by cadaveric material. Not the wound, but the contamination of the wound by cadaveric material was the cause of death. Kolletschka was not the first to die in this fashion. I must acknowledge if Kolletschka's disease and the disease from which I saw so many puerperae die, are identical, then in the puerperae it must be produced by the selfsame engendering cause, which produced it in Kolletschka. In Kolletschka, the specific agent was cadaveric particles, which were introduced into his vascular system. I must ask myself the question: Did the cadaveric particles make their way into the vascular systems of the individuals whom I had seen die of an identical disease? The question I answer in the affirmative. [15, pp. 391–392]

40. Semmelweis therefore concluded that it is through the doctors' and medical students' examinations of the women that cadaveric particles are absorbed into the system. Semmelweis writes that "from the first this seemed to me more than likely, since the fact was known to me that decaying organic matter brought into contact with living organisms produced in them a putrefactive process" [15, p. 393].

41. Semmelweis now had a hypothesis that he could put to the test: Cadaveric material was the *cause* of puerperal fever. The solution was to eliminate the particles by correct washing. The results should be a lower death rate. Since Semmelweis believed that cadaveric particles were not removed by soap and water, because the odor remains, he started using a solution of chlorinated lime, with the idea to eliminate the odor, and

by so doing, to eliminate the particles. He emphasized washing the hands until they squeaked, thinking this would ensure that all particles were removed.

42. An experiment was set up to ensure that no other changes were allowed in the first clinic. The only new factor was the washing of hands in the solution. The immediate result was that the childbed fever rate dropped from 12% to 3% in the first clinic. For the year 1848, the rates of the two divisions were as follows: first division, 1.27%; second division, 1.33% [15, p. 394]. For Semmelweis, the reason that the second clinic always had a lower death rate was now understood; the midwives did not come in contact with cadaveric material.

43. Semmelweis later refined his discovery and concluded that puerperal fever was not a specific disease as everyone had believed; it was a variety of blood poisoning. So childbed fever was not a contagious disease in the usual sense, because a contagious disease produced a contagium by which it spread as the identical disease. For example, smallpox cannot cause a different disease, such as scarlet fever. On this topic, Semmelweis writes:

> This explains why the dispute over the contagiousness or noncontagiousness of childbed fever can never be brought to a satisfactory conclusion, because the contagionists can cite cases where the spread of childbed fever from an ill puerpera to a healthy one could not be denied. And the opponents of the contagion theory can likewise bring forward cases in which the spread of childbed fever did not occur under circumstances where it should have happened if it were a contagious disease. Childbed fever is not a contagious disease, but it is communicable from an ill puerpera to a healthy one by means of *decomposed animal-organic matter*. [15, p. 434]

CHECK YOUR UNDERSTANDING 15D

1. What was Semmelweis's reasoning concerning the hypothesis that something in the atmosphere in the hospital was the cause of the disease? (paragraph 12)

Answer: Since the two clinics had a corridor in common, the atmosphere should be the same in both clinics, and thus the rates of death should be similar as well. Also, the fever occurred more in women admitted on Sundays, Mondays, Wednesdays, and Fridays, which happens to coincide with admissions to the first clinic. Surely the fever did not appear in the hospital's atmosphere only on those 4 days.

2. What was Semmelweis's reasoning concerning the hypothesis that something in the atmosphere outside the hospital was the cause of the disease? (paragraph 13)

3. How did the disease of childbed fever differ from cholera? (paragraph 14)

4. If the epidemic theory was correct, then it could not account for two completely different childbed fever rates in the same city (where medical teaching was conducted). Given this, what was Semmelweis's early conclusion? (paragraph 15)

 ⭐ 5. What was Semmelweis's reasoning regarding the "overcrowding" hypothesis? (paragraph 16)

   6. What experiment did Semmelweis conduct regarding the priest and the ringing of the bell? What were the results of the experiment? (paragraph 17)

   7. What was Semmelweis's reasoning regarding the "poor patients" hypothesis? (paragraph 18)

   8. What was Semmelweis's reasoning regarding the "unmarried young woman" hypothesis? (paragraph 19)

 ⭐ 9. What was Semmelweis's reasoning regarding the hypothesis that "doctors and medical students were *rougher* in handling women than the midwives"? (paragraph 20)

 10. What was Semmelweis's reasoning regarding the "embarrassment" hypothesis? (paragraph 21)

 11. What was Semmelweis's reasoning regarding the "medical treatment and attention" hypothesis? (paragraph 22)

 12. What was Semmelweis's reasoning regarding the "ventilation" hypothesis? (paragraph 23)

 ⭐ 13. What was Semmelweis's reasoning regarding the "linen" hypothesis? (paragraph 24)

 14. What was Semmelweis's reasoning regarding the "food" hypothesis? (paragraph 25)

 15. What was Semmelweis's reasoning regarding the "lateral position" hypothesis? (paragraph 27)

 16. What was Semmelweis's reasoning regarding the "conception process" hypothesis? (paragraph 28)

 ⭐ 17. What was Semmelweis's reasoning regarding the "birth act" hypothesis? (paragraph 29)

 18. What was the "protracted labor" puzzle? (paragraphs 30 and 31)

 19. What important evidence did Semmelweis become aware of regarding newborn children? How did this affect his thinking regarding the idea that childbed fever was a disease that affected only pregnant women? (paragraphs 32 and 33)

 20. What did the government do in the face of the scandal surrounding the first clinic of the Vienna Hospital? What did the commission conclude? What policy was implemented? What was the result? (paragraphs 35 and 36)

 ⭐ 21. Explain how the Kolletschka case affected Semmelweis's thinking. (paragraph 39)

 22. What did Semmelweis conclude? Describe Semmelweis's reasoning. (paragraphs 39 and 40)

23. What was Semmelweis's hypothesis, and how was he going to test it? What did he predict should happen? Did the results confirm the hypothesis? (paragraphs 41 and 42)

24. What refinements did Semmelweis make to his hypothesis? (paragraph 43)

Summary of Semmelweis's Account

- Eliminated epidemic theories.
- Followed the methods of his teachers:
  - Studied the processes of the disease.
  - Did autopsy studies.
  - Was familiar with anatomical findings of childbed fever victims and babies.
- Knew the symptoms of childbed fever.
- Through the similarity of anatomical results, conjectured that babies (male and female) could die from the fever.
- Knew the general symptoms of blood poisoning.
- Common knowledge that an accidental cut during dissection can be fatal.
- Knew that blood poisoning could come from a cut received during an autopsy (through an open wound coming in contact with cadaveric particles).
- Noticed that the autopsy findings in Kolletschka were similar to those who died from childbed fever.
- Noted that Kolletschka died from blood poisoning.
- Made the discovery that childbed fever was *not* a specific disease; it was a form of blood poisoning.

E. INITIAL QUESTIONS

44. At this point the attentive reader may be wondering why it took Semmelweis so long to make the discovery. With so much "obvious" evidence at his disposal, why didn't he make the connection sooner? A quick look at the clues Semmelweis admits having long before the Kolletschka case might seem to support this view:

45. A prolonged pre-birth period almost assuredly led to childbed fever, but not in the second clinic.

46. In the first clinic the patients sickened in rows, but not in the second clinic.

47. Those women giving birth outside the hospital had less chance of contracting the fever.

48. In hospitals where only midwifery was done, the rate of puerperal fever was generally low.

49. Babies, including males, could get puerperal fever.

50. The rate of puerperal fever was always lower in the second clinic.

51. The death rate did go down when the number of students was reduced in the first clinic.

52. Semmelweis tells us that the rate in the second clinic was normally very low, with one exception: "Only in 1842–1843, when in the second division there was one assistant who was engaged in several branches of pathological anatomy, did the mortality, which was otherwise small in that division, go up; in 1842, it rose to 202; in 1843, to 164" [7, p. 53].

53. It has been pointed out that the fact that Semmelweis had such a well-controlled experiment contributed to solving the mystery of childbed fever. Nevertheless, Semmelweis seems to have missed entirely what appears to be *the most obvious difference* (at least to us, looking back)— namely, midwives in the second clinic, doctors and interns in the first clinic. And yet it took the Kolletschka case to jolt Semmelweis out of his slumber.

54. The history of science shows us that simply having certain pieces of evidence does not ensure that someone will make a discovery. In the study of childbed fever, many doctors at the same time Semmelweis was working were in possession of similar facts but nevertheless failed to make the discovery.

55. It has been suggested that the experimental method was the key to Semmelweis's discovery—that is, using controlled experiments to eliminate false causes. However, given all the hints Semmelweis had, and even using controlled experiments to the fullest, Semmelweis still missed the crucial difference: doctors/midwives. In fact, Semmelweis's own account emphasizes the importance of his "seeing" Kolletschka as like a childbed fever victim.

56. Since Semmelweis did not publish anything concerning his discovery until 1858, it has not escaped historians notice that Semmelweis's account may be faulty; nevertheless, no alternative reconstruction has been given. Some work has been done exploring Semmelweis's career after leaving Vienna, as well as the controversy over the precedence of the discovery. This can be seen in regard to another issue, the priority of the discovery. For example:

> It is not that Dr. Holmes considered the disease contagious, while Semmelweis wrote an entire article arguing that it was not. The definitions of "contagion" and "infection" were everywhere so vague at that time that it would be extremely difficult to guess what they actually have meant. The important difference lies rather in that in the same article Semmelweis asserted firmly that puerperal fever was nothing else but a general sepsis or pyemia [blood poisoning]. Dr. Holmes simply did not think of it in these terms [7, p. 32].

57. A few inquiries into the historical accuracy of Semmelweis's discovery have concentrated on the obvious length of time until Semmelweis's first written reconstruction, his bitterness over the lack of acceptance of his discovery, and, recently, the possibility that Semmelweis had Alzheimer's disease [6, 17, 13]. All of this leads to some important

questions concerning Semmelweis's account. Although a few writers have tentatively touched on the Kolletschka case and have questioned its central position as a point of discovery, no one has offered a complete alternative solution to where, when, and how Semmelweis made the discovery. So the Kolletschka case will be the point of departure for our subsequent discussion.

58. Close analysis of the Kolletschka affair reveals many gaps and points the way to a new interpretation of the discovery. Although the leap of the imagination from the Kolletschka case to the *final answer* of the cause of childbed fever might seem immense, Semmelweis tells us that it happened. However, if we take a close look at Semmelweis's own recollection of this crucial time period, then many puzzles immediately arise. For example, Semmelweis tells us that the picture of Kolletschka's death haunted him day and night until the necessary connection struck him. Although he does not give us an exact date for the discovery, from Semmelweis's account it happened quite soon after March 20. If this is so, then Semmelweis never explains why he did not start implementing the use of chlorine lime until the end of May, *2 months after the Kolletschka case*. If he made the discovery soon after looking at Kolletschka's autopsy report, then why did he wait 2 months to test his hypothesis? Semmelweis provides no answer.

59. The two most important clues that Semmelweis had for the discovery were (1) a realization that some babies had the same symptoms as women who died of childbed fever; and (2) the Kolletschka case. Semmelweis tells us that the crucial point came when he noticed that Kolletschka had died of the same symptoms as the women. The emphasis is on connecting Kolletschka with the women and babies. Semmelweis is using analogical reasoning here. The process he gives is this: The first analogy was that the symptoms of the babies and women were similar; the second analogy that the symptoms of Kolletschka were similar to the women. Therefore, in both cases, Semmelweis claims that he made the connection by using the principle of going from the *same effects to the same causes*.

60. If you recall, Semmelweis told us that he noticed early in his search that the uterus after birth could be seen as being like an open wound. He also knew that a cut during an autopsy could prove fatal. The important aspect was not simply the contact with cadaveric material, but the *open wound* coming in contact with cadaveric particles. Semmelweis realized that the second part was the deciding factor. As we saw earlier, he wrote, "Not the wound, but the contamination of the wound by cadaveric material was the cause of death." He had been looking for something that would explain the transmission of childbed fever, and he had eliminated many possible factors. He was struck by the fact that Kolletschka died of an open wound that had come in contact with cadaveric particles. Seeing the uterus *as being wounded* allowed him to realize how the disease could be spread. Just as the key factor with Kolletschka was not simply coming in contact with cadaveric material, but rather being wounded and coming in contact with it, so the wounded uterus coming in contact with cadaveric material through the doctors and interns' many examinations was the answer to the mystery.

What this interpretation does is change Semmelweis's analogical reasoning. We find that the process was this: From an open wound coming in contact with cadaveric material blood poisoning can occur. A wounded uterus coming in contact with cadaveric material can lead to blood poisoning as well. As we can see, this reasoning goes from *same causes to same effects*.

61.   Semmelweis's account places the entire discovery on the Kolletschka case. However, no matter how we try to integrate Semmelweis's narrative with his *actions*, we find many curious incidents. It is therefore appropriate to analyze whether the discovery happened the way Semmelweis reports. In other words, what did Semmelweis know, and when did he know it?

CHECK YOUR UNDERSTANDING 15E

1. What was the crucial difference that everyone had missed? (paragraph 55)
Answer: The crucial difference: The first clinic was staffed by doctors and interns; the second clinic was staffed by midwives.

2. Discuss the "obvious" evidence at Semmelweis's disposal. (paragraphs 45–53)

3. What is the Holmes versus Semmelweis issue regarding the priority of the discovery? (paragraph 56)

4. What are some of puzzles regarding Semmelweis's received view of his discovery? (paragraph 58)

5. What were the two most important clues that Semmelweis had for the discovery? (paragraph 59)

6. What were the two analogies that Semmelweis used? What principle did Semmelweis apply to the analogical reasoning? (paragraph 59)

7. What is "new" interpretation of Semmelweis's analogical reasoning, and how does it change the overall principle behind Semmelweis's reasoning? (paragraph 60)

F. A NEW INTERPRETATION

62.   An important period leading up to the discovery, and the least talked about by Semmelweis, is the 5 months during which he was relieved of his duties as assistant of the first clinic. It is ironic that the 5 months in which he did not have control over the clinic gave him the opportunity to do the necessary historical study that enabled him to make the discovery. Taking into consideration the information Semmelweis tells us he knew prior to the Kolletschka case, and noticing what he did during the 5 months in question, it becomes clear that Semmelweis had enough information to provide him

with a new plan of action. Indeed, it will soon become evident that all Semmelweis had after he got his assistantship back, and after the Kolletschka case, was simply one more conjecture to put to the test. However, it will be argued that he had made *no final discovery directly* after Kolletschka's death.

63. Semmelweis was understandably crestfallen at the prospect of losing his assistantship. After all, it had been understood that he would be given the full-time position, since he had performed so well as a substitute. Losing the position meant that he would have to wait 2 years to resume the search. The prospect of finding the answer must have appeared bleak.

64. Semmelweis had a lot of free time during this period; time to study the history of the Vienna Hospital, whose records revealed something curious. The high death rate had not always been the case at the hospital; in fact, the rate had started going up only when the current head of the department, Dr. Klein, took over in 1822. Before this, Dr. Boer had been in charge for 30 years. Under Boer's direction, from 1789 to 1822, the rate of childbed fever averaged 1.4%. When Klein took control the rate almost immediately jumped to 7.5%, and it remained high [10, pp. 57 & 183–184; 16, pp. 46 & 55; 17, pp. 70–72; 6, p. 47].

65. This rate of childbed fever is interesting, because we can see that when the two clinic system was implemented, the rate in the first clinic became 12%, while the second was 3%. But while the midwives and doctors/students worked together in one clinic the rate averaged out to 7.5%, under Klein. Why had the rate gone up when Klein took over? What changed when Klein assumed control?

66. Semmelweis's inquiries into Boer's history with the Vienna Hospital revealed some important clues. Semmelweis found that Boer had gone to England to study the methods used in combating childbed fever [10, p. 52; 16, p. 55]. Boer came back much impressed and immediately implemented the English methods of cleanliness and the use of disinfectants. Boer had considered childbed fever to be a deposit in the abdominal cavity and defined it pathologically-anatomically as "putrescence of the uterus" [10, p. 55]. Boer dissected cases assiduously and had the purulent discharge matter chemically analyzed. He also was conscientious about publishing truthfully the mortality figures of the clinic each year. These figures were statistically substantial. The number of births in the Vienna Hospital, dating back to 1789, was between 3000 and 4000 annually [10, p. 55].

67. This information fits squarely with Semmelweis's claim that during the 5 months' break he began studying English in the hope of going to Dublin. Additional evidence points to ideas that directly influenced Semmelweis at this time. A Dublin Hospital report, published in 1835, stated that there were over 10,000 deliveries without a single death [14, p. 202]. A routine of cleanliness and disinfection of wards, beds, and equipment with chlorine water was observed. It is probable that Semmelweis was aware of the success reported in Dublin; after all, he tells us, "The fact that the English physicians regarded childbed fever as contagious and use chlorine solutions against it was

certainly well known to me" [7, p. 97]. His interest in their work was coupled with the knowledge that Boer went to England and had been successful when he was in charge.

68. What Boer had done was to suspend the use of cadavers as a teaching device for students in the obstetric department. All teaching was done by using the "phantom model," a mannequin body-machine with an artificial uterus and pelvic canal [10, p. 57; 17, p. 72]. The students, therefore, had no chance of coming in contact with cadavers before examining patients.

69. But when Klein (who was an avowed believer in miasm theory) took over, he immediately changed the routines of Boer. Klein immediately put the phantom model away and had all students learn by actual work on cadavers [6, p. 47]. Since Semmelweis had been trained in this manner, he could not be expected to realize that it had been different in the past. Therefore, the process of compiling statistics and examining the history of the obstetric department provided Semmelweis with crucial information showing the great rise in the death rate after Klein took over.

70. It appears that long before Kolletschka's death Semmelweis had gathered sufficient relevant information to put a new hypothesis to the test. All the work that he did up to this period had enabled him to eliminate many ideas. He had weakened severely the epidemic theory and thus found himself in a position to try ideas connected with contagion theory. But he was cut short before he had a chance to implement anything. However, even if he had not been relieved of his duties, it seems unlikely that he could have gone very far. *It was only after he had gained the information about the phantom model, saw Boer's success rate, and studied the English methods of combating childbed fever that he had a program to implement.* Therefore, when Semmelweis got back his position, he was ready to apply the new information. He did not need the Kolletschka case at all to give him any new ideas, because he already had knowledge that the use of the phantom model was important, plus the fact the English had used disinfectants very successfully. He could apply these facts without any help gained by Kolletschka's death.

71. If we look carefully at Semmelweis's address to the Vienna Medical Society in May 1850, we find that Semmelweis explained in detail the painstaking method he applied to his search. He placed great emphasis on his use of the comparative history of the two clinics and his refutation of alleged causes, and he makes it a point to single out the importance of Boer's success [16, pp. 100–101]. Thus it seems that when Semmelweis started implementing the use of chlorinated lime, he had not made any real breakthrough. All he was doing was testing the English contagion theorists' methods. At this point, Semmelweis had no reason to believe childbed fever was not in fact a specific disease. He states that his sole idea at this time was to *eliminate the cadaveric particles.* He had no idea that the disease could be spread any other way. This is clear in that complications arose that required additional explanation.

72. In October 1847, Semmelweis examined a woman suffering from a "foully discharging cancer of the uterus." This meant that Semmelweis and his students came in contact with the cancerous discharge. The result was that eleven out of twelve women

who delivered along with this woman died [15 p. 396; 6, p. 53]. Semmelweis was very disturbed by this result. How could it have happened? Semmelweis knew that they had washed their hands carefully *before* entering the clinic. He kept constant watch for people coming into the clinic who had been working on cadavers. What had gone wrong?

73. Semmelweis retraced the events leading up to the deaths, and the only thing he could seize on was the fact that the woman with the cancer of the uterus was in the first bed in the clinic that he and the students had examined. He realized that, after having examined her, they had failed to wash their hands again. *But of course there was no reason at the time to do so.* After all, up to this point Semmelweis firmly believed that the disease was caused *only by cadaveric particles*. He had no reason, until now, to think that there was more than one cause. But the latest deaths, and the new facts associated with them, forced Semmelweis to devise a new hypothesis: childbed fever was *not caused only* by cadaveric particles, but by *any* ichorous discharge (putrid matter) originating in living organisms. This explains why Semmelweis was so surprised when the deaths occurred from the woman with the cancerous uterus. Since he originally believed that cadaveric material was the *only* cause, he was unprepared for the latest deaths. This was not, however, a strong enough blow for him to abandon his hypothesis; after all, the death rate had dropped dramatically since he tried his new method. All Semmelweis had to do was to modify his theory to include *any putrid matter*, not just cadaveric material. This dovetailed with contagion theory, because at this point Semmelweis believed that *direct contact* must be made in order for the disease to spread.

74. However, further results would cause Semmelweis to revise his hypothesis even more. In November 1847, a woman was admitted to the clinic with a "severely discharging carious [decaying] knee." The odor and the amount of putrid material pervaded the room. Of course Semmelweis made sure that persons coming in contact with this woman had to wash their hands immediately before examining another patient. Semmelweis had no reason to believe that this would not work. But the odor from the fluid coming from the wound was so strong that nearly everyone in the clinic giving birth at that time died [15, pp. 396–397; 6, p. 53]. Here was another phenomenon that Semmelweis had to absorb into his expanding hypothesis.

75. His first modification came from the necessity to explain how something *other* than cadaveric particles could cause the fever. Now he had to explain why it was *not even necessary* for direct contact to take place. The fact that the air being so fouled with matter was *sufficient* for the disease to be contracted forced Semmelweis to revise his thinking a second time. He had to admit that putrid matter could be absorbed by the internal surface of the uterus whose mucous membrane after delivery was similar to an open wound. Semmelweis's *final conclusion* had to take all of these additional facts into consideration. He had to be able to account for all the various ways that a woman could get childbed fever.

76. The case of the woman with the carious knee was a seemingly unexplainable anomaly for Semmelweis. If puerperal fever was a contagious disease that was received

by *direct contact only* (and Semmelweis's actions up until this point confirm that he believed this), then how could he explain the fact that childbed fever could be received without direct contact? Semmelweis had thought that washing of the hands would eliminate the possibility of spreading the disease. If you eliminate the direct contact, then the disease should not spread. Therefore, the new deaths must surely have been upsetting to Semmelweis. After all his work eliminating the miasm theory, and the success of the contagion approach, he was stuck with something for which he could give no account.

77.   Semmelweis had been confronted with two clear anomalies. It is interesting to see how these anomalies (the deaths from the cancer of the uterus and the carious knee problem) came about. Semmelweis simply began testing the contagion theory by using disinfectants to eliminate cadaveric particles. Although this produced amazing results, it also gave rise to anomalies. However, it would be incorrect to think that the solution to the two new problems was simply a refinement of the initial discovery—that it clinched the fact that puerperal fever was a blood poisoning. From the available evidence, we can conclude that the two anomalies were not simply further clarifications of the discovery, *because Semmelweis did not have the discovery until after he resolved the second anomaly.*

78.   The problem situation kept changing for Semmelweis. It is his work on these new problems that enabled Semmelweis to finally hit upon the discovery. Semmelweis had to explain how childbed fever could be *both* a contagious and a noncontagious disease at the same time. What could he do to make sense of this? Until the second anomaly, Semmelweis was simply following what had been common practice in England for years. But it is his particular insight at this critical juncture that ensures Semmelweis's place as *the* discoverer of the cause of childbed fever.

79.   The idea that childbed fever was a form of blood poisoning was the answer that Semmelweis needed to make sense of all the facts. The final anomaly vanished. The great debate over the status of childbed fever between contagion and miasm theory disappeared. Semmelweis no longer had to explain how the disease fits in with both theories. He was able to eliminate the problem by seeing that the disease was a form of blood poisoning. By doing this, he eliminated the need to explain that childbed fever was a specific disease that had a specific cause. This is precisely what no one else had been able to do. This is Semmelweis's great accomplishment. It is also why the English contagion theorists cannot be given credit for having made the discovery. No one before Semmelweis was able to break out of the trap of seeing childbed fever as being a *specific disease* that affected *only pregnant women*. No one else found that childbed fever was simply a form of blood poisoning.

80.   We can conclude that the final discovery could not have occurred before December 1847, almost 9 months after Kolletschka's death. The problem posed by the first anomaly simply led to an expansion of a *contagion* hypothesis. The second anomaly brought about a completely new problem situation, the resolution of which enabled Semmelweis to make his final discovery.

CHECK YOUR UNDERSTANDING 15F

1. What was the death rate of childbed fever under Dr. Boer's direction? How did it change after Dr. Klein took over? (paragraphs 64 and 65)

Answer: Under Boer's direction the rate of childbed fever averaged 1.4%. When Klein took control the rate almost immediately jumped to 7.5%, and it remained high. When the two-clinic system was implemented the rate in the first clinic became 12%, while the second was 3%.

2. What important clues did Semmelweis find in his examination of the history of the Vienna Hospital under Dr. Boer? (paragraph 66)

3. What additional ideas did Semmelweis find out about the Dublin Hospital, and how did this information influence Semmelweis's thinking? (paragraph 67)

4. What was the "phantom model" procedure? How was this important to Semmelweis's research? (paragraph 68)

5. Describe what Semmelweis knew before the Kolletschka incident. (paragraph 70)

6. What did Semmelweis emphasize in his address to the Vienna Medical Society in May 1850? Why does this support the conjecture that at that time Semmelweis still thought that childbed fever was a specific disease? (paragraph 71)

7. What happened in the clinic when there was a woman suffering from a foully discharging cancer of the uterus? Why would the results be surprising to Semmelweis? (paragraph 72)

8. What was Semmelweis's new hypothesis? Why did he need to modify his original hypothesis? (paragraph 73)

9. What happened in the clinic when a woman was admitted with a severely discharging carious (decaying) knee? Why would the results be surprising to Semmelweis? (paragraph 74)

10. Why did Semmelweis think that washing the hands would eliminate the possibility of spreading the disease, and how did the new facts affect his thinking? (paragraph 75 and 76)

11. Describe the two anomalies that confronted Semmelweis. Why can these be used to conclude that Semmelweis did not have the final discovery of the cause of childbed fever until after he resolved the second anomaly? (paragraphs 77 and 78)

12. What was Semmelweis's final discovery and how did it make sense of all the facts? (paragraphs 79 and 80)

Summary

- In 1784, Joseph II made a decree setting up the lying-in (maternity) hospital of Vienna.
- In 1840, the Vienna Hospital set up two divisions in the obstetric department. The first clinic was staffed by doctors and medical students doing intern work in obstetrics, while the second employed midwives who had no other duties than assisting in the care of the patients and in deliveries.
- When Semmelweis began his investigation, the rates of death from puerperal fever were approximately 12% monthly for the first clinic, but only 3% for the second clinic.
- Until Semmelweis made his discovery, childbed fever (also called "puerperal fever") was universally believed to be a disease peculiar to women.
- Miasm theory postulated that diseases were carried by the air; certain combinations of the basic elements in the atmosphere were potentially harmful to humans.
- Contagion theory held that a contagious disease is one transmissible from individual to individual by immediate or direct contact.
- Infectious: Refers to the causation of the disease.
- Contagious: Refers to the manner of transmission of a disease.
- Semmelweis could not use germ theory as support, because Pasteur's experimental results would not be universally accepted for another 16 years.
- Since Semmelweis was looking for the cause of childbed fever, he began testing some obvious implications of the miasm view.
- Semmelweis's early conclusion was that childbed fever was endemic—a disease that was the result of causes within the hospital.
- Semmelweis came to believe that the symptoms occurred in both female and male babies.
- Semmelweis concluded that it is through the doctors' and medical students' examinations of the women that cadaveric particles are absorbed into the system.
- An experiment was set up to ensure that no other changes were allowed in the first clinic. The only new factor was the washing of hands in the solution. The immediate result was that the childbed fever rate dropped from 12% to 3% in the first clinic.
- Semmelweis used analogical reasoning: The first analogy was that the symptoms of the babies and women were similar; the second analogy was that the symptoms of Kolletschka were similar to the women.
- It was only after he had gained the information about the phantom model, saw Boer's success rate, and studied the English methods of combating childbed fever that he had a program to implement.
- Semmelweis's first modification came from the necessity to explain how something other than cadaveric particles could cause the fever. Then he had to explain why it was not even necessary for direct contact to take place.
- The idea that childbed fever was a form of blood poisoning was the answer that Semmelweis needed to make sense of all the facts.

KEY TERMS

childbed fever   640
miasm theory   640

contagion theory   640
infectious   641

contagious   641
endemic   643

LOGIC CHALLENGE: A RELATIVE PROBLEM

At a party you overhear two conversations. In the first conversation you hear this:

Stu: Who is that man sitting on the couch, the one with the red sweater?
Lou: His name is Drew and he is my nephew.
Sue: He is definitely not my nephew.

You walk over to the couch and hear this:

Pru: By the way, is Lou married?
Drew: No, he is single. He is Sue's biological brother.

No two people at the party have the same name, so each of the conversations are referring to the same persons. The question is: How are Sue and Drew related?

BIBLIOGRAPHY

[1]   Abbott, A. C. *The Hygiene of Transmissible Diseases*, Saunders, 1901.
[2]   Carter, K. Codell. "Semmelweis and His Predecessors," *Medical History*, 25, 1981, pp. 7–72.
[3]   Dawson, Percy. "Semmelweis: An Interpretation," *Annals of Medical History*, 6, 1924, pp. 258–279.
[4]   Fisher, John. *New England Quarterly Journal of Medicine and Science*, 1842–1843, pp. 562–569.
[5]   Galdston, Iago. "*Homines Ad Deos*," *Bulletin of the History of Medicine*, 28, 1954, pp. 515–524.
[6]   Gortvay, Gyorgy, and Imre Zoltan. *Semmelweis, His Life and Work*, Akademiai Kiado, Budapest, 1968.
[7]   Gyorgyey, Ferenc. *Puerperal Fever 1847–1861*, M.S. thesis, Yale University, 1968.
[8]   Hempel, Carl G. *Philosophy of Natural Science*, Prentice-Hall, 1966.
[9]   Howard-Jones, Norman. *The Scientific Background of the International Sanitary Conferences 1851–1938*, World Health Organization, 1975.
[10] Lesky, Erna. *The Vienna Medical School of the 19th Century*, Johns Hopkins University Press, 1976.
[11] Murphy, Frank. "Obstetric Training in Vienna: One Hundred Years Ago," *Bulletin of the History of Medicine*, 21, 1947.
[12] Newsholme, Arthur. *Evolution of Preventive Medicine*, 1927.
[13] Nuland, Sherwin. "The Enigma of Semmelweis: An Interpretation," *Journal of the History of Medicine*, 20, 1979, pp. 255–272.
[14] Peckham, C. H. "A Brief History of Puerperal Infection," *Bulletin of the Institute of the History of Medicine*, 3, 1935, pp. 187–209.
[15] Semmelweis, Ignaz. *The Etiology, the Concept, and the Prophylaxis of Childbed Fever*, translated by Frank Murphy, *Medical Classics*, Vol. 5, 1941.
[16] Sinclair, William. *Semmelweis: His Life and Doctrine*, Manchester University Press, 1909.
[17] Slaughter, Frank. *Immortal Magyar*, Schuman, 1950.
[18] Winslow, C. E. A. *Man and Epidemics*, Princeton University Press, 1952.

Glossary

A

A priori theory of probability: Ascribes to a simple event a fraction between 0 and 1.

A-proposition: A categorical proposition having the form "All S are P."

Abduction: The process that occurs when we infer explanations for certain facts.

Abnormal state: A drastic change in the normal state regarding an object.

Accident: When a generalization is inappropriately applied to the case at hand.

Addition: A rule of inference (implication rule).

Affidavit: A written statement signed before an authorized official.

Affirmative conclusion/negative premise: A formal fallacy that occurs when a categorical syllogism has a negative premise and an affirmative conclusion.

Amphiboly: Ambiguity that arises when a poorly constructed statement muddles the intended meaning.

Analogical argument: The argument lists the characteristics that two (or more) things have in common and concludes that the things being compared probably have some other characteristic in common.

Analogical reasoning: One of the most fundamental tools used in creating an argument. It can be analyzed as a type of inductive argument—it is a matter of *probability*, based on experience, and it can be quite persuasive.

Analogy: To draw an analogy is simply to indicate that there are similarities between two or more things.

Appeal to an unqualified authority: An argument that relies on the opinions of people who have no expertise, training, or knowledge relevant to the issue at hand.

Appeal to force: A threat of harmful consequences (physical and otherwise) used to force acceptance of a course of action that would otherwise be unacceptable.

B

Begging the question: An argument that assumes as evidence in the premises the very thing that it attempts to prove in the conclusion.

Biased sample: An argument that uses a non-representative sample as support for a statistical claim about an entire population.

Biconditional: A compound statement consisting of two conditionals—one indicated by the

Appeal to ignorance: An argument built on a position of ignorance claims either that (1) a statement must be true because it has not been proven to be false or (2) a statement must be false because it has not been proven to be true.

Appeal to pity: A specific kind of emotional plea that relies solely on a sense of pity for support.

Appeal to the people: The avoidance of objective evidence in favor of an emotional response defeats the goal of a rational investigation of truth. The tactic appeals to people's desire to belong to a group.

Appellate courts: Courts of appeal that review the decisions of lower courts.

Argument: A group of statements of which one (the conclusion) is claimed to follow from the others (the premises).

Argument against the person: When a claim is rejected or judged to be false based on alleged character flaws of the person making the claim. A second common form occurs whenever someone's statement or reasoning is attacked by way of a stereotype, such as a racial, sexual, or religious stereotype. A third form involves the use of the circumstances of a person's life to reject his claims.

Argument form: An arrangement of logical operators and statement variables in which a consistent replacement of the statement variables by statements results in an argument.

Association: A rule of inference (replacement rule).

Asymmetrical: Illustrated by the following: If A is the father of B, then B is not the father of A.

word "if" and the other indicated by the phrase "only if." The triple bar symbol is used to translate a biconditional statement.

Bound variables: Variables governed by a quantifier.

C

Categorical imperative: The basic idea is that your actions or behavior toward others should always be such that you would want everyone to act in the same manner.

Categorical proposition: A categorical proposition relates two classes of objects.

Categorical syllogism: A syllogism constructed entirely of categorical propositions.

Causal network: A set of conditions that bring about an effect.

Change of quantifier: The rule allows the removal or introduction of negation signs. (The rule is a set of four logical equivalences).

Childbed fever: Also called *puerperal fever*, was universally believed to be a disease peculiar to women.

Class: A group of objects.

Cogent argument: An inductive argument is cogent when the argument is strong and the premises are true.

Cognitive meaning: Language that is used to convey information has cognitive meaning.

Coincidence: A fallacy that results from the accidental or chance connection between two events.

Common cause fallacy: A mistake that occurs when someone thinks that one event causes another, when in fact both events are the result of a common cause.

Commutation: A rule of inference (replacement rule).

Complement: The set of objects that do not belong to a given class.

Complex question: A single question that actually contains multiple, hidden parts.

Composition: The mistaken transfer of an attribute of the individual parts of an object to the object as a whole.

Compound statement: A statement that has at least one simple statement as a component.

Conclusion: The statement that is claimed to follow from the premises of an argument.

Conclusion indicator: Words and phrases that indicate the presence of a conclusion (the statement claimed to follow from premises).

Conditional: In ordinary language, the word "if" typically precedes the antecedent of a conditional; "only if" typically precedes the consequent of a conditional. The horseshoe symbol is used to translate a conditional statement.

Conditional probability: The calculation of the probability of an event if another event has already happened.

Conditional proof: A method that starts by assuming the antecedent of a conditional statement on a separate line and then proceeds to validly derive the consequent on a separate line.

Conjunction: A compound statement that has two distinct statements (called conjuncts) connected by the dot symbol. Also, a rule of inference (implication rule).

Consequentialism: A class of moral theories in which the moral value of any human action or behavior is determined exclusively by its outcomes.

Consistent statements: Two (or more) statements that have at least one line on their respective truth tables where the main operators are true.

Constructive dilemma: A rule of inference (implication rule).

Contagion theory: Held that a contagious disease is one transmissible from individual to individual by immediate or direct contact.

Contagious: Refers to the *manner of transmission* of a disease.

Contingent statements: Statements that are neither necessarily true nor necessarily false (they are sometimes true, sometimes false).

Contradictories: In categorical logic, pairs of propositions in which one is the negation of the other.

Contradictory statements: Two statements that have opposite truth values on every line of their respective truth tables.

Contraposition: We replace the subject term of a given proposition with the complement of its predicate term, and then replace the predicate term of the given proposition with the complement of its subject term.

Contraposition by limitation: Subalternation is used to change a universal **E**-proposition into its corresponding particular **O**-proposition. We then apply the regular process of forming a contrapositive to this **O**-proposition.

Contraries: Pairs of propositions that cannot both be true at the same time, but can both be false at the same time.

Control group: The group in which the variable being tested is withheld.

Controlled experiment: One in which multiple experimental setups differ by only one variable.

Convergent diagram: A diagram that reveals the occurrence of independent premises.

Conversion: An immediate argument created by interchanging the subject and predicate terms of a given categorical proposition.

Conversion by limitation: We first change a universal **A**-proposition into its corresponding particular **I**-proposition, and then we use the process of conversion on the **I**-proposition.

Copula: The words "are" and "are not" are forms of "to be" and serve to link (to "couple") the subject class with the predicate class.

Correlation: A correspondence between two sets of objects, events, or sets of data.

Counteranalogy: A new, competing argument—one that compares the thing in question to something else.

Counterexample: A counterexample to a statement is evidence that shows the statement is false. A counterexample to an argument shows the possibility that premises assumed to be true do not make the conclusion necessarily true. A single counterexample to a deductive argument is enough to show that the argument is invalid.

D

Decreasing extension: In a sequence of terms where each term after the first denotes a set of objects with fewer members than the previous term.

Decreasing intension: In a sequence of terms where each term after the first connotes fewer attributes than the previous term.

Deductive argument: An argument in which it is claimed that the conclusion follows *necessarily* from the premises. In other words, it is claimed that under the assumption that the premises are true it is *impossible* for the conclusion to be false.

Definiendum: Refers to that which is being defined.

Definiens: Refers to that which does the defining.

Definite description: Describes an individual person, place, or thing.

Definition: A definition assigns a meaning to a word, phrase, or symbol.

Definition by genus and difference: Assigns a meaning to a term (the species) by establishing a genus and combining it with the attribute that distinguishes the members of that species.

Definition by subclass: Assigns meaning to a term by naming subclasses (species) of the class denoted by the term.

De Morgan: A rule of inference (replacement rule).

Deontology: The theory that duty to others is the first and foremost moral consideration.

Dependent premises: Premises are dependent when they act together to support a conclusion.

Disanalogies: To point out differences between two things.

Disjunction: A compound statement that has two distinct statements (called disjuncts) connected by the wedge symbol.

Disjunctive syllogism: A rule of inference (implication rule).

Distributed: If a categorical proposition asserts something definite about every member of a class, then the term designating that class is said to be distributed.

Distribution: A rule of inference (replacement rule).

Divergent diagram: A diagram that shows a single premise supporting independent conclusions.

Division: The mistaken transfer of an attribute of an object as a whole to its individual parts.

Domain of discourse: The set of individuals over which a quantifier ranges.

Double negation: A rule of inference (replacement rule).

E

E-proposition: A categorical proposition having the form "No S are P."

Egoism: The basic principle that everyone should act in order to maximize his or her own individual pleasure or happiness.

Emotive meaning: Language that is used to express emotion or feelings has emotive meaning.

Emotivism: A theory that asserts that moral value judgments are merely expressions of our attitudes or emotions.

Emphasis: A fallacy that occurs when attention is purposely (or accidentally) diverted from the issue at hand.

Empty class: A class that has zero members.

Endemic: A disease that is confined to a specific place.

Enthymemes: Arguments with missing premises, missing conclusions, or both.

Enumerative definition: Assigns meaning to a term by naming the individual members of the class denoted by the term.

Equiprobable: When each of the possible outcomes has an equal probability of occurring.

Equivocation: The intentional or unintentional use of different meanings of words or phrases in an argument.

Exclusive disjunction: An exclusive disjunction is where both disjuncts cannot be true at the same time.

Exclusive premises: A formal fallacy that occurs when both premises in a categorical syllogism are negative.

Existential fallacy: A formal fallacy that occurs when a categorical syllogism has a particular conclusion and two universal premises.

Existential generalization: A rule that permits the valid introduction of an existential quantifier from either a constant or a variable.

Existential import: A proposition has existential import if it presupposes the existence of certain kinds of objects.

Existential instantiation: A rule that permits giving a name to a thing that exists. The name can then be represented by a constant.

Existential quantifier: Formed by putting a backward E in front of a variable, and then placing them both in parentheses.

Experimental group: The group that gets the variable being tested.

Experimental science: Tests the explanations proposed by theoretical science.

Explanation: An explanation provides reasons for why or how an event occurred. By themselves, explanations are not arguments; however, they can form part of an argument.

Exportation: A rule of inference (replacement rule).

Extension: The class or collection of objects to which the term applies. In other words, what the term denotes (its reference).

Extensional definition: Assigns meaning to a term by indicating the class members denoted by the term.

F

Factual dispute: Occurs when people disagree on a matter that involves facts.

Fallacy of affirming the consequent: An invalid argument form; it is a formal fallacy.

Fallacy of ambiguity or diversion: A fallacy that occurs when the meanings of terms or phrases are changed (intentionally or unintentionally) within the argument, or when our attention is purposely (or accidentally) diverted from the issue at hand.

Fallacy of denying the antecedent: An invalid argument form; it is a formal fallacy.

Fallacies of relevance: Fallacies that occur whenever irrelevant premises are offered in support of a conclusion.

Fallacies of unwarranted assumption: Arguments that assume the truth of some unproved or questionable claim.

False cause: A fallacy that occurs when a causal connection is assumed to exist between two events when none actually exists.

False dichotomy: A fallacy that occurs when it is assumed that only two choices are possible, when in fact others exist.

False dilemma: A fallacy that occurs when two choices are asserted, each leading to an unwanted result, but there is a failure to acknowledge that other possibilities exist.

Figure: The middle term can be arranged in the two premises in four different ways. These placements determine the figure of the categorical syllogism.

Finite universe method: The method of demonstrating invalidity that assumes a universe, containing at least one individual, to show the possibility of true premises and a false conclusion.

Formal fallacy: A logical error that occurs in the form or structure of an argument; it is restricted to deductive arguments.

Free variables: Variables that are not governed by any quantifier.

Functional definition: Specifies the purpose or use of the objects denoted by the term.

General conjunction method: The method that is used for calculating the probability of two or more events occurring together, regardless of whether the events are independent or not independent.

General disjunction method: The method that is used for calculating the probability when two or more events are not mutually exclusive.

H

Hasty generalization: A generalization created on the basis of a few instances.

Hypothesis: Provides an explanation for known facts and a way to test an explanation.

Hypothetical syllogism: A rule of inference (implication rule).

I

I-proposition: A categorical proposition having the form "Some S are P."

Identity: A binary relation that holds between a thing and itself.

Illicit major: A formal fallacy that occurs when the major term in a categorical syllogism is distributed in the conclusion but not in the major premise.

Illicit minor: A formal fallacy that occurs when the minor term in a categorical syllogism is distributed in the conclusion but not in the minor premise.

Immediate argument: An argument that has only one premise.

Implication rules: Valid argument forms that are validly applied only to an entire line.

Inclusive disjunction: An inclusive disjunction is where both disjuncts can be true at the same time.

Inconsistent statements: Two (or more) statements that do not have even one line on their respective truth tables where the main operators are true (but they can be false) at the same time.

Increasing extension: In a sequence of terms where each term after the first denotes a set of objects with more members than the previous term.

Increasing intension: In a sequence of terms where each term after the first connotes more attributes than the previous term.

Independent premises: Premises are independent when the falsity of either one would not nullify any support the others would give to the conclusion.

Indictment: A formal accusation presented by a grand jury.

Indirect proof: A method that starts by assuming the negation of the required statement and then validly deriving a contradiction on a subsequent line.

Individual constants: The subject of a singular statement is translated using lowercase letters. The lowercase letters act as names of individuals.

Individual variables: The three lowercase letters, $x, y,$ and z.

Inductive argument: An argument in which it is claimed that the premises make the conclusion *probable*. In other words, it is claimed that under the assumption that the premises are true it is *improbable* for the conclusion to be false.

Infectious: Refers to the *causation* of a disease.

Inference: A term used by logicians to refer to the reasoning process that is expressed by an argument.

Inference to the best explanation: When we reason from the premise that a hypothesis would explain certain facts to the conclusion that the hypothesis is the best explanation for those facts.

Inferential claim: If a passage expresses a reasoning process—that the conclusion follows from the premises—then we say that it makes an inferential claim.

Informal fallacy: A mistake in reasoning that occurs in ordinary language and is different from an error in the form or structure of arguments.

Instantial letter: The letter (either a variable or a constant) that is introduced by universal instantiaton or existential instantiation.

Instantiation: When instantiation is applied to a quantified statement, the quantifier is removed, and every variable that was bound by the quantifier is replaced by the same instantial letter.

Intension: The intension of a term is specified by listing the properties or attributes that the term connotes—in other words, its sense.

Intensional definition: Assigns a meaning to a term by listing the properties or attributes shared by all the objects that are denoted by the term.

Intransitive: Illustrated by the following: If A is the mother of B, and B is the mother of C, then A is not the mother of C.

Invalid deductive argument: An argument in which, assuming the premises are true, it is *possible* for the conclusion to be false. In other words, the conclusion does not follow necessarily from the premises.

Irreflexive: An example of an irreflexive relationship is expressed by the statement "Nothing can be taller than itself."

J

Joint method of agreement and difference: If two or more instances of an event have only one thing in common, while the instances in which it does not occur all share the absence of that thing, then the item is a likely cause.

Justification: Refers to the rule of inference that is applied to every validly derived step in a proof.

L

Lexical definition: A definition based on the common use of a word, term, or symbol.

Linked diagram: A diagram that reveals the occurrence of dependent premises.

Logic: The study of reasoning.

Logical operators: Special symbols that can be used as part of ordinary language statement translations.

Logically equivalent: Two truth-functional statements may appear different but have identical truth tables. When this occurs, they are logically equivalent.

M

Main operator: The operator that has in its range the largest component or components in a compound statement.

Major premise: The first premise of a categorical syllogism (it contains the major term).

Major term: The predicate of the conclusion of a categorical syllogism.

Material equivalence: A rule of inference (replacement rule).

Material implication: A rule of inference (replacement rule).

Mean: A statistical average that is determined by adding the numerical values in the data concerning the examined objects, then dividing by the number of objects that were measured.

Median: A statistical average that is determined by locating the value that separates the entire set of data in half.

Mediate argument: An argument that has more than one premise.

Method of agreement: The method that looks at two or more instances of an event to see what they have in common.

Method of concomitant variations: The method that looks for two factors that vary together.

Method of difference: The method that looks for what all the instances of an event do not have in common.

Method of residues: The method that subtracts from a complex set of events those parts that already have known causes.

Miasm theory: Postulated that diseases were carried by the air; that certain combinations of the basic elements in the atmosphere were potentially harmful to humans.

Middle term: The term that occurs only in the premises of a categorical syllogism.

Minor premise: The second premise of a categorical syllogism (it contains the minor term).

Minor term: The subject of the conclusion of a categorical syllogism.

Misleading precision: A claim that appears to be statistically significant but is not.

Missing the point: When premises that seem to lead logically to one conclusion are used instead to support an unexpected conclusion.

Mode: A statistical average that is determined by locating the value that occurs most.

Modus ponens: A rule of inference (implication rule).

Modus tollens: A rule of inference (implication rule).

Monadic predicate: A one-place predicate that assigns a characteristic to an individual thing.

Mood: The mood of a categorical syllogism consists of the type of categorical propositions involved (**A, E, I,** or **O**) and the order in which they occur.

Mutually exclusive: Two events, such that if one event occurs, then the other cannot.

N

Natural deduction: A proof procedure by which the conclusion of an argument is validly derived from the premises through the use of rules of inference.

Naturalistic fallacy: Value judgments cannot be logically derived from statements of fact.

Naturalistic moral principle: Since it is natural for humans to desire pleasure (or happiness), and to avoid pain, human behavior ought to be directed to these two ends.

Necessary condition: When one thing is essential, mandatory, or required in order for another thing to be realized.

Negation: The word "not" and the phrase "it is not the case that" are used to deny the statement that follows them, and we refer to their use as negation.

Negation method: The method that is used once the probability of an event occurring is known; it is then easy to calculate the probability of the event not occurring.

Negative conclusion/affirmative premises: A formal fallacy that occurs when a categorical syllogism has a negative conclusion and two affirmative premises.

Noncontingent statement: A statement such that the truth values in the main operator column do not depend on the truth values of the component parts.

Nonreflexive: When a relationship is neither reflexive nor irreflexive.

Nonsymmetrical: When a relationship is neither symmetrical nor asymmetrical, then it is nonsymmetrical. Illustrated by the following: If Kris loves Morgan, then Morgan may or may not love Kris.

Nontransitive: Illustrated by the following: If Kris loves Morgan and Morgan loves Terry, then Kris may or may not love Terry.

Nontrivial prediction: The prediction requires reference to background knowledge, which is everything we know to be true.

Normal state: The historical information regarding an object.

Normative: Establishing standards for correct moral behavior; determining norms or rules of conduct.

O

O-proposition: A categorical proposition having the form "Some S are not P."

Obversion: An immediate argument formed by changing the quality of the given proposition, and then replacing the predicate term with its complement.

Operational definition: Defines a term by specifying a measurement procedure.

Opposition: When two standard-form categorical propositions refer to the same subject and predicate classes, but differ in quality, quantity, or both.

Order of operations: The order of handling the logical operators within a truth-functional proposition; it is a step-by-step method of generating a complete truth table.

Ostensive definition: Involves demonstrating the term—for example, by pointing to a member of the class that the term denotes.

P

Particular affirmative: An **I**-proposition. It asserts that at least one member of the subject class is a member of the predicate class.

Particular negative: An **O**-proposition. It asserts that at least one member of the subject class is not a member of the predicate class.

Persuasive definition: Assigns a meaning to a term with the direct purpose of influencing attitudes or opinions.

Plaintiff: The person who initiates a lawsuit.

Population: Any group of objects, not just human populations.

Post hoc fallacy: A fallacy involving either a short-term or long-term pattern that is noticed after the fact.

Precedent: A judicial decision that can be applied to later cases.

Precipitating cause: The object or event directly involved in bringing about an effect.

Precising definition: Reduces the vagueness and ambiguity of a term by providing a sharp focus, often a technical meaning, for a term.

Predicate logic: Integrates many of the features of categorical and propositional logic. It combines the symbols associated with propositional logic with special symbols that are used to translate predicates.

Predicate symbols: Predicates are the fundamental units in predicate logic. Uppercase letters are used to symbolize the units.

Predicate term: The term that comes second in a standard-form categorical proposition.

Prejudicial effect: Evidence that might cause some jurors to be negatively biased toward a defendant.

Premise: The information intended to provide support for a conclusion.

Premise indicator: Words and phrases that help us recognize arguments by indicating the presence of premises (statements being offered in support of a conclusion).

Prescriptive: The term means "to offer advice."

Principle of charity: We should choose the reconstructed argument that gives the benefit of the doubt to the person presenting the argument.

Principle of replacement: Logically equivalent expressions may replace each other within the context of a proof.

Probability calculus: The branch of mathematics that can be used to compute the probabilities of complex events from the probabilities of their component events.

Probative value: Evidence that can be used during a trial to advance the facts of the case.

Proof: A sequence of steps (also called a deduction or a derivation) in which each step is either a premise or follows from earlier steps in the sequence according to the rules of inference.

Proposition: The information content imparted by a statement, or, simply put, its meaning.

Propositional logic: The basic components in propositional logic are statements.

Q

Quality: When we classify a categorical proposition as either affirmative or negative we are referring to its quality.

Quantifier: The words "all," "no," and "some" are quantifiers. They tell us the extent of the class inclusion or exclusion.

Quantity: When we classify a categorical proposition as either universal or particular we are referring to its quantity.

R

Random sample: Where every member of the population has an equal chance of getting into the sample.

Red herring: A fallacy that occurs when someone completely ignores an opponent's position and changes the subject, diverting the discussion in a new direction.

Reflexive: The idea that *anything is identical to itself* is expressed by the reflexive property.

Relational predicate: Establishes a connection between individuals.

Relative frequency theory of probability: The theory that some probabilities can be computed by dividing the number of favorable cases by the total number of observed cases.

Relativism: First, all moral value judgments are determined by an individual's personal beliefs or by a society's beliefs toward actions or behavior. Second, there are no objective or universal moral value judgments.

Remote cause: Something that is connected to the precipitating cause by a chain of events.

Replacement rules: Pairs of logically equivalent statement forms.

Representative sample: A sample that accurately reflects the characteristics of the population as a whole.

Restricted conjunction method: The method that is used in situations dealing with two or more independent events, where the occurrence of one event has no bearing whatsoever on the occurrence or nonoccurrence of the other event.

Restricted disjunction method: The method that is used when two (or more) events are independent of each other, and the events are mutually exclusive.

Rhetorical conditional: A conditional statement that is used to imply an argument.

Rhetorical disjunction: A disjunction that is used to disguise a statement or an implied argument.

Rhetorical language: When we speak or write for dramatic or exaggerated effect; that is, the language we employ may be implying things that are not explicitly said.

Rhetorical question: When a statement is disguised in the form of a question.

Rule-based reasoning: Legal reasoning is also referred to as *rule-based reasoning.*

Rules of inference: The function of rules of inference is to justify the steps of a proof.

Rules of law: The legal principles that have been applied to historical cases.

S

Sample: A subset of a population.

Self-contradiction: A statement that is necessarily false.

Serial diagram: A diagram that shows that a conclusion from one argument is a premise in a second argument.

Simple statement: One that does not have any other statement as a component.

Simplification: A rule of inference (implication rule).

Singular proposition: A proposition that asserts something about a specific person, place, or thing.

Situation ethics: Although there can be general, even objective, moral rules, we should not rigidly apply those rules to every possible situation.

Slippery slope: An argument that attempts to make a final event the inevitable outcome of an initial act.

Sorites: A special type of enthymeme that is a chain of arguments. The missing parts are intermediate conclusions, each of which, in turn, becomes a premise in the next link in the chain.

Sound argument: When logical analysis shows that a deductive argument is valid, and when truth value analysis of the premises shows that they are all true, then the argument is sound.

Standard deviation: A measure of the amount of diversity in a set of numerical values.

Standard-form categorical proposition: A proposition that has one of the following forms: "All S are P," "Some S are P," "No S are P," "Some S are not P."

Standard-form categorical syllogism: A categorical syllogism that meets three requirements: (1) All three statements must be standard-form categorical propositions. (2) The two occurrences of each term must be identical and have the same sense. (3) The major premise must occur first, the minor premise second, and the conclusion last.

Statement: A sentence that is either true or false.

Statement form: A pattern of statement variables and logical operators.

Statement function: An expression that does not make any universal or particular assertion about anything; therefore, it has no truth value. Statement functions are simply patterns for a statement.

Statement variable: A statement variable can stand for any statement, simple or complex.

Stipulative definition: Introduces a new meaning to a term or symbol.

Strategy: Referring to a greater, overall goal.

Straw man: A fallacy that occurs when someone's written or spoken words are taken out of context. It purposely distorts the original argument to create a new, weak argument that can be easily refuted (a straw man that is easily knocked down).

Strong inductive argument: An argument such that if the premises are assumed to be true, then the conclusion is probably true. In other words, if the premises are assumed to be true, then it is improbable that the conclusion is false.

Subalternation: The relationship between a universal proposition (referred to as the *superaltern*) and its corresponding particular proposition (referred to as the *subaltern*).

Subcontraries: Pairs of propositions that cannot both be false at the same time, but can both be true; also, if one is false, then the other must be true.

Subject term: The term that comes first in a standard-form categorical proposition.

Subjectivist theory of probability: The theory that some probability determinations are based on the lack of total knowledge regarding an event.

Sufficient condition: Whenever one event ensures that another event will happen.

Syllogism: A deductive argument that has exactly two premises and a conclusion.

Symmetrical: Illustrated by the following: If A is married to B, then B is married to A.

Synonymous definition: Assigns a meaning to a term by providing another term with the same meaning; in other words, by providing a synonym.

T

Tactics: The use of small-scale maneuvers or devices.

Tautology: A statement that is necessarily true. Also, a rule of inference (replacement rule).

Teleology: The philosophical belief that the value of an action or object can be determined by looking at the purpose or the end of the action or object.

Term: A single word or a group of words that can be the subject of a statement; it can be a common name, a proper name, or even a descriptive phrase.

Theoretical definition: Assigns a meaning to a term by providing an understanding of how the term fits into a general theory.

Theoretical science: Proposes explanations for natural phenomena.

Transitive: Illustrated by the following: If A is taller than B, and B is taller than C, then A is taller than C.

Transposition: A rule of inference (replacement rule).

Truth function: The truth value of a truth-functional compound proposition is determined by the truth values of its components and the definitions of the logical operators involved. Any truth-functional compound proposition that can be determined in this manner is said to be a truth function.

Truth table: An arrangement of truth values for a truth-functional compound proposition that displays for every possible case how the truth value of the proposition is determined by the truth values of its simple components.

Truth value: Every statement is either true or false; these two possibilities are called *truth values*.

Tu quoque: A variety of the *ad hominem* fallacy that is distinguished by the specific attempt of one person to avoid the issue at hand by claiming the other person is a hypocrite.

U

Uncogent argument: An inductive argument is uncogent if either or both of the following conditions hold: the argument is weak, or the argument has at least one false premise.

Undistributed: If a proposition does not assert something definite about every member of a class, then the term designating that class is said to be undistributed.

Undistributed middle: A formal fallacy that occurs when the middle term in a categorical syllogism is undistributed in both premises of a categorical syllogism.

Unintended consequences: Something that is a direct result of an analogy, but that is unacceptable to the person presenting the analogy.

Universal affirmative: An **A**-proposition. It affirms that every member of the subject class is a member of the predicate class.

Universal generalization: A rule by which you can validly deduce the universal quantification of a statement function from a substitution instance with respect to the name of any arbitrarily selected individual (subject to restrictions).

Universal instantiation: A substitution instance of a statement function can be validly deduced from the universally quantified statement by the rule of universal instantiation.

Universal negative: An **E**-proposition. It asserts that no members of the subject class are members of the predicate class.

Universal quantifier: The symbol used to capture the idea that universal statements assert something about every member of the subject class.

Universalizable: When the same principles hold for all people at all times.

Unsound argument: If a deductive argument is invalid, or if at least one of the premises is false (truth value analysis), then the argument is unsound.

Utilitarianism: It can be summed up in the famous dictum "the greatest good for the greatest number."

V

Valid deductive argument: An argument in which, assuming the premises are true, it is *impossible* for the conclusion to be false. In other words, the conclusion follows necessarily from the premises.

Value claim: A judgment that someone (or something) is good or bad, moral or immoral, or better or worse than another person (or thing).

Value judgment: A claim that a particular human action or object has some degree of importance, worth, or desirability.

Venn diagram: A diagram that uses circles to represent categorical proposition forms.

Verbal dispute: Occurs when a vague or ambiguous term results in a linguistic misunderstanding.

Verifiable prediction: One where the prediction, if it is true, must include an observable event.

W

Weak inductive argument: An argument such that if the premises are assumed to be true, then the conclusion is not probably true.

Well-formed formulas: Compound statement forms that are grammatically correct.

Answers to Selected Exercises

CHAPTER 1

Check Your Understanding 1B.1

5. *Premises:*
   (a) True friends are there when we need them.
   (b) They suffer with us when we fail.
   (c) They are happy when we succeed.
   Conclusion: We should never take our friends for granted.
   Although there are no indicator terms, the first statement is the conclusion, the point of the passage, for which the other statements offer support.

9. *Premises:*
   (a) At one time Gary Kasparov had the highest ranking of any chess grand master in history.
   (b) He was beaten in a chess tournament by a computer program called Deep Blue.
   Conclusion: The computer program should be given a ranking higher than Kasparov.
   The indicator word "So" identifies the conclusion. The other statements are offered as support.

13. *Premises:*
   (a) My guru said the world will end on August 6, 2045.
   (b) So far everything he predicted has happened exactly as he said it would.
   Conclusion: The world will end on August 6, 2045.
   The indicator word "because" identifies the premises, so the first statement is the conclusion.

Check Your Understanding 1B.2

5. Argument. The phrase "It follows from the fact that" identifies the premise, which is offered as support for the conclusion "she must be a vegetarian."

9. Argument. The premise "She won the lottery" is offered as a reason to conclude that "she will quit her job soon."

13. Argument. The conclusion is "The handprint on the wall had not been made by the librarian himself." The premises are "there hadn't been blood on his hands," and "the print did not match his (the librarian)."

17. Argument. The first statement, "The idea that space and time may form a closed surface without boundary also has profound implications for the role of God in the affairs of the universe" sets up the goal of the passage. The implied conclusion is that the universe does not need a creator. The

word "So" is not used as a conclusion indicator here; instead it forms part of the premises: "So long as the universe had a beginning, we could suppose it had a creator. But if the universe is really completely self-contained, having no boundary or edge, it would have neither beginning nor end; it would simply be."

21. Argument. The conclusion (as indicated by the word "Thus") is "we do not necessarily keep eBooks in compliance with any particular paper edition."

25. Not an argument. The passage provides a definition of "authoritarian governments" and a definition of "democratic governments." Although there is no direct conclusion, the author's choice of definitions indicates his point of view.

29. Not an argument.

33. Not an argument. The information is offered as advice.

37. Not an argument.

41. Not an argument.

45. Not an argument.

49. Not an argument.

Check Your Understanding 1C

5. Explanation. The first statement establishes that something has already occurred. The statement "It must be because voters are disappointed with the two-party system" is offered as an explanation of the fact.

9. Explanation. In this context, the word "because" indicates an explanation of what the author means by the term "fall."

13. Explanation. The information is offered to explain why "the iPhone and Android are popular."

17. Explanation. The information is offered to explain why Twain "gave up the idea" of making a lecturing trip through the antipodes and the borders of the Orient.

Check Your Understanding 1E

5. Deductive. The first premise tells us something about *all* fires. If both premises are assumed to be true, then the conclusion is necessarily true.

9. Deductive. The first premise tells us something about *all* elements with atomic weights greater than 64. If both premises

are assumed to be true, then the conclusion is necessarily true.

13. Deductive. The first premise specifies the minimum age when someone can legally play the slot machines in Las Vegas. The second premise tells us Sam is 33 years old. If both premises are true, then the conclusion is necessarily true.

17. Inductive. We are told something about *most* Doberman dogs. Also, the use of the word "probably" in the conclusion indicates that it is best classified as an inductive argument.

Check Your Understanding 1F

5. If we let C = *computers*, E = *electronic devices*, and A = *things that require an AC adapter*, then the argument form is the following:

All C are E.
All A are E.
All C are A.

The following substitutions create a counterexample: let C = *cats*, E = *mammals*, and A = *dogs*.

All cats are mammals.
All dogs are mammals.
All cats are dogs.

Both premises are true, and the conclusion is false. Therefore, the counterexample shows that the argument is invalid.

9. If we let U = *unicorns*, I = *immortal creatures*, and C = *centaurs*, then the argument form is the following:

No U are I.
No C are I.
No U are C.

The following substitutions create a counterexample: let U = *cats*, I = *snakes*, and C = *mammals*.

No cats are snakes.
No mammals are snakes.
No cats are mammals.

Both premises are true, and the conclusion is false. Therefore, the counterexample shows that the argument is invalid.

13. We must make sure that whatever birth dates we assign to Fidelix and Gil the premises must turn out to be *true*. Suppose Fidelix was born in 1989 and Gil was born in 1988. Both premises are then true. However, the conclusion is then *false*.

17. If we let S = *strawberries*, F = *fruit*, and P = *plants*, then the argument form is the following:

All S are F.
All S are P.
All F are P.

The following substitutions create a counterexample: let S = *puppies*, F = *mammals*, and P = *dogs*.

All puppies are mammals.
All puppies are dogs.
All mammals are dogs.

Both premises are true, and the conclusion is false. Therefore, the counterexample shows that the argument is invalid.

Check Your Understanding 1G

5. Weak. The fact that it came up heads ten times in a row has no bearing on the next toss; each coin toss is an independent event, each having a 50–50 chance of heads or tails.

9. Strong. If we assume the premises are true, then the conclusion is probably true.

CHAPTER 2

Check Your Understanding 2A

I.
5. head of state, executive officer, elected official, commander-in-chief
9. produces food from photosynthesis, multicellular, rigid cell walls, manufacturing business

II.
5. Socrates, Plato, Aristotle
9. Lake Superior, Lake Tanganyika, Lake Erie

III.
5. Great Pyramid of Giza, Colossus of Rhodes, Lighthouse of Alexandria, Hanging Gardens of Babylon, Statue of Zeus at Olympia, Mausoleum at Halicarnassus, Temple of Artemis at Ephesus
9. January, March, May, July, August, October, December

IV.
5. robin, thrush, bird, flying animal, animal
9. Cherry Jell-O, Jell-O, chilled dessert, dessert, food

Check Your Understanding 2C

5. Synonymous
9. Enumerative
13. Subclass
17. Subclass
21. Operational
25. Enumerative
29. Ostensive
33. Synonymous

Check Your Understanding 2D

5. Theoretical
9. Lexical
13. Precising
17. Stipulative
21. Precising
25. Precising

29. Stipulative
33. Functional
37. Lexical
41. Precising
45. Functional
49. Theoretical

Check Your Understanding 2E

5. The definition uses figurative language (Guideline 7). In addition, it fails to provide the essential meaning of the term (Guideline 2).
9. We can use Guideline 1 to add quotation marks: "Grade point average."
13. We can add quote marks (Guideline 1): "Romanticism."
17. The definitions use ambiguous and vague language (Guideline 6).

Check Your Understanding 2F

5. Cognitive meaning.
9. Both cognitive meaning and emotive meaning. The claims about the wealth of some players provide cognitive meaning. However, an emotional twinge is provided by the claim "I don't feel we owe anybody anything monetarily. Some of these players are wealthier than their bosses."
13. Emotive meaning.

Check Your Understanding 2G

5. Verbal dispute.
9. Verbal dispute.
13. Verbal dispute.
17. Verbal dispute.

CHAPTER 3

Check Your Understanding 3A

I.

5. [1]We should never take our friends for granted. [2]True friends are there when we need them. [3]They suffer with us when we fail, and [4]they are happy when we succeed.

9. [1]At one time Gary Kasparov had the highest ranking of any chess grandmaster in history. However, [2]he was beaten in a chess tournament by a computer program called Deep Blue, so [3]the computer program should be given a ranking higher than Kasparov.

13. [1]The world will end on August 6, 2045. I know this because [2]my guru said it would, and [3]so far everything he predicted has happened exactly as he said it would.

II.

5. [1]Death is not an event in life: we do not live to experience death. [2]If we take eternity to mean not infinite temporal duration but timelessness, then eternal life belongs to those who live in the present. [3]Our life has no end in just the way in which our visual field has no limits.

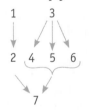

9. Because [1]there is a law such as gravity, [2]the universe can and will create itself from nothing. [3]Spontaneous creation is the reason [4]there is something rather than nothing, [5]why the universe exists, [6]why we exist. [7]It is not necessary to invoke God to light the blue touch paper and set the universe going.

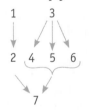

13. [1]The line that I am urging as today's conventional wisdom is not a denial of consciousness. [2]It is often called, with more reason, a repudiation of mind. [3]It is indeed a repudiation of mind as a second substance, over and above body. [4]It can be described less harshly as an identification of mind with some of the faculties, states, and activities of the body. [5]Mental states and events are a special subclass of the states and events of the human or animal body.

17. [1]It has only just begun to dawn on us that in our own language alone, not to speak of its many companions, the past history of humanity is spread out in an imperishable map, just as the history of the mineral earth lies embedded in the layers of its outer crust. But [2] there is this difference between the record of the rocks and the secrets which are hidden in language: [3] whereas the former can only give us knowledge of outward dead things—such as forgotten seas and the bodily shapes of prehistoric animals—[4] language has preserved for us the inner living history of man's soul. [5] It reveals the evolution of consciousness.

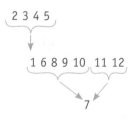

21. [1]It is a commonplace that all religion expresses itself in mythological or metaphorical terms; [2] it says one thing and means another; [3] it uses imagery to convey truth. But [4] the crucial fact about religion is not that it is metaphor, but [5] that it is unconscious metaphor. [6] No one can express any thought without using metaphors, but [7] this does not reduce all philosophy and science to religion, because [8] the scientist knows that his metaphors are merely metaphors and [9] that the truth is something other than the imagery by which it is expressed, whereas [10] in religion the truth and the imagery are identified. [11] To repeat the Creed as a religious act it is necessary not to add "All this I believe in a symbolical or figurative sense": [12] to make that addition is to convert religion into philosophy.

2 3 4 5

1 6 8 9 10   11 12

7

Check Your Understanding 3B

I.

5. *Missing conclusion:* My headache will be relieved.

This makes the argument valid, provided the third premise means that in *all instances* taking aspirin relieves a headache. However, since this interpretation is false, this reconstruction is an unsound argument.

Missing conclusion: My headache will probably be relieved.

This makes the argument strong, provided we interpret the third premise as asserting that *in most cases* taking aspirin relieves a headache. However, we would have to gather data to see if this assertion is true or false. If it is true, then the argument is cogent; if it is false, then the argument is uncogent.

9. *Missing conclusion:* The penicillin pills Jake took will have no effect on his viral infection.

This makes the argument valid. The argument is unsound if any premise is false.

Missing conclusion: The penicillin pills Jake took will probably have no effect on his viral infection.

This makes the argument strong. The argument is uncogent if any premise is false.

13. *Missing premise:* All safe drivers have low insurance rates.

This makes the argument valid.

Missing premise: Most safe drivers have low insurance rates.

This makes the argument strong.

17. *Missing premise:* Earmarks do not benefit just those we represent from our states.

Missing conclusion: Earmarks benefit just those who help us become senators.

This makes the argument valid. However, we would have to gather data to see if the premises are true or false in order to determine if it is a sound argument.

Missing premise: Earmarks do not benefit just those we represent from our states.

Missing conclusion: Earmarks benefit some of those who help us become senators.

This makes the argument strong. However, we would have to gather data to see if this assertion is true or false. If it is true, then the argument is cogent; if it is false, then the argument is uncogent.

II.

5. *Weakens the argument.* If the lamp is not plugged in correctly, then electricity is probably not getting to the lamp.

9. *Strengthens the argument.* If every other electrical fixture in the room works, then electricity is probably getting to the lamp.

13. *Strengthens the argument.* Since the battery is so old, it is likely to be defective or worn out; therefore, we can determine that this new evidence strengthens the argument.

17. *Weakens the argument.* The loose terminal clamp is probably not relaying the battery power; therefore, we can determine that this new evidence weakens the argument.

Check Your Understanding 3C

5. We can reconstruct the argument two ways:

Either you love me or you hate me.
<u>You do not hate me.</u>
You love me.

Either you love me or you hate me.
<u>You do not love me.</u>
You hate me.

False dichotomy: It is possible that the disjuncts in the first premise are both false.

9. <u>You sit around the house all day doing nothing.</u>
    You do not want to get in shape.

The rhetorical force behind the assertion, "you sit around the house all day doing nothing," seems to be indicating that the conclusion should be negative in tone.

13. The force of the statement seems to be indicating a *dilemma*. When interpreted this way, we can reconstruct the argument two ways:

    Either we cut school spending or we raise taxes.
    <u>We will not raise taxes.</u>
    We will cut school spending.

    Either we cut school spending or we raise taxes.
    <u>We will not cut school spending.</u>
    We will raise taxes.

    False dilemma: It is possible that the disjuncts in the first premise are both false.

17. *Rhetorical conditional.* We can consider two possibilities:

    <u>You don't have a retirement counselor.</u>
    You don't want to be financially secure in your retirement years.

    <u>You want to be financially secure in your retirement years.</u>
    You should get a retirement counselor.

21. All three sentences can be rewritten to eliminate the rhetorical aspect of the statements:

    If my God told me to poke the elderly with sharp sticks, that would not make it morally acceptable to others.
    <u>In this age, we know better.</u>
    Wrong-headed decisions do not suddenly become right when defended with religious conviction.

25. The rhetorical aspect can be eliminated and the argument reconstructed in this manner:

    I teach children not to care about anything too much, even though they want to make it appear that they do.
    How I do this is very subtle.
    I do it by demanding that they become totally involved in my lessons, jumping up and down in their seats with anticipation, competing vigorously with each other for my favor.
    When the bell rings I insist that they stop whatever it is that we've been working on and proceed quickly to <u>the next work station.</u>

    Conclusion: The third lesson I teach kids is indifference.

    Indeed, the lesson of the bells is that no work is worth finishing, so do not care too deeply about anything.
    Years of bells will condition all but the strongest to a world that can no longer offer important work to do.
    Bells are the secret logic of schooltime; their argument is inexorable.
    Bells destroy the past and future, converting every interval into a sameness, as an abstract map makes every living mountain and river the same even though <u>they are not.</u>

Conclusion: Bells inoculate each undertaking with indifference.

Check Your Understanding 3D

I.

5. Sufficient condition. Since June has exactly 30 days, if the antecedent is true, then the consequent will be true as well.

9. Sufficient condition. Since 100 pennies is the equivalent of $1, if the antecedent is true, then the consequent will be true as well.

13. Sufficient condition. *If* it is true that I am eating a banana, then it must be true that I am eating a fruit.

II.

5. Necessary condition. June has exactly 30 days. Given this, if this month does *not* have exactly 30 days, then this month is *not* June.

9. Necessary condition. If I do *not* have *at least* the equivalent of $1, then I have *at most* 99 cents. Given this, I do *not* have exactly 100 pennies.

13. Necessary condition. If I am *not* eating a fruit, then I am *not* eating a banana.

CHAPTER 4

Check Your Understanding 4A

I.

5. True. *Tu quoque* is a variety of the *ad hominem* fallacy distinguished by the specific attempt of one person to avoid the issue at hand by claiming the other person is a hypocrite.

9. False. An appeal to an unqualified authority is an argument that relies on the opinions of people who have no expertise, training, or knowledge relevant to the issue at hand.

II.

5. Argument against the person (*ad hominem*): When a claim is rejected or judged to be false based on alleged character flaws of the person making the claim. A second common form occurs whenever someone's statement or reasoning is attacked by way of a stereotype, such as a racial, sexual, or religious stereotype. A third form involves the use of the circumstances of a person's life to reject his claims.

9. Appeal to an unqualified authority: When an argument relies on the opinions of people that have no expertise, training, or knowledge relevant to the issue at hand.

13. Missing the point: When premises that seem to lead logically to one conclusion are used instead to support an unexpected conclusion.

17. Appeal to force: A threat of harmful consequences (physical and otherwise) used to force acceptance of a course of action that would otherwise be unacceptable.

21. Argument against the person (*ad hominem*): When a claim is rejected or judged to be false based on alleged character flaws of the person making the claim. A second common form occurs whenever someone's statement or reasoning is attacked by way of a stereotype, such as a racial, sexual, or religious stereotype. A third form involves the use of the circumstances of a person's life to reject his claims.

25. Argument against the person (*ad hominem*): When a claim is rejected or judged to be false based on alleged character flaws of the person making the claim. A second common form occurs whenever someone's statement or reasoning is attacked by way of a stereotype, such as a racial, sexual, or religious stereotype. A third form involves the use of the circumstances of a person's life to reject his claims.

26. Appeal to ignorance: An argument built on a position of ignorance claims either that (1) a statement must be true because it has not been proven to be false or (2) a statement must be false because it has not been proven to be true.

29. Appeal to the people: The avoidance of objective evidence in favor of an emotional response defeats the goal of a rational investigation of truth.

33. Appeal to an unqualified authority: When an argument relies on the opinions of people that have no expertise, training, or knowledge relevant to the issue at hand.

37. Appeal to the people: The avoidance of objective evidence in favor of an emotional response defeats the goal of a rational investigation of truth.

Check Your Understanding 4B

I.

5. True. A biased sample leaves out members of a subset of the population that will be mentioned in the conclusion.

9. True. When an argument assumes as evidence (in the premises) the very thing that it attempts to prove in the conclusion.

II.

5. Misleading precision: A claim that appears to be statistically significant, but is not.

9. Hasty generalization: A generalization created on the basis of a few instances.

13. Accident: When a generalization is inappropriately applied to the case at hand.

17. Slippery slope: An argument that attempts to make a final event the inevitable outcome of an initial act.

21. Common cause fallacy: The assumption that one event causes another when in fact both events are the result of a common cause.

25. Common cause fallacy: The assumption that one event causes another when in fact both events are the result of a common cause.

29. Begging the question: An argument that assumes as evidence in the premises the very thing that it attempts to prove in the conclusion.

Check Your Understanding 4C

I.

5. False. A straw man fallacy occurs when someone's written or spoken words are taken out of context. It purposely distorts the original argument to create a new, weak argument that can be easily refuted (a straw man that is easily knocked down).

II.

5. Amphiboly: Ambiguity that arises when a poorly constructed statement muddles the intended meaning.

9. Composition: The mistaken transfer of an attribute of the individual parts of an object to the object as a whole.

13. Division: The mistaken transfer an attribute of an object as a whole to its individual parts.

17. Red herring fallacy: A fallacy that occurs when someone completely ignores an opponent's position and changes the subject, diverting the discussion in a new direction.

21. Equivocation: The intentional or unintentional use of different meanings of words or phrases in an argument.

25. Emphasis: A fallacy that occurs when attention is purposely (or accidentally) diverted from the issue at hand.

Check Your Understanding 4D

5. Amphiboly. Two problems: 1. "the only failure" is mentioned, so there is only one kind of failure; but she goes on to say, "the other failure." 2. She then says, "And I did both," so are we to conclude that she failed to try *and* failed to give her best effort?

9. False dilemma. The disjunction offers two choices, each leading to an unwanted result, but neglects to acknowledge that other possibilities exist.

13. Coincidence. A false cause resulting from the accidental or chance connection between two events.

17. Argument from ignorance. The argument is built on a position of ignorance; it claims that a statement must be true because it has not been proven to be false.

21. Begging the question. The argument assumes as evidence in the premises the very thing that it attempts to prove in the conclusion.

25. False dichotomy. The asserted disjunction assumes that only two choices are possible when in fact others exist.

29. Amphiboly. The ambiguity that arises from a misunderstanding of the doctor's statement.

33. Appeal to an unqualified authority. The argument relies on the opinions of people who have no expertise, training, or knowledge relevant to the issue at hand.

37. Appeal to the people. The avoidance of objective evidence in favor of an emotional response.

41. Begging the question. The argument assumes as evidence in the premises the very thing that it attempts to prove in the conclusion.

45. Misleading precision. A claim is made that appears to be statistically significant, but which, upon analysis, is not.

CHAPTER 5

Check Your Understanding 5A

5. Subject term: *malicious murderers*
   Predicate term: *evil people*

This is an example of an **A**-proposition.

9. Subject term: *lottery winners*
   Predicate term: *lucky people*

This is an example of an **E**-proposition.

13. Subject term: *amendments to the U.S. Constitution*
    Predicate term: *unconstitutional acts*

This is an example of an **E**-proposition.

Check Your Understanding 5B

5. Universal negative; subject term distributed; predicate term distributed.
9. Universal affirmative; subject term distributed; predicate term undistributed.
13. Universal negative; subject term distributed; predicate term distributed.

Check Your Understanding 5C

I.
5. True.

II.
5. a. True. Since these fall under *subalternation*, if the universal (in this case an **E**-proposition) is true, then the corresponding particular (in this case an **O**-proposition) must be true, too.

III.
5. Undetermined. No immediate inference can be made about the subaltern of a false **A**-proposition.

IV.
5. c. Undetermined. Since these fall under *subalternation*, if the universal is false, then the corresponding particular could be either true or false.
9. a. True. Since these fall under *subalternation*, if the universal is true, then the corresponding particular must be true.
13. c. Undetermined. Since these fall under *subalternation*, if the particular is true, then the corresponding universal could be either true or false.
17. a. True. Since they are *contradictories*, if one is false, then the other must be true.
21. c. Undetermined. Since they are *subcontraries*, they can both be true at the same time.

Check Your Understanding 5D

5. A. Converse: No people likely to go to prison are greedy politicians.
   B. Obverse: All greedy politicians are non-people likely to go to prison.
   C. Contrapositive: Some non-people likely to go to prison are not non-greedy politicians. (*Valid by limitation*)
9. A. Converse: Some days when banks close are public holidays. (*Valid by limitation*)
   B. Obverse: No public holidays are non-days when banks close.
   C. Contrapositive: All non-days when banks close are nonpublic holidays.
13. A. Converse: No diet-busters are ice cream toppings.
    B. Obverse: All ice cream toppings are non-diet-busters.
    C. Contrapositive: Some non-diet-busters are not non–ice cream toppings. (*Valid by limitation*)
17. A. Converse: Some grease-laden products are French fries. (*Valid by limitation*)
    B. Obverse: No French fries are non-grease-laden products.
    C. Contrapositive: All non-grease-laden products are non–French fries.
21. A. Converse: Some great works of art are tattoos.
    B. Obverse: Some tattoos are not non-great works of art.
    C. Contrapositive: Not valid for **I**-propositions.
25. A. Converse: No acts left unrewarded are good deeds.
    B. Obverse: All good deeds are non-acts left unrewarded.
    C. Contrapositive: Some non-acts left unrewarded are not non-good deeds. (*By limitation*)

Check Your Understanding 5G

5. Let S = *psychics*, and P = *frauds*. All S are P.

9. Let S = *teachers*, and P = *miserable wretches*. All S are P.

13. Let S = *sea creatures*, and P = *bivalves*. All S are P.

17. Let S = *scientific researchers*, and P = *people with impeccable credentials*. Some S are P.

21. Let S = *French pastries*, and P = *baked items*. All S are P.

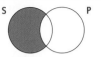

25. Let S = *dogs*, and P = *faithful pets*. All S are P.

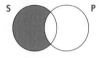

29. Let S = *teachers*, and P = *inspired orators*. All S are P.

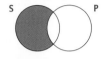

33. Let S = *designer jeans*, and P = *genetically engineered objects*. All S are P.

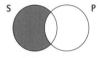

37. Let S = *traffic accidents*, and P = *speeding incidents*. Some S are P.

41. Let S = *ice cream toppings*, and P = *diet-friendly products*. No S are P.

45. Let S = *French fries*, and P = *grease-laden spuds*. All S are P.

Check Your Understanding 5H

5.

Under both the *modern interpretation* and the *traditional interpretation*, in order for conclusion to be true (an **I**-proposition) an X needs to be in the area where S and P overlap. Since this is not the case, this is an invalid argument under both interpretations.

9. The diagram for the premise (an **O**-proposition) is the same for both the *modern interpretation* and the *traditional interpretation*.

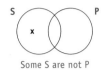

However, in order for conclusion to be true (an **I**-proposition) there needs to be an X in the area where *S* and *P* overlap. Since this is not the case, this is an invalid argument under both interpretations.

13.
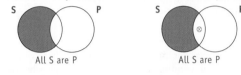

Under both the *modern interpretation* and the *traditional interpretation*, in order for conclusion to be true (an **E**-proposition) the area where *S* and *P* overlap needs to be shaded. Since this is not the case, this is an invalid argument under both interpretations.

17.
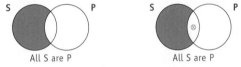

Under the *modern interpretation*, in order for conclusion to be true (an **I**-proposition) there would have to be an X in the area where *S* and *P* overlap. Since there is none, this is an invalid argument.

Under the *traditional interpretation*, in order for conclusion to be true (an **I**-proposition) there would have to be an X in the area where *S* and *P* overlap. As we can see, the assumption of existence symbol (the red circled X) is in the area. Now we need to see if the red circled X represents something that actually exists. Since the *S* stands for *abominable snowmen*, and they do not exist, the assumption of existence symbol does not represent something that actually exists. Therefore, the argument is invalid under the traditional interpretation.

Check Your Understanding 5I

5. All happy people are dancers.
9. Some novels are not satires.
13. Some final exams in calculus are not challenging tests.
17. No young children are protected from the dangers of war.
21. All video game companies are companies that hire game-testers.
25. All people who laugh last are people who laugh best.

29. All persons identical to Marie Curie are persons identical to the winner of Nobel Prizes in two different sciences, and all persons identical to the winner of Nobel Prizes in two different sciences are persons identical to Marie Curie.

33. Some diamond mines are places in California.

37. No best intentions are defeated.

41. All legitimate religions are religions certified by the government.

45. All times you can get electricity in your apartment are times you pay your electric bill.

49. All Orangutans are animals native to Borneo.

53. All improvements made to the gas engine are things that decrease our need for oil.

57. Some people are not people who bowl.

61. All beliefs worth having are beliefs that must withstand doubt.

65. All endings are new beginnings.

69. All people over thirty years are people to be trusted.

73. All people winning at the moment are people who will seem to be invincible.

CHAPTER 6

Check Your Understanding 6B

I.

5. Invalid.

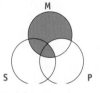

9. Invalid.

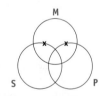

13. Valid.

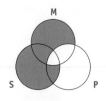

II.

5. Invalid. Let S = *septic tanks*, P = *swimming pools*, and W = *sewers.*

No W are P.
No S are P.
No S are W.

9. Invalid. Let B = *buildings*, P = *poorly constructed domiciles*, and A= *architectural nightmares.*

Some B are P.
Some B are A.
Some A are P.

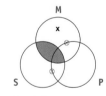

Check Your Understanding 6C

I.

5. Invalid.

9. Invalid.

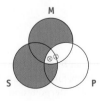

13. Invalid.

II.

5. Invalid. Let S = *septic tanks*, P = *swimming pools*, and W = *sewers*.

    No W are P.
    No S are P.
    Some S are not W.

9. Invalid. Let B = *buildings*, P = *poorly constructed domiciles*, and A = *architectural nightmares*.

    Some B are P.
    No B are A.
    Some A are P.

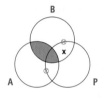

Check Your Understanding 6D

I.

5. A. Major term: independent creatures
   B. Minor term: lovable pets
   C. Middle term: cats
   D. Mood: **OOO**
   E. Figure: **3**

II.

5. Valid under both interpretations.

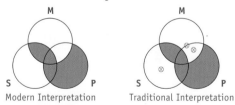

Modern Interpretation   Traditional Interpretation

9. Valid under both interpretations.

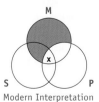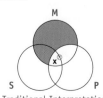

Modern Interpretation   Traditional Interpretation

13. Valid under both interpretations.

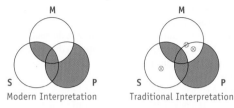

Modern Interpretation   Traditional Interpretation

III.

5. Invalid under the modern interpretation, but provisionally valid under the traditional interpretation.

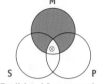

Modern Interpretation   Traditional Interpretation

9. Invalid under the modern interpretation, but provisionally valid under the traditional interpretation.

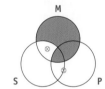

Modern Interpretation   Traditional Interpretation

Check Your Understanding 6E

I.

5. **OOO-3**
9. **AEO-1**

II.

5. All six rules are met.
   Rule 1: The middle term is distributed in the second premise.
   Rule 2: The major term is distributed in the conclusion and in the major premise.
   Rule 3: It does not have two negative premises.
   Rule 4: It has a negative premise and a negative conclusion.
   Rule 5: It has a negative conclusion and a negative premise.
   Rule 6: It does not have universal premises and a particular conclusion.

9. All six rules are met.
   Rule 1: The middle term is distributed in the first premise.
   Rule 2: The major term is not distributed in the conclusion.
   Rule 3: It does not have two negative premises.
   Rule 4: It does not have a negative premise.
   Rule 5: It does not have a negative conclusion.

Rule 6: It does not have universal premises and a particular conclusion.

13. All six rules are met.

Rule 1: The middle term is distributed in the second premise.
Rule 2: The major term is distributed in the conclusion and in the major premise.
Rule 3: It does not have two negative premises.
Rule 4: It has a negative premise and a negative conclusion.
Rule 5: It has a negative conclusion and a negative premise.
Rule 6: It does not have universal premises and a particular conclusion.

III.

5. Some furry creatures are lovable pets. Some eccentric people are lovable pets. So, some eccentric people are furry creatures. Let F = *furry creatures*, L = *lovable pets*, and E = *eccentric people*.

Some F are L.
Some E are L.
Some E are F.

III-2.

Invalid under both interpretations.

(The Venn diagram is the same for both interpretations.) Rule 1 is broken: The middle term is not distributed in at least one premise.

Check Your Understanding 6F.1

I.

5. Some A are non-B.
All C are non-B.
Some C are not A.

The syllogism violates Rule 1: The middle term must be distributed in at least one premise.

The syllogism violates Rule 2: If a term is distributed in the conclusion, then it must be distributed in a premise.

The syllogism violates Rule 5: A negative conclusion must have a negative premise.

The following Venn diagram shows that the syllogism is invalid:

9. No A are B.
All C are A.
All C are B.

The syllogism violates Rule 4: A negative premise must have a negative conclusion.

The following Venn diagram shows that the syllogism is invalid:

13. All C are A.
All A are B.
All B are C.

The syllogism violates Rule 2: If a term is distributed in the conclusion, then it must be distributed in a premise.

The following Venn diagram shows that the syllogism is invalid:

II.

5. Let S = *self-motivated students*, I = *students using their intellectual capabilities*, D = *disinterested students*, non-D = *interested students*.

All S are I.		All S are I.
No D are I.	Rewritten as:	No D are I.
All S are non-D.		No S are D.

The syllogism does not violate any of the six rules.

The following Venn diagram shows that the syllogism is valid:

9. Let P = *preschool children*, S = *severely overweight students*, O = *obese students*, and D = *people susceptible to diabetes*.

Since the term "severely overweight students" and the term "obese students" are synonyms, we can use the same letter for both when we rewrite the syllogism.

Some P are S.		Some P are S.
Some O are D.	Rewritten as:	Some S are D.
Some P are not D.		Some P are not D.

The syllogism violates Rule 1: The middle term must be distributed in at least one premise.

The syllogism violates Rule 2: If a term is distributed in the conclusion, then it must be distributed in a premise.

The following Venn diagram shows that the syllogism is invalid.

Check Your Understanding 6F.2

5. Let R = *refurbished computers*, E = *expensive things*, U = *computers bought by my uncle*.

All U are non-E.
<u>All U are R.</u>   Rewritten as:
No R are E.

All U are non-E.
<u>All U are R.</u>
All R are non-E.

The syllogism violates Rule 2: If a term is distributed in the conclusion, then it must be distributed in a premise.

The following Venn diagram shows that the syllogism is invalid:

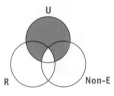

9. Let S = *starvation diets*, E = *effective ways to lose weight*, B = *things that are bad for your heart*.

Some S are E.
<u>All S are B.</u>
Some E are B.

The syllogism does not violate any of the six rules.

The following Venn diagram shows that the syllogism is valid:

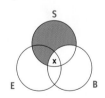

13. Let T = *traditional Western philosophy*, F = *footnotes to Plato*, A = *Asian philosophy*.

All T are F.
<u>No A are T.</u>
No A are F.

The syllogism violates Rule 2: If a term is distributed in the conclusion, then it must be distributed in a premise.

The following Venn diagram shows that the syllogism is invalid:

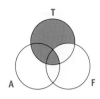

Check Your Understanding 6G

I.

5. Let B = *replaced broken cell phones*, A = *broken cell phones accompanied by a sales slip*, I = *cell phones identical to my broken cell phone*.

Missing conclusion: My broken cell phone will not be replaced.

All R are A.
<u>No I are A.</u>
No I are R.

The syllogism does not violate any of the six rules.

The following Venn diagram shows that the syllogism is valid:

9. Let S = *people who can successfully find their way home*, L = *people who can learn logic*, C = *students in this class*.

Missing conclusion: All the students in this class can learn logic.

All S are L.
<u>All C are S.</u>
All C are L.

The syllogism does not violate any of the six rules.

The following Venn diagram shows that the syllogism is valid:

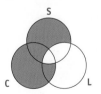

13. Let S = *state laws*, U = *unconstitutional laws*, O = *laws overturned by the Supreme Court*.

Missing premise: All unconstitutional laws are laws overturned by the Supreme Court.

All U are O.
<u>Some S are U.</u>
Some S are O.

The syllogism does not violate any of the six rules.

The following Venn diagram shows that the syllogism is valid:

17. Let A = *airline companies*, G = *companies that take their customers for granted*, R = *companies that refuse to give a refund on a purchase.*
Missing premise: Some airline ompanies are companies that refuse to give a refund on a purchase.

All R are G.
Some A are R.
Some A are G.

The syllogism does not violate any of the six rules.

The following Venn diagram shows that the syllogism is valid:

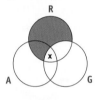

II.

5. Let K = *countries identical with the two Koreas,* W = *countries still technically at war,* and T = *war that ended only with a truce.*
Missing premise. All wars that ended only with a truce are countries still technically at war.

All T are W.
All K are T.
All K are W.

The syllogism does not violate any of the six rules.

The following Venn diagram shows that the syllogism is valid:

9. Let P = *people who failed,* D = *people with dreams of perfection,* and I = *splendid failures to do the impossible.*
Missing premise: All people with dreams of perfection are splendid failures to do the impossible.

All D are I.
All P are D.
All P are I.

The syllogism does not violate any of the six rules.

The following Venn diagram shows that the syllogism is valid:

Check Your Understanding 6H

I.

5. All B are D.   All B are D.
    No E are C.   No E are C.
    No A are non-C.   Rewrite as: All A are C.
    All non-A are non-B.   All B are A.
    All D are non-E.   No D are E.

    No E are C.
    All A are C.
    No A are E. *(Intermediate conclusion)*

The syllogism does not violate any of the six rules.

The following Venn diagram shows that the syllogism is valid:

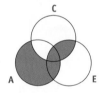

No A are E.
All B are A.
No B are E. *(Intermediate conclusion)*

The syllogism does not violate any of the six rules.

The following Venn diagram shows that the syllogism is valid:

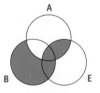

No B are E.
All B are D.
No D are E.

The syllogism violates Rule 2: If a term is distributed in the conclusion, then it must be distributed in a premise.

The following Venn diagram shows that the syllogism is invalid:

9.

    All D are C.
    <u>All C are A.</u>

All four possible categorical statements (**A, E, I, O**) as the conclusion will result in an invalid syllogism.

For example, if either **E** or **O** is used, then the subsequent syllogisms will violate Rule 5: A negative conclusion must have a negative premise. On the other hand, if **A** is used, then the syllogism will violate Rule 2: If a term is distributed in the conclusion, then it must be distributed in a premise. Finally, if **I** is used, then the syllogism will violate Rule 6: Two universal premises cannot have a particular conclusion.

II.

5. Let F = *famous sitcoms*, C = *controversial shows*, M = *shows written for mass audiences*, X = *X-rated movies*.

No F are C.		No F are C.
All F are M.	Rewritten as:	All F are M.
<u>All X are non-M.</u>		<u>No X are M.</u>
All X are C.		All X are C.

    No F are C.
    <u>All F are M.</u>

All four possible categorical statements (**A, E, I, O**) as the conclusion will result in an invalid syllogism.

For example, if either **A** or **I** is used, then the subsequent syllogisms will violate Rule 4: A negative premise must have a negative conclusion. On the other hand, if **E** is used, then the syllogism will violate Rule 2: If a term is distributed in the conclusion, then it must be distributed in a premise. Finally, if **O** is used, then the syllogism will violate Rule 6: Two universal premises cannot have a particular conclusion.

9. Let N = *all neighbors identical to my neighbor*, L = *people who play loud music*, D = *drum sounds*, H = *hearts of songs*, M = *people who play music that has a melody*, and Y = *music that you can hear*.

    All N are L.
    All D are H.
    All N are M.
    All Y are L.
    <u>All M are D.</u>
    All Y are H.

    All D are H.
    <u>All M are D.</u>
    All M are H. *(Intermediate conclusion)*

The syllogism does not violate any of the six rules.

The following Venn diagram shows that the syllogism is valid:

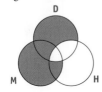

All M are H.
<u>All N are M.</u>
All N are H. *(Intermediate conclusion)*

The syllogism does not violate any of the six rules.

The following Venn diagram shows that the syllogism is valid:

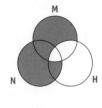

    All N are H.
    <u>All N are L.</u>

All four possible categorical statements (**A, E, I, O**) as the conclusion will result in invalid syllogisms.

For example, if either **E** or **O** is used, then the subsequent syllogisms will violate Rule 5: A negative conclusion must have a negative premise. On the other hand, if **A** is used, then the syllogism will violate Rule 2: If a term is distributed in the conclusion, then it must be distributed in a premise. Finally, if **I** is used, then the syllogism will violate Rule 6: Two universal premises cannot have a particular conclusion.

CHAPTER 7

Check Your Understanding 7A

5. Let C = *My car does look great*, and M = *it gets great gas mileage*: $\sim C \cdot M$

Although you could translate the first statement simply as C (where C = *My car does not look great*), nevertheless, $\sim C$ captures the English more accurately.

9. Let C = *candy is bad for your teeth*, and Q = *tobacco is bad for your teeth*: $C \lor Q$

13. Let T = *Toothpaste is good for your teeth*, and B = *tobacco is good for your teeth*: $T \cdot \sim B$

17. Let R = *My room could use a good cleaning*, and L = *I am too lazy to do anything about it*: $R \cdot L$

21. Let T = *I will leave a big tip*, and E = *the dinner is excellent*: $T \supset E$

25. Let G = *Grover Cleveland was the greatest U.S. president*: $\sim G$

Although you could translate the statement simply as G (where G = *It is false that Grover Cleveland was the greatest U.S. president*); nevertheless, $\sim G$ captures the English more accurately.

29. Let B = *Barbara is going to lose her football bet*, and J = *Johnny will get a night at the ballet*: $B \cdot J$

33. Let D = *driving too fast is hazardous to your health*, and B = *driving without buckling up (is hazardous to your health)*: $D \supset B$

37.   Let *R* = *my room could use a good cleaning*, and *L* = *I am too lazy to do anything about it*: *L* ⊃ *R*

41.   Let *R* = *it rains tomorrow*, and *W*= *I will have to water my plants*: *R* ⊃ ~ *W*

45.   Let *O* = *My car is old*, and *R* = *it is still reliable*: *O* · *R*

49.   Let *T* = *Teaching is a challenging profession*: *T*

Check Your Understanding 7B.1

5.   *L* ⊃ ~ *P*   This is a *WFF.*

9.   [(*P Q*] v ~ *R*   This is not a *WFF. Rule 4: Parentheses* must be used to indicate the main operator.

13. *P Q*   This is not a *WFF.* **Rule 1:** The dot, wedge, and horseshoe must always go between two statements (simple or complex).

Check Your Understanding 7B.2

The *main operator* is circled in each example.

5.   *L* ⊖ ~ *P*

9.   (*P* · *Q*) ⓥ ~ *R*

13. ~ *K* ⊖ ~ *P*

17. [(*M* v *P*) ⊃ (*Q* v *R*)] ⓥ (*S* · ~ *P*)

21. ~ *Q* ⊙ *P*

25. *L* ⊖ (~ *P* ⊃ *Q*)

Check Your Understanding 7B.3

I.

5.   Let *S* = *you can save $100 a month*, *A* = *you can afford the insurance*, and *B* = *you can buy a motorcycle.*

$$S ⊃ (A ⊃ B)$$

The second use of a conditional, *A* ⊃ *B*, must be placed within parentheses so it becomes the consequent of the conditional that has *S* as the antecedent.

9.   Let *W*= *Walter can drive to Pittsburgh next weekend*, *S*= *Sandy can drive to Pittsburgh next weekend*, *J*= *Jessica will come home*, and *F*= *Jennifer is able to arrive on time.*

$$~ (W v S) ⊃ (~ J v F)$$

The antecedent is the negation of a disjunction, and it must be placed within parentheses; the consequent is a disjunction, so it too must be placed within parentheses.

13. Let *D*= *your disc player breaks*, *B*= *I will get you a new one for your birthday* and *F*= *you can see about getting it fixed.*

$$(D ⊃ B) v F$$

The first disjunct is a conditional, so it has to be placed in parentheses.

17. Let *S*= *you will eat a lot of salads*, and *T*= *you will absorb a lot of vitamins.*

$$~ (S ⊃ T) · ~ (T ⊃ S)$$

The main operator is a dot, so parentheses must be placed around each conjunct with the negation sign outside of each set of parentheses.

II.

5.   Let *S* = *a spirit of harmony will survive in America*, and *D* = *each of us remembers that we share a common destiny*: *S* ⊃ *D*

9.   Let *F*= *I have failed*, and *W*= *I've just found 10,000 ways that will work*: ~ *F* · ~ *W*

13. Let *H* = *the only tool you have is a hammer*, and *N* = *you tend to see every problem as a nail*: *H* ⊃ *N*

17. Let *W* = *the fight is won far away from witnesses*, *L* = *the fight is lost far away from witnesses*, and *B* = *when I am behind the lines, in the gym, and out there on the road, long before I dance under those lights*: (*W* · *B*) v (*L* · *B*)

Check Your Understanding 7C

5.   (a) X must be true.

The negation changes the truth value of whatever follows it.

9.   (a) Yes

A disjunction is true if at least one disjunct is true.

13. (c) Y could be true or false. A conditional can be true if the antecedent is true and the consequent true, or if the antecedent is false.

17. (c) Y could be true or false. A biconditional is true when both components have the same truth value (either both true or both false).

Check Your Understanding 7D.1

5.

R	S	Q	(R · S)	v	Q
T	T	T	T		T
T	T	F	T		T
T	F	T	F		T
T	F	F	F		F
F	T	T	F		T
F	T	F	F		F
F	F	T	F		T
F	F	F	F		F

9.

Q	R	P	~	(Q · R)	⊃ P
T	T	T	F	T	T
T	T	F	F	T	T
T	F	T	T	F	T
T	F	F	T	F	F
F	T	T	T	F	T
F	T	F	T	F	F
F	F	T	T	F	T
F	F	F	T	F	F

13.

P	S	R	P ≡ (~ S v ~ R)
T	T	T	F F F F
T	T	F	T F T T
T	F	T	T T T F
T	F	F	T T T T
F	T	T	T F F F
F	T	F	F F T T
F	F	T	F T T F
F	F	F	F T T T

17.

P	Q	R	~ [P ⊃ (Q v R)]
T	T	T	F T T
T	T	F	F T T
T	F	T	F T T
T	F	F	T F F
F	T	T	F T T
F	T	F	F T T
F	F	T	F T T
F	F	F	F T F

Check Your Understanding 7D.2

I.

5.

P	S	R	P v (S v R)
T	F	T	T T

9.

P	Q	R	S	[P v (Q · R)] v ~ S
T	F	T	F	T F T T

II.

5.

P	S	R	Q	[P v (S v R)] ⊃ ~ Q
T	?	F	T	T F F

9.

P	Q	R	S	[P v (Q · R)] ⊃ ~ S
T	T	F	?	T F ?

The antecedent of the conditional is true. However, the truth value of the consequent cannot be determined because the truth value of S is unassigned. Therefore, the truth value for the main operator is undetermined.

Check Your Understanding 7E

5. Tautology

P	Q	(P v ~ P) v Q
T	T	T F T
T	F	T F T
F	T	T T T
F	F	T T T

9. Tautology

R	S	~ (R · ~ R) v ~ (S v ~ S)
T	T	T F F T F T F
T	F	T F F T F T T
F	T	T F T T F T F
F	F	T F T T F T T

13. Tautology

P	P ⊃ P
T	T
F	T

17. Tautology

R	S	(R · ~ R) ⊃ (S v ~ S)
T	T	F F T T F
T	F	F F T T T
F	T	F T T T F
F	F	F T T T T

Check Your Understanding 7F

5. Logically equivalent

P	Q	R	P v (Q · R)	(P v Q) v R
T	T	T	T T	T T
T	T	F	T T	T T
T	F	T	T T	T T
T	F	F	T F	T T
F	T	T	T T	T T
F	T	F	T T	T T
F	F	T	T T	F T
F	F	F	F F	F F

9. Logically equivalent

P	P	~ ~ P
T	T	T F
F	F	F T

13. Logically equivalent

P Q	P ≡ Q	(P · Q) v (~ P · ~ Q)
T T	[T]	T [T] F F F
T F	[F]	F [F] F F T
F T	[F]	F [F] T F F
F F	[T]	F [T] T T T

17. Not logically equivalent

P Q	~ (P · Q)	~ P · ~ Q
T T	[F] T	F [F] F
T F	[T] F	F [F] T
F T	[T] F	T [F] F
F F	[T] F	T [T] T

21. Not logically equivalent

P Q	P ≡ Q	(P ⊃ Q) v (Q ⊃ P)
T T	[T]	T [T] T
T F	[F]	F [T] T
F T	[F]	T [T] F
F F	[T]	T [T] T

25. Not logically equivalent

P Q	P ⊃ Q	~ Q v P
T T	[T]	F T
T F	[F]	T T
F T	[T]	F F
F F	[T]	T T

Check Your Understanding 7G

5. Consistent

T U	T ≡ U	T · U
T T	[T]	[T]
T F	[F]	[F]
F T	[F]	[F]
F F	[T]	[F]

9. Contradictory

C D	C · D	~ C v ~ D
T T	[T]	F [F] F
T F	[F]	F [T] T
F T	[F]	T [T] F
F F	[F]	T [T] T

13. Consistent

M	M v ~ M	M
T	[T] F	[T]
F	[T] T	[F]

17. Consistent

Q R S	(Q ⊃ ~ R) ⊃ S	S ≡ (Q · R)
T T T	F F [T]	[T] T
T T F	F F [T]	[F] T
T F T	T T [T]	[F] F
T F F	T T [F]	[T] F
F T T	T F [T]	[F] F
F T F	T F [F]	[T] F
F F T	T T [T]	[F] F
F F F	T T [F]	[T] F

Check Your Understanding 7H

I.

5. Invalid. Line 2 has the premise true and the conclusion false.

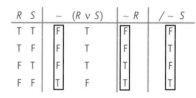

R S	~ R v ~ S	/ ~ R
T T	F [F] F	[F]
T F	F [T] T	[F] √
F T	T [T] F	[T]
F F	T [T] T	[T]

9. Valid

R S	~ (R v S)	~ R	/ ~ S
T T	[F] T	[F]	[F]
T F	[F] T	[F]	[T]
F T	[F] T	[T]	[F]
F F	[T] F	[T]	[T]

13. Valid

S Q R	S v (Q v R)	~ Q	~ R	/ S
T T T	[T] T	[F]	[F]	[T]
T T F	[T] T	[F]	[T]	[T]
T F T	[T] T	[T]	[F]	[T]
T F F	[T] F	[T]	[T]	[T]
F T T	[T] T	[F]	[F]	[F]
F T F	[T] T	[F]	[T]	[F]
F F T	[T] T	[T]	[F]	[F]
F F F	[F] F	[T]	[T]	[F]

II.

5. Valid

P	Q	R	S	(P ⊃ Q)	·	(R ⊃ S)	P v R	/ Q v S
T	T	T	T	T	T	T	T	T
T	T	T	F	T	F	F	T	T
T	T	F	T	T	T	T	T	T
T	T	F	F	T	T	T	T	T
T	F	T	T	F	F	T	T	T
T	F	T	F	F	F	F	T	F
T	F	F	T	F	F	T	T	T
T	F	F	F	F	F	T	T	F
F	T	T	T	T	T	T	T	T
F	T	T	F	T	F	F	T	T
F	T	F	T	T	T	T	F	T
F	T	F	F	T	T	T	F	T
F	F	T	T	T	T	T	T	T
F	F	T	F	T	F	F	T	F
F	F	F	T	T	T	T	F	T
F	F	F	F	T	T	T	F	F

9. Invalid

R	S	R ≡ S	/ R
T	T	T	T
T	F	F	T
F	T	F	F
F	F	T	F √

13. Invalid

P	R	S	~ (R · S)	~ R ⊃ P	/ ~ S
T	T	T	F T	F T	F
T	T	F	T F	F T	T
T	F	T	T F	T T	F √
T	F	F	T F	T T	T
F	T	T	F T	F T	F
F	T	F	T F	F T	T
F	F	T	T F	T F	F
F	F	F	T F	T F	T

17. Invalid

S	Q	R	[(S · Q) · R] ⊃ Q	Q	R	/ ~ S
T	T	T	T T T	T	T	F √
T	T	F	T F T	T	F	F
T	F	T	F F T	F	T	F
T	F	F	F F T	F	F	F
F	T	T	F F T	T	T	T
F	T	F	F F T	T	F	T
F	F	T	F F T	F	T	T
F	F	F	F F T	F	F	T

21. Valid

P	Q	R	P ⊃ (Q v ~ R)	Q ⊃ ~ R	/ P ⊃ ~ R
T	T	T	T T F	F F	F F
T	T	F	T T T	T T	T T
T	F	T	F F F	T F	F F
T	F	F	T T T	T T	T T
F	T	T	T T F	F F	T F
F	T	F	T T T	T T	T T
F	F	T	T F F	T F	T F
F	F	F	T T T	T T	T T

25. Invalid

P	Q	S	(P v Q) ≡ S	/ P
T	T	T	T	T	T
T	T	F	T	F	T
T	F	T	T	T	T
T	F	F	T	F	T
F	T	T	T	T	F √
F	T	F	T	F	F
F	F	T	F	F	F
F	F	F	F	T	F √

III.

5. Invalid. Let *S = we stop interfering in other countries' internal affairs*, and *E = we will find ourselves with more enemies than we can handle*.

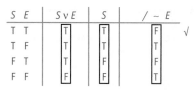

S	E	S v E	S	/ ~ E
T	T	T	T	F √
T	F	T	T	T
F	T	T	F	F
F	F	F	F	T

9. Invalid. Let P = the prosecuting attorney's claims are correct, and G = the defendant is guilty.

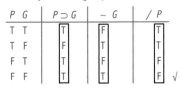

P G	P ⊃ G	~ G	/ P
T T	T	F	T
T F	F	T	T
F T	T	F	F
F F	T	T	F √

13. Invalid. Let U = UFOs exist, and L = there is life on other planets.

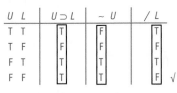

U L	U ⊃ L	~ U	/ L
T T	T	F	T
T F	F	F	F
F T	T	T	T
F F	T	T	F √

17. Invalid. Let V = you take 1000 mg of Vitamin C every day, and C = you will get a cold.

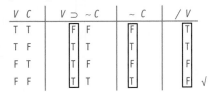

V C	V ⊃ ~ C	~ C	/ V
T T	F F	F	T
T F	T T	T	T
F T	T F	F	F
F F	T T	T	F √

Check Your Understanding 71.1

5. Invalid

P Q R S	[P v (Q v S)] ⊃ R	~P	~Q	~S	/ ~R
F F T F	F F T	T	T	T	F √

9. Valid

P Q R S	~ (P v Q) v ~ (R · S)	P · Q	R	/ ~S
T T T T	F T F F T	T	T	F

The only assignments available to get the conclusion false and the second and third premises true make it impossible to then get the first premise true. Since it is impossible to get all the premises true and the conclusion false at the same time, we have shown that the argument is valid.

13. Although there is only one way to get the conclusion false, there are three ways to get each premise true. Therefore, we might need to explore all the possibilities:

(Option 1)

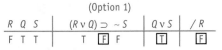

R Q S	(R v Q) ⊃ ~S	Q v S	/R
F T T	T F F	T	F

This assignment of truth values makes the conclusion false, and the second premise true. However, since the first premise is false with this assignment, this cannot give us all true premises and a false conclusion. Therefore, we must try the next option.

(Option 2)

R Q S	(R v Q) ⊃ ~S	Q v S	/R
F T F	T T T	T	F √

This assignment of truth values makes the conclusion false, and all the premises true; therefore, the argument is invalid. (Thus, it is not necessary to try the other option.)

17. Invalid

R Q S	~ (~ R v ~ Q) ⊃ ~ S	Q ⊃ S	/ ~ R ⊃ S
F F F	F T T T T	T	T F √

Check Your Understanding 71.2

5. Invalid. Let C = animals are conscious, P = animals do feel pain, and R = animals do have rights.

C P R	(~ C v ~ P) ⊃ ~ R	~ R	~ P	/ ~ C
T F F	F T T T T	T	T	F √

9. Invalid. Let E = Elvis sold the most records of all time, B = the Beatles sold the most records of all time, and C = I won the contest.

B E C	(E v B) ⊃ ~ C	~ B	/ C
F F F	F T T	T	F √

13. Invalid. Let J = Joyce went south on I-15 from Las Vegas, and L = Joyce got to Los Angeles.

J L	J ⊃ L	~ J	/ ~ L
F T	T	T	F √

17. Valid. Let E = Eddie can vote, and R = he (Eddie) is registered.

R E	E ≡ R	E	/ R
F T	F	T	F

Since the only way to get the conclusion false is for R to be false, and the only way to get the second premise true is for E to be true, it will be impossible to then get the first premise true. Thus, the argument is valid.

Check Your Understanding 71.3

5. Consistent

R P S Q	R v (~ P · S)	Q v ~ P	Q ⊃ ~ P
T F T T	T T T	T T	T T

9. Consistent

M P Q R	~ M v ~ P	~ M v Q	P v R
F T	T T	T T	T

13. Consistent

Q R S	~ (Q ⊃ R) ⊃ S	S v (Q · R)
T	T	T

CHAPTER 8

Check Your Understanding 8B

I.

[5]	3.	~Q	1, 2, MT
[9]	3.	$P \supset Q$	1, 2, DS
[13]	3.	$R \supset P$	1, 2, HS

II.

[5]	3.	$Q \cdot S$	1, 2, DS
[9]	3.	$\sim(T \supset R)$	1, 2, MT
[13]	3.	$\sim(P \cdot \sim R)$	1, 2, MT

III.

[5]	5.	$P \supset S$	1, 4, HS
	6.	$P \supset Q$	3, 5, HS
	7.	Q	2, 6, MP
[9]	5.	$P \supset Q$	3, 4, HS
	6.	$\sim R$	2, 5, MP
	7.	$\sim S$	1, 6, DS

IV.

[5]	5.	$\sim S$	1, 3, DS
	6.	$P \supset Q$	2, 5, MP
	7.	R	4, 6, MP
[9]	5.	$\sim P$	2, 3, MT
	6.	$\sim S$	4, 5, MT
	7.	$P \lor Q$	1, 6, DS
	8.	Q	5, 7, DS

Check Your Understanding 8C

I.

[5]	1.	$\sim P \supset (Q \lor R)$	
	2.	$(\sim P \supset \sim S) \supset \sim L$	
	3.	$(Q \lor R) \supset \sim S$	$/ \sim L$
	4	$\sim P \supset \sim S$	1, 3, HS
	5	$\sim L$	2, 4, MP
[9]	1.	$R \lor S$	
	2.	$\sim(P \lor Q)$	
	3.	$R \supset (P \lor Q)$	
	4.	$S \supset (Q \lor R)$	$/ Q \lor R$
	5.	$\sim R$	2, 3, MT
	6.	S	1, 5, DS
	7.	$Q \lor R$	4, 6, MP
[13]	1.	$P \lor (S \supset Q)$	
	2.	$\sim Q$	
	3.	$P \supset Q$	
	4.	$\sim S \supset R$	$/ R$
	5.	$\sim P$	2, 3, MT
	6.	$S \supset Q$	1, 5, DS
	7.	$\sim S$	2, 6, MT
	8.	R	4, 7, MP

[17]	1.	$Q \supset P$	
	2.	S	
	3.	$(Q \lor \sim R) \supset \sim P$	
	4.	$S \supset (Q \lor \sim R)$	$/ \sim R$
	5.	$Q \lor \sim R$	2, 4, MP
	6.	$\sim P$	3, 5, MP
	7.	$\sim Q$	1, 6, MT
	8.	$\sim R$	5, 7, DS

II.

[5]	1.	$S \supset (C \supset H)$	
	2.	$E \supset S$	
	3.	$E \lor (S \lor C)$	
	4.	$\sim(C \supset H)$	$/ C$
	5.	$\sim S$	1, 4, MT
	6.	$\sim E$	2, 5, MT
	7.	$S \lor C$	3, 6, DS
	8.	C	5, 7, DS
[9]	1.	$(C \lor M) \supset L$	
	2.	$S \supset (\sim E \supset \sim L)$	
	3.	$E \lor S$	
	4.	$\sim E$	$/ \sim(C \lor M)$
	5.	S	3, 4, DS
	6.	$\sim E \supset L$	2, 5, MP
	7.	$\sim L$	4, 6, MP
	8.	$\sim(C \lor M)$	1, 7, MT

Check Your Understanding 8D

I.

[5]	3.	$\sim P \cdot (T \supset U)$	1, 2, Conj
[9]	3.	$P \cdot Q$	1, 2, Conj
[13]	3.	$P \cdot [(R \supset S) \lor Q]$	1, 2, Conj

II.

[5]	2.	P	1, Simp
[9]	3.	$(P \supset Q) \cdot (R \lor S)$	1, 2, Conj
[13]	2.	$(\sim P \lor S)$	1, Simp

III.

[5]	1.	P	
	2.	$(P \lor Q) \supset R$	
	3.	$R \supset S$	$/ S$
	4.	$P \lor Q$	1, Add
	5.	R	2, 4, MP
	6.	S	3, 5, MP
[9]	1.	$P \cdot (S \lor Q)$	
	2.	$(P \lor R) \supset M$	$/ M$
	3.	P	1, Simp
	4.	$P \lor R$	3, Add
	5.	M	2, 4, MP
[13]	1.	$(P \supset Q) \cdot (R \supset S)$	
	2.	$P \lor L$	
	3.	$(L \supset M) \cdot (N \supset K)$	$/ Q \lor M$
	4.	$P \supset Q$	1, Simp

5. $L \supset M$ 3, Simp
6. $(P \supset Q) \cdot (L \supset M)$ 4, 5, Conj
7. $Q \vee M$ 2, 6, CD

[17] 1. $S \vee P$
2. $(R \vee S) \supset L$
3. $(P \vee Q) \supset R$
4. $\sim S$ $/ L$
5. P 1, 4, DS
6. $P \vee Q$ 5, Add
7. R 3, 6, MP
8. $R \vee S$ 7, Add
9. L 2, 8, MP

[21] 1. $R \supset P$
2. $(Q \cdot \sim R) \supset (S \cdot \sim R)$
3. $\sim P$
4. $P \vee Q$ $/ S$
5. Q 3, 4, HS
6. $\sim R$ 1, 3, MT
7. $Q \cdot \sim R$ 5, 6, Conj
8. $S \cdot \sim R$ 2, 7, MP
9. S 8, Simp

[25] 1. $(M \vee N) \supset (P \cdot K)$
2. $(P \vee \sim Q) \supset [(R \supset L) \cdot S]$
3. M $/ P \cdot (R \supset L)$
4. $M \vee N$ 3, Add
5. $P \cdot K$ 1, 4, MP
6. P 5, Simp
7. $P \vee \sim Q$ 6, Add
8. $(R \supset L) \cdot S$ 2, 7, MP
9. $R \supset L$ 8, Simp
10. $P \cdot (R \supset L)$ 6, 9, Conj

[29] 1. $P \cdot \sim Q$
2. $(P \vee \sim R) \supset (\sim S \cdot M)$
3. $(\sim S \cdot P) \supset (P \supset N)$ $/ N$
4. P 1, Simp
5. $P \vee \sim R$ 4, Add
6. $\sim S \cdot M$ 2, 5, MP
7. $\sim S$ 6, Simp
8. $\sim S \cdot P$ 4, 6, Conj
9. $P \supset N$ 3, 8, MP
10. N 4, 9, MP

IV.

[5] 1. $\sim B \vee \sim H$
2. $P \supset S$
3. $(\sim B \supset F) \cdot (\sim H \supset \sim A)$
4. $(F \vee \sim A) \supset \sim S$ $/ \sim P$
5. $F \vee \sim A$ 1, 3, CD
6. $\sim S$ 4, 5, MP
7. $\sim P$ 2, 6, MT

[9] 1. $G \supset C$
2. $U \supset \sim S$
3. G

4. $C \supset U$ $/ \sim S$
5. C 1, 3, MP
6. U 4, 5, MP
7. $\sim S$ 2, 6, MP

Check Your Understanding 8E

I.

[5] 2. $\sim \sim S$ 1, DN
[9] 2. $P \cdot (Q \vee R)$ 1, Dist
[13] 2. $S \cdot (Q \cdot R)$ 1, Assoc

II.

[5] 2. $\sim (P \vee Q)$ 1, DM
[9] 2. $R \vee [S \vee (P \supset Q)]$ 1, Assoc
[13] 2. $\{ [R \supset (P \cdot Q)] \vee L \} \vee M$ 1, Assoc

III.

[5] 1. $P \supset (Q \cdot R)$
2. $\sim Q \cdot S$ $/ \sim P$
3. $\sim Q$ 2, Simp
4. $\sim Q \vee \sim R$ 3, Add
5. $\sim (Q \cdot R)$ 4, DM
6. $\sim P$ 1, 5, MT

[9] 1. $\sim (P \cdot Q)$
2. $(\sim P \vee \sim Q) \supset (R \cdot S)$
3. $(R \vee Q) \supset \sim T$ $/ \sim T$
4. $\sim P \vee \sim Q$ 1, DM
5. $R \cdot S$ 2, 4, MP
6. R 5, Simp
7. $R \vee \sim Q$ 6, Add
8. $\sim T$ 3, 7, MP

[13] 1. $\sim P$
2. $Q \vee (R \cdot P)$ $/ Q$
3. $(Q \vee R) \cdot (Q \vee P)$ 2, Dist
4. $(Q \vee P) \cdot (Q \vee R)$ 3, Com
5. $Q \vee P$ 4, Simp
6. $P \vee Q$ 5, Com
7. Q 1, 6, DS

[17] 1. $P \vee Q$
2. $(R \cdot S) \cdot L$ $/ [(L \cdot R) \cdot P] \vee [(L \cdot R) \cdot Q]$
3. $L \cdot (R \cdot S)$ 2, Com
4. $(L \cdot R) \cdot S$ 3, Assoc
5. $L \cdot R$ 4, Simp
6. $(L \cdot R) \cdot (P \vee Q)$ 1, 5, Conj
7. $[(L \cdot R) \cdot P] \vee [(L \cdot R) \cdot Q]$ 6, Dist

[21] 1. $P \supset \sim \sim R$
2. $P \cdot \sim (S \cdot R)$ $/ \sim S$
3. P 2, Simp
4. $\sim \sim R$ 1, 3, MP
5. $\sim (S \cdot R) \cdot P$ 2, Com
6. $\sim (S \cdot R)$ 5, Simp
7. $\sim S \vee \sim R$ 6, DM
8. $\sim R \vee \sim S$ 7, Com
9. $\sim S$ 4, 8, DS

[25] 1. $\sim(P \cdot Q)$
  2. R
  3. $[S \supset (P \cdot Q)] \cdot (R \supset L)$
  4. $S \vee R$ $/ \sim P \supset (\sim Q \cdot L)$
  5. $(P \cdot Q) \vee L$ 3, 4, CD
  6. L 1, 5, DS
  7. $\sim P \vee \sim Q$ 1, DM
  8. $L \vee \sim P$ 6, Add
  9. $(\sim P \vee \sim Q) \cdot (L \vee \sim P)$ 7, 8, Conj
  10. $(\sim P \vee \sim Q) \cdot (\sim P \vee L)$ 9, Com
  11. $\sim P \vee (\sim Q \cdot L)$ 10, Dist

[29] 1. $P \supset \sim Q$
  2. $P \cdot (R \vee Q)$
  3. $R \supset S$ $/ S$
  4. P 2, Simp
  5. $\sim Q$ 1, 4, MP
  6. $(R \vee Q) \cdot P$ 2, Com
  7. $R \vee Q$ 6, Simp
  8. $Q \vee R$ 7, Com
  9. R 5, 8, DS
  10. S 3, 9, MP

[33] 1. $\sim(J \equiv Q) \cdot R$
  2. $[S \supset (L \cdot M)] \vee (N \cdot J)$
  3. $[S \supset (L \cdot Q)] \supset (J \equiv M)$ $/ (J \vee K) \cdot (R \vee \sim H)$
  4. $\sim(J \equiv Q)$ 1, Simp
  5. $\sim[S \supset (L \cdot M)]$ 3, 4, MT
  6. $N \cdot J$ 2, 5, DS
  7. $J \cdot N$ 6, Com
  8. J 7, Simp
  9. $J \vee K$ 8, Add
  10. $R \cdot \sim(J \equiv M)$ 1, Com
  11. R 10, Simp
  12. $R \vee \sim H$ 11, Add
  13. $(J \vee K) \cdot (R \vee \sim H)$ 9, 12, Conj

IV.
[5] 1. $(\sim A \cdot L) \vee (\sim A \cdot F)$
  2. $\sim F$ $/ L$
  3. $\sim A \cdot (L \vee F)$ 1, Dist
  4. $(L \vee F) \cdot \sim A$ 3, Com
  5. $L \vee F$ 4, Simp
  6. $F \vee L$ 5, Com
  7. L 2, 6, DS

[9] 1. $N \supset (R \cdot M)$
  2. $(N \cdot P) \vee (N \cdot F)$ $/ N \cdot M$
  3. $N \cdot (P \vee F)$ 2, Dist
  4. N 3, Simp
  5. $R \cdot M$ 1, 4, MP
  6. $M \cdot R$ 5, Com
  7. M 6, Simp
  8. $N \cdot M$ 4, 7, Conj

Check Your Understanding 8F

I.
[5] 2. $(R \supset S) \cdot (S \supset R)$ 1, Equiv
[9] 2. $P \supset Q$ 1, Impl
[13] 2. $[(S \vee L) \cdot (Q \vee K)] \vee$
    $[\sim(S \vee L) \cdot \sim(Q \vee K)]$ 1, Equiv

II.
[5] 2. $S \supset P$ 1, Impl
[9] 2. $[(R \vee K) \supset (Q \vee S)] \cdot$
    $[(Q \vee S) \supset (R \vee K)]$ 1, Equiv

III.
[5] 1. $S \supset (P \supset Q)$
  2. $\sim Q$ $/ \sim(S \cdot P)$
  3. $(S \cdot P) \supset Q$ 1, Exp
  4. $\sim(S \cdot P)$ 2, 3, MT
[9] 1. $P \equiv S$ $/ P \supset S$
  2. $(P \supset S) \cdot (S \supset P)$ 1, Equiv
  3. $P \supset S$ 2, Simp
[13] 1. $(S \cdot T) \cdot R$ $/ S$
  2. $S \cdot (T \cdot R)$ 1, Assoc
  3. S 2, Simp

IV.
[5] 1. $\sim Q \supset \sim P$
  2. $(P \cdot R) \supset S$
  3. P $/ Q \vee S$
  4. $P \supset Q$ 1, Trans
  5. Q 3, 4, MP
  6. $Q \vee S$ 5, Add
[9] 1. $\sim P \cdot Q$
  2. $Q \supset (R \supset P)$ $/ \sim R$
  3. $Q \cdot \sim P$ 1, Com
  4. Q 3, Simp
  5. $R \supset P$ 2, 4, MP
  6. $\sim P$ 1, Simp
  7. $\sim R$ 5, 6, MT
[13] 1. $[P \supset (Q \cdot R)] \cdot [S \supset (L \cdot Q)]$
  2. $P \cdot R$ $/ Q \cdot (R \vee L)$
  3. P 2, Simp
  4. $P \vee S$ 3, Add
  5. $(Q \cdot R) \vee (L \cdot Q)$ 1, 4, CD
  6. $(Q \cdot R) \vee (Q \cdot L)$ 5, Com
  7. $Q \cdot (R \vee L)$ 6, Dist
[17] 1. $\sim(P \cdot Q) \supset (R \vee S)$
  2. $\sim P \vee \sim Q$
  3. T $/ (T \cdot R) \vee (T \cdot S)$
  4. $\sim(P \cdot Q)$ 2, DM
  5. $R \vee S$ 1, 4, MP
  6. $T \cdot (R \vee S)$ 3, 5, Conj
  7. $(T \cdot R) \vee (T \cdot S)$ 6, Dist
[21] 1. $(P \vee Q) \vee \sim R$
  2. $[(P \vee Q) \supset Q] \cdot (\sim R \supset S)$

3. ~P   / Q v (S · ~R)
4. Q v S   1, 2, CD
5. P v (Q v ~R)   1, Assoc
6. Q v ~R   3, 5, DS
7. (Q v S) · (Q v ~R)   4, 6, Conj
8. Q v (S · ~R)   7, Dist

[25] 1. ~P ⊃ Q
2. ~R ⊃ ~(~S v P)
3. Q ⊃ ~S   / R
4. ~P ⊃ ~S   1, 3, HS
5. S ⊃ P   4, Trans
6. ~S v P   5, Impl
7. ~~(~S v P)   6, DN
8. ~~R   2, 7, MT
9. R   8, DN

[29] 1. ~R v ~S
2. P v [Q v (R · S)]
3. L ⊃ ~P   / L ⊃ Q
4. (P v Q) v (R · S)   2, Assoc
5. ~(R · S)   1, DM
6. (R · S) v (P v Q)   4, Com
7. P v Q   5, 6, DS
8. ~~P v Q   7, DN
9. ~P ⊃ Q   8, Impl
10. L ⊃ Q   3, 9, HS

[33] 1. S ⊃ Q
2. R · S
3. Q ⊃ (L v ~R)   / L
4. S · R   2, Com
5. S   4, Simp
6. Q   1, 5, MP
7. L v ~R   3, 6, MP
8. R   2, Simp
9. ~~R   8, DN
10. ~R v L   7, Com
11. L   9, 10, DS

[37] 1. Q v (P ⊃ S)
2. S ≡ (R · T)
3. P · ~Q   / P · R
4. P   3, Simp
5. ~Q · P   3, Com
6. ~Q   5, Simp
7. P ⊃ S   1, 6, DS
8. S   4, 7, MP
9. [S ⊃ (R · T)] ·
   [(R · T) ⊃ S]   2, Equiv
10. S ⊃ (R · T)   9, Simp
11. R · T   8, 10, MP
12. R   11, Simp
13. P · R   4, 12, Conj

[41] 1. P v R
2. ~P v (Q · R)

3. R ⊃ (Q · S)   / Q · S
4. R v P   1, Com
5. ~R ⊃ P   4, Impl
6. P ⊃ (Q · R)   2, Impl
7. ~R ⊃ (Q · R)   5, 6, HS
8. ~~R v (Q · R)   7, Impl
9. R v (Q · R)   8, DN
10. (R v Q) · (R v R)   9, Dist
11. (R v R) · (R v Q)   10, Com
12. R v R   11, Simp
13. R   12, Taut
14. Q · S   3, 13, MP

[45] 1. P ⊃ Q
2. Q ⊃ ~(R v P)
3. ~S ⊃ Q
4. S ⊃ (M ⊃ L)
5. R
6. M v P   / L
7. R v P   5, Add
8. ~~(R v P)   7, DN
9. ~Q   2, 8, MT
10. ~P   1, 9, MT
11. P v M   6, Com
12. M   10, 11, DS
13. ~~S   3, 9, MT
14. S   13, DN
15. S · M   12, 14, Conj
16. (S · M) ⊃ L   4, Exp
17. L   15, 16, MP

[49] 1. ~(S ⊃ Q)
2. (M · N) ⊃ (O v P)
3. ~[O v (N · P)]
4. N ≡ ~(Q · R)   / ~(M v Q)
5. ~(~S v Q)   1, Impl
6. ~~S · ~Q   5, DM
7. ~O · ~(N · P)   3, DM
8. ~Q · ~~S   6, Com
9. ~Q   8, Simp
10. ~Q v ~R   9, Add
11. ~(Q · R)   10, DM
12. [N ⊃ ~(Q · R)] ·
    [~(Q · R) ⊃ N]   4, Equiv
13. [~(Q · R) ⊃ N] ·
    [N ⊃ ~(Q · R)]   12, Com
14. ~(Q · R) ⊃ N   13, Simp
15. N   11, 14, MP
16. ~(N · P) · ~O   7, Com
17. ~(N · P)   16, Simp
18. ~N v ~P   17, DM
19. ~~N   15, DN
20. ~P   18, 19, DS
21. ~O   7, Simp

22.	$\sim O \cdot \sim P$	20, 21, Conj
23.	$\sim (O \vee P)$	22, DM
24.	$\sim (M \cdot N)$	2, 23, MT
25.	$\sim M \vee \sim N$	24, DM
26.	$\sim N \vee \sim M$	25, Com
27.	$\sim M$	19, 26, DS
28.	$\sim M \cdot \sim Q$	9, 27, Conj
29.	$\sim (M \vee Q)$	28, DM

V.

[5]
1. $\sim M$ / $\sim G \supset \sim M$
2. $\sim M \vee G$ 1, Add
3. $M \supset G$ 2, Impl
4. $\sim G \supset \sim M$ 3, Trans

[9]
1. $F \supset O$
2. $F \supset W$ / $F \supset (W \cdot O)$
3. $\sim F \vee W$ 2, Impl
4. $\sim F \vee O$ 1, Impl
5. $(\sim F \vee W) \cdot (\sim F \vee O)$ 3, 4, Conj
6. $\sim F \vee (W \cdot O)$ 5, Dist
7. $F \supset (W \cdot O)$ 6, Impl

[13]
1. $\sim (H \vee Y)$
2. $I \supset \sim (\sim Y \vee H)$ / $\sim I$
3. $\sim (Y \vee H)$ 1, Com
4. $\sim Y \cdot \sim H$ 3, DM
5. $\sim Y$ 4, Simp
6. $\sim Y \vee H$ 5, Add
7. $\sim \sim (\sim Y \vee H)$ 6, DN
8. $\sim I$ 2, 7, MT

Check Your Understanding 8G

I.

[5]
1. $(P \cdot Q) \supset S$
2. $P \supset Q$ / $P \supset S$
   3. P *Assumption (CP)*
   4. Q 2, 3, MP
   5. $P \cdot Q$ 3, 4, Conj
   6. S 1, 5, MP
7. $P \supset S$ 3–6, CP

[9]
1. $P \supset (Q \cdot R)$
2. $S \supset (Q \cdot T)$ / $(S \vee P) \supset Q$
   3. $S \vee P$ *Assumption (CP)*
   4. $[S \supset (Q \cdot T)] \cdot [P \supset (Q \cdot R)]$ 1, 2, Conj
   5. $(Q \cdot T) \vee (Q \cdot R)$ 3, 4, CD
   6. $Q \cdot (T \vee R)$ 5, Dist
   7. Q 6, Simp
8. $(S \vee P) \supset Q$ 3–7, CP

[13]
1. $[(P \vee Q) \vee R] \supset (S \vee L)$
2. $(S \vee L) \supset (M \vee K)$ / $Q \supset (M \vee K)$
   3. Q *Assumption (CP)*
   4. $Q \vee P$ 3, Add
   5. $P \vee Q$ 4, Com

   6. $(P \vee Q) \vee R$ 5, Add
   7. $S \vee L$ 1, 6, MP
   8. $M \vee K$ 2, 7, MP
9. $Q \supset (M \vee K)$ 3–8, CP

[17]
1. $Q \supset \sim P$
2. $\sim P \vee (Q \vee R)$ / $P \supset (R \vee \sim S)$
   3. P *Assumption (CP)*
   4. $\sim \sim P$ 3, DN
   5. $Q \vee R$ 2, 4, DS
   6. $\sim Q$ 1, 4, MT
   7. R 5, 6, DS
   8. $R \vee \sim S$ 7, Add
9. $P \supset (R \vee \sim S)$ 3–8, CP

[21]
1. $[(A \cdot B) \cdot C] \supset D$ / $A \supset [B \supset (C \supset D)]$
   2. A *Assumption (CP)*
     3. B *Assumption (CP)*
       4. C *Assumption (CP)*
       5. $A \cdot B$ 2, 3, Conj
       6. $(A \cdot B) \cdot C$ 4, 5, Conj
       7. D 1, 6, MP
     8. $C \supset D$ 4–7, CP
   9. $B \supset (C \supset D)$ 3–8, CP
10. $A \supset [B \supset (C \supset D)]$ 2–9, CP

[25]
1. $(P \vee Q) \supset (R \cdot S)$
2. $(R \vee \sim L) \supset [M \cdot (K \vee N)]$ / $P \supset [R \cdot (K \vee N)]$
   3. P *Assumption (CP)*
   4. $P \vee Q$ 3, Add
   5. $R \cdot S$ 1, 4, MP
   6. R 5, Simp
   7. $R \vee \sim L$ 6, Add
   8. $M \cdot (K \vee N)$ 2, 7, MP
   9. $(K \vee N) \cdot M$ 8, Com
   10. $K \vee N$ 9, Simp
   11. $R \cdot (K \vee N)$ 6, 10, Conj
12. $P \supset [R \cdot (K \vee N)]$ 3–11, CP

[29]
1. $R \supset \sim U$
2. $P \supset (Q \vee R)$
3. $(Q \supset S) \cdot (S \supset T)$ / $P \supset (\sim U \vee T)$
   4. P *Assumption (CP)*
   5. $Q \vee R$ 2, 4, MP
   6. $Q \supset S$ 3, Simp
   7. $(S \supset T) \cdot (Q \supset S)$ 3, Com
   8. $S \supset T$ 7, Simp
   9. $Q \supset T$ 6, 8, HS
   10. $(Q \supset T) \cdot (R \supset \sim U)$ 1, 9, Conj
   11. $T \vee \sim U$ 5, 10, CD
   12. $\sim U \vee T$ 11, Com
13. $P \supset (\sim U \vee T)$ 4–12, CP

[33] 1. $P \supset Q$
2. $(P \cdot Q) \equiv S$ / $P \equiv S$
3. $[(P \cdot Q) \supset S] \cdot$
      $[S \supset (P \cdot Q)]$ 2, Equiv
   4. P *Assumption (CP)*
   5. Q 1, 4, MP
   6. $P \cdot Q$ 4, 5, Conj
   7. $(P \cdot Q) \supset S$ 3, Simp
   8. S 6, 7, MP
9. $P \supset S$ 4–8, CP
   10. S *Assumption (CP)*
   11. $[S \supset (P \cdot Q)] \cdot$
       $[(P \cdot Q) \supset S]$ 3, Com
   12. $S \supset (P \cdot Q)$ 11, Simp
   13. $P \cdot Q$ 10, 12, MP
   14. P 13, Simp
15. $S \supset P$ 10–14, CP
16. $(P \supset S) \cdot (S \supset P)$ 9, 15, Conj
17. $P \equiv S$ 16, Equiv

II.

[5] 1. $L \supset A$
2. $U \supset (P \supset L)$ / $U \supset (P \supset A)$
   3. U *Assumption (CP)*
   4. $P \supset L$ 2, 3, MP
   5. $P \supset A$ 1, 4, HS
6. $U \supset (P \supset A)$ 3–5, CP

Check Your Understanding 8H

I.

[5] 1. $\sim Q \vee P$
2. $\sim (P \vee S)$ / $\sim Q$
   3. $\sim\sim Q$ *Assumption (IP)*
   4. P 1, 3, DS
   5. $P \vee S$ 4, Add
   6. $(P \vee S) \cdot \sim (P \vee S)$ 2, 5, Conj
7. $\sim\sim\sim Q$ 3–6, IP
8. $\sim Q$ 7, DN

[9] 1. $[P \supset (Q \cdot R)] \cdot (S \supset L)$
2. S / L
   3. $\sim L$ *Assumption (IP)*
   4. $(S \supset L) \cdot [P \supset (Q \cdot R)]$ 1, Com
   5. $S \supset L$ 4, Simp
   6. $\sim S$ 3, 5, MT
   7. $S \cdot \sim S$ 2, 7, Conj
8. $\sim\sim L$ 3–7, IP
9. L 8, DN

[13] 1. $\sim P \supset \sim (Q \vee \sim P)$ / P
   2. $\sim P$ *Assumption (IP)*
   3. $\sim (Q \vee \sim P)$ 1, 2, MP
   4. $\sim Q \cdot \sim\sim P$ 3, DM
   5. $\sim\sim P \cdot \sim Q$ 4, Com

   6. $\sim\sim P$ 5, Simp
   7. P 6, DN
   8. $P \cdot \sim P$ 2, 7, Conj
9. $\sim\sim P$ 2–8, IP
10. P 9, DN

[17] 1. $\sim P \cdot \sim T$
2. $\sim (P \cdot \sim Q) \supset R$ / $R \vee T$
   3. $\sim R$ *Assumption (IP)*
   4. $\sim\sim (P \cdot \sim Q)$ 2, 3, MT
   5. $P \cdot \sim Q$ 4, DN
   6. P 5, Simp
   7. $\sim P$ 1, Simp
   8. $P \cdot \sim P$ 6, 7, Conj
9. $\sim\sim R$ 3–8, IP
10. R 9, DN
11. $R \vee T$ 10, Add

[21] 1. $P \supset (\sim P \equiv \sim Q)$
2. $\sim P \vee \sim Q$ / $\sim P$
   3. P *Assumption (IP)*
   4. $\sim\sim P$ 3, DN
   5. $\sim Q$ 2, 4, DS
   6. $\sim P \equiv \sim Q$ 1, 3, MP
   7. $(\sim P \supset \sim Q) \cdot$
       $(\sim Q \supset \sim P)$ 6, Equiv
   8. $(\sim Q \supset \sim P) \cdot$
       $(\sim P \supset \sim Q)$ 7, Com
   9. $\sim Q \supset \sim P$ 8, Simp
   10. $\sim P$ 5, 9, MP
   11. $P \cdot \sim P$ 3, 10, Conj
12. $\sim P$ 3–11, IP

[25] 1. $P \supset Q$
2. $(R \cdot S) \vee L$
3. $L \supset \sim Q$ / $(\sim S \vee \sim R) \supset \sim P$
   4. $\sim S \vee \sim R$ *Assumption (CP)*
     5. P *Assumption (IP)*
     6. $\sim (S \cdot R)$ 4, DM
     7. $\sim (R \cdot S)$ 6, Com
     8. L 2, 7, DS
     9. $\sim Q$ 3, 8, MP
     10. Q 1, 5, MP
     11. $Q \cdot \sim Q$ 9, 10, Conj
   12. $\sim P$ 5–11, IP
13. $(\sim S \vee \sim R) \supset \sim P$ 4–12, CP

[29] 1. $P \supset Q$
2. $\sim R \supset (P \cdot S)$
3. $S \supset \sim Q$ / R
   4. $\sim R$ *Assumption (IP)*
   5. $P \cdot S$ 2, 4, MP
   6. P 5, Simp
   7. Q 1, 6, MP
   8. $\sim\sim Q$ 7, DN
   9. $\sim S$ 3, 8, MT

10. $S \cdot P$	5, Com
11. S	9, Simp
12. $S \cdot \sim S$	8, 9, Conj
13. $\sim \sim R$	4–12, IP
14. R	13, DN

[33]
1. $(P \supset Q) \supset \sim (S \supset R)$	
2. $\sim (P \lor T)$	$/ S$
3. $\sim S$	Assumption (IP)
4. $\sim S \lor R$	3, Add
5. $S \supset R$	4, Impl
6. $\sim \sim (S \supset R)$	5, DN
7. $\sim (P \supset Q)$	1, 6, MT
8. $\sim (\sim P \lor Q)$	7, Impl
9. $\sim \sim P \cdot \sim Q$	8, DM
10. $P \cdot \sim Q$	9, DN
11. P	10, Simp
12. $\sim P \cdot \sim T$	2, DM
13. $\sim P$	12, Simp
14. $P \cdot \sim P$	11, 13, Conj
15. $\sim \sim S$	3–14, IP
16. S	15, DN

II.

[5]
1. $\sim (\sim J \cdot F)$	
2. $\sim J \supset F$	$/ J$
3. $\sim J$	Assumption (IP)
4. F	2, 3, MP
5. $\sim \sim J \lor \sim F$	1, DM
6. $J \lor \sim F$	5, DN
7. $\sim F$	3, 6, DS
8. $F \cdot \sim F$	4, 7, Conj
9. J	3–8, IP

CHAPTER 9

Check Your Understanding 9A

5. $\sim As$
9. $(x) \{Ux \supset [Gx \equiv (Wx \cdot Lx)]\}$
13. $(x) (Cx \supset \sim Ux)$
17. $(x) (Cx \supset Px)$
21. $(x) (Lx \supset Ax)$
25. $(x) (Bx \supset \sim Cx)$
29. $(\exists x) (Sx \cdot \sim Ex)$
33. $(x) (Fx \supset \sim Cx)$
37. $(x) [Wx \supset (Ex \lor Ox)]$
41. $(\exists x) (Tx \cdot Wx) \supset (x) (Tx \supset Ix)$
45. $(x) (Ax \supset Mx)$
49. $(Mt \cdot Ms) \supset \sim (Mf \lor Mr)$
53. $\sim Pp \supset \sim Gp$
57. $(Ds \cdot Da) \cdot (\sim Ps \cdot \sim Pa)$

Check Your Understanding 9B

III.

[5]
1. $(\exists x) Hx$	
2. $(x)(Hx \supset Px)$	$/ (\exists x)(Hx \cdot Px)$
3. Hc	1, EI
4. $Hc \supset Pc$	2, UI
5. Pc	3, 4, MP
6. $Hc \cdot Pc$	3, 5, Conj
7. $(\exists x)(Hx \cdot Px)$	6, EG

[9]
1. $(x)(Ux \supset Sx)$	
2. $(\exists x)(Ux \cdot Tx)$	$/ (\exists x)(Tx \cdot Sx)$
3. $Ua \cdot Ta$	2, EI
4. $Ua \supset Sa$	1, UI
5. Ua	3, Simp
6. Sa	4, 5, MP
7. $Ta \cdot Ua$	3, Com
8. Ta	7, Simp
9. $Ta \cdot Sa$	6, 8, Conj
10. $(\exists x)(Tx \cdot Sx)$	9, EG

[13]
1. $(\exists x) (Px \cdot Qx)$	
2. $(x) (Px \supset Rx)$	$/ (\exists x) (Qx \cdot Rx)$
3. $Pa \cdot Qa$	1, EI
4. Pa	3, Simp
5. $Pa \supset Ra$	2, UI
6. Ra	4, 5, MP
7. $Qa \cdot Pa$	3, Com
8. Qa	7, Simp
9. $Qa \cdot Ra$	6, 8, Conj
10. $(\exists x) (Qx \cdot Rx)$	9, EG

[17]
1. $(x)[\sim (Fx \lor Gx) \supset Hx]$	
2. $(x)(Hx \supset Lx)$	
3. $(x) \sim Fx$	$/ (x)(Gx \lor Lx)$
4. $\sim (Fx \lor Gx) \supset Hx$	1, UI
5. $Hx \supset Lx$	2, UI
6. $\sim (Fx \lor Gx) \supset Lx$	4, 5, HS
7. $\sim \sim (Fx \lor Gx) \lor Lx$	6, Impl
8. $(Fx \lor Gx) \lor Lx$	7, DN
9. $Fx \lor (Gx \lor Lx)$	8, Assoc
10. $\sim Fx$	3, UI
11. $Gx \lor Lx$	9, 10, DS
12. $(x)(Gx \lor Lx)$	11, UG

IV.

[5]
1. $(x) \sim Rx$	
2. $(x) [(Bx \lor Gx) \equiv Rx]$	$/ (\exists x) (Gx \equiv Bx)$
3. $(Ba \lor Ga) \equiv Ra$	2, UI
4. $[(Ba \lor Ga) \supset Ra] \cdot$ $\quad [Ra \supset (Ba \lor Ga)]$	3, Equiv
5. $(Ba \lor Ga) \supset Ra$	4, Simp
6. $\sim Ra$	1, UI
7. $\sim (Ba \lor Ga)$	5, 6, MT
8. $\sim (Ga \lor Ba)$	7, Com

9.	$\sim Ga \cdot \sim Ba$	8, DM
10.	$(\sim Ga \cdot \sim Ba) \vee (Ga \cdot Ba)$	9, Add
11.	$(Ga \cdot Ba) \vee (\sim Ga \cdot \sim Ba)$	10, Com
12.	$Ga \equiv Ba$	11, Equiv
13.	$(\exists x)(Gx \equiv Bx)$	12, EG

Check Your Understanding 9C

I.

5. $\sim (\exists x)(Px \supset Qx)$
9. $\sim (\exists x)(Px \supset Qx)$

II.

[5]
1.	$\sim (\exists x) Gx$	
2.	$(\exists x) Fx \vee (\exists x)(Gx \cdot Hx)$	$/ (\exists x) Fx$
3.	$(x) \sim Gx$	1, CQ
4.	$\sim Gx$	3, UI
5.	$\sim Gx \vee \sim Hx$	4, Add
6.	$\sim (Gx \cdot Hx)$	5, DM
7.	$(x) \sim (Gx \cdot Hx)$	6, UG
8.	$\sim (\exists x)(Gx \cdot Hx)$	7, CQ
9.	$(\exists x)(Gx \cdot Hx) \vee (\exists x) Fx$	2, Com
10.	$(\exists x) Fx$	8, 9, DS

[9]
1.	$\sim (x) Gx$	
2.	$(x)(Fx \supset Gx)$	
3.	$\sim (x) Hx \vee (x) Fx$	$/ (\exists x) \sim Hx$
4.	$(\exists x) \sim Gx$	1, CQ
5.	$\sim Ga$	4, EI
6.	$Fa \supset Ga$	2, UI
7.	$\sim Fa$	5, 6, MT
8.	$(\exists x) \sim Fx$	7, EG
9.	$\sim (x) Fx$	8, CQ
10.	$(x) Fx \vee \sim (x) Hx$	3, Com
11.	$\sim (x) Hx$	9, 10, DS
12.	$(\exists x) \sim Hx$	11, CQ

[13]
1.	$\sim (\exists x) Lx$	
2.	$(\exists y) My$	
3.	$(x)[(Kx \supset \sim Mx) \vee La]$	$/ \sim (y) Ky$
4.	$(x) \sim L$	1, CQ
5.	Ma	2, EI
6.	$\sim La$	4, UI
7.	$(Ka \supset \sim Ma) \vee La$	3, UI
8.	$La \vee (Ka \supset \sim Ma)$	7, Com
9.	$Ka \supset \sim Ma$	6, 8, DS
10.	$\sim \sim Ma$	5, DN
11.	$\sim Ka$	9, 10, MT
12.	$(\exists y) \sim Ky$	11, EG
13.	$\sim (y) Ky$	12, CQ

III.

[5]
1.	$\sim (\exists x)(Hx \vee Gx)$	
2.	$(x)(Fx \cdot \sim Gx) \supset (\exists x) Hx$	$/ \sim (x) Fx$

3.	$(x) \sim (Hx \vee Gx)$	1, CQ
4.	$\sim (Hx \vee Gx)$	3, UI
5.	$\sim Hx \cdot \sim Gx$	4, DM
6.	$\sim Hx$	5, Simp
7.	$(x) \sim Hx$	6, UG
8.	$\sim (\exists x) Hx$	7, CQ
9.	$\sim (x)(Fx \cdot \sim Gx)$	2, 8, MT
10.	$(\exists x) \sim (Fx \cdot \sim Gx)$	9, CQ
11.	$\sim (Fa \cdot \sim Ga)$	10, EI
12.	$\sim Fa \vee \sim \sim Ga$	11, DM
13.	$\sim Fa \vee Ga$	12, DN
14.	$\sim Gx \cdot \sim Hx$	5, Com
15.	$\sim Gx$	14, Simp
16.	$(x) \sim Gx$	15, UG
17.	$\sim Ga$	16, UI
18.	$Ga \vee \sim Fa$	13, Com
19.	$\sim Fa$	17, 18, DS
20.	$(\exists x) \sim Fx$	19, EG
21.	$\sim (x) Fx$	20, CQ

Check Your Understanding 9D

I.

[5]
1.	$(x)(Fx \supset Hx)$	
2.	$(x)(Fx \supset Gx)$	$/ (x)[Fx \supset (Gx \cdot Hx)]$
3.	Fx	Assumption (CP)
4.	$Fx \supset Gx$	2, UI
5.	$Fx \supset Hx$	1, UI
6.	Gx	3, 4, MP
7.	Hx	3, 5, MP
8.	$Gx \cdot Hx$	6, 7, Conj
9.	$Fx \supset (Gx \cdot Hx)$	3–8, CP
10.	$(x)[Fx \supset (Gx \cdot Hx)]$	9, UG

[9]
1.	$\sim (\exists y) Ky \supset \sim (\exists z) Mz$	
2.	$(\exists x)[Hx \supset (y) \sim Ky]$	$/ (x) Hx \supset (z) \sim Mz$
3.	$(x) Hx$	Assumption (CP)
4.	$Ha \supset (y) \sim Ky$	2, EI
5.	Ha	3, UI
6.	$(y) \sim Ky$	4, 5, MP
7.	$\sim (\exists y) Ky$	6, CQ
8.	$\sim (\exists z) Mz$	1, 7, MP
9.	$(z) \sim Mz$	8, CQ
10.	$(x) Hx \supset (z) \sim Mz$	3–9, CP

[13]
1.	$(x)[Gx \supset (Hx \cdot Lx)]$	$/ (x)(Fx \supset Gx) \supset (x)$
		$(Fx \supset Lx)$
2.	$(x)(Fx \supset Gx)$	Assumption (CP)
3.	Fx	Assumption (CP)
4.	$Fx \supset Gx$	2, UI
5.	Gx	3, 4, MP
6.	$Gx \supset (Hx \cdot Lx)$	1, UI
7.	$Hx \cdot Lx$	5, 6, MP
8.	$Lx \cdot Hx$	7, Com
9.	Lx	8, Simp

10. $Fx \supset Lx$	3–9, CP
11. $(x)(Fx \supset Lx)$	10, UG
12. $(x)(Fx \supset Gx) \supset (x)(Fx \supset Lx)$	2–11, CP

[17] 1. $(\exists x)(Dx \lor Mx) \supset (x)Fx$
  2. $(\exists x)Bx \supset (\exists x)(Cx \cdot Dx)$ / $(x)(Bx \supset Fx)$

3. Bx	Assumption (CP)
4. $(\exists x)Bx$	3, EG
5. $(\exists x)(Cx \cdot Dx)$	2, 4, MP
6. $Ca \cdot Da$	5, EI
7. $Da \cdot Ca$	6, Com
8. Da	7, Simp
9. $Da \lor Ma$	8, Add
10. $(\exists x)(Dx \lor Mx)$	9, EG
11. $(x)Fx$	1, 10, MP
12. Fx	11, UI
13. $Bx \supset Fx$	3–12, CP
14. $(x)(Bx \supset Fx)$	13, UG

II.

[5] 1. $(x)(Ux \supset Sx)$
  2. $(\exists x)Sx \supset (\exists x)Ax$ / $\sim(\exists x)Ax \supset \sim(\exists x)Ux$

3. $\sim(\exists x)Ax$	Assumption (CP)
4. $\sim(\exists x)Sx$	2, 3, MT
5. $(x)\sim Sx$	4, CQ
6. $\sim Sx$	5, UI
7. $Ux \supset Sx$	1, UI
8. $\sim Ux$	6, 7, MT
9. $(x)\sim Ux$	8, UG
10. $\sim(\exists x)Ux$	9, CQ
11. $\sim(\exists x)Ax \supset \sim(\exists x)Ux$	3–10, CP

Check Your Understanding 9E

I.

[5] Some dinosaurs were meat-eaters.
Therefore, all dinosaurs were meat-eaters.

[9] Every fruit is a plant.
Therefore, everything is either a fruit or a plant.

II.

[5] A universe containing one individual:

La	Ma	$La \supset Ma$	Ma	/ La
F	T	T	T	F √

[9] A universe containing one individual:

Ha	Fa	Ga	$Ha \supset Fa$	$Fa \supset Ga$	/ $Ga \supset Ha$
F	T	T	T	T	F √

[13] A universe containing one individual:

Ga	La	Ha	$Ga \cdot La$	$Ga \cdot Ha$	/ $La \supset Ha$
T	T	F	T	F	F

A universe containing two individuals:

Ga La Ha Gb Lb Hb	$(Ga \cdot La) \lor (Gb \cdot Lb)$	$(Ga \cdot Ha) \lor (Gb \cdot Hb)$	/ $(La \supset Ha) \cdot (Lb \supset Hb)$
T T F T T	T T	F T T	F F √

III.

[5] 1. $(\exists x)(Cx \cdot \sim Bx)$
  2. $(\exists x)(Wx \cdot Cx)$ / $(\exists x)(Bx \cdot \sim Wx)$

A universe containing one individual:

Ba	Ca	Wa	$Ca \cdot \sim Ba$	$Wa \cdot Ca$	/ $Ba \cdot \sim Wa$
F	T	T	T T	T	F F √

Check Your Understanding 9F.1

5. $(\exists x)\,(y)Dxy$
9. $(x)\,(Rxt \supset Rxd)$
13. $(x)\,(\exists y)\,Cxy$
17. $(x)\,[Gx \supset (\exists y)\,(\exists z)\,(Pyz \cdot Pxy)]$

Check Your Understanding 9F.2

[5] 1. $(x)\,(y)\,(Fxy \supset {\sim} Fyx)$
2. Fba $/ {\sim} Fab$
3. $(y)\,(Fby \supset {\sim} Fyb)$ 1, UI
4. $Fba \supset {\sim} Fab$ 3, UI
5. ${\sim} Fab$ 2, 4, MP

[9] 1. ${\sim} (\exists x)\,[Fx \cdot (\exists y)\,(Fy \cdot Bxy)]$
         $/ (x)\,[Fx \supset (y)\,(Fy \supset {\sim} Bxy)]$
2. $(x) {\sim} [Fx \cdot (\exists y)\,(Fy \cdot Bxy)]$ 1, CQ
3. ${\sim} [Fa \cdot (\exists y)\,(Fy \cdot Bay)]$ 2, UI
4. ${\sim} Fa \vee {\sim} (\exists y)\,(Fy \cdot Bay)$ 3, DM
5. ${\sim} Fa \vee (y) {\sim} (Fy \cdot Bay)$ 4, CQ
6. ${\sim} Fa \vee (y)\,({\sim} Fy \vee {\sim} Bay)$ 5, DM
7. $Fa \supset (y)\,({\sim} Fy \vee {\sim} Bay)$ 6, Impl
8. $Fa \supset (y)\,(Fy \supset {\sim} Bay)$ 7, Impl
9. $(x)\,[Fx \supset (y)\,(Fy \supset {\sim} Bxy)]$ 8, UG

[13] 1. $(x)\,(\exists y)\,(Mx \cdot Py)$ $/ (x)\,Mx$
2. ${\sim} (x)\,Mx$ Assumption (IP)
3. $(\exists x) {\sim} Mx$ 2, CQ
4. ${\sim} Ma$ 3, EI
5. $(\exists y)\,(Ma \cdot Py)$ 1, UI
6. $Ma \cdot Pb$ 5, EI
7. Ma 6, Simp
8. $Ma \cdot {\sim} Ma$ 4, 7, Conj
9. ${\sim}{\sim} (x)\,Mx$ 2-8, IP
10. $(x)\,Mx$ 9, DN

[17] 1. Fa $/ (x)\,[(Gx \cdot Hxa) \supset (\exists y)\,(Fy \cdot Hxy)]$
2. $Gx \cdot Hxa$ Assumption (CP)
3. ${\sim} (\exists y)\,(Fy \cdot Hxy)$ Assumption (IP)
4. $(y) {\sim} (Fy \cdot Hxy)$ 3, CQ
5. ${\sim} (Fa \cdot Hxa)$ 4, UI
6. ${\sim} Fa \vee {\sim} Hxa$ 5, DM
7. ${\sim}{\sim} Fa$ 1, DN
8. ${\sim} Hxa$ 6, 7, DS
9. $Hxa \cdot Gx$ 2, Com
10. Hxa 9, Simp
11. $Hxa \cdot {\sim} Hxa$ 8, 10, Conj
12. ${\sim}{\sim} (\exists y)\,(Fy \cdot Hxy)$ 3-11, IP
13. $(\exists y)\,(Fy \cdot Hxy)$ 12, DN
14. $(Gx \cdot Hxa) \supset (\exists y)\,(Fy \cdot Hxy)$ 2-13, CP
15. $(x)\,[(Gx \cdot Hxa) \supset (\exists y)\,(Fy \cdot Hxy)]$ 14, UG

Check Your Understanding 9G.1

5. $c = k$
9. $(\exists x)\,(Fx \cdot Sx)$

---

13. $(\exists x)\,(\exists y)\,[(Px \cdot Py) \cdot x \neq y]$
17. $Vk \cdot Mk \cdot (x)\,[(Vx \cdot Mx) \supset x = k]$

Check Your Understanding 9G.2

[5] 1. Fb
2. $(x)\,(Fa \supset x \neq a)$ $/ a \neq b$
3. $a = b$ Assumption (IP)
4. $b = a$ 3, Id
5. Fa 1, 4, Id
6. $Fa \supset b \neq a$ 2, UI
7. $b \neq a$ 5, 6, MP
8. $b = a \cdot b \neq a$ 4, 7, Conj
9. $a \neq b$ 3-8, IP

[9] 1. ${\sim} Lb$
2. $(x)\,[Hx \supset (Lx \cdot x = b)]$ $/ {\sim} Ha$
3. Ha Assumption (IP)
4. $Ha \supset (La \cdot a = b)$ 2, UI
5. $La \cdot a = b$ 3, 4, MP
6. La 5, Simp
7. $a = b \cdot La$ 5, Com
8. $a = b$ 7, Simp
9. Lb 6, 8, Id
10. $Lb \cdot {\sim} Lb$ 1, 9, Conj
11. ${\sim} Ha$ 3-10, IP

[13] 1. $(Fb \cdot Gab) \cdot (x)\,[(Fx \cdot Gax) \supset x = b]$
2. $(\exists x)\,[(Fx \cdot Gax) \cdot Hx]$ $/ Hb$
3. $(Fc \cdot Gac) \cdot Hc$ 2, EI
4. $(x)\,[(Fx \cdot Gax) \supset x = b] \cdot (Fb \cdot Gab)$ 1, Com
5. $(x)\,[(Fx \cdot Gax) \supset x = b]$ 4, Simp
6. $(Fc \cdot Gac) \supset c = b$ 5, UI
7. $Fc \cdot Gac$ 3, Simp
8. $c = b$ 6, 7, MP
9. $Hc \cdot (Fc \cdot Gac)$ 3, Com
10. Hc 9, Simp
11. Hb 8, 10, Id

[17] 1. $(Fb \cdot Hab) \cdot (x)\,[(Fx \cdot Hax) \supset x = b]$
2. $(\exists x)\,\{(Fx \cdot Gx) \cdot (y)\,[(Fy \cdot Gy) \supset y = x] \cdot Hax\}$
     $/ (\exists x)\,\{(Fx \cdot Gx) \cdot (y)\,[(Fy \cdot Gy) \supset y = x] \cdot x = b\}$
3. $(Fc \cdot Gc) \cdot (y)\,[(Fy \cdot Gy) \supset y = c] \cdot Hac$ 2, EI
4. $(x)\,[(Fx \cdot Hax) \supset x = b] \cdot (Fb \cdot Hab)$ 1, Com
5. $(x)\,[(Fx \cdot Hax) \supset x = b]$ 4, Simp
6. $(Fc \cdot Hac) \supset c = b$ 5, UI
7. $Fc \cdot Gc$ 3, Simp
8. Fc 7, Simp
9. $Hac \cdot (Fc \cdot Gc) \cdot (y)\,[(Fy \cdot Gy) \supset y = c]$ 3, Com
10. Hac 9, Simp
11. $Fc \cdot Hac$ 7, 10, Conj
12. $c = b$ 6, 11, MP
13. $(Fc \cdot Gc) \cdot (y)\,[(Fy \cdot Gy) \supset y = c]$ 3, Simp
14. $(Fc \cdot Gc) \cdot (y)\,[(Fy \cdot Gy) \supset y = c] \cdot c = b$ 12, 13, Conj
15. $(\exists x)\,\{(Fx \cdot Gx) \cdot (y)$
     $[(Fy \cdot Gy) \supset y = x] \cdot x = b\}$ 14, EG

CHAPTER 10

Check Your Understanding 10A

I.

5. *Premise 1: X*, the Junior, and *Y*, the fifth grader, have the following attributes in common: *a*, eat the same food; *b*, have their own bedrooms; *c*, get the same amount of allowance.
Premise 2: X has *d*: has to do housework.
Conclusion: Therefore, *probably Y* should have *d*: has to do housework.
The structure of the argument:

> *X* and *Y* have *a, b, c,* in common.
> *X* has *d.*
> Therefore, probably *Y* should have *d.*

9. *Premise 1: X*, fruit, and *Y*, Chocolate Peanut Gooies, have the following attributes in common: *a*, provides energy; *b*, roughage; *c*, sugar; *d*, citric acid; *e*, vitamins; *f*, minerals.
Premise 2: X, has *g*: is good for your health.
Conclusion: Therefore, *probably Y* has *g*: is good for your health.
The structure of the argument:

> *X* and *Y* have *a, b, c, d, e, f,* in common.
> *X* has *g.*
> Therefore, probably *Y* has *g.*

13. *Premise 1: X*, fruit trees and vegetables, and *Y*, seaweed, have the following attribute in common: *a*, they are plants.
Premise 2: X has *b*: adding fertilizer helps them to grow better.
Conclusion: Adding fertilizer should help seaweed grow better.
The structure of the argument:

> *X* and *Y* have *a* in common.
> *X* has *b.*
> Therefore, probably *Y* has *b.*

II.

5. *Premise 1:* X, my assertion and belief that between the Earth and Mars there is a china teapot revolving about the sun in an elliptical orbit, and Y, received dogmas, have the following attributes in common: *a*, they are purposely devised to be incapable of disproof by physical and scientific methods; *b*, based on pure belief without any physical evidence to support them; *c*, since the assertions cannot be disproved it is an intolerable presumption on the part of human reason to doubt them.
Premise 2: We know that for X, *d*, I should rightly be thought to be talking nonsense.
Conclusion: Therefore, it is probable that for Y, a received dogma *d*, it should rightly be thought to be talking nonsense.
The structure of the argument:

> *X* and *Y* have *a, b, c* in common.
> *X* has *d.*
> Therefore, probably *Y* has *d.*

Check Your Understanding 10B

I.

5. (a) *Number of entities:* The high school student and the fifth grader.
(b) *Variety of instances:* Just two people are being compared.
(c) *Number of characteristics:* Food; bedroom; allowance.
(d) *Relevancy:* They seem relevant to the question of chores.

9. (a) *Number of entities:* Fruit and Chocolate Peanut Gooies.
(b) *Variety of instances:* It is assumed that many kinds of fruit are referred to in the example.
(c) *Number of characteristics:* Providing energy; roughage; sugars; citric acid; vitamins; minerals.
(d) *Relevancy:* The characteristics listed are relevant to the issue of health.

13. (a) *Number of entities:* Fruit trees, vegetables, and seaweed.
(b) *Variety of instances:* Some are grown on land and some in water.
(c) *Number of characteristics:* All are plants.
(d) *Relevancy:* This characteristic is probably related to plant growth.

II.

5. (a) *Number of entities:* Many received dogmas and one contrived assertion.
(b) *Variety of instances:* Received dogmas differ in their age and popularity.
(c) *Number of characteristics:* Three are mentioned.
(d) *Relevancy:* All the characteristics are relevant to the point being made.

III.

5. Since we are not offered any information regarding the average time it took for the brakes to fail, this does not weaken the argument. The evidence is strong enough to warrant having your brakes replaced.

Check Your Understanding 10C

I.

5. (a) *Disanalogies:* The age difference is considerable when one factors in the probable difference in size, strength, capabilities, stamina, and level of responsibility.
(b) *Counteranalogy:* The high school student is more like the parents. The high school student is nearly an adult, and adults are expected to accept responsibility. They are expected to take care of a house and everything in it. They are expected to relieve children of the burdens of adulthood and let the children be children.
(c) *Unintended consequences:* Since the high school student wants equal treatment, then perhaps the parents should make both children go to bed, or be in the house, at the same time at night. Since the fifth grader is not

permitted to drive the car, then the high school student should not have that privilege either.

9. *(a) Disanalogies:* The candy bar probably contains numerous artificial ingredients whose health benefits may be questioned. Fruit contains no artificial ingredients. The sugar that grows in fruit is not the same as that put in most candy bars.

(b) Counteranalogy: The candy bar is like cotton candy. They both taste good to most people, usually because they contain so much sugar (or artificial sugar substitute). They both provide a quick burst of energy. This kind of energy causes a backlash when its effects wear off. The person usually feels lethargic, and his or her attention and focus is disrupted. Both foods are artificial and not organic natural products. If cotton candy is not healthy, then neither are Chocolate Peanut Gooies.

(c) Unintended consequences: Since the candy bar is just as good as fruit, we can eliminate the need for fruit in our diets and substitute the candy bar to meet our minimum daily requirements.

13. *(a) Disanalogies:* All the plants that the fertilizer worked on were grown on land. It has not yet been tried on plants grown in water.

(b) Counteranalogy: Seaweed grows in saltwater. It has been shown that the fertilizer does not work in saltwater. So, adding the fertilizer will probably not help the seaweed to grow better.

(c) Unintended consequences: The fertilizer alters the genetic structure of the plants. If you alter the genetic structure of seaweed it might disrupt the ecosystem in the sea and prove harmful.

II.

5. *(a) Disanalogies:* The assertion and belief that between the Earth and Mars there is a china teapot revolving about the sun in an elliptical orbit, and received dogmas are different in the main sense that the received dogmas have long histories of being believed; also, received dogmas are usually classified as "religions" and are established beliefs that are protected by many democratic societies. Many received dogmas are a source of comfort and hope for the followers.

(b) Counteranalogy: The teapot belief offers no hope of an afterlife and provides no moral guides to acting as a human. Therefore, it will not offer hope or comfort to people.

(c) Unintended consequences: At most times in history there were scientific hypotheses that could not be tested because the technology was not available. Given this, if we are to discard any belief that cannot be disproved, then some of theoretical science will have to be discarded; for example, if string theory is not testable, then physicists should abandon it.

CHAPTER 11

Check Your Understanding 11E

5. (A) The credibility of a witness may be attacked **or** (B) supported by evidence in the form of opinion **or** (C) reputation, **but** subject to these limitations: (D) the evidence may refer **only** to (E) character for truthfulness **or** (F) untruthfulness, **and** (G) evidence of truthful character is admissible **only** after (H) the character of the witness for truthfulness has been attacked by opinion **or** (I) reputation evidence **or** (J) otherwise.

[A or (B or C)] and [If D, then (E or F)] and
[If G, then (H or I or J)]

9. (A) Evidence of juvenile adjudications is generally **not** admissible under this rule. (B) The court may, **however**, in a criminal case allow evidence of a juvenile adjudication of a witness other than the accused **if** (C) conviction of the offense would be admissible to attack the credibility of an adult **and** (D) the court is satisfied that admission in evidence is necessary for a fair determination of the issue of guilt **or** (E) innocence.

A and [If C and (D or E), then B]

13. (A) Cross-examination should be limited to the subject matter of the direct examination **and** (B) matters affecting the credibility of the witness. (C) The court may, in the exercise of discretion, permit inquiry into additional matters as if on direct examination.

The information in C gives the court the option to allow "inquiry into additional matters" by referring to those matters "as if" they were being conducted on direct examination. In other words, the "additional matters" are to be understood as being *similar to* those under direct examination.

(A and B) and C

17. (A) Extrinsic evidence of a prior inconsistent statement by a witness is **not** admissible **unless** (B) the witness is afforded an opportunity to explain **or** (C) deny the same **and** (E) the opposite party is afforded an opportunity to interrogate the witness thereon, **or** (F) the interests of justice otherwise require. (G) This provision does **not** apply to admissions of a party-opponent as defined in rule 801(d)(2).

{If not [(B or C) and (E or F)], then A} and G

21. (A) At the request of a party (B) the court shall order witnesses excluded so that they cannot hear the testimony of other witnesses, **and** (C) it may make the order of its own motion. This rule does **not** authorize exclusion of (1) (E) a party who is a natural person, **or** (2) (F) an officer **or** (G) employee of a party which is **not** a natural person designated as its representative by its attorney, **or** (3) (H) a person whose presence is shown by a party to be essential to the

presentation of the party's cause, **or** (4) (I) a person authorized by statute to be present.

The use of the word "and" in the phrase "**and** it may make the order of its own motion" is being used to indicate another way that "the court shall order witnesses excluded." In other words, the rule is *not* stating that "the court shall order witnesses excluded" if both A and C occur at the same time; only one of them needs to occur.

[If (A or C), then B] and [If (E or F or G or H or I), then not B]

Check Your Understanding 11G

I.

5. (1) U.S. Common law courts also provided judicial review of the size of damage awards. They deferred to jury verdicts, **but** *they recognized that juries sometimes awarded damages so high as to require correction.*
   (2) If the plaintiff did *not* agree to a reduction in his damages, then Justice Story ordered a new trial.
   (3) The court may grant a new trial for excessive damages; however, it *is indeed an exercise of discretion full of delicacy and difficulty.*
   (4) [**if**] (A) it should clearly appear that the jury have committed a gross error, **or** (B) have acted from improper motives, **or** (C) have given damages excessive in relation to the person **or** (D) the injury, [**then**] (E) it is as much the duty of the court to interfere, to prevent the wrong, as in any other case:

   If (A or B or C or D), then E.

9. (A) An Oregon trial judge, **or** (B) an Oregon Appellate Court, may order a new trial **if** (C) the jury was **not** properly instructed, [**or**] **if** (D) error occurred during the trial, **or if** (E) there is no evidence to support any punitive damages at all:

   If (C or D or E), then (A or B).

But **if** (F) the defendant's only basis for relief is the *amount* of punitive damages the jury awarded, [**then**] (G) Oregon provides no procedure for reducing **or** (H) setting aside that award: If F, then (G or H)

The precedent evidence is then added to: "This has been the law in Oregon at least 1949 when the State Supreme Court announced its opinion in *Van Lom v. Schneiderman*, definitively construing the 1910 amendment to the Oregon Constitution. In that case the court held that it had *no power to reduce or set aside an award* of both compensatory and punitive damages that was admittedly excessive."

13. (A) Oregon's abrogation of a well-established common law protection against arbitrary deprivations of property raises a presumption that its procedures violate the Due Process Clause. (B) As this Court has stated from its first Due Process cases, traditional practice provides a touchstone for constitutional analysis. **Because** (C) the basic procedural protections of the common law have been regarded as so fundamental, [**therefore**] (D) very few cases have arisen in which a party has complained of their denial:

   (B and C), therefore D.

In fact, (E) most of our Due Process decisions involve arguments that traditional procedures provide too little protection **and** (F) that additional safeguards are necessary to ensure compliance with the Constitution. **Nevertheless**, (G) there are a handful of cases in which a party has been deprived of liberty **or** property without the safeguards of common law procedure:

   (E and F) and G.

(H) When the absent procedures would have provided protection against arbitrary **and** inaccurate adjudication, (I) this Court has **not** hesitated to find the proceedings violative of Due Process:

   If H, then I.

17. The Court then begins its response to the argument in 16: (A) The first, limitation of punitive damages to the amount specified, is hardly a constraint at all, **because** (B) there is no limit to the amount the plaintiff can request, **and** (C) it is unclear whether an award exceeding the amount requested could be set aside. (D) See *Tenold v. Weyerhaeuser Co*: Oregon Constitution bars court from examining jury award to ensure compliance with $500,000 statutory limit on noneconomic damages:

   (B, C, D), therefore A.

II.

5. Precedent case example: (A) "The guaranty of the right to jury trial in suits at common law, incorporated in the Bill of Rights as one of the first ten amendments of the Constitution of the United States, was interpreted by the Supreme Court of the United States to refer to jury trial as it had been theretofore known in England; **and so** (B) it is that the federal judges, like the English judges, have always exercised the prerogative of granting a new trial when the verdict was clearly against the weight of the evidence, whether it be **because** (C) excessive damages were awarded **or** (D) for any other reason.

   [A and (C or D)], therefore B.

III.

5. Second, (A) Oberg was **not** allowed to introduce evidence regarding Honda's wealth until he "presented evidence sufficient to justify to the court a prima facie claim of punitive damages. (B) During the course of trial, evidence of the defendant's ability to pay shall **not** be admitted **unless and until** (C) the party entitled to recover establishes a prima facie right to recover [punitive damages]." (D) This evidentiary rule is designed to lessen the risk "that juries will use their verdicts to express biases against big businesses," to take into account "[t]he total deterrent effect of other

punishment imposed upon the defendant as a result of the misconduct":

A and (B only if C).

9. The passage lays out the facts and issues, but the direct conclusion needs to be added:

(A) The Court's opinion in *Haslip* went on to describe the checks Alabama places on the jury's discretion *postverdict*—through excessiveness review by the trial court, **and** appellate review, which tests the award against specific substantive criteria. (B) While postverdict review of that character is **not** available in Oregon, (C) the seven factors against which Alabama's Supreme Court tests punitive awards strongly resemble the statutory criteria Oregon's juries are instructed to apply. **And** (D) this Court has often acknowledged, **and** generally respected, the presumption that juries follow the instructions they are given. (E) As the Supreme Court of Oregon observed, *Haslip* "determined only that the Alabama procedure, as a whole and in its net effect, did **not** violate the Due Process Clause."

A, B, C, D, E

Therefore, [The Honda decision did **not** violate the Due Process Clause.]

13. In short, (A) Oregon has enacted legal standards confining punitive damage awards in product liability cases. (B) These state standards are judicially enforced by means of comparatively comprehensive preverdict procedures but markedly limited postverdict review, (C) for Oregon has elected to make fact-finding, once supporting evidence is produced, the province of the jury . . . (D) The Court today invalidates this choice, largely **because** (E) it concludes that English and early American courts generally provided judicial review of the size of punitive damage awards. (F) The Court's account of the relevant history is **not** compelling.

A and B and C.
E and F.
Therefore D.

17. **Furthermore**, (A) common law courts reviewed punitive damage verdicts extremely deferentially, if at all. (B) See, *Day v. Woodworth*: assessment of "exemplary, punitive, **or** vindictive damages . . . has been always left to the discretion of the jury, as the degree of punishment to be thus inflicted must depend on the peculiar circumstances of each case"; (C) *Missouri Pacific R. Co. v. Humes*: "[t]he discretion of the jury in such cases is **not** controlled by any very definite rules"; (D) *Barry v. Edmunds*: in "actions for torts where no precise rule of law fixes the recoverable damages, it is the peculiar function of the jury to determine the amount by their verdict." (E) True, 19th century judges occasionally asserted that they had authority to overturn damage awards upon concluding, from the size of an award, that the jury's

decision must have been based on "partiality" **or** "passion and prejudice." **But** (F) courts rarely *exercised* this authority.

B, C, D, E, F.
Therefore, A.

21. (A) Oregon's procedures adequately guide the jury charged with the responsibility to determine a plaintiff's qualification for, **and** (B) the amount of, punitive damages, **and on that account** (C) do **not** deny defendants procedural due process; (D) Oregon's Supreme Court correctly refused to rule that "an award of punitive damages, to comport with the requirements of the Due Process Clause, *always* must be subject to a form of postverdict or appellate review" for excessiveness; (E) the verdict in this particular case, considered in light of this Court's decisions in *Haslip* and *TXO*, hardly appears "so 'grossly excessive' as to violate the substantive component of the Due Process Clause," *TXO*. **Accordingly**, (F) the Court's procedural directive to the state court is neither necessary nor proper. (G) The Supreme Court of Oregon has **not** refused to enforce federal law, **and** (H) I would affirm its judgment.

(A and B), therefore C.
Therefore D.
E, therefore (G and H).
Therefore F.

CHAPTER 12

Check Your Understanding 12A
5. Factual claim
9. Personal value claim
13. Moral value claim

Check Your Understanding 12B
5. False
9. False
13. True

Check Your Understanding 12E
5. stealing
   Argument: *Situation ethics:* Stealing is sometimes justified. For example, if a society is corrupt and the economy is such that survival is difficult, then stealing from those who have amassed their wealth through corrupt means is morally justified.
   Discussion of the argument: Stealing is never justified. If a society is corrupt, then all citizens must do their best to change it by moral means. That includes protest and civil disobedience. Stealing simply copies a behavior that is unjustified, no matter who does it and for whatever purpose.

9. animal rights

Argument: *Relativism:* Since there are no universal objective rights even for humans, it stands to reason that animals do not have any rights either. Besides, any "right" is provided by a collective agreement among people with free will, those capable of making rational decisions. There is no evidence that animals act on anything other than instinct; therefore, any talk of "animal rights" is misguided.

Discussion of the argument: Even if there are no universal objective rights, we can still agree to establish certain basic rights for others. For example, most people agree that humans have basic rights regardless of their physical or mental capabilities. Likewise, we can choose to designate certain basic rights to animals.

13. freedom of speech

Argument: *Emotivism:* Even though most people believe that freedom of speech is a fundamental right of all humans, that "social fact" does not make it objective. In other words, people have a strong *emotional* attachment to the idea of freedom of speech, but that in no way makes it an objective fact of the world.

Discussion of the argument: The "social fact" aspect of freedom of speech is important for people to be able to recognize repressive and dictatorial regimes, and to take steps to remedy the situations. The ability to criticize a government through freedom of speech is a sign of a healthy and mature society.

17. birth control

Argument: *Situation ethics:* Birth control is an effective way to control overpopulation, especially in undeveloped countries where children have no real hope of long-term survival. It takes pressure off individual families who may not be able to feed another mouth. It allows people to decide when and if they want to have children, and thereby take better control over their lives.

Discussion of the argument: Birth control can also mean stopping pregnancies for any reason whatsoever. There are many countries where female children are not wanted, so couples take it upon themselves to abort female fetuses. In the future, people might decide to eliminate any fetus if it doesn't conform to their expectations.

Check Your Understanding 12F

5. **Argument:** After more than three years of pressure from shareholders, religious groups and blacks, the Colgate-Palmolive Company announced yesterday that it would rename Darkie, a popular toothpaste that it sells in Asia, and redesign its logotype, a minstrel in blackface. It is plain wrong, and it is offensive. Therefore, the morally right thing dictated that we must change.

Discussion: *Deontology* holds that we have a duty to not offend others. If the toothpaste design and logo offends a group of people, and according to all accounts even shareholders in the company agreed that it is offensive, then the company has the responsibility to change the design.

9. **Argument:** Different cultures have different views on concussions and different views on identifying concussions, or even what the symptoms are that may suggest concussion. We know from research, for example, that the reporting of symptoms varies by language of origin. We have determined that players from different nationalities and cultural backgrounds report concussions in different manners. Different cultures also put more or less importance around different symptoms. One culture may not consider a headache to be important and won't report it, but they will report dizziness. Meanwhile, headaches can be one of the indicators for post-concussion syndrome. [Therefore, we should be more cautious and explore different ways of identifying possible concussion cases.]

Discussion: According to *relativism*, we should not expect people from different cultures, people with different languages, and different nationalities to agree on when a concussion occurred. But since a concussion can be medically defined with some degree of precision, we should apply those medical standards and the appropriate tests to determine the objective aspect of a concussion, instead of relying on people's subjective opinions on whether they think they have suffered a concussion.

CHAPTER 13

Check Your Understanding 13A

5. *Sample:* 6000 urban public high school seniors throughout the United States.

Population: All U.S. high school seniors.

Sample size: The sample is large and taken from throughout the United States. This raises the likelihood that the sample is representative of the population.

Potential bias: The sample excludes private high schools. This reduces the likelihood that the sample is representative of the population, because there may be a significant difference between the two groups' test scores. Their exclusion from the study may bias the results in one direction or another.

Randomness: This is a random sample. This raises the likelihood that the sample is representative of the population. However, it would be better for the researchers to generalize to public school seniors because that is what they studied.

9. *Sample:* The results of the World Series from 1903 to 2008 and the correlation to sales.

Population: Future World Series winners.

Sample size: The sample includes the results from 105 years. The sample is certainly large enough to be representative of

the past winners, since it includes nearly the entire past population. However, since the researchers are projecting into the future, there may be reasons to think that future society may not be the same as that represented in the sample.
Potential bias: The sample clearly shows a past trend. However, since we know that cigarette and liquor sales are affected by many social factors, the extended trend may be a simple correlation and not an indication of any real connection (the issue of *correlation* will be explored further in the next chapter). This allows us to question the likelihood that the sample is representative of the population.
Randomness: In a sense, randomness is not an issue here. If all the World Series results are included, then no data are missing regarding other World Series.

Check Your Understanding 13B

I.
5. Mean: 186.7; Median: 200; Mode: 200

II.
5. Mean: $1200.30; Median: $1000; Mode: $1000

III.
5. Mean: 3.17; Median: 3.16; Mode: 3.16

IV.
5. Mean: 55.29″; Median: 74″; Modes: 74″, 80″

Check Your Understanding 13C

I.
1. The standard deviation is 3.13.
    Step 1: 5.17
    Step 2: –3.17; –2.17; –1.17; –1.17; 2.83; 4.83
    Step 3: 10.05, 4.71, 1.37, 1.37, 8.01, 23.33
    Step 4: 48.84
    Step 5: 9.77
    Step 6: 3.13
5. The standard deviation is 52.41.
    Step 1: 186.7
    Step 2: –86.7; –76.7; 13.3; 13.3; 23.3; 113.3
    Step 3: 7,516.9; 5,882.9; 176.9; 176.9; 542.9; 12,836.9
    Step 4: 13,733.6
    Step 5: 2,746.72
    Step 6: 52.41

II.
1. The standard deviation is 48,093.66
    Step 1: 52,500
    Step 2: –46,500; –10,500; –10,500; 67,500
    Step 3: 2,162,250,000; 110,250,000; 110,250,000; 4,556,250,000
    Step 4: 6,939,000,000
    Step 5: 2,313,000,000

Step 6: 48,093.66
5. The standard deviation is 1,642.90.
    Step 1: 1200.30
    Step 2: –1199.80; –1199.30; –200.30; –200.30; 2799.70
    Step 3: 1,439,520.04; 1,438,320.49; 40,120.09; 40,120.09; 7,838,320.09
    Step 4: 10,796,400.80
    Step 5: 2,699,100.20
    Step 6: 1642.90

III.
1. The standard deviation is 0.72.
    Step 1: 3.15
    Step 2: –1.01; –0.66; 0.11; 0.11; 0.63; 0.84
    Step 3: 1.02; 0.44; 0.01; 0.01; 0.40; 0.71
    Step 4: 2.59
    Step 5: 0.52
    Step 6: 0.72
5. The standard deviation is 0.20.
    Step 1: 3.17
    Step 2: –0.31; –0.21; –0.01; –0.01; 0.09; 0.19
    Step 3: 0.10; 0.04; 0.00; 0.00; 0.01; 0.04
    Step 4: 0.19
    Step 5: 0.04
    Step 6: 0.20

IV.
1. The standard deviation is 18.20.
    Step 1: 61.14
    Step 2: –24.14; –16.14; –13.14; 5.86; 5.86; 16.86; 24.86
    Step 3: 582.74; 260.50; 172.66; 34.34; 34.34; 284.26; 618.02
    Step 4: 1986.86
    Step 5: 331.14
    Step 6: 18.20
5. The standard deviation is 27.22.
    Step 1: 55.29
    Step 2: –31.29; –28.29; –27.29; 18.71; 18.71; 24.71; 24.71
    Step 3: 979.06; 800.32; 744.74; 350.06; 350.06; 610.58; 610.58
    Step 4: 4445.40
    Step 5: 740.90
    Step 6: 27.22

Check Your Understanding 13E

5. First, we are told that the "hundreds of millions of dollars" are wasted, presumably because of late penalties incurred with the IRS. Second, "workers have forgone huge amounts of money in matching 401(k) contributions because they never got around to signing up for a retirement plan." However, no accurate figures are given to support this claim. Third, we are told that "Seventy percent of patients suffering from glaucoma risk blindness because they don't use their

eyedrops regularly." However, no information is given to show how this figure was arrived at; we are not told the kind of study, the sample size, or whether it was random. Fourth, the claim that "Procrastination also inflicts major costs on businesses and governments" has no supporting evidence. Also the term "major costs" is vague. Finally, the claim that "the bankruptcy of General Motors was due in part to executives' penchant for delaying tough decisions" has no supporting evidence.

Check Your Understanding 13G

5. Using the restricted conjunction method we get the following:

$$1/7 \times 1/7 = 1/49$$

9. Using the restricted conjunction method we get the following:

$$1/2 \times 1/2 = 1/4$$

13. Using the restricted conjunction method we get the following:

$$4/15 \times 4/15 = 16/225$$

17. Question 1: 2/52, or 1/26
    Question 2: 4/52, or 1/13
21. $1/4 \times 1/4 \times 1/4 \times 1/4 = 1/256$

25. Let A be the event of drawing a brown sock on the first attempt. The probability, $P(A)$, of this occurring is 4/15. Now *if A occurs*, then there will be only fourteen socks left in the drawer, three of which will be brown (because one brown sock has been removed). The probability of getting a brown sock on the second attempt, called B, is 3/14. We calculate the probability of getting two brown socks in succession as the joint occurrence of A and (B if A), which is the product of the probabilities of their separate occurrence: $4/15 \times 3/14 = 12/210$. Dividing both by 6, we get 2/35.

Check Your Understanding 13I

5. Let A = *graduating with a GPA greater than 3.5*, and B = *scoring above 1200 on the MAD test.*
   $Pr (B, if A) = .70$
   $Pr (B, if {\sim}A) = .25$
   $Pr (A) = .10$
   $.70 \times .10/ Pr (B)$
   $.07/Pr (B)$
   $Pr (B) \quad = (.70 \times .10) + (.25 \times .90)$
   $= .07 \times .23$
   $= .30$
   $Pr (A, if B) \quad = .07/.30 = .23, or\ 23\%$
   Therefore, it is not a strong measure.

CHAPTER 14

Check Your Understanding 14B

I.

5. Sufficient condition
9. Sufficient condition

II.

5. False
9. True

III.

5. The joint method of agreement and difference

IV.

5.

The **Effect**	Dinner	Groceries	Gas	Lent to Friend	Lost the Money
Missing $20					√

The chart displays the *method of agreement*. We can conclude that losing the money is probably causally connected to the missing $20.

9.

Instances of the **Effect**	Batch of Seeds	Soil	Watering Schedule	Amount of Water	Sun	Fertilizer
Plant 1: Twice the pounds as Plant 2.	√	√	√	√	√	√
Plant 2: Half the pounds as Plant 1.	√	√	√	√	√	

The chart displays the *method of difference*. We can conclude that spraying the plant with a fertilizer once a week is probably causally connected to producing twice as many pounds of tomatoes.

13.

Hardness of Egg	Minutes Boiling an Egg							
	3 Runny	4 Thicker	5 Perfect	6 Harder	7 Harder	8 Harder	9 Harder	10 Perfect

The chart displays the *method of concomitant variations*. We can conclude that the number of minutes boiling an egg is probably causally connected to the hardness of the egg.

Check Your Understanding 14G

I.
  5. True.
  9. False.

II.
  5. *Hypothesis 1:* Your friend forgot to water the plants.
     Experiment 1: Check for moisture in the dirt.
     Hypothesis 2: Your plants have contracted a disease.
     Experiment 2: Check with a plant nursery.
  9. *Hypothesis 1:* The service was interrupted and you are both calling at the same time.
     Hypothesis 2: Your mother took another call and accidentally disconnected your call.
     Experiment: Wait for a few minutes and try dialing again.

III.
  5. *Hypothesis:* The battery in Joe's car is dead.
     Experiment: Replace the battery.
     Prediction: If the hypothesis is correct, then the car will start.
     Confirm/Disconfirm: The prediction was true, and the evidence confirms the hypothesis.
     Alternative Explanations: The clamps on either the positive or negative terminal heads might have been loose. If so, the battery might not have been dead or defective. The battery could have (and should have) been tested. It may have simply needed recharging. Without having evidence to rule out these possibilities, we must be careful not to assign too much weight to the existing evidence.
  9. *Hypothesis:* Becky is allergic to her cat.
     Experiment: Two experiments: (A) Becky will give the cat to a neighbor for a day, during which time Becky will see if she stops sneezing. (B) Becky will take allergy medicine to control the sneezing.
     Prediction: For the first experiment, if the hypothesis is correct, then Becky should stop sneezing. For the second experiment, provided the medicine is effective, Becky should stop sneezing.
     Confirm/Disconfirm: Both predictions turned out true, and Becky was convinced that the evidence confirmed her hypothesis.

Alternative Explanations: We are told that the sneezing started about the same time as Becky's husband started using a new flea powder, and the sneezing stopped when he started using the old brand of flea powder. This evidence certainly weakens Becky's hypothesis, but it does not mean that her hypothesis cannot be true. We would have to do additional experiments with combinations of old and new flea powder and the allergy medicine to be able to gather the strongest possible evidence to confirm or disconfirm either Becky's hypothesis or the alternative flea powder hypothesis.

CHAPTER 15

Check Your Understanding 15B
  5. What was the cause of childbed fever, and why did more deaths occur as a result of childbed fever in the first clinic than in the second?

Check Your Understanding 15C
  5. *Infectious* is understood as being distinct from *contagious*, in that the former is the broader of the two. Whereas infectious refers to the *causation* of the disease, contagious refers only to the *manner of transmission*.

Check Your Understanding 15D
  5. It turned out that there was no real difference between the two clinics in terms of number of patients per available area. If anything, the second clinic might at times have been more crowded than the first, because women were becoming aware of the great chance of death that accompanied admission to the first clinic.
  9. Semmelweis responded that the fetal body was much rougher on women through delivery than was the male doctors' examinations.

13. Semmelweis determined that the linen was the same and was laundered at the same place.

17. Semmelweis pointed out that all these effects could be seen in both clinics. The outcomes of the birth act had to be similar in both divisions.

21. "Day and night this picture of Kolletschka's disease pursued me, and with ever increasing determination, I was obliged to acknowledge the identity of the disease, from which Kolletschka died, with that of which I saw so many puerperae die."

Check Your Understanding 15E

5. A realization that some babies had the same symptoms as women who died of childbed fever; and (2) the Kolletschka case.

Check Your Understanding 15F

5. He had weakened severely the epidemic theory and thus found himself in a position to try ideas connected with contagion theory. It was only after he had gained the information about the phantom model, saw Boer's success rate, and studied the English methods of combating childbed fever that he had a program to implement. He already had knowledge that the use of the phantom model was important, plus the fact that the English had used disinfectants very successfully. He could apply these facts without any help gained by Kolletschka's death.

9. Semmelweis made sure that persons coming in contact with this woman had to wash their hands immediately before examining another patient. But the odor from the fluid coming from the wound was so strong that nearly everyone in the clinic giving birth at that time died. Semmelweis could not explain why the deaths had occurred.

Index

Alternate Version
of Chapter 4
with Diagramming

Chapter 4

Informal Fallacies

A. Fallacies of Relevance
B. Fallacies of Unwarranted Assumption
C. Fallacies of Ambiguity or Diversion
D. Recognizing Fallacies in Ordinary Language

We run into arguments everywhere—even when we are not looking for them. For example, you might be watching television, listening to the news, or watching a sporting event when you hear the following:

> For a number of years, seven-time Tour de France bicycle champion Lance Armstrong has been accused of using performance-enhancing drugs. An article in the French newspaper *L'Equipe* alleged that six of Armstrong's urine samples from the 1999 race were retested and found to contain the drug erythropoietin (EPO). If EPO is injected it can give an athlete a tremendous performance boost; however, it had already been banned by the Tour de France in 1999.
>
> Both the newspaper that published the report and the Tour de France race are owned by Amaury Sport Organization (ASO). In his response to the accusation by the newspaper, Armstrong said, "My question is how ASO can own the paper and the race."
>
> Adapted from Philip Hersh, "Armstrong, Defenders Not Forthright," *Chicago Tribune*

Armstrong's response avoided the question of his possible use of the drug, and shifted any potential wrongdoing to ASO. He deflected our attention away by implying that since the newspaper and the race have the same owner, they have formed a conspiracy against him. Of course, Armstrong may be innocent of the drug charge, but his defense did nothing to clarify the issue or advance his cause.

We often encounter arguments that appear to be correct, but on close inspection they lack real merit. Trying to pin down why can be a challenge—or part of the game. Here is an example from a popular television show:

> *Homer*: Not a bear in sight. The Bear Patrol must be working like a charm!
> *Lisa*: That's specious reasoning, Dad.
> *Homer*: Thank you, dear.
> *Lisa*: By your logic I could claim that this rock keeps tigers away.
> *Homer*: Oh, how does it work?
> *Lisa*: It doesn't work.
> *Homer*: Uh-huh.

Lisa: It's just a stupid rock.
Homer: Uh-huh.
Lisa: But I don't see any tigers around, do you?
Homer: Lisa, I want to buy your rock.

From "Much Apu About Nothing," *The Simpsons*

Homer has committed a fallacy, and he is not going to give it up without a fight.

The term "fallacy" derives from a Latin word meaning *to deceive*. (Another label for fallacies is revealing—*non sequitur*, which literally means "it does not follow.") Fallacious arguments are often misleading or deceptive, but they can also be unintentional. They can also be intentionally comic, like in *The Simpsons*. Clearly fallacious reasoning is often used in literature, movies, and jokes to point out the irrelevancy or absurdity of a statement or an argument.

Arguments purport to offer evidence for a conclusion, but they can fail, and some special cases of failure are classified as fallacies. A **formal fallacy** is a logical error that occurs in the form or structure of an argument. Formal fallacies are restricted to deductive arguments, and an understanding of deductive analysis and logical form makes it possible to recognize and understand them. (Formal fallacies are discussed in Chapters 7 and 8.) An **informal fallacy** is a mistake in reasoning that occurs in ordinary language. Rather than an error in the form or structure of an argument, informal fallacies include mistakes of *relevance*, *unwarranted assumption*, and *ambiguity* or *diversion*. We shall meet them all in this chapter. These classifications are simply aids in recognizing similarities among informal fallacies ("family resemblance"), not a rigid method of categorization.

The mistakes that occur in informal fallacies are not always easy to spot. A subtle change in the meaning of words, a shift in the reference of names, or a hidden irrelevancy are just a few of the many ways we can be fooled. In addition, fallacies are sometimes so persuasive because they involve fear, anger, pity, or even admiration. We start by looking at fallacies of relevance.

A. FALLACIES OF RELEVANCE

In **fallacies of relevance**, irrelevant premises are offered in support of a conclusion. Arguments that use irrelevant premises in support of a conclusion suffer from serious flaws in reasoning. Premises must be relevant; they must establish logical, reasonable ties to the conclusion. In addition, many irrelevant premises rely on psychological or emotional appeal for their persuasive force. We can distinguish eight kinds of fallacies of relevance.

1. Argument Against the Person
(ARGUMENTUM AD HOMINEM—"TO THE PERSON")
The truth of a statement and the strength of an argument should be judged on objective grounds. In an **argument against the person**, a claim is rejected or judged

Formal fallacy A logical error that occurs in the form or structure of an argument; it is restricted to deductive arguments.

Informal fallacy A mistake in reasoning that occurs in ordinary language and is different from an error in the form or structure of arguments.

Fallacies of relevance Fallacies that occur whenever irrelevant premises are offered in support of a conclusion.

Argument against the person When a claim is rejected or judged to be false based on alleged character flaws of the person making the claim. A second common form occurs whenever someone's statement or reasoning is attacked by way of a stereotype, such as a racial, sexual, or religious stereotype. A third form involves the use of the circumstances of a person's life to reject his claims.

to be false based on alleged character flaws of the person making the claim. This would be attacking the person, not the person's assertions or arguments, and is commonly referred to by the Latin term *ad hominem*. Generally speaking, people's characters are irrelevant to the determination of the truth or falsity of their claims. An important exception to this rule occurs in sworn testimony. If someone has previously been exposed as a liar based on contradictions in statements given under oath, then there are objective grounds for suspicion about any current or future statements.

Clear cases of *ad hominem* are not difficult to recognize. They divert attention away from the objective truth or falsity of a claim and instead denigrate the character of the person making the claim. Here are some examples:

- Why should I believe what he says about our economy? He is not even a citizen.
- You can't accept her advice. She is so old she has no idea what goes on in today's world.
- Why would you listen to him? He's too young to have any wisdom about life.

In all these cases, the reason to reject someone's statement or position is based on irrelevant information. Another common form of *ad hominem* occurs whenever someone's statement or reasoning is attacked by way of a stereotype, such as a racial, sexual, or religious stereotype. It can be subtle rather than overtly dismissive. But it will not advance your cause. A reference to any kind of stereotype is irrelevant to the determination of the truth or falsity of a person's claim or argument.

Another form of the *ad hominem* fallacy involves the use of the circumstances of a person's life to reject his claims. Circumstances are different from character. For example, political affiliation, educational institution, place of birth, religious affiliation, and income are circumstances connected to people's lives. When we insinuate that someone's circumstances dictate the truth or falsity of the claim, then we are once again attacking the person rather than the claim. Here is an example:

Of course Senator Hilltop thinks my administration's tax proposals are bad for the country. After all, his political party lost the last election, and everyone knows that losers are jealous.

Paraphrasing and diagramming the argument can help with the analysis:

[1] Senator Hilltop thinks my administration's tax proposals are bad for the country. [2] His political party lost the last election. [3] Members of the losing party are always jealous of the winning party.

2   3   The premises attack Senator Hilltop's party affiliation and nega-
         tively stereotype the senator and his party.

1

Now suppose that Senator Hilltop has provided reasons for why he is against the tax proposals. If so, then the foregoing argument is an instance of *ad hominem*, because it attacks the person and not the person's reasons.

The following two arguments illustrate the same point:

- You don't want cars to get better gas mileage because you are a stockholder in the three major gasoline companies. If cars get better gas mileage, then your stock dividends will go down.
- You are against euthanasia because you are a physician. You make money only if terminally ill people are kept alive as long as possible.

A special kind of *ad hominem* argument is called "poisoning the well." In these instances, the attack against the person occurs before opponents have a chance to present their case. The attacker mentions something about the opponent's character or life and uses that information to warn the audience not to believe anything they hear or read. For example:

> Before you read her article "Stop All Wars," you should know that she was arrested six times for protesting in front of the Pentagon and White House. She also has been investigated by the FBI for possible ties to peace movements in other countries, some of which resulted in violence. It is crystal clear that these kinds of people are dangerous and want to destroy our Constitution and take away our basic freedoms. We must not let them.

Once again, it is important to recognize that any criticism of a person's argument should be restricted to their argument and should not be based on *ad hominem* attacks. All *ad hominem* fallacies rest on the same kind of reasoning error—the rejection of a statement or argument by criticizing a person's character or circumstances. In all cases, neither the truth of the claim nor the strength of the argument is ever considered on logical or factual grounds.

2. *Tu Quoque*

A variety of the *ad hominem* fallacy known as **tu quoque** (meaning "you, too" or "look who's talking") is distinguished by the specific attempt of one person to avoid the issue at hand by claiming the other person is a hypocrite. For example:

> [1] You have been lecturing me about not joining a gang. But Dad, [2] you were a gang member, and [3] you never went to jail. So, [4] I'll make my own decision about joining a gang.

Premises 1, 2, and 3 are used to imply the following: [5] *Dad, you are a hypocrite.* This result is then used to reject Dad's arguments: [6] *I can disregard your lectures.* The reconstructed argument can be diagrammed as follows:

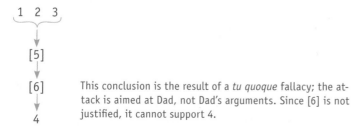

This conclusion is the result of a *tu quoque* fallacy; the attack is aimed at Dad, not Dad's arguments. Since [6] is not justified, it cannot support 4.

Tu quoque A variety of the *ad hominem* fallacy that is distinguished by the specific attempt of one person to avoid the issue at hand by claiming the other person is a hypocrite.

We can see that [6] is the result of the *tu quoque* fallacy. This fallacious result is then used as justification, and ultimately as support for 4. But since [6] is itself not justified, any further use of it is also unjustified. The fallacy occurs because the argument attacks Dad; therefore, it fails to address Dad's arguments.

Another example comes from the political world. If a U.S. senator criticizes the human rights failings of China by offering a detailed description of recorded UN inquiries, a Chinese representative might say the following:

> The senator should look in his own backyard. What about the complete disregard of the universal rights of people who the U.S. government incarcerates without any recourse to courts or even to a lawyer? What about the U.S. policy of spying on its own citizens without a court order? The senator should not throw stones when he lives in a glass house. The senator quotes many of his pronouncements from the Bible, so let me remind him that "whoever is without sin let him cast the first stone."

Other than stringing together a number of clichés, this response offers no rational rebuttal of the assertions of human rights violations. Of course, the senator might respond with his own cliché: Two wrongs don't make a right.

Instances of *tu quoque* fallacies occur quite often in personal arguments within families. For example, a child might say the following:

> Dad, I don't know why you keep pressuring me to give up smoking. You keep showing me statistics proving that smoking is bad for my health, that it will shorten my life, that it costs too much money. But you started smoking at my age and only recently quit. How can you honestly tell me to stop?

Since there are many good reasons to support the conclusion that someone should stop smoking, these reasons must be rationally argued against. To attack the person making the argument rather than the argument is to commit the fallacy.

3. Appeal to the People

(ARGUMENTUM AD POPULUM)

Appeal to the people
The avoidance of objective evidence in favor of an emotional response defeats the goal of a rational investigation of truth. The tactic appeals to people's desire to belong to a group.

Some arguments or claims rely on the arousal of a strong emotional state or psychological reaction. In an **appeal to the people**, the avoidance of objective evidence in favor of an emotional response defeats the goal of a rational investigation of truth. This fallacious tactic has been used by tyrants and bigots throughout history, with devastating social effects. It often appeals to a mob mentality, to an "us against them" attitude, with a fixation on fear or hate. Exposing the fallacy can sometimes be the first step in defeating this potentially harmful social ill. Another term that has come to be associated with this fallacy is the "bandwagon effect," which derives its name from the emotions involved in joining a movement merely because it is popular (to "jump on the bandwagon").

The fallacy of appealing to the people is a common thread that also runs through much of today's advertising campaigns. Slick ads are created in order to arouse a desire to attain the product. Such products are often displayed being used by beautiful, successful, and happy people. The obvious implication is that if you use this product, you will be transformed into one of the lucky ones, the ones living life to the fullest. The ads push psychological buttons: the need to belong to a group, the desire to be respected, the desire to be successful, and so on. The emotional reasons for buying products are powerful tools that are understood and effectively used by corporations to sell their products.

Pollsters for political groups also use this tactic. They can manipulate poll questions so that the appeal to an emotional response overrides the rational grounds for a person's belief. Here is an example of a rhetorical, or loaded, question:

> [1] Public schoolteachers are demanding a pay raise and threaten to strike if they don't get it. [2] A prolonged strike will jeopardize our children's future. In addition, [3] some economists predict that any substantial pay raise will result in an unbalanced budget, [4] which in turn will lead to an increase in taxes. Although [5] the school year lasts only 180 days, the teachers get paid 12 months a year, whether or not school is in session. So are you for or against a pay raise for public school teachers?

Since the final sentence is a rhetorical question, it needs to be rewritten before we assign it a numeral: [6] *You should be against a pay raise for public school teachers.* We can now diagram the argument.

1 2 3

4 5   The language employed is meant to appeal to the emotions
        of taxpayers and voters. The terms "demanding," "threaten,"
        "prolonged strike," and "jeopardize" are used to evoke a
[6]   sense of dire consequences and to provoke anger.

The argument offers only several negative consequences of a teachers' pay raise, but only as possibilities, not as facts. Also, the mention of higher taxes fuels the emotions of many voters.

4. Appeal to Pity

(ARGUMENTUM AD MISERICORDIAM—"FROM PITY OR GUILT")

A specific kind of emotional plea is the **appeal to pity**. For example, a defense attorney may attempt to get the jury to sympathize with the defendant prior to deliberation. If the defendant is found guilty, then the appeal may be addressed to the judge, asking for a light sentence based on the effects that a harsh sentence would have on the defendant's family. On the other side, the prosecution may appeal to the jury to sympathize with the victim, not the defendant. The prosecutor may appeal to the judge to consider the emotional devastation inflicted on the victim's family. In this way, he may persuade the judge to sentence the defendant to the maximum penalty allowed by law. However, trials are, ideally, rational decision-making processes. The image of justice as a blindfolded person holding a set of scales emphasizes the goal of

Appeal to pity A specific kind of emotional plea that relies solely on a sense of pity for support.

an objective weighing of the evidence. If pity is substituted for evidence and the rule of law, then the judgment is fallacious.

Here is a classic example:

> [1] Your honor, before you sentence my client for the murder of his parents, I ask you to consider his situation. [2] He is an orphan. [3] Perhaps you can give him the lightest punishment possible.

1   2   The premises provide no objective evidence for a light punish-
          ment. The argument is ironic since the premises ask the judge to
          pity the defendant because he is a self-caused orphan.
3

Many charities arouse a sense of pity, and perhaps even guilt, when they solicit pledges of support. These charities know that people do not always act rationally and in their own long-term best interests. Nevertheless, any cause worthy of support should have rational, legitimate reasons, which, when understood, should be sufficient to get people to give. In addition to evoking our human sense of compassion for those who are suffering, a *legitimate* argument will not have to rely solely on pity to support its conclusion.

5. Appeal to Force

(ARGUMENTUM AD BACULUM—"APPEAL TO THE STICK")

Appeal to force A threat of harmful consequences (physical and otherwise) used to force acceptance of a course of action that would otherwise be unacceptable.

The threat of physical harm, an **appeal to force**, can sometimes cause us to accept a course of action that otherwise would be unacceptable. There are cases where witnesses and jurors have been threatened with physical harm to themselves or to their families if they go against the defendant. Voters have been pressured into changing their vote by the threat of violence.

However, the threat need not be so overt and directly physical. For example, a large company may send out the following memo to its employees:

> [1] If the workers of this company do not agree to a 25% cut in salary, then the company may have to shut its doors. Therefore, [2] the workers of this company must agree to a 25% cut in salary.

Here is a diagram and analysis of the argument.

1   The premise is an obvious threat. As such, it does not, by itself, pro-
      vide objective evidence for the conclusion.

2

If the company is in bad financial shape, then there should be objective evidence to present to the workers. The evidence would have to show that without the pay cut the company would be forced to close. However, without this evidence, the threat by the company to close its doors unless its employees vote to take a pay cut results in an instance of the fallacy of appeal to force.

Another example illustrates the same point. A parent may threaten a child with loss of privileges or being grounded in order to achieve desired results:

You had better get straight A's on your next report card. If you don't, then we will have to punish you. You will be not allowed to go out with your friends for an entire month.

It is not difficult to imagine perfectly legitimate reasons why students should get good grades. Rational, objective evidence can be used as support for why students should do well in school. Anytime an overt or implied threat is used to convince someone to make a decision, in the absence of supporting evidence for the conclusion, the rational decision-making process is subverted.

6. Appeal to Ignorance
(ARGUMENTUM AD IGNORANTIAM—"ARGUING FROM IGNORANCE")

An **appeal to ignorance** (lack of knowledge) makes one of two possible mistakes: (1) a claim is made that a statement must be true because it has not been proven to be false, or (2) a claim is made that a statement must be false because it has not been proven to be true. Both claims are unjustified. An example of the first kind of mistake is this:

> UFOs exist because nobody has proven that they don't exist.

Here is an example of the second kind of mistake:

> [1] There is no life anywhere else in the universe. [2] We have never received signals from any part of space.

Here is the diagram of the argument:

> 2   The conclusion is based on a single factor—the lack of signals from
>   outer space. But our failure to have detected any signals may signify
>   our ignorance of sophisticated methods of detection. Also, the abil-
> 1   ity to send signals is not a necessary requirement for life to exist.

Appeal to ignorance
An argument built on a position of ignorance claims either that (1) a statement must be true because it has not been proven to be false or (2) a statement must be false because it has not been proven to be true.

If substantial evidence is available to decide an issue, then the fallacy does not arise. For example, after thorough investigation, if no credible evidence is found linking a suspect to a crime, then we are justified in claiming the suspect is not guilty precisely because no evidence exists to prove guilt.

7. Missing the Point
(IGNORATIO ELENCHI—"IRRELEVANT PROOF")

The fallacy of **missing the point** occurs when premises that seem to lead logically to one conclusion are used instead to support an unexpected conclusion. A conclusion "misses the point" or "comes out of left field" when the premises do not adequately prepare us for it. For example:

> Hey Mom, guess what I found out? If we buy a second car, the insurance will only be an additional $400 a year! Let's go get one before the insurance company changes the rate.

Missing the point
When premises that seem to lead logically to one conclusion are used instead to support an unexpected conclusion.

The first sentence is not part of the argument, so we can disregard it when we number the relevant statements. This will form the basis for constructing the diagram of the argument.

[1] If we buy a second car, the insurance will only be an additional $400 a year. [2] Let's go get one before the insurance company changes the rate.

1   The evidence regarding the cost of the insurance may not be in
     dispute, but the gap between the premises and conclusion is so great
     that the conclusion becomes, in a sense, irrelevant.

2

The need for a second car has not been adequately established; nor has the family's financial situation been determined.

8. Appeal to an Unqualified Authority

(ARGUMENTUM AD VERECUNDIAM—"APPEAL TO REVERENCE OR RESPECT")

Arguments often rely on the opinions of experts, specialists whose education, experience, and knowledge provide relevant support for a claim. The appeal to expert testimony strengthens the probability that the conclusion is correct, as long as the opinion falls within the realm of the expert's field. On the other hand, arguments that rely on the opinions of people who have no expertise, training, or knowledge relevant to the issue at hand **appeal to an unqualified authority**.

The most prevalent fallacious use of inappropriate authority is in advertisements and commercials. Athletes, movie and television stars, and former politicians endorse products to boost sales. The consumer is expected to respect the famous personalities and trust their opinion.

Here is an example:

> [1] I'm Nick Panning, quarterback of the Los Angeles Seals. [2] I've been eating *Oaties* for breakfast since I was a kid. [3] *Oaties* provides nutrition and vitamins and helps build strong bones. [4] *Oaties* tastes great. [5] You should get some for your kids today.

Here is a diagram of the argument:

1   2   3   4   Merely being famous does not qualify someone to
                  pronounce the merits of a product. An athlete gener-
                  ally has no expertise of the nutritional value of a
          5   breakfast cereal.

On the other hand, a person with a Ph.D. in nutrition would presumably be in a good position to offer a fair assessment of the breakfast cereal (provided the opinion is not based on monetary compensation).

Albert Einstein, the famous physicist, was asked to be the first president of Israel. He humbly declined, stating that he had no idea how to run a country. Such modesty is rare.

Summary of Fallacies of Relevance

1. Argument against the person (*ad hominem*)

When a claim is rejected or judged to be false based on alleged character flaws of the person making the claim. A second common form occurs whenever someone's

---

Appeal to an unqualified authority
An argument that relies on the opinions of people who have no expertise, training, or knowledge relevant to the issue at hand.

statement or reasoning is attacked by way of a stereotype, such as a racial, sexual, or religious stereotype. A third form involves the use of the circumstances of a person's life to reject his claims.

2. *Tu quoque*

A variety of the *ad hominem* fallacy in which one person attempts to avoid the issue at hand by claiming the other person is a hypocrite.

3. Appeal to the people

The avoidance of objective evidence in favor of an emotional response defeats the goal of a rational investigation of truth. The tactic appeals to people's desire to belong to a group.

4. Appeal to pity

A specific kind of emotional plea that relies solely on a sense of pity for support.

5. Appeal to force

A threat of harmful consequences (physical and otherwise) used to force acceptance of a course of action that would otherwise be unacceptable.

6. Appeal to ignorance

An argument claiming either that (1) a statement must be true because it has not been proven to be false or (2) a statement must be false because it has not been proven to be true.

7. Missing the point

When premises that seem to lead logically to one conclusion are used instead to support an unexpected conclusion.

8. Appeal to an unqualified authority

An argument that relies on the opinions of people who have no expertise, training, or knowledge relevant to the issue at hand.

CHECK YOUR UNDERSTANDING 4A

I. Determine whether each statement is true or false.

1. The appeal to an unqualified authority occurs when an argument relies on the experience, training, or knowledge of people who are experts relevant to the issue at hand.

Answer: False. The fallacy occurs when an argument relies on the opinions of people who have *no* expertise, training, or knowledge relevant to the issue at hand.

2. The appeal to pity is a specific kind of *ad hominem* fallacy.

3. An appeal to ignorance occurs when a person's character or circumstances are used to reject their claims.

4. The appeal to force uses rational reasons in support of a controversial position.

⭐ 5. *Tu quoque* is a variety of the *ad hominem* fallacy distinguished by the specific attempt of one person to avoid the issue at hand by claiming the other person is a hypocrite.

6. The fallacy of missing the point occurs in an argument where premises that seem to lead logically to one conclusion are used instead to support an unexpected conclusion.

7. An appeal to the people is not considered a specific kind of *ad hominem* fallacy.

8. An argument that claims either (1) a statement must be true because it has not been proven to be false or (2) a statement must be false because it has not been proven to be true is called *ad hominem*.

⭐ 9. A threat of harmful consequences (physical and otherwise) used to force acceptance of a course of action that would otherwise be unacceptable is called an appeal to an unqualified authority.

10. *Ad hominem* fallacies occur when an argument uses character flaws or circumstances of people's lives to reject their claims.

II. Each of the following passages contains a fallacy of relevance. Determine the fallacy that best fits each case. Explain your answer.

1. Biology 1 was easy for me. Physics 1 was no problem. I think I'm going to change my major to social work.

Answer: Missing the point. This is an example of an argument that does not work because the premises seem to head in one direction (the person does well in natural science courses), but the conclusion heads in another direction (changing to a social work major).

2. This team beat us 64–0 last year. So we need to go out and give them a taste of their own medicine and see how they like it. Are you ready to fight?

3. If we don't raise gasoline prices, then we can't afford to explore for new oil reserves. In that case our dependency on foreign oil will bankrupt the major gasoline companies. The price will skyrocket and will be out of the reach of most people.

4. Maybe you didn't know that she is an orphan. Her outrageous behavior should be excused because of her background.

⭐ 5. I saw him play football, and he is ferocious on the field; he tackles everything in sight. Don't hire him to tutor young kids; he's too violent.

6. That must be a great product for men since a former senator and presidential candidate endorsed it.

7. I believe that we are reincarnated. No one has ever been able to prove that after death our spirits don't move on to another baby.

8. He is an atheist. He cannot possibly have anything relevant to say on ethical issues.

★ 9. That guy plays a doctor on my favorite TV show. I saw him in a commercial where he said that Asperalinol was great for migraine headaches. It must really work, so the next time you go to a drugstore pick me up a bottle.

10. I know that Senator Wickhaven has been found guilty of harassment, but did you know that he was twice wounded in the Korean War? Since he has suffered so much for our country, he should not be punished for this crime.

11. If you don't break off your relationship with him, your mother and I will disinherit you.

12. She did not vote in the last election. Anything she suggests about how our country should be run cannot possibly be of any concern to us.

★ 13. Mr. Crabhouse is a hard grader. Not only that, he forces you to attend class, participate in discussions, and do homework. He actually expects us to think about the material outside of class. So you can believe that his class teaches students nothing about real life.

14. My uncle drinks a six-pack of beer a day, so I couldn't believe it when he lectured me on the dangers of alcohol. He's one to talk! Nothing he says about drinking can be true because he cannot stop drinking himself.

15. I know that we haven't looked for the missing money in the attic, but I'm sure that it is there.

16. I know that he did not do well on the exams; nevertheless, you should give him an A for the course. After all, he is taking 18 credits and is holding down a full-time job.

★ 17. Of course you should pay us for protection. After all, if you don't, we will have to break your arms, wreck your business, and harass your customers.

18. I would not believe anything he says in his book. He is constantly on TV, on the radio, and in magazines trying to promote it so it will become a best seller.

19. Aliens from another planet must have built the great pyramids of Egypt because there is no record of how they were actually constructed.

20. He has taken one psychology course, so he must be wrong when he claims that gambling is addictive.

★ 21. That physician is a male. He couldn't possibly know anything about female health problems.

22. I know that deep inside you love her. Draw on that undying love, and forget that she spent all the money on losing lottery tickets.

23. Statistics show that people with a college degree earn 50% more during their lifetime than those without a degree. So, you should begin investing in blue chip stocks.

24. I am going to vote for the incumbent, Senator Loweman, because my chemistry teacher said he is the best candidate.

⭐ 25. Since that sports reporter is a female, her analysis of what caused our team to lose the game is irrelevant.

26. Even though neither of us was at home when it happened, the dog must have broken the window by jumping on it. You have not shown me any other way that it could have happened.

27. He is a college student. That is enough to convince me that he drinks alcohol excessively.

28. The advertisement showed the latest Nobel Prize winner in literature drinking that new wine, Chateau Rouge. It must taste divine.

⭐ 29. I know you don't want to become a lawyer. However, your mother and I would be so proud to finally have a professional in the family. We would die happy if you go to law school.

30. I know your cousin recommends taking vitamins every day. After all, she's a pharmacist; what do you expect her to tell you?

31. He failed his final exam, so don't blame him for getting drunk and destroying his dorm room.

32. She is a chess grand master, so she can't be very beautiful.

⭐ 33. Look, the picture of the Olympic basketball team is on this cereal. It must be good for athletes.

34. Scientific experiments have never proved conclusively that there are not any ghosts; therefore, I firmly believe that they do exist.

35. He eats meat, so we should not invite him to speak at our seminar on animal rights.

36. I like chocolate. I like ice cream. Therefore, I'll take a hot dog for lunch.

⭐ 37. Your next-door neighbor works on his car day and night. You said you can't get any rest from the noise, so if you want him to stop, then let's steal his car and trash it out of town.

38. I have not decided if you can go to the concert tonight. I would like to see how much you contribute to this household. We will see what happens if you clean the house, wash the car, and do the grocery shopping today.

39. You can't give me an F on the exam. If you do, my mother and father will be so upset they will have to be hospitalized.

40. You tell me to wear a seat belt when I drive because it will protect me in case I get in an accident. I never saw you wear one when you drive, so why should I wear one?

B. FALLACIES OF UNWARRANTED ASSUMPTION

Fallacies of unwarranted assumption exhibit a special kind of reasoning error: they assume the truth of some unproved or questionable claim. The fallacies become apparent when the assumptions and lack of support are exposed. We can distinguish twelve kinds of fallacies of unwarranted assumption. (We continue our numbering of fallacies from the previous section.)

> **Fallacies of unwarranted assumption** Arguments that assume the truth of some unproved or questionable claim.

9. Begging the Question

(PETITIO PRINCIPII—"ASSUMPTION AT THE BEGINNING")

One type of the fallacy of **begging the question** assumes as evidence the very thing that it attempts to prove in a conclusion. In other words, the conclusion of an argument is smuggled into the premises. This can occur if the premises are confusing, complex, or obscure. It can occur even if the conclusion is assumed as an undeclared premise. Cases of begging the question can go unnoticed because they often sound so convincing. This should not be surprising; in many cases, the conclusion is already assumed in the premises, so on the surface it might appear to be a strong argument. However, premises can legitimately support conclusions only by providing reasons that are independent of the claim in the conclusion. No one would be fooled by the following argument:

> **Begging the question** An argument that assumes as evidence in the premises the very thing that it attempts to prove in the conclusion.

> My brother has difficulty sleeping. Therefore, my brother has difficulty sleeping.

Since the conclusion merely restates the information in the premise, the argument is valid. However, the premise offers no independent or "new" information that would allow us to see that the conclusion has been well supported. Is the following argument any better?

> My brother suffers from insomnia. Therefore, my brother has difficulty sleeping.

At first sight it might appear that the information about insomnia offers an independent, good reason to accept the conclusion. However, close analysis reveals that the word "insomnia" means *having difficulty sleeping*. In other words, the premise contains the same information as the conclusion, so the argument begs the question.

Now let's consider this argument:

> [1] Jane has the highest GPA among all the seniors in my school. [2] There are 300 graduating seniors in my class. Therefore, [3] no senior has a higher GPA than she.

Numbering the statements provides the basis for a diagram of the argument.

> 1   2
> ⌣
> ↓   Premise 1 and the conclusion say the same thing. They both as-
> 3   sert that Jane has the highest GPA among seniors. In fact, the
>   second premise becomes irrelevant; the number of graduating
>   seniors has no bearing on the conclusion.

The conclusion is already assumed in the premises; it is merely worded differently. Obviously, if the claim is true in the premises, it will be true in the conclusion. The argument begs the question because it assumes what it intends to prove.

A different kind of fallacy of begging the question occurs when a premise needs independent support for its acceptance. For example, if your argument relies on a controversial or unsubstantiated premise, then you are assuming information that is by itself unwarranted and that could be unacceptable to those you are trying to convince. Consider this argument:

> The murder of a human being is always wrong. Abortion is the murdering of an embryo or fetus, both of which are human beings. Therefore, abortion is always wrong.

Most people would probably accept the first premise. If clarity is needed, we could offer a definition of "murder" as "the unjustified taking of the life of a human being." Our discussion might exempt cases of self-defense, legitimate police activity while protecting the citizenry, and certain military engagements. However, the second premise presents a greater challenge. The assertion that an embryo or fetus is a human being is often the central point on which opposing positions regarding abortion rest. Someone who disagrees with the conclusion of the argument can point out that the second premise "begs the question," in that it presents as a good reason what is in fact an unwarranted assumption: an embryo or fetus is a human being. The fallacious nature of the argument is not based on the underlying logic, because if both premises are true, then the argument is valid. The fallacy occurs because the truth of the second, controversial, premise has been assumed. The argument lacks sufficient additional, independent reasons to make the second premise acceptable and warranted.

Another type of begging the question is *circular reasoning*. Here is an example:

> You can believe him because he never lies. Furthermore, since he always tells the truth, he is someone that you can believe.

Paraphrasing the argument reveals the problem:

> ¹You can believe him. ² He never lies. ³ He always tells the truth. ⁴ He is someone that you can believe.

If you look closely, you can see that 2 and 3 say the same thing. Saying that someone never lies is the same thing as saying that he or she always tells the truth. Also, 1 and 4 say the same thing; they both say that you can believe him. The argument can be captured in a diagram that reveals how the statements are related to each other.

As we can see in the diagram, 1 is used to support 2, and then 2 is used to support 1. The argument goes in a circle.

10. Complex Question

Complex question
A single question that actually contains multiple, hidden parts.

The fallacy of **complex question** occurs when a single question actually contains multiple, hidden parts. The questioner tries to force a single answer that, in turn, is used against the respondent. For example, suppose you are asked the following question:

Do you still cheat on your taxes?

Answering either *yes* or *no* is an admission that you did, in fact, cheat on your taxes. The key words that create the complex question are "still cheat." If you answer "Yes," then the questioner can conclude that you currently cheat on your taxes and you have done so in the past. On the other hand, even if you never cheated on your taxes, answering "No," is an admission that you once did cheat on your taxes, but you no longer do. Therefore, the questioner can use this as evidence to support the conclusion that you cheated on your taxes. Here is what the questioner's argument would like:

[1] I asked you if you still cheated on your taxes. [2] You said "No." Therefore, [3] by your own admission you did cheat on your taxes.

Here is a diagram of the argument:

1   2   The premises rely on the fact that the complex question
         contained two distinct questions that should have been asked
         separately: A. Did you ever cheat on your taxes? B. Do you now
3   cheat on your taxes?

The ability to recognize that there are actually two questions at work here allows us to avoid the trap of the complex question. Once the questions are separated an innocent person can answer "No" to question A (Did you ever cheat on your taxes?) and "No" to question B (Do you now cheat on your taxes?). This prevents the questioner from drawing an unjustified conclusion.

Complex questions can be used to trap us in unacceptable situations. For example, suppose someone asks,

Aren't you going to do something about your child's terrible behavior?

This complex question presupposes the following: (1) you agree that your child's behavior needs correcting and (2) you are going to correct it. Therefore, if you answer "Yes" to the complex question, you have admitted the child's behavior needs correcting. However, if you answer "No" to the complex question, then you have, once again, admitted the behavior needs correcting. You simply are not going to do anything about it.

11. Biased Sample

In the fallacy of **biased sample**, an argument uses a nonrepresentative sample as support for a statistical claim about an entire population. A representative sample occurs when the characteristics of a sample are correctly identified and matched to the population under investigation. For example, consider this argument:

[1] Evidence shows that approximately 85% of all Americans believe that abortion is morally wrong. [2] Recently, a sample of Catholics revealed that 85% believe that abortion is morally wrong.

Biased sample An argument that uses a nonrepresentative sample as support for a statistical claim about an entire population.

Here is a diagram of the argument:

2   The sample surveyed only Catholics, but the conclusion generalizes
     to all Americans.

1

This illustrates how a sample may intentionally or unintentionally exclude segments of the entire population. This results in a nonrepresentative sample, and the argument commits the fallacy of biased sample.

Here is another example:

A survey of 100 seniors at our university showed that 90% do not oppose a parking fee increase that will go into effect next year. Therefore, we can report that nearly all the students do not oppose a parking fee increase.

The sample surveyed only seniors at the university, but the conclusion generalizes to all students. Since seniors are unlikely to be affected by an increase in parking fees next year, the sample intentionally or unintentionally excluded segments of the entire population. The resulting biased sample does not provide good evidence for the conclusion. (Chapter 13 returns to statistical arguments.)

12. Accident

(RIGID APPLICATION OF A GENERALIZATION)

Accident When a generalization is inappropriately applied to the case at hand.

The fallacy of **accident** arises when a generalization is inappropriately applied to the case at hand. In fact, many generalizations have exceptions—a special case that does not fall under the general rule. We often make allowances for circumstances that permit breaking a rule. Therefore, to rigidly apply an otherwise acceptable generalization, even in the face of known exceptions, is to commit the fallacy of accident. For example, suppose someone says the following:

1 I can't believe that the police didn't give the driver of that ambulance any citations. 2 The driver was speeding. 3 The driver went through a red light. 4 The ambulance swerved from lane to lane without using any turn signals.

Here is a diagram of the argument:

2 3 4   It is true that under nonemergency circumstances the
           driver's behavior would be subject to penalties. However,
           exceptions apply to ambulance drivers, firefighters, and to
1   the police when they are responding to emergencies.

Similarly, you probably would be excused if you had to rush a seriously injured person to the hospital. Therefore, the speaker in the foregoing example has rigidly applied an otherwise acceptable generalization in the face of known exceptions. The unwarranted assumption in this case is that there are no exceptions to the rule.

13. Hasty Generalization
(CONVERSE ACCIDENT)

Fallacies can occur from the mistaken application of generalizations. For example, it is not unusual for someone to have a few negative experiences with members of a group and then quickly stereotype that group by assigning derogatory characteristics to the entire group. However, it is improbable that such a small sample will be representative of an entire group of humans. Any argument that concludes with a generalization based on a few instances would be terribly weak, and it is an example of the fallacy of **hasty generalization**. For example, consider this argument:

> [1] I saw a fraternity guy act rudely to a fast-food employee in the food court at lunch today. [2] Probably most fraternity and sorority members are rude and arrogant.

Hasty generalization
A generalization created on the basis of a few instances.

Here is a diagram of the argument:

> 1   The premise reports the observation of a single instance. However,
>   the conclusion generalizes the observed behavior to most fraternity
>   and sorority members.
> 2

We are not justified in saying that all or most members of a class of people have a certain characteristic simply because the characteristic was observed in one or a few members of the class. The evidence is not adequate to make such a generalization, so the premise cannot provide a good reason to support the conclusion.

Here is another example:

> The first two students whose exams I graded each got an A. Thus, I expect all 50 students in the class to get A's on the exam.

The teacher is probably being overly optimistic. Although it is possible that all 50 students will get an A on the exam, the fallacy of hasty generalization is apparent in this case. The conclusion follows from the unwarranted assumption that the grades of 2 students are a representative sample and can therefore be generalized to all 50 students in the class.

14. Misleading Precision

A fallacy of **misleading precision** occurs when a claim appears to be statistically significant but is not. Often statistics are used misleadingly. The following is an example that we might find in an advertisement:

Misleading precision A claim that appears to be statistically significant but is not.

> [1] Our cookies contain 30% less fat, so [2] you should start eating them if you want to lose weight.

Here is a diagram of the argument:

> 1   It is fair to ask, "30% less fat than what?" The asserted percentage
>   is relative to some other item, and we need to know what that is in
>   order to know if this product is really significantly lower in fat than
> 2   competing products of the same type.

The argument does not stand up to scrutiny. It might also be the case that the cookies have 30% less fat than they did before, but they still might contain much more fat than is allowed for someone trying to lose weight.

Here is another example of the kind of claim we might find in an advertisement:

> In order to clear out our inventory, we have reduced our used car prices by 20%. These prices won't last forever, so you better hurry in and buy one of these cars before the sale ends.

In this example we need to ask, "Reduced by 20% from what?" The car dealership might have used an outdated markup price no longer in effect in order to get an artificial reduction. Another possibility is that the dealer might have recently tried raising the cost of used cars and, if sales were slow, simply returned the car prices to their previous level.

The fallacy of misleading precision can even occur in a seemingly straightforward scientific claim. For example, consider the following:

> The full moon affects people in strange ways. We have found that you have a 100% greater chance of being physically assaulted during a full moon than at any other time of the month.

In order to evaluate the argument, we need to know the average rate of physical assault over an extended period of time. For example, suppose we find that the average physical assault rate per month is 1 out of every 10,000 persons. According to the argument, the full moon rate would then be 2 out of every 10,000 persons. Although the statistics do show that you have a 100% greater chance of being physically assaulted during a full moon, nevertheless the greater chance is not statistically significant. Whenever statistics are used without a reference or comparison group, you should try to determine if this is an instance of misleading precision.

15. False Dichotomy

False dichotomy A fallacy that occurs when it is assumed that only two choices are possible, when in fact others exist.

The fallacy of **false dichotomy** (*dichotomy* means "to cut in two parts") occurs when it is assumed that only two choices are possible, when in fact others exist. Examples can often be found in television programs where two or more self-proclaimed intellectuals shout insults at each other for a half hour at a time. At some point, we might hear the following:

> Either you agree with me or you are an idiot.

The arguer assumes that we will flesh out the appropriate conclusion. Let's look at two possible argument reconstruction scenarios:

Either you agree with me or you are an idiot.	Either you agree with me or you are an idiot.
<u>You are not an idiot.</u>	<u>You do not agree with me.</u>
You agree with me.	You are an idiot.

The two reconstructions create deductive arguments. In fact, both arguments are valid. Let's look at the argument form for the first reconstruction. If we let A = *you agree with me*, and I = *you are an idiot*, then we get this result:

```
A or I
Not I
A
```

If we assume that the first premise is true, then there are only two options, A or I. Next, if we assume that the second premise is true, then option I is eliminated. Therefore, A follows necessarily.

However, the question of soundness yields interesting results. An evaluation of the truth content of the first premise reveals a major problem. The first premise offers only two alternatives, but surely there are more than these two possibilities. The first premise provides the necessary ingredient for an instance of the fallacy of false dichotomy because the asserted disjunction assumes that only two choices are possible, when, in fact, others exist. If we add even one more possibility, we can reconstruct a new argument:

```
Either you agree with me, or you are an idiot, or your position is correct.
You do not agree with me.
You are not an idiot.
Your position is correct.
```

In the original argument the speaker used a false dichotomy to try to trap us into agreeing with his position. Revealing the fallacy allows us to analyze and evaluate the argument in a comprehensive manner. Of course, the opponent might have tried to turn the tables on the speaker by responding rhetorically, "If I have to agree with you, then I really am an idiot."

16. False Dilemma

A special kind of false dichotomy is the fallacy of false dilemma (*dilemma* means "double proposition"). When we are confronted with a choice between two alternatives, both of which will lead to unwanted results, then we are facing a dilemma. For example, suppose you promise to help someone at a certain time and date, and later you realize that you had already made a promise to another person for that same time. If it is not possible to fulfill both promises, then your dilemma is choosing which person to hurt, that is, which promise you will break. Situations like these are sometimes referred to as "being between a rock and a hard place." In these instances someone is likely to advise you to "choose the lesser of two evils." (For a powerful example of a dilemma, you should read *Sophie's Choice*, by William Styron.)

However, the term "dilemma" is often misapplied, as in these examples:

A. I just won the lottery, but now I have a dilemma. Should I take the five million in one lump sum or spread it out over 20 years?

B. My parents are buying me a car for graduation, so now my dilemma is whether to choose a BMW or a Porsche.

Since neither of these cases contains a choice that would lead to an unwanted result, these are clearly not dilemmas.

The fallacy of **false dilemma** occurs when two choices are asserted, each leading to an unwanted result, but there is a failure to acknowledge that other possibilities exist. For example, a person defending the Patriot Act and its potential infringement on certain basic freedoms might say the following:

> Either we give up some traditional basic freedoms or we lose the war on terror.

The argument is missing a premise and the conclusion. Since the person is defending the Patriot Act, the missing premise is "No one wants to lose the war on terror," and the missing conclusion is "We must give up some traditional basic freedoms."

Let's reveal the argument form. If we let G = *we give up some traditional basic freedoms*, and L = *we lose the war on terror*, then we get this result:

G or L   Premise 1 fails to acknowledge that other possibilities
Not L   exist; thus it sets up a false dilemma.
G

If we are captured by the passionate nature of the assertion and its implications, then we seem to be facing a dilemma. According to the assertion there are only two choices. If we don't want to lose the war on terror, then we must conclude that we are willing to give up some traditional basic freedoms. On the other hand, if we are not willing to give up some traditional basic freedoms, then we must conclude that we will lose the war on terror. However, once we see that this is really an instance of the fallacy of false dilemma, we can reject the entire notion of having only two choices in the matter. We can argue that it is possible to win the war on terror without giving up traditional basic freedoms.

FALSE CAUSE FALLACIES

Fallacies of false cause are a special subset of fallacies of unwarranted assumption. These fallacies include *coincidence*, post hoc *fallacy*, *common cause fallacy*, and *slippery slope*. As we will see in Chapter 14, cause-effect patterns help us to understand the world and to predict future events. However, fallacies of **false cause** occur when a causal connection is assumed to exist between two events when none actually exists. Since causal claims require strong evidence, a cause-effect claim based on insufficient evidence commits the fallacy of false cause.

Consider the following argument:

> I told you not to trust him. After all, he was born under the sign of Aquarius in the year of the Rabbit. He can't help himself: the stars dictate his behavior.

Astrology places human behavior under the influence of the planets and stars. It claims that we are causally connected to astral influences that occurred at the time of our birth and continue throughout our lives. Of course, these causal claims do not have any credible scientific evidence in their support; they are based mostly on anecdotal evidence. In addition, the general personality traits associated with astrology can be applied to anyone.

False dilemma A fallacy that occurs when two choices are asserted, each leading to an unwanted result, but there is a failure to acknowledge that other possibilities exist.

False cause A fallacy that occurs when a causal connection is assumed to exist between two events when none actually exists.

17. Coincidence

A fallacy of **coincidence** results from the accidental or chance connection between two events. For example, suppose someone says the following:

> [1] I can prove that some dreams let us see into the future. [2] Last week, I dreamed that my cousin Charlie was in a terrible car wreck. [3] Just now, I got a phone call from my cousin Charlie's wife saying that he is in the hospital because he was in a car accident.

Here is a diagram of the argument:

2   3   The coincidence can be explained by recognizing that we
⎵⎵⎵   have thousands of dreams a year, a few of which are likely to
↓   resemble real events. Also, the vast majority of dreams do not
1   connect to real events, but we tend to forget that important
fact.

If someone dreams that a relative or friend is injured or dies and a similar event actually happens, then the dream might be interpreted as being *caused* by the future event. However, a belief in "backward causality" (a future event causing the present dream) violates a fundamental principle of science: causes must precede effects.

It is normal and helpful for us to look for connections between events; that's how we learn about the world. Scientific results are achieved by correctly identifying cause-effect connections. This is how we are able to discover the cause of diseases, how and why things deteriorate over time, how to develop helpful drugs, how certain genes are connected to risk factors, and many other types of knowledge. However, not every connection that we happen to notice reveals a true cause-effect relationship. When unwanted things happen to us, it is reasonable to seek out the cause, but we must recognize that many things we connect in our day-to-day life are just coincidences.

Superstitions develop over time when instances of individual coincidences get passed from one person to another. After a few instances are noticed, it often becomes accepted that a cause-effect relationship exists. However, this is a self-sustaining result: only positive connections are recognized; negative instances are overlooked. A scientific approach would record the number of positive and negative instances to see if there is truly a causal connection. Instead of this, anecdotal evidence that recognizes only positive instances gets passed on, thus reinforcing the superstition. The type of fallacious reasoning that develops over time from a few coincidences is related to the *post hoc* fallacy, our next topic.

18. *Post Hoc* Fallacy

Another type of false cause fallacy, the ***post hoc*** fallacy, concerns a pattern that is noticed "after the fact." (The full name of this type of fallacy is called *post hoc, ergo propter hoc*, which means "after the fact, therefore because of the fact.") It is not unusual for someone to find either a short-term or long-term pattern and to make a causal connection between two things. The fallacy lies in mistaking the statistical pattern, or *correlation*, for cause and effect.

Coincidence A fallacy that results from the accidental or chance connection between two events.

Post hoc fallacy A fallacy involving either a short-term or long-term pattern that is noticed after the fact.

For example, we might read the following:

> [1] Researchers have discovered that, for over 30 years, there has been a definite pattern connecting the party affiliation of the U.S. president and specific soft drink sales. [2] During the years when a Democrat was president, Morphiacola topped all soft drink sales. [3] When a Republican was president, Opiacola was number one in sales. [4] If you are an investor, we advise you to put your money on the soft drink company based on who is in the White House.

Here is a diagram of the argument:

1   2   3   The premises fail to provide the necessary support for a
              true causal claim. Arguments that use *post hoc* reasoning
              fall prey to the mistake of confusing a correlation with a
4   cause.

Fallacies of this type can be persuasive, because unlike a mere coincidence, a regular pattern seems to have emerged. Although every cause-effect relationship reveals a strong correlation, not all strong correlations reveal cause-effect relationships. For example, there is a strong correlation between wearing bathing suits and getting wet, but wearing a bathing suit does not cause us to get wet. (For more details on the difference between a *correlation* and a *cause*, see Chapter 14.)

The pattern in the cola argument was between the party in the White House and the type of cola having the most sales. Patterns like these are also referred to as *trends* and are often the basis for gambling purposes. For example, in baseball, the National League may win four straight All-Star games. In football, the American Conference might win three consecutive Super Bowls. In roulette, a red number may come up six times in a row. However, trends are temporary, and unless some definite cause-effect relationship is independently discovered that would *explain* the trend, we should not expect the trend to continue indefinitely.

19. Common Cause Fallacy

Common cause fallacy
A mistake that occurs when someone thinks that one event causes another, when in fact both events are the result of a common cause.

The **common cause fallacy** occurs when one event is believed to cause a second event, when in fact both events are the result of a common cause. For example, someone might claim that the falling barometer is the cause of a storm, when in fact both events are caused by a change in atmospheric pressure. The following illustration reveals the common cause fallacy:

Atmospheric Pressure

Falling Barometer ◄——×——► Storm

The two downward arrows indicate that the atmospheric pressure is the common cause of both the falling barometer and the storm. The arrow with the large X through it shows the fallacious cause-effect claim.

Another example of the fallacy occurs when someone mistakenly thinks that a rash is causing a fever. It is quite possible that both the rash and the fever have a common cause: a virus.

20. Slippery Slope

Some complex arguments attempt to link events in such a way as to create a chain reaction. The idea is to create a series of occurrences whereby the first link in a chain leads directly to the next, and so on, until the final result is achieved. A **slippery slope** fallacy attempts to make a final event the inevitable outcome of an initial act. We are then urged to stop the chain reaction before it has a chance to begin, by preventing the first act from ever happening. For example, consider the following argument:

> [1] If you start smoking marijuana for pleasure, then you will need more and more to achieve the expected high. [2] You will begin to rely on it whenever you feel depressed. [3] Eventually you will experiment with more powerful drugs that act faster and last longer. Of course, [4] the amount of drug intake will have to increase to achieve the desired results. [5] At this point, the addiction will take hold and will lead to a loss of ambition, a loss of self-esteem, the destruction of your health, and the dissolution of all social ties. Therefore, [6] you should not start smoking marijuana.

Slippery slope An argument that attempts to make a final event the inevitable outcome of an initial act.

Here is a diagram of the argument:

```
1
↓
2       Slippery slope arguments rely on a kind of causal network where each
↓       step in the chain causes the next step. However, the alleged inevi-
3       tability of the final act needs to be supported by providing specific
↓       objective evidence for the supposed causal network.
4
↓
5
↓
6
```

Each link in the chain of arguments requires relevant evidence for its connection to the next link in the chain. Until this is objectively established, the argument need not be accepted.

Summary of Fallacies of Unwarranted Assumption

9. Begging the question
An argument that assumes as evidence in the premises the very thing that it attempts to prove in the conclusion.

10. Complex question
A single question that actually contains multiple, hidden parts.

11. Biased sample
An argument that uses a nonrepresentative sample as support for a statistical claim about an entire population.

12. Accident
When a generalization is inappropriately applied to the case at hand.

13. Hasty generalization
A generalization created on the basis of a few instances.

14. Misleading precision
A claim that appears to be statistically significant, but is not.

15. False dichotomy
A fallacy that occurs when it is assumed that only two choices are possible, when in fact others exist.

16. False dilemma
A fallacy that occurs when two choices are asserted, each leading to an unwanted result, but there is a failure to acknowledge that other possibilities exist.

17. Coincidence
A special kind of false cause that results from the accidental or chance connection between two events.

18. *Post hoc* fallacy
A type of false cause fallacy involving either a short-term or long-term pattern that is noticed after the fact. This type of false cause fallacy is also called *post hoc, ergo propter hoc* ("after the fact, therefore because of the fact").

19. Common cause fallacy
The assumption that one event causes another, when in fact both events are the result of a common cause.

20. Slippery slope
An argument that attempts to make a final event the inevitable outcome of an initial act.

CHECK YOUR UNDERSTANDING 4B

I. Determine whether each statement is true or false.

1. A complex question is a single question that actually contains multiple, hidden parts.

Answer: True.

2. A hasty generalization occurs whenever a generalization leaves out members of a subset of the population that is referred to in the conclusion.

3. When a claim is made that appears to be statistically significant but which, upon analysis, is not, is an example of the fallacy of misleading precision.

4. A coincidence is a special type of false cause fallacy concerning a short-term pattern that is noticed after the fact.

⭐ 5. A biased sample leaves out members of a subset of the population that is referred to in the conclusion.

6. An argument that attempts to make a final event the inevitable outcome of an initial act is called *post hoc*.

7. To rigidly apply an otherwise acceptable generalization, even in the face of known and understood exceptions, is to commit the fallacy of common cause.

8. An argument that offers only two alternatives when in fact more exist is an example of a biased sample.

⭐ 9. An argument that assumes as evidence the very thing that it attempts to prove in the conclusion begs the question.

10. A slippery slope fallacy concerns a short-term pattern that is noticed after the fact.

11. An argument that offers two choices each of which leads to an undesirable outcome is an example of false dilemma.

12. A claim that appears to be statistically significant, but which upon analysis is not, is the fallacy of accident.

II. Each of the following passages contains a fallacy of unwarranted assumption. Determine the fallacy that best fits each case. Explain your answer.

1. Do you still plagiarize your research papers from the Internet?
Answer: Complex question: A single question that actually contains multiple, hidden parts.

2. This car gets the highest gas mileage of any car on the market. So, you can't buy a more fuel efficient car at any cost.

3. That ambulance didn't even stop for the red light. It went zooming right through! If I did that, I would get a citation. Life just isn't fair.

4. All the people in my fraternity think that hazing is not a problem. So, I'm sure that the entire student population agrees with us on this issue.

⭐ 5. Last week's poll showed the incumbent senator had 52% of the votes and the challenger had 48%. This week's poll shows the incumbent ahead 54% to 46%. So, we can safely say that the incumbent will get at least 53% of the votes on Election Day.

6. I met two people from that state, and they both were rude. There must be something in the drinking water of that state that makes all the people from there so rude.

7. Have you stopped stealing money from your parents' wallets?

8. The label on that cheesecake says that it has 40% fewer calories. If I eat that cheesecake regularly, then I should lose some weight.

⭐ 9. I don't recommend that you eat at that restaurant. I did not like the breakfast I had there last week. I'm sure that all of their meals are of poor quality.

10. That is the type of movie you hate; lots of jokes and slapstick. So, you will hate it.

11. Ninety-five percent of a sample of registered Republicans in this state said that they will vote for the Republican nominee for Congress from their district. I predict that the Republican nominee will definitely get around 95% of the total vote this fall.

12. Everything written in that book is 100% accurate. It has to be, since nothing in it is false.

★ 13. When I need to travel to another city I have to buy my own airplane ticket. The president of the United States has Air Force One to take him wherever he wants to go, and he doesn't have to pay a penny. Why can't I have a deal like that?

14. The advertisement for that DVD player claims that it has 50% fewer moving parts. You should buy it; it is less likely to break down in the future.

15. He is a very honest individual because he is not dishonest.

16. My horoscope said I would meet someone new. Today my company hired a really good-looking salesperson, and we will be working closely together. Now do you see why I read my horoscope every day?

★ 17. If you don't clean your room, then the dirt and dust will build up. Before you know it, bacteria grow. Whatever you touch in your room will then spread bacteria, which will contaminate the entire house. We will all wind up in the hospital, terminally ill.

18. On seven different occasions it rained the day after I washed my car. I washed my car today, so take your umbrella with you tomorrow.

19. I had two station wagons, and they both were lemons. I'm sure that there is something in the design of station wagons that makes them all terrible vehicles.

20. Every football player at Crestfallen High School can run 2 miles in under 15 minutes. They have good physical education teachers, so the students at that school must be in great physical condition.

★ 21. She began making $100,000 the year after she graduated from college, and when she took an IQ test, she scored 20 points higher than when she was in high school. See, I told you: money makes people smarter.

22. My bill at the restaurant was $4.29. I played the number 429 on the lottery today, and it came up. Therefore, it was my destiny to play that number today and win.

23. That politician never tells the truth because every time he tries to explain why he did something wrong, he fabricates a story.

24. Do you still look for discarded food in dumpsters?

★ 25. Every time the barometer drops below 30, it rains. It has some mysterious power over the weather, I guess.

26. Either we cut school funding or we raise taxes. Nobody wants to cut school funding, so we must raise taxes.

27. For the last 50 years, whenever the American League won the World Series, there was a recession that year, but when the National League won, stock prices went up. There must be some unknown economic force at work that we don't understand.

28. That fire engine was going over 60 mph in a 35-mph zone. The police should give the driver a ticket.

★ 29. I have certain inalienable rights because they have never been taken away from me.

30. If you drop out of one course this semester, you will have less than a full-time load. It will take you longer to graduate. It will delay your getting a job another year, meaning that you won't get promoted as fast as others who graduated on time. So, you can expect to lose approximately $100,000 during your lifetime.

31. Whenever I step in the shower, either my phone rings or someone knocks on the door. I'll have to change my bathing habits, I suppose.

32. Either you love your country or you are a traitor. I'm sure you are not a traitor. Therefore, you must love your country.

C. FALLACIES OF AMBIGUITY OR DIVERSION

A **fallacy of ambiguity or diversion** occurs when the meanings of terms or phrases are changed (intentionally or unintentionally) within the argument, or when our attention is purposely (or accidentally) diverted from the issue at hand. Fallacies of ambiguity depend on the fact that words or phrases can have many different meanings, and context is crucial. Ambiguity, vagueness, or any unclear use of a term can seriously affect the understanding, analysis, and evaluation of an argument. We can distinguish seven kinds of fallacies of ambiguity and diversion. (We will continue to number the fallacies starting from the previous section.)

> **Fallacy of ambiguity or diversion** A fallacy that occurs when the meanings of terms or phrases are changed (intentionally or unintentionally) within the argument, or when our attention is purposely (or accidentally) diverted from the issue at hand.

21. Equivocation

To shift the meaning of a term during the course of an argument is to commit the fallacy of **equivocation**. For example, someone might say the following:

> My older brother tries hard to be cool. I told him he has the personality of a cucumber. Since a refrigerator is a good place to keep things cool, he should spend some time there.

> **Equivocation** The intentional or unintentional use of different meanings of words or phrases in an argument.

The word "cool" obviously has numerous meanings that tend to sort themselves out in the context of particular sentences.

Equivocation can also occur when *relative terms* are misused, such as "big" and "small." For example:

> I was told that he is a big man on campus (BMOC). But look at him; he's no more than 5'7" tall.

The equivocation is compounded by the fact that the term "big" in BMOC does not refer to height. Here are two other examples of the fallacy:

- Judy said she had a hot date last night. Therefore, the air conditioning in her apartment must not have been working.
- That looks like a hard outfit to get into. So maybe you should wash it in some fabric softener.

The world of politics offers numerous examples of equivocation. A major issue discussed quite often during presidential campaigns is employment. For example, a recent administration had to respond to a huge loss of manufacturing jobs during its time in office. To counteract the statistics showing a loss of jobs, the administration proposed that some fast-food workers should be reclassified from service workers to manufacturing workers. Under the new definition, anyone who cooked a burger, placed it on a bun, added condiments, and put it in a wrapper was engaged in manufacturing a product. There would thus have been a gain in manufacturing jobs over the previous four years. Of course, once the opposing political party found out about the idea, it was quickly dropped.

An earlier administration hatched a similar idea. The federal government normally defines the "unemployed" as only those people who are actively collecting government unemployment checks. Under this definition, people who have either exhausted their checks or are on welfare are not unemployed. The unemployment rate is then calculated by finding the number of unemployed and comparing this with the total number of those employed. In addition, the entire military did not count toward the unemployment rate. In other words, the military was considered neither employed nor unemployed. Again, just before a presidential election, a scheme was considered. It was proposed that all active military personnel should be considered employed. This would have seriously reduced the unemployment rate, favoring the incumbent administration. Once again, the idea was exposed and abandoned.

22. Amphiboly

Amphiboly Ambiguity that arises when a poorly constructed statement muddles the intended meaning.

Amphiboly ("irregular speech") is ambiguity that arises when a poorly constructed statement muddles the intended meaning. Premises and a conclusion appear to be true, because two different interpretations are being used. If we retain one meaning throughout the argument, we can usually spot the mistake:

- He was shot in the train in the back in the sleeping car.
- She watched the monkey eating a banana.
- Sipping on cold coffee, the corpse lay in front of the tired detective.
- Cursing his bad luck, the DVD player refused to work for Eddie.

In the first example, we can conclude either that (1) the bullet is lodged in the victim's back or (2) the shooting occurred in the sleeping car, which is in the back of the train. In the second example, we can conclude either that (1) the monkey was eating a banana or (2) the person watching the monkey was eating a banana. In the third example, either (1) the detective was sipping on cold coffee or (2) the corpse was sipping on coffee at the time of death. In the final example, either (1) Eddie was cursing his bad luck or (2) the DVD player was cursing its bad luck and refused to play.

Amphiboly relies on the confusion caused by grammatical errors. For example:

> *John*: In my backyard a bird did not see my cat hunched on all fours ready to pounce but suddenly he flew away.
> *Barb*: I didn't know cats could fly.

23. Composition

In the fallacy of **composition**, an attribute of the individual parts of an object is mistakenly transferred to the entire object. For example, suppose someone said the following of a 7-foot-tall basketball player:

> All the cells in his body are tiny. Thus, he is tiny.

Composition The mistaken transfer of an attribute of the individual parts of an object to the object as a whole.

The mistake is taking an attribute that is true of the parts and erroneously applying it to the whole. The fallacy can also occur when the conclusion is not necessarily untrue, but merely in doubt:

> The bricks in this building are sturdy, so the building must be sturdy.

Even if the individual bricks are sturdy (the premise), the building may not be sturdy (the conclusion). Here are three other examples of the fallacy of composition:

- The thread you are using is easily torn, so the garment you are making will be easily torn.
- Each ingredient you are using tastes delicious. Therefore, the cake has to taste delicious.
- I understand every word in the poem, so I must understand what the poet is getting at.

We must be careful not to misapply this fallacy. Not every argument that reasons from parts to a whole is fallacious. For example:

> Every thread of material of which this shirt is composed is red, so the shirt is red.

This argument does not commit the fallacy of composition; in fact, it is a strong argument. Here is another legitimate use of composition:

> Since every piece of my sewing machine is made from steel, it follows that my sewing machine is steel.

Compare the fallacious examples with the legitimate ones. You can see that fallacies here are not mistakes in the structure of an argument. Rather, the context of an argument, together with our knowledge of the world, is often needed to distinguish fallacious from nonfallacious informal arguments.

All of the examples of the composition fallacy so far have concerned a possible mistaken identity—of parts of an object with the whole object (a body, a building, a garment, a cake, and a poem). However, another kind of composition fallacy occurs when the attributes of individual members of a class are mistakenly applied to the collection of objects itself. This mistake occurs when we confuse the *distributive* and *collective* use of terms. "Distributive" refers to the individual members of a group. In the statement "Motorcycles are noisy," the term "noisy" is being used distributively to refer to individual motorcycles. "Collective" refers to the group as a whole. In the statement "Motorcycles make up only 5% of all vehicles on U.S. roadways," the phrase "make up only 5% of all vehicles on U.S. roadways" is being used collectively to refer to the class of all motorcycles, not to individual motorcycles. This type of composition fallacy is revealed in the following argument:

> More noise is produced by a motorcycle than by a car. Therefore, more noise is produced on U.S. roadways by motorcycles than by cars.

24. Division

Division The mistaken transfer of an attribute of an object as a whole to its individual parts.

In the fallacy of **division**, an attribute of an object as a whole is mistakenly transferred to its individual parts. The fallacy of division is the opposite of the fallacy of composition. For example, suppose someone said the following of a 7-foot-tall basketball player:

> He is huge, so he must have huge cells.

The mistake is taking an attribute that is true of the whole object and erroneously applying it to the parts that make up the object. Here are three other examples of the fallacy:

- She is intelligent, so she must have smart brain cells.
- The garment is strong, so the individual threads must be strong.
- The cake tastes burnt, so you must have used burnt ingredients.

As with the fallacy of composition, we must be careful not to misapply the fallacy of division. Not every argument that reasons from the whole object to its parts is fallacious. For example:

> That is a wooden chair, so the legs are made of wood.

This argument does not commit the fallacy of division; in fact, it is a strong argument. Here is another example of a legitimate use of division:

> The book he is reading is made of paper. Therefore, the pages of the book are made of paper.

All the examples of the fallacy so far have concerned a possible mistaken identity of an object (a body, a person's intelligence, a garment, and a cake) with its parts. However, a second kind of division fallacy is similar to the second kind of composition fallacy. This occurs when attributes of a collection of objects are mistakenly applied to the individual members of that class. As before, the mistake occurs when the distributive and collective uses of terms are confused. In the statement "Bald eagles are disappearing," the term "disappearing" is being used collectively to refer to the class of bald eagles; individual members may still live full lives. The second type of division fallacy can be recognized in the following argument:

> My teacher said that bald eagles are disappearing. I remember seeing a bald eagle down at the zoo. Let's hurry down to see it before it disappears.

25. Emphasis

Fallacies of **emphasis** (also called *accent*) can occur when attention is purposely (or accidentally) diverted from the issue at hand. In other words, statements or arguments intending one thing are subtly distorted in order to shift the emphasis to another issue. The use of emphasis occurs in everyday conversation as well, as in this discussion:

> *Jenn*: He did win an Academy Award for best actor.
> *Jess*: You might think he did, but you're wrong.
> *Jenn*: I don't think; I know.
> *Jess*: I don't think you know either.

Jess twists the meaning of a key phrase by changing the emphasis of Jenn's claim. This emphasis seems to refute Jenn's claim of knowledge. The same kind of mistake occurs in the next passage:

> *Mary Lynn*: Lee Ann, you will wash the car this afternoon.
> *Lee Ann*: I will?
> *Mary Lynn*: I'm glad you agree.

Lee Ann's question is turned into an assertion by Mary Lynn's change of emphasis. Although these particular verbal changes are fairly easy to spot, they nevertheless reveal the possibility of altering meaning by shifting emphasis at a key point.

Emphasis A fallacy that occurs when attention is purposely (or accidentally) diverted from the issue at hand.

26. Straw Man Fallacy

There are two major kinds of fallacies of emphasis. The first, called the **straw man** fallacy, often occurs when someone's written or spoken words are taken out of context. This effectively creates a new argument, which can be easily refuted. The new argument is so weak that it is "made of straw." This tactic is common in the political arena. Candidates distort the views of their opponents by clipping a small piece out of a speech or interview. Taken out of context, a word or phrase might give an impression directly opposite from that of the original. For example, a person running for public office might say the following:

> I oppose the law that requires teaching intelligent design as an alternative to evolutionary theory in public school biology classes. Evolution is an established scientific theory and deserves to be taught in a science class. Intelligent design is not a scientific theory, and it should not be taught in a science class.

Straw man A fallacy that occurs when someone's written or spoken words are taken out of context. It purposely distorts the original argument to create a new, weak argument that can be easily refuted (a straw man that is easily knocked down).

An opponent of this candidate might criticize her position this way:

> She is against the new law that mandates teaching intelligent design along-
> side the theory of evolution. It should be obvious to anyone that she really
> wants to eliminate religious beliefs. She wants us to destroy one of the basic
> principles of the Constitution of the United States.

A straw man argument has been created by several steps. The opponent takes the original statement and adds an unjustified premise, "It should be obvious to anyone that what she really wants to do is to eliminate all religious beliefs." The fallacy concludes that "She wants us to destroy one of the basic principles of the Constitution of the United States."

Distortions of this kind are not limited to politics. It is not difficult to extract passages from an article to make it appear that the author is contradicting herself.

27. Red Herring Fallacy

Red herring A fallacy that occurs when someone completely ignores an opponent's position and changes the subject, diverting the discussion in a new direction.

The second type of fallacy of emphasis, the **red herring** fallacy, occurs when some-one completely ignores an opponent's position. By changing the subject, the red herring "throws one off the scent," diverting the discussion in a new direction. For example:

> Many people criticize TV as turning America into an illiterate society. How can
> we criticize the very medium that is the envy of countries all over the world?
> The entertainment quality and variety of TV programs today are greater than
> ever before, not to mention the enormous number of cable options available
> to members of the viewing audience.

Rather than presenting evidence, the passage shifts the emphasis to the entertain-ment value of TV. This diversion ignores the question of whether TV is causing Amer-ica to become an illiterate society. The red herring argument has ignored the crucial issue at hand.

In 2003, a photograph purported to show that Jose Santos, the jockey of Kentucky Derby winner Funny Cide, was carrying an illegal object. The picture showed a dark spot in Santos's hand. Some concluded that a "battery" was used to provide an electri-cal shock through the whip, causing the horse to run faster. But those who emphasized the dark spot deemphasized or overlooked the film of the race. It clearly shows Santos switching hands with his whip more than once. As one commentator remarked, hold-ing a battery while performing these tricky maneuvers would make Santos one of the world's best magicians. A thorough analysis of the available information exonerated the jockey.

Summary of Fallacies of Ambiguity or Diversion

21. Equivocation
The intentional or unintentional use of different meanings of words or phrases in an argument.

22. Amphiboly

Ambiguity that arises when a poorly constructed statement muddles the intended meaning.

23. Composition

The mistaken transfer of an attribute of the individual parts of an object to the object as a whole.

24. Division

The mistaken transfer of an attribute of an object as a whole to its individual parts.

25. Emphasis

A fallacy that occurs when attention is purposely (or accidentally) diverted from the issue at hand.

26. Straw man fallacy

A fallacy that occurs when someone's written or spoken words are taken out of context. It purposely distorts the original argument to create a new, weak argument that can be easily refuted (a straw man that is easily knocked down).

27. Red herring fallacy

A fallacy that occurs when someone completely ignores an opponent's position and changes the subject, diverting the discussion in a new direction.

CHECK YOUR UNDERSTANDING 4C

I. Determine whether each statement is true or false.

1. The fallacy of composition occurs when an attribute of the individual parts of an object are transferred to the entire object.

Answer: True.

2. The red herring fallacy occurs when someone's words are taken out of context to create an argument that distorts the person's position.

3. A mistake of interpretation that occurs because of the grammar or syntax of a statement is called the fallacy of emphasis.

4. A fallacy of equivocation can happen only if the argument intentionally uses different meanings of words or phrases.

⭐ 5. A straw man fallacy is a mistake in grammar.

6. To mistakenly transfer an attribute of the individual parts of an object to the entire object is to commit the fallacy of division.

7. A fallacy of emphasis occurs when a word has a different meaning in the premises than it has in the conclusion.

8. A fallacy of equivocation mistakenly transfers an attribute of the individual parts of an object to the entire object.

II. Each of the following passages contains a fallacy of ambiguity or diversion. Determine the fallacy that best fits each case. Explain your answer.

1. Each grain of sand is hard, so your sand castle will be hard.

Answer: Composition: The mistake is in the transfer of an attribute of the individual parts of the object to the object as a whole.

2. *Sam:* I think you broke my watch.
   Joe: I did?
   Sam: Well since you admit it, now I know you did it.

3. He's a real pain the neck. Cortisone shots help relieve neck pain. Maybe a good dose of cortisone will change his attitude.

4. She is very beautiful. I bet even her appendix is lovely.

⭐ 5. Just waiting to be eaten, he noticed the cake in the corner.

6. My father said that the Super Bowl halftime show was a real disaster. That's interesting because I read in the newspaper that the federal government has relief funds available for victims of disasters. Maybe my dad can apply for some relief funds.

7. If you are going to have that fruit juice tomorrow morning, then you better start shaking the bottle right now. I read the label, and it recommends that you shake the contents well before using.

8. I read that cars in the United States consume more gasoline each year than trucks. I guess that means that my car uses more gasoline each year than that tractor trailer over there.

⭐ 9. I know for a fact that the acrylic paints that Vincent van Gogh used to create this portrait were very inexpensive. So even though his painting is hanging in a museum, it can't be very expensive.

10. I heard that he got injured in that building in the rear.

11. My mother, a professional poker player, always told me that having one pair is better than nothing. Of course, in the game of poker nothing beats a royal flush. It follows that my one pair beats your royal flush.

12. He said that walking around the corner the Eiffel Tower suddenly took his breath away. I didn't know those famous Parisian landmarks roamed the streets.

⭐ 13. According to the census data, the population of that city is 10% atheists. My Uncle Sam lives there, so he must be 10% atheist.

14. In physics class we learned that elementary particles have little or no mass. My $150 physics textbook is made up of elementary particles, thus it has little or no mass.

15. I hear that Walter is handling some hot stocks right now. The new asbestos gloves I bought protect your hands from hot objects. Maybe I should give them to Walter for protection.

16. Sitting in the front seat of the car, the cow stared intently into Jim's eyes. Of course, from this we can conclude that it was a very large car indeed.

17. My mother wants me to take piano lessons because studies show that early music training helps students in math. But pianos cost a lot of money, and even if we could afford one, our apartment is too small.

18. Evolution is a biological law of nature. All civilized people should obey the law. Therefore, all civilized people should obey the law of evolution.

19. Chicken eggs do not weigh very much. So if I eat an omelet made from fifty eggs, it will not weigh very much.

20. My boss caught me playing video games on my office computer during work hours. He said that it was a violation of office policies, and he warned me to stop or I would be fired. Pretty soon he will try to eliminate coffee breaks or even going to the bathroom. He doesn't have the right to take away all my benefits.

21. The sign says that there is no mass on Sunday. But my science teacher said that mass is the same as energy. So I guess there is no energy on Sunday either.

22. Sitting in front of the open window, the freshly mowed grass satisfied Robert.

23. Each page of the encyclopedia weighs practically nothing, so the encyclopedia weighs practically nothing.

24. You have chosen great paint colors; therefore, your house will look great.

25. *Walter:* You will help me with my homework.
    Sandy: I will?
    Walter: I knew you would cooperate.

26. That comedian is a real ham. Of course, ham and eggs are good for breakfast. So, if that comedian added some eggs to his act, it would make a good breakfast.

27. The house is poorly constructed, so the material it is made of must be poorly constructed as well.

28. The stone hit the window. The force broke it into a thousand pieces.

D. RECOGNIZING FALLACIES IN ORDINARY LANGUAGE

The examples of informal fallacies analyzed so far have been constructed to reveal clearly the mistake in reasoning. They were meant to be fairly easy to recognize—once you understand the underlying techniques. However, when you read something or hear someone talk, then detecting any informal fallacies may be a bit more challenging. A writer who has a fluid prose style can sometimes produce a persuasive passage merely by dazzling you with her brilliant writing style. A great speaker can mesmerize his audience with the mere sound of his voice, so much so that we overlook the substance of what it being said.

For example, the great actor Laurence Olivier gave an emotional acceptance speech at the Academy Awards:

> Mr. President and Governors of the Academy, Committee Members, fellows, my very noble and approved good masters, my colleagues, my friends, my fellow-students. In the great wealth, the great firmament of your nation's generosity, this particular choice may perhaps be found by future generations as a trifle eccentric, but the mere fact of it—the prodigal, pure, human kindness of it—must be seen as a beautiful star in that firmament which shines upon me at this moment, dazzling me a little, but filling me with warmth and the extraordinary elation, the euphoria that happens to so many of us at the first breath of the majestic glow of a new tomorrow. From the top of this moment, in the solace, in the kindly emotion that is charging my soul and my heart at this moment, I thank you for this great gift which lends me such a very splendid part in this, your glorious occasion.

This short speech left most of the audience in awe, in part because Olivier was considered perhaps the greatest Shakespearian actor and in part because of his dramatic delivery. Few people went back to read the words, which, although poetic and emotional, do not contain much of substance. The moral of the story is that we have to be careful when we encounter either impressive-sounding speech or beautifully crafted written material. This is especially true if the passages contain arguments.

Some fallacies occur because the emotional attachment to a belief overrides the demands of a clear, rational, well-supported argument. Here is one example:

PROFILES IN LOGIC

Arthur Schopenhauer

Arthur Schopenhauer (1788–1860) is not generally regarded as a logician or a mathematician, but rather as a philosopher who devoted his life to, as he tells us, "debunking charlatans, windbags, and claptrap." Schopenhauer firmly believed that fallacies should be exposed whenever they appear. In *The Art of Controversy*, he remarks that "it would be a very good thing if every trick could receive some short and obviously appropriate name, so that when a man used this or that particular trick, he could be at once reproached for it." Indeed, hundreds of fallacies have been recognized, described, and named.

Schopenhauer is often called the philosopher of pessimism because he thought that human experience is filled with all manner of brutality, pain, and suffering. Humans are compelled to hate, love, and desire, with only temporary escapes—philosophic contemplation, art (especially music), and sympathy for the plight of others.

In addition, Schopenhauer was one of the first Western philosophers to recognize and incorporate ideas from Eastern religions, such as Buddhism. In his system of thought, we are asked to "see ourselves in all existence."

> Our acceptance of abortion does not end with the killing of unborn human life; it continues on to affect our attitude toward all aspects of human life. This is most obvious in how quickly, once we accept abortion, then comes the acceptance of infanticide, the killing of babies who after birth do not come up to someone's standard of life worthy to be lived, and then on to euthanasia of the aged. If human life can be taken before birth, there is no logical reason why human life cannot be taken after birth.   Francis Schaeffer, *Who Is for Life?*

The author's position about abortion is clear. However, the attempt to discredit any acceptance of abortion leads the author to commit the slippery slope fallacy. No evidence is offered in the passage to support the (assumed) link in the chain of reasoning that "once we accept abortion, then comes the acceptance of infanticide." Similarly, the author provides no support for the next (assumed) link in the chain, namely the claim that "and then on to euthanasia of the aged." This example points out the importance of separating a belief from the possible reasons in support of a belief. It also illustrates the need to guard against the quick acceptance (or rejection) of a position based solely on our emotional attachment to a position.

Fallacies are not just the result of an emotional attachment to a moral question or to a controversial political viewpoint. In fact, they can occur in a scientific study:

> Winning the Nobel Prize adds nearly two years to your lifespan, and it's not because of the cash that goes with it. The status alone conferred on a scientist by the world's most famous prize is enough to prolong his life; in fact, the status seems to work a *health-giving magic*. The study compared Nobel Prize winners with scientists who were nominated, but did not win. The average lifespan for the winners was just over 76 years, while those who had merely been nominated lived on average for 75.8 years. The researchers found that since the amount of actual prize money won had no affect on longevity, therefore the sheer status of the award is the important factor in extending lifespan.
> Donald MacLeod, "Nobel Prize Winners Live Longer," *Education Guardian*

Quite often, a single piece of research gets widespread coverage because it seems to indicate some new and exciting discovery. However, advances in science occur through repeated and exhaustive trials in which many groups of researchers try to eliminate every possible explanation for an effect, leaving only one answer. Therefore, preliminary results, or studies with limited data need to be carefully weighed. In this example, a correlation has been found, but the difference in longevity between the two groups is small. The argument to support the claim that "status causes the Nobel Prize winners to live longer" could be an instance of the *post hoc* fallacy—or simple coincidence.

Although emotional appeals are a powerful way to sway public opinion, unfortunately some of those appeals are fallacious. Most of us try to balance our feelings with our reason, but it is not always easy. Strong emotions can sometimes override rational thinking and lead to disastrous results. This can be seen in the increase in political anger in the United States and the way it is broadcast over the airwaves. Incivility is on view almost daily, and rudeness, discourteous behavior, and disrespect can escalate into violence.

Many people have begun pleading for a less heated and less passionate climate in the public arena. The call is for a reduction in unhelpful rhetoric—in thinly veiled acts of retaliation, in blatant threats, in the exaggeration of apocalyptic social and political consequences, in direct insults, in misinformation and outright lies, and in an unhealthy disregard of intellectual thought and the role of reason. We can replace the negative and destructive tone with constructive and reasonable debate. Issues can be discussed based on facts and the merits of the arguments, without resorting to emotionally charged language that does nothing to advance the correctness of a position.

The call for a reduction in highly charged political discourse reached a high point following the shooting of a member of Congress in 2011. However, another member of Congress objected:

> We can't use this as a moment to try to stifle one side or the other. We can't use this as a moment to say, one side doesn't have a right to talk about the issues they are passionate about.

The response sets up a *straw man* by claiming that the advocates for a reduction in emotional rhetoric are saying that "one side doesn't have a right to talk about the issues they are passionate about." The speaker is arguing against a position that no one holds.

The principles of reason, intellectual honesty, and analysis that we applied to short examples can be adapted to longer passages as well. In fact, the next *Check Your Understanding* allows you to apply those principles to recent events and to historically important cases, many of which are examples of extended arguments.

CHECK YOUR UNDERSTANDING 4D

The following passages were taken from various sources. Use your understanding of all the fallacies that were presented in this chapter to determine which fallacy best fits the passage. In some cases a passage may contain more than one fallacy. Explain your answers.

1. You can't speak French. Petey Bellows can't speak French. I must therefore conclude that nobody at the University of Minnesota can speak French.

   Max Shulman, "Love Is a Fallacy"

Answer: Hasty generalization. The conclusion about the entire university is based on two instances.

2. It's a mistake because it is in error.

   William Safire, "On Language: Take My Question Please!"

3. Police authorities are finding the solution of murders more and more difficult because the victims are unwilling to cooperate with the police.

   Radicalacademy.com

4. Either man was created just as the Bible tells us, or man evolved from inanimate chemicals and random chance.

   Skeptic.org

⭐ 5. I always said the only failure is when you fail to try. I guess the other failure would not be giving your best effort. And I did both.

Martina Navratilova, quoted in Telegraph.co.uk

6. Do you favor the United States Army abolishing the affirmative-action program that produced Colin Powell?

Bill Clinton, quoted in the *New York Times*

7. It is the case that either the nobility of this country appear to be wealthy, in which case they can be taxed, or else they appear to be poor, in which case they are living frugally and must have immense savings, which can be taxed.

"Morton's Fork," *Encyclopedia Britannica*

8. I don't like spinach, and I'm glad I don't, because if I liked it I'd eat it, and I just hate it.

Clarence Darrow, in *Clarence Darrow: A One-Man Play*

⭐ 9. I often read the Mexico enablers justify the 800,000 Mexicans illegally crossing the U.S. border each year, rationalizing this with a statement such as, "well it is either they stay in Mexico and starve, or risk their lives crossing the border."

"The Fulano Files," at Fulanofiles.blogspot.com

10. To be an atheist, you have to believe with absolute certainty that there is no God. In order to convince yourself with absolute certainty, you must examine all the Universe and all the places where God could possibly be. Since you obviously haven't, your position is indefensible.

Infidels.org

11. Near-perfect correlations exist between the death rate in Hyderabad, India, from 1911 to 1919, and variations in the membership of the International Association of Machinists during the same period.

David Hackett Fischer, *Historians' Fallacies*

12. I hardly think that 58 is the right age at which to talk about a retirement home unless there are some serious health concerns. My 85-year-old mother power-walks two miles each day, drives her car safely, climbs stairs, does crosswords, and reads the daily paper.

Letter to the editor, *Time*

⭐ 13. For the natives, they are near all dead of the smallpox, so as the Lord hath cleared our title to what we possess.

John Winthrop, governor, Massachusetts Colony, 1634

14. He's not a moron at all, he's a friend. My personal relations with the president are extremely good.

Canadian prime minister Jean Chrétien, quoted in the *Canadian Press*

15. Why opium produces sleep: Because there is in it a dormitive power.

Molière, *The Imaginary Invalid*

16. My opponent wants to sever the Danish church from the state for his own personal sake. His motion is an attempt to take over the church and further his ecumenical theology by his usual mafia methods.

Charlotte Jorgensen, "Hostility in Public Debate"

⭐ 17. I do not have much information on this case except the general statement of the agency that there is nothing in the files to disprove his Communist connections.

Richard H. Rovere, *Senator Joe McCarthy*

18. We took the Bible and prayer out of public schools, and now we're having weekly shootings practically. We had the '60s sexual revolution, and now people are dying of AIDS.   Christine O'Donnell, quoted in the *New Statesman*

19. How is education supposed to make me feel smarter? Besides, every time I learn something new, it pushes some old stuff out of my brain. Remember when I took that home winemaking course, and I forgot how to drive?
    Homer Simpson, "Secrets of a Successful Marriage," *The Simpsons*

20. The community of Pacific Palisades is extremely wealthy. Therefore, every person living there is extremely wealthy.   Peter A. Angeles, *Dictionary of Philosophy*

★ 21. Dear Friend, a man who has studied law to its highest degree is a brilliant lawyer, for a brilliant lawyer has studied law to its highest degree.
    Oscar Wilde, *De Profundis*

22. The most stringent protection of free speech would not protect a man in falsely shouting fire in a theater and causing a panic.
    Oliver Wendell Homes, Supreme Court Opinion, *Schenk v. United States*

23. Twenty seven years ago, Luis Alvarez first proposed that the Cretaceous–Tertiary extinction event was caused by an asteroid that struck the earth 65.5 million years earlier. This means the dinosaurs died out 65,500,027 years ago.
    Worldlingo.com

24. Should we not assume that just as the eye, hand, the foot, and in general each part of the body clearly has its own proper function, so man too has some function over and above the function of his parts?   Aristotle, *Nicomachean Ethics*

★ 25. We will starve terrorists of funding, turn them one against another, drive them from place to place, until there is no refuge or rest. And we will pursue nations that provide aid or safe haven to terrorism. Every nation, in every region, now has a decision to make. Either you are with us, or you are with the terrorists.
    George W. Bush, Sept. 20, 2001, in an address to Congress

26. You may be interested to know that global warming, earthquakes, hurricanes, and other natural disasters are a direct effect of the shrinking numbers of Pirates since the 1800s. For your interest, I have included a graph of the approximate number of pirates versus the average global temperature over the last 200 years. As you can see, there is a statistically significant inverse relationship between pirates and global temperature.   Bobby Henderson, "Open Letter to Kansas School Board"

27. Following a tip-off from hospital administrators, investigators looked into a series of "suspicious" deaths or near deaths in hospital wards where a certain nurse had worked from 1999 to 2001, and they found that the nurse had been physically present when many of them took place. The nurse is serving a life sentence for seven murders and three attempted murders.
    Mark Buchanan, *New York Times*

28. Gerda Reith is convinced that superstition can be a positive force. "It gives you a sense of control by making you think you can work out what's going to happen next," she says. "And it also makes you feel lucky. And to take a risk or to enter into a chancy situation, you really have to believe in your own luck. In that sense, it's a very useful way of thinking, because the alternative is fatalism, which is to say, 'Oh, there's nothing I can do.' At least superstition makes people do things."

David Newnham, "Hostages to Fortune"

★ 29. *Doctor:* I can't find the cause of your illness, but frankly I think it's due to drinking.
Patient: Then I'll come back when you are sober.

Anonymous—used by many comedians

30. Morality in this nation has worsened at the same time that adherence to traditional Christian beliefs has declined. Obviously, the latter has caused the former, so encouraging Christianity will ensure a return to traditional moral standards.

About.com

31. Whether deconstruction is an art or a science, a malady or a Catch-22, it would seem to belong at honours level in university degrees. School is for basics and knowledge, certainly accompanied by critical thinking, but not in a milieu where all is relative and there are no absolutes for young people who do not have the intellectual maturity to cope with the somewhat morbid rigour of constant criticism and questioning of motives. If you go on deconstructing for long enough you will become a marshmallow or a jelly.

Kenneth Wiltshire, "In Defense of the True Values of Learning"

32. *Dan Quayle:* I have far more experience than many others that sought the office of vice president of this country. I have as much experience in Congress as Jack Kennedy did when he sought the presidency. I will be prepared to deal with the people in the Bush administration, if that unfortunate event would ever occur.
Lloyd Bentsen: I served with Jack Kennedy; I knew Jack Kennedy; Jack Kennedy was a friend of mine. Senator, you're no Jack Kennedy.

The 1988 U.S. vice presidential debates

★ 33. I call this the "Advertiser's Fallacy" because it's so prevalent in commercials, such as the one where a famous baseball slugger gives medical advice on erectile dysfunction (that should pick up the hit count!). No. See a properly qualified doctor for ED, see Rafael Palmiero only if you want to improve your baseball swing.

Joe McFaul, "Law, Evolution, Science, and Junk Science"

34. Recently, we highlighted a British journalist's story about the underside of Dubai's startling ascent. Some in Dubai called foul, including one writer who wants to remind Britons that their own country has a dark side. After all, what to think of a country in which one fifth of the population lives in poverty?

Freakonomics.com, "Dubai's Rebuttal"

35. The anti-stem-cell argument goes like this: If you permit scientists to destroy human embryos for the purpose of research, [then it goes] from there to killing human fetuses in order to harvest tissue, and from there to euthanizing disabled or terminally ill people to harvest their organs, and from there to human cloning and human-animal hybrids, and if making chimeras is okay, well then Dr. Frankenstein must also be okay, and Dr. Mengele, too, and before you know it, it's one long hapless inevitable slide from high-minded medicine to the Nazis.

Marty Kaplan, in an article at Huffingtonpost.com

36. The first mate on a ship decided to celebrate an occasion with some rum. Unfortunately he got drunk. The captain saw him drunk and when the first mate was sober, showed him the following entry in the ship's log: *The first mate was drunk today.*

"Captain please don't let that stay in the log," the mate said. "This could add months or years to my becoming a captain myself."
"Is it true?" asked the captain, already knowing the answer.
"Yes, it is true" the mate said.
"Then if it is true it has to go in the log. That's the rule. If it's true it goes into the log. End of discussion," said the captain sternly.
Weeks later, it was the first mate's turn to make the log entries. The first mate wrote: *The ship seems in good shape. The captain was sober today.*

Adapted from "The Captain Was Sober Today," at Blogs.rassak.com

★ 37. These are the times that try men's souls. The summer soldier and the sunshine patriot will in this crisis shrink from the service of his country; but he that stands it now deserves the love and thanks for man and woman. Tyranny, like hell, is not easily conquered; yet we have this consolation with us, that the harder the conflict, the more glorious the triumph. What we obtain too cheap, we esteem too lightly; 'tis dearness only that gives everything its value. Heaven knows how to put a proper price upon its goods; and it would be strange indeed, if so celestial an article as freedom should not be highly rated. Britain, with an army to enforce her tyranny, has declared that she has a right (not only to tax) but "to bind us in all cases whatsoever," and if being bound in that manner is not slavery, then there is no such thing as slavery upon earth.   Thomas Paine, *The Crisis*

38 It is argued that in these tragic cases the great value of the mental health of a woman who becomes pregnant as a result of rape or incest can best be safeguarded by abortion. It is also said that a pregnancy caused by rape or incest is the result of a grave injustice and that the victim should not be obliged to carry the fetus to viability. This would keep reminding her for nine months of the violence committed against her and would just increase her mental anguish. It is reasoned that the value of the woman's mental health is greater than the value of the fetus. In addition, it is maintained that the fetus is an aggressor against the woman's integrity and personal life; it is only just and morally defensible to repel an aggressor even by killing him if that is the only

way to defend personal and human values. It is concluded, then, that abortion is justified in these cases.

Andrew Varga, *The Main Issues in Bioethics*

39. If the Iraqi regime is able to produce, buy, or steal an amount of highly-enriched uranium a little larger than a single softball, it could have a nuclear weapon in less than a year. And if we allow that to happen, a terrible line would be crossed. Saddam Hussein would be in a position to blackmail anyone who opposes his aggression. He would be in a position to dominate the Middle East. He would be in a position to threaten America. And Saddam Hussein would be in a position to pass nuclear technology to terrorists. Knowing these realities, America must not ignore the threat gathering against us. Facing clear evidence of peril, we cannot wait for the final proof—the smoking gun—that could come in the form of a mushroom cloud.

President George W. Bush, October 8, 2002

40. A person apparently hopelessly ill may be allowed to take his own life. Then he may be permitted to deputize others to do it for him should he no longer be able to act. The judgment of others then becomes the ruling factor. Already at this point euthanasia is not personal and voluntary, for others are acting on behalf of the patient as they see fit. This may well incline them to act on behalf of other patients who have not authorized them to exercise their judgment. It is only a short step, then, from voluntary euthanasia (self-inflicted or authorized), to directed euthanasia administered to a patient who has given no authorization, to involuntary euthanasia conducted as a part of a social policy.

J. Gay Williams, "The Wrongfulness of Euthanasia"

41. Once, many National Football League (NFL) teams played on Thanksgiving; to this day, high school teams play championship or rivalry games on Thanksgiving. In the 1950s, the old NFL began a tradition of having only one game on turkey day, always at Detroit. In the 1960s, a Cowboys' home date was added on Thanksgiving, to help the Dallas expansion franchise become established. Detroit and Dallas have been the traditional hosts since. There's no larger reason—the reason is, "We do it that way because that's the way we do it."

Gregg Easterbrook, ESPN.com's Page 2

42. If I were to suggest that between the Earth and Mars there is a china teapot revolving about the sun in an elliptical orbit, nobody would be able to disprove my assertion provided I were careful to add that the teapot is too small to be revealed even by our most powerful telescopes. But if I were to go on to say that, since my assertion cannot be disproved, it is an intolerable presumption on the part of human reason to doubt it, I should rightly be thought to be talking nonsense. If, however, the existence of such a teapot were affirmed in ancient books, taught as the sacred truth every Sunday, and instilled into the minds of children at school, hesitation to believe in its existence would become a mark of eccentricity and entitle the doubter to the attentions of the psychiatrist in an enlightened age or of the Inquisitor in an earlier time.

Bertrand Russell, "Is There a God?"

43. *Dorothy:* Are you doing that on purpose, or can't you make up your mind?
Scarecrow: That's the trouble. I can't make up my mind. I haven't got a brain—just straw.
Dorothy: How can you talk if you haven't got a brain?
Scarecrow: I don't know. But some people without brains do an awful lot of talking, don't they?
Dorothy: I guess you're right.   From the movie *The Wizard of Oz*

44. To cast abortion as a solely private moral question is to lose touch with common sense. How human beings treat one another is practically the definition of a public moral matter. Of course, there are many private aspects of human relations, but the question whether one human being should be allowed fatally to harm another is not one of them. Abortion is an inescapably public matter.   Helen M. Alvaré, *The Abortion Controversy*

★ 45. Consider a precise number that is well known to generations of parents and doctors: the normal human body temperature of 98.6 degrees Fahrenheit. Recent investigations involving millions of measurements have revealed that this number is wrong; normal human body temperature is actually 98.2 degrees Fahrenheit. The fault, however, lies not with Dr. Wunderlich's original measurements—they were averaged and sensibly rounded to the nearest degree: 37 degrees Celsius. When this temperature was converted to Fahrenheit, however, the rounding was forgotten, and 98.6 was taken to be accurate to the nearest tenth of a degree. Had the original interval between 36.5 degrees Celsius and 37.5 degrees Celsius been translated, the equivalent Fahrenheit temperatures would have ranged from 97.7 degrees to 99.5 degrees.   John Allen Paulos, *A Mathematician Reads the Newspaper*

Summary

- Formal fallacy: A logical error that occurs in the form or structure of an argument and is restricted to deductive arguments.
- Informal fallacy: A mistake in reasoning that occurs in ordinary language and is different from an error in the form or structure of arguments.
- Fallacies of relevance: Occur whenever irrelevant premises are offered in support of a conclusion.
- Argument against the person (*ad hominem*): Occurs when a claim is rejected or judged to be false based on alleged character flaws of the person making the claim. A second common form occurs whenever someone's statement or reasoning is attacked by way of a stereotype, such as a racial, sexual, or religious stereotype. A third form involves the use of the circumstances of a person's life to reject his claims.
- *Tu quoque:* A variety of the *ad hominem* fallacy that is distinguished by the specific attempt of one person to avoid the issue at hand by claiming the other person is a hypocrite ("you, too" or "look who's talking").

- Appeal to the people: The avoidance of objective evidence in favor of an emotional response defeats the goal of a rational investigation of truth. The tactic appeals to people's desire to belong to a group.
- Appeal to pity: A specific kind of emotional plea that relies solely on a sense of pity for support.
- Appeal to force: A threat of harmful consequences (physical and otherwise) used to force acceptance of a course of action that would otherwise be unacceptable.
- An argument built on a position of ignorance claims either that (1) a statement must be true because it has not been proven to be false or (2) a statement must be false because it has not been proven to be true.
- Missing the point: Occurs when premises that seem to lead logically to one conclusion are used instead to support an unexpected conclusion.
- Appeal to an unqualified authority: Occurs when an argument that relies on the opinions of people who have no expertise, training, or knowledge relevant to the issue at hand.
- Fallacies of unwarranted assumption: Assume the truth of some unproved or questionable claim.
- Begging the question: Occurs when an argument assumes as evidence in the premises the very thing that it attempts to prove in the conclusion.
- Complex question: A single question that actually contains multiple, hidden parts.
- Biased sample: An argument that uses a nonrepresentative sample as support for a statistical claim about an entire population.
- Accident: The fallacy that arises when a generalization is inappropriately applied to the case at hand.
- Hasty generalization: A generalization created on the basis of a few instances.
- Misleading precision: Occurs when a claim appears to be statistically significant but is not.
- False dichotomy: Occurs when it is assumed that only two choices are possible, when in fact others exist.
- False dilemma: Occurs when two choices are asserted, each leading to an unwanted result, but there is a failure to acknowledge that other possibilities exist.
- False cause: Occurs when a causal connection is assumed to exist between two events when none actually exists.
- Coincidence: A fallacy that results from the accidental or chance connection between two events.
- *Post hoc* fallacy: Involves either a short-term or long-term pattern that is noticed after the fact.
- Common cause fallacy: A mistake that occurs when someone thinks that one event causes another when in fact both events are the result of a common cause.
- Slippery slope: The attempt to make a final event the inevitable outcome of an initial act.
- Fallacy of ambiguity or diversion: Occurs when the meanings of terms or phrases are changed (intentionally or unintentionally) within the argument,

or when our attention is purposely (or accidentally) diverted from the issue at hand.

- Equivocation: The intentional or unintentional use of different meanings of words or phrases in an argument.
- Amphiboly: Ambiguity that arises when a poorly constructed statement muddles the intended meaning ("irregular speech").
- Composition: When an attribute of the individual parts of an object is mistakenly transferred to the entire object.
- Division: When an attribute of an object as a whole is mistakenly transferred to its individual parts.
- Emphasis: Occurs when attention is purposely (or accidentally) diverted from the issue at hand.
- Straw man: A fallacy that occurs when someone's written or spoken words are taken out of context. It purposely distorts the original argument to create a new, weak argument that can be easily refuted (a straw man that is easily knocked down).
- Red herring: When someone completely ignores an opponent's position and changes the subject, diverting the discussion in a new direction.

KEY TERMS

LOGIC CHALLENGE: A CLEVER PROBLEM

In a certain faraway country (long, long, ago), prisoners to be executed were either shot or hanged. Prisoners were allowed to make one statement. If their statement turned out to be true, then they were hanged. If their statement turned out to be false, then they were shot. That is, until one clever prisoner put an end to the practice of execution. The prisoner made her one statement, upon which the judge was forced to set her free. What statement did she make?